The Enduring Vision

THE Enduring Vision

A HISTORY OF THE AMERICAN PEOPLE

VOLUME ONE: TO 1877

Concise Sixth Edition

PAUL S. BOYER
University of Wisconsin, Madison

CLIFFORD E. CLARK, JR.
Carleton College

SANDRA MCNAIR HAWLEY
San Jacinto College

JOSEPH F. KETT
University of Virginia

ANDREW RIESER
State University of New York, Dutchess Community College

NEAL SALISBURY
Smith College

HARVARD SITKOFF
University of New Hampshire

NANCY WOLOCH
Barnard College

WADSWORTH
CENGAGE Learning

Australia • Brazil • Japan • Korea • Mexico • Singapore • Spain • United Kingdom • United States

WADSWORTH
CENGAGE Learning

Editor-in-Chief: P. J. Boardman

Publisher: Suzanne Jeans

Senior Sponsoring Editor: Ann West

Senior Developmental Editor: Lisa Kalner
Williams

Assistant Editor: Megan Curry

Senior Marketing Manager: Katherine Bates

Marketing Communications Manager:
Christine Dobberpuhl

Senior Content Project Manager: Jane Lee

Art and Design Manager: Jill Haber

Cover Design Director: Tony Saizon

Senior Photo Editor: Jennifer Meyer Dare

Composition Buyer: Chuck Dutton

Print Buyer: Paula Vang

Permissions Manager, Images: Jennifer Meyer
Dare

Permissions Manager, Text: Katie Huha

Editorial Assistant: Laura Collins

Cover image: *View of the South East Prospect
of the City of Philadelphia* by Peter Cooper
on a signboard, 1720. Credit: Library
Company of Philadelphia.

For product information and technology assistance, contact us at
Cengage Learning Academic Resource Center, 1-800-354-9706

For permission to use material from this text or product, submit all requests online
at **www.cengage.com/permissions**. Further permissions questions can be emailed
to **permissionrequest@cengage.com**

Library of Congress Control Number: 2008939229

ISBN-13: 978-0-547-22281-3

ISBN-10: 0-547-22281-5

Wadsworth
25 Thomson Place
Boston, MA 02210
USA

Cengage Learning products are represented in Canada by Nelson Education, Ltd.

For your course and learning solutions, visit **academic.cengage.com**

Purchase any of our products at your local college store or at our preferred online
store **www.ichapters.com**

Printed in Canada
1 2 3 4 5 6 7 12 11 10 09 08

Contents

7

Launching the New Republic, 1788–1800   145

8

Jeffersonianism and the Era of Good Feelings, 1801–1824   170

9

The Transformation of American Society, 1815–1840   193

13

Immigration, Expansion, and Sectional Conflict, 1840–1848   278

14

From Compromise to Secession, 1850–1861   301

15

Crucible of Freedom: Civil War, 1861–1865   324

16

The Crisis of Reconstruction, 1865–1877   353

Maps

Charts, Graphs, and Tables

M uch has changed in America and the world since we began planning *The Enduring Vision* more than two decades ago. Some of these developments have been welcome and positive; others deeply unsettling. This new Concise Sixth Edition fully documents all of these changes, as well as the continuities that offer reassurance for the future.

The Concise Sixth Edition builds on the underlying strategy that has guided us from the beginning. We want our history to be not only comprehensive and illuminating, but also lively, readable, and true to the lived experience of earlier generations of Americans. Within a clear political and chronological framework, we integrate the best recent scholarship in all areas of American history. Our interest in social and cultural history, which shapes our own teaching and scholarship, has suffused *The Enduring Vision* from the outset, and it remains central. We integrate the historical experience of women and men of all regions, ethnic groups, and social classes who make up the American mosaic.

New Interpretations, Expanded Coverage

In recent years, American historians have emphasized how deeply our history is embedded within a larger global context. In the Concise Sixth Edition we have underscored the wider context of American history throughout the narrative. From the origins of agriculture two millennia ago to the impact of globalization today, we have emphasized how the social, economic, and political developments central to our historical experience emerge with fresh new clarity when viewed within a broader world framework.

As in earlier editions, coverage of environmental history, the land, and the West is fully integrated into the narrative, and treated analytically, not simply "tacked on" to a traditional account. We also incorporate the best of the new political history, stressing the social, cultural, and economic issues at stake in political decisions and debates.

We again offer extensive coverage of medicine and disease, from the epidemics brought by European explorers and settlers to today's AIDS crisis, bioethics debates, and controversies over health-care financing. We also give careful attention to religious history, from the spiritual values of pre-Columbian communities to the political activism of contemporary conservative Christian groups.

Visual Resources and Aids to the Student

The layout of this edition has changed from previous editions. A new one-column format allows for more seamless integration of images and a smoother narrative flow. Each chapter begins with Focus Questions that correspond to the major sections of the chapter to give students a preview of the key topics to be covered. These questions are briefly answered at the end of the chapter in the "Chapter Summary." Throughout the chapters, students get assistance from key terms that are boldfaced in the text and defined in the margins; "Checking In" boxes at the end of each section summarize the key points in that section.

SUPPLEMENTARY RESOURCES

A wide array of supplements accompanies this text to help students master the material and guide instructors in teaching from *The Enduring Vision, Concise Sixth Edition*. For details on viewing or ordering these materials, please consult your Cengage Learning sales representative.

Instructor Tools

The **Instructor Website** (found at **www.cengage.com/history/boyer/enduringconcise6e**) offers the *Instructor's Guide*, an online manual including Instructional Techniques and Resources, Historical Investigations for students, and for each chapter, chapter themes, lecture suggestions, print and nonprint resources, and a guide to using the Enduring Voices document sets. Also available on the Instructor Website are primary sources with instructor notes, PowerPoint slides for classroom presentation, and personal response system slides. A computerized testing program, available on CD-ROM, provides flexible test-editing capabilities.

Instructors who adopt *The Enduring Vision, Concise Sixth Edition* also receive access to **HistoryFinder**, a powerful search engine and primary source repository that helps instructors create rich and exciting classroom presentations. This online tool offers thousands of online resources, including art, photographs, maps, primary sources, multimedia content, and Associated Press interactive modules. HistoryFinder's assets can easily be searched by keyword or from pull-down menus by topic, media type, or by Wadsworth/Cengage Learning textbook. Instructors can then browse, preview, and download resources straight from the website.

Student Tools

The **Student Website** (found at **www.cengage.com/history/boyer/enduringconcise6e**) contains a variety of tutorial resources including ACE quizzes with practice feedback, interactive maps, primary sources, chronology exercises, flashcards, and MP3 chapter summaries.

The **American History Resource Center** offers hundreds of primary sources such as speeches, letters, legal documents and transcripts, poems, maps, simulations, timelines, and additional images that bring history to life—along with interactive assignable exercises. A map feature using Google Earth coordinates helps students learn geography by comparing traditional textbook maps with an aerial view of the location today.

ACKNOWLEDGMENTS

Any book, and this one in particular, is the result of the hard work of many people. As always, the editorial staff at Houghton Mifflin has been outstanding. Particularly deserving of thanks are Ann West, Lisa Kalner Williams, and Bob Greiner.

Sandra Hawley thanks her daughter, Lee Anne Hawley, who as ever, has been invaluable in multiple ways. Great thanks are owed as well to Lisa LaDay Morris, Patricia Piper, Dorothy White, Larry Kallus, Eric Johnson, Melanie Welavir, and Tony Sisk for their continuing support.

Andrew Rieser acknowledges Sandra McNair Hawley and the co-authors for handing him a superb text from which to whittle down the second volume; and he thanks Paul S. Boyer for his support and friendship.

CHAPTER 1

Native Peoples of America

TO 1500

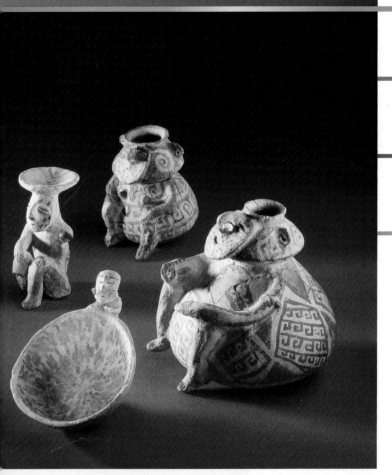

Hohokam Ceramics, ca. A.D. 1000

CHAPTER PREVIEW

The First Americans, c. 13,000–2500 B.C.
How did environmental change shape the transition from Paleo-Indian to Archaic ways of life?

Cultural Diversity, c. 2500 B.C.–A.D. 1500
What were the principal differences among the Native American cultures that emerged after 2500 B.C.?

North American Peoples on the Eve of European Contact
What common values did Native Americans share despite their vast diversity?

The history of the Americas began thousands of years before Christopher Columbus's first voyage. Over that time, an indigenous American history unfolded, separate from that of the Old World of Africa, Asia, and Europe.

Some Native Americans eked out their existence in precarious environments, whereas others enjoyed prosperity; some lived in small bands, but others dwelt in large cities; some believed that the first humans came from the sky, and others thought that they originated underground. Wherever and however they lived, and whatever they believed, native peoples together made North America a human habitat and gave it a history.

CL This icon will direct you to the website where you can Prepare for Class, Improve Your Grade, and Ace the Test: **www.cengage.com/history/boyer/ enduringconcise6e**

1

THE FIRST AMERICANS, C. 13,000–2500 B.C.

How did environmental change shape the transition from Paleo-Indian to Archaic ways of life?

Precisely how and when the Western Hemisphere was settled remains uncertain. Although many Indians believe that their ancestors originated in the Americas, most scientific theories point to the arrival of peoples from northeastern Asia during the last Ice Age (c. 33,000–10,500 B.C.), when land linked Siberia and Alaska. As the Ice Age waned, Native Americans adapted to environments that ranged from tropical to frigid and developed diverse cultures that nonetheless had many elements in common.

Peopling New Worlds

Monte Verde, Chile Site of human habitation by 12,000 B.C.

Bering land bridge link between Northeast Asia and far Northwest North America during late Ice Age

Scientists now believe that the earliest migrants from Asia traveled by boat along the coastline around 13,000 B.C. Recent archaeological finds at **Monte Verde, Chile,** reveal evidence of human habitation by 12,000 B.C. Later migrants reached the Americas by crossing the **Bering land bridge** and fanned out in the interior as melting glaciers opened the way for eastward and southward migration.

Most Native Americans descend from these early migrations, but a later surge of migration brought Athapaskan (ath-a-PAS-kan)-speaking peoples to the Americas about 7000 B.C. Their descendants include the Apaches and Navajos. The arrival of non-Indian Inuits, Aleuts, and Eskimos after 3000 B.C. completed the peopling of the Americas.

Paleo-Indians Earliest peoples of the Americas, 13,000–8000 B.C.

Most **Paleo** (PAY-lee-oh)-**Indians** lived in small bands of fifteen to fifty people. The band lived together for the summer but split into smaller groups of one or two families for fall and winter. Although they moved constantly, they remained within informal boundaries except when they traveled to favored quarries to obtain jasper or flint for making tools. Here they encountered other bands, with whom they traded and joined in religious ceremonies. Most Paleo-Indians practiced **reciprocity,** the mutual bestowing of gifts and favors rather than competition for resources.

reciprocity mutual bestowing of gifts and favors rather than competition for resources

By 9000 B.C. many big-game species, including mammoths and mastodons, had vanished. Paleo-Indian hunters contributed to this extinction, as did a warming climate and environmental changes. Human beings were major beneficiaries of these changes.

Archaic Societies

Climatic warming continued until about 4000 B.C. with dramatic effects for North America. Sea levels rose, flooding the shallow continental shelf, and glacial runoff filled the Great Lakes, the Mississippi River basin, and other waters. As the glaciers receded northward, so did the cold, icy arctic or subarctic environments that had covered much of what is now the United States. Treeless plains and evergreen forests yielded to deciduous forests in the East, grassland prairies on the Plains, and desert in much of the West. An immense range of plants and animals covered the landscape.

Archaic peoples Native Americans from 8000–2500 B.C.

The **Archaic** (ar-KAY-ick) **peoples,** as archaeologists term native North Americans from 8000 B.C. to sometime after 2500 B.C., lived off wide varieties of smaller

Chronology

c. 13,000 b.c.	People present in America
c. 10,500–9000 b.c.	Paleo-Indians spread throughout Western Hemisphere
c. 9000 b.c.	Extinction of big-game mammals
c. 8000 b.c.	Archaic era begins
c. 7000 b.c.	Athapaskan-speaking peoples arrive in North America
c. 5000 b.c.	First domesticated plants grown
c. 3000 b.c.	First maize grown in Mesoamerica
c. 3000–2000 b.c.	Eskimo and Aleut peoples arrive in North America
c. 2500 b.c.	Archaic societies yield before diverse cultures; first maize grown in North America
c. 1200 b.c.	Poverty Point flourishes in Louisiana
c. 400–100 b.c.	Adena culture flourishes in Ohio Valley
c. 250 b.c.	Hohokam culture begins in Southwest
c. 100 b.c.	Anasazi culture begins in Southwest
c. 100 b.c.–a.d. 600	Hopewell culture thrives in Midwest
c. a.d. 1	Rise of chiefdoms on Northwest Coast and in California
c. 100–700	Teotihuacán flourishes in Mesoamerica
c. 600–1400	Mayan kingdoms flourish
c. 700	Mississippian culture begins; Anasazi expansion begins
c. 900	Urban center arises at Cahokia
c.1000	Norse attempt, and fail, to colonize Vinland
c. 1200	Anasazi and Hohokam peoples disperse in Southwest
c. 1200–1400	Cahokia declines; inhabitants disperse
1428	Rise of Aztec empire
1438	Rise of Inca empire
1492	Christopher Columbus reaches Western Hemisphere

mammals, fish, and wild plants rather than big game. Greater efficiency in hunting and gathering permitted larger populations to inhabit smaller areas. In rich areas, such as the East and Midwest, large populations lived in villages for virtually the entire year. For example, a year-round village that flourished near present-day Kampsville, Illinois, from 3900 to 2800 B.C. supported 100 to 150 people. Its residents procured fish and mussels from local lakes to supplement the deer, birds, nuts, and seeds available in the surrounding area.

Over time, Archaic Americans sharpened distinctions between women's and men's roles. Generally men fished and hunted while women foraged for wild plant products. However, both genders apparently served as religious healers. As they foraged for wild plants, gatherers—usually women in North America—gradually learned

Map 1.1   The Peopling of the Americas

Scientists postulate two probable routes by which the earliest peoples reached America. By 9500 B.C., they had settled throughout the Western Hemisphere.

how to cultivate some plants and then developed tools for digging and grinding, as well as effective methods of drying and storing seeds.

The most sophisticated of these early farmers lived in highland valleys in **Mesoamerica,** particularly Tehuacán (teh-wha-CAHN). By 3000 B.C. they were cultivating squash, gourds, beans, chili peppers, and fruits. At the same time Tehuacán farmers began the long process of domesticating a lowlands plant called teosinte, which ultimately became maize (maze), or corn. Maize agriculture spread rapidly; by 2500 B.C. maize was cultivated as far north as modern New Mexico and as far south as the Amazon basin.

At the same time, Indians in the Andes were already cultivating potatoes, while their counterparts along the Pacific coast harvested squash, beans, and peppers. Initially these domesticated plants constituted only a small part of the Native American diet, essentially a supplement to meat, fish, and wild plants. Centuries would pass before stable societies based primarily on agriculture emerged.

CULTURAL DIVERSITY, C. 2500 B.C.–A.D. 1500

What were the principal differences among the Native Americans that emerged after 2500 B.C.?

After 2500 B.C. many Native Americans moved far beyond the ways of their Archaic ancestors. The most far-reaching changes occurred among peoples whose environments permitted them to produce food surpluses, by cultivating crops or other means. Intensive farming radically changed the environment, and larger populations linked by trade and religion evolved into formal confederacies, and even hierarchical states joined by political and religious systems.

Mesoamerica and South America

Mesoamerican farmers rapidly developed more sophisticated agricultural systems, improving both the quality and the quantity of their crops. In turn, the higher yields and improved nutrition led to the emergence of maize-based farming societies throughout Mesoamerica during the next eight centuries.

By 2000 B.C. some Mesoamerican farming societies were trading surplus crops to their nonfarming neighbors. Trade led to the development of wealthy and powerful urban centers that dominated surrounding communities. These chiefdoms generally dominated relatively small areas, but some developed into centralized states complete with taxes, public works, and armies. The capital of the largest early state, Teotihuacán (tehoh-tee-whah-KAHN), about fifty miles northeast of modern Mexico City, housed a population of one hundred thousand people. At its center was a complex of pyramids over which towered the Sun Pyramid, the largest structure in the Americas prior to the arrival of the Spanish. From A.D. 100 to 700, Teotihuacán dominated the Valley of Mexico, with trade networks extending throughout modern Mexico; its influence on the religion, government, and culture of its neighbors was enormous.

Mesoamerica Roughly, land extending from modern Mexico to Colombia; Central America plus Mexico

CHECKING IN

- Historians believe that most Native Americans descended from northeast Asian peoples who arrived in the Americas from around 33,000 to 9000 B.C.
- Paleo-Indians, the earliest peoples of the Americas, lived in small groups and were mainly hunters.
- Climatic warming created favorable environments for expansion, including the emergence of agriculture by 5000 B.C.

Sun Pyramid, Teotihuacán

Built over several centuries, this pyramid remained the largest structure in the Americas until after the Spanish arrived.

As Teotihuacán declined, the Maya (MY-uh) rose. Living in kingdom-states that flourished from southern Mexico to Honduras, the Maya developed a highly accurate calendar; a numerical system; and a system of phonetic, hieroglyphic writing. Mayan codices (singular, codex)—formed from bark paper glued into long folded strips—recorded religious ceremonies, historical traditions, and astronomical observations.

In the fifteenth century two powerful empires emerged: the Aztecs of Mexico and the Inca of Peru. In 1428 the Aztecs began asserting control over Lake Texcoco in the Valley of Mexico and its surrounding communities. After 1450 Aztec expansion became increasingly bloody, as Aztec priests maintained that their gods demanded to be served human blood and hearts; warriors sought captives for human sacrifice.

Tenochtitlán (teh-knowtch-teet-LAN), the Aztec capital, at its peak had some two hundred thousand inhabitants. At the center of the city was a massive temple complex. The Aztecs borrowed freely from other Mesoamerican societies, taking writing from Teotihuacán and the calendar from the Maya. To support the capital's population, the Aztecs developed intensive agriculture based on artificially created islands anchored in Lake Texcoco; Aztec engineers developed an elaborate irrigation system to provide fresh water for both people and crops.

The Aztecs collected taxes from conquered peoples living within a hundred miles of the capital; from those farther away, they exacted tribute. Aztec trading networks extended far from Tenochtitlán, reaching as far north as the American Southwest. However, by the early sixteenth century rebellions had flared up within the Aztec empire.

Far to the south, the Inca empire was expanding as well. After 1438 Inca conquest created an empire that stretched along the Andes and its adjacent areas. The Inca were highly successful farmers, producing enormous quantities of potatoes, maize, beans, and meats. They constructed terraced irrigation systems on their uneven terrain, perfected freeze-drying and other preservation techniques, and built a vast network of roads and bridges.

The arrival of the Spanish would destroy both empires.

The Southwest

The Southwest (the modern American Southwest and most of northern Mexico) is an arid region of diverse landscapes; however, various peoples managed to establish stable supplies of water and to become farmers. Although maize had reached the Southwest as early as 2500 B.C., not until the introduction of drought-resistant strains of the plant around 400 B.C. did large agricultural societies emerge. The two most influential of these were the **Hohokam** (ho-HO-kum) and the **Anasazi** (an-uh-SAW-zee).

Hohokam Early agricultural society of Southwest

Anasazi Pueblo culture that dominated Southwest from 100 B.C.–A.D. 1200

Hohokam culture emerged in the third century B.C. when ancestors of Pima and Tohono O'odham Indians began farming in the Gila (HEE-la) River and Salt River valleys of southern Arizona. The Hohokam people built elaborate canal systems for irrigation that enabled them to harvest two crops each year. The construction and maintenance of the canals demanded large, coordinated work forces. The Hohokams therefore built permanent villages of several hundred residents, and many such communities were joined in confederations linked by canals. The central village in each confederation coordinated labor, trade, and religious and political life for all.

The Hohokam way of life drew on Mesoamerican materials and ideas. From about the sixth century A.D., the larger Hohokam villages had ball courts and platform mounds like those in Mesoamerica, and ball games became major public events. Mesoamerican art influenced Hohokam artists, who used clay, stone, turquoise, and shell. Archaeologists have found Mesoamerican items, such as rubber balls, macaw feathers, and copper bells, at Hohokam sites.

Anasazi culture originated during the first century B.C. in the Four Corners area where Arizona, New Mexico, Colorado, and Utah meet. Although they adopted village life and agriculture late, the Anasazis expanded rapidly in the eighth century A.D. and came to dominate a wide area. Modern Pueblo Indians are descendants of the Anasazi.

The Anasazis had a distinctive architecture. They constructed their early dwellings, round pit houses, in the shape of *kivas* (KEE-vahs), the partly underground, circular structures where Anasazi men conducted religious ceremonies. Anasazi-style apartments and kivas are characteristic of the architecture of the modern-day Pueblo Indians of the Southwest.

kiva A large chamber, often wholly or partially underground, in an Anasazi and later a Pueblo Indian village; used for religious ceremonies and other purposes

From the tenth through the mid-twelfth century, an unusually wet period, the Anasazis expanded over much of today's New Mexico and Arizona. Village populations grew to a thousand or more. In **Chaco** (CHAH-ko) **Canyon** in northwestern New Mexico, a cluster of twelve villages forged a powerful confederation numbering fifteen thousand people. Perfectly straight roads radiated from the canyon to satellite pueblos up to sixty-five miles away. The builders carved out stairs or footholds in the sides of steep cliffs. The canyon was a major trade center, importing and exporting a wide range of materials from and to Mesoamerica, the Great Plains, the Mississippi Valley, and California.

Chaco Canyon Center of powerful Anasazi confederation, A.D. 900–A.D. 1200

Devastating droughts in the late twelfth and thirteenth centuries destroyed classic Anasazi culture. Suddenly, the amount of farmland was drastically reduced for a population that had grown rapidly during the preceding centuries. The Indians abandoned the great Anasazi centers and scattered. Other large agricultural communities, such as those of the Hohokam, also dispersed when droughts came, clearing the way for the arrival of the non-farming Navajos and Apaches at the end of the thirteenth century.

The Eastern Woodlands

Long before they developed agriculture, Indians of the Eastern Woodlands, the vast forests from the Mississippi Valley to the Atlantic coast, experimented with village life and political centralization. By 1200 B.C. about five thousand people had concentrated in a single village at Poverty Point on the Mississippi River in Louisiana. Two large mounds flanked the village, and six concentric embankments—the largest over

Primary Source:
Cahokia

mound-building culture Eastern Woodlands societies, which flourished 1200 B.C.–A.D. 1400; included Poverty Point, Adena, Hopewell, and Mississipian

Cahokia Major mound-building "supercenter," A.D. 900–A.D. 1200

half a mile in diameter—surrounded it. During the spring and autumn equinoxes, a person standing on the larger mound could watch the sun rise directly over the village center. Solar observations formed the basis for these Indians' religious beliefs as well as for their calendar.

Poverty Point lay at the center of a large political and economic unit. It imported quartz, copper, obsidian, crystal, and other sacred materials from long distances and distributed them to nearby communities. These communities almost certainly supplied the labor for the earthworks. The Olmec peoples of Mesoamerica clearly influenced the design and organization of Poverty Point. The settlement flourished for only three centuries and then declined, for reasons that are unclear. A different **mound-building culture,** the Adena, emerged in the Ohio Valley in the fifth century B.C. Adena villages rarely exceeded four hundred inhabitants, but the Adena people spread over a wide area and built hundreds of mounds, most of them containing graves that reflected an individual's social standing.

During the first century B.C., Adena culture evolved into a more developed and widespread culture known as Hopewell. Hopewell ceremonial centers, larger and more elaborate than those of the Adena, mushroomed along the Ohio River and Illinois River valleys. Some centers contained two or three dozen mounds within enclosures of several square miles. The graves of the elite contained elaborate burial goods: freshwater pearls, copper ornaments, mica, quartz, and other sacred substances. Hopewell artisans used raw materials from throughout America east of the Rockies. Through trade networks Hopewell influence spread to communities as distant as places in modern-day Wisconsin, Florida, and New York.

The people who created the sophisticated Hopewell culture were primarily hunter-gatherers, not farmers. Although they did grow some crops, agriculture became a dietary mainstay for Woodlands people only between the seventh and twelfth centuries A.D.

The first full-time farmers in the East were the Mississippians, who lived on the flood plains of the Mississippi River and its major tributaries. Their culture, beginning sometime around A.D. 700, blended elements of the Hopewell culture and ideas from Mesoamerica with their own traditions. Mississippian towns, containing hundreds or even thousands of people, were built around open plazas like those of central Mexico. Religious temples and elite residences stood atop large mounds next to the plazas. Religious ceremonies focused on worship of the sun as the source of agricultural fertility. Chiefs claimed to be related to the sun, and when they died, wives and servants were killed to accompany them to the afterlife. Artisans produced sophisticated work in clay, stone, shell, copper, and wood, largely for religious and funeral rituals.

By the tenth century most Mississippian centers were part of larger confederacies based on trade and shared religious beliefs. Powerful "supercenters" and their chiefs dominated these confederacies. The most powerful confederacy revolved around the magnificent city of **Cahokia** (ka-HO-kee-uh), near modern St. Louis; its influence extended from the Appalachians to the edge of the Plains and from the Great Lakes to the Gulf of Mexico.

After A.D. 1200 Cahokia and other valley centers experienced shortages of food and other resources. Densely concentrated societies had taxed a fragile environment with a fluctuating climate. Competition for suddenly scarce resources led to debili-

Cahokia Mounds
This contemporary painting conveys Cahokia's grand scale. Not until the late eighteenth century did another North American city (Philadelphia) surpass the population of Cahokia, c. 1150.

tating warfare. Survivors fled to the surrounding prairies. By the fifteenth century, their descendants lived in villages linked by reciprocity instead of coercion. After 2500 B.C. many Native Americans moved far beyond the ways of their Archaic ancestors. The most far-reaching changes occurred among peoples whose environments permitted them to produce food surpluses, by cultivating crops or other means. The Spanish later encountered them as the forerunners of the Cherokee, Creek, and other Southeastern Indian peoples.

The Mississippians profoundly affected native culture in the Eastern Woodlands. They spread not only new strains of corn and beans but also the techniques and tools to cultivate them. Only northern New England and the upper Great Lakes had growing seasons too short for corn to become a reliable crop.

Woodlands tribes employed slash-and-burn techniques, which were environmentally sound as well as economically productive. Indian men systematically burned hardwood forests to form open expanses of land. The grass and berry bushes that flourished there attracted deer and other game, and some areas of the ash-enriched soil were planted in corn, beans, and pumpkins. After several years of abundant harvests, yields declined, and the Indians repeated the process on another area; ground cover eventually restored the fertility of the abandoned areas, permitting the Indians to return.

CL Interactive Map:
Culture Areas of
Native Americans
and Locations of Selected
Tribes, A.D. 1500

Nonfarming Societies

Along the Pacific coast, from Alaska to southern California, improvements in the production and storage of food enabled Indians to develop more settled ways of life than their Archaic forebears. From the Alaskan panhandle to northern California, natives spent brief periods each year catching salmon and other fish. The Northwest Coast Indians dried and stored enough fish to last the year, and their seasonal movements gradually gave way to settled life in permanent villages of cedar-plank houses. On the Columbia Plateau, Indians built villages of pit houses and ate salmon through the summer. They left these communities in spring and fall for hunting and gathering.

By A.D. 1 many Northwest Coast villages numbered several hundred people. Trade and warfare strengthened the power of chiefs and other leaders, whose families had greater wealth and prestige than commoners. Leading families proclaimed their status in elaborate totem poles depicting supernatural beings linked to their ancestors and in potlatches, ceremonies in which the Indians gave away or destroyed much of their material wealth. The artistic and architectural achievements of Northwest Coast Indians awed Europeans.

At about the same time, Indians farther south, along the coast and in the interior valleys of what is now California, began to live in villages of one hundred or more people. Acorns dominated their diet, supplementing game, fish, and plants. After the fall harvest, Indians ground the acorns into meal, leached them of bitter tannic acid, and then roasted, boiled, or baked the nuts before eating or storing them.

The end of the Archaic period produced little change in the forbidding aridity of the Great Basin, encompassing present-day Nevada, western Utah, southern Idaho, and eastern Oregon. The area continued to support small hunting-and-gathering bands.

To the east of the Great Basin lay the grasslands of the Great Plains, too dry to support large human settlements but ideal for herds of game animals such as antelope, deer, and elk. Primary among the Great Plains animals were the buffalo, which served nomadic hunters as an ambulatory supermarket. In addition to meat, buffalo provided hides for clothing and tipis, bones and horn for tools and arrowheads; Indians used most other buffalo parts as well. Following the great herds on foot, nomadic tribes killed individual animals with spears and arrows, but also stampeded hundreds at a time over cliffs.

During and after the Mississippian era, some Eastern Woodlands tribes migrated to the lower river valleys of the Plains, where they established permanent villages and relied upon farming as well as hunting.

In western Alaska, the Aleuts arrived around 3000 B.C., bringing within them sophisticated tools and weapons from their Siberian homeland. Most importantly, the Aleuts introduced the bow and arrow to the Americas. Over several thousand years, they spread eastward across Canada as far as Greenland.

The first verified contacts between Europe and America came when the **Norse** colonized Greenland in the 980s. The Norse traded with the Aleuts for furs and walrus ivory. In 1001 Leif Ericson led a group of Norse who planted a small settlement in **Vinland,** now known as Newfoundland. However, the Norse quickly settled into a pattern of hostility with local Indians. By 1015 the Norse had abandoned their

CHECKING IN

- Powerful states, such as the Maya, Aztec, and Inca empires, developed in Mesoamerica and Peru.
- Pueblo society, featuring sophisticated agriculture and irrigation, developed in the Southwest.
- The Eastern Woodlands saw an increase of mound builders in Mississippian centers such as Cahokia.
- Along the Pacific coast, nonfarming societies flourished.

Norse also known as Vikings, were a warrior culture from Scandinavia

Vinland site of first known attempt at European settlement in the Americas

Vinland settlement, although the Greenland settlements endured almost until the end of the fifteenth century; it would be later Europeans who would reap, at the expense of the native peoples, the fruits of a "new world."

NORTH AMERICAN PEOPLES ON THE EVE OF EUROPEAN CONTACT

What common values did Native Americans share despite their vast diversity?

In 1492 the Western Hemisphere numbered about 75 million people, clustered thickly in Mexico and Central America, the Caribbean islands, and Peru. Between 7 and 10 million Native Americans lived north of Mexico. Sparse nomad populations inhabited the Great Basin, the high plains, and the northern forests. Denser concentrations, however, thrived along the Pacific coast, in the Southwest and Southeast, in the Mississippi Valley, and along the Atlantic coast. Speaking many diverse languages and dialects, these people constituted several hundred Indian nations and tribes.

Despite the vast diversity of Native American cultures, they shared many characteristics. Kinship, reciprocity, and communal control of resources lay at the base of Indian societies, while trade ensured that the bow and arrow, ceramic pottery, and certain religious practices existed in almost all Indian societies.

Kinship and Gender

Kinship and gender cemented societies north of Mesoamerica together. Ties to cousins, aunts, and uncles created complex patterns of social obligation.

Kinship bonds were more important in Indian society than the bonds within **nuclear families;** that is, among married couples and their children. Indians did not necessarily expect spouses to be bound together forever, but kinship lasted for life. Customs regulating marriage varied, but strict rules prevailed. In most cultures young people married in their teens, generally after a period of sexual experimentation. Strong ties of residence and deference bound each couple to one or both sets of parents, producing what social scientists call **extended families.**

In some Native American societies such as the Iroquois, the extended families of women took precedence over those of men. A new husband moved in with [h]is wife's extended family. The mother's oldest brother was the primary male auth[ority] figure in a child's life. In many ways, a husband and father was simply the [guest of] his wife's family. Other Indian societies recognized men's extended famil[ies as pri]mary, while still others did not distinguish sharply between the status [of male and] female family lines.

In addition, kinship was the basis for armed conflict. Indian [societies] considered homicide a matter to be resolved by the extended fa[mily of the victim] and the perpetrator. If the perpetrator's family offered a gift t[hat the victim's family] considered appropriate, the question was settled. If not, [the victim's family would] avenge the killing by armed retaliation. Chiefs or other leaders [might mediate] disputes within the same village or tribe, but disputes between me[mbers of different] groups could escalate into war. Densely populated societies that compe[ted]

nuclear fam[ily]
couples ar[

Map
Today
would [

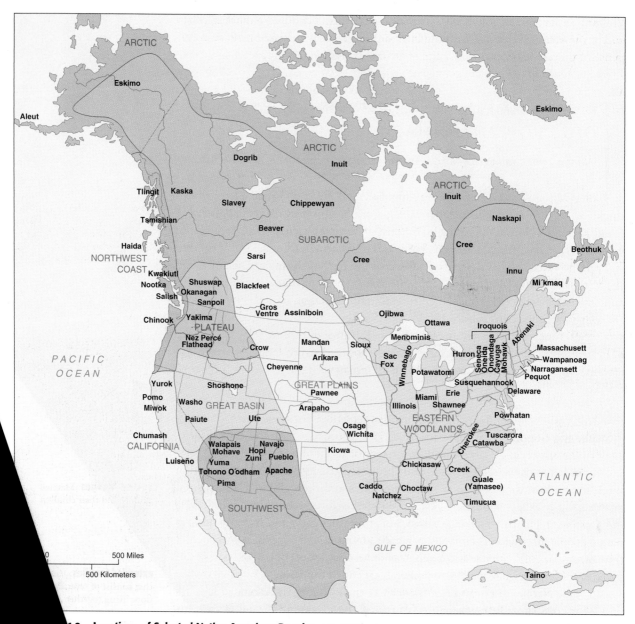

1.2 Locations of Selected Native American Peoples, A.D. 1500

Indian nations were well established in homelands across the continent when Europeans first arrived. Many combine with others or move in later centuries, either voluntarily or because they were forced.

resources, as on the California coast, and centralized societies that attempted to dominate trade networks through coercion, such as the Hopewell culture, experienced frequent and intense warfare. However, warfare remained a low-level affair in most of North America. An exasperated New England officer, writing of his efforts to win Indian allies in the early seventeenth century, described a battle between two Indian groups as "more for pastime than to conquer and subdue enemies." He concluded that "they might fight seven years and not kill seven men."

Among almost all agricultural Indians except those in the Southwest (where men and women shared the work), women did most of the cultivating. With women producing most of the food supply, some communities gave women more power than European societies did. Among the Iroquois of what today is upstate New York, for example, women collectively owned the fields, distributed food, and played a major role in selecting chiefs. In New England, women sometimes served as *sachems*, or chiefs.

Spiritual and Social Values

Native American religions revolved around the conviction that nature was alive, pulsating with spiritual power—*Manitou* (MAN-ih-too) in the Algonquian language. A mysterious, awe-inspiring force that affected human life for both good and evil, such power united all nature in an unbroken web. Manitou encompassed "every thing which they cannot comprehend," wrote the English Puritan leader Roger Williams. Belief in supernatural power led most Indians to seek constantly to conciliate all the spiritual forces in nature: living things, rocks, water, the sun and moon, even ghosts and witches.

manitou Powerful spiritual force that Algonquian-speaking Indians believed pervaded all of nature. Other Native American languages had comparable terms.

Native Americans had several ways of gaining access to spiritual power. One was dreaming; most Native Americans took seriously the visions that came to them in sleep. They also sought access to the supernatural by using physical ordeals to alter their consciousness. Young men gained recognition as adults through a vision quest—a solitary venture that entailed fasting and waiting for the appearance of a spirit that would endow them with special powers. Girls went through comparable rituals at the onset of menstruation, to initiate them into the spiritual world from which female reproductive power flowed. Entire communities often engaged in collective power-seeking rituals, such as the Sun Dance (see Chapter 17).

Indians normally relied on those with special powers to communicate with unseen spirits. These medicine men and women were healers who used medicinal plants and magical chants to cure illnesses. They also interpreted dreams, guided vision quests and other ceremonies, invoked war or peace spirits, and figured prominently in community councils.

Native American societies demanded cooperation. From early childhood, Indians learned to be accommodating and reserved—careful not to reveal their feelings before they could sense those of others. Indian parents generally punished by shaming. Communities made decisions by consensus, and leaders articulated slowly emerging agreements in passionate oratory. All Indian cultures possessed a strong sense of order. Custom, the demands of social conformity, and the rigors of nature strictly regulated life. Everyday affairs mingled with the spiritual world at every turn. Nature and the supernatural could be frightening. Indians feared ghosts and believed that nonconformists could invoke evil spirits by witchcraft, the most dreaded crime in Indian cultures.

The principle of reciprocity remained strong. Although it involved mutual give-and-take, the purpose of reciprocity was not equality, but the

Huron War Leader

Warfare among the Iroquois and neighboring Hurons was intense by the time Europeans arrived. Warriors wore wooden shields to protect themselves from enemy arrows.

CHECKING IN

- Kinship ties bound virtually all Native Americans.
- In most Native American societies, gender roles were clear: women farmed and men hunted.
- Native Americans lived in a world permeated by spiritual power that they could tap into through various rituals.
- Indian societies generally demanded cooperation and order from their members.
- Reciprocity dominated political and social relationships among individuals and between leaders and their followers.

maintenance of equilibrium and interdependence among individuals of unequal power and prestige.

Most leaders' authority depended on the obligations they bestowed, rather than on coercion. The distribution of gifts obligated members of the community to support them and to accept their authority. In the same way, powerful communities distributed gifts to weaker neighbors who reciprocated with tribute in the form of material goods and submission.

Chapter Summary

DOWNLOAD THE MP3 AUDIO FILE OF THE CHAPTER SUMMARY TO LISTEN TO ON THE GO.

How did environmental change shape the transition from Paleo-Indian to Archaic ways of life? (page 2)

Ancestors of most Native Americans reached North America from around 33,000 to 10,500 B.C. The earliest known human settlements date to around 12,000 B.C. Paleo-Indians and their Archaic descendants developed diverse societies, with agriculture appearing in Mesoamerica as early as 5000 B.C.

What were the principal differences among the Native American cultures that emerged after 2500 B.C.? (page 5)

From 2500 B.C. to A.D. 1500 diverse Native American societies based on agriculture proliferated and adapted to widely varying environments. Among the most prominent were the centralized Mesoamerican societies, such as the Maya and the Aztec; the Inca of the Peruvian Andes; the Pueblo societies of what is now the southwestern United States; and the Eastern Woodlands mound builders of Hopewell, Adena, and Cahokia. Nonfarming societies like those of the Pacific Northwest also prospered. The vast grasslands of the Great Plains were home to nomadic hunters dependent on the great buffalo herds.

KEY TERMS

Monte Verde, Chile (p. 2)
Bering land bridge (p. 2)
Paleo-Indians (p. 2)
Reciprocity (p. 2)
Archaic peoples (p. 2)
Mesoamerica (p. 5)
Hohokam (p. 6)
Anasazi (p. 6)
kiva (p. 7)
Chaco Canyon (p. 7)
mound-building culture (p. 8)
Cahokia (p. 8)
Norse (p. 10)
Vinland (p. 10)
nuclear family (p. 11)
extended family (p. 11)
manitou (p. 13)

What common values did Native Americans share despite their vast diversity? (page 11)

Despite their diversity, the majority of these societies shared several common characteristics. In most, kinship played a critical social and political role, with extended families assuming greater importance than nuclear families. Gender also played a major role in organizing most societies, with women doing the farming and men primarily hunting. Indians believed that nature was spiritual as well as physical and sought to live in accord with the supernatural. Most peoples sought orderly societies and relied on reciprocity to maintain stability.

Native Americans never saw themselves as single people. It was Europeans who emphasized differences between themselves and the Indians, a name bestowed by Christopher Columbus, who thought he had landed in the Indies. This new America, in which people were categorized according to continental ancestry, was radically different from the one that flourished for thousands of years before 1492.

CHAPTER 2

The Rise of the Atlantic World

1400–1625

Bartholomew Goswald Trading with Wampanoag Indians at Martha's Vineyard, Massachusetts (New England, 1602), by Theodore De Bry, 1634

CHAPTER PREVIEW

African and European Backgrounds
What major changes were reshaping the African and European worlds in the fifteenth and sixteenth centuries?

Europe and the Atlantic World, 1440–1600
What was the Atlantic world, and how did it emerge?

Footholds in North America, 1512–1625
How did European exploration, conquest, and colonization of North America begin?

At ten o'clock on a moonlit night the tense crew spotted a glimmering light. At two o'clock the next morning came the shout "Land! Land!" It was October 12, 1492. At daybreak Christopher Columbus went ashore, the royal standard of Spain fluttering, knelt to give thanks, and rose to claim for Spain the island that he named San Salvador.

Columbus's crew quickly began trading with the local Taino Indians for golden ornaments. To the Tainos their trade with the Spanish was an exchange between equal partners. But Columbus believed that the Spanish were entitled to rule the Indians and to provide them with Christianity and European civilization whether they wanted these things or not.

Columbus's meeting with the Tainos was a critical step in the formation of an Atlantic world. After 1492, peoples from Europe, Africa, and North and South America became intertwined in elaborate webs of trade, colonization, religion, and war. These interchanges constantly challenged customary ways of thinking and acting. They also led to far-reaching environmental changes, as not only people but also plants and animals crossed the Atlantic in both directions, a process known as the "Columbian exchange." European nations sought to increase their wealth and power by conquering and exploiting the inhabitants of the Americas, whom they deemed noncivilized.

In much of what is now Latin America, the arrival of the Europeans led to conquest. In the future United States and Canada, however, European mastery came more slowly; more than one hundred years would pass before self-sustaining colonies were established there.

AFRICAN AND EUROPEAN BACKGROUNDS

What major changes were reshaping the African and European worlds in the fifteenth and sixteenth centuries?

Even before the emergence of the Atlantic world in the fifteenth and sixteenth centuries, the four continents bordering the Atlantic were changing. In the Americas, societies rose and fell (see Chapter 1). In Africa and Europe, the growth of long-distance trade enabled some states to flourish as a market economy developed alongside older social and religious customs. In Europe, ambitious monarchs joined forces with merchants to propel territorial expansion, the population nearly doubled, societies grew unstable, and an intellectual revolution, the Renaissance, spawned a religious revolution, the Reformation.

West Africa: Tradition and Change

Before the beginning of Atlantic travel, the only link between sub-Saharan Africa and the Mediterranean was a broad belt of grassland, or **savanna,** which separates the desert from the forests to the south. Here caravan trade stimulated the rise of kingdoms and empires whose size and wealth rivaled those of any in Europe.

savanna Rich grasslands where West African civilizations prospered

The richest grassland kingdoms rose in West Africa, with its ample stores of gold. Chief among these in the fifteenth century was Mali, whose Muslim rulers enjoyed access to a network of wealthy Muslim rulers and merchants. Mali's wealth rested on the careful cultivation of trade, and its fame extended throughout Africa, Europe, and the Middle East. Its best-known city, Timbuktu, was famed for its intellectual and academic vitality and its beautiful architecture.

Mali fell victim to internal strife early in the fifteenth century, however; a successor state, Songhai (SONG-high), prospered for less than a century before it was absorbed by Morocco.

Interactive Map: Africa and Its Peoples, c. 1400

To the south of the savanna empires lay a region of small states and chiefdoms. During the first millennium A.D., coastal West Africa was relatively insignificant. During the first millennium A.D., Islamic states arose in Senegambia (seh-nuh-GAM-bee-ah), at Africa's westernmost bulge, and in Guinea's (GINN-ee) coastal forests. The best-known state was Benin (BEH-nin), where artisans fashioned magnificent ironwork for centuries.

Near the Congo River still farther south, four major kingdoms had arisen by the fifteenth century. The most powerful of these kingdoms was Kongo.

When most European nations adopted gold as the standard for their currency in the fifteenth century, gold-rich Guinea's population soared. Thousands of

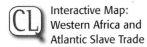

Interactive Map: Western Africa and Atlantic Slave Trade

newcomers from the savanna and Central Africa surged into Africa's "Gold Coast," and new states emerged to capitalize on the precious metal. None was as extensive or powerful as Mali or Ghana at their height.

West African leaders wielded sharply different amounts and kinds of political power. Grassland emperors claimed semigodlike status, which they only thinly disguised if adopting Islam. Rulers of smaller kingdoms depended on their ability to persuade, to conform to custom, and sometimes to redistribute wealth justly among their people.

In West Africa, kinship groups knit societies together. Parents, aunts, uncles, distant cousins, and those who shared clan ties formed networks of mutual obligation. In centuries to come, the tradition of strong extended families would help enslaved Africans to endure the breakup of nuclear families by sale. The region's high mortality rate from famine and tropical disease epidemics was a driving force behind marriage. Children were an essential part of the labor force, contributing to a family's wealth by increasing its food production and the amount of land it cultivated. Men of means frequently married more than one wife in order to produce more children; women generally married soon after puberty.

Both men and women farmed. The high ratio of land to people enabled African farmers to shift their fields periodically and thus maintain high soil quality and productivity. In areas of coastal rain forest, food crops such as yams, sugar cane, bananas, and eggplant flourished; so, too, did cotton. On the grasslands, cattle raising and fishing complemented the cultivation of millet, sorghum, and rice.

By the fifteenth century the market economy took in many small farmers, who traded surplus crops for other food and cloth. Artisans wove cotton or raffia palm leaves, made clothing and jewelry, and crafted tools and religious objects.

Mali Horseman, c. 13th–14th century

This terra-cotta figure originated in Mali, one of several powerful empires in West Africa before the arrival of Europeans.

Religion permeated African life. People believed that another world lay beyond the one they perceived through their five senses, a world to which the souls of most people passed at death. Deities spoke to mortals through a variety of means, including priests, dreams, "speaking shrines," and magical charms. West African religions emphasized the importance of continuous revelations; consequently, there was no fixed dogma or hierarchy like those that characterized both Islam and Christianity. African religion also emphasized ancestor worship, venerating ancestors as spiritual guardians. Religious motifs saturated African art. West Africans used their ivory, cast-iron, and wood sculptures in ceremonies reenacting creation myths and honoring spirits. A strong moralistic streak ran through African folktales. Oral reciters transmitted these stories in dramatic public presentations with ritual masks, dance, and music of complex rhythmic structure. West African art and music powerfully influenced twentieth-century art and jazz.

Chronology

c. 1400–1600	European Renaissance
c. 1400–1600	Coastal West African kingdoms rise and expand
1440	Portuguese slave trade in West Africa begins
1488	Bartolomeu Días reaches the Cape of Good Hope
1492	Christian "reconquest" of Spain; Columbus lands at San Salvador
1498	Vasco da Gama rounds the Cape of Good Hope and reaches India
1517	Protestant Reformation begins in Germany
1519–1521	Hernán Cortés leads conquest of Aztec empire
1519–1522	Magellan's expedition circumnavigates the globe
1532–1536	Spanish conquest of Inca empire
1534	Church of England breaks from Roman Catholic church
1539–1543	De Soto attempts conquests in southeastern America
1541–1542	Cartier attempts to colonize eastern Canada
1558	Elizabeth I becomes queen of England
1565	St. Augustine founded by Spanish
1585–1590	English colony of Roanoke established, then disappears
1588	England defeats the Spanish Armada
1598	Oñate founds New Mexico
1603	James I becomes king of England
1607	English found colonies at Jamestown and Sagadahoc
1608	Champlain founds New France
1609	Henry Hudson explores the Hudson River
1610–1614	First Anglo-Powhatan War
1614	New Netherlands colony founded
1619	Large exports of tobacco from Virginia begin; House of Burgesses, first elected assembly In English North America, established in Virginia; first Africans arrive in Virginia
1620	Plymouth colony founded
1622–1632	Second Anglo-Powhatan War
1624	James I revokes Virginia Company's charter

Among Africans, Islam appealed primarily to merchants trading with Muslim North Africa and to grassland rulers eager to consolidate their power. By 1400, Islam had just begun to affect the daily lives of grassland cultivators and artisans.

European Culture and Society

When Columbus reached the Americas in 1492, Europe was approaching the height of a cultural revival known as the **Renaissance,** a rebirth of classical Greek and Roman culture. Intellectuals and poets believed that their age marked a return to the ideals

Renaissance "Rebirth" of classical Greek and Roman culture that swept Europe from the fifteenth to the seventeenth century

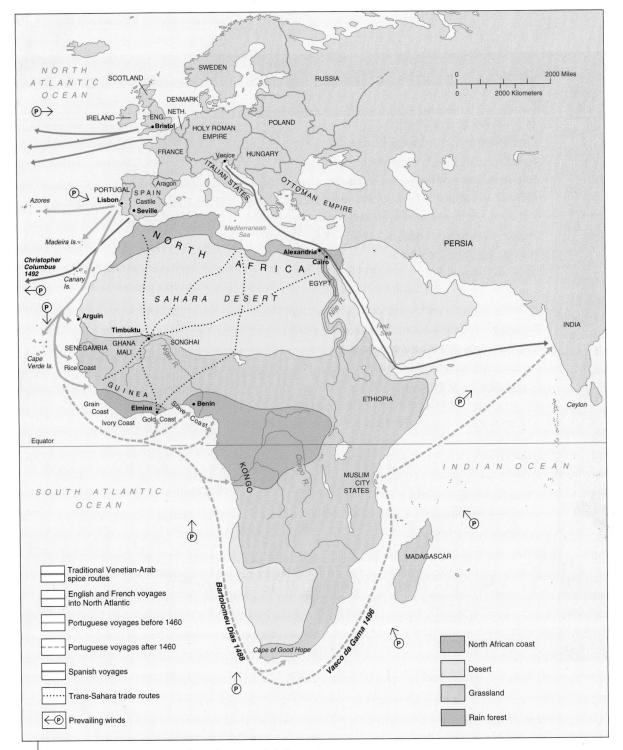

Map 2.1   Europe, Africa, and Southwestern Asia in 1500

During the fifteenth century, Portugal led the way in integrating Europe with Africa in a new Atlantic world. Several voyages near the end of the century extended Europe's reach to India and the Americas.

Legend:
- Traditional Venetian-Arab spice routes
- English and French voyages into North Atlantic
- Portuguese voyages before 1460
- Portuguese voyages after 1460
- Spanish voyages
- Trans-Sahara trade routes
- ←(P) Prevailing winds

- North African coast
- Desert
- Grassland
- Rain forest

of the ancient Greeks and Romans. The writings of Muslim, Eastern Orthodox, and Jewish scholars provided a treasure trove of ancient texts in philosophy, science, medicine, geography, and other subjects. Scholars strove to reconcile Christian faith and ancient philosophy, to explore the mysteries of nature, to map the world, and to explain the motions of the heavens. Renaissance painters and sculptors created works based on close observations of nature and attention to perspective.

At the same time, European society quivered with tension. The era's artistic and intellectual creativity stemmed partly from intense social and spiritual stress, as Europeans groped for stability by glorifying order, hierarchy, and beauty. A concern for power and rank, or "degree," dominated European life in the fifteenth and sixteenth centuries. Gender, wealth, inherited position, and political power affected every European's status, and few people lived beyond the reach of some political authority's claim to tax and rule. But this order was shaky. Conflicts between ranks, between religions, and between rich and poor threatened the balance, making Europeans cling all the more eagerly to order and hierarchy.

Change lay at the heart of these conflicts. By the end of the fifteenth century, strong national monarchs in France and England had unified their realms and reduced the power of both the nobility and the Catholic church. On the Iberian Peninsula, the marriage of King Ferdinand of Aragon and Queen Isabella had created the Spanish monarchy and a unified Spain.

Seventy to eighty percent of Europeans were peasants. Taxes, rents, and other dues to landlords and church officials were heavy. Poor harvests or war drove even well-to-do peasants to starvation.

By 1600 dramatic growth was driving up the population to 100 million. Food supplies, however, did not rise as rapidly. Peasant families survived on pitifully low yields of wheat, barley, and oats. Plowing, sowing, and harvesting together, they also grazed livestock on jointly owned "commons." But with new land at a premium, landlords, especially the English gentry, began to "enclose" the commons, thus making them private property. Peasants with no *written* title to their lands were particularly vulnerable.

Land scarcity and population growth worsened peasants' circumstances, as did a "little Ice Age" that lasted more than four centuries, drastically reducing the food supply. Hunger and malnutrition were widespread, and full-scale famine struck in some areas. Population growth led to increased demand for wood and thus to deforestation of large areas; the subsequent disappearance of wild foods and game accelerated the exodus of rural Europeans to towns and cities.

Although numerous, European towns usually contained only a few thousand inhabitants. London, a great metropolis of 200,000 people by 1600, was an exception. Large or small, towns were dirty and disease ridden, and townspeople lived closely packed with their neighbors. People of the times saw towns as centers of opportunity, and immigration from the countryside swelled urban populations.

The consequences of rapid population growth were acute in England, where the population doubled from 2.5 million in 1500 to 5 million by 1620. Some members of the gentry grew rich selling wool, but because of technological stagnation, per capita output and household income among textile workers fell. In effect, more workers competed for fewer jobs as European markets for English cloth diminished and as food prices rose. Land **enclosure** aggravated unemployment; large numbers

enclosure English practice of fencing off what had been common grazing land; left many peasants impoverished of unemployed workers and displaced farmers wandered the countryside, seeming to threaten law and order. A handful of English writers began to speculate that overseas colonies could serve in effect as a safety valve.

As in the New World and Africa, traditional society in Europe rested on long-term, reciprocal relationships. Reciprocity required the upper classes to act with self-restraint and dignity, and the lower classes to show deference to their "betters." It demanded strict economic regulation, too, to ensure that sellers charged a "just" price—one that covered costs and allowed the seller to profit but barred him from taking advantage of buyers' and borrowers' misfortunes or of shortages to make "excessive" profits.

Yet the ideals of traditional economic behavior had been withering for centuries. By the sixteenth century, nothing could stop the practices of charging interest on borrowed money and of increasing prices in response to demand. New forms of business organization, such as the **joint-stock company,** the ancestor of the modern corporation, steadily spread. Demand for capital investment grew, and so too did the supply of accumulated wealth. Gradually, a new economic outlook arose that justified the unimpeded acquisition of wealth and unregulated economic competition. Its adherents insisted that individuals owed one another only the money necessary to settle each market transaction. This "market economy" capitalism stood counter to traditional demands for the strict regulation of economic activity to ensure social reciprocity and to maintain "just prices."

> **joint-stock company** Forerunner of modern corporation; way to raise large sums of money by selling shares in an enterprise

Sixteenth- and seventeenth-century Europeans were ambivalent about economic enterprise and social change. A restless desire for opportunity kept life simmering with competitive tension. However, even those who prospered still sought the security and prestige of traditional social distinctions, and the poor longed for the age-old values that they hoped would restrain irresponsible greed.

Fundamental change in European society could also be seen in the rising importance of the nuclear family. Each member of the family—father, mother, children—had specific roles. The father exercised supreme authority; the wife bore and reared children, and assisted her husband in the unending labor of providing for the family's subsistence. Children were laborers from an early age. The family was thus the principal economic unit in European society and the household, the primary social organization. Those who lived outside a household were viewed with extreme suspicion and became easy targets for accusations of theft or even witchcraft. Although a father enjoyed full authority over his family in theory, his dependence on his wife's work often limited his authority in practice.

Religious Upheavals

Sixteenth-century Europeans believed in the biblical explanation of the origins of the world and its peoples. Christianity taught that Jesus Christ, God's Son, redeemed sinners through His crucifixion and resurrection. As real as God to European Christians was the devil, Satan, who lured people to damnation by tempting them to do evil. Many sixteenth-century Europeans also believed in witchcraft, magic, and astrology.

Although Jewish and Muslim European minorities shared Christians' worship of a single supreme being, based on the God of the Old Testament, hatred and violence often marred their shared history. European Christians had conducted Crusades against Muslims in the Middle East; each side saw the conflict as "holy war" or "jihad" and labeled the other "infidel." At the same time as the Catholic empires of Spain and Portugal drove Muslims from their territory, the Islamic Ottoman empire conquered much of the Balkans and menaced Central Europe. In 1492 the Spanish completed the "reconquest" of the Iberian peninsula from Muslims and forced Jews to convert or leave.

The medieval Christian church taught that Christ had founded the church to save sinners from hell. Every time a priest said Mass, Christ's sacrifice was repeated, and divine grace flowed to sinners through sacraments that priests alone could administer—especially baptism, confession, and the Eucharist (YOU-kar-ist), or communion. In most of Europe the "church" was a huge network of clergymen set apart from laypeople by ordination into the priesthood and by the fact that they did not marry. The pope, the "vicar (representative) of Christ," topped this hierarchy. His authority reached throughout most of central and western Europe.

The papacy wielded awesome spiritual power. Fifteenth- and sixteenth-century popes claimed the authority to dispense extra blessings, or "indulgences," to repentant sinners in return for "good works," such as donating money to the church. Indulgences also promised time off from future punishment in purgatory. Given people's anxieties over sin, indulgences were enormously popular.

But the sale of indulgences provoked charges of materialism and corruption. In 1517 Martin Luther, a German friar, attacked the practice. When the papacy tried to silence him, Luther broadened his criticism to include the Mass, priests, and the pope. His revolt sparked the **Protestant Reformation,** which changed Christianity forever.

Protestant Reformation Split of reformers from Roman Catholic church; triggered by Martin Luther

To Luther, the selling of indulgences was evil not only because it bilked people but also because the church did harm by falsely assuring people that they could "earn" salvation by doing good works. Luther believed instead that God alone chose whom to save and that believers should trust only God's love, not the word of priests and the pope. Luther's own spiritual struggle and experience of being "reborn" constituted a classic conversion experience—the heart of Protestant religion as it would be preached and practiced for centuries in England and North America.

Later reformers also abandoned Catholicism. For example, the French theologian **John Calvin** insisted on the doctrine of predestination, in which an omnipotent God "predestined" most sinful humans to hell, saving only a few to exemplify his grace. Both Calvinists and Lutherans, as the followers of the two Reformation leaders came to be called, were horrified by radical Protestants, such as the Anabaptists, who criticized the rich and powerful and restricted baptism to adults who had undergone a conversion.

John Calvin Early Protestant theologian who believed in "predestination"

Despite such differences, Protestants shared much common ground. Reading the Bible became an essential element of faith; translations into living languages made the Bible accessible, and the newly invented printing press allowed for wide circulation. Protestantism thus fostered education. Protestants also rejected the idea that priests had special powers; each individual had to assume responsibility for his or her own spiritual and moral condition. Finally, many Protestants felt displaced by the rapidly changing European world and yearned for greater simplicity. Thus Protestantism condemned the replacement of traditional reciprocity by marketplace values.

Challenged by the rise of Protestantism, the Catholic Church displayed remarkable resilience. Indeed, the papacy vigorously attacked church corruption and combated Protestant viewpoints. This Catholic revival, known as the Counter-Reformation, created the modern Roman Catholic church.

The Reformation also split Europe geographically. Many northern and western European areas, including England, most of the German states, the Netherlands, and parts of France, became predominantly Protestant; most southern European states—Portugal, Spain, and Italy—and most of France remained Roman Catholic.

The Reformation in England, 1533–1625

England's Reformation began when King Henry VIII, anxious for a male heir, tried to annul his marriage to Catherine of Aragon. When the pope refused to do so, Henry persuaded Parliament to annul the marriage and then to proclaim him "supreme head" of the Church of England (the Anglican church).

Religious strife troubled England for over a century after Henry's break with Rome. Under his son Edward VI (ruled 1547–1553), however, the English church veered sharply toward Protestantism. Then Henry's daughter Mary assumed the throne in 1553 and tried to restore Catholicism, in part by burning several hundred Protestants at the stake.

The reign of Mary's successor, Elizabeth I, who became queen in 1558, marked a crucial watershed. Most English people were now Protestant; *how* Protestant was the question. A militant Calvinist minority, the **Puritans,** demanded wholesale "purification" of the Church of England from "popish abuses." As Calvinists, they affirmed salvation by predestination, denied Christ's presence in the Eucharist, and believed that a learned sermon was the heart of true worship. They wished to free each congregation from outside interference and encouraged lay members to participate in parish affairs.

Puritans English followers of Calvin, dissenters from established Church of England

Puritanism appealed mainly to the growing middle sectors of English society—the gentry, university-educated clergymen and intellectuals, merchants, shopkeepers, artisans, and well-to-do farmers. Self-discipline had become central to both the worldly and the spiritual dimensions of these people's lives, and from their ranks would come the settlers of New England (see Chapter 3). Puritanism attracted few of the titled nobility, who enjoyed their wealth and privilege, and few of the desperately poor, who were struggling for mere survival.

Queen Elizabeth distrusted Puritan militancy until the pope declared her a heretic in 1570 and urged Catholics to overthrow her. By courting influential Puritans and embracing militant anti-Catholicism, Elizabeth maintained most Puritans' loyalty. But after her death, religious tensions came to a boil.

Under Elizabeth, most Puritans expected to transform the Church of England into independent congregations of "saints." However, Stuart monarchs James I (ruled 1603–1625) and Charles I (ruled 1625–1649) bitterly opposed Puritan efforts to eliminate the office of bishop. Recognizing that Puritan attacks on bishops were a direct threat to his throne, James snapped, "No bishop, no king." Nonetheless, he quietly tolerated Calvinists who did not dissent loudly.

CHECKING IN

- In the fifteenth century the West African savanna fragmented politically, and Islam gained a foothold.
- From the fourteenth to seventeenth centuries, Europe was undergoing major changes. The Renaissance, the rise of nation-states, population growth, the emergence of a market economy, and the Reformation set the stage for territorial expansion and conflict.
- In the throes of religious transformation, Reformation England saw the rise of Puritanism.

EUROPE AND THE ATLANTIC WORLD, 1440–1600

What was the Atlantic world, and how did it emerge?

At the start of the fifteenth century, European wealth was concentrated in the Mediterranean city-states, such as Venice. By the seventeenth century, much of this wealth had shifted to the Atlantic states, where monarchs were consolidating their power over vast territories in Europe and the Americas. Portugal and Spain emerged as the first great Atlantic powers, driving a new European imperialism across the oceans of the world. From this imperialism would emerge both a transatlantic slave trade and the colonization of new lands; these in turn would lead to a new Atlantic world.

Portugal and the Atlantic, 1440–1600

Merchants realized that they could increase their profits by trading directly with Asia and Africa. Leading the shift from a Mediterranean to an Atlantic world was Portugal.

Improved maritime technology permitted this European expansion. In the early fifteenth century, shipbuilders added the triangular Arab sail to their heavy cargo ships, creating a highly maneuverable ship, the caravel, to sail the stormy Atlantic. Further, the growing use of the compass and astrolabe permitted mariners to calculate their bearings on the open sea. Hand in hand with the technological advances of this "maritime revolution," Renaissance scholars corrected ancient geographical data and drew increasingly accurate maps.

Led by **Prince Henry "the Navigator,"** Portugal was first to capitalize on these developments. Henry encouraged Portuguese seamen to pilot their caravels farther down the African coast searching for weak spots in Muslim defenses and for trade opportunities. By the time of Henry's death, the Portuguese had built a profitable slaving station at Arguin; shortly afterward, they had penetrated south of the equator. In 1488 Bartolomeu Días reached Africa's southern tip, the Cape of Good Hope, opening the possibility of direct trade with India, and in 1498 Vasco da Gama led a Portuguese fleet around the cape and on to India. For more than a century the Portuguese remained an imperial presence in the Indian Ocean and the East Indies (modern Indonesia). But far more significantly, they brought Europeans face to face with black Africans.

Prince Henry "the Navigator"
Member of Portuguese royal family who encouraged exploration of Africa, searched for routes to Asia

The "New Slavery" and Racism

Slavery was well established in fifteenth-century West Africa, as elsewhere. The grassland emperors as well as individual families depended on slave labor. But most slaves or their children were absorbed into African families over time. First Arabs, and then Europeans, however, turned African slavery into an intercontinental business.

The Portuguese exploited existing African commercial and social patterns, often trading slaves and local products to other Africans for gold. The local African kingdoms were too strong for the Portuguese to attack, and black rulers traded—or chose not to trade—according to their own self-interest.

African View of the Portuguese, c. 1650–1700

A carver in the kingdom of Benin, on Africa's west coast, created this salt holder depicting Portuguese officials and their ship.

"new slavery" Harsh form of slavery based on racism; arose as a result of Portuguese slave trade with Africa

Interactive Map: Major Transatlantic Explorations, 1000–1587

The coming of the Portuguese slavers changed West African societies. Small kingdoms in Guinea and Senegambia expanded to "service" the trade, and some of their rulers became rich. Farther south, in modern Angola, the kings of Kongo used the slave trade to consolidate their power and adopted Christianity. African kings and their communities used the slave trade to dispose of "undesirables," including troublesome slaves, lawbreakers, and persons accused of witchcraft. But most slaves were simply victims of raids or wars. Muslim and European slave trading greatly stimulated conflicts among communities in Africa.

Europeans had used slaves since ancient Greece and Rome, but ominous changes took place in European slavery once the Portuguese began making voyages to Africa. First, the new slave trade was a high-volume business that expanded at a steady rate as Europeans colonized the Western Hemisphere and established plantation societies there. Between 1500 and 1600, perhaps 250,000 African slaves would reach the New World, and 50,000 would perish en route. Between 1601 and 1621, 200,000 more would arrive. Before the Atlantic slave trade ended in the nineteenth century, nearly 12 million Africans would be shipped across the sea. Slavery on this scale had been unknown since the Roman Empire. Second, African slaves received exceptionally harsh treatment. In medieval Europe, slaves had primarily performed domestic service, but by 1450 the Portuguese and Spanish had created large slave-labor plantations on their Atlantic and Mediterranean islands. Using African slaves who toiled until death, these plantations produced sugar for European markets. Enslaved Africans became property rather than persons of low status, consigned to endless, exhausting, mindless labor. By 1600 the **"new slavery"** had become a brutal link in an expanding commerce that ultimately would encompass all major Western nations.

Finally, race became the explicit basis of the "new slavery." Africans' blackness and alien religion dehumanized them in European eyes. As racial prejudice hardened, Europeans found it easy to justify black slavery. European Christianity, moreover, made few attempts to soften slavery's rigors. Because the victims of the "new slavery" were physically distinctive and culturally alien, slavery became a lifelong, hereditary, and despised status.

To America and Beyond, 1492–1541

The fascinating, contradictory figure of Christopher Columbus (1451–1506) embodied Europeans' varied motives for expansion. The son of an Italian weaver, Columbus became obsessed by the idea that Europeans could reach Asia by sailing westward across the Atlantic. Combining an overestimation of Asia's eastward thrust with an underestimation of the earth's circumference, he concluded that the world was much smaller than it actually is and that the open-sea distance from Europe to Asia was roughly three thousand miles, not the actual twelve thousand miles. Religious fervor led Columbus to dream of carrying Christianity around the globe, but he also hungered for wealth and glory.

Europeans had ventured far into the Atlantic before Columbus: besides the early Norse, fifteenth-century English fishing boats may have reached North America's coast. What distinguished Columbus was his persistence in hawking his "enterprise of the Indies" around Europe's royal courts. In 1492 the rulers of newly united Spain,

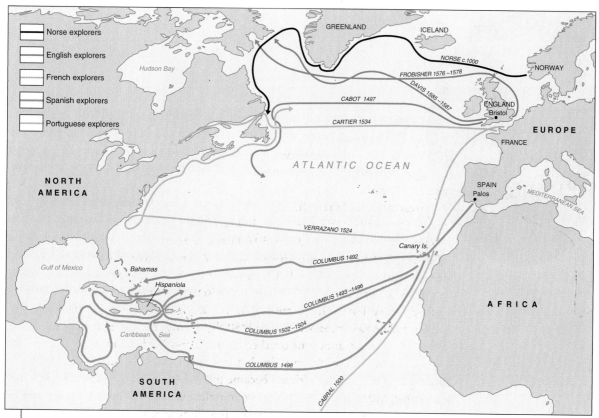

Map 2.2   Major Transatlantic Explorations, 1000–1587
Following Columbus's 1492 voyage, Spain's rivals soon began laying claim to parts of the New World based on the voyages of Cabot for England, Cabral for Portugal, and Verrazano for France. Later English and French exploration focused on finding a passage to Asia around or through Canada.

Isabella of Castile and Ferdinand of Aragon, accepted Columbus's offer, hoping to break a threatened Portuguese monopoly on Asian trade. Picking up the westerly trade winds, Columbus's three small ships made landfall within a month off the North American coast at a small island that he named San Salvador.

Word of Columbus's discovery fired Europeans' imagination. It also induced the Spanish and Portuguese to sign the **Treaty of Tordesillas** (tore-day-SEE-yuss) in 1494, dividing all future discoveries between themselves. Columbus made three further voyages, in the course of which he established Spanish colonies but never fulfilled his promise of reaching Asia. Meanwhile, England's Henry VII (ruled 1485–1509) ignored the Treaty of Tordesillas and sent an Italian navigator known as **John Cabot** westward across the northern Atlantic in 1497. Cabot claimed Nova Scotia, Newfoundland, and the rich Grand Banks fisheries for England, but he vanished at sea on a second voyage. Eighty years would pass before England capitalized on Cabot's voyage.

The more Europeans explored, the more apparent it became that a vast landmass blocked the western route to Asia. In 1500 the Portuguese claimed Brazil, and

Treaty of Tordesillas Agreement in which Portugal and Spain divided between them all future discoveries in the non-Christian world

John Cabot Italian explorer who established English claims to the New World

Christopher Columbus

Christopher Columbus around the time of his first voyage to the Americas.

other voyages outlined a continuous coastline from the Caribbean to Brazil. In 1507 a publisher brought out a collection of voyagers' tales, including one from the Italian Amerigo Vespucci (ves-POO-chee). A shrewd marketer, the publisher devised a catchy name for the new continent: America.

Getting past America to Asia remained the early explorers' goal. In 1513 the Spaniard Vasco Núñez de Balboa crossed the narrow isthmus of Panama and chanced upon the Pacific Ocean. In 1519 the Portuguese mariner Ferdinand Magellan, sailing under the Castilian flag, began a voyage around the world through the stormy straits at South America's southern tip, now named the Straits of Magellan. He crossed the Pacific to the Philippines, only to die fighting with natives. One of his five ships and fifteen emaciated sailors returned to Spain in 1522, the first people to have sailed around the world.

| **Spain's Conquistadors, 1492–1526** |

Columbus was America's first slave trader and the first Spanish *conquistador* (cone-KEES-ta-dohr), or conqueror. On Hispaniola he enslaved native people and created *encomiendas* (en-cohmee-EN-dahs), grants for both land and the labor of the Indians who lived on it.

From the beginning, *encomienderos,* those given the encomiendas, harshly exploited the native people. As disease, overwork, and malnutrition killed thousands of Indians, Portuguese slave traders supplied shiploads of Africans to replace them. Although shocked Spanish friars sent to convert the Native Americans reported the Indians' exploitation, and King Ferdinand attempted to forbid the practice, no one worried about African slaves' fate. Spanish settlers were soon fanning out across the Caribbean in pursuit of slaves and gold. In 1519 the young nobleman **Hernán Cortés** (core-TEZ) (1485–1547) led a small band of Spaniards to the Mexican coast. Destroying his boats and enlisting Indian allies, he marched inland to conquer Mexico.

Upon reaching the Aztec capital of Tenochtitlán (see Chapter 1), the Spanish were stunned by its size and wealth. The Spanish raided the imperial palace and treasury, melting down all the gold they could find. But the Aztecs regrouped and recaptured the city. Then an epidemic of smallpox, which the Aztecs and other Indians were ill equipped to resist, plus reinforcements from Cuba, enabled Cortés to defeat the Aztecs. By 1521 the Spanish had begun to build Mexico City on the ruins of Tenochtitlán. Within twenty years, Central America lay at the Spaniards' feet. Thus was New Spain born.

Over the remainder of the sixteenth century, conquistadors and officials established a great Spanish empire stretching from Mexico to Chile. The Inca empire represented the most important conquest, thanks to smallpox and Inca unfamiliarity

Hernán Cortés Spanish conqueror of Aztec empire

CL Primary Source: Spanish Monk Pleads for Better Treatment of the Indians with European weapons. The human cost of the Spanish empire was enormous. When Cortés landed in 1519, central Mexico had been home to between 13 and 25 million people. By 1600 the population had shrunk to 700,000. Peru and other regions witnessed similar devastation in the greatest demographic disaster in world history.

Map 2.3   The Spanish and Portuguese Empires, 1610

By 1610 Spain dominated Latin America, including Portugal's possessions. Having devoted its energies to exploiting Mexico and the Caribbean, Spain had not yet expanded into what is now the United States, aside from establishing outposts in Florida and New Mexico.

The Columbian Exchange

The Spanish conquest came at enormous human cost. Disease, not war or slavery, was the greatest killer. Native Americans lacked resistance to European and African infections, especially the deadly, highly communicable smallpox. From the first years of contact with Europeans, terrible epidemics decimated Indian communities. In the West Indies the native population vanished within a half-century, and disease opened the mainland for conquest as well.

The **"Columbian exchange"**—the biological encounter of the Old and New Worlds—went beyond deadly germs. Europeans brought horses, cattle, sheep, swine, chickens, wheat, coffee, sugar cane, and numerous fruits and vegetables with them, as well as an astonishing variety of weeds. African slaves carried rice and yams across the Atlantic. The list of American gifts to Europe and Africa was equally impressive: it included corn, white and sweet potatoes, many varieties of beans, tomatoes, squash, pumpkins, peanuts, vanilla, chocolate, avocados, pineapples, chilis, tobacco, and turkeys. European weeds and domesticated animals often overwhelmed indigenous plant life and drove away native animals, especially in North America. Settlers' crops, intensively cultivated on land never allowed to lie fallow, frequently exhausted American soil. Nonetheless, the worldwide exchange of food products enriched human diets and made possible enormous population growth. Today, nearly 60 percent of all food crops worldwide trace their roots to the Native American garden.

"Columbian exchange"
Exchange of people, plants, animals within the Atlantic world as a result of European voyages

Another dimension of the emergence of the Atlantic world was the mixing of peoples. Within Spain's empire, a great human intermingling occurred. From 1500 to 1600 about 300,000 Spaniards immigrated to the New World, 90 percent of them male. A racially mixed population developed, particularly in towns. Spaniards fathered numerous children with African or Indian mothers; most of the former were slaves. Such racial mixing would occur, although far less commonly, in French and English colonies as well.

The Americas supplied seemingly endless wealth for Spain. West Indian sugar plantations and Mexican sheep and cattle ranches enriched many. Much of Spain's wealth, however, was dug from the silver mines of Mexico and Peru. After 1540, enormous amounts of silver flowed across the Atlantic, far more than the small Spanish economy could absorb, setting off inflation that eventually engulfed Europe. But, bent on dominating Europe, Spanish kings needed even more silver to pay for their ships and armies. Several times they went bankrupt, and in the 1560s their efforts to squeeze more taxes from their subjects provoked revolt in Spain's Dutch provinces. In the end, gaining access to American wealth cost the Spanish dearly.

FOOTHOLDS IN NORTH AMERICA, 1512–1625

How did European exploration, conquest, and colonization of North America begin?

Spain's New World wealth attracted other Europeans. Throughout the sixteenth century, they sailed the North American coast, exploring, fishing, trading for furs, and smuggling. But, except for a Spanish fort at St. Augustine, Florida, all sixteenth-century attempts at colonizing North America failed. Unrealistic dreams of easy wealth and pliant Indians brought French, English, and Spanish attempts to grief. Only the ravaging of the Indians by disease, declining Spanish power, and rising French, Dutch, and English power finally made colonization possible.

In 1607–1608 the English and French established permanent colonies. By 1614 the Dutch had followed. Within a generation, North America's modern history took shape as each colony developed an economic orientation and its own approach to Native Americans.

Spain's Northern Frontier

The Spanish built their New World empire by subduing the Aztecs, Inca, and other Indian states. The dream of finding even more wealth drew would-be conquistadors to lands north of Mexico.

Earliest came Juan Ponce de León (wahn PON-say deh lee-OWN), the conqueror of Puerto Rico, who trudged through Florida in search of gold and slaves twice, in 1512–1513 and in 1521, and then died in an Indian skirmish. The most astonishing early expedition began when three hundred explorers left Florida in 1527 to explore the Gulf of Mexico. Indian attacks whittled their numbers until only a handful survived. Stranded in Texas, the survivors, led by Cabeza de Vaca (cuh-BAY-zuh deh VAH-cah), moved from Indian tribe to tribe, at first as slaves, later as traders and medicine men. They finally made their way south to Mexico in 1536.

As de Soto roamed the Southeast, the Southwest drew others with dreams of conquest, lured by rumors that the fabled Seven Golden Cities of Cíbola (SEE-bow-lah) lay north of Mexico. In 1538 an expedition sighted the Zuñi (ZOO-nyee) pueblos and assumed them to be the golden cities.

For decades after these failures, Spain's principal interest in the lands north of Mexico lay in establishing a few strategic bases in Florida to keep out intruders. In 1565 Spain planted the first successful European settlement on mainland North America, the fortress of St. Augustine. Spanish missionaries moved north from the fortress to establish religious missions as far north as the Chesapeake (CHESS-uh-peak) Bay, but Indian resistance and epidemic disease ended their efforts shortly before 1600.

Navajo View of Spanish Colonizers

This pictograph—a painting or drawing on rock—was sketched in the early colonial period in Cañón del Muerto, Arizona. Cabeza de Vaca inspired other would-be conquerors. In 1539–1543 Hernando de Soto and his party blundered from Tampa Bay to the Appalachians and back to southern Texas, scouring the land for gold and harrying the Indians. Although de Soto died without finding gold or conquering any Indians, his and other expeditions touched off epidemics that destroyed most of the remaining Mississippian societies.

Meanwhile, in the 1580s, the Spanish had returned to the southwestern pueblo country, preaching Christianity and scouting for wealth. In 1598 Juan de Oñate (oh-NYAH-tee) led five hundred Spaniards into the upper Rio Grande Valley, where he proclaimed the royal colony of New Mexico. When Acoma Indians refused his demands for provisions in December 1598, Oñate ordered massive retaliation. In January, Spanish troops captured the pueblo, killing more than eight hundred inhabitants. Oñate then forced surviving men to have one foot cut off and sent them, along with women and children, to become servants.

The new colony barely survived. In 1606 the Spanish replaced Oñate because of his excessive brutality. Determined to succeed, by 1630 Franciscan missionaries had established more than fifty pueblo missions stretching along the Rio Grande and had converted about 20,000 Indians.

Colonizing Canada

France made its first attempt at colonizing North America in 1541, when ten ships sailed into the St. Lawrence Valley. Having alienated many of the Indians along the St. Lawrence in two previous expeditions, Jacques Cartier built a fortified settlement on Indian land and thus ended all possibility of peaceful Indian-French relations. Steady Indian attacks and scurvy (for which the Indians could have shown them a cure) drove the French off within two years.

This fiasco underlined one Spaniard's view that "this whole coast as far [south] as Florida is utterly unproductive." In 1562 French Huguenots (HYEW-guh-nots) (Calvinists) made the next French attempt at colonization, establishing a base in modern South Carolina. Two years later they founded a settlement in Florida, which

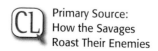
Primary Source:
How the Savages
Roast Their Enemies

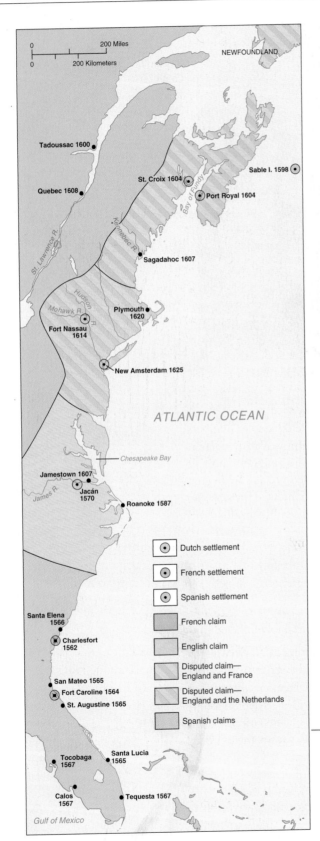

Map 2.4   European Imperial Claims and Settlements in Eastern North America, 1565–1625

By 1625, four European nations contended for territory on North America's Atlantic coast. Except for St. Augustine, Florida, all settlements established before 1607 had been abandoned by 1625.

the Spanish quickly destroyed. These failures, as well as a civil war between French Catholics and Huguenots, ended France's first attempts at colonization.

Meanwhile, French and other European fishermen worked the teeming Grand Banks off the coast of Newfoundland. Going ashore to dry their catch, French sailors bartered with Indians for beaver pelts; by the late sixteenth century, as European demands for beaver hats soared, a French-dominated fur trade blossomed.

Most traders, unlike explorers or colonizers, recognized the need for reciprocity in dealing with Native Americans; consequently, trade flourished. Glass beads were a mainstay of this trade, for Indians believed that the beads possessed spiritual power comparable to that of quartz, mica, and other sacred substances. To deter potential competitors, the French dispatched Samuel de Champlain to establish the colony of New France at Quebec in 1608. Familiar with Indian politics and diplomacy, Champlain built alliances with the Montagnais (MON-tan-yay) and Algonquins (al-GON-kwins) of the St. Lawrence and with the Hurons of the lower Great Lakes by promising to help them defeat their enemies the Mohawks.

In July 1609 Champlain and Indian allies encountered a substantial Mohawk force near the southern tip of Lake Champlain (which the explorer had named for himself). In the ensuing Battle of Lake Champlain, more than fifty Mohawks died and a dozen were captured. The battle marked the beginning of a deadly era of trade, diplomacy, and warfare. Through their alliance with the Hurons, the French gained access to the thick beaver pelts of the interior in exchange for European goods and protection against the Mohawks and other Iroquois. These economic and diplomatic arrangements defined the course of New France's history for the rest of the seventeenth century.

England and the Atlantic World, 1558–1603

When Elizabeth I became queen in 1558, England, a second-rank power, stood on the sidelines as Spain and France grappled for European supremacy. Religious division and domestic instability preoccupied the English. They hoped to cure the country's economic woes by founding colonies overseas, but Spain blocked the way.

Meanwhile, England's position in Ireland had deteriorated. By 1565 English troops were fighting to impose Elizabeth's rule throughout the island, where a Protestant English government was battling Irish Catholic rebels aided by Spain. In a war that ground on through the 1580s, English troops drove the Irish clans from their strongholds and established "plantations," or settlements, of Scottish and English Protestants. The English resorted to a "scorched earth policy" of starvation and mass slaughter to break the Irish spirit. Elizabeth's generals justified these atrocities by calling the Irish "savages." The Irish experience gave England strategies that it later used against North American Indians, whose customs, religion, and methods of fighting seemed to absolve the English from guilt in waging exceptionally cruel warfare.

England had two objectives in the Western Hemisphere in the 1570s. The first was to find the northwest passage to Asia, preferably one lined with gold. The second, as Sir Francis Drake said, was to "singe the king of Spain's beard" by raiding Spanish fleets and cities. The search for a northwest passage proved fruitless, but the English did stage spectacularly successful and profitable privateering raids against the Spanish. The most breathtaking enterprise of the era was Drake's voyage around the world in 1577–1580 in quest of sites for colonies.

In 1587 Sir Walter Raleigh, dreaming of founding an American colony where English, Indians, and even blacks freed from Spanish slavery could live together amicably, sponsored a colony on **Roanoke** Island, off the modern North Carolina coast. An earlier attempt (1585–1586) had failed, in part because the colonists refused to grow their own food, expecting the Indians to feed them, and wore out their welcome. One hundred ten colonists, many of them members of families, reached Roanoke in late summer 1587. Almost immediately the colony's leader, John White, returned to England for more supplies, leaving the settlers behind.

Roanoke Site of first English attempt at New World colonization; failure

Spain's attempt to crush England with the Great Armada in 1588 prevented White from returning to Roanoke until 1590. When he did, he found only rusty armor, moldy books, and the word CROATOAN (CROW-uh-tan) carved into a post. To this day, no one knows exactly what happened to the "Lost Colony," although they were probably living among the nearby Croatoan Indians. The miserable failure at Roanoke would postpone the establishment of English colonies for seventeen more years.

However, England's victory over the Spanish Armada in 1588 preserved English independence and confirmed its status as a major Atlantic power.

Failure and Success in Virginia, 1603–1625

Two events opened the way for English colonization: peace with Spain and the emergence of the joint-stock company. In the peace between England and Spain, concluded in 1604 by Elizabeth's successor, James I (ruled 1603–1625), the Spanish not only agreed to peace but also renounced their claims to Virginia, leaving England a free hand. At the same time, the development of joint-stock companies, which could amass money through sales of stock, created a way for potential colonizers to raise large sums of money with limited risk for the individual investor.

On April 10, 1606, James I granted charters to two separate joint-stock companies, one based in London and the other in Plymouth. The **Virginia Company of Plymouth** received a grant extending from modern Maine to the Potomac River; the **Virginia Company of London** received a grant from Cape Fear north to the Hudson River. The grants overlapped, with the land in question to go to the first successful colonizer. Both companies dispatched colonists in 1607.

The Virginia Company of Plymouth sent 120 men to Sagadahoc at the mouth of the Kennebec River in Maine. The following year, the colony disintegrated, the victim of Indian hostility (generally provoked) and the hard Maine winter. The company subsequently became dormant. The Virginia Company of London dispatched 105 settlers to a site on the James River near Chesapeake Bay that they named **Jamestown.** But the first colonists, who included many members of the gentry, hunted for gold and failed to plant crops. When relief ships arrived in January 1608, they found only 38 survivors.

Near anarchy reigned at Jamestown until September 1608, when desperate councilors, representatives of the Virginia Company of London, turned to a brash soldier of fortune, Captain **John Smith.** Only twenty-eight, Smith found that his experiences fighting the Spanish and the Turks had prepared him well to assume control in Virginia. By instituting harsh discipline, organizing the settlers, and requiring them to build houses and plant food, he ensured Jamestown's survival. During the winter of 1608–1609, Smith lost just twelve men out of two hundred.

Smith also became the colony's best diplomat. After local Indians captured him late in 1607, Smith displayed such impressive courage that Powhatan (pow-uh-TAN), the leader of the nearby Powhatan Confederacy, arranged an elaborate ceremony in which Pocahontas, his daughter, "saved" Smith's life during a mock execution. This gesture was meant to remind the English that Powhatan's people were the stronger force and that reciprocity rather than force should govern their dealings with one another. Powhatan expected that the English would become his allies against local tribal enemies. Smith maintained satisfactory relations with the Powhatan Confederacy partly through his personality and partly through calculated demonstrations of English military strength.

When serious injuries forced Smith to return to England in 1609, discipline again crumbled. Expecting the Indians to furnish corn, the settlers had not laid away enough food for winter. One colonist reported that Jamestown residents ate dogs, cats, rats, and snakes in order to survive. He gruesomely added that "many besides fed on the corpses of dead men." Of the 500 residents at Jamestown in September 1609, only 100 lived to May 1610. An influx of new recruits and the imposition of military rule, however, enabled Virginia to win the First Anglo-Powhatan War (1610–1614) and, by 1611, to expand west to modern Richmond. The English population remained small—only 380 by 1616—and produced nothing of value for the stockholders.

Tobacco saved Virginia. **John Rolfe,** an Englishman who married Pocahontas, perfected a salable variety of tobacco for planting there, and by 1619 Virginia was ex-

---

Virginia Company of Plymouth Received charter to establish colonies from Chesapeake Bay northward

Virginia Company of London Received charter to establish colonies from Chesapeake Bay southward; founded Jamestown

Jamestown First successful English colony, established in 1607

John Smith Soldier of fortune who "saved" Jamestown by establishing order, good relations with Indians

John Rolfe Brought tobacco to Jamestown, thus ensuring its economic survival porting large, profitable amounts of the crop. Thereafter the Virginia Company poured supplies and settlers into the colony.

To attract labor and capital, the company awarded fifty-acre land grants ("headrights") to anyone paying his or her own passage or that of a laborer. By financing the passage of indentured servants, planters could accumulate large tracts of land. Thousands of single young men and a few hundred women became indentured servants, choosing the uncertainty of Virginia over poverty in England. In return for their passage, they worked a fixed term, usually four to seven years.

In 1619 the Virginia Company ended military rule and provided for an elected assembly, the **House of Burgesses.** Although the company could veto the assembly's actions, 1619 marked the beginning of representative government in North America. However, Virginia still faced three serious problems. First, local officials systematically defrauded shareholders, in the process sinking the company deeply into debt. Second, the colony's death rate soared. Malnutrition, salt poisoning, typhus, and dysentery (from drinking polluted river water), killed thousands of immigrants. Third, Indian relations worsened. After Powhatan's death in 1618, the new leader, Opechancanough (oh-peh-can-CUH-noo), worried about the relentless expansion of the English colony. In 1622 the Indians killed 347 of the 1,200 settlers in a surprise attack. With their livestock destroyed, spring planting impossible, and disease spreading through crowded stockades, hundreds more colonists died in the ensuing months.

The Virginia Company sent more men, and Governor Francis Wyatt took the offensive. Using tactics developed during the Irish war, Wyatt destroyed the Indians' food supplies, conducted winter campaigns to drive them from their homes when they would suffer most, and fought (according to John Smith) as if he had "just cause to destroy them by all means possible." By 1625 the English had won the Second Powhatan War, and the Indians had lost their best chance of forcing out the intruders.

But the struggle bankrupted the Virginia Company. After receiving complaints about its management, James I revoked its charter and made Virginia a royal colony in 1624. Only five hundred Old World settlers lived there, including a handful of Africans who had been brought in since 1619. With its combination of fabulous profits, unfree labor, and massive mortality, Virginia was truly a land of contradictions.

Primary Source:
A Virginia Case
Involving Runaway
Indentured Servants

House of Burgesses First elected representative legislature in New World, in Virginia; first met in 1619

New England Begins, 1614–1625

After Virginia, the next permanent English settlements appeared in New England. Along the coast, a terrible epidemic had devastated the Indian population by about 90 percent in 1616–1618. In 1620 the Virginia Company of London granted a patent for a settlement to a group of English merchants, who dispatched eighteen families (102 people) in a small, leaky ship, the *Mayflower.* The colonists promised to send back lumber, furs, and fish for seven years, after which they would own the tract.

The expedition's leaders, and half its members, belonged to a small religious community from the northern English town of Scrooby. Separatist Puritans, they had earlier fled to the Netherlands to practice their religion freely. Fearing that their children were adopting Dutch ways, they decided to immigrate to America.

In November 1620 the *Mayflower* landed at **Plymouth,** outside the bounds of Virginia. Because they had no legal right to be there, the leaders forced the adult

Plymouth Colony established by Pilgrims in Massachusetts

Mayflower Compact Agreement signed by Pilgrims to govern themselves

males in the group to sign the **Mayflower Compact** before they landed. By this document they constituted themselves a "civil body politic"—a civil government—under James I's sovereignty and established the colony of Plymouth Plantation.

Weakened by their journey and unprepared for winter, half the Pilgrims, as they were later called, died within four months. Two Indians helped the others to survive: Squanto, a local Patuxet, and Samoset (SAM-oh-sett), an Abenaki (aah-beh-NAH-key) from Maine who had traded with the English. To stop the Pilgrims from stealing their food, the Indians taught the newcomers how to grow corn. Squanto and Samoset also arranged an alliance between the Pilgrims and the local Wampanoag (wahm-puh-NO-ag) Indians, who were headed by Chief Massasoit (MASS-uh-soyt).

Plymouth's relations with the Indians soon worsened. Learning of the Virginia massacre of 1622, the Pilgrims militarized their colony and threatened their Indian "allies" with their monopoly of firepower. Within a decade, Plymouth had attracted several hundred colonists and had become economically self-sufficient. After they abandoned communal farming for individually owned plots, prosperous farmers produced corn surpluses that they traded for furs. Prosperity allowed Plymouth's elite to buy out the colony's London backers.

Plymouth colony had three lasting influences. It constituted an outpost of Puritans dissenting from the Church of England, proved that a self-governing society could exist in New England, and foreshadowed the aggressive methods that would give Europeans mastery over the Indians. Plymouth represented the vanguard of a massive migration of Puritans to New England in the 1630s (see Chapter 3).

New Amsterdam Dutch colony that would become New York

A "New Netherland" on the Hudson, 1609–1625

The Dutch-speaking provinces of the Netherlands were among the most fervently Calvinist regions of Europe. Ruled by the Spanish during the sixteenth century and alienated by high taxes and religious intolerance, the Dutch rebelled in 1566. More than forty years later, in 1609, Spain and the Dutch Republic signed a truce. By then the Netherlands was a wealthy commercial power whose empire stretched from Brazil to South Africa to Taiwan. It would play a key role in colonizing North America.

In 1609 Henry Hudson sailed up the broad, deep river that today bears his name, and in the next year Dutch ships sailed up the Hudson to trade with Indians. In 1614 they began their New Netherland colony by establishing Fort Nassau at the site of modern Albany, New York, and in 1625 planted another fort on an island at the mouth of the Hudson. Within two years, Peter Minuit, director-general of the colony, bought the island from local Indians, named it Manhattan, and began a settlement christened **New Amsterdam.**

Furs, particularly beaver pelts, became the New Netherlanders' chief economic staple. The Mohawks, as well as the other nations of the Iroquois Confederacy, became the Dutch colonists' chief suppliers of furs and soon found themselves embroiled in competition with the French-supported Hurons.

CHECKING IN

- Pushing northward from their New World empire, Spanish explorers roamed the American Southwest, and conquistadors conquered the Pueblo Indians.

- Early French colonies based on agriculture barely survived, but the French fur trade with Indians of the interior prospered.

- The first English colony, Roanoke, failed, but Jamestown and Plymouth survived despite hardship.

- The Dutch established New Amsterdam at the mouth of the Hudson River and relied on the fur trade.

Chapter Summary

DOWNLOAD THE MP3 AUDIO FILE OF THE CHAPTER SUMMARY, AND LISTEN TO IT ON THE GO.

What major changes were reshaping the African and European worlds in the fifteenth and sixteenth centuries? (page 17)

The fifteenth and sixteenth centuries were times of tumultuous change in both West Africa and Europe. In the West African savannah, powerful kingdoms such as Mali gave way to more fragmented political structures. In Europe, the Renaissance, the Reformation, a population boom, and the emergence of the market economy created new tensions as well as new opportunities. In England, the Reformation led to the rise of Puritanism, which found itself in a tense relationship with the monarchy.

What was the Atlantic world, and how did it emerge? (page 25)

The Atlantic world began to open as Portuguese explorers traveled along the African coast; one sad result of this was the "new slavery," based primarily on race. Spanish explorers such as Columbus, Balboa, and Magellan opened the way for the creation of an empire that would encompass both the Aztecs and the Inca in the Americas. Plants, animals, drugs, and diseases crossed the Atlantic in both directions in the "Columbian exchange."

How did European exploration, conquest, and colonization of North America begin? (page 30)

The Spanish explored large parts of North America, conquered the Pueblo Indians of the Southwest, and incorporated them into their empire. Although France attempted to plant agricultural colonies, its primary success lay in establishing the fur trade with the Indians of the interior. After failure at Roanoke, Englishmen successfully planted colonies at Jamestown in Virginia and at Plymouth in Massachusetts. The Dutch established New Amsterdam.

KEY TERMS

savanna (p. 17)
Renaissance (p. 19)
enclosure (p. 21)
joint-stock company (p. 22)
Protestant Reformation (p. 23)
John Calvin (p. 23)
Puritans (p. 24)
Prince Henry "the Navigator" (p. 25)
"new slavery" (p. 26)
Treaty of Tordesillas (p. 27)
John Cabot (p. 27)
Hernán Cortés (p. 28)
"Columbian exchange" (p. 29)
Roanoke (p. 33)
Virginia Company of Plymouth (p. 34)
Virginia Company of London (p. 34)
Jamestown (p. 34)
John Smith (p. 34)
John Rolfe (p. 34)
House of Burgesses (p. 35)
Plymouth (p. 35)
Mayflower Compact (p. 36)
New Amsterdam (p. 36)

CHAPTER 3

The Emergence of Colonial Societies

1625–1700

Sir William Berkeley

CHAPTER PREVIEW

Chesapeake Society
How did tobacco shape the Chesapeake colonies?

Puritanism in New England
What was the "New England Way," and what challenges did it endure?

The Spread of Slavery: The Caribbean and Carolina
Why and how did plantation agriculture shape slavery in the Caribbean and Carolina?

The Middle Colonies
How did diversity distinguish the Middle Colonies?

Rivals for North America: France and Spain
How did the French and Spanish empires develop in the seventeenth century?

The seventeenth century witnessed a flood of English migration across the Atlantic. In 1600 no English person lived along the North American seacoast. By 1700, however, about 225,000 people of English birth or ancestry were dwelling in what would become the United States. Large numbers of Dutch, French, Spanish, Irish, Scottish, and German settlers joined them. A second wave carried 300,000 West Africans to the English colonies, about 10 percent of whom arrived in North America. Whereas English immigrants to America hoped to realize economic opportunity or religious freedom, Africans and their descendants were owned by others. The majority of Africans taken to the English colonies went to West Indies sugar plantations. A third demographic upheaval, the depopulation and uprooting of Native Americans, made these two other migrations possible. Epidemic disease did much of the work of destroying the Indians, but warfare played an important role as well. About 1 million Indians had died as a result of contact with Europeans by 1700.

Indian depopulation and European and African immigration transformed North America in the seventeenth century. Europeans expanded their territorial domains and established colonial societies from the St. Lawrence River to the Rio Grande, increasing the continent's cultural diversity.

English immigrants, and English capital, ensured that England would dominate the East Coast as well as the Caribbean; by 1700 the English would force out the Dutch and leave France and Spain with lands less attractive to colonists. Four distinct regions emerged within England's mainland colonies: New England, the Chesapeake, Carolina, and the Middle Colonies, each shaped by its environment, the motives of white immigrants, and the concentrations of enslaved Africans.

CHESAPEAKE SOCIETY

How did tobacco shape the Chesapeake colonies?

Thanks to the tobacco boom of the 1620s, the English colonies on the Chesapeake Bay—Virginia and Maryland—were the first in North America to prosper. They shared similar economies, populations, and patterns of growth that gave them a distinct regional identity. Chesapeake society was highly unequal and unstable. Life for most colonists was short and living conditions poor. Not until English colonists seized large amounts of Native American land to grow tobacco and shifted from white indentured servants to black slaves did they finally achieve stability.

State and Church in Virginia

James I planned to rule Virginia through appointed officials, but Virginians petitioned repeatedly for the restoration of their elected assembly, the first in the New World. James I's successor, Charles I, grudgingly relented in 1628, but only to induce the assembly to tax tobacco exports so as to transfer the cost of government from the crown to Virginia's taxpayers. After 1630, seeking more taxes, Virginia's royal governors called regular assemblies. During the 1650s the assembly split into two chambers, the elected House of Burgesses and the appointed Governor's Council.

View of Jamestown, 1625
As Virginia's tobacco production boomed, the capital expanded beyond the fort that had originally confined it.

Primary Source:
Indentured Servant's
Confession

Local government officials were appointed, rather than elected, during Virginia's first quarter-century. In 1634 Virginia adopted England's county-court system. Appointed by the royal governor, justices of the peace acted as judges, set local tax rates, paid county officials, and oversaw the construction and maintenance of roads, bridges, and public buildings. Thus unelected county courts became the basic unit of local government south of New England.

In contrast to Puritan New England, Virginia had the Church of England as its established church. Anglican vestries governed each parish; elected vestrymen handled church finances, determined poor relief, and investigated complaints against the minister. Taxpayers were legally obliged to pay fixed rates to the Anglican church. Because of the large distances between settlements and churches, as well as a chronic shortage of clergymen, few Virginians regularly attended services. In 1662 Virginia had just ten ministers to serve its forty-five parishes.

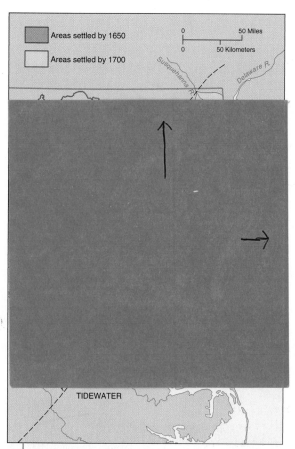

Areas settled by 1650

Areas settled by 1700

0   50 Miles
0   50 Kilometers

Susquehanna R.

Delaware R.

TIDEWATER

Map 3.1   Chesapeake Expansion, 1607–1700

The Chesapeake colonies expanded slowly before midcentury. By 1700, Anglo-Indian wars, a rising English population, and an influx of enslaved Africans permitted settlers to spread throughout the tidewater.

State and Church in Maryland

Beginning in the 1630s, grants by the crown to reward English politicians replaced joint-stock companies as the primary mechanism of colonization. The first such grant, or proprietorship, went in 1632 to Lord Baltimore (Cecilius Calvert); he named the large tract east of Chesapeake Bay "Maryland" in honor of England's Queen Henrietta Maria. Lord Baltimore enjoyed broad power, lessened only by the stipulations that an elected assembly had to approve all laws and that the crown would control both war and trade.

With Charles I's consent, Baltimore intended to make Maryland a refuge for England's Catholics, who could neither worship in public nor hold political office and who had to pay tithes to the Anglican church. To make Maryland a haven, Baltimore tried to install the old English manor system. In theory, a manor lord would employ a Catholic priest as chaplain and allow others to hear Mass and to receive the sacraments on the manor. In practice, this arrangement never worked, for relatively few Catholics settled in Maryland, which was overwhelmingly Protestant from the beginning. Cheap land lured settlers who did not need to become tenants on the manors, and Baltimore's scheme fell apart. By 1675 all sixty of Maryland's nonproprietary manors had become plantations.

Religious tension gradually developed in Maryland society. The Protestant majority dominated the elected lower house of government, but many Catholics had become large landowners, held high public office, and dominated the appointive upper house. Until 1642, Catholics and Protestants shared the chapel at St. Mary's, the capital, but they began to argue over its use. As antagonisms in-

Chronology

1628	Massachusetts Bay colony founded
1630–1642	"Great migration" to North America
1633	First English settlements in Connecticut
1634	Lord Baltimore founds Maryland
1636	Roger Williams founds Providence, Rhode Island; Harvard College established
1637	Antinomian crisis in Massachusetts Bay; Pequot War in Connecticut
1638	New Sweden established
1642–1648	English Civil War
1644–1646	Third Anglo-Powhatan War in Virginia
1649	Maryland's Act for Religious Toleration; King Charles I beheaded
1655	New Netherland annexes New Sweden
1660	Restoration in England; Charles II becomes king
1661	Maryland defines slavery as a lifelong, inheritable racial status
1662	Half-Way Covenant adopted
1664	English conquer New Netherland; establish New York and New Jersey
1670	Charles Town, Carolina, established; Virginia defines slavery as a lifelong, inheritable racial status
1675–1676	King Philip's War in New England
1675–1676	Bacon's Rebellion in Virginia
1680	Pueblo Revolt begins in New Mexico
1681	William Penn founds Pennsylvania
1682	La Salle claims Louisiana for France
1691	Spain establishes Texas
1692–1693	Salem witchcraft trials
1692–1700	Spain "reconquers" New Mexico
1698	First French settlements in Louisiana

tensified, Baltimore drafted, and the assembly passed, the Act for Religious Toleration (1649).

Unfortunately, the toleration act did not secure religious peace. In 1654 the Protestant majority barred Catholics from voting; ousted Governor William Stone, a pro-tolerance Protestant; and repealed the Toleration Act. Stone raised an army, both Protestant and Catholic, to regain the government but met defeat at the Battle of the Severn River in 1655. The victors imprisoned Stone and hanged three Catholic leaders. Maryland remained in Protestant hands until 1658. Although Lord Baltimore was restored to control that year (ironically, at the command of English Puritans), Protestant resistance to Catholic political influence continued to cause problems in Maryland.

Primary Source:
Marcy Freeman
Headstone

Death, Gender, and Kinship

So few women immigrated to the Chesapeake that, before 1650, only one-third of male servants could find brides and then only after completing their indenture. Female scarcity gave women an advantage in negotiating favorable marriages. Many female indentured servants married prosperous planters who paid off their remaining time of service.

Death ravaged Chesapeake society and left domestic life exceptionally fragile. In 1650 malaria joined the killer diseases typhoid, dysentery, and salt poisoning as the marshy lowlands of the tidewater Chesapeake became fertile breeding grounds for the mosquitoes that spread malaria. Life expectancy in the 1600s was twenty years lower in the Chesapeake than in New England. Servants died at appalling rates; 40 percent were dead within a decade of arrival and 70 percent before reaching age fifty.

Chesapeake widows often enjoyed substantial property rights. The region's men wrote wills giving their wives perpetual and complete control of their estate, so that their own children could inherit it. Although a widow in such circumstances had a degree of economic independence, she faced enormous pressure to remarry, particularly a man who could produce income by farming her fields.

The lopsided sex ratio and high death rates contributed to slow population growth in the Chesapeake. Although perhaps 100,000 English immigrated to the Chesapeake between 1630 and 1700, the white population was just 70,000 in 1700. In contrast, the benign disease environment and more balanced gender ratio of New England allowed that region's 28,000 white immigrants to burgeon to 91,000 during the same time period. Change came gradually as children acquired childhood immunities, life spans lengthened, and the sex ratio evened out. By 1720 most Chesapeake residents were native born.

Tobacco Shapes a Region, 1630–1670

Chesapeake settlers were scattered across the landscape. A typical community included only twenty-four families in a twenty-five-square-mile area, a mere six people per square mile. (In contrast, New England often had five hundred people squeezed onto one square mile.) Most Chesapeake inhabitants lived in a world of few friendships and considerable isolation; typical was Robert Boone, a Maryland farmer, who died at age seventy-nine "on the same Plantation where he was born in 1680, from which he never went 30 miles in his Life."

Isolated Chesapeake settlers shared a life governed by one overriding factor: the price of tobacco. After an initial boom, tobacco prices plunged 97 percent in 1629 before stabilizing at 10 percent of their original high. Tobacco was still profitable as long as it was grown on fertile soil near navigable water. As a result, 80 percent of Chesapeake homes were located along a riverbank. Wealthy planters built wharves that served as depots for tobacco exports and distribution centers for imported goods. Consequently a merchant class was slow to materialize, and towns grew painfully slowly; by 1678 St. Mary's, Maryland's capital, had just thirty scattered houses.

Chesapeake society became increasingly unequal. A few planters used the headright system to build up large landholdings and to profit from their servants' labor. Wretchedly exploited—and poorly fed, clothed, and housed—servants faced a bleak future even when their indenture ended. Although some were able to claim fifty acres of land in Maryland, the majority who went to Virginia had no such prospects. Indeed, in Virginia after 1650 most riverfront land was held by large planters and speculators, and upward mobility became virtually impossible.

In 1660 Chesapeake tobacco prices plunged 50 percent, setting off a depression that lasted fifty years. Despite losses, large planters earned some income from rents, interest on loans, and shopkeeping, and many landowners scrambled to sell corn and cattle in the West Indies. A typical family in this depression era lived in a small wooden shack, slept on rags, and ate mush or stew cooked in their single pot. Ex-servants in particular became a frustrated and embittered underclass that seemed destined to remain landless and poor.

Bacon's Rebellion, 1675–1676

By the 1670s these bleak conditions had locked most Virginia landowners into a losing battle against poverty and had left the colony's freedmen in despair. Both groups were capable of striking out in blind rage if an opportunity to stave off economic disaster presented itself. In 1676 this human powder keg exploded in violence.

Virginians had been free of serious conflict with the Indians since the end of the Third Anglo-Powhatan War in 1646. By 1653 tribes encircled by English settlements had begun agreeing to remain within boundaries set by the government—in effect, on reservations. White settlement continued to expand northward to the Potomac River, and by 1675 whites outnumbered Indians by a ten-to-one ratio.

In June 1675 a dispute between some Doeg (Dohg) Indians and a Virginia farmer escalated. A force of Virginia and Maryland militia pursuing the Doegs murdered fourteen friendly Susquehannocks (suss-kweh-HAN-nocks) and later executed five of their chiefs. The violence was now unstoppable. Although Governor William Berkeley proposed defending the frontier with a costly system of forts, small farmers preferred the cheaper solution: a war of extermination against the Indians. Some three hundred settlers elected Nathaniel Bacon, a distant relative of Berkeley and a member of the Royal Council, to lead them against nearby Indians in April 1676. The expedition found only peaceful Indians but slaughtered them anyhow.

Returning to Jamestown in June 1676, Bacon asked for authority to wage war "against all Indians in general." The legislature voted for a program designed to appeal to both hard-pressed taxpayers and landless ex-servants. All Indians who had left their village without permission (even if fleeing Bacon) were declared enemies, and their lands were forfeited. Bacon's troops could seize any "enemy" property and enslave Indian prisoners.

But Governor Berkeley soon had second thoughts about the slaughter and recalled Bacon and his thirteen hundred men. Forbidden to attack Indians, Bacon's forces turned against the government and burned Jamestown. The rebels offered freedom to any servants or slaves owned by Berkeley's allies who would join them, and then looted enemy plantations. What had begun as Indian warfare was now a social rebellion. Before the uprising could proceed further, however, Bacon died of dysentery in late 1676, and his followers dispersed.

Bacon's Rebellion revealed a society under deep internal stress. Begun as an effort to displace escalating tensions among whites onto the Indians, it became an excuse to plunder other whites. This rebellion was an outburst of pent-up

Bacon's Rebellion Uprising that showed deep stresses within the Virginia colony frustrations by marginal taxpayers and ex-servants driven to desperation by the tobacco depression.

From Servitude to Slavery

Chesapeake whites drew racial boundaries between themselves and the region's growing African population and tried to avert class conflict by substituting black slaves for white servants.

Racial slavery developed in three stages. From 1619 to 1640, Anglo-Virginians carefully distinguished between whites and blacks in official documents but did not assume that every African sold was a slave for life. Some Africans gained their freedom, and a few even owned their own farm.

By 1640 blacks and some Indians were being treated as slaves, and their children inherited their status. Thus their situation had become inferior to that of indentured white servants. In the final phase, after 1660, laws defined slavery as a lifelong, inheritable status based on color. By 1705 strict legal codes defined the place of slaves in society and set standards of racial etiquette.

Slavery was a system for blacks and Indians only. Whites never enslaved their white enemies; rather, they reserved the complete denial of human rights for nonwhites. To stabilize Chesapeake society and to defuse the resentment of poor whites, planter elites created a caste system based on race. This system simultaneously defined nonwhites as unfit for freedom and created a common, exclusive identity among whites.

Slavery grew slowly in the Chesapeake, with fewer than a thousand slaves in Virginia and Maryland as late as 1660. By 1680, however, the slave population had grown to twelve thousand; by 1700 slaves would make up nearly one-fourth of the Chesapeake population and much of the labor force.

Preparing a Slave Voyage
Africans weep as relatives or friends are taken to a slave vessel.

The rise of a direct slave trade with Africa increased the growing gap between whites and blacks. Before 1690, most blacks in the Chesapeake, having spent long periods in West African ports or other American colonies, were familiar with English ways and spoke some English. They could carve out space for themselves as free landowners. After 1690, as slaves poured into the Chesapeake directly from the West African interior, language and culture became barriers rather than bridges, reinforcing increased racism among whites.

Racism was enforced by the changing composition of the white population, increasingly American-born and evenly distributed between male and female. Whites shared a sense of common racial identity vis-à-vis an increasingly fragmented and seemingly alien black population.

By 1700 the Chesapeake had been transformed; profits had fallen, but life expectancy had risen. As nonwhites' condition deteriorated, Virginia and Maryland expanded their territories, and their white colonists flourished.

PURITANISM IN NEW ENGLAND

What was the "New England Way," and what challenges did it endure?

As England's religious and political environment grew worse for the Puritans in the 1620s, many of them became interested in colonizing New England. Large-scale Puritan migration would begin in 1630, as the intensely religious Puritans built a community based on religious ideals, the first utopian society in America.

In almost every way—the place of religion, economies, class structure, local communities, and living standards—New England contrasted sharply with the Chesapeake colonies. Both, however, shared English nationality and a determination to expand at Native Americans' expense.

Map 3.2   English Migration, 1610–1660
During the first phase of English transatlantic migration, the West Indies attracted more than twice as many colonists as went to the Chesapeake, and over four times as many as settled in New England.

A City upon a Hill, 1628–1632

Upon ascending the throne in 1625, Charles I scrapped James's policy of tolerance toward the Puritans and began a systematic campaign to eliminate Puritan influence within the Church of England. In response to continual harassment, in 1628 several Puritan merchants obtained a charter to settle north of the Separatist colony at Plymouth. Organized as the Massachusetts Bay Company, they moved the seat of their colony's government to New England, paving the way for Massachusetts to be self-governing.

In 1630 the company dispatched a "great fleet," eleven ships and seven hundred passengers, to New England. As the ships crossed the Atlantic, Governor John Winthrop delivered a lay sermon, "A Model of Christian Charity," in which he explained how and why the new colony would differ from England itself.

Winthrop boldly announced that "we shall be as **a city upon a hill,** the eyes of all people are upon us." The settlers would build a godly community whose compelling example would shame England. The English government would then truly reform the church, and a revival of piety would create a nation of saints. Denouncing economic jealousy, Winthrop explained that God intended "in all times some must be rich and some poor." The rich would practice charity and mercy, and the poor show their faith in God's will by practicing patience and fortitude. In a godly state, the government would prevent the greedy among the rich from exploiting the poor and the lazy among the poor from burdening their fellow citizens.

By 1631, thirteen hundred more settlers had arrived, and the colony was moving toward both economic and political stability. Most of the new colonists were land-owning farm families of modest means, who had neither indentured servants nor slaves. More than fifteen thousand colonists had settled in New England by 1642.

Massachusetts established a broad-based political system, permitting every adult male church member to vote; the widespread suffrage contrasted sharply with England itself, where property requirements restricted the vote to less than 30 percent of adult males. Within a few years of their arrival, the colonists had established a bicameral legislature, the General Court, with an appointed Governor's Council as the upper house and two delegates from each town as the lower house.

a city upon a hill John Winthrop's vision of the Puritan settlement in New England as a model for the world

New England Ways

Self-governing Puritan congregations ignored the authority of Anglican bishops. Male "saints," as Puritans termed those who had been saved, ran each congregation. By majority vote they chose ministers, elected a board of elders to handle finances, and decided who were saints. Thus control of New England churches was broadly based.

The clergy quickly asserted its power in New England's religious life. In England, Puritans had focused on their common opposition to Anglican practices. In America, however, theological differences began to undermine the harmony that Winthrop had envisioned. Puritan ministers struggled to define orthodox practices—**the "New England Way"**—that strengthened their authority at the expense of the laypersons (nonclergy).

Education was a key means of establishing orthodoxy. Like most Protestants, Puritans insisted on familiarity with the Bible and, thus, literacy. Education should begin in childhood and be promoted by each colony.

In 1647 the Massachusetts Bay colony passed the **Old Deluder Act** because "one chief project of that old deluder, Satan [is] to keep men from knowledge of the Scriptures." Every town of fifty or more households was to appoint one teacher from whom all children could receive instruction, and every town of one hundred households or more was to maintain a grammar school with a teacher capable of preparing students for university-level learning. This law, echoed by other Puritan colonies, was New England's first step toward public education, although attendance remained optional and boys were more likely to be taught reading and writing than girls.

the "New England Way" Puritan orthodoxy that was supposed to govern the Massachusetts Bay colony

Old Deluder Act Law requiring Puritan towns to establish and maintain schools; foundation of public education in New England

An educated clergy was essential, so in 1636 Massachusetts founded Harvard College to produce learned ministers. In its first thirty-five years, the college turned out 201 graduates, 111 of them ministers. These alumni made New England the only American colony with a college-educated elite during the seventeenth century.

Although agreeing that the church must be free of state control, Winthrop and other Massachusetts Bay leaders insisted that a holy commonwealth required cooperation between church and state. Therefore, the colony required all adults to attend services and pay tithes to support their local church. Massachusetts thus had a state-sponsored or "established" religion. Some Puritans, however, dissented from their leaders' vision of social order and religious conformity. **Roger Williams,** who arrived in America in 1631, argued that civil government had to remain absolutely uninvolved with religious matters. Williams opposed compulsory church service and interference with private religious beliefs because he feared that the state would eventually corrupt the church and its saints.

Roger Williams Dissenter seen as a threat to the New England Way; ultimately banished; founded Rhode Island

Believing that the purpose of the colony was to protect true religion and to prevent heresy, political authorities declared Williams's opinions subversive and banished him in 1635. Williams went south to the edge of Narragansett Bay to a place that he later named Providence, which he purchased from the Indians. A steady stream of dissenters drifted to the group of settlements near Providence, forming Rhode Island in 1647. The only New England colony to practice religious toleration, Rhode Island grew to eight hundred settlers by 1650.

Anne Hutchinson presented the second major challenge to the New England Way. "A woman of haughty and fierce carriage, of a nimble wit and active spirit," Hutchinson maintained that her fellow Puritans were too certain that they could tell whether or not a person was a saint on the basis of his or her behavior. She reminded them that their creed stressed predestination, not good works, and argued that New England's ministers had gone astray.

Anne Hutchinson Dissenter feared not only for her theology but also because she challenged gender roles; banished from Massachusetts

Hutchinson's ideas directly attacked the clergy's authority to interpret and teach Scripture; critics charged that her beliefs would delude individuals into imagining that they were accountable only to themselves. Her followers were labeled "antinomians," meaning those opposed to the rule of law. Anne Hutchinson bore the additional liability of being a woman challenging traditional male roles in church and state. Her gender made her seem an especially dangerous foe. "You have stepped out of your places; you [would] rather have been a husband than a wife, a preacher than a hearer. . . ." one of her foes railed against her.

Massachusetts Bay split into pro- and anti-Hutchinson forces. Her opponents prevailed, bringing Hutchinson to trial for sedition in 1637 before the Massachusetts Bay legislature (the General Court) and then for heresy before a panel of ministers. Hutchinson's knowledge of Scripture was so superior to that of her inquisitors that she might well have been acquitted had she not claimed to communicate directly with the Holy Spirit. Because Puritans believed that God had ceased to make matters of faith known by personal revelation since New Testament times, Hutchinson was condemned by her own words. Banished from the colony along with other antinomians, Hutchinson settled in Rhode Island and then moved to New Netherland, where she was killed in that colony's war with Indians in 1643. Her banishment effectively ended the last challenge capable of splitting congregationalism and ensured the survival of the New England Way for two more generations.

New restrictions on women's independence and on equality within Puritan congregations followed antinomianism's defeat. Increasingly, women were prohibited from assuming the kind of public religious role claimed by Hutchinson and were even required to relate their conversion experiences in private to their minister rather than publicly, before their congregation.

Towns, Families, and Farm Life

To ensure that colonists would settle in communities with congregations, all New England colonies provided for the establishment of towns by awarding a grant of land to several dozen landowning church members. These men laid out the settlement, organized its church, distributed land among themselves, and established a town meeting. At the center of each town was the meetinghouse, which served as both church and town hall.

Local administration lay in the hands of the town meeting, which resulted in a highly decentralized authority over political and economic decisions. Each town determined its own qualifications for voting and for holding office; most allowed all male taxpayers, including nonsaints, to participate.

Most towns attempted to maintain communities of tightly clustered settlers by distributing only as much land as was necessary for each family to support itself. The remaining land would be distributed to future generations as needed. Forcing residents to live close together was an attempt to foster social reciprocity. New England's generally compact system of settlement made people interact with each other and established an atmosphere of mutual watchfulness that promoted godly order.

Despite the restriction of their public roles after the antinomian crisis, women remained a social force in their communities. Remaining at home while husbands and older sons tended the families, fields, and business, women exchanged goods—a pound of butter for a section of spun wool, for example—advice, and news. Women confided in one another, creating a community of women that helped enforce morals and protect the poor and vulnerable.

Puritans defined matrimony as a contract, not a sacrament; they were thus married by justices of the peace rather than ministers. As a civil institution, marriage could be dissolved by the courts in cases of desertion, bigamy, adultery, or physical cruelty. However, New England courts saw divorce as a remedy only for extremely wronged spouses, such as the Plymouth woman who found that her husband also had wives in Boston, Barbados (bar-BAY-dose), and England.

New England wives enjoyed significant legal protections against spousal violence and nonsupport and had more freedom to escape a failed marriage than their English counterparts. But they suffered the legal disabilities borne by all women under English law. A wife had no property rights independent of her husband except by premarital agreement. Only if there were no other heirs, or if a will so specified, would a widow receive control of household property, although law entitled her to lifetime use of one-third of the estate.

New England's families enjoyed greater stability and lived longer lives than their English counterparts. The region's cold climate limited the impact of disease, especially in winter when limited travel between towns slowed the spread of infection. Easy access to land contributed to a healthy diet, which strengthened resistance to disease and lowered death rates associated with childbirth. Life expectancy for Puritan men reached sixty-five, and women lived nearly that long. These life spans were ten years or more longer than those in England. More than 80 percent of all infants survived long enough to marry. Because so many of the twenty thousand immigrants who arrived in New England between 1630 and 1642 came as members of families, an even sex ratio and a rapid natural increase of population followed.

Families were economically interdependent. Male heads of family managed the household's crops and livestock, conducted its business transactions, and represented it at town meetings. Wives bore and nurtured children, and performed or oversaw work in the house, garden, and barn. Sons depended on parents to provide them with acreage for a farm, and parents encouraged sons to stay at home and work in return for a bequest of land later on. Young males often tended their father's fields until their late twenties before receiving their own land. The average family, raising four sons to adulthood, could count on thirty to forty years of work if their sons delayed marriage until age twenty-six.

There were other benefits. Prolonged dependence for sons ensured that the family line and property would continue in the hands of capable, experienced men. Although daughters performed vital labor, they would marry into another family. Young women with many childbearing years ahead of them were the most valuable potential wives, and first-generation women tended to marry by the age of twenty-one.

Economic and Religious Tensions

Saddled with a short growing season, rocky soil salted with gravel, and an inefficient system of land distribution that forced farmers to cultivate widely scattered strips, the colonists nevertheless managed to feed their families and to keep ahead of their debts. Few grew wealthy from farming. For wealth, New Englanders turned lumbering, shipbuilding, fishing, and rum distilling into major industries that employed perhaps one-fifth of all adults full time. As its economy diversified, New England prospered.

While most Puritans shared Winthrop's view of community, self-discipline, and mutual obligation, a large minority had come to America for prosperity and social mobility. The most visibly ambitious colonists were merchants, whose activities fueled New England's economy but whose way of life challenged its ideals.

Merchants fit uneasily into a religious society that equated financial shrewdness with greed. New England ministers attempted to curtail the acquisitive impulses transforming England itself. Merchants clashed with political leaders, who were trying to regulate prices so that consumers would not suffer from the chronic shortage of manufactured goods that afflicted New England. In 1635 the General Court forbade the sale of any item above 5 percent of its cost. Led by Robert Keayne, merchants protested that they needed to sell some goods at higher rates to offset losses incurred by shipwreck and inflation. In 1639 authorities fined Keayne for selling nails at 25 percent above cost and forced him to apologize in front of his congregation.

Keayne symbolized the fear that a headlong rush for prosperity would lead New Englanders to forget that they were their brothers' keepers. Controversies like these were part of a struggle for the New England soul. At stake was the Puritans' ability to insulate their city upon a hill from a market economy that threatened to strangle the spirit of community within a harsh world of frantic competition.

Other changes further undermined Winthrop's vision. After 1660 farmers voted themselves larger amounts of land and consolidated their scattered parcels of land. Farmers began to leave town centers to live on their outlying tracts. Friction grew between townspeople and "outlivers," whose distance from the town center limited their influence over town affairs. John Winthrop's vision of a society sustained by reciprocity was slowly giving way to the materialistic, acquisitive society that the original immigrants had fled in England.

As New England struggled for stability and conformity, old England fell into chaos and civil war. Alienated by years of religious harassment, Puritans gained control of the revolt, beheaded Charles I in 1649, and governed without a king for more than a decade. In 1660 a provisional English government recalled the Stuarts and restored Charles II to the throne.

The Stuart Restoration left American Puritans without a mission. Having conquered a wilderness and built their city upon a hill, they found that the eyes of the world were no longer fixed on them.

An internal crisis also gripped New England. First-generation Puritans had believed that they held a covenant, a holy contract, with God to establish a scripturally ordained church and to charge their descendants with its preservation. However, understandably reluctant to submit to a public review of their spirituality, relatively few second-generation Puritans were willing to join the elect by making the required conversion relation before the congregation. This generation also rejected the ritual of public conversion relation as an unnecessary source of division and bitterness that undermined Christian fellowship.

Half-Way Covenant Law to admit nonsaints to church membership; major blow to New England Way

Because Puritan churches baptized only babies born to saints, first-generation Puritans faced the prospect that their own grandchildren would remain unbaptized unless the standards for church membership were lowered. They solved their dilemma in 1662 through a compromise known as the **Half-Way Covenant,** which permitted the children of all baptized members, including nonsaints, to be baptized. Church membership would pass down from generation to generation, but nonsaints would be "half-way" members, unable to take communion or to vote in church affairs. When forced to choose between a church system founded on a pure membership of the elect and one that embraced the entire community, New Englanders opted for worldly power over spiritual purity.

The Half-Way Covenant marked the end of the New England Way. Most adults chose to remain in "half-way" status for life, and the saints became a shrinking minority in the third and fourth generations. By the 1700s there were more female than male saints in most congregations. But because women could not vote in church affairs, religious authority stayed in male hands.

Expansion and Native Americans

In contrast to the settlement of Virginia, the Puritan colonization of New England initially met little resistance from Native Americans, whose numbers had been drastically reduced by disease. Between 1616 and 1618 an epidemic had killed 90 percent of New England's coastal Indians, and a second epidemic in 1633–1634 inflicted comparable casualties on Indians throughout the Northeast. By 1675, New England's Native American population had shrunk from 125,000 in 1600 to about 10,000. During the 1640s, Massachusetts Bay passed laws prohibiting Indians from practicing their own religion and encouraging missionaries to convert them to Christianity. The Massachusetts Indians surrendered much of their independence and moved into "praying towns," such as Natick, a reservation established by the colony.

The expansion of English settlement farther inland, however, aroused Indian resistance. As settlers moved into the Connecticut River Valley, beginning in 1633, friction developed with the Pequots, who controlled the trade in furs and wampum with New Netherland. After tensions escalated into violence, the English waged a ruthless campaign against the Pequots, using tactics similar to those devised to break Irish resistance (see Chapter 2). In a predawn attack, troops led by Captain John Mason surrounded and set fire to a Pequot village at Mystic, Connecticut, and then cut down all who tried to escape. Several hundred Pequots, mostly women and children, were killed. By late 1637, Pequot resistance was crushed, and English settlement of the new colonies of Connecticut and New Haven could proceed unimpeded.

Indians felt the English presence in many ways. The fur trade, initially beneficial to Native Americans of the interior, became a burden. Once Indians began hunting for trade instead of for their subsistence needs alone, they quickly depleted the supply of beavers and other fur-bearing animals. Because English traders advanced trade goods on credit before the hunting season began, many Indians fell into debt. Traders increasingly took Indian land as collateral and sold it to settlers.

English townspeople, eager to expand their agricultural output and provide for their sons, voted themselves much larger amounts of land after 1660. For example, Dedham, Massachusetts, had distributed only three thousand acres from 1636 to 1656; by 1668 it had allocated another fifteen thousand acres. Many farmers built homes on their outlying tracts, crowding closer to the Indians' settlements and hunting, fishing, and gathering areas.

Expansion put pressure on the natives and the land alike. By clearing trees for fields and for use as fuel and building material, the colonists were altering the entire ecosystem by the mid-1600s. Deer no longer grazed freely, and the wild plants on which the Indians depended for food and medicine could not grow. Clear-cutting trees not only dried the soil but also brought frequent flooding. Encroaching white settlers allowed their livestock to run wild, according to English custom. Pigs damaged Indian cornfields and shellfish-gathering sites. Cattle and horses devoured native grasses, which the settlers replaced with English varieties.

Powerless to reverse the alarming decline of population, land, and food supplies, many Indians became demoralized. Some turned to alcohol, which became increasingly available during the 1660s despite colonial attempts to suppress its sale to Native Americans. Interpreting the crisis as one of belief, other Indians converted to Christianity. By 1675 Puritan missionaries had established about thirty "praying towns." Although missionaries struggled to convert the Indians to "civilization"—English culture and ways of life—most Indians integrated the new faith with their native cultural identities, reinforcing the hostility of settlers who believed that all Indians were irrevocably "savage" and heathen.

Anglo-Indian conflict became acute in the 1670s because of pressure on the Indians to sell their land and to accept missionaries and the legal authority of English courts. Tension was especially high in the Plymouth colony, where Puritans had engulfed the Wampanoag tribe and forced a series of humiliating concessions from their leader, Metacom (MEH-tuh-comb), or "King Philip," the son of the Pilgrims' onetime ally, Massasoit.

In 1675 Plymouth hanged three Wampanoags for killing a Christian Indian. Then several other Wampanoags were shot while burglarizing a farmhouse, touching off the conflict known as **King Philip's War.** In response to the escalation of violence, Metacom organized two-thirds of the Native Americans, including a few praying Indians, into a military alliance. The war raged across New England. Metacom's forces, as well armed as the Puritans, devastated the countryside, wiping out twelve of New England's ninety towns and killing six hundred colonists. The following year, 1676, saw the tide turn as Puritan militia destroyed their enemies' food supplies and sold hundreds of captives into slavery, including Metacom's wife and child. Perhaps five thousand Indians starved or died in battle, including Metacom himself.

King Philip's War reduced southern New England's Indian population by almost 40 percent and eliminated open Indian resistance to white expansion. It also deepened whites' hostility toward all Native Americans, even the Christian Indians who had fought against King Philip. In 1677 ten praying towns were disbanded, and all Indians were restricted to the remaining four. Missionary work ceased.

King Philip's War Last major war between Indians and New England settlers; reduced Indian population by nearly 40 percent; ended Indian resistance

Salem Witchcraft, 1691–1693

Nowhere in New England did the conflicts dividing white New Englanders converge more forcefully than in Salem, Massachusetts. Trade made Salem prosperous but destroyed the relatively equal society of the first generation. Such divisions were especially sharp in Salem Village, an economically stagnant district north of Salem Town; those who lived in the eastern section farmed richer soils and benefited from Salem Town's commercial expansion, whereas those in the less fertile western half did not share this prosperity and lost the political influence that they had once held.

In late 1691 several Salem Village girls encouraged an African slave woman, Tituba (TEE-too-bah), to tell fortunes and talk to them about sorcery. When the girls began behaving strangely, villagers assumed that they were victims of witchcraft. Pressed to identify their tormenters, they named two local white women and Tituba.

To this point the incident was not unusual; witchcraft beliefs remained strong in seventeenth-century Europe and its colonies. Generally, witches were women whose greed, pride, envy, or discontent supposedly drove them to sign pacts with the devil and use his supernatural power of evil to torment neighbors by causing illness, destroying property, or "possessing" their victims' minds and bodies. Witnesses also usually accused these women of unfeminine behavior. A disproportionate number of the 342 accused witches in New England were women who had inherited or stood to inherit more property than the usual one-third of a husband's estate. In other words, most accused witches were assertive women who had or might have more economic power and independence than many men. To New Englanders, who felt it necessary to limit both female independence and economic individualism, they were dangerous. In most earlier witchcraft accusations, there was only one defendant, and the case never went to trial. However, the **Salem witchcraft trials** would lead to a colonywide panic.

Salem witchcraft trials Hysteria that delivered final blow to New England Way, revealing social divisions

By April 1692 the girls had denounced two prosperous farm wives long considered saints in the local church and identified the village's former minister as a wizard (male witch). Fear of witchcraft soon overrode doubts about the girls' credibility and led local judges to ignore legal bans on "spectral evidence," testimony that a spirit resembling the accused had been seen tormenting a victim. Thereafter, charges multiplied until the jails overflowed with accused witches.

The pattern of hysteria and accusations reflected Salem Village's internal divisions. Most charges came from the western side of the village and were lodged against people from the eastern village and in Salem Town. Two-thirds of all accusers were girls aged eleven to twenty, and more than half of them had lost one or both parents in conflicts between Indians and settlers in Maine. They and other survivors had fled to Massachusetts, where most worked as servants in other families' households. They most frequently named as witches middle-aged wives and widows—women who had escaped the poverty and uncertainty that they themselves faced.

Those found guilty of witchcraft tried to stave off death by implicating others. As the pandemonium spread, fear dissolved ties of friendship and family. A minister was condemned by his granddaughter, a mother by her seven-year-old daughter, and a husband and father by his wife and daughter. Fifty saved themselves by confessing, but twenty were condemned and executed.

By late 1692, doubts about the charges were surfacing. Clergymen objected to the emphasis on spectral evidence, crucial to most convictions. By accepting such evidence in court, minister Increase Mather warned, the Puritans had fallen victim to a deadly game of "blind man's buffet" set up by Satan and were "hotly and madly mauling one another in the dark." In October, Governor William Phips forbade any further imprisonments for witchcraft. One hundred were still in jail, and two hundred more stood accused. In early 1693 Phips ended the terror by pardoning all those who were convicted or suspected of practicing witchcraft.

The witchcraft hysteria marked the end of Puritan New England. Colonists reaching maturity after 1692 would reject the ideals of earlier generations and become "Yankees" who shrewdly pursued material gain. True to their Puritan roots, they would retain their forceful convictions and self-discipline, giving New England a distinctive regional identity that would endure.

Primary Source: Cotton Mather on the Education of His Children

CHECKING IN

- John Winthrop proclaimed that Puritans would build a "city upon a hill" in the New World, a godly community that would be an example to the world.

- Threats to Puritan orthodoxy, the "New England Way," included religious dissenters Roger Williams and Anne Hutchinson and the growth of a market economy.

- White expansion steadily displaced New England's Native Americans; New Englanders celebrated the massacre of the Pequots, and later resistance, culminating in the bitter and costly King Philip's War, proved futile.

- The Half-Way Covenant relaxed standards for church membership and marked the beginning of the end of the New England Way.

- The Salem witchcraft hysteria delivered the final blow to the New England Way, revealing deep social divisions.

THE SPREAD OF SLAVERY: THE CARIBBEAN AND CAROLINA

Why and how did plantation agriculture shape slavery in the Caribbean and Carolina?

As European colonies expanded on the mainland, an even larger wave of settlement swept the West Indies. Between 1630 and 1642 nearly two-thirds of the English who emigrated to the Americas went to the Caribbean. Beginning in the 1640s both the French and the English followed the Spanish, Portuguese, and Dutch in using slave labor to produce sugar on large plantations.

After 1670 large numbers of English islanders migrated to the Chesapeake and to Carolina, carrying with them the habits and prejudices of plantation slave-holding. By 1710 the population of Carolina, like that of the Caribbean colonies, was predominantly black and enslaved.

Sugar and Slaves: The West Indies

Initially, the English West Indies developed along lines similar to Virginia, with tobacco the dominant crop. Because a single worker could tend only three acres of tobacco, tobacco farming demanded a large population. By 1640 more colonists lived on England's five West Indian islands than in all of Virginia.

Tobacco, requiring little equipment beyond a curing shed, was cheap to raise, and tobacco cultivation gave individuals with little money a chance at upward mobility. Through the 1630s the West Indies remained a society with a large percentage of independent landowners, an overwhelmingly white population, and no extreme inequality of wealth.

Sugar cane soon changed that, revolutionizing the islands' economy and society. Encouraged by Dutch merchants, wealthy English planters began to raise this enormously lucrative crop. The demand for labor soared because sugar required triple the labor force of tobacco. African slaves soon replaced indentured white servants in the fields. Most planters preferred black slaves to white servants because they could be driven harder and maintained more cheaply. Also, African slaves could better withstand the tropical diseases of the Caribbean, they had no rights under contract, and they toiled until they died. Although slaves initially cost two to four times more than indentured servants, they were an economical long-term investment. Some English immigrants to the Caribbean copied the example already set by the Spanish and enslaved both Indians and Africans.

By 1670 the sugar revolution had transformed the British West Indies into a predominantly black and slave society. In 1713 slaves outnumbered whites by four to one; the slave population had leaped from 40,000 in 1670 to 130,000 in 1713, with the white population remaining stable at 33,000. Meanwhile, driven from the Indies by high land prices, thousands of English settlers went north to the mainland, settling in Carolina.

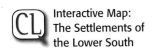 Interactive Map: The Settlements of the Lower South

Rice and Slaves: Carolina

In 1663 Charles II bestowed the swampy coast between Virginia and Spanish Florida on several English supporters, making it the first of several Restoration colonies. The proprietors named their colony Carolina in honor of Charles (*Carolus* in Latin).

Settlers from New England and the West Indies had established outposts along the northern Carolina coast in the 1650s; the proprietors organized them into a separate district with a bicameral legislature. In 1669 one of the proprietors, Anthony Ashley Cooper, accelerated settlement by offering immigrants fifty-acre headright grants for every family member, indentured servant, or slave they brought in. The next year, two hundred white Barbadians and their slaves began the settlement of

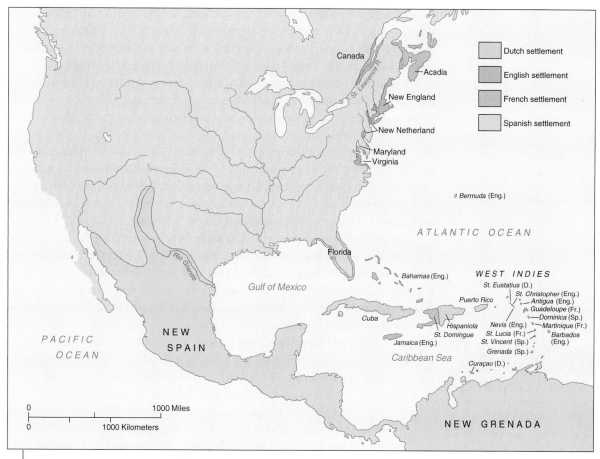

Map 3.3 The Caribbean Colonies, 1660

By 1660 nearly every West Indian island had been colonized by Europeans and was producing sugar with slave labor.

southern Carolina near modern Charleston, "in the very chops of the Spanish." In the settlement they called Charles Town, they formed the colony's nucleus, with a bicameral legislature distinct from that of the northern district.

Cooper and his secretary, John Locke, devised an intricate plan for Carolina's settlement and government. Their Fundamental Constitutions of Carolina attempted to ensure the colony's stability by decreeing that political power and social rank should accurately reflect settlers' landed wealth. Thus they invented a three-tiered nobility that would hold two-fifths of all land, make laws through a council of nobles, and dispense justice through manorial courts.

In the early years, Carolina's population consisted mainly of small landowners who saw little reason to follow the complex system drawn up on the other side of the Atlantic. Southern Carolinians raised livestock, and colonists in northern Carolina exported tobacco, lumber, and pitch. In neither north nor south did the people realize enough profit to maintain slaves, so self-sufficient white families predominated. But southern Carolinians eagerly sought a cash crop. In the early 1690s they found it—rice. Rice cultivation enriched the few settlers with capital enough to acquire the dikes, dams, and slaves necessary to grow it. By earning annual profits of 25 percent, successful rice planters within a generation became the only colonial mainland elite whose wealth rivaled that of the Caribbean sugar planters.

Treated inhumanely, white indentured servants did not survive in the humid rice paddies swarming with malaria-carrying mosquitoes. Thus planters imported an ever-growing force of African slaves, who possessed two major advantages. First, some had cultivated rice in Africa and possessed expertise vital to teaching whites how to raise the unfamiliar crop. Second, many Africans were immune to malaria and yellow fever, which were endemic in coastal regions of West Africa, and which they carried to North America. (Tragically, the antibody against malaria also tends to produce the sickle-cell trait, an often-fatal genetic condition.) These two factors made commercial rice production possible in Carolina.

The typical rice planter, with 130 acres in cultivation, needed sixty-five slaves. Demand drove the proportion of slaves in southern Carolina's population from 17 percent in 1680 to 67 percent in 1720, when the region officially became South Carolina. By 1776 the colony, with at least 100,000 slaves, would have more bondsmen than any other mainland colony in the eighteenth century. It would be Britain's only eighteenth-century mainland colony with a black majority.

As the black majority increased, whites relied on force and fear to control their slaves. In 1696 Carolina adopted the galling restrictions and gruesome punishments of the Barbados slave code. Bondage in the mainland colony grew as cruel and harsh as in the West Indies.

White Carolinians' attitudes toward Native Americans likewise hardened. The most vicious result was the trade in Indian slaves. White Carolinians armed allied Indians, encouraged them to raid and capture unarmed Indians to the south and west, and sold the captives to the West Indies during the 1670s and 1680s. A recent study estimates that the Carolina traders enslaved tens of thousands of Indians. Once shipped to the West Indies, most Native Americans died because they lacked immunities to European and tropical diseases.

CHECKING IN

- The English Caribbean colonies became dependent on sugar, which required a large labor force.
- Plantations appeared in the Caribbean, and slavery spread.
- South Carolina became wedded to a cash crop (rice), plantations, and slavery.
- Northern Carolinians exported tobacco, lumber, and pitch.

THE MIDDLE COLONIES

How did diversity distinguish the Middle Colonies?

The Dutch and the Swedish established small commercial outposts between the Chesapeake and New England. The Dutch took over New Sweden, and in turn England seized New Netherland in 1664; by 1681 England had used this territory as the basis for New York, New Jersey, and Pennsylvania, creating a fourth colonial region, the Middle Colonies.

Precursors: New Netherland and New Sweden

New Netherland became North America's first multiethnic society. Barely half the settlers were Dutch; most of the rest comprised Germans, French, Scandinavians, and Africans, both free and slave. In 1643 the population included Protestants, Catholics, Jews, and Muslims, speaking eighteen European and African languages. Religion counted for little (in 1642 the colony had seventeen taverns but not a single place of worship). The trading company that had established the settlement struggled to control the settlers, whose get-rich-quick attitude sapped company profits as private individuals traded illegally in furs. Eventually, the company legalized the private trade.

Privatization rapidly increased the number of guns in the hands of New Netherland's Iroquois allies, giving them a distinct advantage over other tribes. As overhunting depleted local fur supplies and smallpox epidemics raged, the Iroquois encroached on Huron territory for pelts and captives (who were adopted into Iroquois families to replace the dead). After 1648 the Dutch-armed Iroquois attacked French settlements along the St. Lawrence.

Although the Dutch had allied with the inland Iroquois, relations with the nearer Indian neighbors were terrible. With greedy settlers and military weakness, New Netherland largely had itself to blame. In 1643 an all-out war erupted when Governor Willem Kiefft ordered the massacre of previously friendly Indians. By 1645 the Dutch had temporarily prevailed, but only by enlisting English help and inflicting atrocities. The fighting cut New Netherland's Indian population from sixteen hundred to seven hundred.

Another European challenger, Sweden, distracted the Dutch in their war with the Native Americans. In 1638 Sweden had planted a small fur-trading colony in the lower Delaware Valley that was diverting furs from New Netherland. In 1655 the Dutch colony's stern soldier-governor, Peter Stuyvesant (STY-vuh-sant), marched against New Sweden, whose four hundred residents peacefully accepted Dutch annexation. But New Netherland paid dearly for its victory.

Although tiny, the Dutch and Swedish colonies were significant. Above all, they bequeathed a religious and ethnic diversity that would continue in England's Middle Colonies.

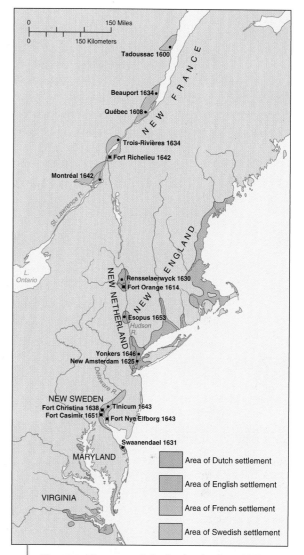

Map 3.4 European Colonization in the Middle and North Atlantic, c. 1650

North of Spanish Florida, four European powers competed for territory and trade with Native Americans in the early seventeenth century. Swedish and Dutch colonization was the foundation on which England's Middle Colonies were built.

English Conquests: New York and New Jersey

Like the Carolinas, New York and New Jersey originated with Restoration-era proprietors hoping to grow rich from rents collected from settlers within a hierarchical society. New York marginally achieved this dream, but New Jersey did not.

In 1664, at war with the Dutch Republic, Charles II attacked the Dutch colony of New Netherland. Four hundred poorly armed Dutch civilians under Governor Peter Stuyvesant surrendered peacefully. Charles II made his brother James, Duke of

York, proprietor of the new English colony and renamed it New York. With James's ascension to the throne in 1685, he converted New York into a royal colony. By 1700 immigration had swelled the population to twenty thousand, of whom just 44 percent were descended from the original Dutch settlers.

New York's governors rewarded their influential political supporters with large land grants. By 1703 five families held 1.75 million acres, which they carved into manors and rented to tenants. By 1750 the enormous income they earned from rents had made the New York estate owners a landed elite second in wealth only to the Carolina rice planters.

Ambitious plans collided with American realities in New Jersey, also carved out of New Netherland. In 1664 the Duke of York awarded a group of supporters New Jersey, at the time inhabited by a few hundred Dutch and Swedes and several thousand Delaware Indians. Within a decade thousands of troublesome New England Puritans settled in New Jersey, and the proprietors sold the region to Quakers, who split the territory into East and West Jersey.

The Jerseys' Quakers, Anglicans, Puritans, Scottish Presbyterians, and Dutch Calvinists quarreled with one another and got along even worse with the proprietors. The governments collapsed between 1698 and 1701, and in 1702 the disillusioned proprietors surrendered their political powers to the crown, which made New Jersey a royal colony.

William Penn Quaker who tried to establish Pennsylvania as a "peaceable kingdom" that reflected Quaker ideals of tolerance

Quaker Pennsylvania

In 1681 Charles II paid off a huge debt by appointing a supporter's son, **William Penn,** as proprietor of the last unallocated tract of American territory at the king's disposal. Penn, a Quaker, thus founded the colony as a "holy experiment" based on the teachings of the English preacher George Fox. Penn also hoped for financial gain.

Quakers in late-seventeenth-century England stood well beyond the fringe of respectability. Challenging conventional foundations of social order, they appealed to those at the bottom of the economic ladder. But they also attracted some well-educated, well-to-do individuals disillusioned by the quarreling of rival religious faiths, including significant numbers of merchants. The members of this radical religious sect, which had been born in war-torn England during the 1640s and 1650s, called themselves the Society of Friends, but most others dubbed them Quakers.

At the heart of their founder George Fox's theology was the belief that the Holy Spirit, or "Inner Light," could inspire every soul. Mainstream Christians found this claim highly suspicious. In their religious services ("meetings"), Quakers sat silently until the Inner Light prompted one of them to speak. Quakers believed that the Inner Light could "speak in the female as well as the male," and they thus accorded women unprecedented equality.

Quaker behavior often seemed disrespectful to government and to the social elite, and thus aroused hostility. For example, Quakers refused to tip their hat to their social betters, insisting that spiritual state, not wealth or status, deserved recognition. Their refusal to bear arms appeared unpatriotic and cowardly, yet they faced persecution and imprisonment with courage.

Care and planning made the Quaker migration to Pennsylvania one of the most successful initial transplantations of Europeans in any North American colony. After sending an advance party, Penn arrived in 1682. He named his new capital Philadelphia, the "City of Brotherly Love." Within five years, eight thousand English Quakers had joined him. Quakers migrated in family groups, and their high birthrate led to rapid population growth. (Pennsylvania's religious toleration attracted not only Quakers but also many other religious groups: Presbyterians, Baptists, Anglicans, and Catholics from England, and Lutherans and radical sectarians from Germany.)

A victim of persecution, Penn hated intolerance and arbitrary governance. He offered Quakers the opportunity to make laws according to their ideals. His Frame of Government (constitution) featured a strong executive branch (a governor and governor's council) and a lower chamber (the assembly) with limited power. Friends, a majority in the colony, dominated the assembly, and Penn generally named Quakers to other positions. To prevent wrangling and to achieve an orderly disposition of property, Penn personally oversaw land sales. He also designed a grid plan for Philadelphia, the "city of brotherly love," reserving park areas to keep it a "greene country towne." Penn sought peace with Native Americans by reassuring the Indians that the Quakers wished "to live together as Neighbours and Friends" and by buying land from them fairly.

Pennsylvania seemed an ideal colony—intelligently organized, well financed, tolerant, open to all industrious settlers, and at peace with the Indians. Rich lands and a lengthy growing season produced bumper crops. West Indian demand for grain generated widespread prosperity. By 1700 Philadelphia had become a major port. In 1704 counties along the lower Delaware River, where Swedes and Dutch had settled long before Penn, gained the right to elect their own legislature and became the colony of Delaware.

However, by this time Penn's "peaceable kingdom" had bogged down in human bickering. In 1684 Penn had returned to England, and during his fifteen-year absence the settlers had quarreled incessantly. Struggles between pro- and anti-Penn forces deadlocked the government. Penn's return in 1699 restored some order, but before leaving again in 1701, he made the legislature unicameral (one chamber) and allowed it to initiate measures.

Meanwhile, religious controversy erupted in the 1690s, when prominent Quaker preacher George Keith urged the Quakers to adopt a formal religious creed. Doing so would have changed the democratically functioning Quakers into a conventional clergy-dominated church. In 1692 a majority of Quakers rejected Keith's views, and he joined the Church of England. Keith's departure began a major decline in the Quaker share of Pennsylvania's population. In 1748 Penn's sons, who inherited the proprietorship, would become Anglican, and Anglicans thereafter would hold the highest political offices, although Friends would still dominate the colony's assembly.

Before they were a quarter-century old, the Middle Colonies had demonstrated that English America could benefit by encouraging pluralism. New York and New Jersey successfully integrated Dutch and Swedish populations; Pennsylvania, New Jersey, and Delaware refused to require residents to support any official church. But the virtual completion of English claim staking along the Atlantic Coast had set England on a collision course with France and Spain, which were also vying for American territory.

CHECKING IN

- The Dutch established New Netherland (later called New York) and took over Swedish colonies to the south.
- The Dutch colonies, seized by England in 1664, brought a tradition of religious and ethnic diversity and tolerance to the English empire.
- William Penn established the Pennsylvania colony as a refuge for Quakers, who suffered persecution.
- Penn tried to create a "peaceable kingdom" in Pennsylvania, encouraging good relations with Indians and religious tolerance.

RIVALS FOR NORTH AMERICA: FRANCE AND SPAIN

How did the French and Spanish empires develop in the seventeenth century?

Unlike England, with its compact seacoast colonial settlements in North America, France and Spain had cast enormous nets of widely separated trading posts and missions across the interior. The two Catholic nations had converted many Indians to Christianity and made them trading partners and allies. By 1720, scattered missionaries, fur traders, and merchants had spread French and Spanish influence across two-thirds of today's United States.

France Claims a Continent

After briefly losing Canada to England (1629–1632), France resumed and extended its colonization there. Initially a privately held company, the Company of New France issued extensive tracts to large landlords, who in turn imported indentured servants or rented out small tracts. Nonetheless, Canada's harsh winters and short growing season sharply limited their numbers.

More successful were the traders and missionaries who spread beyond the settlements and relied on stable relations with the Indians to succeed. The lucrative opportunities offered by trade converted many would-be farmers into traders.

Jesuit missionaries followed the traders into the interior, spreading French influence westward to the Great Lakes. Ursuline nuns ministered to Native American women and girls nearer Quebec, ensuring that Catholic piety and morality reached all members of Indian families.

Under King Louis XIV (personally reigned 1661–1715), France sought to subordinate its American colony to French interests, following the doctrine of *mercantilism*. According to this doctrine, colonies should serve as sources of raw materials and as markets for manufactured goods so that the colonial power did not have to depend on rival nations for trade. The French hoped that New France would increase the fur trade, provide agricultural surpluses to ship to France's West Indies colonies, and export timber for those colonies and for the French navy. To achieve this, the French government transformed New France into a royal colony, confronted and sought to stifle the Iroquois, and encouraged French immigration to Canada.

The Iroquois had long limited French colonial profits by intercepting convoys of fur pelts. In the 1660s Louis XIV had dispatched French troops to New France. The French army had burned Mohawk villages. Sobered by the destruction, the Iroquois Confederacy had made a peace that permitted New France's rapid expansion of fur exports.

The French crown energetically built up New France's population, primarily by sending indentured servants to New France; army members stationed there were encouraged to stay, become farmers, and marry the "king's girls," female orphans shipped over with dowries. After 1673, however, immigration dwindled. Colonists who returned to France—more than two-thirds of the immigrants—told horrifying tales of disease, Canada's hard winter, and "savage" Indians. Natural increase would replace immigration as the chief source of population growth, guaranteeing slow development for New France.

Even male immigrants who stayed did not always fulfill the French vision of sturdy farmers. Many of them struck out westward from the St. Lawrence Valley, becoming *coureurs de bois* (koo-RUHR duh BWAH), independent and sometimes disreputable fur traders. These French traders obtained furs from the Indians in exchange for European goods, including guns. The coureurs lived and married among the Indians, forging for France a precarious empire based on alliances with Canadian and Great Lakes Indians. Alarmed by the rapid expansion of England's colonies, France sought to contain the English colonies and prevent Spain from linking Florida with New Mexico by dominating the North American heartland.

As early as 1672, fur trader Louis Jolliet and Jesuit missionary Jacques Marquette became the first Europeans known to have reached the upper Mississippi; they later paddled twelve hundred miles downstream to the Mississippi's junction with the Arkansas. Ten years later, the Sieur de La Salle, an ambitious dreamer and adventurer, descended the entire Mississippi to the Gulf of Mexico, ultimately claiming the entire Mississippi basin—half the territory of the present-day United States—for Louis XIV.

Having asserted title to Louisiana, as La Salle christened this empire, the French began settling its southern gateway. The first colonizers arrived on the Gulf Coast in 1698; within a year, the French had erected a fort near modern Biloxi, Mississippi; in 1702 the French founded a trading post where De Soto had faltered and called it Mobile. But Louisiana's growth would be delayed for another decade.

> **coureurs de bois** French fur traders who spread throughout the French empire in North America

New Mexico: The Pueblo Revolt

After 1625 Spanish colonization in North America expanded on early bases in New Mexico and Florida. Although the colonies needed ties with friendly Native Americans to obtain land, labor, and security, such friendly relations proved hard to come by.

The Spanish sought to rule New Mexico by subordinating the Pueblo Indians to their authority. Franciscan missionaries established churches in the native communities (pueblos) and tried to force the Indians to attend Mass and observe Catholic rituals and morality. Spanish landowners received *encomiendas* that allowed them to exploit Indian labor. Finally, the Spanish drove a wedge between the Pueblo Indians and their nonfarming trade partners, the Apaches (uh-PATCH-ees) and the Navajos (NAV-uh-hoes). Corn once used for trade was now claimed as tribute by the Spanish. In response, the Apaches raided both pueblos and Spanish settlements, driving most of the pueblo dwellers to stronger ties with the Spanish.

Spanish rule began to chafe, especially after 1660. Drought withered Pueblo crops, leaving populations vulnerable to disease and starvation. The Pueblo population plummeted from eighty thousand in 1600 to barely seventeen thousand by the 1670s. Compounding the misery, Apaches riding horses stolen from the Spanish raided and plundered the pueblos. Desperate Indians turned to traditional beliefs and ceremonies to restore the

Diego de Vargas

As the newly appointed governor of New Mexico, Vargas led Spain's reoccupation of New Mexico, beginning in 1692.

spiritual balance and bring rainfall and peace. Determined to suppress this "witch-craft," Franciscan missionaries entered sacred kivas, destroyed religious objects, and publicly whipped native religious leaders and their followers.

In 1675 Governor Juan Francisco Treviño ordered the kivas sacked and religious leaders arrested. Three leaders went to the gallows; a fourth hanged himself; forty-three others were jailed, whipped, and sentenced to be sold as slaves.

Indian resentment against the Spanish blazed, and Pueblo leaders began planning to overthrow the Spanish. At the head of the revolt was **Popé** (poe-PAY), who had been arrested in 1675. Other leaders included disillusioned Christian converts and individuals of mixed Pueblo-Spanish ancestry. Most had tried to reconcile Christianity and Spanish rule with their Indian identity, but the deteriorating conditions and Spanish intolerance had turned them against Catholicism.

The Pueblo Revolt began in August 1680 as Popé and cohorts attacked Spanish colonists residing near Taos and killed sixty-eight of the seventy who lived there. Joined by Indians from neighboring pueblos, they laid siege to New Mexico's capital, Santa Fe. The rebels destroyed the churches and killed nearly four hundred colonists and missionaries. The Spanish fled, not to return for twelve years. They left behind them large numbers of livestock and horses, around which many Native Americans would build new ways of life.

Led by a new governor, Diego de Vargas, the Spanish returned in 1692, using both violence and threats of violence to reestablish their rule. Spanish control of New Mexico remained limited as the Europeans abolished the encomiendas and reined in the Franciscans. Pueblo suspicion of the Spanish remained, but there were no more revolts. Instead, the Indians accepted the limited Spanish control and sustained their cultural identity within the boundaries of colonial rule.

Florida and Texas

The Spanish fared no better in Florida. Periodic rebellions swept the Spanish settlements, and beginning in the 1680s, Indian slave raiders, allied with the English, killed or captured thousands of Florida natives and sold them to English slave traders. Even before a new round of warfare erupted in Europe at the turn of the century, Spain was ill prepared to defend its beleaguered North American empire.

English expansion threatened Florida, while the French establishment of Louisiana dashed Spanish hopes of linking Florida to New Mexico. To offset the French, Spanish authorities proclaimed the province of Tejas (Texas) in 1691, but no permanent Spanish settlements appeared there until 1716.

Popé Leader of Pueblo Revolt against Spanish in 1680

CHECKING IN

- France created a New World empire that encompassed North America from the Appalachians to the Rockies.
- The French empire rested primarily on trade with Native Americans rather than on conquest and displacement.
- Spanish policies led to the Pueblo revolt in 1680, but the Spanish reestablished control by 1700.
- The Spanish tried to establish frontiers in Texas and Florida, but their presence there was weak and scattered.

Chapter Summary

 DOWNLOAD THE MP3 AUDIO FILE OF THE CHAPTER SUMMARY, AND LISTEN TO IT ON THE GO.

KEY TERMS

Bacon's Rebellion (p. 43)

a city upon a hill (p. 46)

the "New England Way" (p. 46)

Old Deluder Act (p. 46)

Roger Williams (p. 47)

Anne Hutchinson (p. 47)

Half-Way Covenant (p. 50)

King Philip's War (p. 52)

Salem witchcraft trials (p. 52)

William Penn (p. 58)

coureurs de bois (p. 61)

Popé (p. 62)

How did tobacco shape the Chesapeake colonies? (page 39)

Unlike New England with its diversified economy, the Chesapeake colonies became dependent on a single cash crop, tobacco. Tobacco shaped the Chesapeake region by leading to the plantation system and dependence on African slavery, which developed gradually in the seventeenth century.

What was the "New England Way," and what challenges did it endure? (page 45)

Puritans established "a city upon a hill" in Massachusetts Bay to serve as a model to the world. The "New England Way"—a society based on religion—was threatened by dissenters Roger Williams and Anne Hutchinson and by the rise of a market economy. White expansion steadily displaced New England's Native Americans, and from the Pequot War to the bitter and costly King Philip's War resistance was crushed. The Half-Way Covenant marked the beginning of the end for the New England Way by relaxing standards for church membership, and the Salem witchcraft hysteria delivered the final blow, revealing deep social divisions.

Why and how did plantation agriculture shape slavery in the Caribbean and Carolina? (page 53)

Dependent on sugar cane, the Caribbean colonies evolved a harsh form of plantation slavery, while rice created a similarly harsh system in southern Carolina, which became the only mainland colony with a black majority population. Carolinians also enslaved tens of thousands of Indians.

How did diversity distinguish the Middle Colonies? (page 56)

The Middle Colonies followed yet another path of development. The Dutch New Netherland colony, conquered and incorporated by the English, contributed a strong history of religious and ethnic diversity. William Penn's "holy experiment" in Pennsylvania flourished, although it gradually moved away from some of its founder's ideals. Nonetheless, it, too, maintained both religious and economic diversity.

How did the French and Spanish empires develop in the seventeenth century? (page 60)

In contrast to the fairly compact English settlements, the French empire became a far-flung web stretching from the Appalachians to the Rockies, dependent almost exclusively on trade and thus on good relations with Native Americans. After suppressing the Pueblo Revolt in the late seventeenth century, the Spanish tried to establish their imperial frontiers in Texas and Florida, but both remained only lightly settled.

CHAPTER 4

The Bonds of Empire

1660–1750

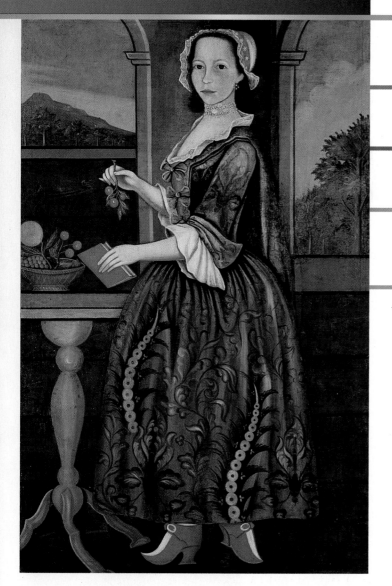

Mrs. Harme Gansevoor

CL This icon will direct you to the website where you can Prepare for Class, Improve Your Grade, and Ace the Test:
www.cengage.com/history/boyer/
enduringconcise6e

CHAPTER PREVIEW

Rebellion and War, 1660–1713
How did the Glorious Revolution shape relations between England and its North American colonies?

Colonial Economies and Societies, 1660–1750
What were the most important consequences of British mercantilism for the mainland colonies?

Competing for a Continent, 1713–1750
What factors explain the relative success of the British, French, and Spanish empires in North America?

Public Life in British America, 1689–1750
How did politics, the Enlightenment, and religious movements shape public life in the colonies?

Two men, George Whitefield and Benjamin Franklin, exemplified the major cultural currents that swept across the Atlantic from Europe to the colonies in the mid-eighteenth century. The embodiment of the powerful revival of piety that reinvigorated Protestantism on both sides of the ocean, Whitefield also demonstrated and reinforced the close ties that bound England and the colonies. Franklin, considered the leading American scientist of his time, personified the faith in reason known as the Enlightenment.

Born on opposite sides of the Atlantic, both men moved easily in English and colonial society, leaving behind provincialism for careers that brought them renown on both sides of the Atlantic. Their lives illustrate the increasingly close ties between England and her mainland colonies, ties that strengthened as the political and economic bonds of the empire grew tighter. This new imperial relationship enabled the Anglo-American colonies to achieve a level of growth and prosperity unequalled elsewhere in the Americas.

REBELLION AND WAR, 1660–1713

How did the Glorious Revolution shape relations between England and its North American colonies?

After the Restoration, England undertook a concerted effort to expand overseas trade and to subordinate its colonies to English commercial interests and political authority. The fall of the Stuart dynasty in 1689 and a succession of international wars hindered but did not halt this effort.

Royal Centralization, 1660–1688

The sons of a king executed by Parliament, the last Stuart monarchs, Charles II and James II, disliked representative government. Beginning in the mid-1670s, they tried to rule England as much as possible without Parliament and eyed American colonial assemblies suspiciously.

As Duke of York during his brother Charles's rule, James showed his disdain for colonial assemblies almost as soon as he became the proprietor of New York. Calling elected assemblies "of dangerous consequence," he forbade legislatures to meet from 1664 to 1682. In Charles's twenty-five-year reign, more than 90 percent of the governors whom he appointed were army officers, a serious violation of the English tradition of holding the military accountable to civilian authority. When James became king, he continued the policy.

Ever resentful of outside meddling, New Englanders resisted such centralization of power. In 1661 the Massachusetts assembly declared its citizens exempt from all English laws and royal decrees except declarations of war.

Provoked, Charles moved to break the Puritan establishment's power. In 1679 he carved a new royal territory, New Hampshire, from Massachusetts. In 1684 he declared Massachusetts a royal colony and revoked its charter, the very foundation of the Puritan city upon a hill.

James II went further. In 1686 the new king merged five separate colonies—Massachusetts, New Hampshire, Connecticut, Rhode Island, and Plymouth—into the **Dominion of New England,** later adding New York and the Jerseys. Under the new system, these colonies' legislatures ceased to exist. Sir Edmund Andros, a former army officer, became the Dominion's governor.

Dominion of New England
James II's attempt to tighten royal control of colonies by creating a new political entity

Andros's arbitrary actions ignited burning hatred in Massachusetts. He limited towns to one annual meeting and jailed prominent citizens to crush protests. He forced a Boston Puritan congregation to share its meetinghouse with an Anglican minister. Confronted by outraged colonists, he snapped "You have no more privileges left you than not to be sold for slaves."

Tensions also ran high in New York, where Catholics held high political and military posts under the Duke of York's rule. Anxious colonists feared that these

Chronology

1651–1733	England enacts Navigation Acts
1660	Restoration of the English monarchy
1686–1689	Dominion of New England
1688–1689	Glorious Revolution in England
1689	Uprisings in Massachusetts, New York, and Maryland; royal authority established English Bill of Rights
1689–1697	King William's War (in Europe, War of the League of Augsburg)
1690	John Locke, *Essay Concerning Human Understanding*
1701	Iroquois Confederacy agrees to remain neutral in future wars between England and France
1702–1713	Queen Anne's War (in Europe, War of the Spanish Succession)
1711–1713	Tuscarora War in Carolina
1715–1716	Yamasee War in Carolina
1716	San Antonio de Bexar founded
1718	New Orleans founded
1732	Georgia founded
1735	John Peter Zenger acquitted of seditious libel in New York; Jonathan Edwards leads revival in Northampton, Massachusetts
1739	Great Awakening begins with George Whitefield's arrival in British colonies; Stono Rebellion in South Carolina
1739–1740	Anglo-Spanish War
1739–1748	King George's War (in Europe, the War of the Austrian Succession)
1743	Benjamin Franklin founds American Philosophical Society
1750	Slavery legalized in Georgia

Catholic officials would betray the colony to France. When Andros's local deputy allowed harbor forts to deteriorate, New Yorkers suspected the worst.

The Glorious Revolution in England and America, 1688–1689

The Protestant majority in England also worriedly monitored Stuart displays of pro-Catholic sympathies. The Duke of York himself became a Catholic in 1676, and Charles II converted on his deathbed. Both rulers violated English law by allowing Catholics to hold high office and to worship openly.

In 1688 James's second wife bore a son, who would be raised—and perhaps would rule—as a Catholic. Aghast at the idea, English political leaders asked James's Protestant daughter Mary and her husband, William of Orange (the Dutch Republic's leader), to intervene. When William and Mary led a small army to England in November 1688, royal troops defected to them, and James II fled to France.

This nearly bloodless coup, the **"Glorious Revolution,"** created a "limited monarchy" as defined by England's **Bill of Rights** of 1689. The monarchs promised to summon Parliament annually, to sign its bills, and to respect civil liberties. Neither

"Glorious Revolution" Overthrow of James II in favor of William and Mary

Bill of Rights Drastically limited kingly power; vindicated limited representative government

Sir Edmund Andros and Boston Broadside Urging Him to Surrender, 1689
News of the Glorious Revolution in England quickly undermined Andros's authority within the Dominion of New England. Shortly after town authorities issued this public warning to Andros, Boston's militia arrested him

the English nor Anglo-Americans would ever forget this vindication of limited representative government. News of the Glorious Revolution electrified Massachusetts Puritans, who arrested Andros and his councilors. Acting in the name of William and Mary, the Massachusetts elite resumed its own government. The new monarchs allowed Connecticut and Rhode Island to resume election of their own governors and permitted Massachusetts to absorb the Plymouth colony. But Massachusetts enjoyed only a partial victory. The colony's new royal charter of 1691 reserved to the crown the appointment of the governor. Moreover, property ownership replaced church membership as the criterion for voting. Worst of all, the Puritan colony had to tolerate Anglicans and all other Protestants, who were proliferating in the port towns.

New York's counterpart to the anti-Stuart uprising was Leisler's Rebellion. In May 1689 the city militia, under Captain Jacob Leisler (LIES-luhr), had seized the harbor's main fort and called elections for an assembly. Andros's deputy, his authority strangled, sailed for England. In 1691 Leisler, still riding high, denied newly arrived English troops entry to key forts for fear that they were loyal to James II. But after a brief skirmish, Leisler was arrested and charged with treason. Elite New Yorkers, many of whom Leisler had arrested, packed the jury, and both he and his son-in-law were convicted and hanged.

Arbitrary government and fears of Catholic plots had also brought turmoil to Maryland by 1689, where the Protestant-dominated lower house and the Catholic upper chamber were feuding. When the Glorious Revolution toppled James II, Lord Baltimore, away in England, dispatched a courier to Maryland, commanding obedience to William and Mary. But the courier died en route.

Protestant rebel John Coode organized the Protestant Association to secure Maryland for William and Mary. In July 1689 Coode and his coconspirators seized the capital, removed Catholics from office, and requested that the crown take over the colony. Maryland became a royal province in 1691 and made the Church of England its established religion in 1692. Catholics, making up less than one-fourth of the population, lost the right to vote and to worship in public. In 1715 the fourth Lord Baltimore joined the Church of England and regained his proprietorship.

The revolutionary events of 1688–1689 reestablished the colonies' legislative government and ensured Protestant religious freedom. William and Mary allowed colonial elites to reassert local control and encouraged Americans to identify their interests with England, laying the foundation for an empire based on voluntary allegiance, not raw force.

A Generation of War, 1689–1713

The Glorious Revolution ushered in a quarter-century of war that convulsed both England and the colonies. In 1689 England joined a European coalition against France's Louis XIV and plunged into the War of the League of Augsburg (which Anglo-Americans called **King William's War**).

In 1690 the war spread to North America, as New Yorkers and New Englanders launched an invasion of England's enemy, New France. The invasion deteriorated into cruel but inconclusive border raids by both sides. The Iroquois, allied to the English, bore the brunt of the war. French forces, enlisting the aid of virtually every other tribe from Maine to the Great Lakes, played havoc with Iroquois land and peoples. By 1700 one-fourth of the Iroquois warriors had been killed or taken prisoner, or had fled to Canada. By comparison, English and Dutch casualties were fewer than nine hundred, and the French probably lost no more than four hundred. In 1701 the Iroquois agreed to let Canada's governor settle their disputes with other Indians and to remain neutral in future Anglo-French wars. Thereafter, playing French and English off against each other, the Iroquois maintained control of their lands, rebuilt their population, and held the balance of power along the Great Lakes.

In 1702 a new European war pitted England against France and Spain. During what the colonists called **Queen Anne's War,** Anglo-Americans became painfully aware of their own military weakness. French and Indian raiders from Canada destroyed New England towns, while the Spanish invaded southern Carolina and nearly took Charles Town in 1706. Colonial vessels fell to French and Spanish warships. English forces, however, gained control of the Hudson Bay region, Newfoundland, and Acadia (henceforth called Nova Scotia). The peace signed in 1713 allowed Britain to keep these lands but left the French and Indians in control of their interior.

King William's War European war that spilled over into North America (1689-1697)

Queen Anne's War European war that spilled over into North America

CHECKING IN

- After the Restoration, Britain attempted to tighten control over the colonies.
- The Glorious Revolution drove James II from the throne in 1688.
- The colonies regained their legislative rights.
- Protestant religious freedom was ensured.
- European wars from 1689 to 1713 played out in part in North America and strengthened colonial ties to England.

These wars had a profound political consequence. Anglo-Americans, realizing how much they needed the protection of the Royal Navy and identifying with England's leadership in the Protestant cause, became more loyal than ever to the English crown.

COLONIAL ECONOMIES AND SOCIETIES, 1660–1750

What were the most important consequences of British mercantilism for the mainland colonies?

The arrival of peace in 1713 shifted the competition among England, France, and Spain from the military to the economic. Britain and France sought to integrate their colonies into single colonial empires; Spain attempted to do so but found its power north of Mexico and the Caribbean severely limited.

mercantilism Political/economic theory that self-sufficiency was the way to national prosperity; tied colonial economies to the mother country

Navigation Acts Series of laws meant to make colonies conform to the ideas of mercantilism

Mercantilist Empires in America

A set of political-economic assumptions known as **mercantilism** supplied the framework for the new imperial economies. The term refers to European policies aimed at guaranteeing prosperity by making the European country (England, France, or Spain) as self-sufficient as possible by eliminating its dependence on foreign suppliers, damaging its foreign competitors' commerce, and increasing the national stock of gold and silver by selling more goods abroad than it bought.

A series of **Navigation Acts** governing commerce between Britain and its colonies embodied mercantilism. In 1651 the English Parliament passed the first Navigation Act to exclude the Dutch from English trade. During the Restoration, Parliament enacted the Navigation Acts of 1660 and 1663; they barred colonial merchants from exporting such commodities as sugar and tobacco to anywhere but England and from importing goods on non-English ships. Another major measure, the Molasses Act of 1733, sought to integrate Caribbean sugar growers into the imperial economy by slapping heavy import taxes on non-British imports and thus creating in effect a protective tariff.

By 1750 a long series of Navigation Acts was affecting the colonial economy in four major ways. First, the laws limited imperial trade to British-owned ships whose crews were three-quarters British (broadly defined to include all colonists, even blacks). This new shipping restriction helped Britain to become Europe's foremost shipping nation and laid the foundations for an American merchant marine. By the 1750s Americans owned one-third of all imperial vessels. The swift growth of the merchant marine diversified the colonial economy and made it more self-sufficient. The expansion of colonial shipping hastened urbanization. By 1770 New York, Philadelphia, Boston, and Charleston had become major ports.

Second, the Navigation Acts barred the colonies' export of "enumerated goods" unless they first passed through England or Scotland. Among these were tobacco, rice, furs, indigo, and naval stores (masts, hemp, tar, and turpentine). Parliament did not restrict grain, livestock, fish, lumber, or rum, which constituted 60 percent of colonial exports. To sweeten the deal, Parliament gave American tobacco a monopoly in British markets; it also eased the burden of customs duties on both tobacco and rice. Despite the restrictive laws, planters' profits dropped only 3 percent.

Third, the navigation system encouraged economic diversification. Parliament paid modest bounties to Americans producing silk, iron, dyes, hemp, lumber, and other products that Britain would otherwise have had to import from foreign countries. Parliament also erected protective tariffs against foreign goods. In addition, the trade laws forbade Anglo-Americans from competing with British manufacturing of certain products, especially clothing. There were no restrictions on the production of iron, and by the eve of the Revolution, 250 ironworks were in production.

Finally, the Navigation Acts made the colonies a protected market for low-priced consumer goods from Britain. As a result, the share of British exports bound for America rose from just 5 percent in 1700 to almost 40 percent by 1760. Mercantilism gave rise to a "consumer revolution" in British America.

Britain's fellow mercantilists in France and Spain enjoyed no such growth or prosperity. France's Canadian colonies had few materials other than furs to export, and they imported primarily wine and brandy. The French government actually lost money in the fur trade by sending sizable amounts of cloth, firearms, and other manufactured commodities to its Indian allies; the large army that France kept stationed in North America was also a drain on the French treasury. French Canada continued to lack the private investment, commercial infrastructure, consumer market, and manufacturing capacity that British North America was rapidly developing. The French did achieve some economic success in the West Indies, where sugar planters (in defiance of mercantilist principles) turned their cane into molasses and then sold much of the molasses to New England merchants. Louisiana remained unprofitable, a drain on French resources.

Spain's economic record was even more dismal. The revival of the Spanish and Latin American economies during the eighteenth century did not extend north of Mexico, where many Spanish colonists turned to smuggling goods to and from Spain's rivals as a source of income. These economic successes and failures mirrored what was happening in the European mother countries. In both France and Spain, most wealth was in the form of land held by the nobility and the Catholic Church; there was almost no liquidity. In contrast, England's economy was a commercial-mercantile one. More and more wealth was in the hands of merchants, who used it as capital to invest in commercial enterprises, trade, and manufacturing. Britain's navy protected that trade, while the Bank of England ensured a stable money supply. Great Britain was well on the way to becoming the world's first industrial nation, and its colonies benefited accordingly; indeed, the colonies' per capita income from 1650 to 1770 rose twice as fast as that of Britain.

Population Growth and Diversity

Demographic differences reinforced Britain's economic advantages. By 1750 the British North American colonies boasted more than 1.1 million inhabitants; the French colonies, 60,000; and the Spanish colonies, an almost negligible 19,000.

Potential Spanish immigrants generally chose the wealthier Latin American colonies as their destination. Spain saw its settlements north of Mexico primarily as a buffer against French or English expansion and consequently maintained a heavy military presence there.

Poverty kept most French people from immigrating, and tales of harsh Canadian winters and wretched Louisiana conditions often deterred those who might otherwise have tried their luck in the New World. French Canada's population growth was primarily the result of natural increase; to populate Louisiana, the French government dispatched paupers and criminals and encouraged the large-scale importation of slaves. By 1732 two-thirds of lower Louisiana's 5,800 people were slaves.

Unlike their French and Spanish rivals, the British colonies could offer potential immigrants ample farmland and a healthy imperial economy. Equally important, the British willingly accepted non-British immigrants—as long as they were not Catholics—including a handful of Jews. Thus British North America had a much deeper pool of potential immigrants.

Primary Source:
Main Sources of
African Slaves

Natural increase fueled population growth. After 1700, when life expectancy and family size in the South rose to parallel those of the North, Anglo-America's growth far outpaced Britain's. In 1700 England's population outnumbered the colonies' by

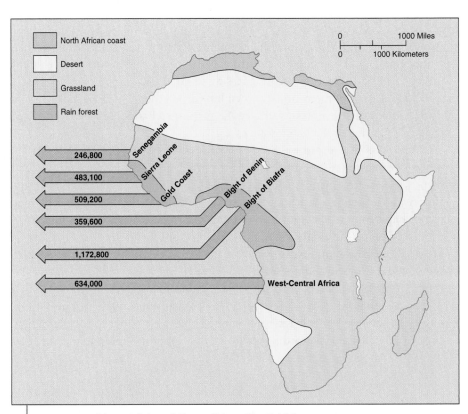

Map 4.1   African Origins of Slaves Shipped by British, 1692–1807
Virtually all slaves brought to English North America came from West Africa, between Senegambia and West-Central Africa. Most were captured or bought inland and marched to the coast, where they were sold to African merchants who in turn sold them to European slave traders.

twenty to one; by 1775 the ratio would be only three to one. Nevertheless continuing immigration contributed significantly to colonial population growth. In the forty years after Queen Anne's War, 350,000 newcomers had reached the colonies.

Between 1630 and 1700 approximately two thousand English settlers arrived in the colonies annually, constituting 90 percent of all European immigrants. After 1713 the flood slowed to a trickle of five hundred English immigrants a year. Rising employment and wages in England made emigration less attractive, but economic hardships elsewhere in the British Isles and on the Continent guaranteed a steady stream of immigrants, greatly increasing ethnic diversity among white North Americans.

 Primary Source: Excerpts of Virginia Law on Indentured Servitude

More than 100,000 newcomers in this era were from Ireland. Two-thirds of these were "Scots-Irish," the descendants of sixteenth-century Scottish Presbyterian settlers of northern Ireland. The Scots-Irish generally immigrated as complete families. In contrast, 90 percent of Irish Catholic immigrants were unmarried males who, once in America, often abandoned their faith to marry Protestant women.

Germany contributed some 125,000 settlers, the majority seeking escape from desperate poverty. One-third were "redemptioners" who had sold themselves or their children as indentured servants. Lutherans and Calvinists predominated, but a significant minority belonged to small, pacifist sects that desired above all to be left alone.

Indentured servants had to work one to four years for a master who might exploit them cruelly. Servants could be sold or rented out, beaten, kept from marrying, and sexually harassed; attempted escape usually meant an extension of service. At the end of their term, most collected "freedom dues," which helped them to marry and acquire land.

The piedmont, a broad, rolling upland stretching along the eastern slope of the Appalachians, drew many immigrants seeking open land. Upper New York, Pennsylvania, and Maryland attracted large numbers of Germans and Scots-Irish. Charles Town became a popular gateway for immigrants who later moved westward to the Carolina piedmont to become small farmers. In 1713 few Anglo-Americans lived more than fifty miles from the Atlantic, but by 1750 one-third of the colonists resided in the piedmont.

Map 4.2   Immigration and British Colonial Expansion, to 1755
Black majorities emerged in much of the Chesapeake tidewater and the Carolina-Georgia low country. Immigrants from Germany, Ireland, and Scotland predominated among the settlers in the piedmont. A significant Jewish population emerged in the seaports.

Not all of the white immigrants came voluntarily. Between 1718 and 1783 some thirty thousand English convicts arrived in North America; some were murderers, most were poor petty criminals. They were sold as servants. Relatively few committed crimes in the colonies, and some established themselves as successful backcountry farmers.

There were no volunteers among the 140,000 enslaved Africans who constituted the largest single group of newcomers. Most were from Africa's west coast, and all had survived a sea crossing of sickening brutality known as the **Middle Passage.** Ship captains closely calculated how many slaves they could jam into their vessels. Kept below deck in near-darkness, surrounded by filth and stench, numbed by depression, the Africans frequently fell victim to disease.

By mid-century blacks constituted 20 percent of the North American colonies' population. Although slavery remained primarily a southern institution, 15 percent of all slaves lived north of Maryland; by 1750 one in seven New Yorkers was a slave.

West Indian and Brazilian slave buyers outbid Anglo-Americans, who of necessity not only bought a higher proportion of female slaves but also protected their investments by maintaining slaves' health. As a result, slaves in British mainland colonies, more often than their Caribbean or Brazilian counterparts, formed fami-

Middle Passage Brutal and often fatal slave journey from Africa to the Americas

Architect's Plan of a Slave Ship
This plan graphically depicts the crowded, unsanitary conditions under which enslaved Africans were packed like cargo and transported across the Atlantic.

lies and lived longer. Natural increase among African-Americans almost equaled that of whites, and in some places American-born slaves outnumbered those born in Africa.

Rural White Men and Women

Because the vast majority of colonial landowners had just enough acreage for a working farm, most could not provide land for their children when they married. Moreover, with longevity increasing, children often did not receive their inheritances until middle age or later, and because families were large, a farmer's wealth was typically divided into small portions. Under these circumstances, a young man typically worked from about age sixteen to age twenty-three as a field hand to save money just to buy farm equipment, and a young husband generally had to rent land until he reached his mid-thirties.

The payment of mortgages was slow. A farmer could expect to earn 6 percent cash income per year, which barely equaled mortgage interest. After making a down payment of one-third, a husband and wife generally paid the next third through their inheritances. The final third would be paid when the children reached their teens and helped to double the regular farm income. Most colonial parents found themselves free of debt only as they reached their late fifties.

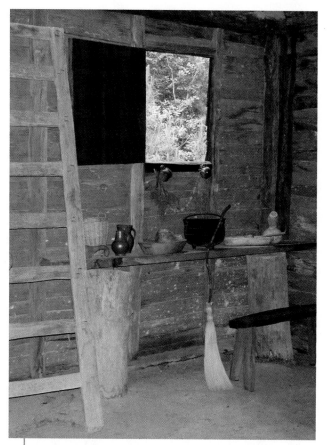

Poor Farmer's House
Many poor Chesapeake farmers lived in a single room with a dirt floor, no interior walls, an unglazed window, and minimal furnishings.

Rural families depended somewhat on barter and much more on what wives and daughters manufactured: soap, preserved food, knitted goods, yarn, and the products of dairy, orchard, and garden. However, legal constraints bound colonial women. A woman's most independent decision was her choice of a husband. Once married, she lost control of any goods or money she brought into the marriage. Nevertheless, widows controlled substantial property—an estimated 8 to 10 percent of all property in eighteenth-century Anglo-America—and some ran large estates or plantations.

Colonial Farmers and the Environment

As English settlement expanded, the environment east of the Appalachians changed rapidly. Eighteenth-century settlers cleared forest land to plant crops in its fertile soil. New England farmers also cleared from their land innumerable large rocks, debris from the last Ice Age. The felled trees provided timber to construct houses, barns, and fences and were burned as fuel for cooking and heating. Urban dwellers bought their firewood and construction timber from farmers and planters.

deforestation Removal of trees that had devastating ecological impact

Removal of trees (**deforestation**) deprived large forest creatures, such as bears, panthers, and wild turkeys, of their habitat, while the planted land provided free lunch for rabbits, mice, and possums. Deforestation removed protection from wind and sun, producing warmer summers and harsher winters, and, ironically, reinforcing the demand for firewood. By hastening the runoff of spring waters, deforestation led to heavier flooding and, where water could not escape, to larger swamps. Volatile temperatures and water levels rapidly reduced the number of fish in colonial streams and lakes.

Deforestation also dried and hardened the soil; colonial crops had even more drastic effects. Native Americans had rotated their crops to protect against soil depletion, but many colonial farmers lacked enough land to do so—and many more were unwilling to sacrifice short-term profits for long-term benefits. Tobacco yields in the Chesapeake region declined in fields planted only three or four consecutive years. As Chesapeake tobacco growers abandoned tidewater fields and moved to the piedmont, they hastened erosion. By 1750, to remain productive, many shifted from tobacco to wheat.

Well-to-do Europeans had already turned to conservation and "scientific farming." North American colonists ignored such techniques. Some could not afford to implement them, and virtually all believed that America's vast lands, including those still held by Indians, would sustain them and future generations indefinitely.

The Urban Paradox

Cities were colonial America's economic paradox. Although they shipped the livestock, grain, and lumber that enriched the countryside, at the same time they were caught in a downward spiral of declining opportunity.

After 1740 many among the 4 percent of colonists in cities found economic success elusive. Philadelphia, New York, and Boston faced escalating poverty. The cities' poor rolls, moreover, always bulged with the survivors of mariners lost at sea; unskilled, landless men; and women (often widows) and children from the countryside. High population density and poor sanitation left colonial cities vulnerable to the rapid spread of contagious diseases. As a result, half of all city children died before age twenty-one, and urban adults averaged ten fewer years of life than rural residents.

Even the able-bodied found cities economically treacherous. Traditionally, artisans trained apprentices and employed them as journeymen until they could open their own shops. After 1750, however, more employers released their workers when business slowed. And from 1720 onward, recessions hit frequently, creating longer spells of unemployment.

After 1700 urban poverty became a major problem. In Boston, for example, the proportion of the population too poor to pay taxes climbed steadily. New York did not build its first poorhouse until 1736, but 4 percent of its population needed public assistance by 1772. The percentage of Philadelphia families listed as poor jumped from 3 percent in 1720 to 11 percent by 1760.

Wealth remained highly concentrated. New York's wealthiest 10 percent owned about 45 percent of the property throughout the eighteenth century; Boston and Philadelphia followed similar patterns.

In the South, most cities were little more than large towns, although Charles Town was North America's fourth-largest city. South Carolina's capital offered gracious living to wealthy planters during the months of heat and insect infestations on their plantations. But shanties on the city's outskirts sheltered a growing crowd of destitute whites. Like their counterparts in northern port cities, Charles Town's poor whites competed for work with urban slaves whose masters rented out their labor. Racial tensions simmered.

Middle-class urban women faced less manual drudgery than their rural counterparts. Nonetheless, they managed complex households, often including servants and other nonfamily members. Although they sewed, knitted, and raised poultry and vegetables, urban women generally purchased their cloth and most of their food. Household servants, usually young single women or widows, helped with cooking, cleaning, and laundering. Wives also worked in family businesses, usually located in the owner's home.

Widows and less affluent wives took in boarders and often spun and wove cloth for local merchants. As grim conditions in Boston forced many widows with children to look to the community for relief, more prosperous Bostonians scorned them.

Slavery

Masters could usually afford to keep slaves healthy, but they rarely made their human chattels comfortable. Slave upkeep generally cost 60 percent less than the maintenance of indentured servants. White servants ate two hundred pounds of beef or pork a year; slaves, fifty pounds. A master would spend as much providing beer and hard cider for a servant as food and clothing for a slave. Adult slaves received eight quarts of corn and one pound of pork weekly and were expected to grow vegetables and raise poultry.

Slaves worked for a longer portion of their lives than whites. Slave children worked part time from the age of seven and full time as early as eleven. African-American women performed hard work alongside men and tended tobacco and rice crops even when pregnant. Most slaves toiled until they died, although those in their sixties rarely did hard labor.

As the number of Creole (American-born) slaves grew, sharp differences between them and African-born blacks arose. Creoles enjoyed the advantage of knowing the English language, the local environment, and the ways of their masters. They often translated this advantage into greater autonomy. Wealthier planters in particular used African-born slaves as field hands while training Creoles to perform household duties, such as repairing and driving carriages, preparing and serving meals, sewing, and caring for their children.

Both Africans and Creoles maximized opportunities within this harsh system. House slaves demanded that guests tip them for shining shoes and stabling horses; they also expected gifts on holidays. In the Carolina and Georgia rice country, the task system gave slaves some control of their work. Under tasking, each slave spent half a day caring for one-quarter acre, after which his or her duties ended. Ambitious slaves used the rest of the day to keep hogs or to grow vegetables for sale in Charles Town.

The gang system used on tobacco plantations gave Chesapeake slaves less free time than their counterparts in Carolina. However, despite Carolina slaves' greater autonomy, racial tensions ran high, especially as blacks began to outnumber whites. For example, a law of 1735 imposed severe restrictions on slave clothing. Of far greater concern were large gatherings of blacks uncontrolled by whites. In 1721 Charles Town enacted a 9:00 p.m. curfew for blacks. Slaves responded with increased instances of arson, theft, flight, and violence.

By mid-century, slaves constituted 20 percent of New York City's population and formed a majority in Charles Town and Savannah. Skilled urban slaves hired themselves out and kept part of their wages. By 1770 one-tenth of Savannah's slaves were living in rented rooms away from their owners. Despite substantial personal freedom, they remained slaves.

Stono Rebellion Failed South Carolina slave uprising

Tensions erupted in 1739 when a slave uprising known as the **Stono Rebellion** jolted South Carolina. Stealing guns and ammunition from a store at the Stono River Bridge, one hundred slaves headed for Florida crying, "Liberty!" Along the way they burned seven plantations and killed twenty whites. Within a day, however, mounted militiamen surrounded the runaways, cut them down, and spiked a rebel head on every milepost back to Charles Town. Whites expressed their fears in a new slave code stipulating constant surveillance and discipline for slaves, and requiring legislative approval for manumission (the freeing of individual slaves). The Stono Rebellion thus accelerated South Carolina's emergence as a racist and fear-ridden society.

Racial tensions wracked cities as well as plantations. In 1712 rebellious slaves in New York City killed nine whites; as a result, thirteen slaves were hanged, one was starved to death, three were burned at the stake, one was broken on the wheel, and six committed suicide. In 1741 a wave of thefts and fires attributed to slaves in New York led to the torture and hanging of thirteen slaves, the burning of thirteen more, and the sale of seventy to the West Indies.

The Rise of the Colonial Elites

For white colonial Americans, wealth defined status. "A man who has money here, no matter how he came by it, he is everything," wrote a Rhode Islander in 1748. Once wealthy, a man was expected to be responsible, dignified, and generous, and to act as a community leader—to act like a gentleman. His wife was expected to be a skillful household manager and a refined, respectful hostess—a lady.

Before 1700 class structure in the colonies was relatively invisible; the rural elite spent its resources on land, servants, and slaves instead of on conspicuous luxuries. A traveler visiting one of Virginia's richest planters noted that his host owned only "good beds but no curtains and instead of cane chairs . . . stools made of wood." After 1720, however, the display of wealth became more ostentatious. The greater gentry—the richest 2 percent of the population—built splendid estate homes. The lesser gentry, or the second-wealthiest 2 to 10 percent, lived in more modest field-stone or wood-frame houses, and middle-class farmers typically inhabited one-story wooden buildings with four small rooms.

The gentry also exhibited their wealth after 1720 by imitating European "refinements." They wore costly English fashions, drove carriages, and bought expensive china, books, and furniture. They pursued a gracious life by studying foreign languages, learning formal dances, and cultivating polite manners.

CHECKING IN

- After 1713, competition for North America shifted from the military to the economic realm as Britain embraced mercantilism.

- Prosperity boomed in the English colonies.

- The English colonies saw rapid population growth, in part from immigration.

- The differences between rural and urban life sharpened, and the number of colonial elites arose.

- Slavery became more important both economically and socially.

COMPETING FOR A CONTINENT, 1713–1750

What factors explain the relative success of the British, French, and Spanish empires in North America?

█ Europeans transformed North America in the first half of the eighteenth century as they expanded their territorial claims, opened new areas for settlement, and engaged in more intensive trade and warfare with Native Americans. In turn, Native Americans often welcomed trade but resisted Europeans who tried to settle nearby.

Interactive Map: Immigration and Frontier Expansion, to 1755

France and the American Heartland

Louisiana became a principal focus of France's imperial efforts. New Orleans, established in 1718, became the colony's capital and port. France hoped to use the Choctaw Indians as allies, but by the 1730s the tribe had become bitterly divided between pro-English and pro-French factions.

Louisiana's sluggish export economy forced settlers and slaves to find other means of support. Like the Indians, they hunted, fished, gathered wild plants, and cultivated gardens. And Indian, white, and black Louisianans traded with one another. Indians provided corn, tallow, and, above all, deerskins to merchants in return for blankets, axes, chickens, guns, and alcohol. Indians from west of the Mississippi brought horses and cattle, usually stolen from Spanish ranches in Texas. West African slaves, familiar with cattle from their homelands, managed many of Louisiana's herds; some became rustlers and illicit traders of beef.

French settlements in Upper Louisiana, usually referred to as Illinois (but also including parts of Missouri), were somewhat better off. Wheat became Illinois's major export, a more stable and profitable crop than the plantation commodities grown farther south. However, the colony's remote location limited exports and attracted few whites. It continued to depend on Native American allies to defend it from Indian enemies.

French attention also turned to the Ohio Valley, which, thanks to Iroquois neutrality, had become a refuge for dislocated Native American tribes, such as the Kickapoos, Shawnees, and Delawares. To counter growing English influence and to secure commercial and diplomatic ties with the Indians, the French expanded their trade. Several French posts, including Detroit, ballooned into sizable villages of Indian, French, and mixed-ancestry residents. Although the French were generally more successful than the English among the Indians, they never won over the Carolina-backed Chickasaws, and waged brutal warfare against the Mesquakies at Detroit and the Natchez in Louisiana. The French sold captives seized in these wars as slaves in their mainland colonies and in the West Indies. By 1744 French traders had explored as far west as North Dakota and Colorado, buying beaver pelts and Indian slaves on the Great Plains. These traders and their competitors spread trade goods, including guns, to Native Americans throughout central Canada and the Plains. Meanwhile, Indians in the southern Plains and the Great Basin had acquired horses from the thousands left behind by fleeing Spaniards after the Pueblo Revolt of 1680. Horses and guns enabled tribes such as the Lakota Sioux and the Comanche to move onto the Plains and build a new, highly mobile way of life based on the pursuit of the buffalo. By 1750, France claimed an immense territory but their domain was precariously dependent on relations with Native Americans.

Native Americans and British Expansion

The depopulation and dislocation of Native Americans made possible the colonies' rapid expansion. Epidemic diseases, environmental changes, war, and political pressure opened new land for Europeans. In Carolina, imperial wars and the trade in Indian slaves soon produced violence. Between 1711 and 1713, clashes between the Tuscaroras and white settlers led to the death or enslavement of about one-fifth of the tribe; most survivors migrated northward to upstate New York to become the sixth nation of the Iroquois Confederacy. Settler abuses against Indians continued, leading the Yamasees and several allied nations to attack English settlements in 1715 and 1716. Only by relying on the aid of the Cherokees and by arming four hundred slaves did the colony crush the uprising.

The defeat of the Yamasees in turn left their Catawba allies wedged uncomfortably between the English to the south and the Iroquois to the north. They turned to the English for help. In return for land and promises to defend the colony against other Indians, the Catawbas received guns, food, and clothing. Although this gave the Catawbas at least temporary security, the rapidly increasing white population and the competition for resources sharply limited Catawba autonomy.

To the North, the Iroquois tried to accommodate the English and consolidate their own power. Late in the seventeenth century, the Iroquois had entered into a series of agreements, known as the **Covenant Chain,** to relocate Indians whose lands the colonists desired. These tribes were moved to areas of New York and Pennsylvania, on the periphery of the Iroquois homeland, where they served as buffers against English expansion. In that way, and by incorporating the Tuscaroras into their confederacy, the Iroquois created a center of Native American power distinct from, but cooperative with, the British.

Covenant Chain Treaties by which Iroquois agreed to relocate displaced tribes to the periphery of Iroquois lands

 Interactive Map: The Indian Confederacies

In similar fashion, Pennsylvania coerced the Delawares into selling more than fifty thousand acres between 1729 and 1734. Then the colony's leaders produced a fraudulent treaty, dated to 1686, that required the Delawares to cede twelve hundred square miles of land. The Iroquois forced the Delawares to move to the upper Ohio Valley while the proprietors made a huge profit by selling the Delawares' land. Indians elsewhere along the westward-moving frontier faced pressure from settlers on one side and the Iroquois on the other.

British Expansion in the South: Georgia

In 1732 Parliament chartered a new colony, Georgia. It was to be a refuge for debtors, whose settlement would buffer South Carolina against attacks from Spanish Florida. Further, the new English colony would export expensive commodities, such as wine and silk.

James Oglethorpe Founder of Georgia colony

James Oglethorpe, who dominated the provincial board of trustees, shaped Georgia's early years. He established the port of entry, Savannah, in 1733. By 1740 nearly three thousand colonists resided in Georgia. Almost half were non-English immigrants from Germany, Switzerland, and Scotland, and most had their overseas passage paid by the government. A small number of Jews were among the early settlers. Thus Georgia began as the last English colony.

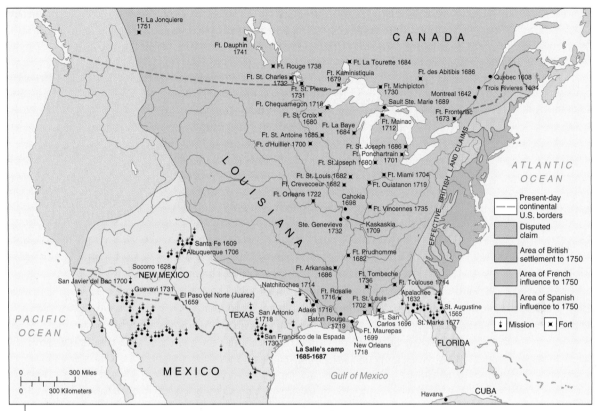

Map 4.3   French and Spanish Occupation of North America, to 1750
Spanish and French occupation depended on ties with Native Americans. By contrast, British colonists had dispossessed Native peoples and densely settled the eastern seaboard.

Idealism and concerns about security led Oglethorpe to ban slavery from Georgia. Oglethorpe thought that slavery degraded blacks, made whites lazy, and presented a terrible risk. Parliament thus made Georgia the only colony where slavery was forbidden.

Oglethorpe's well-intentioned plans failed. Few debtors arrived because of Parliament's restrictions on their release from prison. Limitations that Oglethorpe had secured on settlers' rights to enlarge or sell their holdings discouraged immigrants, as did the ban on slavery. Georgia exported neither wine nor silk; only rice proved profitable. After a decade of struggle against economic reality, Oglethorpe yielded. In 1750 slavery became legal, and restrictions on landholdings ended. As a result, Georgia boomed.

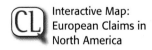
Interactive Map: European Claims in North America

Spain's Borderlands

While trying to maintain an empire in the face of Native American, French, and British adversaries, Spain spread its language and culture over much of North America, especially the Southwest. To repopulate New Mexico with settlers after the Pueblo Revolt (see Chapter 3), Spain handed out huge land grants and constructed fortifications, primarily for defense against, first, the Apaches and later, the Comanches (cuh-MAN-cheese).

Livestock-raising *ranchos* (ranches) monopolized vast amounts of land along the Rio Grande and blocked the establishment of further towns. On these ranchos, mounted herders of cattle and sheep (*vaqueros*) (vah-CARE-ohs) created the way of life later adopted by the American cowboy, featuring lariat and roping skills, cattle drives, and roundups.

By 1750 New Mexico numbered about 14,000, more than half of them Pueblos. Integrated into New Mexico society, most Pueblos practiced both Catholicism and their traditional religion and helped to defend the colony. Most Apaches had fled to Mexico or made peace with the Spanish to gain support against raids by Utes (yoots) and Comanches from the north.

To counter growing French influence among the Comanches and other Native Americans on the southern plains, Spain colonized Texas. In 1716 the Spanish established four missions. The most successful of the missions was at San Antonio de Bexar (day beh-HAR), where friars constructed a fortified building known as the Alamo. The Spanish presence in Texas remained light, however; by mid-century only 1,200 Spaniards lived there, under constant threat of Indian raids.

Spain's position in Florida was only slightly less precarious. As early as 1700, when 1700 English had settled in the Carolinas, only 1500 Spanish were in Florida, a discrepancy that would continue to widen. To some extent, trade with the Creeks helped offset this numerical difference. But Florida's trade profits remained slim because it lacked cheap, desirable trade goods.

Florida gained more at English expense through its recruitment of escaped slaves from Carolina. In 1693 the Spanish monarch, Charles II, had decreed that any English-owned slaves who reached Florida and became Catholic would be freed. Word of this spread back to the Carolinas, prompting more slaves to flee to Florida. Eventually the Spanish would recruit an all-black militia unit and build a fortified village for the former slaves and their families.

By 1750 the French and Spanish empires had reached their limits in North America. Spain controlled much of the Southeast and Southwest, and France claimed the Mississippi, Ohio, and Missouri river valleys. Spain also maintained a precarious hold on Florida. Both empires, spread thin, depended heavily on Indian goodwill. In contrast, British North America, compact and wealthy, was densely populated by whites and was generally antagonistic toward Native Americans.

CHECKING IN

- The French remained lightly scattered over their North American empire and dependent on maintaining good relations with the Indians.
- British expansion continued to push Indians westward.
- Spain extended its control in the Southwest and established a light presence in Texas.
- Early in the eighteenth century, continental European wars again spread to North America.

The Return of War, 1739–1748

Imperial rivalries between England on the one hand and France and Spain on the other prevailed after 1713. In 1739 Britain launched a war against Spain. James Oglethorpe led a massive but unsuccessful assault on St. Augustine in 1740; Spanish troops and refugee slaves from South Carolina likewise failed in a counterattack on Georgia two years later. By then, the Anglo-Spanish War had merged with one in Europe, the War of the Austrian Succession (1739–1748), known as King George's War to the colonists. In this conflict, four thousand New Englanders besieged the French fortress at Louisbourg, at the mouth of the St. Lawrence, and captured it after seven intense weeks of fighting. But the war was inconclusive, and in 1748 Britain returned Louisbourg to the French under terms of the peace treaty ending the conflict.

Public Life in British America, 1689–1750

How did politics, the Enlightenment, and religious movements shape public life in the colonies?

During the early and middle eighteenth century, the ties linking Britain and its colonies extended far beyond the movement of goods and peoples. England's new Bill of Rights was the foundation of government and politics in the colonies. English thinkers inspired the Enlightenment, and English preacher George Whitefield (WHIT-field) sparked a generation of colonists to transform the practice of Protestantism in British America. Significantly, these developments involved many more colonists than before as active participants in politics, in intellectual discussions, and in new religious movements. This wider participation signaled the emergence of a broad Anglo-American "public."

Colonial Politics

The most important political development after 1700 was the rise of the assembly as the dominant force in colonial government. Except in Connecticut and Rhode Island, the crown or proprietors chose colonial governors, who in turn named a council, or upper legislative house. Only in the lower house, or assembly, could members of the gentry assert their interests. Until 1689 governors and councils drafted laws, and the assemblies generally followed passively. Thereafter, assemblies assumed a more central role in politics, as colonial leaders argued that their legislatures should exercise the same rights as Parliament's House of Commons, believing that colonial governors should be as restricted as England's monarchs were. Parliament's victory in the Glorious Revolution convinced Americans that their governors should defer to the assemblies.

The lower houses refused to permit meddling in their procedures, took control over taxes and budgets, and kept a tight rein on the salaries of governors who received no salary from Britain and remained vulnerable to such financial pressure. This power of the purse often forced governors to sign laws opposed by the crown.

Moreover, Britain's lack of interest in colonial politics allowed the assemblies to take considerable power. The Board of Trade, established by Parliament in 1696 to monitor American affairs, had neither the staff, the energy, nor the vision to maintain royal authority by supporting embattled governors. This political vacuum allowed the colonies to become self-governing in most respects except for regulating trade, printing money, and declaring war. Colonial autonomy, reinforced by self-assertive assemblies, would haunt British authorities when they attempted to exercise more direct rule after 1763 (see Chapter 5).

The colonial elite dominated politics as well as society. Governors appointed members of the greater gentry to serve on councils and as judges in the highest courts. The upper gentry, along with militia majors and colonels, also dominated among the representatives elected to the legislatures' lower houses (the assemblies). Members of the lesser gentry sat less often in the legislatures, but they commonly served as justices of the peace in the county courts.

Outside New England, property restrictions barred 80 percent of white men from running for the assembly. In any case, few ordinary citizens could have afforded the high costs of elective office. Assemblymen received meager living expenses, which did not cover the cost of staying at the capital, much less make up for six to ten weeks of missed work. Consequently, political leadership fell to a small number of wealthy families with a tradition of public service.

The colonies generally set liberal qualifications for male voters, but all excluded women, blacks, and Indians from voting. In seven colonies, voters had to own land (usually forty to fifty acres), and in the others they had to have enough property to furnish a house and to work a farm. Most of the 40 percent who could not meet these requirements were indentured servants, single sons living with parents, or young men just beginning family life. Most white males in Anglo-America could vote by age forty, whereas across the Atlantic, two-thirds of all Englishmen and 90 percent of Irishmen could never vote.

Rural voting participation was low, averaging 45 percent. Governors called elections randomly so that after years without an election, one could be called on short notice. Voters in isolated areas often did not know of an upcoming election. Voting took place at the county seat, and many voters did not risk traveling long distances over poor roads to reach the voting place. In many colonies voters stated their preference publicly, often face to face with the candidates, a practice that discouraged dissenters. There were no political parties to stimulate popular interest or to mobilize voters. Candidates nominated themselves and ran on their reputation, not on the issues.

In view of these factors, political indifference was widespread. For example, to avoid paying legislators' expenses, many Massachusetts towns refused to elect assemblymen. From 1731 to 1760, one-third of South Carolina's elected assemblymen neglected to take their seats. Apathy might have been even greater had not candidates plied voters with alcohol. George Washington dispensed almost two quarts of liquor for each voter when he was first elected to Virginia's assembly in 1758.

Competitive politics first developed in the northern seaports. Wealthy colonists aligned themselves with or against royal and proprietary governors. To gain advantage over rivals, some factions courted artisans and small shopkeepers whose fortunes had stagnated or declined as the distribution of wealth favored the rich.

John Peter Zenger Central figure in a trial that opened the way for freedom of the press

In 1735 New York became the site of a celebrated trial. Newspaper printer **John Peter Zenger** was charged with seditiously libeling the colony's governor. Zenger's acquittal on the charge broadened political discussion and participation beyond a small circle of elites. It also established truth as a defense against the charge of libel, opening the way toward greater freedom of the press in the future.

The Enlightenment

If property and wealth were keys to political participation and office-holding, literacy and education enabled Anglo-Americans to participate in the transatlantic world of ideas and beliefs. Eighteenth-century Anglo-America was probably the world's most literate society. Ninety percent of New England's adult white males and 40 percent of its women could write well enough to sign documents. In other colonies the literacy rate varied from 35 to 50 percent. In contrast, in England it stood at just over 30 percent. Nevertheless, ordinary Americans' reading encompassed only a few books: an almanac, a psalter, and the Bible.

Members of the gentry, well-to-do merchants, and educated ministers lived in a world of print culture. Although costly, books and writing paper opened eighteenth-century European civilization to men and women of these classes who could read. And a rich, exciting world it was. Great advances in natural science seemed to explain the laws of nature, human intelligence appeared poised to triumph over ignorance and prejudice, and life itself would surely become more pleasant. For those with time to read and think, an age of optimism and progress had dawned: the **Enlightenment.**

Enlightenment ideals combined confidence in reason with skepticism about beliefs not based on science or logic. Enlightenment thought drew on the work of the English physicist **Sir Isaac Newton** (1642–1727), who explained how gravitation ruled the universe. Newton's work demonstrated the harmony of natural laws and stimulated others to search for rational principles in medicine, law, psychology, and government.

No American more embodied the Enlightenment spirit than **Benjamin Franklin** (1706–1790). Born in Boston, Franklin migrated to Philadelphia at age seventeen, bringing considerable assets: skill as a printer, ambition, and insatiable curiosity. In 1732 Franklin began publishing *Poor Richard's Almanack,* a collection of proverbs that made him famous. By age forty-two he had saved enough money to retire from printing and devote himself to science and community service.

To Franklin, science and community service were intertwined; true science would make everyone's life more comfortable. For example, his experiments in flying a kite during a thunderstorm proved that lightning was electricity and led to the invention of the lightning rod. In 1743 Franklin organized the American Philosophical Society to encourage "all philosophical experiments that let light into the nature of things, tend to increase the power of man over matter, and multiply the conveniences and pleasures of life." By 1769 the society had blossomed into an intercolonial network of amateur scientists.

Although some plantation owners, among them Thomas Jefferson, championed the Enlightenment, it flourished in the seaboard cities, where the latest ideas from Europe circulated and gentlemen and artisans met in small societies to investigate nature. To these individuals, the Royal Society in London, the foremost learned society in the English-speaking world, represented the ideal. The Enlightenment thus initially strengthened ties between British and colonial elites. Its adherents envisioned progress as gradual and proceeding from the top down. Just as Newton inspired the scientific bent of Enlightenment intellectuals, the English philosopher **John Locke's** *Essay Concerning Human Understanding* (1690) led many to embrace "reasonable" or "rational" religion. Locke contended that ideas are not inborn but are acquired by investigation of, and reflection on, experience. Enlightenment intellectuals believed that the study of the

Enlightenment Intellectual revolution that elevated reason, science, and logic

Sir Isaac Newton British scientist whose ideas lay at the heart of the Enlightenment

Benjamin Franklin American who embodied Enlightenment ideas

John Locke British philosopher who explained how reason functions

Benjamin Franklin
This earliest known portrait of Franklin dates to about 1740, when he was a rising leader in bustling Philadelphia.

harmony and order of nature provided the best argument for God, a rational Creator. A handful insisted that where the Bible conflicted with reason, one should follow reason. Those—including Franklin and Jefferson—who took the argument furthest were called **Deists**. They concluded that God, having created a perfect universe, did not miraculously intervene in its workings but instead left it alone to operate according to natural law.

Deists Rationalists who insisted that the universe operates by natural law

Most colonists influenced by the Enlightenment considered themselves Christians but feared Christianity's excesses, particularly persecution in the name of religion and "enthusiasts" who emphasized emotion over reason. Mindful of Locke's caution that no human can be absolutely certain of anything but his or her own existence, they distrusted zealots and sectarians, and believed that religion's value lay in the encouragement of virtue and morality, not in theological hair splitting.

In 1750 the Enlightenment's greatest contributions to American life lay in the future, when Anglo-Americans would draw on the Enlightenment's revolutionary ideas as they declared independence and created a new nation. In the meantime, a series of religious revivals known as the Great Awakening would challenge the Enlightenment's most basic assumptions.

The Great Awakening

Rationalists viewed the world as orderly and predictable. Many Americans, however, had neither worldly goods nor orderly and predictable lives. The result was a spiritual longing that neither traditional religion nor Enlightenment philosophy could satisfy.

A quickening of religious fervor in scattered places in the 1730s became passionate revivalism throughout Anglo-America in 1739. This **"Great Awakening"** cut across lines of class, status, and education. Above all, the Great Awakening represented an unleashing among ordinary people of anxiety about sin and longing for assurances of salvation. Some revivalists were steeped in Enlightenment ideas but for all, religion was primarily a matter of emotional commitment.

"Great Awakening" Protestant revival movement that emphasized each person's urgent need for salvation by God

In contrast to rationalists, who stressed the human potential for betterment, the ministers of the Great Awakening emphasized the corruption of human nature, the fury of divine wrath, and the need for immediate repentance. Congregationalist minister **Jonathan Edwards** of Northampton, Massachusetts drove home this message with breathtaking clarity. In 1735 during a revival Edwards preached his great sermon "Sinners in the Hands of an Angry God." "The God that holds you over the pit of Hell, much as one holds a spider or other loathsome insect over the fire, abhors you," Edwards intoned. "His wrath toward you burns like fire; He looks upon you as worthy of nothing else but to be cast into the fire."

Jonathan Edwards Revivalist preacher whose sermon "Sinners in the Hands of an Angry God" summarized Great Awakening beliefs

Other colonial ministers—Presbyterian William Tennent and Dutch Reformed Theodore Frelinghuysen—had anticipated Edwards's themes. Pulling the diverse threads of revival together was the arrival in 1739 of the charismatic English cleric **George Whitefield.** A man of overpowering presence and a booming voice, Whitefield attracted some crowds exceeding 20,000. On a tour through the colonies, Whitefield inspired thousands, mainly young adults, to seek salvation.

George Whitefield English preacher who toured the colonies and played a major role in the Great Awakening

Whitefield's powerful allure awed even his critics. But divisions over the revivals developed in Whitefield's wake. For example, after leaving Boston in October 1740,

Whitefield invited Gilbert Tennent (William's son) to follow "in order to blow up the divine flame lately kindled there." Denouncing Boston's established clergy as "dead Drones" and lashing out at elites, Tennent built a following among the poor and downtrodden.

Exposing colonial society's divisions, Tennent and other radicals corroded support for revivals among established ministers and officials. Increasingly, lines hardened between the revivalists, the "New Lights," and the rationalist clergymen, or "Old Lights," who dominated the Anglican, Presbyterian, and Congregational churches. In 1740 Gilbert Tennent hinted that most Presbyterian ministers lacked saving grace and were bound for hell, and he urged parishioners to abandon them for the New Lights. By sowing doubts about ministers, Tennent undermined one of the foundations of the social order: if people could not trust their ministers, whom *could* they trust? Old Light rationalists fired back. In 1742 Charles Chauncy, a Boston Congregationalist, condemned revivals as an epidemic of the "enthusiasm" that enlightened intellectuals so hated. Chauncy especially blasted enthusiasts who mistook the ravings of their overheated imagination for direct communications from God.

The Great Awakening thus split American Protestantism. In 1741 Old and New Light Presbyterians formed rival branches that reunited in 1758 when the revivalists emerged victorious. The Anglican church lost many members to New Light Presbyterians and Baptists. Congregationalists also splintered badly; by 1760 New Lights had seceded from one-third of all churches and formed separate parishes.

The Great Awakening peaked in New England in 1742, but New Lights made steady gains into the 1770s, and the revival's long-term effects far exceeded its immediate impact. First, the revival started a decline in the influence of older sects, such as the Quakers, Anglicans, and Congregationalists. In turn, the number of Presbyterians and Baptists increased after 1740, and that of Methodists rose steadily after 1770. These churches have since dominated American Protestantism. Second, the Great Awakening stimulated the founding of new colleges unscarred by religious wars. The College of New Jersey (Princeton, 1746), King's College (Columbia, 1754), the College of Rhode Island (Brown, 1764), Queen's College (Rutgers, 1766), and Dartmouth (1769) trace their roots to this era. Third, the revival drew many African-Americans and Native Americans to Protestantism for the first time. Its oral and communal nature, and its emphasis on piety rather than learning, incorporated aspects of both groups' traditional cultures. The Great Awakening marked the emergence of black Protestantism as New Lights reached out to slaves. Meanwhile, a few New Light preachers, Indian as well as white, became missionaries to Indians. Still, nonwhites faced discrimination, even among New Lights.

The Great Awakening, moreover, gave women added prominence in colonial religion. For several decades, ministers had praised women—the majority of church members—as the embodiment of Christian piety. Now some New Light sects, mainly Baptist and Congregationalist, granted women the right to speak and vote in church meetings. Some women, like Anne Hutchinson a century earlier, presided over prayer meetings that included women, men, and sometimes even slaves. Although some of these women's activities were suppressed, none was prosecuted, as Hutchinson had been. The Great Awakening also fostered religious tolerance by blurring theological differences among New Lights. Indeed, revivalism's emphasis on inner experience,

- Elected assemblies, dominated by colonial elites, became increasingly powerful.
- Political participation and competition were more evident in cities than in the countryside.
- The Enlightenment, with its optimism and strong emphasis on rationality, spread widely among colonial elites.
- At the same time, the Great Awakening expressed widespread religious longings, and new Protestant denominations challenged older ones.

rather than on doctrinal fine points, emphasized Protestants' common experiences and promoted the coexistence of denominations.

Historians disagree about whether the Great Awakening had political effects. Although New Lights flayed the wealthy, they neither advocated a social revolution nor developed a political ideology. Yet, by empowering ordinary people to criticize those in authority, the revivals helped to lay the groundwork for political revolutionaries a generation later who would preach that royal government had grown corrupt and unworthy of obedience.

Chapter Summary

DOWNLOAD THE MP3 AUDIO FILE OF THE CHAPTER SUMMARY TO LISTEN TO ON THE GO.

How did the Glorious Revolution shape relations between England and its North American colonies? (page 66)

After the Restoration of the Stuart kings to England's throne, the British government attempted to tighten control over the colonies with measures such as the Navigation Acts and the Dominion of New England. When the Glorious Revolution drove James II from England, the colonies regained control of their own legislatures. England's wars on the continent of Europe spread to the New World, raising colonists' recognition of their own military weakness and strengthening their bonds to England.

What were the most important consequences of British mercantilism for the mainland colonies? (page 70)

The Navigation Acts, passed in response to a quickening sense of mercantilism in England, sought to control colonial trade. The primary effect was to increase colonial prosperity. Britain's colonies welcomed immigrants, and their population soared. Slavery became increasingly widespread, as did fears of slave rebellion. Population growth was a major factor in deforestation, which in turn stimulated westward movement away from depleted soils. Increased prosperity also contributed to the rise of colonial elites, but the poverty rate rose among ordinary city dwellers.

KEY TERMS

Dominion of New England *(p. 66)*
"Glorious Revolution" *(p. 67)*
Bill of Rights *(p. 67)*
King William's War *(p. 69)*
Queen Anne's War *(p. 69)*
mercantilism *(p. 70)*
Navigation Acts *(p. 70)*
Middle Passage *(p. 74)*
deforestation *(p. 76)*
Stono Rebellion *(p. 78)*
Covenant Chain *(p. 80)*
James Oglethorpe *(p. 80)*
John Peter Zenger *(p. 84)*
Enlightenment *(p. 85)*
Sir Isaac Newton *(p. 85)*
Benjamin Franklin *(p. 85)*
John Locke *(p. 85)*
Deists *(p. 86)*
"Great Awakening" *(p. 86)*
Jonathan Edwards *(p. 86)*
George Whitefield *(p. 86)*

What factors explain the relative success of the British, French, and Spanish empires in North America? (page 79)

The first half of the eighteenth century saw renewed competition among the French, the British, and the Spanish for control of North America. France and Spain maintained sparse settlement and relied on good relations with Indians. English expansion created renewed problems for Native Americans.

How did politics, the Enlightenment, and religious movements shape public life in the colonies? (page 83)

The same time frame saw an explosion of colonial interest in politics and other elements of public life, such as intellectual discussion and new religious movements. Politics was far more an urban than a rural phenomenon; its chief feature was the rise of the colonial assembly. The Enlightenment brought the growth of rationalism and the religious movement known as Deism. At the same time, Protestant ministers, such as Jonathan Edwards, sought to restore religious enthusiasm. New denominations, such as Unitarians, Baptists, and Methodists, appeared. Women played a larger role in religion, and the questioning of authority was encouraged.

Roads to Revolution

CHAPTER 5

1750–1776

A View of the Town of Concord, 1775

This icon will direct you to the website where you can Prepare for Class, Improve Your Grade, and Ace the Test: **www.cengage.com/history/boyer/ enduringconcise6e**

By 1763 Britain had defeated France, its chief competitor for preeminence in North America, and stood at the height of eighteenth-century imperial power. British rule ran undisputed from the Atlantic seacoast to the Mississippi River and from northernmost Canada to the Florida straits. Ironically, this greatest of British triumphs would turn into one of the greatest of British defeats.

The imperial reorganization that war and conquest made necessary after 1763 radically altered Britain's relationship with its American colonies. Conflict arose between Britain and the colonies when Parliament, as it searched for ways to pay off the enormous debt accumulated during the war, attempted to tighten control over colonial affairs. The colonists, accustomed to legislating for themselves, resisted this effort to centralize decision making in London. American leaders interpreted Britain's clampdown as calculated antagonism, intended to deprive them of both prosperity and relative independence.

Conflict spilled out beyond constitutional issues. In port cities, crowds of poor and working people engaged in direct, often violent demonstrations against British authority. Settlers in the backcountry invoked the ideas of urban radicals when resisting large landowners and distant colonial governments dominated by elites. These movements reflected political and economic tensions within the colonies as well as growing defiance of elites by ordinary colonists. The growing participation of white women reflected impatience with restraints imposed by traditional gender norms. Nonwhites, both African-American and Native American, often perceived the colonists as greater threats to their liberty than the British. Within Britain itself many opposed the government's colonial policies.

Colonial resistance to British policies also reflected democratic stirrings in America and throughout the North Atlantic world. Among the products of this democratic urge were both the American Revolution, which erupted in 1776, and the French Revolution, which began in 1789 and sparked unrest over much of Europe and the Americas.

Despite their apprehension, colonial politicians expressed their opposition peacefully from 1763 to 1775 through legislative resolutions and commercial boycotts. Even after fighting erupted, the colonists agonized for more than a year about whether to sever their political relationship with England—which even native-born Americans sometimes referred to affectionately as "home." Of all the world's colonial peoples, none became rebels more reluctantly than Anglo-Americans did in 1776.

TRIUMPH AND TENSIONS: THE BRITISH EMPIRE, 1750–1763

How did Britain and its colonies view their joint victory over France in the Seven Years War?

King George's War (see Chapter 4) did nothing to avert a showdown between Britain and France. The conflict resumed in 1756 and ended in 1763. Known as the **Seven Years' War,** it was a major turning point in both American and European history.

Seven Years' War Major French-English conflict known in North America as the French and Indian War

A Fragile Peace, 1750–1754

Because neither Britain nor France emerged from King George's War as the dominant power in North America, each prepared for another war. The Ohio Valley became the tinderbox for conflict. When France started building a chain of forts to regain control of the Virginia and Pennsylvania Indian trade, Virginia sent a twenty-one-year-old surveyor, George Washington, to demand that the French abandon their forts. In 1754 French troops drove Washington and his militiamen back to their homes.

Map 5.1   The Seven Years' War in North America, 1754–1760
After experiencing major defeats early in the war, Anglo-American forces turned the tide against the French by taking Fort Duquesne and Louisbourg in 1758. After Canada fell in 1760, the fighting shifted to Spain's Caribbean colonies.

In mid-1754 seven colonies sent delegates to Albany, New York, to coordinate their mutual defense with British officials. The Albany Congress persuaded the wary Iroquois to support the British and endorsed a plan for a colonial confederation, the Albany Plan of Union, often seen as a predecessor to the federal system under the Constitution. However, the plan collapsed because no colonial legislature would surrender control over its powers of taxation.

The Seven Years' War in America, 1754–1760

Although France and Britain remained at peace in Europe until 1756, Washington's unsuccessful conflict with the French had created a virtual state of war in North America. In 1754 Britain dispatched General Edward Braddock and one thousand regulars to take Fort Duquesne (doo-KAIN), at the headwaters of the Ohio River.

Chronology

1740–1748	King George's War
1754	Albany Congress
1756–1763	Seven Years' War
1760	George III becomes king of Great Britain; Writs of assistance
1763	Proclamation of 1763; Treaty of Paris divides France's North American empire between Britain and Spain
1763	Pontiac leads Indian uprising in Ohio Valley and Great Lakes
1764	Sugar Act
1765	Stamp Act followed by colonial resistance; First Quartering Act
1766	Stamp Act repealed; Declaratory Act
1767	Revenue Act (Townshend duties); American Board of Customs Commissioners created
1768	Massachusetts circular letters; John Hancock's ship *Liberty* seized by Boston customs commissioner; St. George's Fields massacre in London; First Treaty of Fort Stanwix
1770	Townshend duties, except tea tax, repealed; Boston Massacre
1772	Somerset decision in England
1772–1774	Committees of correspondence formed
1773	Tea Act and Boston Tea Party
1774	Coercive Acts and Quebec Act (Intolerable Acts); First Continental Congress meets in Philadelphia and adopts Suffolk Resolves
1775	Battles of Lexington and Concord; Lord Dunmore offers freedom to Virginia slaves joining British forces; Olive Branch Petition; Battles at Breed's Hill and Bunker Hill; King and Parliament declare colonies to be in rebellion
1776	Thomas Paine, *Common Sense*; Declaration of Independence

Scornful of colonial soldiers and friendly Native Americans, Braddock expected his disciplined regulars to make short work of the French. On July 9, 1755, about 850 French and Indians ambushed Braddock's 2,200 Britons and Virginians near Fort Duquesne. After three hours of steady fire, the British regulars broke and retreated, leaving Washington's Virginians to cover the withdrawal. Nine hundred regular soldiers and colonists died, including Braddock.

In 1756–1757 New France's daring commanding general, Louis Joseph Montcalm, maintained the offensive. Anglo-Americans outnumbered Canadians twenty to one, but Montcalm benefited from large numbers of French regulars, Indian support, and full-scale mobilization of the Canadian population. The Anglo-American colonies supported the war grudgingly, providing few and usually poorly trained troops. French-armed Shawnees, Delawares, and Mingos struck hard at settlers in Western Pennsylvania, Maryland, and Virginia. These attacks halted English expansion and prevented the three colonies from joining the war against France for three years.

However, 1758 proved a turning point for the British. First, Indian support for the French evaporated. (Preferring competitive trade to warfare, most Indians hoped that neither European power would drive out the other.) Indian withdrawal enabled

Britain to capture Fort Duquesne easily and win control of the Ohio Valley. Second, British minister William Pitt took over Britain's military affairs. The imaginative and single-minded Pitt reinvigorated the military campaign. Hard pressed in Europe by France and its allies (which after 1761 included Spain), Pitt believed that mobilizing colonial forces was the key to crushing New France. Keeping fewer than 4,000 British regulars in North America, he promised that Parliament would bear the cost of maintaining colonial troops.

Pitt's offer to free Americans from the war's financial burden generated unprecedented support. In 1758 and again in 1759 the colonies organized 40,000 troops. As a result, Britain took the offensive and captured Louisbourg and Fort Duquesne in 1758, and Quebec in September 1759. In 1760, with Montreal's surrender, French resistance ended.

Treaty of Paris of 1763 Treaty by which France ceded virtually its entire North American empire to Britain and Spain

The End of French North America, 1760–1763

In the **Treaty of Paris of 1763,** France ceded all its territories on the North American mainland. Several thousand French colonists, scattered from Quebec to Louisiana, became British or Spanish citizens. However, one group, the Acadians (uh-KAY-dee-uns) of Nova Scotia, suffered tremendous dislocation. The British deported the Acadians, nearly 5 percent of Canada's French population, to more southerly colonies, such as Pennsylvania and Maryland. Impoverished and facing intense anti-French, anti-Catholic prejudice, most fled to Louisiana, where they became known as the "Cajuns."

Under the Treaty of Paris, Britain received all French lands east of the Mississippi; Spain acquired the port of New Orleans and all French lands west of the Mississippi. Spain traded Florida to Britain in return for Cuba. Thus Spain's New World empire actually increased in size, but France's virtually vanished, shrinking to a handful of islands. Britain's North American empire quadrupled in size.

The effects of King George's War and the Seven Years' War were mixed. On one hand, shedding their blood in a common cause led British and Americans to rely on each other as never before. However, the conclusion of both wars led to misunderstanding, suspicion, and hostility between the former compatriots.

Anglo-American Friction

During the war, British officers complained that colonial troops not only fought poorly but also tended to return home, even in the midst of campaigns, when their term was up or when their pay lagged. In turn, colonial soldiers complained that British officers treated their troops "little better than slaves."

Tensions flared as well between British officers and colonial civilians. Officers groused about colonial unwillingness to provide food or shelter; colonists resented the officers' arrogance. Moreover, Pitt's promise to reimburse the colonies for their military expenses enraged Britons. Wartime spending had brought substantial profits to colonial farmers, artisans, and merchants. And some merchants had continued their illicit trade with the French West Indies, simultaneously violating the Navigation Acts *and* trading with the enemy. Britain's national debt had nearly doubled during the war, to more than £132 million. In contrast, the total colonial debt amounted to less than £2 million. Staggering under debt and taxes, the British thought it outrageous to repay the Americans for defending themselves.

Colonists felt equally burdened. Wartime profits had gone to pay for British goods accelerating the "consumer revolution" that had been underway for several decades (see Chapter 4). The wartime boom ended when peace returned. Now accustomed to a new middle-class lifestyle, colonists went into debt, and British creditors obliged by extending repayment terms from six months to a full year. Newly prosperous colonists found themselves in debt and even bankruptcy, and many began to suspect Britain of plotting to "enslave" the colonies to protect its own merchants and manufacturers.

The new revenue measures followed the ascension to the British throne of George III (reigned 1760–1820). The new king was determined to play a major role in government, but he proved ill suited to the task of building political coalitions or pursuing consistent policies. Until 1774, George III made frequent abrupt changes in government leadership that destabilized politics in Britain and exacerbated relations with the colonies.

Map 5.2   European Territorial Claims, 1763

The Treaty of Paris (1763) divided France's North American empire between Britain and Spain. Britain in 1763 established direct imperial authority west of the Proclamation line.

Frontier Tensions

Worse, Britain's victory over the French generated new Anglo-Indian conflicts that drove the British debt even higher. No longer able to play the two imperial powers off against each other, Indians feared the consequences. They were right. To cut costs after the war, the British had stopped distributing food and ammunition to their Indian allies. Meanwhile, colonial squatters were moving onto Indian lands, raising both fears and tensions.

In early 1763 the Delaware Indian religious prophet Neolin called for Indians to repudiate European culture, goods, and alliances. **Pontiac,** an Ottawa Indian, and other leaders forged an anti-British coalition that sacked eight British forts and besieged British positions at Detroit and Pittsburgh. Short on food and ammunition, suffering a smallpox epidemic (deliberately spread by the British), and recognizing that the French would not return, the Indians surrendered in early fall.

But the British victory over the Indians was indecisive. Hoping to end the frontier fighting, the British government issued the **Proclamation of 1763,** which asserted royal control of land transactions, settlements, and trade of non-Indians west of the Appalachians, and recognized existing Indian land titles everywhere west of the "proclamation line," which ran down the crest of the Appalachian Mountains. Although the policy calmed Indian fears, it angered the colonies by subordinating their western land claims to imperial authority and slowing colonial expansion.

Pontiac Ottawa chief who created short-lived anti-British coalition among Native Americans

Proclamation of 1763 An attempt to end Indian problems by preventing westward movement by colonists

Pontiac's rebellion also led the British government to station ten thousand regular troops in North America to occupy the western lands that France had ceded and to intimidate the Indians. The cost of administering British North America reached almost £440,000 yearly. Britons believed it perfectly reasonable for the colonists to help offset this expense. The colonists, however, struggling with their own postwar economic recession, saw it as none of their responsibility.

Although partially offsetting the colonies' unfavorable balance of payments with Britain, these troops raised fears of a peacetime "standing army" that could threaten American liberty. With the French menace gone, increasing numbers of colonists viewed Indian lands to the west as the key to future prosperity. The British troops that enforced the Proclamation Act of 1763 thus became, not protectors, but threats to that future.

IMPERIAL AUTHORITY, COLONIAL OPPOSITION, 1760–1766

What was imperial reorganization, and how did it change relations between Britain and the North American colonies?

Even as the Seven Years' War wound down, tensions developed between Britain and its colonies, largely the result of Britain's plans to finance its greatly enlarged empire by a series of revenue measures whose enforcement bypassed local authorities and seemed a dangerous extension of Parliamentary powers. The success of protest and opposition movements after the Stamp Act revealed a widening gulf between British and colonial ideas about the proper relationship between the empire and its colonies.

The Writs of Assistance, 1760–1761

writ of assistance A general search warrant of dubious legality

To halt American trade with the enemy in the French West Indies during the Seven Years' War, Britain had cracked down on colonial smuggling. In 1760 the royal governor of Massachusetts authorized the use of the **writ of assistance** to seize illegally imported goods. A general search warrant, the writ permitted customs officials to enter any ship or building where smuggled goods might be hidden. Because it required no evidence of probable cause for suspicion, the writ was considered unconstitutional by most English legal authorities.

The writ of assistance proved a powerful weapon against smuggling. Merchants in Boston, the colonies' smuggling capital, hired James Otis to challenge the device's constitutionality. The former prosecuting attorney for Boston's vice-admiralty court, Otis had resigned to protest the use of the writ. Before Massachusetts' highest court in 1761, he argued that "an act against the Constitution is void"—even an act of Parliament. But the court, noting the use of an identical writ of assistance in England, ruled against the merchants.

Despite having lost his case, Otis had stated with clarity the colonial conception of Parliament's role under the British constitution. Most British politicians assumed that Parliament's laws themselves were part of the unwritten constitution and that Parliament could in effect alter the constitution at will. But, like most colonists, Otis believed that Parliament had no authority to violate the traditional "rights of Englishmen" by authorizing illegal searches and seizures in private homes.

The Sugar Act, 1764

In 1764, three years after Otis's court challenge, Parliament passed the **Sugar Act** to offset part of Britain's North American military expenses. In ending the longstanding exemption of colonial trade from revenue-raising measures, the Sugar Act triggered new tension between Britain and the colonies. The Navigation Acts, in contrast, had been intended not to raise revenue but to benefit the imperial economy by controlling trade.

Sugar Act Act passed by British Parliament that placed new taxes and restrictions on colonists' trade

The Sugar Act amended the Molasses Act of 1733, which constituted a 6-pence-per-gallon tariff on French-produced molasses. Colonists commonly bribed customs inspectors 1½ pence per gallon to look the other way when they unloaded smuggled molasses. In designing the Sugar Act, British officials, well aware of the widespread bribery, wrongly assumed that the colonists would willingly pay a lower, 3-pence-per-gallon tax.

Colonists found other features of the Sugar Act equally objectionable. The act stipulated that the colonists had to export certain raw commodities *through Britain* instead of going directly to foreign ports, as they had been doing. It also complicated the requirements for shipping colonial goods. A captain had to fill out a confusing series of documents certifying the legality of his trade. The absence of any document left his cargo liable to seizure. The law's petty regulations made it virtually impossible for many colonial shippers to avoid committing technical violations of the act.

Finally, the Sugar Act discarded many traditional English protections for a fair trial. First, the law allowed customs officials to transfer smuggling cases from the colonial courts, in which juries decided the outcome, to vice-admiralty courts, in which a judge delivered the verdict. Because the act awarded vice-admiralty judges 5 percent of any confiscated cargo, it gave them a financial incentive to find defendants guilty. Second, until 1767 the law required all cases to be heard in the vice-admiralty court at Halifax, Nova Scotia. The law also reversed normal procedure by presuming the guilt of the accused and requiring the defendant to prove innocence.

The Sugar Act was no idle threat—the navy enforced it vigorously. A Boston resident complained that "no vessel hardly comes in or goes out but they find some pretence to seize and detain her."

Americans continued to smuggle molasses rather than pay the three-pence tax until 1766, when the British lowered the duty to a penny, making it cheaper to pay the tax than to smuggle. After that, the tax brought in about £30,000 a year.

Generally, opposition to the Sugar Act remained fragmented; the act provoked most opposition in the most heavily affected colonies—Massachusetts, New York, and Pennsylvania. Other colonies, unaffected, protested very little.

The Stamp Act Crisis, 1765–1766

Revenues raised by the Sugar Act did little to ease Britain's financial crisis. Britons groaned under the second-highest tax rates in Europe and looked resentfully at the lightly taxed colonists, who paid an average of one shilling per person compared to their twenty-six shillings per person.

Stamp Act Revenue measure that provoked open opposition by colonists

In March 1765, to force colonists to pay a larger share of imperial expenses, Parliament passed the **Stamp Act.** The law obliged Americans to purchase and use specially marked or stamped paper for newspapers, customs documents, wills, contracts, and other public legal documents. Violators faced prosecution in vice-admiralty courts, without juries. Unlike the Sugar Act, which was an *external* tax levied on imports, the Stamp Act was an *internal* tax levied directly on property, goods, and services in the colonies. External taxes regulated trade and fell primarily on merchants and ship captains, but internal taxes were designed to raise revenue and had far wider effects. The Stamp Act would tax anyone who made a will, bought or sold property, purchased newspapers, or borrowed money.

William Pitt and others objected to such an internal tax, arguing that the colonies taxed themselves through their elected assemblies. But to Grenville and his supporters the tax seemed a small price for the benefits of empire, especially because Britons had paid a similar tax since 1695. Grenville agreed with Stamp Act opponents that Parliament could not tax British subjects unless they enjoyed representation in that body. He contended, however, that the colonists, like many other British adult males who did not vote for members of Parliament, were *virtually* represented. According to the theory of virtual representation, every member of Parliament considered the welfare of *all* subjects, not just his constituents, in deciding issues. Whether or not they voted in parliamentary elections, all imperial subjects, including Americans, could depend on each member of Parliament to protect their well-being.

Grenville and his supporters also held that the colonial assemblies were local governments, with no powers other than those Parliament allowed them. This view clashed directly with the stance of the many colonists who had argued for decades that their assemblies exercised legislative power equivalent to that of Britain's House of Commons.

The Stamp Act caused many colonists to believe that they had to confront parliamentary taxation head on or surrender any claim to meaningful self-government.

New Hampshire Stamp Act Protest

In order to frighten stamp tax collectors into resigning their posts, crowds in colonial cities and towns would parade an agent's effigy through the streets.

However much they admired Parliament, few Americans thought that it represented them. Although virtual representation might apply to England and Scotland, they argued, it certainly did not extend across the Atlantic. In the American view, unless a lawmaker shared his constituents' interests, he would have no personal stake in opposing bills contrary to their welfare. Thus the colonists favored *actual,* rather than virtual, representation.

To the colonists, the Stamp Act demonstrated both Parliament's indifference to their interests and the shallowness of virtual representation. Nonetheless, they conceded that Parliament possessed *limited* powers of legislation, and they accepted the parliamentary regulation of imperial trade.

In a speech opposing the Sugar Act, James Otis had expressed Americans' basic argument: "that by [the British] Constitution, every man in the dominions is a free man; that no parts of His Majesty's dominions can be taxed without consent; that every part has a right to be represented in the supreme or some subordinate legislature." In essence, the colonists saw the empire as a loose federation (union) in which their legislatures possessed considerable autonomy.

Patrick Henry, a twenty-nine-year-old Virginia lawyer with a gift for fiery oratory, expressed the rising spirit of resistance in late May 1765. He persuaded Virginia's House of Burgesses to adopt four relatively mild resolutions denying Parliament's power to tax the colonies, but the House rejected three stronger ones. Garbled accounts of Henry's resolutions and speeches—he probably never said, "Give me liberty or give me death"—electrified other colonists.

Meanwhile, active resistance took shape outside elite political circles. In Boston by late summer, middle-class artisans and businessmen had created the Loyal Nine to fight the Stamp Act. They recognized that the stamp distributors, who alone could sell the specially watermarked paper, represented the law's weak link. If public pressure could force them to resign before the tax went into effect on November 1, the Stamp Act would not work.

Boston's preeminence in opposing Parliament was no accident. Bostonians lived primarily by trade and distilling, and in 1765 they were not living well. The heavy tax on molasses burdened rum producers, and the Sugar Act's trade restrictions dried up the wine import business and interfered with the direct export of New England products to profitable overseas markets. Moreover, its shipbuilding and fishing industries were declining; taxes, unemployment, and poverty had skyrocketed; and the city was recovering from a disastrous fire that had left every tenth family homeless.

This widespread economic distress produced an explosive situation. It was easy to blame British policy for hard times. Furthermore, poor and working-class Bostonians were accustomed to gathering in large crowds to express themselves politically. The morning of August 14, 1765, found a likeness of Boston's stamp distributor, Andrew Oliver, swinging from a tree. Oliver did not take the hint to resign, so at dusk several hundred Bostonians demolished a new building of his at the dock. The mob then surged toward Oliver's house and vandalized it. Surveying his devastated home the next morning, Oliver announced his resignation.

Anger against the Stamp Act unleashed spontaneous, contagious violence. For example, in late August, rioting Bostonians demolished the elegant home of Lieutenant Governor and Chief Justice Thomas Hutchinson.

Sons of Liberty Groups to resist Stamp Act; formed by elites in an attempt to curb violence

Stamp Act Congress Assembly where representatives from nine colonies met to discuss resistance to Stamp Act

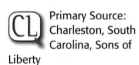

Primary Source: Charleston, South Carolina, Sons of Liberty

Declaratory Act Parliamentary assertion of right to legislate for the colonies

At the same time, groups calling themselves **Sons of Liberty** were forming throughout the colonies. Elite leaders of these groups sought to curb violence, fearful that attacks on one set of elites could lead to attacks on all elites. The Sons of Liberty focused their actions against property and carefully left avenues of escape for their victims; they forbade their members to carry weapons in order to avoid harming royal soldiers or officials.

In October 1765 representatives from nine colonies met in New York City in the **Stamp Act Congress.** There the colonies agreed on, and boldly articulated, the principle that Parliament had no authority to levy taxes outside Britain or to deny any person a jury trial. The united front of the Stamp Act Congress was far more effective than the one earlier intercolonial meeting, the Albany Congress of 1754. But although they emboldened and unified the colonies, declarations of principle like the Stamp Act Congress resolutions seemed futile to many colonists, in view of Parliament's earlier refusal to consider their objections to the stamp duties.

By late 1765 most stamp distributors had resigned or fled, and without the watermarked paper required by law, most customs officials and court officers refused to perform their duties. In response, legislators compelled them to resume operations by threatening to withhold their pay. At the same time, merchants obtained sailing clearances by insisting that they would sue if their cargoes spoiled while delayed in port. By late December the colonial courts and harbors were again functioning.

In these ways colonial elites assumed control of the public outcry against the Stamp Act. Respectable gentlemen kept an explosive situation under control by taking over leadership of local Sons of Liberty, by coordinating protest through the Stamp Act Congress, and by having colonial legislatures resume normal business. But the Stamp Act remained in effect. To force its repeal, New York's merchants agreed on October 31, 1765, to boycott all British goods. Others followed. Because the colonies purchased 40 percent of England's manufactures, this nonimportation strategy triggered panic within England's business community.

The Declaratory Act, 1766

The Marquis of Rockingham, who had succeeded George Grenville as prime minister, hesitated to advocate repeal, but parliamentary support for repeal gradually grew—the result of practicality, not principle. In March 1766 Parliament revoked the Stamp Act. Simultaneously, however, Parliament passed the **Declaratory Act,** affirming parliamentary power to legislate for the colonies "in all cases whatsoever."

Because Americans interpreted the Declaratory Act as merely a face-saving measure on Parliament's part, they ignored it. In truth, however, the House of Commons intended that the colonists take the Declaratory Act literally to mean that they were not exempt from *any* parliamentary statute, including a tax law. The Stamp Act crisis thus ended in a fundamental disagreement between Britain and America over the colonists' political rights.

Although philosophical differences between Britain and America remained unresolved, most colonists put the events of 1765 behind them. Still loyal to "Old England," Anglo-Americans concluded that their resistance to the law had slapped Britain's leaders back to their senses, but they would examine future British policies and actions more deeply.

Ideology, Religion, and Resistance

The Stamp Act crisis had revealed a chasm between the colonies and Great Britain. For the first time, some Anglo-Americans saw a sinister quality in the imperial relationship with Britain. To understand these perceptions, some educated colonists turned to philosophers, historians, and political writers. Many more looked to religion.

Educated colonists were familiar with John Locke and other Enlightenment political thinkers. Locke argued that, in a state of nature, people enjoyed the "natural rights" of life, liberty, and property. To form governments to protect these rights, people entered into a "social contract." A government that encroached on natural rights broke its contract with the people. In such cases the people could resist their government. To many colonial readers, Locke's concept of natural rights justified opposition to Parliament's arbitrary legislation.

Colonists also read European writers who portrayed concentrations of executive power as threats to liberty. Some balanced Locke's emphasis on the rights of the individual with an emphasis on subordinating individual interests to the good of the people as a whole. Looking to the Greeks and Romans, these "republican" theorists admired the sense of civic duty of the Roman republic. Like the early Romans, they maintained that a free people had to practice "public virtue." An elected leader of a republic would commend obedience "more by the virtue of the people than by the terror of his power."

The political writers read most widely in the colonies included a group known as oppositionists. According to John Trenchard and Thomas Gordon, among others, Parliament—the freely elected representatives of the people—formed the foundation of England's unique political liberties and protected them against the inherent corruption and tyranny of executive power. Most members of Parliament, they held, no longer represented the true interests of their constituents; instead, they had sold their souls for financial gain and joined a "conspiracy against liberty."

Influenced by such ideas, a number of colonists believed they detected a diabolical conspiracy underlying British policy. Joseph Warren of Massachusetts observed that the Stamp Act "induced some to imagine that the minister designed by this to force the colonies into a rebellion, and from thence to take occasion to treat them with severity and, by military power, to reduce them to servitude."

Beginning with the Stamp Act crisis, many Protestant clergymen summoned their flock to stand up for God and liberty. Clergymen who exalted the cause of liberty exerted an enormous influence on popular opinion. Far more Americans heard or read sermons than had access to newspapers or pamphlets. A popular theme was how God sent the people woes only to strengthen and sustain them until victory. Moreover, protest leaders' calls to boycott British luxuries meshed neatly with ministers' traditional warnings against frivolity and wastefulness.

CHECKING IN

- The young British king George III was ill suited to the job.
- War and imperial expansion left Britain with staggering debt, and the British concluded that colonists should pay their fair share.
- Parliament passed a series of laws to rationalize control over the colonies, such as the Proclamation of 1763 and the Sugar Act, which colonists found distasteful.
- The Stamp Act, clearly intended to raise revenues, instead raised open resistance.
- Colonists welcomed repeal of the Stamp Act and unwisely ignored the Declaratory Act.

RESISTANCE RESUMES, 1766–1770

In what ways did resistance to the Townshend duties differ from earlier colonial resistance efforts?

Repeal of the Stamp Act temporarily quieted colonial protests, but Britain's search for new revenue soon revived them. Most colonists became convinced that the Stamp Act had been not an isolated mistake, but part of a deliberate design to undermine colonial self-government. Meanwhile growing numbers of English people likewise protested their government's policies.

Opposing the Quartering Act, 1766–1767

In August 1766 George III dismissed the Rockingham government and summoned William Pitt, an opponent of taxing the colonies, to form a cabinet. However, Pitt's health collapsed in March 1767, and Charles Townshend, the chancellor of the exchequer (treasurer), became the effective leader.

Quartering Act Required colonial legislatures to provide supplies to British troops

Just as Townshend took office, a conflict arose with the New York legislature over the **Quartering Act** of 1765, which ordered colonial legislatures to pay for certain goods used by British soldiers stationed within their borders—candles, windowpanes, mattress straw, and a small liquor ration. The act applied only to troops in settled areas, not to those on the frontier, and it did not force citizens to accept soldiers in private homes. The law aroused resentment, however, because it constituted an *indirect* tax. In other words, although it did not empower royal officials to collect money directly from the colonists, it obligated assemblies to raise revenue by whatever means they considered appropriate. The act fell lightly on all the colonies except New York, where more soldiers were stationed than in any other province. New York refused to grant the supplies.

New York's resistance unleashed a torrent of anti-American feeling in Parliament, still bitter after revoking the Stamp Act. Townshend responded by drafting the New York Suspending Act, which threatened to nullify all laws passed by the colony after October 1, 1767, if it refused to vote the supplies. By the time George III signed the measure, New York had already appropriated the funds. Nonetheless, the conflict over the Quartering Act demonstrated that British leaders would not hesitate to defend Parliament's authority through the most drastic of all steps: interfering with American self-government.

Crisis over the Townshend Duties, 1767

This new wave of British resentment toward the colonies coincided with an outpouring of frustration over the government's failure to cut taxes from wartime levels. Discontent seethed among the landed gentry, whose members took advantage of their domination of the House of Commons to slash their own taxes in 1767. This move cost the government £500,000 and prompted Townshend to propose laws that would tax imports entering America and increase colonial customs revenues.

Townshend sought to tax the colonists by exploiting a loophole in their arguments against the Stamp Tax. Americans had emphasized their opposition to *inter-*

nal taxes but had said nothing about *external* taxes—Parliament's right to tax imports as they entered the colonies. Townshend interpreted this silence as evidence that the colonists accepted Britain's right to impose external taxes. Parliament passed Townshend's Revenue Act of 1767 (popularly called the **Townshend duties**) in the summer. The new law taxed glass, paint, lead, paper, and tea imported into the colonies.

Townshend duties More Parliamentary attempts to raise revenues from the colonies

On the surface, Townshend's case for external taxation was convincing, as the colonists had long accepted parliamentary regulation of trade and had in principle acknowledged taxation as a form of regulation. But the Townshend duties differed significantly from what Americans considered a legitimate way of regulating trade through taxation. To the colonists, charging a duty was a lawful way for British authorities to control trade only if it excluded foreign goods by making them prohibitively expensive. The Revenue Act of 1767, however, set moderate rates that did not price goods out of the colonial market; clearly, its purpose was to collect money for the treasury. Thus, from the colonial standpoint, Townshend's duties were taxes just like the Stamp Act duties.

Townshend had an ulterior motive for establishing an American source of revenue. Traditionally, colonial legislatures set colonial royal governors' salaries and often refused to pay them until the governors signed bills that they opposed. Townshend hoped that the Revenue Act would establish a fund to pay governors' and other royal officials' salaries, freeing them from the assemblies' control. In effect, he would strip the assemblies of their most potent weapon, the power of the purse, and tip the balance of power away from elected representatives and toward appointed royal officials.

The Revenue Act never yielded the income that Townshend had anticipated. Of all the items taxed, only tea produced any significant revenue—£20,000 of the £37,000 expected. And because the measure would serve its purpose only if the colonists could afford British tea, Townshend eliminated £60,000 in import fees paid on East Indian tea entering Britain before transshipment to America. On balance, the Revenue Act *worsened* the British treasury's deficit by £23,000. By 1767 Britain's financial difficulties were more an excuse for political demands to tax the colonies than a driving force. From Parliament's standpoint, the conflict with America was becoming a test of national will over the *principle* of taxation.

Primary Source: William Shepherd Attempts to Collect Customs Duties

The Colonists' Reaction, 1767–1769

Resistance to the Revenue Act remained weak until December 1767, when John Dickinson published *Letters from a Farmer in Pennsylvania*. These twelve essays, which appeared in nearly every colonial newspaper, emphasized that Parliament had no right to tax trade for the simple purpose of raising revenue. No tax designed to produce revenue could be considered constitutional unless a people's elected representatives voted for it. Dickinson's writings convinced Americans that their arguments against the Stamp Act also applied to the Revenue Act.

In early 1768 the Massachusetts assembly asked Samuel Adams to draft a "circular letter" to other legislatures. Possessing a flair for the push and shove of local politics, Adams had helped organize the Sons of Liberty in Boston. Adams's circular letter denounced taxation without representation and the threat to self-governance posed by Parliament's making governors and royal officials independent of the legislatures. Nevertheless, the document acknowledged Parliament as the "supreme legislative Power over the whole Empire" and advocated no illegal activities.

Virginia's assembly warmly approved Adams's eloquent measure and sent out a more strongly worded letter of its own, urging all the colonies to oppose imperial policies that would "have an immediate tendency to enslave them." But most colonial legislatures reacted indifferently to these letters. In fact, resistance might have disintegrated had not the British government overreacted to the circular letters.

Indeed, parliamentary leaders saw even the mild Massachusetts letter as "little better than an incentive to Rebellion." Disorganized because of Townshend's sudden death in 1767, the king's Privy (PRIH-vee) Council (advisers) directed Lord Hillsborough, the first appointee to the new post of secretary of state for the colonies, to express the government's displeasure. Hillsborough ordered the Massachusetts assembly to disown its letter, forbade all overseas assemblies to endorse it, and commanded royal governors to dissolve any legislature that violated his instructions.

The tactic backfired. Protesting Hillsborough's bullying, many legislatures previously indifferent to the Massachusetts letter adopted it enthusiastically. The Massachusetts House of Representatives voted ninety-two to seventeen not to recall its letter. The number 92 immediately acquired symbolic significance for Americans; colonial politicians on more than one occasion drank 92 toasts in tipsy salutes to Massachusetts' action. Royal governors responded by dismissing legislatures in Massachusetts and elsewhere, playing into the hands of Samuel Adams and others who wished to ignite widespread opposition to the Townshend duties.

Increasingly outraged, the colonists still needed an effective means of pressuring Parliament for repeal. Nonimportation seemed especially promising because it offered an alternative to violence and would distress Britain's economy. Thus in August 1768 Boston's merchants adopted a nonimportation agreement, and the tactic spread southward. "Save your money, and you save your country!" trumpeted the Sons of Liberty, who reorganized after two years of inactivity. However, not all colonists supported nonimportation. Many merchants continued to import British goods until early 1769. The boycott probably kept out about 40 percent of British imports, while encouraging colonists to resist British policies more actively.

Women and Colonial Resistance

Nonimportation convinced the British—and the colonists—that all Americans were determined to sustain resistance, and it demonstrated that the American cause rested on foundations of impeccable morality and sensible moderation. It also provided a unique opportunity for women to join the protest.

White women had been gradually widening their participation in public affairs for several decades. For example, women far outnumbered men among white church members, and they were hailed as superior to most men in piety and morality. During the Stamp Act crisis, upper-class women had attended political rallies and expressed their political opinions in discussion and correspondence.

Calling themselves Daughters of Liberty, upper-class female patriots assumed a highly visible role during the Townshend crisis. Convinced that colonial women could exert a persuasive moral influence on public opinion, American leaders encouraged them to protest the Revenue Act's tax on tea. Accordingly, in early 1770 more than three hundred "mistresses of families" in Boston denounced the consumption of the beverage. In some ways nonconsumption was more effective than nonimportation, for the colonists' refusal to consume imports would chill merchants' economic incentive to import British goods.

Nonconsumption agreements therefore became popular and were extended to include other goods, mainly clothes. Again, women played a vital role, because the boycott would fail unless the colonists replaced British imports with apparel of their own making. Responding to leaders' pleas for an expansion of domestic cloth production, women of all social ranks organized spinning bees. These attracted intense publicity as evidence of American determination to fight parliamentary taxation. Spinning bees not only helped to undermine the masculine prejudice that women had no place in public life, but also endowed spinning and weaving, previously considered routine tasks, with political virtue. Female activities such as spinning bees and tea boycotts dramatically demonstrated that American protests extended beyond a few male merchants and crowds of angry men into the heart of American households and congregations. For many colonists, the area of supposed feminine virtues widened from religion to include politics. Women's participation showed that colonial protests reached into the heart of American households and were leading to broader popular participation in politics.

Board of Customs Commissioners Officials sent to oversee collection of taxes; their corruption a target for colonial anger

Customs "Racketeering," 1767–1768

Townshend also sought to increase revenues by extending British surveillance of colonial trade. In 1767 he induced Parliament to create the American **Board of Customs Commissioners** to strictly enforce the Navigation Acts. The new law increased the number of port officials, funded a colonial coast guard to catch smugglers, and provided money for secret informers. The law quickly drew protests because of the ways it was enforced and because it reversed the traditional legal process by assuming the accused to be guilty until proven otherwise.

The act also included new provisions that awarded an informer one-third of the value of all goods and ships appropriated through a conviction of smuggling. The fact that fines could be tripled under certain circumstances provided an even greater incentive to seize illegal cargoes. Smuggling cases were heard in vice-admiralty courts where the probability of conviction was extremely high. The prospect of accumulating a small fortune proved too tempting to most commissioners.

Revenue agents commonly perverted the law by filing charges for technical violations of the Sugar Act, even when no evidence existed of intent to conduct illegal trade. They most often exploited the provision that declared any cargo illegal unless it had been loaded or unloaded with a customs officer's written authorization.

John Hancock

A prominent anti-British merchant, Hancock was also a popular political leader in pre-Revolutionary Boston.

(Photograph © 2007 Museum of Fine Arts, Boston. *John Hancock,* 1765, John Singleton Copley, American, 1738–1815. Oil on canvas, 100.01 x 124.78 cm (39 3/8 x 49 1/8 in.). Museum of Fine Arts, Boston. Deposited by the City of Boston, L-R 30.76d.)

Customs commissioners also fanned anger by invading sailors' traditional rights. Long-standing maritime custom allowed crews to supplement their income by making small sales between ports. Anything stored in a sailor's chest was considered private property, exempt from the Navigation Acts. But after 1767, revenue agents treated such belongings as cargo, thus establishing an excuse to seize the entire ship. Under this policy, crewmen saw arrogant inspectors break open their trunks and then lost trading stock worth several months' wages. Sailors waited for chances to get even. Not surprisingly, after 1767 inspectors increasingly fell victim to riots dominated by vengeful sailors.

In these ways the commissioners embarked on a program of "customs racketeering" that constituted legalized piracy. This program fed an upsurge in popular violence. Above all, customs commissioners' use of informers provoked retaliation. The *Pennsylvania Journal* in 1769 scorned these agents as "dogs of prey, thirsting after the fortunes of worthy and wealthy men."

Nowhere were customs agents and informers more detested than in Boston, where citizens retaliated in June 1768. When customs agents seized colonial merchant John Hancock's sloop *Liberty* on a technicality, a crowd tried to prevent the towing of Hancock's ship and then began assaulting customs officials. Swelling to several hundred, the mob drove all revenue inspectors from the city. To appease angry colonists momentarily, British officials dropped the charges against Hancock.

John Wilkes British opponent of King George III who became a hero to American colonists

Wilkes and Liberty, 1768–1770

In addition to colonial opposition to the Revenue Act, British merchants and artisans, hit hard by the exclusion of 40 percent of imports, also demanded repeal of the Townshend duties. Their protests became part of a larger movement in the 1760s against the policies of George III and a Parliament dominated by wealthy landowners. **John Wilkes,** a fiery London editor whose newspaper regularly and irreverently denounced the king, became both leader and focal point of the protest. A member of Parliament, Wilkes was tried for seditious libel and acquitted, to great popular acclaim. George III's government then shut down his newspaper and persuaded members of the House of Commons to deny Wilkes his seat. After publishing another slashing attack on the king, Wilkes fled to Paris.

In 1768 Wilkes returned to England, defying an arrest warrant, and again ran for Parliament. By then, government policies, including the Townshend Acts, had unleashed a flood of protests against the "obnoxious" government ministers. Manufacturers, merchants, and artisans all rallied around the cry "Wilkes and Liberty."

When the newly elected Wilkes was once again arrested, twenty to forty thousand angry "Wilkesites" massed on St. George's Fields, outside the prison where he was being held. Soldiers and police opened fire on rock-throwing demonstrators, killing eleven. The "massacre of St. George's Fields" furnished martyrs to the protesters, and Wilkes received enormous outpourings of public support from the North American colonies as well as from Britain. From his prison cell, Wilkes maintained a regular correspondence with Boston's Sons of Liberty, and Bostonians cheered his release from prison in April 1770 with a massive celebration.

CHECKING IN

- The Quartering Act showed colonists that Parliament was willing to interfere with their self-government.
- The Townshend duties failed to raise revenues, but their intent to do so angered colonists even more.
- Colonial reaction to Parliament united in the protests of John Dickinson, the Massachusetts circular letter, and nonimportation agreements; women played an important public role in implementing nonimportation.
- The Board of Customs Commissioners sent to Boston to oversee collection of taxes were often corrupt and became a target for colonial anger.
- John Wilkes became a symbol of the dangers posed by a too-powerful government.

The Wilkes furor sharpened the political ideas of government opponents on both sides of the Atlantic. English voters sent petitions to Parliament proclaiming that its refusal to seat Wilkes was an affront to the electorate's will and calling "virtual representation" a sham. Emboldened by the "Wilkes and Liberty" movement, William Pitt and others forcefully denounced the government's colonial policies. The colonists themselves concluded that Parliament and the government represented a small but powerful minority whose authority they could legitimately question.

THE DEEPENING CRISIS, 1770–1774

In what ways did colonists' views of parliamentary authority change after 1770?

After 1770 the imperial crisis took on ominous new dimensions. Colonists and British troops clashed on the streets of Boston. Resistance leaders in the colonies developed ways to systematically coordinate their actions and policies. After the defiance manifested in the Boston Tea Party, Britain was determined to subordinate the colonies once and for all. Adding to the general tension were several violent conflicts that erupted in the western backcountry.

The Boston Massacre, 1770

British authorities responded to the violence directed at customs commissioners by dispatching four thousand British troops to Boston in 1768. But the violence only escalated, intersecting with intracolonial tensions and extending the crisis beyond the port cities.

Crackling with tension, Boston took on the atmosphere of an occupied city. Armed soldiers and resentful civilians traded insults, and off-duty soldiers undercut local laborers by working for lower wages. Many of the soldiers were Irish Catholics, especially galling to the mainly Protestant Bostonians.

Bostonians' resentment of British authority boiled over on February 22, 1770, when a customs informer fired birdshot at several children throwing rocks at his house and killed an eleven-year-old boy. Samuel Adams organized a burial procession to maximize the horror over a child's death, relying on grief to unite the community in opposition to British policies. "My Eyes never beheld such a funeral," wrote his cousin John Adams. "A vast Number of Boys walked before the Coffin, a vast Number of Women and Men after it. . . . This Shows there are many more Lives to spend if wanted in the Service of their country."

The Boston Massacre, 1770
Engraving by Paul Revere.

Primary Source:
Boston Gazette
Describes the
Boston Massacre

Boston Massacre Confrontation between colonists and British troops in which five colonists were shot and killed

Although the army had played no part in the shooting, it became a target for Bostonians' rage. A week after the funeral, tension erupted at the guard post protecting the customs office. When an officer tried to disperse a crowd led by Crispus Attucks, a seaman of African and Native American ancestry, the mob responded with a barrage of flying objects. One soldier, knocked down by a block of ice, fired, and then the others opened fire. Their volley killed five people, including Attucks.

Royal authorities moved quickly to defuse the crisis by isolating the army on a fortified island in the harbor and putting soldiers who had fired on trial. Patriot leader John Adams defended the accused British troops by claiming that they had been provoked by a "motley rabble," an accusation that resonated with Boston's "respectable" middle-and upper-class elites. Only two soldiers were found guilty; they received the relatively mild punishment of branding on their thumbs.

Burning hatred underlay the **Boston Massacre**—a name designed to invoke the St. George's Fields massacre two years earlier. For the first time colonists had to confront the stark possibility that a tyrannical British government was determined to coerce and suppress them through armed force.

The Committees of Correspondence, 1772–1773

committees of correspondence Local committees established throughout colonies to coordinate anti-British actions

In the fall of 1772 Lord North prepared to implement Townshend's goal of paying royal governors from customs revenues, freeing them from the control of the colonial assemblies. With representative government deeply threatened, Samuel Adams persuaded Boston's town meeting to request that every Massachusetts community appoint people to exchange information and coordinate measures to defend colonial rights. Within a year, most Massachusetts communities had established **committees of correspondence,** and the idea spread throughout New England.

The committees of correspondence, the colonists' first attempt to maintain close political cooperation over a wide area, allowed Samuel Adams to conduct a campaign of political education for all New England. He sent messages for each local committee to read at its town meeting, which debated the issues and adopted formal resolutions. The system made tens of thousands of citizens consider evidence that their rights were being endangered and committed them to take a stand. Adams's most successful venture in whipping up public alarm came in June 1773, when he published letters from the governor of Massachusetts, Thomas Hutchinson, obtained by Benjamin Franklin, advocating "an abridgment of what are called English liberties" and "a great restraint of natural liberty." The Hutchinson correspondence confirmed Americans' suspicions that a plot was afoot to destroy their basic freedoms.

Patrick Henry, Thomas Jefferson, and Richard Henry Lee had proposed in March 1773 that Virginia establish committees of correspondence, and by early 1774 a communications web linked leaders from all the colonies.

In contrast to the brief, intense Stamp Act crisis, the dissatisfaction spawned by the Townshend duties persisted and gradually poisoned relations between Britain and America. In 1765 strong ties of loyalty and affection had disguised the depth of the division over taxation. By 1773, however, colonial allegiance was becoming tenuous.

Conflicts in the Backcountry

On the Appalachian frontier, tensions among natives, recent settlers, and colonial authorities underlined a continuing sense of emergency. Rapid population growth had spurred the migration of people and capital to the frontier where colonists sought access to Indian lands.

Tension flared into violence in Pennsylvania's backcountry. Settlers in and around the town of Paxton blamed the Pennsylvania assembly, which was dominated by Quakers, for failing to provide military protection and for denying them equal representation in the assembly. The "Paxton Boys," as they were known, believed all Native Americans were their racial enemies. After laying waste to two villages of peaceful Conestoga Indians, killing and scalping men, women, and children, in February 1764 about 200 Paxton Boys headed for Philadelphia with plans to kill Christian Indian refugees there. A government delegation headed by Benjamin Franklin met the armed mob on the outskirts of the city and promised that the assembly would consider their grievances. Appeased, the Paxton Boys returned home.

Land pressures and the lack of adequate revenue from the colonies left the British government helpless to enforce the Proclamation of 1763. Speculators, squatters, hunters, and thieves trespassed on Native American lands, often leading Indians to respond violently, while the British withdrew troops that might have maintained order.

Under such pressures, Britain and the Iroquois, in the Treaty of Fort Stanwix (1768), turned land along the Ohio River that was occupied by the Shawnees, Delawares, and Cherokees over to the Virginia and Pennsylvania governments, resolving the two colonies' overlapping land claims in Ohio at the Indians' expense. The Shawnees assumed leadership among the Ohio Indians, who, with the Cherokees, were convinced that appeasement would not stop colonial expansion.

The treaty heightened rather than eased frontier tensions, especially in the Ohio country. Colonists moving westward into what they called Kentucky collided with Shawnee and Mingo Indians, and in 1774 Virginia launched Lord Dunmore's War. After Virginia's victory at Point Pleasant, Virginia gained uncontested rights to all land south of the Ohio River in exchange for giving up all claims north of the river. Resentment continued to fester on both sides, and fighting would resume when war broke out between Britain and the colonies.

Interactive Map: Indian Land Cessions, 1768–1799

Other frontier disputes led to conflict among the colonists themselves. Settlers in western Massachusetts in the early 1760s, for example, found their titles challenged by New Yorker landlords. In 1766, threatened with eviction, the New Englanders staged an armed uprising. And in 1769 New Hampshire settlers calling themselves the Green Mountain Boys began guerrilla warfare against other New York landlords. The independent government they formed ultimately became that of Vermont.

Expansion also provoked conflict between frontier settlers and their own colonial governments. In North Carolina, westerners, who were underrepresented in the assembly, found themselves exploited by dishonest officeholders appointed by eastern politicians. Twenty-five hundred armed westerners, known as Regulators, clashed with thirteen hundred North Carolina militia on May 16, 1771, at the battle of Alamance Creek. Although the Regulator uprising disintegrated, it crippled the colony's subsequent ability to resist British authority. A Regulator movement also arose in South Carolina, in this case to counter the government's unwillingness to prosecute bandits who terrorized the settlers. Fearful that the colony's slave population might revolt if the militia was dispatched, South Carolina's government yielded to the Regulators by establishing new courts and allowing jury trials in recently settled areas.

Although unrelated, these episodes reflected the tensions generated by a land-hungry white population willing to use violence against Native Americans, other colonists, and British officials.

The Tea Act, 1773

Smuggling and nonconsumption had taken a heavy toll on Britain's East India Company, the holder of the legal monopoly on importing tea into the British Empire. By 1773, as tons of tea rotted in warehouses, the East India Company was teetering on the brink of bankruptcy. But Lord North could not let the company fail because, by maintaining British authority in India at its own expense, the East India Company had become a vital component in the British imperial structure.

If the company could control the colonial market, North reasoned, it could increase its profits, and its survival would be guaranteed. Americans consumed vast amounts of tea but by 1773 were purchasing just one-quarter of it from the company. In May 1773, to save the beleaguered East India Company, Parliament passed the **Tea Act,** which eliminated all import duties on tea entering England and thus lowered the selling price to consumers. To reduce the price further, the Tea Act also permitted the company to sell tea directly to consumers rather than through wholesalers. These provisions reduced the cost of East India Company tea in the colonies to well below the price of smuggled tea. Parliament expected economic self-interest to overcome American scruples about buying taxed tea.

But the Tea Act alarmed many Americans, who recognized that the revenues raised by the law would place royal governors' purses beyond the reach of the colonial assemblies. The law also threatened to seduce Americans into accepting parliamentary taxation in return for a frivolous luxury. The committees of correspondence decided to resist the importation of tea by pressuring the East India Company's agents to refuse acceptance or by preventing the landing of East India Company cargoes.

In Boston on November 28, 1773, the first ship came under jurisdiction of the customhouse, to which duties would have to be paid within twenty days, or the cargo would be seized from the captain and the tea would be claimed by the company's agents and placed on sale. When Samuel Adams, John Hancock, and others asked customs officers to issue a special clearance for the ship's departure (to avoid the seizure and sale), Governor Hutchinson refused.

On the evening of December 16, 1773, Samuel Adams convened a meeting in Old South Church, at which he told five thousand citizens about Hutchinson's insistence on landing the tea, warned them that the grace period would expire in a few hours, and proclaimed that "this meeting can do no more to save the country." About fifty young men disguised as Indians and armed with "tomahawks" headed for the wharf, followed by the crowd.

Tea Act Attempt to bail out East India Company that heightened tensions between England and colonists

Thousands lined the waterfront to watch them heave forty-five tons of tea overboard; for an hour the only sounds echoing through the crisp, moonlit night were the steady chop of hatchets breaking open wooden chests and the soft splash of tea on the water. Their work finished, the participants left quietly. The town lapsed into a profound hush—"never more still and calm," according to one observer.

TOWARD INDEPENDENCE, 1774–1776

What led most colonists in 1776 to abandon their loyalty to Britain and choose national independence?

The calm that followed the Boston Tea Party was the calm before the storm. The British government was more determined than ever to quash colonial insubordination, whereas colonial leaders were equally determined to defend self-government and liberty. The empire and its American colonies were on a collision course, but the colonists hesitated at a declaration of independence. In the meantime, African-Americans, both free and slave, pondered how to realize their own freedom.

Liberty for African-Americans

Throughout the imperial crisis, African-American slaves quickly responded to calls for liberty and equality. In 1772 a British court decision electrified much of the black population. A Massachusetts slave, James Somerset, whose master had taken him to England, sued for his freedom; Lord Chief Justice William Mansfield ruled that Parliament had never explicitly established slavery and that therefore no court could compel a slave to obey an order depriving him of his liberty.

Although the decision applied only in England, Massachusetts slaves petitioned the legislature to apply it in their colony as well. In the Chesapeake area, dozens of slaves ran away from their masters and sought passage on ships bound for England. As Anglo-American tensions mounted in 1774, many slaves began to anticipate the arrival of British troops as their path to liberation. White Chesapeake colonists began to fear that war would lead to slave rebellion.

Bearing out such fears in 1775, Virginia's royal governor, **Lord Dunmore,** promised freedom to any slave who enlisted in the cause of restoring royal authority. Nearly a thousand slaves responded to Dunmore's proclamation before angry colonists forced him to flee the colony. Perhaps more important, both whites and blacks began to see a clear link between British forces and slave liberation.

Lord Dunmore Royal governor of Virginia who promised freedom to slaves who fought to restore royal authority

The "Intolerable Acts"

Boston's "Tea Party" enraged the British. Only "New England fanatics" could imagine that cheap tea oppressed them, fumed Lord North. A Welsh member of Parliament declared that "the town of Boston ought to be knocked about by the ears, and destroy'd." The great orator Edmund Burke pled in vain for the one action that could end the crisis: "Leave America . . . to tax herself." But the British government swiftly asserted its authority through the passage of four Coercive Acts, known as

Intolerable Acts Laws intended to punish Massachusetts for Boston Tea Party and strengthen royal authority

the Intolerable Acts to the colonists, which, along with the Quebec Act, became known to many colonists as the **"Intolerable Acts."**

The first Coercive Act, the Boston Port Bill, was passed on April 1, 1774. It ordered the navy to close Boston Harbor unless the town arranged to pay for the ruined tea by June 1. The impossibly short deadline was meant to ensure the harbor's closing, which would plunge Boston into economic distress. The second Coercive Act, the Massachusetts Government Act, revoked the Massachusetts charter and made the colony's government less democratic. The upper house would be appointed for life by the crown, not elected annually by the assembly. The royal governor gained absolute control over the appointment of judges and sheriffs. Finally, the new charter limited town meetings to one a year. Although these changes brought Massachusetts government into line with that of other colonies, the colonists interpreted them as assaults on representative government.

The final two Coercive Acts—the Administration of Justice Act and a new Quartering Act—rubbed salt into the wounds. The first of these permitted any person charged with murder while enforcing royal authority in Massachusetts to be tried in England or in another colony. The second went beyond the Quartering Act of 1765 by allowing the governor to requisition *empty* private buildings for quartering, or housing, troops. These measures, coupled with the appointment of General Thomas Gage, Britain's military commander in North America, as governor of Massachusetts, struck New Englanders as proof of a plan to place them under military despotism.

Americans learned of the unrelated Quebec Act at the same time as the Coercive Acts. Intended to cement loyalty to Britain among conquered French-Canadian Catholics, the law established Roman Catholicism as Quebec's official religion. Protestant Anglo-Americans, who associated Catholicism with arbitrary government, took alarm. Furthermore, the Quebec Act gave Canada's governor sweeping powers but established no legislature. The law extended Quebec's territorial claims south to the Ohio River and west to the Mississippi, a vast area populated by Indians and some French, and claimed by several colonies.

The Intolerable Acts convinced New Englanders that the crown planned to corrode traditional English liberties throughout North America. Once the Coercive Acts destroyed these liberties in Massachusetts—many believed—the Quebec Act would serve as a blueprint for extinguishing representative government in other colonies. Parliament would replace all colonial governments with ones like Quebec's. Elected assemblies, freedom of religion for Protestants, and jury trials would vanish.

Intended only to punish Massachusetts, the Coercive Acts thus pushed most colonies to the brink of revolution. Repeal of these laws became the colonists' nonnegotiable demand. The Declaration of Independence would refer to these laws six times in listing colonial grievances justifying the break with Britain.

The First Continental Congress

Continental Congress Major step toward resistance to Britain and unity among colonies

In response to the Intolerable Acts, the committees of correspondence of every colony but Georgia sent delegates to a **Continental Congress** in Philadelphia. The fifty-six delegates who assembled on September 5, 1774, included the colonies' most prominent politicians: Samuel and John Adams of Massachusetts; John Jay of New York; Joseph Galloway and John Dickinson of Pennsylvania; and Patrick Henry, Richard Henry

Lee, and George Washington of Virginia. They were determined to find a way to defend American rights without war.

The Continental Congress endorsed the Suffolk (SUFF-uk) Resolves, extreme statements of principle that proclaimed that the colonies owed no obedience to the Coercive Acts, advocated a provisional government until restoration of the Massachusetts charter, and vowed that defensive measures should follow any attack by royal troops. The Continental Congress also voted to boycott British goods after December 1, 1774, and to stop exporting goods to Britain and its West Indies possessions after September 1775. This agreement, called the Continental Association, would be enforced by locally elected committees of "observation" or "safety." But not all the delegates embraced such bold defiance. Jay, Dickinson, Galloway, and other moderates who dominated the contingent from the Middle Colonies feared that a confrontation with Britain would spawn internal colonial turmoil. They vainly opposed nonimportation and unsuccessfully sought support of a plan for an American legislature that would share with Parliament the authority to tax and govern the colonies.

Finally, the delegates summarized their principles and demands in a petition to George III. They conceded to Parliament the power to regulate colonial commerce but argued that parliamentary efforts to impose taxes, enforce laws through admiralty courts, suspend assemblies, and revoke charters were unconstitutional. By addressing the king rather than Parliament, Congress was imploring George III to end the crisis by dismissing the ministers responsible for passing the Coercive Acts.

From Resistance to Rebellion

Most Americans hoped that resistance would jolt Parliament into renouncing its claims of authority over the colonies. But tensions between American radicals and moderates ran high.

To solidify defiance, American resistance leaders used coercion against waverers and loyalists ("Tories"). Committees elected to enforce the Continental Association became vigilantes, compelling merchants to burn British imports, browbeating clergymen who preached pro-British sermons, and pressuring Americans to free themselves of dependence on British imports by adopting simpler diets and homespun clothing. In colony after colony, moreover, the committees assumed governmental functions by organizing volunteer military companies and extralegal legislatures. By spring 1775 colonial patriots had established provincial "congresses" that rivaled existing royal governments.

In April 1775 armed conflict erupted in Massachusetts. Citizens had collected arms and organized militia units ("minutemen") to respond instantly in an emergency. The British government ordered Massachusetts's governor, Thomas Gage, to quell the "rude rabble" and to arrest the patriot leaders. Aware that most of these had fled Boston, Gage, on April 19, 1775, sent 700 British soldiers to seize colonial military supplies stored at **Concord.** Two couriers, William Dawes and Paul Revere, alerted nearby towns of the British troop movements. At **Lexington** on the road to Concord, about seventy minutemen faced the British on the town green. After a confused skirmish in which eight minutemen died and a single redcoat was wounded, the British marched to Concord. They found few munitions but encountered a swarm of armed Yankees. When some minutemen mistakenly concluded that the

Concord Skirmish between colonists and British troops a few hours after Concord

Lexington One of first armed conflicts between Britain and colonists town was being burned, they exchanged fire with British regulars and touched off a running battle that continued most of the sixteen miles back to Boston. By day's end the redcoats had lost 273 men. These engagements awakened the countryside. Within a day, some 20,000 New Englanders were besieging the British garrison in Boston.

Three weeks later, the Continental Congress reconvened in Philadelphia. Most delegates still opposed independence and agreed to send a "loyal message" to George III. The resulting Olive Branch Petition presented three demands: a cease-fire in Boston, repeal of the Coercive Acts, and negotiations to establish guarantees of American rights. Yet the same delegates who pleaded for peace voted to establish an "American continental army" and to appoint George Washington as commander, measures that the British could only see as rebellious.

The Olive Branch Petition reached London along with news of the Continental Army's formation and of the battles of Breed's Hill and Bunker Hill just outside Boston. Although the British dislodged the Americans in the clashes, they suffered 2,200 casualties, compared to colonial losses of only 311. After Bunker Hill the British public wanted retaliation, not reconciliation. In August, George III proclaimed New England to be in a state of rebellion and in December, Parliament declared all of the colonies rebellious, outlawing all British trade with them and subjecting their ships to seizure.

Common Sense

Most Americans still clung to hopes of reconciliation. Even John Adams, who believed separation inevitable, said that he was "fond of reconciliation, if we could reasonably entertain Hopes of it on a constitutional basis."

The majority of Americans who resisted independence blamed evil ministers, rather than the king, for unconstitutional measures and expected saner heads to rise to power in Britain. On both counts they were wrong. Americans exaggerated the influence of Pitt, Burke, Wilkes (who finally took his seat in 1774), and their other friends in Britain. In March 1775, when Burke proposed that Parliament acknowledge the colonists' right to raise and dispose of taxes, a thumping majority of Parliament voted him down. In August, George III declared the colonies to be in "open and avowed rebellion," and in December Parliament outlawed all trade with them.

Americans' sentimental attachment to the king, the last emotional barrier to independence, crumbled in January 1776 with the publication of Thomas Paine's *Common Sense.* Paine had immigrated to the colonies from England in 1774 with a penchant for radical politics and a gift for plain and pungent prose. Paine told Americans what they had been unable to bring themselves to say: that at the root of the conspiracy against American liberty was not corrupt politicians but the very institutions of monarchy and empire. Further, America did not need its British connection. "The commerce by which she [America] hath enriched herself are the necessaries of life, and will always have a market while eating is the custom in Europe," Paine argued. And, he pointed out, the events of the preceding six months had made independence a reality. Finally, Paine linked America's awakening nationalism with a sense of religious mission: "We have it in our power to begin the world over again. A situation, similar to the present, hath not happened since the days of Noah until now." America, Paine wrote, would be a new *kind* of nation, a model re-

Common Sense Brilliant pamphlet by Thomas Paine that summarized pro-independence arguments public free of oppressive European beliefs and corrupt institutions.

Common Sense, "a landflood that sweeps all before it," sold more than 100,000 copies in three months, one copy for every fourth or fifth adult male in the colonies. By spring 1776 Paine's pamphlet had dissolved lingering allegiance to George III and removed the last psychological barrier to independence.

Declaring Independence

Even as colonists absorbed Paine's views, the military conflict between Britain and the colonies escalated, further diminishing the prospects of reconciliation. In May 1775 colonial troops captured Fort Ticonderoga and Crown Point on the key route connecting New York and Canada. Six months later Washington ordered Colonel Henry Knox, in civilian life a book seller and in war the army's senior artillery officer, to bring the cannons captured at Ticonderoga to reinforce the siege of Boston. Using crude sleds, Knox and his men hauled fifty-nine cannons through dense forest and over snow-covered mountains, one of the Revolution's great feats of endurance. The Ticonderoga cannon forced the British to evacuate Boston on March 17, 1776.

Regrouping, the British planned an assault on New York to drive a wedge between New England and the other colonies. Washington countered by moving his forces there in April 1776. Other military moves quickened the drift toward all-out war. A two-pronged assault on Canada by the colonists failed, as did a British offensive in the southern colonies.

Thomas Paine
Having arrived in the colonies less than two years earlier, Paine became a best-selling author with the publication of *Common Sense* (1776).

Stimulated by Paine's soaring rhetoric, local gatherings throughout the colonies, ranging from town meetings to militia musters, passed resolutions favoring American independence.

Most of New England was already in rebellion, and Rhode Island declared itself independent in May 1776. The Middle Colonies hesitated to support revolution because they feared, correctly, that the war would largely be fought over control of Philadelphia and New York. The South began to press for separation. In April, North Carolina authorized its congressional delegates to vote for independence, and in June, Virginia followed suit. On July 2 the Continental Congress formally adopted the Virginia resolution and created the United States of America.

The drafting of a statement to justify the colonies' separation from England fell to Virginia's Thomas Jefferson. Congress made two important changes to Jefferson's first draft: it inserted the phrase "pursuit of happiness" instead of "property" in the document's most famous sentence, and it deleted a condemnation of George III for forcing the slave trade on unwilling colonists. Congress then approved Jefferson's manuscript on July 4, 1776. Even though parliamentary authority had been the focal

www.cengage.com/history/boyer/enduringconcise6e

Declaration of Independence
Document drafted primarily by Thomas Jefferson presenting American Revolution as struggle for universal principles

point of dispute since 1765, the **Declaration of Independence** never mentioned Parliament by name because Congress was unwilling to imply that Parliament held any authority over America. Jefferson instead focused on George III, citing "repeated injuries and usurpations" against the colonies.

Like Paine, Jefferson elevated colonial grievances to a struggle of universal dimensions. In the tradition of Enlightenment thought, Jefferson argued that Britain had violated its contract with the colonists, giving them the right to replace it with a government of their own. His emphasis on the equality of all individuals and their natural entitlement to justice, liberty, and self-fulfillment expressed the Enlightenment's deep longing for government that rested on neither legal privilege nor the exploitation of the majority by the few—and deliberately ignored the existence of slavery.

Jefferson addressed the Declaration of Independence as much to Americans uncertain about the wisdom of independence as to world opinion. Above all, he wanted to convince his fellow Americans that social and political progress was impossible within the British empire. But the declaration did not address the status of blacks, poor white men, and women. All thirteen of the new states countenanced slavery, severely restricted the rights of free blacks, used property qualifications to determine voting rights, and relegated women to second-class status. Jefferson also put Indians beyond the pale when he accused the king of having unleashed "the merciless Indian savages" on innocent colonists.

Thus the declaration expressed the sentiments of a minority of colonists at the same time that it set out the hopes of thousands upon thousands more. The struggle for independence from Britain had merged with a quest for equality and personal independence that would eventually transcend class, race, and gender. The declaration never claimed that perfect justice and equal opportunity existed; instead, it challenged the revolutionary generation and all who followed to bring this ideal closer to reality.

CHECKING IN

- The Coercive (or Intolerable) Acts pushed the colonies to the brink of war.
- Members of the First Continental Congress proclaimed that parliamentary taxation of the colonies was unconstitutional but stopped short of declaring independence.
- The battles of Lexington and Concord transformed colonial resistance from words into an armed struggle.
- Thomas Paine's *Common Sense* universalized American ideals and prodded colonies toward independence.
- In the Declaration of Independence, Thomas Jefferson proclaimed the colonies to be defending universal natural rights.

Chapter Summary

DOWNLOAD THE MP3 AUDIO FILE OF THE CHAPTER SUMMARY, AND LISTEN TO IT ON THE GO.

How did Britain and its colonies view their joint victory over France in the Seven Years War? (page 91)

Great Britain emerged victorious in the Seven Years' War against France; in 1763 France ceded almost all of her North American empire to Britain, quadrupling the size of the British empire in North America. Ironically, this triumph would also provide the framework for friction between England and its colonies.

KEY TERMS

Seven Years' War *(p. 91)*
Treaty of Paris of 1763 *(p. 94)*
Pontiac *(p. 95)*
Proclamation of 1763 *(p. 95)*
writ of assistance *(p. 96)*
Sugar Act *(p. 97)*

What was imperial reorganization, and how did it change relations between Britain and the North American colonies? (page 96)

Attempts at imperial reorganization in the early 1760s were intended to help defray the enormous costs of England's victory by increasing revenues from the colonies, but the attempts succeeded primarily in alienating the colonists. After open resistance boiled over in the Stamp Act crisis, Parliament backed down a bit but insisted that it had complete authority over the colonies.

In what ways did resistance to the Townshend duties differ from earlier colonial resistance efforts? (page 102)

Controversy between England and the colonies continued with measures such as the Quartering Act and the Townshend duties. Colonial protests found shape in the work of John Dickinson and a hero in the person of John Wilkes. In an attempt to increase tax revenues, Britain created a Board of Customs Commissioners, but many of the commissioners were corrupt, and the board became the target of colonial anger.

In what ways did colonists' views of parliamentary authority change after 1770? (page 107)

The Boston Massacre brought a temporary lull in conflict between England and the colonies, but Lord North's attempt to aid the East India Company led to the Boston Tea Party. Colonists defied Britain's continued revenue-raising measures.

What led most colonists in 1776 to abandon their loyalty to Britain and choose national independence? (page 111)

In response to the Tea Party, Parliament passed a series of Coercive Acts—known to the colonists as the Intolerable Acts—which spawned the First Continental Congress and the beginning of fully coordinated colonial resistance. In 1775 the battles of Lexington and Concord transformed the friction between England and the colonies into armed conflict. Thomas Paine's *Common Sense* ridiculed the arguments against independence and portrayed the colonial struggle as one of universal principles on which Thomas Jefferson elaborated in the Declaration of Independence.

KEY TERMS continued

Stamp Act *(p. 98)*
Sons of Liberty *(p. 100)*
Stamp Act Congress *(p. 100)*
Declaratory Act *(p. 100)*
Quartering Act *(p. 102)*
Townshend duties *(p. 103)*
Board of Customs Commissioners *(p. 105)*
John Wilkes *(p. 106)*
Boston Massacre *(p. 108)*
committees of correspondence *(p. 108)*
Tea Act *(p. 110)*
Lord Dunmore *(p. 111)*
Intolerable Acts *(p. 112)*
Continental Congress *(p. 112)*
Concord *(p. 113)*
Lexington *(p. 113)*
Common Sense *(p. 114)*
Declaration of Independence *(p. 116)*

CHAPTER 6

Securing Independence, Defining Nationhood

1776–1788

Trumbull, "George Washington"

This icon will direct you to the website where you can Prepare for Class, Improve Your Grade, and Ace the Test:
www.cengage.com/history/boyer/ enduringconcise6e

The Revolutionary era would teach Americans a hard lesson: that *proclaiming* a new nation, as they had done so proudly in 1776, was much easier than *making* a new nation, which they struggled to do from 1776 to 1788.

Before 1775 the outlook of inhabitants of the different colonial regions had been narrow. With little opportunity and less necessity to work together, each colonist had regarded his own colony as superior to all others. But eight years of war transformed the colonists' narrow view and turned them into American citizens.

Independence and peace in 1783, however, gave Americans a false security. Major problems remained unsolved. Americans were divided over how to distribute political power. Not until 1787 would they begin to overcome these challenges.

THE PROSPECTS OF WAR

What were the comparative advantages of the British and the colonists when the Revolution began?

The Revolution was both a struggle that pitted Americans against Britain and a civil war between Americans. Those opposed to independence represented one of several factors in Britain's favor as the war began; others included a larger population and superior military resources and preparation. The colonies, on the other hand, were far from Britain and enjoyed the intense commitment to independence from patriots and the Continental Army.

Loyalists and Other British Sympathizers

When independence came in July 1776, many colonists remained unconvinced of its necessity. About 20 percent of all whites actively opposed the rebellion or supported it only when threatened with fines and imprisonment. These opponents of the Revolution called themselves **loyalists,** but **Whigs** (supporters of the Revolution) labeled them Tories.

loyalist Colonist who supported the British

Whig Supporter of the Revolution

Loyalists, like Whigs, typically opposed parliamentary taxation of the colonies. Many loyalists thus found themselves fighting for a cause with which they did not entirely agree; as a result, many switched sides during the war. But loyalists believed that separation was illegal and was not necessary to preserve the colonists' constitutional rights. Above all, they revered the crown and equated any failure to defend their king with a sacrifice of personal honor.

The mutual hatred between Whigs and Tories was intense. Each side saw its cause as sacred, and those who opposed it as traitors. The worst atrocities of the war were committed by Americans against each other.

Loyalist strength in an area depended on how well prominent local Whigs had convinced voters that the king and Parliament were endangering representative government. From 1772 to 1776, elites in New England, Virginia, and South Carolina mobilized citizens by organizing public meetings and repeatedly explaining the issues. The majority opted for resistance; by 1776 loyalists constituted barely 5 percent of whites in these areas. In contrast, elites in New York and New Jersey remained reluctant to declare allegiance to either side, and their indecision resulted in divided communities. These two states provided half of the 21,000 Americans who would fight in loyalist units.

A second major factor in loyalist strength was the geographic distribution of recent British immigrants, who identified closely with their homeland. These newcomers included thousands of British veterans of the French and Indian War who had remained in the colonies, usually in New York. Further, the 125,000 British immigrants who arrived between 1763 and 1775 formed major centers of loyalist sympathy. In New York, Georgia, and the Carolina piedmont, where these newcomers clustered, loyalists probably constituted 25 to 40 percent of the white population in 1776.

Black slaves and Native Americans also widely supported the British. As in Virginia, hundreds of South Carolina slaves sought refuge on British ships before the outbreak of war. During the war itself, at least 20,000 slaves would run away from southern plantations to sign on as laborers or soldiers in the Royal Army. Deeply alienated from white society, southern slaves realized that the Revolution would not benefit them. In contrast, most African-Americans in the North supported the rebels in hopes of hastening their own liberation.

Finally, most Indians, recognizing the threat that expansion-minded colonists posed, likewise supported the British. Of the handful of tribes that sided with the colonists, the most prominent were two Iroquois tribes, the Oneidas (oh-NIE-duhs) and the Tuscaroras (tuss-kuh-ROR-uhs).

The Opposing Sides

Britain entered the war with what should have been two major advantages. First, Britain's 11 million people greatly outnumbered the 2.5 million colonists, one-third of whom were either slaves or loyalists. Second, Britain possessed the world's largest navy and one of its best armies. During the war, the army's size more than doubled, from 48,000 to 111,000 men, and Britain hired 30,000 Hessian (HESH-un) mercenaries and enlisted 21,000 loyalists to supplement its own fighting force.

Despite a smaller population, the new nation mobilized about 220,000 troops—compared to the 162,000 Britons, loyalists, and Hessians who served in the British army. However, most Americans served only a short term; the nation would have been hard pressed without the contributions of its French allies in the late stages of the war. Further, peacetime budget cuts after 1763 had weakened British sea power and thus Britain's ability to crush the rebellion. Midway through the war, half of Britain's ships languished in dry dock, awaiting repairs. In addition, during the war U.S. Navy ships and privateers would capture more than 2,000 British merchant vessels and 16,000 crewmen. Seriously overextended, the navy barely kept the army supplied and never effectively blockaded American ports.

Maintaining public support presented another serious problem for Britain. The war more than doubled the British national debt, adding to the problems of a people already paying record taxes. Resentful of this tax burden, the politically influential landed gentry would not vote against their pocketbooks forever.

The new United States faced different but equally severe problems. First, one-fifth of its population was openly pro-British. Second, state militias lacked the training to fight pitched battles. Their hit-and-run guerrilla tactics could not bring victory, nor could avoiding major battles and allowing the British to occupy population centers. Moreover, the U.S. dependence on guerrilla warfare would convince potential European allies that the Americans could not drive out the British and would doom American efforts to gain foreign loans, diplomatic recognition, and military allies.

The Continental Army would thus have to fight in European fashion, relying on precision movements of mass formations of troops and rapid maneuvers to crush an enemy's undefended flank or rear. Attackers would need exceptional skill in close-order drill. After advancing within musket range, opposing troops would stand upright and fire at each other until one line weakened. Discipline, training, and nerve would be essential if soldiers were to hold their line as comrades fell around them.

In contrast to Britain, which had a well-trained army with a tradition of bravery under fire, the Continental Army had neither an inspirational heritage nor experi-

Chronology

1776	British troops evacuate Boston; British defeat American forces under George Washington in fighting around New York City; American victory in Battle of Trenton
1777	British surrender at Saratoga; British occupy Philadelphia; Congress approves Articles of Confederation
1778	France formally recognizes the United States; France declares war on Britain; British evacuate Philadelphia; British occupy Savannah; Joseph Brant leads Iroquois attacks in western Pennsylvania and New York
1779	Spain declares war on Britain; George Rogers Clark recaptures Vincennes
1780	British seize Charles Town
1781	Articles of Confederation become law; Battle of Yorktown; British General Charles Cornwallis surrenders
1782	Paris peace negotiations begin
1783	Peace of Paris; Newburgh Conspiracy
1784	Spain closes New Orleans to American trade; Economic depression begins
1785	Ordinance of 1785
1786	Congress rejects Jay-Gardoqui Treaty; Joseph Brant organizes Indian resistance to U.S. expansion; Virginia adopts Thomas Jefferson's Statute for Religious Freedom
1786–1787	Shays's Rebellion in Massachusetts
1787	Northwest Ordinance; Philadelphia Convention; federal Constitution signed
1788	Alexander Hamilton, James Madison, and John Jay, *The Federalist*; Federal Constitution ratified

enced officers in 1775. In the war's early years, it suffered heartbreaking defeats. However, to win, the Continentals did not have to destroy the British army but only to prolong the rebellion until Britain's taxpayers lost patience. Until then, American victory depended on the ability of one man to keep his army fighting despite defeat—**George Washington.**

George Washington Commander of the Continental Army; main factor in American success

Few generals looked and acted the role as much as Washington. He spoke with authority and comported himself with dignity. At six feet two inches, he stood a half-foot taller than an average contemporary. Powerfully built, athletic, and hardened by a rugged outdoor life, he could inspire troops to heroism.

Washington's military experience had begun at age twenty-two when he had commanded a Virginia regiment raised to resist French claims in the Ohio Valley (see Chapter 5). Vastly outnumbered, he had lost his first battle. A year later, at Braddock's defeat, Washington had assumed the point of greatest danger, had two horses shot out from under him, and had his hat shot off and his coat ripped by bullets. But Washington's mistakes and lost battles had taught him lessons that easy victories might not have. He had discovered the dangers of overconfidence and the need for determination. He had also learned that Americans fought best when led by example and treated with respect.

In 1758, with Virginia's borders secured, Washington had resigned his commission and become a tobacco planter. He had sat in the House of

CHECKING IN

- At the war's start, the British enjoyed major advantages in population, economic development, and military preparedness.

- However, British supply lines were long and popular support for the war short-lived.

- Americans had no trained army when the war began.

- Americans did not have to defeat the British; they just had to prolong the rebellion.

- Washington kept his army fighting despite defeats; this experience taught him the need for determination and earned him enormous respect among Americans.

Burgesses, where others respected him and sought his opinion. An early opponent of parliamentary taxation, he had also served in the Continental Congress. In the eyes of the many who valued his advice and his military experience, Washington was the logical choice to head the Continental Army.

WAR AND PEACE, 1776–1783

How did the war unfold?

Each side initially won important victories in the North. West of the Appalachians, revolutionary forces prevailed over the British and their Indian allies. However, it was the American and French victory at Yorktown in 1781 that decided the war and gained British recognition of American independence.

Shifting Fortunes in the North, 1776–1778

In March 1776 the British evacuated Boston and moved south to New York, which they wished to use as a base for conquering New England. Under two brothers, General William Howe and Admiral Richard, Lord Howe, 130 warships carried 32,000 troops to New York City in the summer of 1776. Defending the city were 18,000 poorly trained soldiers under Washington. On August 27, 15,000 British troops nearly annihilated 10,500 American troops on Long Island, just across the river from New York City. But Washington executed a masterly night evacuation, saving 9,500 troops and most of his artillery from capture.

In mid-September 1776 the Continental Army numbered 16,000 men. Over the next three months the British killed or took prisoner one-quarter of these troops and drove the survivors across New Jersey. By early December, when Washington retreated from New Jersey into Pennsylvania, he commanded fewer than 7,000 men fit for duty.

With the British within striking distance of Philadelphia, Washington took the offensive before military and national morale collapsed. On Christmas night 1776 he attacked a Hessian garrison at **Trenton,** New Jersey, and captured nearly 1,000 Germans with the loss of only 4 men. On January 3, 1777, Washington attacked Princeton, New Jersey, killing or capturing one-third of his 1,200 British opponents and losing only 40. The American victories at Trenton and Princeton had important consequences. First, they boosted civilian and military morale. Second, they undermined the Howes' plans to rally loyalists and skeptics to Britain's cause and forced the British evacuation of New Jersey in early 1777.

New Jersey's militia meanwhile drove thousands of New Jersey loyalists, who had been plundering Whig property, into British-held New York, where many joined the Royal Army. The New Jersey militia became a police force dedicated to rooting out political dissent. It disarmed known loyalists, jailed their leaders, and constantly watched suspected Tories. Facing constant danger of arrest, most loyalists who remained in New Jersey bowed to the inevitable and swore allegiance to the Continental Congress.

Shortly after the battles of Trenton and Princeton, the Marquis de Lafayette (mar-KEE deh lah-fay-ETT), a young French aristocrat, joined Washington's staff.

Primary Source: Washington Crossing the Delaware

Trenton New Jersey battle where Washington took a thousand Hessian prisoners on Christmas Night, 1776; vital to improve national morale

Map 6.1 The War in the North, 1775–1778
During the early years of the war, most of the fighting took place from Philadelphia northward.

Lafayette was twenty years old, idealistic, brave, infectiously optimistic—and closely connected to the French court. His arrival indicated that France might recognize American independence and declare war on Britain. However, the French first wanted proof that the Americans could win a major battle.

That victory came quickly. In summer 1777 the British planned a two-pronged attack to crush New York State and isolate New England. Two British columns, one from Montreal and the other from Quebec, were to link up near Albany.

Nothing went according to British plans. The first British column, moving south from Montreal under Lieutenant Colonel Barry St. Leger, encountered a Continental

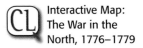
Interactive Map:
The War in the
North, 1776–1779

force holding a chokepoint at Fort Stanwix. Unable to defeat the rebels after a three-week siege, the British retreated north. Meanwhile, the second British column, led by General John Burgoyne, became stranded in western New York, his supply lines overextended and his 8,300 troops depleted by combat and hunger. General Horatio Gates of the Continental Army gathered a force of 17,000 rebels and attacked Burgoyne near **Saratoga.** Burgoyne's troops, surrounded and outnumbered, surrendered on October 17, 1777.

Saratoga American victory in 1777 that convinced the French to support the revolutionaries

Saratoga was the war's turning point, as important diplomatically as militarily. Already pro-American and favorably impressed by the shrewd diplomacy of Benjamin Franklin as American ambassador, the French court received news of the victory at Saratoga as proof that the Americans could win the war and thus deserved diplomatic recognition. In February 1778 France formally recognized the United States. Four months later, France went to war with Britain. Spain and Holland ultimately joined the war as French allies.

The colonies' allies made their presence felt. Between 1779 and 1781 Spanish troops prevented the British from taking the Mississippi Valley, and beginning in 1781 French troops contributed to rebel victories. Moreover, Britain sent thousands of soldiers to Ireland and the West Indies to guard against a French invasion, further stretching already depleted manpower reserves. The French and Spanish navies, which together approximately equaled the British fleet, won several large battles and punctured the Royal Navy's blockade.

In late August 1777 British General Howe landed eighteen thousand troops near Philadelphia. With Washington at their head and Lafayette at his side, sixteen thousand Continentals paraded through the imperiled city.

The armies collided on September 11, 1777, at Brandywine Creek, Pennsylvania. After the Continentals crumbled in the face of superior British discipline, Congress fled Philadelphia, allowing Howe to occupy it. In early October Howe defeated the Americans a second time, at Germantown. In four bloody weeks 20 percent of the Continentals were killed, wounded, or captured. In December 1777 the eleven thousand Continental survivors marched to their winter headquarters at **Valley Forge,** chilled to the bone and short even of shoes. Washington later recalled, "You might have tracked the army from White Marsh to Valley Forge by the blood of their feet." As the British rested comfortably in Philadelphia, eighteen miles away, the Continentals huddled, exhausted and hungry, in crude huts.

Valley Forge Winter camp of Continental Army, 1777–1778; one of lowest points of war

The army slowly regained its strength but still lacked training. At Saratoga the Americans had enjoyed overwhelming numbers. But meeting Howe on an even basis, the Continentals had lost badly—twice. The key skills of marching and maneuvering were nonexistent. Then in February 1778 a German soldier of fortune and drillmaster, Friedrich von Steuben, reached Valley Forge. An administrative genius and immensely popular with an amazing ability to swear forcefully in several languages, he almost singlehandedly turned the U.S. army into a formidable fighting force.

Just how formidable became clear in June 1778 at Monmouth Court House, New Jersey. The battle blazed for six hours, with the Continentals throwing back Britain's finest troops. The British finally broke off contact and slipped away under cover of darkness. Never again would they win easy victories against the Continental Army.

Map 6.2   The War in the West, 1776–1782
The war's western front was closely tied to Native American's defense of their homelands against expansionist settlers.

The Battle of Monmouth ended the contest for the North. Clinton occupied New York, which the Royal Navy made safe from attack. Washington kept his army on watch nearby, while Whig militia hunted down the last few Tory guerrillas.

The War in the West, 1776–1782

West of the Appalachians and along New York and Pennsylvania's western borders, a different kind of war unfolded. The numbers engaged along the frontier were small, but the stakes were enormous. In 1776 few Anglo-Americans had any clear idea of the country's western boundaries. By 1783, when the Peace of Paris concluded the war, the new nation would claim the Mississippi River as its western border. So, although the frontier campaigns would not determine the war's outcome, they would significantly shape the future of the United States.

Frontier fighting first erupted in the South when Cherokees had begun attacking frontier settlements from Virginia to Georgia in 1776. Within a year, retaliatory expeditions had burned most Cherokee towns and forced the Cherokees to cede most of their lands in South Carolina and large tracts in North Carolina and Tennessee. Kentucky saw fierce fighting as rebels under Colonel George Rogers Clark established control of the Ohio River Valley from Pittsburgh to the Mississippi after defeating both the British and Native Americans.

In the East, pro-British Iroquois under the gifted Mohawk leader Joseph Brant devastated the New York and Pennsylvania frontiers in 1778. General John Sullivan led a Continental force, with Tuscarora and Oneida allies, against the Iroquois. Victorious at what is now Elmira, New York, in 1779, Sullivan and his forces burned two dozen Iroquois villages and destroyed a million bushels of corn. The Iroquois fled north to Canada, and hundreds starved to death. Sullivan had destroyed the heartland of the Iroquois; their population declined by one-third during the Revolutionary War.

American Victory in the South, 1778–1781

After 1778 the British focus shifted to the South. France and Spain's entry had embroiled Britain in an international struggle that raged from India to Gibraltar and from the West Indies to the North American mainland. If the British could secure the South, they could easily shuffle forces between the West Indies and the mainland. And the South looked like an easy target: Clinton expected a southern invasion to tap a huge reservoir of loyalist support. British strategy called for seizing key southern ports and, aided by loyal militiamen, moving back north, pacifying one region after another.

At first the plan unfolded smoothly. Sailing from New York with 4,000 men, General Clinton captured Charles Town, South Carolina, in May 1780. He left the mopping-up operation to **Lord Charles Cornwallis.** Clinton's miscalculation of loyalist strength rapidly became apparent. Southern Tories used the British occupation to take revenge for their harsh treatment under rebel rule, and patriots struck back. The war engulfed the lower South and became intensely personal, with individuals choosing sides not for political reasons but for simple revenge.

Lord Charles Cornwallis
British general whose surrender at Yorktown in 1781 effectively ended Revolutionary War

The southern campaign also sparked a renewed exodus of slaves; 25,000 Georgia and South Carolina slaves sought freedom in British-held territory. The British had no intention of emancipating slaves and made every effort to return them to their owners. Nonetheless, fear of slave rebellion caused many former loyalists to abandon their British ties and welcome the rebels' return to power.

Meanwhile, battles between British troops and Continental regulars led to a string of Continental defeats. America's worst loss of the entire war came at Camden, South Carolina, in August 1780. General Horatio Gates's combined force of professionals and militiamen faced Cornwallis's army. The militiamen fled after the first volley, and the badly outnumbered Continentals were overrun. Washington sent General Nathanael Greene to confront Cornwallis. Under Greene, the rebels lost three major battles in 1781 but won the campaign nonetheless. Greene gave the patriot militiamen the protection that they needed to hunt down loyalists, stretched British supply lines until they snapped, and inflicted heavy casualties. Greene's dogged resistance forced Cornwallis to abandon the Carolina backcountry and to lead his battered troops into Virginia.

Still secure in New York, Clinton wanted Cornwallis to return to Charles Town, but Cornwallis established a base at Yorktown, Virginia, where the York and James

Map 6.3 The War in the South, 1778-1781
The South was the setting for the final, decisive phase of the war, culminating in the British surrender at Yorktown in October 1781.

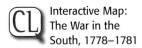

Interactive Map: The War in the South, 1778–1781

rivers empty into Chesapeake Bay. He hoped to fan out into Virginia and Pennsylvania but never got the chance. On August 30, 1781, a French fleet dropped anchor and landed troops near Yorktown. Lafayette joined them, and Washington led his Continental Army south to tighten the noose. Trapped and besieged at Yorktown, Cornwallis's 6,000 troops surrendered to 8,800 Americans and 7,800 French on October 19, 1781.

Peace at Last, 1782–1783

"Oh God!" Lord North exclaimed on hearing of Yorktown. "It's all over." Indeed, Cornwallis's surrender had extinguished Britain's overtaxed people's will to fight and forced the government to begin peace negotiations. Talks opened in Paris in June

Primary Source: Socioeconomic Profile of Loyalist Claimants

1782, with John Adams, Benjamin Franklin, and John Jay as America's principal diplomats.

Military realities largely dictated the terms of the peace treaty. Britain recognized American independence and promised the evacuation of all royal troops from U.S. soil. The British had little choice but to award the new nation the vast territory east of the Mississippi, for by 1783 twenty thousand Anglo-American settlers lived west of the Appalachians, and George Rogers Clark's victories had given Americans control of the Northwest.

The settlement—the Peace of Paris—favored the United States but left some problems unresolved. In a separate treaty Britain transferred East and West Florida back to Spain, but the designated boundaries were ambiguous. Further, although the United States promised to urge state legislatures to compensate loyalists for property losses, several states would later refuse to comply. Completely left out of the treaty—and on their own—were the Native Americans who had supported the British. Indian leaders were outraged; many did not acknowledge the new nation's sovereignty over their territory.

Independence carried a heavy price. At least 5 percent of free males—white, black, and Native American—aged sixteen to forty-five had died fighting the British. And the peace left two important issues unsettled: what kind of society the United States would become and what sort of government it would possess.

THE REVOLUTION AND SOCIAL CHANGE

How did the war affect relationships among Americans of different classes, races, and genders?

Two forces shaped the Revolution's social effects: the principles articulated in the Declaration of Independence and the dislocations caused by the war. These factors combined to force questions of class, gender, and race into public discussion. Popular attitudes about the rights of non-elite white men and of white women and the future of slavery shifted somewhat. Except for slaves in northern states, there was little prospect of substantive change in their status; nevertheless, the discussions ensured that these issues would be debated in the future. However, for Native Americans, the Revolution was a step backward.

Egalitarianism Among White Men

Between 1700 and 1760 social relations between elites and common people had grown more formal, distant, and restrained. Members of the colonial gentry lived sumptuously to emphasize their position. By the late 1760s, however, many in the upper class were wearing homespun clothing in support of boycotts of British goods. When the Virginia planters organized militia companies in 1775, they dressed in plain hunting shirts so that even the poorest farmer would not find his humble appearance too embarrassing for him to enlist. Elites maintained the appearance, if not the substance, of equality.

The war accelerated the erosion of class differences by forcing gentry-officers to respect ordinary men serving as privates. Indeed, the soldiers demanded to be treated with consideration, especially in light of the ringing statement of the Declaration of Independence that "all men are created equal."

The men who expected officers to recognize their worth as individuals carried their new self-esteem and insistence on respect back into civilian life. Personal pride gradually translated into political behavior and beliefs, and candidates took care not to scorn the common people. The war thus fundamentally democratized Americans' political assumptions. The gentry's sense of social rank also diminished as they met men who rose through ability and observed middle-class farmers and artisans handling duties previously thought above their station. In short, revolutionary-generation Americans insisted that virtue and sacrifice, not wealth, defined worth. They came to see the "natural aristocracy"—those who demonstrated fitness for government service by their personal accomplishments—as ideal candidates for political office. This natural aristocracy included self-made men such as Benjamin Franklin. The wealthy could still be elected to office, but not if they flaunted their wealth. This new emphasis on equality did not extend to propertyless men, women, or nonwhites, but it undermined the assumption that birth and wealth conferred a special claim to public office. Nor did the war change the distribution of wealth in the nation; the American upper class seems to have owned about as much of the national wealth in 1783 as it did in 1786.

White Women in Wartime

White women broadened their involvement in the anti-British cause, creating a wide range of activities during the war. Female "camp followers," many of them soldiers' wives, cooked, laundered, and nursed the wounded for both sides. A few women disguised themselves as men and joined the fighting. Women who remained at home managed families, households, farms, and businesses on their own. Despite—and because of—enormous struggles, women gained confidence in their ability to think and act on matters traditionally reserved for men. Although women's public roles and visibility increased during the Revolution, the question was to what extent the new nation would make these gains permanent.

As in all wars, women's public roles and visibility heightened during the Revolution. In 1779, a number of women, including Franklin's daughter Sally Franklin Bache, organized a campaign to raise money for the troops. They likened their role to Joan of Arc and other female heroes who had saved their people, and they proclaimed that American women were "born for liberty" and would never "bear the irons of a tyrannic government."

The most direct challenge to established gender relations came from Abigail Adams. "In the new Code of Laws..."' she wrote to her husband John in 1776, "I desire that you would Remember the Ladies." Abigail made it clear that women saw that the arguments against arbitrary British rule also applied to gender relations. "We will not have ourselves bound by any Laws in which we have no voice, or Representation." Despite his high regard for his wife's intellect, John Adams dismissed her plea as an effort to extend rights and power to the unworthy. The assumption that women were naturally dependent continued to dominate discussions of the female role. For that reason, married women's property remained, in Abigail's bitter words, "subject to the control and disposal of our partners."

Although the war ended in 1783, discussions of women's roles in the new republic would continue.

PHILLIS WHEATLEY NEGRO SERVANT to Mr JOHN WHEATLEY, of BOSTON.

Phillis Wheatley, African-American Poet

Though a slave, Wheatley was the best-known poet in America at the time of the Revolution. Despite her fame, she died in poverty in 1784.

antislavery movement
Opposition to slavery that began slowly during revolutionary period

A Revolution for Black Americans

The wartime condition of African-Americans contradicted the ideals of equality and justice for which Americans fought. About 500,000 black persons, composing one-fifth of the total population, inhabited the United States in 1776. All but 25,000 were slaves. Free blacks could not vote, lived under curfews, and lacked the guarantees of equal justice afforded to even the poorest white criminal.

The war nevertheless presented new opportunities to African-Americans. Some slaves took advantage of the confusion of war to run off and pose as freemen. A 1775 ban on black soldiers was collapsing by 1777. All states but Georgia and South Carolina eventually recruited blacks. Approximately 5,000 African-Americans, mainly from the North, served in the Continental Army. Most were slaves serving with their masters' consent, usually in racially integrated units.

Manpower demands, not a white commitment to equal justice, largely opened these opportunities. In fact, until the mid-eighteenth century, most in the Western world saw slavery as part of the natural order. By the 1760s, however, some American opposition to slavery had blossomed. The Quakers led the way; by 1779 most Quaker slave owners had freed their slaves. The Declaration of Independence's broad assertion of natural rights and human equality spurred a larger attack on slavery. By 1804 all the states from Pennsylvania north, except New Hampshire, had begun phasing out slavery.

The **antislavery movement** reflected the Enlightenment's emphasis on gradual change. By priming public opinion to favor a weakening of the institution over time, leaders sought to bring about its demise. Most state abolition laws provided for gradual emancipation, typically declaring free all children born of a slave woman after a certain date, often July 4. Furthermore, revolutionary leaders did not press for decisive action against slavery in the South, where the institution was embedded in the economy.

Although slavery gnawed at Whig consciences even in the South, no state south of Pennsylvania abolished slavery. Most, however, passed laws making it easier to free slaves. Between 1775 and 1790 the number of free blacks in Virginia and Maryland rose from 4,000 to 21,000, or about 5 percent of all African-Americans residing there.

These "free persons of color" faced a future of destitution and second-class citizenship. Most had used up their cash savings to purchase their freedom and were past their physical prime. They found few whites willing to hire them or to pay equal wages. Most free blacks remained poor laborers or tenant farmers. But a few became landowners or skilled artisans. Benjamin Banneker of Maryland, a self-taught mathematician and astronomer, served on the survey team that laid out Washington, D.C., and published a series of almanacs. Phillis Wheatley, a slave in a Boston merchant family, gained her freedom in 1773, the same year her poems were published to acclaim in England. Several of these poems linked the liberty sought by white Americans with a plea for the liberty of slaves.

One of the most prominent free blacks to emerge during the Revolutionary period was Prince Hall of Boston. After gaining his freedom in 1770, Hall took a leading role among Boston blacks protesting slavery. During the war he formed a separate African-American Masonic lodge, initiating a movement that spread to other northern communities and became an important source of community support for black Americans. In 1786 he petitioned the Massachusetts legislature for support of a plan that would enable interested blacks "to return to Africa, our native country…where we shall live among our equals and be more comfortable and happy than we can be in our present situation." Later activists would echo his call for blacks to "return to Africa."

Most states granted important civil rights to free blacks during and after the Revolution. For example, male free blacks who met property qualifications gained the right to vote everywhere by the 1780s. Most northern states repealed or stopped enforcing curfews and other restrictive laws; most also guaranteed free blacks equal treatment in court.

The Revolution neither ended slavery nor brought equality to free blacks, but it did begin a process by which slavery could be extinguished. In half the nation, public opinion no longer condoned human bondage, and southerners increasingly saw slavery as a necessary evil, implicitly admitting its immorality. The shift proved short-lived, as the trend toward egalitarianism faded in the 1790s.

Native Americans and the Revolution

Revolutionary ideology held out at least abstract hope for African-Americans and women, but it made no provisions for the many Indians who sought to maintain political and cultural independence. Moreover, in an overwhelmingly agrarian society, the Revolution's promise of equal economic opportunity for all set the stage for territorial expansion beyond settled areas, thereby threatening Indian lands. Even where Indians retained land, the influx of settlers posed dangers in the form of deadly diseases, farming practices hostile to Indian subsistence, and alcohol. Indians were all the more vulnerable because during the wars between 1754 and 1783, their population east of the Mississippi had fallen by about half, and many villages had been uprooted.

In the face of these uncertainties, Native Americans continued to incorporate aspects of European culture into their lives. From the early colonial period, they had adopted European-made goods of cloth, metal, and glass while retaining some of their traditional clothing, tools, and weapons. Indians also participated in the American economy by occasionally working for wages or selling food, craft items, and other products.

Thus Native Americans did not hold stubbornly to traditional ways, but they did insist on retaining control of their communities and ways of life. In the Revolution's aftermath, it remained doubtful that the new nation would accommodate Native Americans on these terms.

CHECKING IN

- Egalitarianism among white males increased as a result of the war.
- The war offered free African-Americans some gains in opportunities and rights, but most still faced a future of uncertainty and second-class citizenship.
- Northern states provided for the eventual end of slavery, and an antislavery movement began.
- Women built on their contributions during the war to play a larger public role.
- Native Americans were left in an ambiguous and threatened position.

FORGING NEW GOVERNMENTS, 1776–1787

How did Americans translate revolutionary principles into effective governments?

Despite their unity against British authority, the revolutionaries differed sharply among themselves over basic questions of social and political order. Elite republicans feared democracy as "mob rule," and urban workers feared that elites profited at their expense. Rural colonists emphasized decentralization of power. The revolutionaries' early attempts at creating state and national governments reflected these conflicts.

From Colonies to States

Political conflicts within the new states magnified the prewar struggle between more radical democratic elements and elites who wanted to minimize popular participation. While the new state constitutions retained colonial precedents favoring the wealthy elites, they also laid the foundations for republican government in America.

In establishing the revolutionary state governments, the patriots relied heavily on the colonial experience. For example, most favored bicameral legislatures. Colonial legislatures in the royal provinces had consisted of two houses: an appointed upper chamber (council) and an elected lower chamber (assembly). These two-part legislatures resembled Parliament's division into the House of Lords and the House of Commons, and symbolized the assumption that a government should represent aristocrats and commoners separately. Eleven of the thirteen new legislatures in the 1780s were bicameral. Likewise, few questioned the long-standing practice of setting property requirements for voters and elected officials. Property ownership, most people argued, enabled voters and officeholders to think and act independently.

Americans generally agreed, too, that their elected representatives should exercise independent judgment rather than simply carry out the popular will. The idea of political parties as instruments for identifying and mobilizing public opinion was alien to the Revolutionary era, which equated parties with "factions"—selfish groups that advanced their interests at the expense of the public good. Candidates campaigned on the basis of their reputation and qualifications, not the issues. In general, they did not present voters with a clear choice between policies calculated to benefit rival interest groups. Thus voters did not know how candidates stood on specific issues and found it hard to influence government actions.

As in the colonial era, most legislative districts were bicameral, and most were divided equally among all counties or towns, regardless of population distribution. A minority of voters normally elected a majority of assemblymen. The most radical constitution, Pennsylvania's, tried to establish election districts roughly equal in population so that a minority of voters could not elect a majority of legislators. Nine states reduced property requirements for voting, but none abolished them. In most states the majority of officeholders continued to be appointed.

The persistence of these features should not obscure the pathbreaking nature of the **state constitutions.** First, their adoption required ratification by the people. Second, they could be changed only by popular vote. Above all, counter to the Brit-

state constitutions Written frameworks of government that defined the people as sovereign ish view of a constitution as a body of customary practices, the state constitutions were *written* compacts that defined and limited rulers' powers. As a final check on government power, the revolutionary constitutions contained bills of rights outlining fundamental freedoms beyond government control. Governments would no longer serve as the final judge of the constitutionality of their activities.

Contrary to political elites' predilections, the imperial crisis of the 1760s and 1770s had pulled them into a democratic tide. The assemblies, the most democratic parts of colonial government, had led the fight against British policy. Colonists had embarked on the Revolution dreading executive officeholders and convinced that they could not trust even elected governors. Their recent experience seemed to confirm that those in power tended to become corrupt or dictatorial.

Accordingly, the state constitutions strictly limited executive power. In most states the governor became an elected official, and elections were held far more frequently than before—usually every year. In the majority of states, legislatures, not governors, appointed judges and other officials. Stripped of the veto and most appointive powers, governors became figureheads.

Having weakened the executive branch and vested more power in the legislatures, the state constitutions also made the legislatures more responsive to the will of the people. Nowhere could the governor appoint the upper chamber. Eight states allowed voters to select *both* houses of the legislature. Pennsylvania and Georgia abolished the upper house and substituted a unicameral (one-chamber) legislature. The Whigs' assault on executive power reflected bitter memories of arbitrary royal governors.

But Revolutionary leaders considered themselves republicans, not democrats. To them, "**democracy**" suggested mob rule and the concentration of power in the hands of an ignorant mass. "**Republicanism**" presumed that government would be entrusted to leaders chosen for their talents and wisdom. Most republicans believed that government should balance the interests of different classes to prevent any one group from gaining absolute power. They also rejected monarchy—having blasted one king in the Declaration of Independence, they were not about to enthrone another. Nonetheless, republicans had difficulty reconciling their preference for strong, elite leadership with most Americans' pervasive distrust of executive power.

"democracy" Fully representative government; feared by revolutionary generation as mob rule

"republicanism" Ideal of early revolutionaries that government should be entrusted to leaders chosen for wisdom

Initially, elites had to accept state governments dominated by elected legislatures. Gradually, however, well-to-do landowners, merchants, and lawyers reasserted their desire for centralized authority and the political prerogatives of wealth. For example, in 1780 an elite-dominated convention in Massachusetts pushed through a constitution with stiff property qualifications for voting and holding office and a strong governor with considerable appointment and veto power. Georgia and Pennsylvania had reverted to bicameral legislatures by 1790. Other states raised property qualifications for the upper chamber to make room for men of "Wisdom, remarkable integrity, or that Weight which arises from property."

Troubled far less by differences among social classes and restrictions on the expression of popular will than by the prospect of tyranny, some elites nevertheless feared that deep-seated and permanent social divisions could jeopardize republican liberty. In Virginia between 1776 and 1780, Thomas Jefferson drafted a series of bills to promote equality.

These years also witnessed the end of most state-established churches. Religiously conservative New Hampshire, Connecticut, and Massachusetts resisted this reform until 1817, 1818, and 1833, respectively, but in every state where the Anglican church was established, such status was abolished by 1786. Jefferson's Statute for Religious Freedom (1786) resoundingly defended religious freedom. "Truth is great," he proclaimed, "and will prevail if left to itself."

In 1782 Thomas Paine wrote that the American Revolution was intended to ring in "a new era and give a new turn to human affairs." In this ambitious declaration, Paine expressed the heart of the republican ideal: that *all* political institutions would be judged by whether they served the public good, not the interests of a powerful few. More than anything else, this way of thinking made American politics revolutionary.

Formalizing a Confederation, 1776–1781

Articles of Confederation First American national government; all power held by states

Americans' first national government reflected their fears of centralized authority. In 1776 John Dickinson drafted a proposal for a national government, and in 1777 Congress sent a weakened version of this document, the **Articles of Confederation,** to the states for ratification.

The Articles reserved to each state "its sovereignty, freedom and independence" and made Americans citizens of their states first and of the United States second. John Adams later explained that the Whigs never thought of "consolidating this vast Continent under one national Government" but created instead "a Confederacy of States, each of which must have a separate government."

Under the Articles, the national government consisted of a unicameral Congress, elected by the state legislatures, in which each state had one vote. Congress could request funds from the states but could not tax without every state's approval, nor could it regulate interstate or overseas commerce. The Articles provided for no executive branch. Rather, congressional committees oversaw financial, diplomatic, and military affairs. Nor was there a judicial system by which the national government could compel allegiance to its laws.

Disputes over state claims to western lands, their contributions to Congress, and their representation delayed ratification of the Articles for four years. Only in February 1781—six months before Cornwallis's surrender at Yorktown—did the last state, Maryland, agree to ratification.

Finance, Trade, and the Economy, 1781–1786

Perhaps the greatest challenge facing the Confederation was putting the nation on a sound financial footing. Winning the war cost $160 million, far more than taxation could raise. The government borrowed from abroad and printed paper money, called continentals. But from 1776 to 1791 lack of public faith in the government destroyed 98 percent of the continentals' value—an inflationary disaster. Congress turned to Robert Morris, a wealthy Philadelphia merchant who became the nation's superintendent of finance in 1781. Morris proposed a national import duty of 5 percent to finance the congressional budget and to guarantee interest payments on the war debt, but the duty failed to pass because one state, Rhode Island, rejected it.

In 1783, hoping to panic the country into creating a regular source of national revenue, Morris and New York congressman Alexander Hamilton engineered a dangerous gamble, later known as the **Newburgh Conspiracy.** They secretly persuaded some army officers, encamped at Newburgh, New York, to threaten a coup d'état unless the treasury obtained the taxation authority necessary to raise funds for their pay, which was months late. George Washington forestalled the conspiracy by appealing to his officers' honor.

When peace came in 1783, Morris found it impossible to fund the government adequately. After New York blocked another congressional tax measure sent to the states, state contributions to Congress fell steadily. By the late 1780s the states lagged 80 percent behind in providing the funds that Congress requested.

Nor could the Confederation pry trade concessions from Britain. Before independence, New England had depended heavily on exports to the West Indies. After independence, Britain had slapped strict limitations on U.S. commerce, allowing British shippers to increase their share of the Atlantic trade at American expense. This loss of trade contributed to an economic depression that gripped the nation beginning in 1784.

New Englanders suffered greatly in these hard times. While facing high taxes to pay off war debts, they also confronted tightening credit and the loss of major overseas markets and even whaling grounds. Despite opening new routes and smuggling, by 1791 the number of seamen in fishing and whaling had fallen by more than 40 percent.

Southerners also faced major problems as the markets for tobacco and rice failed to rebound to their prewar levels. As a result they were left with thousands of underemployed slave laborers. On the other hand, mid-Atlantic farmers actually grew more prosperous from exporting grain to famine-stricken areas of Europe, and the region quickly recovered from the Revolution's ravages.

The Confederation and the West, 1785–1787

The postwar settlement and administration of western lands posed another formidable challenge to the new government. Settlers and speculators were determined to possess these lands, and Native Americans were equally determined to keep them out. At the same time, Britain and Spain sought to contain the new nation's territorial expansion.

After the states surrendered claims to more than 160 million acres north of the Ohio River, Congress, in the **Ordinance of 1785,** established uniform procedures for surveying the region. The law made the basic unit of settlement a township six miles square, subdivided into thirty-six sections of 640 acres each, with one section reserved as a source of income for public schools. A subsequent law, the **Northwest Ordinance** of 1787, defined the land north of the Ohio River as the Northwest Territory, provided for its later division into states, and forbade slavery in the territory. The Northwest Ordinance outlined three steps for admitting states to the Union. First, Congress would appoint a territorial governor and judges. Second, as soon as five thousand adult males lived in a territory, the people would write a temporary constitution and elect a legislature. Third, when the population reached sixty thousand, the settlers would write a state constitution, which Congress would approve before granting statehood.

Newburgh Conspiracy Threatened mutiny that showed how deeply some were concerned about weakness of national government

Primary Source: Gouverneur Morris Warns Against Democratic Revolution

Ordinance of 1785 Law that laid framework for settling western lands

Northwest Ordinance Law that provided for creating new states

The Ordinance of 1785 and the Northwest Ordinance became the Confederation's major contributions to American life. They set the principles for surveying the frontier, allowed territorial self-government at an early stage of settlement, and provided reasonable standards for statehood. They became models for organizing territories west of the Mississippi River and established precedents for banning slavery from certain territories.

The Northwest Territory offered enough rich land to guarantee future citizens landownership, thus satisfying the republican belief that opening the West would prevent the rise, east of the Appalachians, of a large class of tenant farmers and poor laborers lacking the property needed to vote. Such a development would poison politics through class conflict and undermine republican equality. However, standing in the way of such republican dreams were some 150,000 Native Americans already inhabiting the western territories and struggling to preserve their way of life.

Joseph Brant, by Gilbert Stuart, 1786
The youthful Mohawk leader was a staunch ally of the British during the Revolutionary War, and thereafter resisted U.S. expansion in the Northwest.

At postwar treaty negotiations, U.S. commissioners told Native Americans, "You are a subdued people....We claim the country by conquest." Under threat of continued warfare, some Indian leaders initially yielded. Through treaties the Iroquois lost about half their land in New York and Pennsylvania, and the Delawares and Shawnees were obliged to recognize American sovereignty over their lands. But most Indians repudiated the treaties, denying that their negotiators had the authority to give up their nations' lands.

The Indians' resistance also stemmed from their confidence that the British would provide the arms necessary to defy the Americans. Britain had refused to abandon seven forts along the nation's northwestern frontier, ostensibly because Tories remained uncompensated for property losses. In April 1784 the British colonial office secretly ordered Canada's governor to hold onto the forts, hoping to reestablish Britain's claim to the Northwest Territory.

The Mohawk Joseph Brant initially sought to lead Indian resistance to white settlement. Courageous, skilled in diplomacy, and well educated, he organized the northwestern Indians into a military alliance in 1786 to keep out white settlers. But Brant and his followers, who had relocated beyond American reach in Canada, could not win support from Native Americans on U.S. soil. Militia raids launched by Kentuckians and others gradually forced the Indian evacuation of southern Indiana and Ohio. In spring 1788, some fifty New Englanders sailed down the Ohio River in a bulletproof barge symbolically named the *Mayflower* to found the town of Marietta.

A few months later a second group of latter-day pilgrims established a settlement on the Ohio at the site of modern Cincinnati.

The Confederation faced similar problems in the Southeast, where Spain and its Indian allies worked to block American encroachment on their land. The Spanish found an ally in the shrewd Creek leader **Alexander McGillivray,** who was determined to regain Creek territory held by Georgia. McGillivray negotiated a secret treaty with Spain that promised the Creeks weapons to protect themselves "from the Bears and other fierce Animals." In 1786, after Creeks expelled occupants of the disputed lands, Georgia quickly accepted McGillivray's offer of a cease-fire.

The Spanish also attempted to prevent American infiltration by denying western settlers permission to ship crops down the Mississippi River to New Orleans. After the Spanish closed New Orleans to Anglo-American commerce in 1784, John Jay went to Spain to negotiate trading privileges at New Orleans. Although he failed to win concessions, he returned with a treaty that opened Spanish markets to eastern merchants at the price of relinquishing American export rights through New Orleans. In 1786 Congress rejected this Jay-Gardoqui Treaty, but westerners and southerners, whose interests seemed to have been sacrificed to benefit northern commerce, felt betrayed.

Consequently westerners talked openly of secession; many accepted Spanish gold, although most pocketed the badly needed cash in exchange for vague promises of goodwill. As the young Andrew Jackson (the future U.S. president) noted, making some arrangement with the Spanish seemed "the only immediate way to obtain peace with the Savage [Indians]."

Alexander McGillivray Creek leader determined to retain his people's territory

CHECKING IN

- Individual states, in drafting their state constitutions, served as workshops for the creation of new republican forms of government.
- Americans made their first national government under the Articles of Confederation deliberately weak, leaving most power to the states.
- National finances remained shaky, but prosperity returned quickly to the mid-Atlantic.
- The Ordinance of 1785 and Northwest Ordinance represented the new government's major accomplishment.
- Indian resistance and Spain's closing of the port of New Orleans hampered Americans' movement westward.

TOWARD A NEW CONSTITUTION, 1786–1788

What were the principal issues dividing supporters and opponents of the new federal Constitution?

Despite the United States' enormous strides in establishing itself as an independent nation, impatience with the national government's limitations continued to grow among those seeking to establish the Republic on a more solid economic and military footing. Impatience became anxiety when protesting Massachusetts farmers defied local authorities. A national convention called to consider amendments to the Articles of Confederation instead created a radical new frame of government, the Constitution; its ratification in 1788 set a new course for America.

Shays's Rebellion, 1786–1787

The Jay-Gardoqui Treaty revealed deep-seated tensions beneath the surface appearance of American national unity. New England, which had never recovered from the loss of its West Indies markets, remained mired in the depression that had begun in 1784. Dominated by commercially minded elites, the Massachusetts legislature voted in 1786 to pay off its revolutionary debt, necessitating a huge tax hike. Compounding these difficulties was a shortage of the specie (gold and silver coin) demanded by bankers, merchants, and tax collectors. Thousands of small family farmers groaned under this cycle of debt.

In contrast, the mid-Atlantic and southern states enjoyed rising prosperity, thanks to increased tobacco and food exports, and were easily paying off their war debts. Despite this general prosperity, a growing minority of nationalists were unhappy with the Confederation. Merchants and shippers wanted a strong central government that could secure trading privileges abroad and ensure America's standing in an Atlantic economy that was still dominated by Britain. Land speculators and western settlers wanted a more activist policy against Spain, Britain, and Native Americans. Urban artisans hoped for a stronger national government that would protect them from foreign competition by imposing high tariffs.

This tinderbox flared first in Massachusetts. Farmers in the western part of the state, already struggling with a narrow profit margin and facing demands for payment in specie, which they lacked, held public meetings to discuss "the Suppressing of tyrannical government." This time, however, tyranny stemmed from the state house in Boston. Late in 1786, Daniel Shays, a Revolutionary War officer and hard-pressed farmer, led two thousand angry men in an attempt to shut down the courts and prevent foreclosures and tax auctions. Although routed by the state militia, Shays's followers won control of the Massachusetts legislature in 1787, cut taxes, and secured a pardon for Shays.

Shays's Rebellion Uprising by Massachusetts farmers that convinced many Americans their government was too weak

Although **Shays's Rebellion** caused little bloodshed and never raised a serious threat of anarchy, critics of the Confederation painted it and similar, less radical movements elsewhere as a taste of the disorder to come under the weak national government. By threatening to seize weapons from a federal arsenal at Springfield, Massachusetts, the Shaysites had unintentionally reminded nationalists how vulnerable to "mobocracy" the United States had become. Meanwhile, rumors that Spain had offered westerners export rights at New Orleans if they would secede from the Union sowed fears that the United States was on the verge of coming apart.

Instead of igniting a popular uprising, Shays's Rebellion encouraged aggressive nationalists to push for wholesale reform of the Republic's legal and institutional structure. Delegates from five states had met at Annapolis, Maryland, intending to discuss ways to promote interstate commerce. With chaos looming in Massachusetts, they called instead for a general convention to propose amendments to the Articles of Confederation. Congress asked the states to appoint delegations to meet in Philadelphia.

The Philadelphia Convention, 1787

In May 1787 fifty-five delegates, from every state but Rhode Island, began gathering at the Pennsylvania State House (later called Independence Hall) in Philadelphia. Among them were men of established reputation—George Washington, Benjamin Franklin, Robert Morris—as well as talented newcomers, such as Alexander Hamilton and James Madison. Most were wealthy, were in their thirties or forties, and had legal training. Nineteen owned slaves. Most important, they shared a "continental" or "nationalist" perspective. Thirty-nine had served in Congress and knew firsthand the weaknesses of the Articles. They were convinced that, without a strong national government, the country would fall victim to foreign aggression or simply disintegrate.

The convention immediately closed its sessions to the press and public and kept no official journal. Chaperones were appointed to accompany the aged and talkative Ben Franklin to dinner parties lest he disclose what was happening. Although these measures opened the convention to charges that it was acting undemocratically, even conspiratorially, the delegates thought secrecy essential to ensure freedom of debate.

Two basic issues confronted the convention. First, should the delegates merely tinker with the Articles, or should they draw up a new frame of government? Second, how could any government balance the conflicting interests of large and small states? Thirty-six-year-old James Madison of Virginia proposed answers to both questions.

Madison's **Virginia Plan,** introduced by fellow Virginian Edmund Randolph in late May, boldly called for a national government, not a confederation of states. It gave Congress virtually unrestricted rights of legislation and taxation, power to veto state laws, and authority to use military force against states. The Virginia Plan specified a bicameral legislature and made representation in both houses of Congress proportional to each state's population. The houses would jointly name the country's president and judges. But opposition to Madison's plan surfaced immediately, particularly to his call for proportional representation, which favored Virginia, the largest state.

On June 15, William Paterson of New Jersey offered a counterproposal, the **New Jersey Plan.** It featured a unicameral legislature in which each state had one vote, just as under the Articles. It went even further than the Virginia Plan by defining congressional laws and treaties as the "supreme law of the land."

The New Jersey Plan exposed the convention's greatest problem: the question of representation. The Virginia Plan gave the four largest states—Virginia, Massachusetts, New York, and Pennsylvania—a majority in both houses. The New Jersey Plan allowed the seven smallest states, with only 25 percent of the U.S. population, to control Congress. By early July the convention was stalemated. To end the impasse, the delegates appointed a "grand committee" dedicated to compromise. This panel adopted a proposal by the Connecticut delegation: an equal vote for each state in the upper house and proportional representation in the lower house. The convention accepted the compromise on July 17 and in two months overcame the remaining hurdles.

As finally approved on September 17, 1787, the Constitution of the United States was an extraordinary document. In addition to reconciling the interests of large and small states, it balanced the delegates' desire for a strong national government against their fear of tyranny and interference with the states' sovereignty. It increased national authority in several ways. It vested in Congress the authority to levy and

James Madison

Although one of the Philadelphia Convention's youngest delegates, Madison of Virginia was among its most politically astute. He played a central role in the Constitution's adoption.

Virginia Plan Madison's blueprint for new national government; favored large states

New Jersey Plan Counterproposal to Virginia Plan that favored small states collect taxes, to regulate interstate commerce, and to conduct diplomacy. Under the Constitution, all acts and treaties of the United States would become "the supreme law of the land." State officials would have to uphold the Constitution, even against acts of their own state. The national government could use military force against any state.

The Constitution's framers restrained the new national government in two key ways. First, they established a **separation of powers** among the three distinct branches within the government—the legislative, the executive, and the judicial. Second, they designed a system of **checks and balances** to prevent one branch from dominating the others. States' equal representation in the Senate offset proportional representation by population in the House, and each chamber could block measures passed by the other. Further, the president could veto acts of Congress, but to prevent capricious use of the presidential veto, a two-thirds majority in each house could override a veto. The president would conduct diplomacy, but only the Senate could ratify treaties. The president appointed his cabinet, but only with Senate approval. Congress could, by joint vote, remove the president and his appointees from office, but only for "high crimes," not for political disagreements.

To further guarantee the independence of each branch, the Constitution provided that the members of one branch would not choose those of another, except judges, whose independence was protected by lifetime appointments. For example, an electoral college, composed of members chosen by the various state legislatures, would select the president. State legislatures would also elect senators, whereas popular vote would determine delegates to the House of Representatives.

In addition to checks and balances, the Constitution embodied a form of **federalism**—a system of shared power and dual lawmaking by the state and national governments—to limit central authority. Not only did the state legislatures have a key role in electing the president and senators, but the Constitution could be amended by the votes of three-fourths of the state legislatures. Federalism assumed that the national government would limit its activities to foreign affairs, national defense, regulation of commerce, and coining of money. Most other political matters were left to the states. The states could otherwise act autonomously on purely internal matters, including slavery.

The Philadelphia Convention faced a dilemma: were slaves property or persons? In general, southern states regarded slaves as property; however, because slaves constituted substantial portions of the southern population, southern delegates wanted to count them as persons in determining representation in the lower house. Many northern delegates from the states that were abolishing slavery hesitated to give southern states a political edge by counting as persons slaves who had neither civil nor political rights. At the same time, northern delegates, themselves property owners, balked at questioning southern notions of property rights. Thus they agreed to the **three-fifths clause,** allowing three-fifths of all slaves to be counted for congressional representation and forbade any state's people from taking action to prevent the return of runaway slaves to another state. The Constitution did limit slavery by not repudiating the Northwest Ordinance's restrictions on slavery and by permitting Congress to ban the importation of slaves after 1808.

Although leaving much authority to the states, the Constitution established a national government clearly superior to the states in several spheres and abandoned

separation of powers The establishment of three distinct branches of government

checks and balances Constitutional system designed to prevent any one branch of government from dominating the other two

federalism System of shared power between state and national governments

three-fifths clause Provided that three-fifths of slaves were to be counted in determining congressional representation the notion of a confederation of virtually independent states. Having thus strengthened national authority, the convention faced the issue of **ratification.** Two factors argued against submitting the Constitution to the state legislatures for ratification. First, the state legislatures would probably reject the Constitution, which shrank their power relative to that of the national government. Second, most of the framers believed that the government had to rest on the consent of the American people themselves. The Constitution's opening words—"We the people of the United States"—embodied this view. In the end, the Philadelphia Convention provided for ratification by special state conventions composed of delegates elected by the people. Approval by nine such conventions would enable the new government to operate.

Under the Constitution, the framers expected the nation's "natural aristocracy" to continue exercising political leadership; but did they also intend to rein in the democratic currents that the Revolution had set in motion? In one respect they did—by curtailing the power of popularly elected state legislatures. However, the Constitution did not try to control faction and disorder by suppressing liberty—a "remedy," wrote Madison, that would have been "worse than the disease." The House of Representatives did provide one crucial democratic element in the new government. Equally important, the Constitution recognized the American people as the ultimate source of political legitimacy. By making the Constitution amendable and by dividing political power among competing branches of government, the framers made it possible for the national government to be slowly democratized.

The Struggle over Ratification, 1787–1788

At first the Constitution had little national support. Many Americans hesitated to accept the idea of a radically restructured government. To quiet fears of centralized national authority, the Constitution's supporters shrewdly dubbed themselves **Federalists,** a term implying that the Constitution successfully balanced the relationship between state and national governments.

The Constitution's opponents became known as Antifederalists, a negative-sounding name that conveyed little of their fears that the Constitution would *not* balance the power of the state and national governments.

Antifederalist arguments reflected the deep-seated Anglo-American suspicion of any concentration of power, a suspicion that had driven events from the Stamp Act Congress through the War of Independence and the early years of the new republic. Unquestionably, the Constitution gave the national government unprecedented authority in an age when most writers on politics agreed that the sole means of preventing despotism was restraining the power of government officials. Distant from the people, especially in an era when news traveled slowly, the national government would be far less responsive to the popular will than state governments would be. Furthermore, no one could be sure that the untried scheme of checks and balances would work. And the Constitution contained no guarantees that the new government would protect the liberties of individuals or the states. The absence of a bill of rights prompted Madison's nationalist ally and fellow Virginian George Mason, the author of the first state bill of rights in 1776, to oppose the Constitution.

The Antifederalists confronted several major disadvantages. For one thing, the Federalists included most of the country's wealthiest and most honored men,

ratification Approval by state conventions of new federal Constitution

Federalists Name supporters of new Constitution gave themselves during ratification struggle

Map 6.4   Federalist and Antifederalist Strongholds, 1787–1790

Federalists drew their primary backing from densely populated areas while Antifederalist support was strongest among small farmers in interior regions. However, some westerners advocated a strong central government that would push back Native Americans.

Federalist majority (for ratification)

Antifederalist majority (against ratification)

Evenly divided

Unsettled or politically unorganized

Interactive Map: Federalist and Antifederalist Strongholds, 1787–1790

including Washington and Franklin. In addition, the majority of newspapers were Federalist and did not hesitate to bias their reporting. Finally, the Antifederalists, largely drawn from state and local leaders, lacked their opponents' contacts and experience at the national level. Ultimately, however, Federalist superiority in funds and political organizing proved decisive. The Antifederalists failed to create a sense of urgency among their supporters, assuming that most would automatically rally to them. However, only one-quarter of the voters turned out to elect delegates to the state ratifying conventions, and most had been mobilized by Federalists.

Federalist delegates prevailed in eight state conventions between December 1787 and May 1788, in all cases but one by margins of two-thirds or more. Such lopsided voting in favor of the Constitution reflected Federalist aggressiveness more than popular support. In a Pennsylvania Antifederalist's words, the Federalists rammed through approval in some states "before it can be digested or deliberately considered." Only Rhode Island and North Carolina rejected the Constitution; Rhode Island would not enter the Union until 1790.

But unless the large states of Virginia and New York ratified, the new government would be unworkable. Antifederalism ran high in both, especially among small farmers, who believed that the Constitution favored city dwellers and moneyed interests. Prominent Antifederalists included New York's governor George Clinton and Virginia's Richard Henry Lee, George Mason, Patrick Henry, and future president James Monroe.

On June 21, 1788, the Constitution became the law of the land when the ninth state, New Hampshire, ratified. Debate continued in Virginia, where the Federalists won wide support from settlers in the western part of the state who wanted a strong national government capable of ending Indian raids along the Ohio River. Western Virginians' votes, combined with Madison's logic and tidewater planters' support, ruled the day. On June 25, the Virginia delegates ratified by a narrow 53 percent majority.

The struggle was even hotter in New York. Antifederalists controlled the state convention and probably would have voted down the Constitution had not news arrived of New Hampshire's and Virginia's ratification. Federalists, led by Alexander Hamilton and John Jay, hinted strongly that, if the convention rejected the Constitution, New York City would secede and join the Union alone, leaving upstate New York a landlocked enclave. Alarmed, a number of Antifederalists switched sides, and New York ratified on July 26 by a 30 to 27 vote.

Despite the defeat, the Antifederalists left an important legacy. At Antifederalist insistence, the Virginia, New York, and Massachusetts conventions ratified the Constitution with requests that the new charter be amended to include a bill of rights protecting Americans' basic freedoms. Widespread support for a bill of rights made it a major item on the new government's agenda, even as states were choosing members of Congress and presidential electors were unanimously designating George Washington president of the United States.

Antifederalists' objections in New York also stimulated one of the greatest works of political analysis ever written: *The Federalist,* a series of eighty-five newspaper articles by Alexander Hamilton, James Madison, and John Jay. Although ***The Federalist* papers** did little to influence the New York vote, they provided a glimpse of the framers' intentions in designing the Constitution and thus powerfully shaped the American philosophy of government. The Constitution, insisted *The Federalist*'s authors, had two main purposes: to defend minority rights against majority tyranny and to prevent a stubborn minority from blocking measures necessary for the national interest. There was no reason to fear that the Constitution would allow a single economic or regional interest to dominate. In the most profound essay in the series, Federalist No. 10, Madison argued that the nation's size and diversity would neutralize the attempts of factions to steer unwise laws through Congress.

Madison's analysis was far too optimistic, however. The Constitution did indeed afford enormous scope for special interests to influence government. The great challenge for Madison's generation would be maintaining a government that provided equal benefits to all, but special privileges to none.

***The Federalist* papers** Series of essays designed to explain new Constitution, convince people to support it

CHECKING IN

- For many, Shays's Rebellion catalyzed fears that the national government was too weak.
- Two major questions faced the Philadelphia Convention. First, should they tinker with the Articles of Confederation or start anew? Second, how could they balance the interests of the large and small states while creating a sufficiently strong national government?
- The Constitution created a new framework, federalism, allowing shared power between state and national governments, and embodied the separation of powers and checks and balances as a way to protect against too strong a government.
- Ratification of the Constitution was won, but not automatically, with Antifederalists voicing loud opposition.
- The ratification struggle left an important legacy in *The Federalist* papers, which helped shape the American philosophy of government.

Chapter Summary

 DOWNLOAD THE MP3 AUDIO FILE OF THE CHAPTER SUMMARY, AND LISTEN TO IT ON THE GO.

What were the comparative advantages of the British and the colonists when the Revolution began? (page 119)

Although the British enjoyed huge advantages in military preparedness and manpower at the war's start, their supply lines were long and their population, tax weary. The colonists eventually forged a professional army and defeated them. The most important key to American victory was George Washington's leadership, especially his determination to continue to fight.

How did the war unfold? (page 122)

Initially, the Continental Army suffered several defeats. Saratoga was the turning point of the war, because the colonial victory there convinced the French to support the Revolution with money, men, and ships. When the British surrendered at Yorktown, it was to a mixed French and American force.

How did the war affect relationships among Americans of different classes, races, and genders? (page 128)

Most wars bring major social changes; the Revolution was no exception. By war's end, white males enjoyed considerably more equality, slavery was clearly being rejected in the northern states, and women had played a significant public role. However, the war only worsened the position of Native Americans.

How did Americans translate revolutionary principles into effective governments? (page 132)

In creating their constitutions, the new states served as workshops for experimenting with various forms of republican government. At the national level the Articles of Confederation created a weak government that almost immediately faced tremendous economic and diplomatic problems. However, the Articles succeeded in formulating the Northwest Ordinance, a blueprint for future expansion.

What were the principal issues dividing supporters and opponents of the new federal Constitution? (page 137)

The new Constitution represented the triumph of nationalism and provided a strong central government, although its framework of federalism seemed to leave considerable power in the hands of the states. Its ratification was far from assured, but it enjoyed the support of respected men such as Franklin, Jefferson, and Washington; in the end, the Federalists achieved ratification. The most important legacy of the struggle for ratification was *The Federalist* papers, which laid a foundation for an American philosophy of government.

KEY TERMS

loyalist *(p. 119)*

Whig *(p. 119)*

Trenton *(p. 122)*

Saratoga *(p. 124)*

Valley Forge *(p. 124)*

Lord Charles Cornwallis *(p. 126)*

antislavery movement *(p. 130)*

state constitutions *(p. 132)*

"democracy" *(p. 133)*

"republicanism" *(p. 133)*

Articles of Confederation *(p. 134)*

Newburgh Conspiracy *(p. 135)*

Ordinance of 1785 *(p. 135)*

Northwest Ordinance *(p. 135)*

Alexander McGillivray *(p. 137)*

Shays's Rebellion *(p. 138)*

Virginia Plan *(p. 139)*

New Jersey Plan *(p. 139)*

separation of powers *(p. 140)*

checks and balances *(p. 140)*

federalism *(p. 140)*

three-fifths clause *(p. 140)*

ratification *(p. 141)*

Federalists *(p. 141)*

The Federalist papers *(p. 143)*

CHAPTER 7

Launching the New Republic

1788–1800

Judith Sargent Stevens (Murray)

CHAPTER PREVIEW

Constitutional Government Takes Shape, 1788–1796
What role did George Washington play in translating the Constitution from words into government?

Hamilton's Domestic Policies, 1789–1794
What were the major components of Hamilton's blueprint for the new nation?

The United States in a Wider World, 1789–1796
How did the new nation deal with France, Spain, and Britain?

Parties and Politics, 1793–1800
Why and how did political parties emerge by 1800?

Economic and Social Change
What major economic and social changes characterized the new republic?

During the 1790s Americans fought bitterly over the political and economic course the new nation should take, and these conflicts were heightened by sharply different reactions to the French Revolution. By 1798, voters had split into two distinct parties, each viewing the other as a threat to liberty. Only when the election of 1800 had been decided—by the narrowest of margins—did it seem certain that the United States would endure.

CONSTITUTIONAL GOVERNMENT TAKES SHAPE, 1788–1796

What role did George Washington play in translating the Constitution from words into government?

Given the social and political divisions among Americans, compounded by their fears of centralized authority, success at implementing the new Constitution was anything but guaranteed. Would Americans accept the results of a national election? Would the three branches of the new government function effectively? Would a Bill of Rights, which several states had made a condition of ratification, amend the Constitution?

Implementing Government

The first order of business in putting the new government into practice was the election of a president and Congress. These first elections swept the Federalists into power with eighteen of twenty seats in the Senate and fifty-four of fifty-nine in the House. The electoral college unanimously chose George Washington as the first president and John Adams as the vice president.

The choice of Washington was hardly a surprise. His leadership during the Revolutionary War and the Constitutional Convention had earned him a reputation as a national hero. Given his reputation, Washington was able to calm Americans' fears of presidential power.

Traveling slowly over the new nation's miserable roads, the men entrusted with launching the federal experiment assembled in New York, the new national capital, in March 1789. Washington did not arrive until April 23 and took his oath of office a week later.

The Constitution was vague about the executive departments, mentioning only in passing that the president must obtain the Senate's "advice and consent" to his nominees to head these bureaus. Otherwise, Congress was free to determine the organization and accountability of what became known as the cabinet. The first cabinet consisted of five departments, headed by the secretaries of state, treasury, and war and by the attorney general and postmaster general. The Senate narrowly defeated a proposal to forbid the president from dismissing cabinet officers without its approval. This outcome reinforced the president's authority to make and carry out policy; it also made the president a more equal partner of Congress by strengthening the separation of powers.

The Federal Judiciary and the Bill of Rights

The Constitution authorized Congress to establish federal courts below the level of the Supreme Court but provided no plan for their structure. In 1789 many citizens feared that federal courts would ride roughshod over local customs. Every state had a blend of judicial procedures suited to its needs, and any attempt to force the states to abandon their legal heritage would have produced counterdemands for narrowly

Chronology

1788	First elections under the Constitution
1789	First Congress convenes in New York; George Washington sworn in as first president; Judiciary Act; French Revolution begins
1790	Alexander Hamilton submits his Reports on Public Credit and National Bank to Congress; Treaty of New York
1791	Bank of the United States granted a twenty-year charter; Bill of Rights ratified; Slave uprising begins in French colony of Saint Domingue; Hamilton submits his Report on Manufactures to Congress
1792	Washington reelected president
1793	Fugitive Slave Law; *Chisholm* v. *Georgia*; French planters flee slave rebellion in Saint Domingue for the United States; France declares war on Britain and Spain; Citizen Genêt arrives in United States; Washington's Neutrality Proclamation; First Democratic societies established
1794	Whiskey Rebellion; Battle of Fallen Timbers
1795	Treaty of Greenville; Jay's Treaty
1796	John Adams elected president; Treaty of San Lorenzo (Pinckney's Treaty) ratified
1797	Washington's Farewell Address
1798	XYZ Affair; Alien and Sedition Acts; Eleventh Amendment to the Constitution ratified
1798–1799	Virginia and Kentucky Resolutions
1798–1800	United States fights Quasi-War with France
1800	Gabriel's rebellion in Virginia; Thomas Jefferson elected president

restricting federal justice. In passing the **Judiciary Act of 1789,** Congress quieted popular apprehensions by establishing in each state a federal district court that operated according to local procedures. As the Constitution stipulated, the Supreme Court exercised final jurisdiction. Congress's compromise respected state traditions while offering wide access to federal justice.

Judiciary Act of 1789 Establishes Federal court system

Behind the movement for a bill of rights lay Americans' long-standing fear that a strong central government would lead to tyranny. Many Antifederalists believed that the best safeguard against tyranny would be to strengthen the powers of the state governments at the expense of the federal government, but many more Americans wanted simply to guarantee basic personal liberties. From the House of Representatives, James Madison played the leading role in drafting the ten amendments that became known as the **Bill of Rights** when ratified in December 1791.

Bill of Rights First ten amendments to the Constitution; guaranteed personal liberties

Madison insisted that the first eight amendments guarantee personal liberties, not strip the national government of authority. The First Amendment safeguarded the most fundamental freedoms of expression—religion, speech, press, and political activity. The Second Amendment ensured that each state could form its own militia. Like the Third Amendment, it sought to protect citizens from what Americans saw as the most sinister embodiment of tyranny: standing armies. The Fourth through Eighth Amendments limited the police powers of the states by guaranteeing fair treatment in legal and judicial proceedings. The Ninth and Tenth Amendments reserved to the people or to the states powers not allocated to the federal government, but Madison headed off proposals to limit federal power more explicitly. In general, the Bill of Rights imposed no serious check on the Framers' nationalist objectives. The ten amendments were submitted to the states and ratified by December 1791.

With the Bill of Rights in place, the federal judiciary established its authority. In the case of *Chisholm* (CHIZZ-um) v. *Georgia* (1793), the Supreme Court ruled that a nonresident could sue a state in federal court. In 1796 the Court declared its right to determine the constitutionality of federal statutes in *Hylton* (HILL-ton) v. *United States* and to strike down state laws in *Ware* v. *Hylton*. But in 1794, Congress decided that the *Chisholm* case had encroached too far on states' authority and overturned the decision through a constitutional amendment. Ratified in 1798, the Eleventh Amendment revised Article III, Section 2, so that private citizens could not undermine states' financial autonomy by using federal courts to sue another state's government in civil cases and claim money from that state's treasury.

By endorsing the Eleventh Amendment, Congress expressed its recognition that federal power could threaten vital local interests. The same awareness had ruptured the nationalist coalition that had written the Constitution, secured its ratification, and dominated the first Congress. Alexander Hamilton had embarked on a bold program that alienated many nationalists by demonstrating that federal policies could be shaped to reward special interests.

CHECKING IN

- Americans remained suspicious of executive power, and thus of the presidency.
- George Washington was unanimously chosen president by the first electoral college.
- Although the Constitution did not spell out the organization of the executive branch, Washington named five department heads who formed his first cabinet.
- The Judiciary Act of 1789 helped allay state fears concerning federal courts.
- The Bill of Rights guaranteed personal liberties.

HAMILTON'S DOMESTIC POLICIES, 1789–1794

What were the major components of Hamilton's blueprint for the new nation?

Alexander Hamilton Washington's chief adviser, architect of major plans for American future

Washington's reluctance to become involved with legislation enabled Secretary of the Treasury **Alexander Hamilton** to set domestic priorities. Hamilton emerged as an imaginative and dynamic statesman by formulating a sweeping program to strengthen the federal government and promote national economic development.

Hamilton and His Objectives

Born in the West Indies in 1755, Hamilton had arrived in New York in 1772 to enroll at King's College (now Columbia University), where he had passionately defended American rights. He entered the Continental Army in 1775 and rose quickly to become a member of Washington's staff and a confidante of the commander in chief. The brilliant Hamilton gained extraordinary influence over the future president. He was a forceful advocate of a strong national government and an economic environment attractive to investment.

Hamilton's financial policies had two goals: to strengthen the nation against foreign enemies and to lessen the threat of disunion. The possibility of war with Britain, Spain, or both presented the most immediate danger. To finance a war, the

Republic would have to borrow, but because Congress under the Articles had failed to redeem or pay interest on the revolutionary debt, the nation had little credit.

Hamilton also feared that the Union might disintegrate because he believed that Americans tended to think first of local loyalties and interests. To him, the Constitution represented a close victory of national over state authority. Now he worried that the states might reassert power over the new government. If they succeeded, he doubted that the nation could prevent ruinous trade discrimination between states, deter foreign aggression, and avoid civil war.

Charming and brilliant, vain and handsome, a notorious womanizer, thirsty for fame and power, Hamilton exemplified the worldly citizens whose fortunes he hoped to link to the Republic's future. To his opponents, however, Hamilton embodied the dark forces luring the Republic to doom—a man who, Jefferson wrote, believed in "the necessity of either force or corruption to govern men."

Alexander Hamilton by John Trumbull, 1792
Hamilton's self-confident pride shines through clearly in this portrait, painted at the height of his influence in the Washington administration.

Establishing the Nation's Credit

In 1789 Congress directed the Treasury Department to evaluate the revolutionary debt. Hamilton seized the opportunity to devise policies to strengthen the nation's credit, enable it to defer paying its debt, and entice the upper class to place its prestige and capital at the nation's service. In January 1790, Congress received his **Report on the Public Credit.** It listed $54 million in U.S. debt: $42 million owed to Americans and the rest to foreigners. Hamilton estimated that, on top of the national debt, the states had debts of $25 million that the United States had promised to reimburse.

Hamilton recommended that the federal government "fund" the national debt by raising $54 million in new securities to honor the revolutionary debt. Purchasers of these securities could choose from several combinations of federal "stock" and western lands. Those who wished could retain their original bonds and earn 4 percent interest. All these options would reduce interest payments on the debt. Creditors would approve this reduction because their investments would become more valuable and secure. The report proposed that the federal government use the same means for the "assumption" of state debts remaining from the Revolution.

Hamilton exhorted the government to use the money earned by selling federal lands in the West to pay off the $12 million owed to Europeans as soon as possible, but he suggested that the remaining $42 million owed to Americans be made a permanent debt. If the government paid only the interest on its bonds, investors would hold them for long terms. The sole burden on taxpayers would be the small annual interest. Thus the United States could uphold its credit at minimal expense without ever having to pay off the debt itself.

A permanent debt, Hamilton believed, would tie the economic fortunes of the nation's creditors to the government. In an age of notoriously risky investments, the

Report on the Public Credit
Hamilton's plan to ensure support for the new government by maintaining permanent debt

federal government would protect the savings of wealthy bondholders through conservative policies but still pay an interest rate competitive with that of the Bank of England. The guarantee of future interest payments would link the interests of the moneyed class to those of the nation.

Hamilton's proposals provoked controversy. Many members of Congress objected that those least deserving reward would gain the most. The original owners of more than 60 percent of the debt certificates issued by the Continental Congress had long since sold them at a loss, often out of dire necessity. To Hamilton's surprise, Madison became a chief opponent of reimbursing current holders at face value. Sensing disapproval of the plan in Virginia, Madison tried but failed to obtain compensation for original owners who had sold their certificates. Hamilton's policy generated widespread resentment by rewarding rich profiteers while ignoring wartime sacrifice by ordinary citizens.

Opposition to assuming the state debts also ran high, especially in the South. But Hamilton saved his proposal by exploiting Virginians' desire to relocate the national capital in their region. They hoped that moving the capital would keep Virginia the nation's largest, most influential state. Essentially, Hamilton traded the votes necessary to locate the capital along the Potomac for enough votes to win his battle for assumption.

Enactment of the Report on the Public Credit reversed the nation's fiscal standing. By 1792 the United States' soaring fiscal reputation allowed some U.S. bonds to sell at 10 percent above face value.

Creating a National Bank

Having restored full faith in greatly undervalued certificates, Hamilton had in effect expanded the capital available for investment. Now he intended to direct that money toward projects to diversify the national economy through a federally chartered bank.

Report on the National Bank
Hamilton's proposal to create the Bank of the United States

In his **Report on the National Bank** in 1790 Hamilton proposed that the Bank of the United States raise $10 million through a public stock offering. Fully four-fifths of the control of the bank would fall to private hands. Private investors could purchase shares by paying for three-quarters of their value in government bonds. In this way the bank would capture a substantial portion of the recently funded debt and make it available for loans; it would also receive steady interest payments from the treasury. Shareholders would profit handsomely.

Hamilton argued that the bank would cost taxpayers nothing and greatly benefit the nation. It would provide a safe place for federal deposits, make inexpensive loans to the government when taxes fell short, and relieve the scarcity of hard cash by issuing paper notes. Further, the bank would regulate the business of state banks and, above all, provide much-needed credit for economic expansion.

Hamilton also called for American economic self-sufficiency. An admirer of the way that factory expansion had stimulated British wealth, he wanted to encourage industrialization in the United States. His **Report on Manufactures** of December 1791 advocated protective tariffs on imports to foster domestic manufacturing, which would in turn attract immigrants and create national wealth.

Report on Manufactures
Hamiltonian plan for tariffs, encouragement of industrialization

Hamilton's critics denounced the national bank as a dangerous scheme that gave a small elite special power to influence the government. These critics believed that the Bank of England had undermined the integrity of the government in Britain. Shareholders of the Bank of the United States could just as easily become tools of unscrupulous politicians. Members of Congress who owned bank stock would likely vote in support of the bank even at the cost of the national good.

Constitutional issues presented the bank's opponents with their strongest argument. The Constitution did not authorize Congress to issue charters of incorporation; in fact, the constitutional convention had rejected such a proposal. Unless Congress adhered to a "strict interpretation" of the Constitution, critics argued, the central government might oppress the states and trample individual liberties.

Congress approved the bank by only a thin margin. Dubious about its constitutionality, Washington asked Jefferson and Hamilton for advice. Jefferson distrusted banking and did not want to extend government power beyond the letter of the Constitution. But Hamilton urged Washington to sign the bill. Because Article I, Section 8, of the Constitution specified that Congress could enact all measures "necessary and proper," Hamilton contended that the only unconstitutional activities were those *forbidden* to the national government. Washington accepted Hamilton's argument, and in February 1791 the Bank of the United States obtained a twenty-year charter. Washington's acceptance of a "loose interpretation" of the Constitution marked an important victory for advocates of an active, assertive national government.

Emerging Partisanship

Hamilton built a political base by appealing to people's economic self-interest. His "rescue" of the national credit provided huge gains for speculators, merchants, and other urban "moneyed men" who by 1790 held most of the revolutionary debt. As holders of bank stock, these same groups had reason to use their prestige on behalf of national authority. Moreover, federal assumption of state debts liberated taxpayers from crushing burdens in New England, New Jersey, and South Carolina, while Hamilton's promotion of industry, commerce, and shipping won favor with the Northeast's budding entrepreneurs and hard-pressed artisans.

Hamilton's economic program sowed dissension in areas where it provided little advantage. Resentment ran high among those who felt that the government was rewarding special interests. Southerners especially detested Hamilton's program. Southern states had generally paid off their revolutionary debts, and few southerners still held revolutionary certificates. Moreover, the Bank of the United States had few southern stockholders and allocated little capital for southern loans.

Hamilton's plan offered little to the West, where agriculture promised exceptional profit once the right of export through New Orleans was guaranteed. Even in New York and Pennsylvania, Hamilton's policies generated some dissatisfaction. Resentment of a supposedly national program that benefited eastern "moneyed men" and Yankees who refused to pay their debts gradually united westerners, southerners, and many people in the mid-Atlantic into a political coalition. Challenging the Federalists for control of the government, these opponents called for a return to true Republicanism.

With Hamilton presenting his measures as "Federalist," Jefferson, Madison, and their supporters began calling themselves "Republicans." They reached out to former

Antifederalists whose ranks had been fatally weakened after the election of 1788. In 1791 they supported the establishment of an opposition newspaper, *The National Gazette*. The paper's editor, Philip Freneau, attacked Hamilton relentlessly, accusing him of try to create an aristocracy and a monarchy in America. In response Hamilton, using pseudonyms, attacked Jefferson as an enemy of President Washington.

Although partisanship intensified as the election of 1792 approached, there was no organized political campaigning. Most voters saw organized factions, or parties, as inherently corrupt. The Constitution's Framers had neither wanted nor planned for political parties. In addition, Washington, by appearing to be above partisan disputes, remained supremely popular.

Washington was unanimously chosen for a second term; by a fairly close margin, John Adams was again chosen vice president.

The Whiskey Rebellion

Whiskey Rebellion Tax protest by western farmers that gave Washington and Hamilton the opportunity to assert the power of national government

Hamilton's program helped to ignite a civil insurrection called the **Whiskey Rebellion.** Severely testing federal authority, this uprising posed the young republic's first serious crisis.

To augment national revenue, Hamilton had proposed an excise tax on domestically produced whiskey. He maintained that such a tax would not only distribute the expense of financing the national debt evenly but also improve the country's morals by lowering liquor consumption. Although Congress passed Hamilton's program in March 1791, many doubted that Americans, who drank an average of six gallons of hard liquor per adult per year, would submit tamely to sobriety.

Western Pennsylvanians found the new tax especially burdensome. Unable to ship their crops to world markets through New Orleans, most local farmers habitually distilled their rye or corn into alcohol, which could be carried across the Appalachians at a fraction of the price charged for bulky grain. Hamilton's excise tax, equal to 25 percent of whiskey's retail value, would wipe out frontier farmers' profit.

Because the law specified, in addition, that federal courts would try all cases of alleged tax evasion, any western Pennsylvanian indicted for noncompliance would have to travel three hundred or so miles to Philadelphia. Not only would the accused face a jury of unsympathetic easterners, but he would also have to shoulder the cost of a long journey and lost earnings, as well as fines and penalties if convicted.

In a scene reminiscent of colonial protests against Britain, large-scale resistance erupted in July 1794. Roving bands torched buildings, assaulted tax collectors, and raised a flag symbolizing an independent country that they hoped to create from six western counties.

Echoing elites' denunciation of colonial protests, Hamilton blasted the rebellion as simple lawlessness. Washington concluded that a federal failure to respond strongly would encourage outbreaks in other frontier areas. The president accordingly mustered 12,900 militiamen to march west under his command, but opposition evaporated once the troops reached the Appalachians. Of 150 suspects later seized, 20 were sent in irons to Philadelphia.

The Whiskey Rebellion was a milestone in determining the limits of public opposition to federal policies. In the early 1790s many Americans as-

CHECKING IN

- Alexander Hamilton devised an ambitious plan to *create* a strong economy and a strong central government. To this end, he proposed federal funding of the national debt from the revolutionary period and creation of a permanent debt.
- Hamilton proposed and achieved a national bank.
- To encourage manufacturing, Hamilton advocated a protective tariff.
- The Whiskey Rebellion gave Washington and Hamilton an opportunity to reinforce national authority.

sumed that it was still legitimate to protest unpopular laws by using the methods that they had employed against British policies. By firmly suppressing the first major challenge to national authority, President Washington served notice that citizens could change the law only through constitutional procedures—by making their dissatisfaction known to their elected representatives and, if necessary, by electing new representatives.

THE UNITED STATES IN A WIDER WORLD, 1789–1796

How did the new nation deal with France, Spain, and Britain?

By 1793 disagreements over foreign affairs had become the primary source of friction in American public life. The division created by controversy over Hamilton's economic program hardened into ideologically oriented factions that disagreed vehemently over whether American foreign policy should favor industrial and mercantile interests or those of farmers, planters, and small businessmen. Complicating American policy making was the French Revolution, which had electrified all Europe in 1789 and touched off a series of wars between France and its neighbors that would last until 1815.

As part of the Atlantic world, the United States could not avoid entanglement in these wars, despite the desire of most Americans to remain uninvolved. Increasingly, foreign policy became caught up in domestic politics, intensifying the emerging partisanship.

Spanish Power in Western North America

Spain enjoyed a brief resurgence of imperial success in the late eighteenth century. Stimulated by its acquisition of Louisiana, the Spanish built new presidios in northern Mexico, New Mexico, and Texas at which they stationed more troops and coordinated the actions of civilian and military authorities. By 1800 the Apaches, Navajos, and Comanches had agreed to cease their raids in New Mexico and Texas, but the success of the truce depended on Spain's ability to strengthen and broaden its imperial position in North America.

These reforms were part of a larger Spanish effort to counter potential rivals for North American territory and influence. Russian fur traders had made substantial inroads along the Northwest Coast as early as the 1740s, and British and American traders followed in the 1780s. All three nations used American furs in the rapidly burgeoning and hugely profitable China trade, and their mounting influence threatened Spain's northwestern frontier.

To counter these threats, Spain flung colonists and missionaries northward along the Pacific coast. Efforts to encourage large-scale Mexican immigration to **"Alta California"** failed. The colony became a chain of religious missions, several presidios, and a few large ranches. Franciscan missionaries tried to convert coastal Indians to Catholicism and "civilize" them by imposing harsh discipline and putting them to work in vineyards and other enterprises. However, epidemic and venereal

"Alta California" Spanish colony on Pacific coast, dominated by missions diseases carried by the Spanish raged among the native coastal tribes; between 1769 and 1830 the Indian population plummeted from about 72,000 to about 18,000.

Having strengthened its positions in Texas, New Mexico, and California, Spain turned its attention to the area later known as Arizona in hopes of dominating North America from the Pacific to Louisiana. However, resistance from Native Americans such as the Hopi (HOE-pee) and the Yuma (YOU-muh) thwarted these hopes.

Challenging American Expansion, 1789–1792

East of the Mississippi River, on the trans-Appalachian frontier, rivalries also multiplied. Spain, Britain, the United States, and Native Americans jockeyed for advantage in an area that all considered central to their interests.

President Washington tried to keep tight control of foreign policy. Recognizing that the complex western problems would not easily yield, he pursued patient diplomacy to "preserve the country in peace if I can, and to be prepared for war if I cannot." The prospect of peace improved in 1789 when Spain unexpectedly opened New Orleans to American commerce. Secessionist sentiment subsided.

In the 1790s the Spanish bribed many well-known political figures in Tennessee and Kentucky, including James Wilkinson, one of Washington's former generals. The admission of Vermont (1791), Kentucky (1792), and Tennessee (1796) as states was meant in part to strengthen their flickering loyalty to the Union.

Washington then moved to weaken Spanish influence in the West by neutralizing Spain's most important ally, the Creek Indians. The Creeks numbered more than twenty thousand, including perhaps five thousand warriors, and were fiercely hostile toward Georgian settlers, whom they called "the greedy people who want our lands." Under the terms of the 1790 Treaty of New York, American settlers could occupy the Georgia piedmont but not other Creek territory. Washington insisted that Georgia restore to the Chickasaws and Choctaws, Creek allies, a vast area along the Mississippi River that Georgia had already begun selling off to land speculators.

Washington tried to force peace through military action against Britain's Indian allies in the Northwest. But two military campaigns, in 1790 and 1791, failed to force peace and cost the United States eleven hundred men.

Washington's frontier policy was in shambles. Matters worsened in 1792 when the Spanish persuaded the Creeks to renounce the Treaty of New York and resume hostilities. Ultimately, the damage to U.S. prestige from these setbacks convinced many Americans that only an alliance with France could counterbalance the combined strength of Britain, Spain, and the Indians.

France and Factional Politics, 1793

One of the most momentous events in history, the French Revolution, began in 1789. Many Americans watched sympathetically as the French abolished nobles' privileges, wrote a constitution, and repelled invading armies. In 1793, after becoming a republic, France proclaimed a war of all peoples against all kings and unleashed a "Reign of Terror," executing not only the king but also dissenting revolutionaries.

Americans were bitterly divided in their views of the French Revolution and how the United States should respond to it. Republicans such as Jefferson supported it as an assault on monarchy and tyranny. Federalists like Hamilton denounced France as a "mobocracy" and supported Great Britain in resisting efforts to sow revolution abroad.

White southern slave owners were among France's fiercest supporters. In 1791 slaves in the French colony of Saint Domingue (san doh-MIN-geh) rebelled against slavery and against French rule, a bloody uprising that took a heavy death toll among French planters and sent thousands fleeing to the United States. Fearful southern whites believed that the British had intentionally sparked the bloodshed and would do the same in the American South.

Northern Federalists damned revolutionary France as an abomination. Conservative and religiously oriented, New Englanders detested the French government's disregard for civil rights and its adoration of reason over the worship of God. Middle Atlantic businessmen, perhaps less religious but no less conservative, condemned French leaders as evil radicals who incited the poor against the rich.

After 1790, economics sharpened differences between northern and southern reactions to the French Revolution. Growing antagonism toward France among northern merchants reflected their awareness that their prosperity depended on good relations with Britain. Northerners argued that the United States could win valuable concessions by demonstrating friendly intentions toward Britain.

Southerners had no such reasons to favor Britain. They perceived American reliance on British commerce as a menace to national self-determination, and they wished to divert most U.S. trade to France. Southern spokesmen, such as Jefferson and Madison, demanded discriminatory duties on British cargoes. These recommendations threatened ties with Britain, which sold more manufactured goods to the United States than to any other country. If Congress adopted trade retaliation, Hamilton predicted, "an open war between the United States and Great Britain" would result.

Pro-French feelings were also high in the western states, especially after France went to war against Spain and Great Britain in 1793. Westerners hoped that a French victory would remove Spanish and British roadblocks to expansion, put an end to Indian wars, and open the Mississippi for navigation.

After declaring war with Spain and Britain in 1793, France sought to embroil the United States in the war and to strengthen the treaty of alliance between the two nations. France dispatched Edmond Genêt (zhe-NAY) as minister to the United States with orders to recruit American mercenaries to conquer Spanish territories and to attack British shipping. Much to France's disgust, President Washington issued a proclamation of neutrality on April 22, 1793.

Meanwhile, **Citizen Genêt** (as he was known in French revolutionary style) had arrived on April 8. He found numerous southern volunteers for his American Foreign Legion despite official U.S. neutrality. Making generals of George Rogers Clark of Kentucky and Elisha Clarke, Genêt ordered them to seize New Orleans and St. Augustine. Clark openly defied the neutrality proclamation by advertising for recruits, and Clarke drilled three hundred soldiers along the Florida border. However, the French failed to provide adequate funds for either campaign, and in 1794 both expeditions disintegrated.

However, Genêt did not need funds to outfit privateers, whose crews were paid from captured plunder. By summer 1793 nearly one thousand Americans were at sea in a dozen ships flying the French flag. These privateers seized over eighty British ships and towed them to American ports, where French consuls sold the ships and cargoes at auction.

Citizen Genêt French minister to United States who ignored U.S. neutrality and recruited Americans to fight British and Spanish

Diplomacy and War, 1793–1796

Although Washington swiftly closed the nation's harbors to Genêt's buccaneers, the episode provoked an Anglo-American crisis. Britain decided that only a massive show of force would deter American aggression. Thus on November 6, 1793, Britain's Privy Council issued orders confiscating foreign ships trading with the French islands in the Caribbean. The orders were kept secret until most U.S. ships carrying winter provisions to the Caribbean left port so that their captains would not know that they were sailing into a war zone. The Royal Navy seized more than 250 U.S. ships.

Meanwhile, the U.S. merchant marine suffered another galling indignity—the drafting of its crewmen into the Royal Navy. Thousands of British sailors had fled to American ships looking for an easier life than the tough, poorly paying British system. In late 1793 British naval officers began inspecting American crews for British subjects, whom they then impressed (forcibly enlisted) as the king's sailors. Overzealous commanders sometimes exceeded orders by taking U.S. citizens—and in any case Britain did not recognize its former subjects' right to adopt American citizenship. Impressment struck a raw nerve in most Americans.

The British, along with Spain and Native Americans, also challenged the United States for control of the West. In February 1794, Canada's governor denied U.S. claims north of the Ohio River and urged Indians to destroy every white settlement in the Northwest. Britain soon erected Fort Miami near Toledo, Ohio. That same year, Spain encroached on U.S. territory by building Fort San Fernando at what is now Memphis, Tennessee.

Hoping to halt the drift toward war, Washington launched a desperate diplomatic initiative, sending Chief Justice John Jay to Great Britain and Thomas Pinckney to Spain. The president also authorized General Anthony Wayne to negotiate a treaty with the Indians of the Ohio Valley.

The Indians scoffed at Washington's peace offer until "Mad Anthony" Wayne led three thousand regulars and militiamen deep into their homeland, ravaging every village in reach. On August 20, 1794, Wayne's troops routed four hundred Shawnees at the Battle of Fallen Timbers, two miles from Britain's Fort Miami. In August 1795 Wayne compelled twelve Ohio Valley tribes to sign the Treaty of Greenville, which opened most of Ohio to white settlement and temporarily ended Indian hostilities.

Wayne's success allowed John Jay a major diplomatic victory in London: a British promise to withdraw troops from American soil. Jay also gained American access to West Indian markets, but only by bargaining away U.S. rights to load cargoes of sugar, molasses, and coffee from the Caribbean. On other points the British remained unyielding. Few Americans would interpret **Jay's Treaty** as preserving peace with honor.

Jay's Treaty left Britain free not only to violate American neutrality but also to restrict U.S. trade with French ports. Moreover, Jay did not succeed in ending impressment. He also failed to gain compensation for slaves taken by the British during the Revolution, an outcome especially galling to southerners. In 1795 the Federalist-dominated Senate ratified the treaty by just one vote.

Jay's Treaty probably represented the most that a weak, politically divided United States could extract from Britain. A major achievement for the

Jay's Treaty Agreement that opened some British markets to Americans but otherwise accomplished little

CHECKING IN

- Spanish power enjoyed a brief resurgence in the 1790s, and Spain strengthened its position in the West and the Southeast.
- Washington countered Spanish expansion by neutralizing its Indian allies and making peace with other tribes.
- The French Revolution produced a deep split in American opinion.
- Citizen Genêt tried to embroil the United States in war against the British.
- Jay's Treaty stimulated American trade with the British Empire, and Pinckney's Treaty resolved many tensions with Spain.

Washington administration, Jay's Treaty also stimulated American trade as British governors in the West Indies used the treaty's ratification as an excuse to open their harbors to U.S. ships. Within a few years of 1795, American exports to the British Empire had shot up 300 percent.

On the heels of Jay's Treaty came an unqualified diplomatic triumph engineered by Thomas Pinckney. Ratified in 1796, the 1795 **Treaty of San Lorenzo** (also called **Pinckney's Treaty**) with Spain gave westerners unrestricted, duty-free access to world markets via the Mississippi River. Spain also promised to recognize the thirty-first parallel as the United States' southern boundary, to dismantle all fortifications on American soil, and to discourage Indian attacks against western settlers.

By 1796 the Washington administration had defended the nation's territorial integrity, restored peace to the frontier, opened the Mississippi for western exports, reopened British markets to U.S. shipping, and kept the nation out of a European war. However, as the outcry over Jay's Treaty showed, foreign policy had left Americans far more divided in 1796 than in 1789.

Treaty of San Lorenzo (Pinckney's Treaty) Agreement that gave Americans access to the Mississippi and to the Gulf of New Mexico via New Orleans

PARTIES AND POLITICS, 1793–1800

Why and how did political parties emerge by 1800?

By the time of Washington's reelection, controversies over domestic and foreign policy had led to the formation of two distinct political factions. During the president's second term, these factions became formal political parties, Federalists and Republicans, which waged a bitter battle culminating in the election of 1800.

Ideological Confrontation, 1793–1794

The French Revolution led many Americans to reassess their political values. The revolution's radical turn in 1793–1794, which sent thousands to the guillotine, polarized public opinion, generally along regional lines. Federalists trembled at the thought of "mob rule" in the nation's future. Citizen Genêt's recruitment of hundreds of Americans to fight for France reinforced their fears. Federalists worried that all of this was just the tip of a revolutionary iceberg.

By the mid-1790s Federalist leaders had concluded that it was dangerous to involve the public deeply in politics. The people were undependable, too easy a prey for rabble-rousers like Genêt. Federalists saw democracy as "government by the passions of the multitude" and argued that personal merits, not policy, should decide elections. Elected officials, they maintained, should rule in the people's name but be independent of direct popular influence.

A very different perspective on government and politics surfaced in urban areas and in the South, **Republicanism.** Republican ideology stressed the corruption inherent in a powerful government dominated by a few highly visible men. Southern Republicans insisted that only the distribution of power among virtuous, independent citizens would protect liberty.

It might seem strange to see southern slave owners embracing Republicanism, with its emphasis on equality and liberty, but southerners saw no such anomaly.

Republicanism Ideology that stressed the dangers of powerful government; embraced by Jefferson, Madison

They understood that the liberty and equality that they advocated were intended for white men only, no matter how universal the terms in which the ideas were expressed. With their own labor force consisting of enslaved blacks, not free wage workers, southern elites did not fear popular participation in politics.

Ambition also drove Jefferson, Madison, and like-minded Americans to rouse ordinary citizens' concerns about civic affairs. Although the awe in which Washington was held precluded open criticism of him or his policies, Jefferson, Madison, and other Republicans hoped to hold the Federalists accountable to a public that could remove them from office for misguided or unpopular policies.

Jefferson's increasing frustration prompted him to resign from Washington's cabinet in 1793, widening the political split. Each side saw itself as the guardian of republican virtue and the other as an illegitimate "faction." In 1793–1794 opponents of Federalist policies began organizing Democratic (or Republican) societies; these societies formed primarily in seaboard cities as well as in the rural South and West. They drew into their ranks planters, small farmers and merchants, artisans, distillers, and sailors.

The Republican Party, 1794–1796

Neither Jefferson nor Madison belonged to a Democratic society. However, the clubs' criticism of the administration galvanized into political activity many who would later support Jefferson's and Madison's Republican party.

In 1794, party development reached a decisive stage. Shortly after Washington aligned himself with Federalist policies, supporters of Jefferson who had begun to call themselves Republicans won a slight majority in the House of Representatives. The election signaled their transformation from a faction to a broad-based party, the Republican party, capable of coordinating nation-wide political campaigns.

Federalists and Republicans alike used the press to mold public opinion. American journalism came of age in the 1790s as the number of newspapers multiplied from 92 to 242. By 1800 newspapers had perhaps 140,000 paid subscribers (about one-fifth of the eligible voters), and their secondhand readership probably exceeded 300,000. Newspapers of both camps cheerfully engaged in fear mongering and character assassination. Republicans stood accused of plotting a reign of terror and scheming to turn the nation over to France. Federalists faced charges of favoring hereditary aristocracy and planning to establish an American dynasty by marrying off John Adams's daughter to George III. But despite the mutual distrust thus created, newspaper warfare stimulated citizens to become politically active.

Accusations that he secretly supported a plot to establish a monarchy enraged Washington. Alarmed by the furor over Jay's Treaty, Washington dreaded the nation's polarization into hostile factions. Lonely and surrounded by mediocre men after Hamilton returned to private life, Washington decided in spring 1796 to retire after two terms and called on Hamilton to give a sharp political twist to a farewell address.

In his farewell message Washington vigorously condemned political parties. Partisan alignments, he insisted, endangered the Republic's survival, especially if they became entangled in foreign policy disputes. Aside from fulfilling existing treaty obligations and maintaining foreign commerce, the United States had to avoid "political connection" with Europe and its wars. If the United States gathered its strength under "an efficient government," it could defy any foreign challenge; but if it was drawn into Europe's quarrels and corruption, the republican experiment would be doomed. Washington and Hamilton thus turned the central argument of Republicanism against their Republican critics. They also evoked a vision of a United States virtuously isolated from foreign intrigue and power politics, an ideal that would remain a potent inspiration for long thereafter.

Washington left the presidency in 1797 and died in 1799. He went out amid a barrage of criticism. The nation's political division into Republicans and Federalists meanwhile hardened into a two-party system.

The Election of 1796

As the election of 1796 approached, the Republicans cultivated a large, loyal body of voters, the first time since the Revolution that the political elite had effectively mobilized ordinary Americans. The Republican constituency included the Democratic societies, workingmen's clubs, and immigrant-aid associations.

Immigrants became a prime target for Republican recruiters. During the 1790s the United States absorbed twenty thousand French refugees from Saint Domingue and sixty thousand Irish. Although few immigrants could vote, the Irish exerted critical influence in Pennsylvania and New York, where public opinion was so closely divided that a few hundred voters could tip the balance.

In 1796 the presidential candidates were Vice President John Adams, whom the Federalists supported, and the Republicans' Jefferson. Republican strength in the South offset Federalist strength in New England, leaving Pennsylvania and New York as crucial swing states where the Irish vote might tip the scales. In the end Jefferson carried Pennsylvania but not New York and lost the presidency by three electoral votes. The Federalists kept control of Congress. But Jefferson became vice president under the constitutional provision (later changed by the Twelfth Amendment) that the candidate receiving the most electoral votes would become president and the candidate finishing second would become vice president.

President Adams's brilliance, insight, and idealism have seldom been equaled among American presidents. He was more comfortable, however, with ideas than with people, more theoretical than practical, and rather inflexible. He inspired trust and admiration but could not inspire the public. As Benjamin Franklin observed, Adams was "always an honest man, often a wise one, but sometimes, and in some things, absolutely out of his senses." Adams's reserved and often stubborn personality left him ill-suited to govern, and he proved unable to unify the country.

John Adams

Adams presided over—and contributed to—the division of American voters into two political parties during the late 1790s.

The French Crisis, 1798–1799

French provocations produced a sharp anti-Republican backlash. France had already recognized Jay's Treaty as an American attempt to assist the British in their war against France. Learning of Jefferson's defeat, the French ordered the seizure of American ships; within a year they had plundered more than three hundred U.S. vessels. The French also ordered that every American captured on a British naval ship, even those involuntarily impressed, be hanged.

Seeking to avoid war, Adams dispatched a peace commission to France. The French foreign minister, Charles de Talleyrand (sharl duh TAL-ee-rahn), refused to meet with the Americans, instead promising through three unnamed agents ("X, Y, and Z") that talks could begin after he received $250,000 and France obtained a $12 million loan. This barefaced demand for a bribe became known as the **XYZ Affair.** Outraged Americans adopted the battle cry "Millions for defense, not one cent for tribute."

XYZ Affair French demand for bribes from American negotiators; triggered great anger

The XYZ Affair discredited Republican foreign policy views. The party's leaders compounded the damage by refusing to condemn French aggression and opposing Adams's call for defensive measures. While Republicans tried to excuse French behavior, the Federalists rode a wave of patriotism to an enormous victory in the 1798 congressional elections.

Congress responded to the XYZ Affair by arming fifty-four ships to protect U.S. commerce. The new warships joined what became known as the Quasi (KWAH-zee) War—an undeclared Franco-American naval conflict in the Caribbean from 1798 to 1800, during which U.S. forces seized ninety-three French privateers while losing just one ship. By early 1799 the French no longer posed a serious threat at sea.

Meanwhile, the Federalist-controlled Congress tripled the regular army to ten thousand men in 1798, with an automatic expansion of land forces to fifty thousand in case of war. But the risk of a land war with France was minimal. What Federalists actually wanted was a strong military force ready in case of a civil war, for the crisis had produced near-hysterical fears that French and Irish malcontents were hatching treasonous conspiracies.

The Alien and Sedition Acts, 1798

The Federalists insisted that the possibility of war with France demanded stringent legislation to protect national security. In 1798 the Federalist Congress passed four measures known collectively as the **Alien and Sedition Acts.** Although President Adams neither requested nor wanted the laws, he deferred to Congress and signed them.

Alien and Sedition Acts Federalist-supported measures to suppress Republican supporters of Jefferson

The least controversial of the four laws, the Alien Enemies Act, was designed to prevent wartime espionage or sabotage. It outlined procedures for determining whether a hostile country's citizens, when staying in America, posed a threat to the United States; if so, they would be deported or jailed. It also established principles to respect the rights of enemy citizens. This law would not be used until the War of 1812.

The second of the laws, the Alien Friends Act, authorized the president to expel foreign residents whose activities he considered dangerous. It required no proof of guilt. Republicans maintained that the law's real purpose was to deport immigrants critical of Federalist policies. Republicans also denounced the third law, the Naturalization Act. This measure increased the residency requirement for U.S. citizenship from five to fourteen years (the last five continuously in one state) to reduce Irish voting.

Finally came the Sedition Act, the only one of these measures enforceable against U.S. citizens. Although its alleged purpose was to punish attempts to encourage the violation of federal laws or to seed a revolution, the act defined criminal activity so broadly that it blurred distinctions between sedition and legitimate political discussion. Thus it forbade an individual or a group "to oppose any measure or measures of the United States"—wording that could be interpreted to ban any criticism of the party in power. Another clause made it illegal to speak, write, or print any statement that would bring the president "into contempt or disrepute." A newspaper editor could therefore face imprisonment for criticizing Adams or his cabinet. However one regarded it, the Sedition Act interfered with free speech. The Federalists wrote the law to expire in 1801 so that it could not be used against them if they lost the next election.

The real target of all this Federalist repression was the opposition press. Four of the five largest Republican newspapers were charged with sedition just as the election of 1800 was getting under way. The attorney general used the Alien Friends Act to drive Irish journalist John Daly Burk underground. After failing to deport Scottish editor Thomas Callender, an all-Federalist jury sent him to prison for criticizing the president. Federalist leaders hoped that a small number of highly visible prosecutions would intimidate journalists and candidates into silence during the election. The attorney general charged seventeen persons with sedition and won ten convictions.

Vocal criticism of Federalist repression erupted only in Virginia and Kentucky. In summer 1798, militia commanders in these states mustered their regiments to hear speeches demanding that the federal government respect the Bill of Rights. Entire units signed petitions denouncing the Alien and Sedition Acts. Young men stepped forward to sign the documents on drumheads, a pen in one hand and a gun in the other. Older officers who had fought in the Continental Army looked on approvingly. It was not hard to imagine rifles replacing quill pens as the men who had led one revolution took up arms again.

Ten years earlier, opponents of the Constitution had warned that giving the national government extensive powers would endanger freedom. By 1798 these predictions seemed to have come true. Shocked Republicans realized that, with the Federalists in control of all three branches of government, neither the Bill of Rights nor the system of checks and balances protected individual liberties. In this context, the doctrine of states' rights was advanced as a way to prevent the national government from violating freedoms.

James Madison and Thomas Jefferson anonymously wrote two manifestos on states' rights that the assemblies of Virginia and Kentucky endorsed in 1798. Madison's **Virginia Resolutions** and Jefferson's **Kentucky Resolutions** proclaimed that state legislatures retained both their right to judge the constitutionality of federal actions and an authority called interposition, which enabled them to protect the liberties of their citizens. A set of Kentucky Resolutions adopted in November 1799 added that states could "nullify"—declare invalid—objectionable federal laws. Although most states did not endorse the resolutions, their passage demonstrated the potential for disunion in the late 1790s.

Virginia and Kentucky Resolutions Jefferson's and Madison's resolutions stressing states' rights and the power of nullification in response to Alien and Sedition Acts

National leaders acted as if a crisis were imminent. Vice President Jefferson hinted that events might push the southern states into secession from the Union; President Adams hid guns in his home. The election of 1800 would take place in an atmosphere charged with tension.

The Election of 1800

In the election campaign, the parties once again rallied around the Federalist Adams and the Republican Jefferson. Moderate leadership in both parties ensured that the nation would survive the tumultuous election. Jefferson and Madison discouraged radical activity, while Adams rejected demands that he ensure victory by deliberately sparking an insurrection or asking for a declaration of war against France.

"Nothing but an open war can save us," declared a high (extreme) Federalist. But when the president discovered the French willing to seek peace in 1799, he proposed a special diplomatic mission. Adams obtained Senate approval for his envoys only by threatening to resign and thus making Jefferson president. High Federalists tried unsuccessfully to dump Adams. Hamilton denounced him as a fool, but this tactic backfired when most New Englanders rallied around the president.

Adams's negotiations with France did not achieve a settlement until 1801, but the expectation of normal relations prevented Federalists from exploiting charges of Republican sympathy for the enemy. With the immediate threat of war removed, voters grew resentful that, in just two years, taxes had soared 33 percent to support an army that had done virtually nothing. As the danger of war receded, voters gave Federalists less credit for standing up to France and more blame for ballooning the national debt by $10 million.

High Federalists spitefully withheld the backing that Adams needed to win the presidency. Republicans successfully mobilized voters in Philadelphia and New York who were ready to forsake the Federalists. Voter turnouts more than doubled those of 1788, rising from 15 percent to 40 percent, and in hotly contested New York and Pennsylvania, more than half the eligible voters participated. Conveniently overlooking Adams's own unconventional religious views, Federalists urged citizens to vote for "GOD—AND A RELIGIOUS PRESIDENT" and rejected "JEFFERSON—AND NO GOD!" Nonetheless, thousands of Baptists, Methodists, and other churchgoers voted for Jefferson.

Adams lost the presidency by just eight electoral votes, but Jefferson's election was not assured. Because all seventy-three Republican electors voted for Jefferson and his running mate, Aaron Burr of New York, the Electoral College deadlocked in a Jefferson-Burr tie. The deadlock put the election into the House of Representatives, where six days and thirty-five ballots produced no result. Burr, now dreaming of becoming president himself, looked for Federalist support but was thwarted by Alexander Hamilton, who saw Jefferson as "by far not so dangerous a man." One Federalist abandoned Burr and gave Jefferson the presidency by history's narrowest margin.

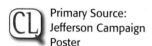

Primary Source: Jefferson Campaign Poster

CHECKING IN

- Federalists viewed the French Revolution with alarm, but Jefferson and his supporters initially viewed it optimistically.
- The XYZ Affair alienated many Americans and hardened party lines between Federalists and Republicans.
- Jefferson's supporters became the Republican party by the mid-1790s; the election of 1796 was the first party-based election.
- In the Alien and Sedition Acts, the Federalists attempted to suppress the Republican party.
- Jefferson's victory in the election of 1800 showed that the party system was firmly entrenched.

ECONOMIC AND SOCIAL CHANGE

What major economic and social changes characterized the new republic?

During the new nation's first twelve years, the spread of economic production for markets transformed the lives of many Americans in ways whose outcome remained uncertain in 1800. At the same time, many Americans were rethinking questions of gender and race in American society.

The fierce political struggles that took place during this period primarily involved white males, those who had the right to vote and the guarantee of at least minimal civil rights. For those not both white and male, the struggle was to achieve minimal rights or at least to survive.

Producing for Markets

For centuries the family household had been the scene of virtually all economic production. Family members, apprentices, servants, and even slaves were all part of this household economy; nearly everyone worked at what was either temporarily or permanently "home." In the late eighteenth century, the vast majority of households consisted of a farmer and his family, which usually included seven children. Husband and sons worked in the fields while wives, daughters, and young sons maintained the barns and gardens near the house and provided food and clothing for the family. Women bore and reared the children as well. Most families produced only what they needed and a small surplus for barter.

After the American Revolution, this began to change in heavily settled regions of the Northeast. Prosperous farmers began to sell their surplus—produce, meat, and dairy products—to urban customers. To improve milk yields, many farmers began to concentrate on breeds of cattle known as good producers. Farmwomen, often referred to as "dairymaids," focused on milking the cattle and churning butter, much in demand by urban consumers.

Poorer farmers found other ways to produce for commercial markets. Young men and young couples moved west, while unmarried daughters frequently remained at home and spun and wove cloth. Enterprising merchants began catering to an emerging urban market for cloth as well as selling to southerners who wanted the cheapest possible material for slave clothing. Merchants would supply raw flax (for linen), wool, and cotton to mothers and daughters in farm households, returning in a few weeks to pay the women cash for their handiwork. A similar system emerged in the shoe industry, where prosperous shoemakers began supplying leather to others and paying them for the finished product.

Numerous other enterprises emerged, employing both men and women to satisfy needs, such as making nails, that self-contained households could not have met.

Spurring on these new industries was an ambitious, aggressive class of businessmen, originally merchants, who invested their profits in factories, ships, government bonds, and banks. Private banks appeared in Philadelphia, Boston, and New York during the 1780s. English artisans were encouraged to immigrate to the United States, bringing with them knowledge of the latest industrial technologies. In 1791 New York and Philadelphia merchants established the Society for the

Encouragement of Useful Manufactures, which attempted to demonstrate the potential of large-scale industrial enterprises by building a factory town at Paterson, New Jersey. The first formal association for trading government bonds appeared in New York City in 1791; it ultimately became the New York Stock Exchange.

For many Americans, the choice between manufacturing and farming was moral as well as economic. Hamilton's aggressive support of entrepreneurship and industrialization embodied his larger vision for America—and contradicted that of Jefferson. While Hamilton admired efficiently run factories in which a few managers supervised large numbers of workers, Jefferson idealized white landowning family farmers, the "yeomen," as bulwarks of republican virtue and liberty. For Hamilton, capital, technology, and managerial discipline were the surest roads to national order and wealth. On the other hand, Jefferson saw land as the key to prosperity and liberty for all. The argument over the relative merits of these two ideals would remain constant in American politics for at least another two centuries.

White Women in the Republic

Along with the growing importance of women's economic roles, discussions of Republicanism raised larger questions of women's equality. Neither the Revolution nor republican state constitutions had substantially altered the legal position of white women. Some states made it easier for women to obtain divorces, but only New Jersey allowed women to vote. In 1807, however, New Jersey disenfranchised both women and free blacks.

Throughout American life, social change and republican ideology combined to challenge traditional attitudes toward women's rights. Americans increasingly recognized the right of a woman to choose her husband. In the Northeast, young women increasingly became pregnant as a way to force their father's consent to marriage. Pregnancy and marriage allowed young women to gain economic support in a region where the westward exodus of young men was increasingly leaving a growing number of women single.

White women also had fewer children than their mothers and grandmothers. Both declining farm sizes and urbanization contributed to the shrinkage; in one Massachusetts town, for example, the average number of children a woman bore declined from nine per marriage in 1750 to six by 1800. Some women were clearly finding relief from the nearly endless cycle of pregnancy and nursing that had consumed their grandmothers.

Republican notions of male-female relations began to change. "I object to the word 'obey' in the marriage-service," wrote one woman. "The obedience between man and wife is, or ought to be mutual." Divorce petitions filed by women increas-

Advocating Women's Rights, 1792

In this illustration from an American magazine for women, the "Genius of the Ladies Magazine" and the "Genius of Emulation" present Liberty with a petition based on British feminist Mary Wollstonecraft's *Vindication of the Rights of Woman.*

ingly cited lack of mutuality as the cause for divorce. A few women also challenged the double standard that allowed men to engage in extramarital affairs while condemning their female partners.

The subordination of women to men increasingly became the subject of debate. Poet and essayist **Judith Sargent Murray** wrote that both genders had equal intellectual ability and deserved equal education. "We can only reason from what we know," she argued, "and if an opportunity of acquiring knowledge hath been denied us, the inferiority of our sex cannot fairly be deduced from there." Women should not rush into marriage but should first improve their minds so that they could instill republican ideals in their children.

Judith Sargent Murray Poet; early feminist

The idea of "republican motherhood" emphasized the necessity of educating white women so that they could inculcate republican virtues in their children, male as well as female. In the 1780s private academies for women began to emerge in cities. In 1789 Massachusetts forbade any town to exclude girls from its elementary schools.

By itself the expansion of educational opportunities for white women had a limited effect, because women were generally still confined to "the narrow circle of domesticity." Republican assertions of male and female moral and intellectual equality provoked scattered calls for political equality, although the great struggle for women's political rights would begin only in the next century. Women could indeed be virtuous wives and mothers, but the world outside their home offered them few opportunities to apply their education.

Land and Culture: Native Americans

Native Americans were excluded from the benefits brought by growing prosperity. By 1795 most eastern Indian tribes had suffered severe reductions in population and territory, owing to battle, famine, and disease. From 1775 to 1795 the Cherokees declined from sixteen thousand to ten thousand and the Iroquois, from nine thousand to four thousand. Between 1775 and 1800 Indians forfeited more land than the area inhabited by whites in 1775. Settlers crowded Indians onto reservations (often illegally), liquor dealers and criminals trespassed on Indian lands, and government agents and missionaries pressured Indians to abandon their lands and cultures. Demoralized and unable to strike back, Indians often sank into alcoholism, and their settlements were plagued by despair and violence.

While not hesitating to use force against Native Americans who resisted U.S. authority, Washington and his Secretary of War, Henry Knox, sought to use the government as an intermediary between Indians and non-Indians. Congress enacted this policy gradually in a series of **Indian Trade and Intercourse Acts** (1790–1796), which became permanent in 1834. The acts prohibited the transfer of tribal lands to outsiders unless authorized by Congress or in formal treaties; the acts required that traders be licensed by the federal government, defined murder and other abuses by non-Indians as federal crimes, and promoted programs that would "promote civilization" among Native Americans. "Civilization" meant Anglo-American culture, private property, and a strictly agricultural way of life. By abandoning communal land ownership and seasonal migrations for hunting, gathering, and fishing, Knox argued, Indians would no longer need most of the land they were trying to protect, thereby making it available for whites.

Indian Trade and Intercourse Acts Series of laws designed to promote better relations between Indians and whites

Interactive Map: Western Land Claims after American Independence

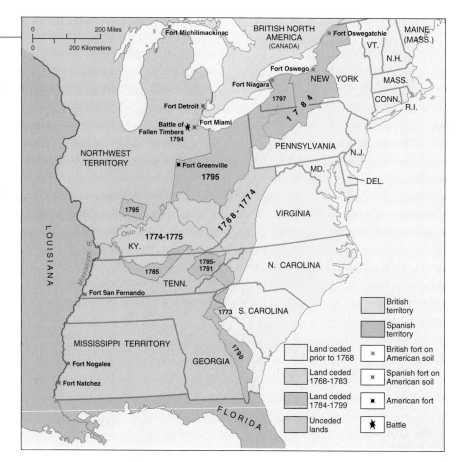

Map 7.1   Indian Land Cessions, 1768–1799

During the last third of the eighteenth century, Native Americans were forced to give up extensive home-lands throughout the east-ern backcountry and further west in the Ohio and Tennessee river valleys.

Among the most devastated tribes in the 1790s were the Seneca Iroquois. A majority of surviving Iroquois had moved to Canada after the Revolution; those who stayed were pressured to sell their land, or were simply defrauded of it, leaving them isolated from one another on tiny reservations. Unable to practice their traditional occupations, Seneca men frequently resorted to heavy drinking that led to violence.

Beginning in 1799 a Seneca Iroquois prophet, Handsome Lake, led his people in a creative effort to resolve the crisis. He preached against alcoholism among the Iroquois by appealing to their religious traditions. He welcomed Quaker missionaries who taught Euro-American agricultural methods to Iroquois men who were no longer able to hunt and trade. Many Iroquois men welcomed the change. Iroquois women who resisted because they stood to forfeit their collective ownership of farm-land, their control of the food supply, and their place in tribal councils were accused of witchcraft. Among the Iroquois, as with most Indians, the conflict between tradition and new ways proceeded fitfully.

African-American Struggles

The Republic's first years marked the high tide of African-Americans' revolutionary-era success in bettering their lot. Although racism persisted, Jefferson's eloquent words "all men are created equal" awakened many white consciences. In 1790, 8 percent of

African-Americans enjoyed freedom. By 1800, 11 percent were free. State reforms meanwhile attempted to improve slaves' conditions. In 1791 the North Carolina legislature declared that the "distinction of criminality between the murder of a white person and one who is equally an human creature, but merely of a different complexion, is disgraceful to humanity" and authorized the execution of whites who murdered slaves. By 1794 most states had outlawed the Atlantic slave trade.

Hesitant measures to ensure free blacks' legal equality appeared in the 1780s and early 1790s. Most states dropped restrictions on their freedom of movement, protected their property, and allowed them to enroll in the militia. All but three states either permitted free blacks to vote or made no specific attempts to exclude them. But before the 1790s ended, the trend toward lessening the social and legal distances between the races ended. Abolitionist sentiment ebbed, slavery became more entrenched, and whites demonstrated reluctance to accept free blacks as fellow citizens.

Federal law led the way in restricting the rights of African-Americans. In 1790 congressional procedures for naturalizing aliens limited eligibility to foreign whites. The federal militia law of 1792 allowed states to exclude free blacks. The navy and marine corps forbade nonwhite enlistments in 1798. By 1807 Delaware, Maryland, Kentucky, and New Jersey had stripped free blacks of the vote. Although free blacks enjoyed rights in some areas, the number of places treating them as the political equals of whites dropped sharply in the early 1800s.

Some free blacks rose above these disadvantages, and a few gained recognition among whites. One of the best-known was Benjamin Banneker of Maryland, a self-taught mathematician and astronomer. Banneker was one of three surveyors who laid out the new national capital in Washington, D.C., and after 1791 he published a series of widely read almanacs. Sending a copy of one to Thomas Jefferson, Banneker chided the future president for holding views of black inferiority that contradicted his ringing words in the Declaration of Independence.

Faced with growing constriction of their freedom and opportunities, free African-Americans turned to one another for support, especially through religious channels. During the 1780s Richard Allen and Absalom Jones formed the Free African Society of Philadelphia, whose members pooled their resources to aid one another and other blacks in need. When the white-dominated Methodist church they attended restricted black worshippers to the gallery, Allen and Jones and their followers formed their own congregation. Comparable developments in other northern communities would lead to the establishment of the African Methodist Episcopal Church (see Chapter 9).

In 1793 a yellow fever epidemic, swept Philadelphia, leaving about four thousand dead. Most affluent whites fled. Allen and Jones organized a relief effort in which African-Americans tended to the sick and buried the dead of both races. Their only reward was a vicious publicity campaign wrongly accusing blacks of profiting at whites' expense.

An especially revealing symptom of changing attitudes occurred in 1793 when Congress passed the **Fugitive Slave Law.** The law required judges to award possession of a runaway slave on a formal request by a master or his representative. Accused runaways were denied jury trials and sometimes were refused permission to present evidence. Slaves' legal status as property disqualified them from claiming these constitutional privileges, but the Fugitive Slave Law denied even *free* blacks the

Interactive Map: African American Population, 1790

Fugitive Slave Law Required return of runaway slaves; denied blacks any constitutional protections legal protections guaranteed to them under the Bill of Rights. White Americans clearly found it easy to forget that the Constitution had not limited citizenship to their race.

The bloody slave revolt on Saint Domingue undermined the trend toward abolition and reinforced the kinds of fears that spawned racism. Reports of the slaughter of French slaveholders made white Americans more reluctant to criticize slavery and helped to transform the image of blacks from that of victims of injustice to one of potential menaces. In August 1800 a planned insurrection of more than one thousand slaves in Richmond, Virginia, kindled smoldering white fears. The militia put down the conspiracy and executed thirty-five slaves, including the leader, Gabriel. **Gabriel's rebellion** fanned fears of future revolts. Isolated uprisings occurred in the United States for years after, and rumors persisted that a massive revolt was brewing. Antislavery sentiment diminished rapidly. The antislavery movement would not recover from the damage inflicted by the Saint Domingue revolt until the early 1830s.

A technological development strengthened slavery. In the 1790s, demand in the British textile industry stimulated the cultivation of cotton in coastal South Carolina and Georgia. Here the soil and climate were ideal for growing long-staple cotton, whose fibers could be separated easily from its seed. In the South's upland and interior regions, however, only short-staple cotton thrived. Its seed clung tenaciously to the fibers and defied cleaning. In 1793 a New Englander, Eli Whitney, invented a **cotton gin** which efficiently cleaned short-staple cotton. Improved by others, Whitney's machine removed a major obstacle to cotton cultivation, gave plantation slavery a new lease on life, and undermined the doubts of those who considered slavery economically outmoded. Thus, by the time Thomas Jefferson became president in 1801, free blacks had suffered a subtle erosion of their political gains, and slaves stood no closer to freedom.

Gabriel's rebellion Failed slave rebellion in Virginia

cotton gin Invention that made cleaning of southern cotton fast and cheap

CHECKING IN

- By 1800 the market economy was beginning to challenge traditional household economies.
- White women gained educational but few other opportunities.
- The status of Native Americans continued to decline.
- The early Republic moved slowly toward ending slavery, but the slave revolt on Saint Domingue and Gabriel's rebellion in Virginia halted progress.
- The invention of the cotton gin in 1793 transformed southern agriculture and entrenched slavery firmly in the South.

Chapter Summary

DOWNLOAD THE MP3 AUDIO FILE OF THE CHAPTER SUMMARY, AND LISTEN TO IT ON THE GO.

What role did George Washington play in translating the Constitution from words into government? (page 146)

As president, Washington worked hard to lessen fears of the government by balancing his cabinet among competing sectional interests. He also established the precedent of serving only two terms. The Judiciary Act of 1789, which left room for state practice, and the Bill of Rights, which guaranteed personal liberties, underscored his commitment to the ideals of the Revolution.

KEY TERMS

Judiciary Act of 1789 *(p. 147)*

Bill of Rights *(p. 147)*

Alexander Hamilton *(p. 148)*

Report on the Public Credit *(p. 149)*

Report on the National Bank *(p. 150)*

Report on Manufactures *(p. 150)*

What were the major components of Hamilton's blueprint for the new nation? (page 148)

Alexander Hamilton, as Washington's secretary of the treasury, devised a blueprint for America's future; among other things, Hamilton advocated creation of a permanent debt, establishment of a national bank, and strong support for industrial development.

How did the new nation deal with France, Spain, and Britain? (page 153)

Spain attempted to expand its North American holdings, but Washington countered by neutralizing its Indian allies. The French Revolution proved a source of contention in the United States, especially with the arrival of Citizen Genêt and his scheme to enlist Americans to fight on France's behalf. To try to relieve tensions, Americans undertook diplomatic missions. Jay's Treaty solved few problems but stimulated the American economy by opening American trade with the British Empire. Pinckney's Treaty resolved tensions with Spain.

Why and how did political parties emerge by 1800? (page 157)

The emergence of political parties clarified and intensified debate over the shape of the nation's future. Frightened by Jefferson's Republican supporters, the Federalists supported the Alien and Sedition Acts. The split over the French Revolution was only one of a series of major issues on which the two parties disagreed.

What major economic and social changes characterized the new republic? (page 163)

The market economy began to transform society. White women enjoyed modest gains in educational but not political opportunities, and Native Americans saw their condition continue to deteriorate. There were some moves toward ending slavery, especially in the northern states, but a series of events essentially put a halt to this—namely, the revolution in Saint Domingue, Gabriel's rebellion in Virginia, and the invention of the cotton gin.

KEY TERMS continued

Whiskey Rebellion *(p. 152)*

"Alta California" *(p. 153)*

Citizen Genêt *(p. 155)*

Jay's Treaty *(p. 156)*

Treaty of San Lorenzo (Pinckney's Treaty) *(p. 157)*

Republicanism *(p. 157)*

XYZ Affair *(p. 160)*

Alien and Sedition Acts *(p. 160)*

Virginia and Kentucky Resolutions *(p. 161)*

Judith Sargent Murray *(p. 165)*

Indian Trade and Intercourse Acts *(p. 165)*

Fugitive Slave Law *(p. 167)*

Gabriel's rebellion *(p. 168)*

cotton gin *(p. 168)*

CHAPTER 8

Jeffersonianism and the Era of Good Feelings

1801 – 1824

War of 1812 Scene

CHAPTER REVIEW

The Age of Jefferson
How did Jefferson's philosophy shape policy toward public expenditures, the judiciary, and Louisiana?

The Gathering Storm
How did the United States slide into war with Great Britain?

The War of 1812
What were the most important consequences of the War of 1812?

The Awakening of American Nationalism
What were the major developments in domestic and foreign affairs during the "Era of Good Feelings"?

O n March 4, 1801, Thomas Jefferson walked from his boarding house to the Capitol for his inauguration, ostentatiously avoiding the pomp and ceremony he thought had grown out of hand under Washington and Adams.

Adams himself, still bitter after the tumultuous election of 1800, was not in Washington for the ceremony.

In his inaugural address, Jefferson struck a conciliatory note, assuring the Federalists that their rights would be respected. Despite the divisiveness of the recent election, he proclaimed that "we are all republicans, we are all federalists." He referred, not to the contending political parties, but to his hope that all Americans who accepted the federal Union and representative government could work harmoniously.

Jefferson's ideals cast a lengthy shadow over the period from 1801 to 1825. His purchase of the Louisiana Territory nearly doubled the size of the United States. And his successors, James Madison and James Monroe, ruled under his belief that governments were strong only to the extent that they earned the affection of a contented people. The Federalist party, deserted by voters, collapsed and disintegrated.

But harmony proved elusive. Events in Europe continued to roil American politics. Even ending all trade with Europe did not allow the United States to remain clear of European wars; the policy, in fact, led to war between Britain and the United States in 1812.

With the Federalist party a declining force, factionalism tore at the Republican party. Ominously, in 1819 and 1820 Republicans split along sectional lines over the extension of slavery into Missouri.

THE AGE OF JEFFERSON

How did Jefferson's philosophy shape policy toward public expenditures, the judiciary, and Louisiana?

Narrowly elected, Jefferson saw his popularity rise in his first term as he scaled down seemingly unnecessary government expenditures. Increasingly confident of public support, he worked to loosen the Federalist grip on appointed offices, especially in the judiciary, and purchased Louisiana. Both political calculation and also his philosophy of government, known as Jeffersonianism, guided his moves.

Jefferson and Jeffersonianism

A man of extraordinary attainments, Jefferson spoke fluent French, read Latin and Greek, and studied several Native American languages. For more than twenty years he was president of America's foremost scientific society, the American Philosophical Society. He designed Monticello (mon-te-CHELL-oh), his mountaintop mansion in Virginia, and spent forty years overseeing its construction. Fascinated by gadgets, he invented a device for duplicating his letters and a revolving book stand. His personal library of seven thousand books was the foundation of the Library of Congress. His public career was luminous: principal author of the Declaration of Independence, governor of Virginia, ambassador to France, secretary of state, vice president, and ultimately president.

Yet Jefferson was, and remains, a controversial figure. In 1802 a former supporter, James Callender, wrote a newspaper account in which he named **Sally Hemings,** a house slave at Monticello, as Jefferson's mistress. The light-skinned and lovely slave was the daughter of Jefferson's own father-in-law. Recent DNA tests have led most scholars to think it likely that Jefferson, a widower, was the father of at least one of her four surviving children.

Callender's story did Jefferson little damage in Virginia. Jefferson acted according to the rules of white Virginia gentlemen by never acknowledging any of Sally's children as his own. Although he freed two of her children (the other two ran away), he never freed Sally, nor did he ever mention her in his correspondence. Yet the story of Sally fed the charge that Jefferson was a hypocrite, for throughout his career he condemned the "race mixing" that he seems to have practiced.

Sally Hemings Jefferson's slave rumored to be his mistress and mother of several of his children

Jefferson did not believe that blacks and whites could live permanently side by side, and he greatly feared a race war so vicious that it could be suppressed only by a dictator. Only by colonizing blacks in Africa, he believed, could America avert revolution and chaos.

High taxes, standing armies, and public corruption could also threaten American liberty, he believed, by making government the master rather than the servant of the people. To prevent the United States from sinking into tyranny, Jefferson advocated that state governments retain great authority because they were immediately responsive to popular will.

Popular liberty required popular virtue, he believed, virtue being the disposition to place public good above private interest and to exercise vigilance in keeping government under control. To Jefferson, the most vigilant and virtuous people were educated farmers, accustomed to acting and thinking with sturdy independence. Least vigilant were the inhabitants of cities, which he saw as breeding grounds for mobs and as menaces to liberty.

Jefferson's "Revolution"

Jefferson described his election as a revolution, but the revolution he sought was to restore the liberty and tranquility that he thought the United States had enjoyed in its earliest years and to reverse what he saw as a drift into despotism. The $10 million growth in the national debt under the Federalists alarmed Jefferson and his secretary of the treasury, Albert Gallatin. They rejected Alexander Hamilton's argument that debt strengthened the government by giving creditors a stake in its health. Just paying interest on the debt would require taxes, which would suck money from industrious farmers, the backbone of the Republic. The money would then fall into the hands of creditors, parasites who leeched off interest payments. Increased tax revenues might also tempt the government to establish a standing army, always a threat to liberty.

To Jefferson and Gallatin, federal economy outweighed the importance of military preparedness; Gallatin calculated that, by holding the line on expenditures, the government could pay off the national debt in sixteen years. A lull in the war between France and England that had threatened American shipping in the 1790s convinced Jefferson that minimal military preparedness was a sound policy.

While cutting back funds for the army, Jefferson was ready to use the navy to gain respect for the American flag. In 1801 he ordered a naval squadron into action against the so-called Barbary (BAR-burr-ee) pirates of North Africa. Jefferson calculated that going to war would be cheaper than continuing to pay tribute to protect peace. In 1805 the United States concluded a peace treaty with Tripoli (TRIP-oh-lee); the war had cost roughly half of the annual tribute fee.

Jefferson and the Judiciary

In his first inaugural address, Jefferson reminded Americans that they agreed on far more than they disagreed about. "We are all republicans," he proclaimed, "we are all federalists." However, conflicts over the judiciary derailed Jefferson's hopes of conciliation with moderate Federalists. The first sticking point was the Judiciary Act of

Chronology

1801	Thomas Jefferson's inauguration
1802	Repeal of the Judiciary Act of 1801; Yazoo land compromise
1803	*Marbury* v. *Madison*; conclusion of the Louisiana Purchase
1804	Impeachment of Justice Samuel Chase; Aaron Burr kills Alexander Hamilton in a duel; Jefferson elected to a second term
1804–1806	Lewis and Clark expedition
1805	British court declares broken voyages illegal
1807	*Chesapeake* affair Embargo Act passed
1808	James Madison elected president
1809	Non-Intercourse Act passed; Embargo Act repealed
1811	Battle of Tippecanoe
1812	United States declares war on Britain; Madison reelected to a second term; General William Hull surrenders at Detroit
1814	British burn Washington, D.C.; Hartford Convention; Treaty of Ghent signed
1815	Battle of New Orleans
1816	James Monroe elected president; Second Bank of the United States chartered
1817	Rush-Bagot Treaty
1818	British-American Convention of 1818 sets U.S.-Canada border in West; Andrew Jackson invades West Florida
1819	Adams-Onís (Transcontinental) Treaty; *Dartmouth College* v. *Woodward*; *McCulloch* v. *Maryland*
1820	Monroe elected to a second term
1820–1821	Missouri Compromise
1823	Monroe Doctrine

1801, which reduced the size of the Supreme Court and created sixteen new federal judgeships, all of which John Adams had filled with Federalists in last-minute "midnight appointments." Given the bitterness created by Federalist zeal in enforcing the Alien and Sedition Acts, to Jefferson this was further proof that his opponents saw the court system as a battering ram to attack Republicanism.

Chief Justice John Marshall, an arch-Federalist appointed by John Adams and the reputed author of the Judiciary Act of 1801, did little to erase Jefferson's suspicions. In **Marbury v. Madison** (1803), Marshall and the Court ruled that Congress had exceeded its constitutional authority in writing the Judiciary Act of 1789. This decision was the first time that the Court had overturned an act of Congress, an important step on the way to establishing the principle of **judicial review.** Jefferson accepted this principle, which was destined to become highly influential.

Even as the *Marbury* decision was pending, Republicans had taken the offensive against the judiciary, moving to impeach two Federalist judges, John Pickering and Samuel Chase. Pickering was quickly removed from office, but Chase presented difficulties. He was an ardent Federalist who had zealously enforced the Alien and

Marbury v. Madison Supreme Court decision that set the framework for judicial review

judicial review Principle that Supreme Court can review and reject measures passed by Congress

Man of the People

Jefferson thought of himself as a working politician and man of the people, not as an aristocratic figurehead. Foreign diplomats in the United States were often shocked when Jefferson greeted them dressed in everyday working clothes and carpet slippers.

Sedition Acts. Nonetheless, the Constitution specified that judges could be impeached only for treason, bribery, and "high Crimes and Misdemeanors." Was impeachment a solution for excessive political partisanship, Chase's fundamental sin? Ultimately Chase was impeached in 1804, but the Senate narrowly failed to convict him, in part because moderate Republicans had begun to doubt that impeachment was the cure for judicial partisanship.

Chase's acquittal ended Jefferson's skirmishes with the judiciary. Unlike his radical followers, Jefferson objected neither to judicial review nor to an appointed judiciary; he merely challenged Federalist use of judicial power for political goals. Yet there was always a gray area between law and politics. To Federalists, there was no conflict between protecting the Constitution and advancing their party's cause. Nor did Federalists use their domination of the courts to undo Jefferson's "revolution" of 1800; the Marshall Court, for example, upheld the constitutionality of the repeal of the Judiciary Act of 1801.

The Louisiana Purchase

Jefferson's goal of avoiding foreign entanglements would remain beyond reach as long as European powers held large territories in North America. In the Treaty of San Ildefonso (san eel-duh-FON-soh) (1800), a weakened Spain had returned the vast Louisiana Territory to France, which, under Napoleon Bonaparte, was emerging as Europe's strongest military power. Jefferson was appalled.

The president had long imagined that the inevitable expansion of a free and virtuous American people would create an "empire of liberty." Spain was no obstacle, but Napoleonic France posed a real danger; Jefferson knew that Bonaparte's capacity for mischief was boundless. If Bonaparte gave England a free hand in the Mediterranean in exchange for a license for French expansion in North America, the United States could be sandwiched between British Canada and French Louisiana.

Bonaparte's real goal was different but no less dangerous to American interests. Sure of his destiny as a conqueror, he dreamed of re-creating a French New World empire bordering the Caribbean and the Gulf of Mexico. The island of Saint Domingue (modern Haiti and the Dominican Republic) would be the fulcrum of the empire, and Louisiana its breadbasket. Before this dream could become reality, however, the French would have to subdue Santo Domingo, where a bloody slave rebellion had led to the creation of a government under the black statesman Toussaint L'Ouverture (too-SAN loo-ver-TOOR). Napoleon accordingly dispatched an army to reassert French control and to reestablish slavery, but yellow fever and fierce resistance by the former slaves doomed the French forces.

In the short run, Jefferson worried most about New Orleans, the only outlet for farmers along the Mississippi and Ohio river systems. Spain had temporarily

Map 8.1   The Louisiana Purchase and the Exploration of the West
The explorations of Lewis and Clark demonstrated the vast extent of the area purchased from France.

granted Americans the right to park their produce there while awaiting transfer to seagoing vessels.

Concern turned to alarm when the Spanish colonial administrator in New Orleans prohibited the deposit of American produce in that city. Most Americans assumed (wrongly) that the order had come from Napoleon, who had not yet taken formal possession of Louisiana. A concerned Jefferson wrote that "the day that France takes possession of N. Orleans . . . we must marry ourselves to the British fleet and nation."

The combination of France's failure to subdue Santo Domingo and the termination of the American right of deposit at New Orleans stimulated two crucial decisions, one by Jefferson and the other by Napoleon, that led to the American purchase of Louisiana. First, Jefferson nominated James Monroe and Robert R. Livingston to negotiate with France for the purchase of New Orleans and as much of the Floridas as possible. Meanwhile, Napoleon had concluded that his Caribbean empire was not worth the cost. In addition, he planned to resume war in Europe and needed cash—

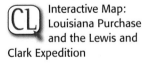

Interactive Map:
Louisiana Purchase
and the Lewis and
Clark Expedition

so he decided to sell *all* of Louisiana. The American commissioners and the French government settled on a price of $15 million. Thus the United States bought this immense, uncharted territory. No one knew its exact size, but the **Louisiana Purchase** virtually doubled the area of the United States.

Louisiana Purchase Jefferson's purchase of interior of North America from France; virtually doubled size of United States

Jefferson found himself caught between ideals and reality. He believed in strict construction—the doctrine that the Constitution should be interpreted according to its letter—but recognized that doubling the size of the Republic would guarantee land for American farmers, the backbone of the nation and the true guardians of liberty. Strict construction was not an end in itself but a means to promote republican liberty. If that end could be achieved in some way other than by strict construction, so be it. Political considerations also figured in Jefferson's calculations. Federalists generally opposed the Louisiana Purchase because it would decrease the relative importance of their strongholds on the eastern seaboard. As the leader of the Republican party, the president saw no reason to hand the Federalists an issue by dallying over ratification of the treaty.

The Election of 1804

The main threat to Jefferson's reelection in 1804 was not the Federalists, who were dispirited and lacked a popular national issue, but Aaron Burr, his own vice president, who had tried to take advantage of a tie in the Electoral College to gain the presidency in 1800. The Twelfth Amendment had clarified the electoral process but had not eliminated Burr's conniving; he had spent much of his vice presidency in intrigue with the Federalists. The Republicans dispensed with the threat by unceremoniously dumping him from the ticket in 1804 in favor of George Clinton. In the election the Federalist nominees, Charles C. Pinckney and Rufus King, carried only two states. Jefferson's overwhelming victory brought his first term to a fitting close; between 1801 and 1804 the United States had doubled its territory, started to pay off its debt, and remained at peace. President Jefferson basked in the sun of success.

The Lewis and Clark Expedition

Louisiana dazzled Jefferson's imagination. Americans knew virtually nothing about the immense territory, not even its western boundary. A case could be made for the Pacific Ocean, but Jefferson was content to claim that Louisiana extended at least to the mountains west of the Mississippi, mountains that few Americans had seen. Thus the Louisiana Purchase was both a bargain and a surprise package.

Even before the purchase, Jefferson had planned an exploratory expedition. He had chosen Lieutenant Meriwether Lewis, his personal secretary, as commander and had sent him to Philadelphia for a crash course in zoology, astronomy, and botany. Lewis was to trace the Missouri River to its source, cross the western highlands, and follow the best water route to the Pacific. Although Jefferson stressed commercial possibilities in requesting congressional funding for the expedition, he probably cared more about advancing scientific knowledge.

Leaving St. Louis in May 1804, Lewis, his second-in-command, William Clark, and about fifty others followed the Missouri and then the Snake and Columbia rivers. In the Dakota Country they hired a French-Canadian fur trader, Toussaint Charbonneau (SHAR-bun-noh), as guide and interpreter. Charbonneau proved less than ideal, but his shortcomings were offset by his wife, Sacajawea (sock-a-ja-WAYah), a sixteen-year-old Shoshone (show-SHOW-nee) stolen by a rival tribe and then married to Charbonneau. During the expedition, the presence of Sacajawea's newborn son helped to persuade skeptical tribes of Lewis and Clark's peaceful intent; she also showed the whites how to forage for wild plants, often their only food, by raiding the dens where rodents stored them.

Despite this establishment of their peaceful intent, Lewis and Clark faced obstacles. The expedition brought them into contact with numerous tribes, each with a history of warring on other tribes and carrying on its own internal feuds. Reliant on Indians for guides, packers, and interpreters, Lewis and Clark had to become diplomats as well as explorers. Jefferson had instructed them to assert American sovereignty over the Purchase. They distributed medals and uniforms to chiefs ready to support American authority and staged military parades and displays of their weapons, which included cannons. But no tribe had a single chief, and Lewis and Clark sometimes miscalculated, thinking a minor chief to be head of an entire tribe. Yet their diplomacy was generally successful, less because they were sophisticated ethnographers than because they avoided violence.

After reaching the Pacific in November 1805, the expedition returned to St. Louis. The explorers had collected vast amounts of scientific information, including the disturbing fact that more than 300 miles of mountains separated the Missouri from the Columbia. Nonetheless, the **Lewis and Clark expedition** stimulated interest in the West. The expedition also produced a sprinkling of tall tales about gigantic Indians, a mountain composed of salt, and soil too rich to grow trees. Tragically, Meriwether Lewis would die of gunshot wounds, perhaps self-inflicted, without ever returning to Washington.

Lewis and Clark expedition
Two-year exploration of newly acquired territory; a scientific treasure trove

CHECKING IN

- President Jefferson feared too strong a central government and saw educated farmers as the backbone of Republicanism.
- The Jefferson administration rejected the Hamiltonian idea of a permanent national debt and downplayed military preparedness.
- Despite qualms about its constitutionality, Jefferson eagerly carried out the Louisiana Purchase.
- With apparent success in both domestic and foreign policy, Jefferson easily won reelection in 1804.
- The Lewis and Clark expedition collected large amounts of scientific data and sparked interest in the West.

THE GATHERING STORM

How did the United States slide into war with Great Britain?

In gaining Louisiana, the United States had benefited from the European powers' preoccupation with their own struggles. But between 1803 and 1814, the Napoleonic Wars turned the United States into a pawn in a chess game played by others and made Jefferson's second term far less successful than his first.

Europe was not Jefferson's only problem. He had to deal with a plot to dismantle the United States, hatched in the inventive and perverse mind of Aaron Burr, as well as face down challenges from within his own party.

Challenges on the Home Front

Aaron Burr suffered a string of reverses in 1804. Dropped from the 1804 ticket, he began to scheme with a faction of high Federalists who were plotting to form a "Northern Confederacy" that would include Nova Scotia, New England, New York, and even Pennsylvania. To advance their plot, the Federalists helped Burr to gain the Federalist nomination for governor of New York. Alexander Hamilton, who had thwarted Burr's grab for the presidency in 1800 by supporting Jefferson, now foiled Burr a second time by allowing publication of his "despicable opinion" of Burr. After his defeat in the New York election, Burr challenged Hamilton to a duel and mortally wounded him at Weehawken, New Jersey, on July 11, 1804.

Indicted in two states for murdering Hamilton, Burr next hatched a scheme so audacious that not even his opponents could believe that he was capable of such treachery. Burr allied himself with General James Wilkinson, the unsavory military governor of the Louisiana Territory, who had been taking Spanish money since the 1780s. Their plot had several dimensions: they would create an independent confederacy of western states, conquer Mexico, and invade West Florida. The scheming duo presented the plot imaginatively. To westerners they said that it had the covert support of the Jefferson administration; to the British, that it was a way to attack Spanish lands; and to the Spanish, that it would open the way to dividing up the United States.

In the fall of 1806 Burr and some sixty followers made their way down the Ohio and Mississippi rivers to join Wilkinson at Natchez (NATCH-ezz). Wilkinson was not there. In October Jefferson, who described Burr as a crooked gun that never shot straight, denounced the conspiracy. Wilkinson abandoned the conspiracy and proclaimed himself a loyal Jeffersonian. Former vice president Burr panicked and tried to flee to West Florida, but was captured and returned to Richmond to stand trial for treason. Chief Justice John Marshall presided and advised the jury that the prosecution had to prove actual treasonable acts—an impossible task because the conspiracy had never reached fruition. The jury returned a "not proved" verdict, which Marshall entered as "not guilty." Still under indictment for the murder of Hamilton, Burr fled to Europe, where he tried but failed to involve Napoleon in a grand scheme that would be the prelude to a proposed Anglo-French invasion of the United States.

Jefferson also faced a challenge from a group of fellow Republicans known as the Quids (kwids).* Their leader was John Randolph of Virginia, an eccentric man of acerbic wit. Randolph still subscribed to the "country ideology" of the 1770s, which celebrated the wisdom of the farmer against rulers and warned against governments' tendency to encroach on liberty. Originally, Jefferson had shared these beliefs, but he had recognized them as an ideology of opposition, not of power; once in office, he therefore compromised. In contrast, Randolph remained frozen in the 1770s, denouncing every change as decline and proclaiming that he would throw all politicians to the dogs, but he had too much respect for dogs.

Not surprisingly, Randolph turned on Jefferson. First, he blasted the president for backing a compromise in the Yazoo land scandal. In 1795 the Georgia legislature had sold the huge Yazoo tract (35 million acres composing most of present-day Alabama and Mississippi) for a fraction of its value to land companies that had bribed virtually the entire legislature. The next legislature canceled the sale, but many investors had already bought land, some of them in good faith. In 1802 a federal commission compromised with an award of 5 million acres to the Yazoo investors. To Randolph, the compromise was itself a scandal—further evidence of the decay of republican virtue.

---

* Quid: A name taken from the Latin *tertium quid,* or "third thing"; roughly, a dissenter.

The Suppression of American Trade and Impressment

Burr's acquittal and Randolph's taunts shattered the aura of invincibility that had surrounded Jefferson. Now foreign affairs posed even sharper challenges. As Britain and France resumed their war, the United States prospered at Britain's expense by carrying sugar and coffee from the French and Spanish Caribbean colonies to Europe. This trade not only provided Napoleon with supplies but also drove down the price of sugar and coffee from British colonies by adding to the glut of these commodities on the world market. The British concluded that their economic problems stemmed from American prosperity.

Fueling this boom was the re-export trade, which created conflicts with Britain. According to the British Rule of 1756, any trade closed during peacetime could not be opened during war. For example, France usually restricted the sugar trade to French ships during peacetime and thus could not open it to American ships during war. The U.S. response to the Rule of 1756 was the "broken voyage," by which U.S. ships would carry French sugar or coffee to American ports, unload it, pass it through customs, and then re-export it as *American* produce. Britain tolerated this dodge for nearly a decade but in 1805 initiated a policy of total war toward France, including the strangulation of French trade. In the *Essex* case (1805), a British court declared broken voyages illegal.

Next came a series of British trade decrees ("Orders in Council"), through which Britain intended to blockade part of continental Europe and thus staunch the flow of any products that might aid the French war effort. French counterdecrees followed, proclaiming the British Isles blockaded. In effect, if Americans obeyed the British regulations, they would violate the French rules, and vice versa. In total war, however, there was no room for neutrality, so both Britain and France seized U.S. ships.

To these provocations the British added **impressment.** At issue was Britain's seizing purported Royal Navy deserters from American merchant ships and subsequently forcing them back into service. British sailors had reason to be discontented with their navy. Discipline on the Royal Navy's "floating hells" was often brutal and the pay low; sailors on American ships earned up to five times more than those on British ships. At a time when war raised the demand for sailors, the Royal Navy suffered a high rate of desertion to American ships.

Impressed sailors led harrowing lives that included frequent escapes and recaptures. One seaman endured impressment eleven times. Another, facing his third recapture, drowned himself rather than spend another day in the Royal Navy. Impressment was, moreover, galling to American pride, for even though many deserters had become American citizens, the British impressed them anyway. The British also impressed U.S.-born seamen, including those who could prove their American birth; between 1803 and 1812, six thousand Americans were impressed.

The *Chesapeake* incident heightened British-American tensions. In June 1807 a British warship, HMS *Leopard,* attacked an American frigate, the USS *Chesapeake,* just off Virginia. The British boarded the vessel and seized four supposed deserters. One, an actual deserter, was later hanged; the other three, former Britons, had "deserted" only from impressment and were now American citizens. Public outrage mounted; Jefferson claimed that he had not seen so belligerent a spirit in America since 1775.

impressment British practice of taking deserters and others from American ships for service in the Royal Navy

CL Primary Source: British Impressment

Boarding and Taking of the American Ship *Chesapeake*

The loss of the frigate *Chesapeake* to HMS *Leopard* in 1807 and the dying words of its commander, James Lawrence, inspired the motto "Don't Give Up the Ship," which was emblazoned on the battle flag of Captain Oliver Hazard Perry.

The Embargo Act of 1807

Yet while making some preparations for a possible war, Jefferson sought peace, first by engaging in fruitless negotiations with Britain to gain redress for the *Chesapeake* and then by steering the **Embargo Act** through Congress in December 1807.

Embargo Act Jefferson's attempt at "peaceable coercion" by suspending American trade with France and England

By far the most controversial legislation of Jefferson's presidency, the Embargo Act prohibited vessels from leaving American harbors for foreign ports. Technically, it prohibited only exports, but it stopped imports as well, for few foreign ships would enter American ports if they had to leave empty. Jefferson defended the embargo as "peaceable coercion," a way of forcing France and especially Britain to respect American neutrality. But it did not work. Although British trade with the United States plummeted, the British opened new markets in South America. France's Napoleon, for his part, treated the act as a joke, seizing American ships and then informing the United States that he was only helping to enforce the embargo.

The United States itself felt the harshest effects. Thirty thousand seamen lost their jobs, hundreds of merchants went bankrupt, and debtors swelled the jail population. Unable to export produce or to sell it at a decent price in the cities, farmers suffered as well. New England suffered most; in Massachusetts, which accounted for a third of foreign trade, the embargo was a calamity.

Yet there were benefits. Unable to export goods, merchants used their capital to begin manufacturing. In 1808 the United States had only fifteen cotton textile mills; by the end of 1809 eighty-seven more had been built. But merchants already ruined or seamen driven to soup kitchens took little comfort. Nor could New Englanders forget that the source of their misery was one of the "Virginia lordlings," "Mad Tom" Jefferson, who knew little about New England and loathed cities, the foundation of the region's prosperity.

James Madison and the Failure of Peaceable Coercion

With Jefferson's blessing, the Republicans nominated James Madison and George Clinton for the presidency and vice presidency in 1808. The Federalists renominated Charles C. Pinckney and Rufus King, the same ticket that had failed in 1804. In 1808 the Federalists staged a modest comeback, but Madison handily won the presidency, and the Republicans continued to control Congress.

The Federalists' revival, modest as it was, rested on two factors. First, the Embargo Act gave them the national issue that they had long lacked. Second, younger Federalists had abandoned their elders' gentlemanly disdain for campaigning and deliberately imitated such vote-winning techniques as barbecues and mass meetings, which had worked for the Republicans.

To some contemporaries, "Little Jemmy" Madison, five feet four inches tall, seemed a weak figure compared to Jefferson. In fact, Madison's intelligence and capacity for systematic thought equaled Jefferson's. He had the added advantage of being married to Dolley Madison. A striking figure in her turbans and colorful dresses, Dolley arranged receptions at the White House in which she charmed Republicans, and even some Federalists, into sympathy with her husband's policies.

Like Jefferson, Madison believed that American liberty rested on the virtue of the people and that virtue was critically tied to the growth and prosperity of agriculture. Madison also recognized that agricultural prosperity depended on trade—farmers needed markets. The British West Indies, dependent on the United States for much lumber and grain, struck Madison as both a natural trading partner and a tempting target. Madison reasoned that the United States could force Britain to its knees before Americans would suffer severe losses.

The American embargo, however, was coercing no one. Increased trade between Canada and the West Indies made a shambles of Madison's plan to pressure Britain. On March 1, 1809, Congress replaced the Embargo Act with the weaker, face-saving Non-Intercourse Act, which opened U.S. trade to all nations except Britain and France and authorized the president to restore trade with either of those nations if it stopped violating neutral rights. But neither nation complied. Meanwhile, American shippers kept up their profitable trade with the British and French, despite the restrictions. In May 1810 Congress substituted a new measure, Macon's Bill No. 2, for the Non-Intercourse Act. This legislation reopened trade with both belligerents, France and Britain, and then offered a clumsy bribe to each: if either nation repealed its restrictions on neutral shipping, the United States would halt all trade with the other. None of these steps worked. France and Britain believed that, when great powers (like themselves) went to war, there could be no neutrals. Weak nations like the United States should stop babbling about moral ideals and neutral rights, and seek the protection of a great power.

As peaceable coercion became a fiasco, Madison came under fire from militant Republicans demanding more aggressive policies. Primarily southerners and westerners, the militants were infuriated by insults to the American flag. In addition, economic recession between 1808 and 1810 had convinced the firebrands that British policies were wrecking their regions' economies. The election of 1810 brought several young militants, christened **"war hawks,"** to Congress. Led by Henry Clay of Kentucky, who preferred war to the "putrescent pool of ignominious peace," the war hawks included John C. Calhoun of South Carolina, Richard M. Johnson of Kentucky, and William R. King of North Carolina—all future vice presidents. Clay was elected Speaker of the House.

"war hawks" Members of Congress elected from western states in 1810 who wanted war with Britain

Tecumseh and the Prophet

More emotional and pugnaciously nationalistic than Jefferson or Madison, the war hawks called for expelling Britain from Canada and Spain from the Floridas. Their demands merged with westerners' fears that the British in Canada were recruiting Indians to halt the march of U.S. settlement. In reality, American policy, not British meddling, was the source of bloodshed on the frontier.

Jefferson believed that Indians and whites could live peacefully together only if the Indians became farmers—and farmers required far less land than nomadic hunters. However, the march of white settlement was steadily shrinking Indian hunting grounds, and some Indians were willing to sign away land in return for blankets, guns, and liquor.

No American was more eager to acquire Indian lands than William Henry Harrison, governor of the Indiana Territory. Harrison realized that Indiana would not become a state without more residents, and the best way to attract more residents was to offer them Indian land. In September 1809 Harrison rounded up a delegation of half-starved Indians who ceded millions of acres of land along the Wabash (WAH-bash) River for two cents an acre; none of the Indians actually lived on the land.

Tecumseh

No fully authenticated portrait of Tecumseh exists, but whites described him as handsome and dominant. Believing that Indian lands were not the possessions of individual tribes to negotiate away, but collectively belonged to all Indians, Tecumseh was a formidable opponent of white expansion.

This treaty, the Treaty of Fort Wayne, outraged numerous tribes. Among the angriest were **Tecumseh** (tuh-CUM-suh), the Shawnee chief, and his brother Lalawéthica (la-la-WAY-thuh-kuh). In 1805 Lalawéthica had had a frightening dream, a vision of drunken Indians who were tormented for eternity. Overnight he was transformed from a drunken misfit into a preacher. He gave up liquor and began beseeching surrounding tribes to return to the old ways and avoid contact with whites. Now known as the Prophet, he took a new name, Tenskwatawa (tens-KWAH-tah-wah), the "open door" through which Indians could achieve salvation. Shawnees responded to his message.

In the meantime, Tecumseh had tried to build a coalition of several tribes to stem the tide of white settlement. He insisted that Indian lands belonged collectively to all the tribes and could not be sold by splinter groups. Failing to reach a settlement with Tecumseh or the Prophet, Harrison concluded that it was time to attack the Indians. His target was a Shawnee encampment near the mouth of the Tippecanoe (TIP-pee-cun-oo) River. With Tecumseh absent and recruiting more followers, the Prophet launched an attack on Harrison's forces in November 1811. Outnumbered two to one and short of ammunition, Tenskwatawa's force was beaten off after inflicting heavy casualties.

Although a small engagement, the Battle of Tippecanoe had far-reaching effects. Harrison became a national hero and ultimately rode his reputation to the White House. The Prophet was discredited, but his brother Tecumseh became recognized as a leader among the western tribes. Finally, Tecumseh concluded that an alliance with the British was the only way to stop the spread of American settlement.

Tecumseh Shawnee leader who tried to build a coalition of several western tribes; allied with British in War of 1812

Congress Votes for War

By spring 1812 President Madison had concluded that war was inevitable, and he sent a war message to Congress on June 1. Ironically, an economic slump prompted Britain to repeal its Orders in Council on June 23, but by then Congress had declared war. Neither the war hawks nor westerners held the key to the vote in favor of war; the votes of Republicans in states like Pennsylvania, Maryland, and Virginia were the decisive force in propelling the declaration of war through Congress. Opposition came mainly from Federalist strongholds in New England and New York.

Madison, in his war message, listed impressment, the presence of British ships in U.S. waters, and British violation of neutral rights as wrongs that justified war. None of these complaints fully explains why America declared war in 1812. Neither do continuing Indian problems (blamed on the British) along the frontier. A more important underlying cause for the war was the economic recession that affected the South and West after 1808. Finally, it was critical that Madison, rather than Jefferson, was president. Jefferson had believed that Britain was motivated primarily by its desire to defeat Napoleon; time was on America's side, Jefferson thought, for once the war in Europe ended, the provocations would stop. Madison held that Britain's real motive was to strangle American trade and thus to eliminate the United States as a trading rival.

CHECKING IN

- In his second term, Jefferson faced challenges from Aaron Burr and John Randolph.
- Impressment became a major issue between the United States and Great Britain.
- Jefferson tried "peaceable coercion" through the Embargo Act; it was a failure.
- "War hawks" from the western states, with their eyes on Canada, demanded more aggressive policies.
- James Madison ultimately asked Congress for a declaration of war because he saw Great Britain as a long-term threat to the United States.

THE WAR OF 1812

What were the most important consequences of the War of 1812?

Although American warships would win a few sensational duels with British men-of-war, the U.S. Navy simply could not challenge the Royal Navy on the high seas, or even prevent a British blockade of the American coast. Madison thus shifted his sights to Canada, whose small population made it seem an easy mark. Jefferson, for example, saw the conquest of Canada as "a mere matter of marching."

Little justified such optimism. Although the British remained preoccupied with the Napoleonic wars in Europe, they enlisted Native Americans as their allies—and used fear of these "uncontrollable savages" to force American surrenders. American militias were often Sunday soldiers who "hollered for water half the time, and whiskey the other." Few understood what the war was about, and fewer still cared.

On to Canada

From the summer of 1812 to the spring of 1814, the Americans launched a series of unsuccessful attacks on Canada. They began in July 1812 when the sixty-year-old general William Hull led an American army from Detroit into Canada. Tecumseh cut his supply lines, and Hull, unnerved, retreated to Detroit. The British commander played on Hull's fears by warning that he might not be able to control the Indians, and Hull promptly surrendered two thousand men to thirteen hundred British and Native American troops.

In two other thrusts in 1812, the United States fared no better. American forces were defeated by the British and their Mohawk allies at the Battle of Queenston, and plans to attack Montreal collapsed when the New York militia refused to advance into Canada.

Renewed U.S. offensives and subsequent reverses in 1813 convinced the Americans that they could not retake Detroit while the British controlled Lake Erie. During winter 1812–1813 U.S. captain Oliver Hazard Perry built ships and outfitted them with captured cannons, and on September 10, 1813, the homemade American fleet destroyed a British squadron at Put-in-Bay on the western end of Lake Erie; "we have met the enemy, and they are ours," Perry triumphantly reported. The British then pulled out of Detroit, but American forces under General William Henry Harrison overtook and defeated a combined British-Indian force at the Battle of the Thames (thaymes) on October 5. Tecumseh, a legend among whites, died in the battle. Perry's and Harrison's victories cheered Americans, but efforts to invade Canada continued to falter.

The British Offensive

With fresh reinforcements from Europe, where Napoleon had abdicated in April, Britain took the offensive in the spring of 1814. Britain's main offensive thrust was meant to split the New England states, which were skeptical of the war, from the rest of the country. General Sir George Prevost headed a force of ten thousand British veterans, the largest and best-equipped British force ever sent to North America. They advanced

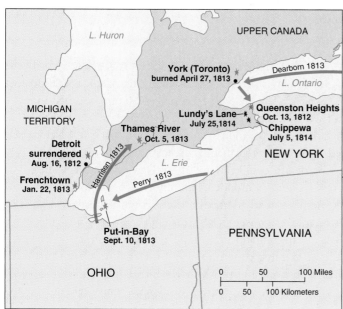

Map 8.2   Major Battles of the War of 1812

Most of the war's major engagements occurred on or near the United States' northern frontier, but the Royal Navy blockaded
the entire Atlantic coast, and the British
army penetrated as far south as Washington
and New Orleans.

readily down Lake Champlain until they reached the entrenched American forces at Plattsburgh; after his fleet met defeat on September 11, Prevost abandoned the campaign.

Ironically, Britain's most spectacular success began as a diversion from Prevost's offensive. A British army that had come up from Bermuda entered Chesapeake Bay and on August 24, 1814, met a larger American force at Bladensburg, Maryland. The Battle of Bladensburg deteriorated into the "Bladensburg Races" as the American troops fled, virtually without firing a shot. The British then descended on Washington, D.C. Madison, who had witnessed the Bladensburg fiasco, fled into the Virginia hills. His wife, Dolley, loaded her carriage before joining her husband. British troops ate the supper prepared for the Madisons and then burned the presidential mansion and other public buildings in the capital. Beyond embarrassing and angering Americans, the Washington raid accomplished little, for after a failed attack on Baltimore, the British broke off the operation.

The Treaty of Ghent, 1814

Treaty of Ghent Treaty that ended War of 1812, restoring *status quo ante bellum*

Napoleon's abdication had made Britain's primary goal a lasting European peace, and thus the British had little to gain by prolonging a minor war in America. The **Treaty of Ghent,** signed on Christmas Eve, 1814, restored the *status quo ante bellum:*[*] the United States neither gained nor lost territory. The fixing of the Canadian-American border was referred to a joint commission for future settlement. Impressment was left hanging, but the end of the European war made neutral rights a dead issue.

Ironically, America's most dramatic victory came on January 8, 1815, two weeks after the treaty had been signed but before word of it had reached America. A British force had descended on New Orleans. U.S. troops commanded by General Andrew ("Old Hickory") Jackson, legendary as a fierce Indian fighter, shredded the line of advancing redcoats, inflicting more than two thousand casualties while suffering only thirteen of their own.

The Hartford Convention

Hartford Convention Federalist meeting that showed seeming disloyalty in time of war; began downfall of the party

Although it meant nothing in terms of the war, the Battle of New Orleans proved devastating for the Federalist party. The Federalists' comeback had continued into the election of 1812, when their candidate, DeWitt Clinton, an antiwar Republican, had carried all of New England except Vermont, along with New York and New Jersey. American military setbacks had intensified Federalist disdain for Madison. He seemed to epitomize a decade of Republican misrule at New England's expense. The Louisiana Purchase, constitutionally dubious, had reduced the importance of New England, the Embargo Act had nearly destroyed the region's commerce, and "Mr. Madison's War" had brought fresh misery in the form of the British blockade. A few New England Federalists began to talk of secession from the Union.

In late 1814 a special Federalist convention met in Hartford, Connecticut. Although some supported secession, moderates took control and passed a series of resolutions expressing New England's grievances. Convinced that New England was

---

[*] *Status quo ante bellum:* Latin for "the state of affairs before the war."

becoming a permanent minority in a nation dominated by southern Republicans who failed to understand the region's commercial interests, the **Hartford Convention** leaders proposed a series of constitutional amendments: to abolish the three-fifths clause, which allowed southerners to count slaves as a basis for representation; to require a two-thirds vote of Congress to declare war and to admit new states into the Union; to limit the president to a single term; to prohibit the election of two successive presidents from the same state; and to bar embargoes lasting more than sixty days. These proposals were as bold as their timing was disastrous. News of the peace and of Jackson's victory at New Orleans dashed Federalist hopes of gaining popular support, while the states' rights emphasis of the convention smelled of treason to many delegates. The restoration of peace stripped the Federalists of their primary grievance. In the presidential election of 1816, James Monroe, Madison's hand-picked successor and another Virginia Republican, swept the nation over negligible Federalist opposition. Four years later he would receive every electoral vote but one. The Federalists were finished as a force in national politics.

CHECKING IN

- The United States failed in its attempts to invade Canada.
- When the war in Europe ended, Britain launched a major offensive in the United States, which included the ransacking of Washington, D.C.
- The Treaty of Ghent ended the war with a restoration of the *status quo ante bellum*.
- At the Hartford Convention, dissatisfied Federalists toyed with the idea of secession, a move ultimately fatal to them as a political party.
- The war produced a hero in Andrew Jackson and a renewed sense of nationalism and confidence throughout the nation.

THE AWAKENING OF AMERICAN NATIONALISM

What were the major developments in domestic and foreign affairs during the "Era of Good Feelings"?

The United States emerged from the War of 1812 bruised but intact. In its first major war since independence, the American republic had demonstrated that it could fight on even terms against a major power and that republics could conduct wars without becoming despotisms. The war also produced several major symbols of American nationalism: the presidential mansion, whitewashed to hide smoke damage, became the White House; Britain's failed attack on Fort McHenry in Baltimore Harbor inspired Francis Scott Key's "Star-Spangled Banner"; and the Battle of New Orleans made Andrew Jackson a national hero and reinforced legends about the prowess of American frontier people and their "long rifles." Much of the legend spun around the Battle of New Orleans was untrue, but Americans loved it nonetheless, especially because it confirmed their conviction that amateur soldiers and militiamen could outfight a professional army.

Madison's Nationalism and the Era of Good Feelings, 1817–1824

The War of 1812 had three major political consequences. First, it eliminated the Federalists as a national political force. Second, it went far toward convincing the Republicans that the nation was strong and resilient, capable of fighting a war while maintaining liberty. Third, with political rivals removed, the Republicans began to embrace some Federalist ideas. Both President Madison and Henry Clay became advocates of federal support for internal improvements, tariff protection for new industries, and the creation of a new national bank; Clay christened these ideas the American System and proclaimed that they would make the nation economically self-sufficient. In 1816 Congress chartered the Second Bank of the United States and enacted a moderate tariff, but federally supported internal improvements were more difficult. Madison vetoed an internal improvements bill in 1817, believing that a constitutional amendment was necessary to authorize such improvements.

As Republicans adopted positions they once had disdained, an **"Era of Good Feelings"** dawned. Coined by a Boston newspaper editor, the term describes both of James Monroe's presidential administrations. Compared to Jefferson and Madison, Monroe was neither brilliant, polished, nor wealthy, but he wanted to heal America's political divisions, and he tried to avoid political controversies. Yet the good feelings were paper-thin, and Madison's veto of the internal improvements bill showed that disagreements lingered about the role of the federal government under the Constitution. The continuation of slavery was arousing sectional animosities that no phrase could paper over. Not surprisingly, the postwar consensus unraveled rapidly.

"Era of Good Feelings" Period of one-party politics during administration of James Monroe

John Marshall and the Supreme Court

In 1819 Jefferson's old antagonist John Marshall, still chief justice, issued two opinions that stunned Republicans. The first case, **Dartmouth College v. Woodward,** focused on New Hampshire's attempt to transform a private corporation, Dartmouth College, into a state university. Marshall concluded that Dartmouth's original charter was a contract and thus was protected under the constitutional prohibition against state interference in contracts. Marshall's ruling had enormous implications. In effect, Marshall said that, once a state had chartered a college or business, that state surrendered its power to alter the charter and, in large measure, its authority to regulate the beneficiary.

Dartmouth College v. Woodward Supreme Court decision that strengthened charters, corporations

A few weeks later, the chief justice handed down an even more momentous decision in **McCulloch v. Maryland.** At issue was whether the state of Maryland had the power to tax a national corporation—specifically, the Baltimore branch of the Second Bank of the United States. Marshall focused on two issues. First, did Congress have the power to charter a national bank? The Constitution, Marshall conceded, did not explicitly grant this power, but the broad sweep of enumerated powers implied the power to charter a bank. This was a clear enunciation of a broad, or "loose," construction (interpretation) of the Constitution. The second issue revolved around whether a state could tax an agency of the federal government that was located within its borders. Marshall argued that any power of the national government, enumerated or implied, was supreme within its sphere. States could not interfere with the exercise of federal power; thus Maryland's attempt to tax the bank was plainly unconstitutional.

McCulloch v. Maryland Supreme Court decision that bolstered broad construction; restated national supremacy over states

The *McCulloch* decision dismayed many Republicans. The bank, initially supported by Madison and Monroe, had triggered the Panic of 1819 by tightening credit. Distressed western farmers angrily blamed the bank for their dilemmas. And now Marshall's decision placed the hated bank beyond the reach of any state government. The Constitution, Marshall said, was the creation not of state governments but of the people of *all* the states and thus overrode state laws. The decision was as much an attack on state sovereignty as a defense of the bank itself.

Like Jefferson, most Republicans considered the Union a compact among states and saw state governments as the guarantors of popular liberty. In Republican eyes, the *Dartmouth* and *McCulloch* cases stripped state governments of the power to impose the will of their people on corporations and thus threatened liberty.

The Missouri Compromise, 1820–1821

The controversy over statehood for Missouri highlighted the fragility of the Era of Good Feelings. Carved from the Louisiana Purchase, Missouri had attracted many southerners who expected to use slaves to grow cotton and hemp. By 1819 slaves made up 16 percent of the territory's inhabitants.

Interactive Map: Missouri Compromise, 1820–1821

In February 1819 the House of Representatives considered a bill to admit Missouri as a slave state. A New York Republican offered an amendment that prohibited the further introduction of slaves into Missouri and provided for the emancipation, at age twenty-five, of all slave offspring born after Missouri joined the Union. Following rancorous debate, the House accepted the amendment and the Senate rejected it. Both chambers voted along sectional lines.

Before this, slavery had not been a major source of the nation's sectional divisions, which tended to pit New England against the South and West. But the Missouri

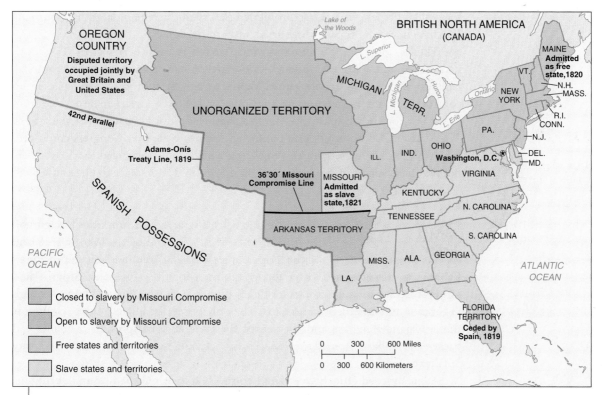

Map 8.3   The Missouri Compromise, 1820–1821

The Missouri Compromise temporarily quelled controversy over slavery by admitting Maine as a free state and Missouri as a slave state and by prohibiting slavery in the remainder of the Louisiana Purchase north of 36°30'.

question, which Jefferson called "a fire bell in the night [which] awakened me and filled me with terror," thrust slavery into the center of long-standing national divisions.

Several factors drove the slavery issue to the forefront. In 1819 the Union had eleven free and eleven slave states; the admission of Missouri would upset this balance to the advantage of the South. Equally important, northerners worried that admitting Missouri as a slave state would set a precedent for the extension of slavery into the northern part of the Purchase. The slave states of Alabama, Mississippi, and Louisiana, already carved from the Purchase with little controversy, were south of Missouri, which was on the same latitude as the free states of Ohio, Indiana, and Illinois. Finally, the disintegration of the Federalists as a national force reduced the need for unity among Republicans, leaving the room to heed sectional pressures more than calls for party loyalty.

Virtually every issue that would wrack the Union in the next forty years was present in the Missouri controversy: southern charges that the North was conspiring to destroy the Union and to end slavery; northern accusations that southerners were conspiring to extend slavery. For a while, leaders doubted that the Union would survive the crisis; the words *disunion* and *civil war* were freely uttered, Henry Clay wrote.

Missouri Compromise An attempt to end slavery controversy by bringing Missouri and Maine into Union, drawing line limiting slavery across the Louisiana Purchase

A series of congressional agreements known collectively as the **Missouri Compromise** resolved the crisis. To balance the number of slave states and free states, Congress in 1820 admitted Maine as a free state and Missouri as a slave state; to forestall a further crisis, it also prohibited slavery in the remainder of the Louisiana Purchase north of 36°30′, Missouri's southern border.

The Missouri Compromise was widely viewed as a southern victory. The South had gained admission of Missouri, whose acceptance of slavery was controversial, while the North had merely gained Maine, whose rejection of slavery sparked no controversy. But at the same time, the South had allowed slavery to be banned from a vast territory north of 36°30′, an area that would not long remain a wilderness. The Missouri Compromise also reinforced the principle that Congress could prohibit slavery in some territories. Southerners had implicitly agreed that slaves were not like other forms of property that could be moved from place to place at will.

Foreign Policy Under Monroe

"Good feelings" also characterized American foreign policy from 1816 to 1824. The end of the War of 1812 and of the Napoleonic Wars had removed most Federalist-Republican disagreements over foreign policy. Moreover, President Monroe had as his secretary of state an extraordinary diplomat, John Quincy Adams, a tough negotiator and an ardent nationalist. The only Federalist in the Senate to support the Louisiana Purchase and the son of the last Federalist president, Adams had backed the embargo, joined the Republican party, and helped to negotiate the Treaty of Ghent.

Adams moved quickly to strengthen the peace with Great Britain. During his term the Rush-Bagot Treaty of 1817 demilitarized the Great Lakes, and the British-American Convention of 1818 fixed the Canadian-American boundary and restored U.S. fishing rights off Newfoundland. With its northern border secure, the United States could turn its attention southward and westward.

Adams was equally successful with the Spanish, who still owned East Florida and claimed West Florida. It had never been clear whether the Louisiana Purchase included West Florida. Acting as if it did, the United States in 1812 had simply added a slice of West Florida to the state of Louisiana and another piece to the Mississippi Territory. Using the pretext that it was a base for Seminole Indian raids and a refuge for fugitive slaves, Andrew Jackson, now a military commander in the South, invaded West Florida in 1818, hanged two British subjects, and captured Spanish forts. Although Jackson had acted without explicit orders, Adams supported the raid, guessing correctly that it would panic the Spanish into further concessions. In 1819 Spain agreed to the Adams-Onís (or Transcontinental) Treaty, ceding East Florida to the United States, renouncing all claims to West Florida, and agreeing to a border that ran north along the Sabine River (separating Spanish Texas from Louisiana), then west along the Red and Arkansas rivers to the Rockies, and then along the forty-second parallel to the Pacific. Finally, the United States had a legitimate claim to the Pacific coast.

The Monroe Doctrine, 1823

John Quincy Adams believed that God and nature had ordained that the United States would eventually span the entire continent of North America. While negotiating the purchase of Florida, he made it clear to Spain that the United States might seize what it could not purchase—including Texas and Mexico. Besides, Spain had other concerns, primarily anticolonial revolutions that had erupted in South America. However, Britain's foreign minister, George Canning, proposed a joint U.S.-British statement opposing European interference in South America and pledging that neither nation would annex any part of Spain's New World empire.

Adams shared Canning's opposition to European intervention in the New World but rejected his insistence on a joint Anglo-American pledge never to annex any of Spain's former territories. Adams wanted the United States to declare policy on its own rather than "come in as a cock boat in the wake of the British man-of-war." In addition, the American secretary of state wanted to keep open the possibility of annexing Texas or Cuba.

This was the background of the **Monroe Doctrine,** as President Monroe's message to Congress on December 2, 1823, became known. Written largely by Adams, the message announced three key principles: that U.S. policy was to avoid European wars unless American interests were involved, that the "American continents" were not "subjects for future colonization by any European power," and that the United States would construe any European attempt at colonization as an "unfriendly act."

Europeans widely derided the Monroe Doctrine as a unilateral pronouncement by a United States that could not enforce it. Fear of Britain's Royal Navy, not the Monroe Doctrine, prevented European intervention in South America. Nonetheless, the doctrine had two major implications. First, in pledging not to interfere in European wars, the United States in effect declined to support any future revolutionary movements in Europe. Second, by keeping open options to annex territory in the Americas itself, the United States was claiming for itself a preeminent position in the New World.

Primary Source:
Monroe Doctrine

Monroe Doctrine Statement that proclaimed U.S. primacy in the New World

CHECKING IN

- As the Federalist party faded as a national force, Monroe's years in the White House became known as the Era of Good Feelings.

- John Marshall's Supreme Court strengthened the power of the central government with critical rulings on the nature of charters, the use of implied powers, and the limits of state power.

- The Missouri Compromise showed how dangerous the issue of slavery was.

- Through a series of treaties, the United States consolidated its northern and southern borders.

- Although derided by other nations, the Monroe Doctrine represented a major step toward American domination of the Western Hemisphere.

Chapter Summary

 DOWNLOAD THE MP3 AUDIO FILE OF THE CHAPTER SUMMARY, AND LISTEN TO IT ON THE GO.

How did Jefferson's philosophy shape policy toward public expenditures, the judiciary, and Louisiana? (page 171)

Jefferson brought with him to the White House a well-defined set of ideas about the necessity for tightly controlled central government, payment of the national debt, and downsizing the American military. Nonetheless, when offered the chance to buy Louisiana, an action not specified in the Constitution, Jefferson eagerly jumped at the chance to rid the New World of France. His sponsorship of the Lewis and Clark expedition exemplified his interest in science and his hope for practical results from science.

How did the United States slide into war with Great Britain? (page 177)

Despite the success of his first term, Jefferson struggled throughout his second term. He faced problems with both Aaron Burr and John Randolph, and saw relations with Great Britain steadily worsen. His attempts at "peaceable coercion" were fruitless, and "war hawks" from the western states became increasingly vocal and powerful. James Madison, Jefferson's successor, saw Britain as a continuing threat to the United States; his declaration of war was based much more on that long-term fear than on short-term problems such as impressment.

What were the most important consequences of the War of 1812? (page 184)

The War of 1812 saw few American successes, but in the Treaty of Ghent, Great Britain essentially restored the *status quo ante bellum*. Nonetheless, the war produced at least one major hero, Andrew Jackson, and spawned a renewed sense of confidence and nationalism. With the Federalist party evaporating as a political force, the nation entered what was known as the "Era of Good Feelings."

What were the major developments in domestic and foreign affairs during the "Era of Good Feelings"? (page 187)

During the Monroe administration, the United States consolidated its northern and southern borders, saw a broad interpretation of the Constitution put in place by the Marshall court, and confronted and then dodged the issue of slavery with the Missouri Compromise. Finally, the Monroe Doctrine represented a major step toward American domination of the Western Hemisphere.

CHAPTER 9

The Transformation of American Society

1815–1840

Woolen Mills, Lowell, c. 1840

Alexis de Tocqueville Young Frenchman whose *Democracy in America* provides rich insight into the United States in the 1830s

This icon will direct you to the website where you can Prepare for Class, Improve Your Grade, and Ace the Test: **www.cengage.com/history/boyer/ enduringconcise6e**

CHAPTER PREVIEW

Westward Expansion
What caused the surge of westward migration after the War of 1812?

The Growth of the Market Economy
What changes were linked to the rise of the market economy?

Industrial Beginnings
Why did industrialization begin to take hold?

Equality and Inequality
In what ways did inequality actually increase?

The Revolution in Social Relationships
How did the rise of the market economy and industrialization change relationships within families and communities?

The years 1815 to 1840 saw rapid, often disorienting changes that affected both those who followed the frontier westward and those who stayed in the East. Viewed superficially, these changes might seem to have had little effect on the way Americans lived. Whether in 1815 or in 1840, most Americans dwelled outside the cities, practiced agriculture for a living, and traveled on foot or by horse. In 1831 two young Frenchmen, **Alexis de Tocqueville** (duh TOKE-vill) and Gustave de Beaumont (BOH-mont), arrived in the United States wanting to learn as much as they could about the "half-civilized, half-wild" American republic. Tocqueville's two-volume *Democracy in America*, published in 1835 and 1840, is still considered a masterpiece of insight into the American character.

Tocqueville and Beaumont had come at a time when everything seemed to be changing for these restless Americans who appeared to live in the middle of "an always moving stream." Improvements in transportation were stimulating inter-regional trade and migration to the trans-Appalachian west, encouraging an unprecedented development of towns and cities, and transforming social relationships. Farmers increasingly raised crops to sell in distant markets, while the new urban dwellers formed a market for farm products as well as the products of the new factories that were springing up in the industrializing East.

To Tocqueville, Americans seemed to have only one goal: "that of getting rich." White Americans were an industrious and democratic people, but they treated non-whites harshly. While recognizing slavery as a blot on American society, Tocqueville noted that whites treated one another as equals and that they all shared a passion for getting ahead.

WESTWARD EXPANSION

What caused the surge of westward migration after the War of 1812?

In 1790 the vast majority of the non-Indian population of the United States lived east of the Appalachian Mountains; by 1840 one-third were living between the Appalachians and the Mississippi River, defined as the West. These Americans rapidly developed a distinctive western culture.

Most Americans came west dreaming of a better version of the life they had known in the East. Several factors fed this dream: the growing power of the federal government, its often-ruthless removal of Indians from the path of white settlements, and a boom in the prices of agricultural commodities.

The Sweep West

This westward movement occurred in several thrusts. Americans leapfrogged the Appalachians after 1791 to bring four new states into the Union by 1803: Vermont, Kentucky, Tennessee, and Ohio. From 1816 to 1821 momentum carried settlers farther west, even across the Mississippi River, and six more states entered: Indiana, Mississippi, Illinois, Alabama, Maine, and Missouri. Ohio's population soared from 45,000 in 1800 to more than 1.5 million by 1840, and Michigan's from 5,000 in 1810 to 212,000 in 1840.

Pioneers usually migrated as families. To get their crops to market, at first most clustered along the Ohio-Mississippi river system. Only when canals spread in the 1820s and 1830s did they venture any distance from rivers. In addition, pioneers often clustered with people who hailed from the same region back east. For example, when New Englanders found southerners already well entrenched in Indiana, they chose to settle in Michigan.

Western Society and Customs

These new westerners craved sociability. Even before towns sprang up, farm families joined their neighbors for sports and festivities. Men met for games that tested strength and agility: wrestling, lifting weights, pole jumping (for distance, not height), and

Chronology

1790	Samuel Slater opens his first Rhode Island mill
1793	Eli Whitney invents the cotton gin
1807	Robert R. Livingston and Robert Fulton introduce the steamboat *Clermont* on the Hudson River
1811	Construction of the National Road begins at Cumberland, Maryland
1813	Establishment of the Boston Manufacturing Company
1816	Second Bank of the United States chartered
1817	Construction of the Erie Canal started; Mississippi enters the Union
1819	Economic panic, ushering in four-year depression; Alabama enters the Union
1820–1850	Growth of female moral-reform societies
1820s	Expansion of New England textile mills
1824	*Gibbons v. Ogden*
1828	Baltimore and Ohio Railroad chartered
1830	Indian Removal Act passed by Congress
1831	*Cherokee Nation v. Georgia;* Alexis de Tocqueville begins visit to the United States
1832	*Worcester v. Georgia*
1834	First strike at the Lowell mills
1835–1838	Trail of Tears
1837	Economic panic begins a depression that lasts until 1843
1840	System of production by interchangeable parts perfected

hammer throwing. Women usually combined work and play in quilting and sewing bees, carpet tackings, and even goose and chicken pluckings. At "hoe-downs" and "frolics," the settlers danced to a fiddler's tune.

Western farm households usually practiced a clear gender division of labor. Men performed the heavy work, such as cutting down trees and plowing fields. Women cooked, spun and wove, and tended their large families. They also often helped with the butchering, scooping out the innards, and hanging hearts and livers to dry. There was nothing dainty about the work of pioneer women.

Most western sports and customs were eastern transplants, but the West developed a character of its own. Eastern elegance yielded to western lack of refinement—and made westerners targets for easterners' contemptuous jibes.

Westerners responded that at least they were honest democrats, not soft would-be aristocrats. Pretension got short shrift. A sojourner at a tavern who hung a blanket to cover his bed from public gaze might find it ripped down; a woman who sought privacy in a crowded room might be dismissed as "stuck up."

The Far West

Exploration carried some Americans even farther west. Zebulon Pike explored the Spanish Southwest in 1806. By 1811, in the wake of Lewis and Clark, the New York merchant John Jacob Astor had founded a fur-trading post at the mouth of the Columbia

River in the Oregon Country. At first, whites relied on the Native Americans for furs, but in the 1820s such "mountain men" as Kit Carson and Jedediah Smith penetrated deep beyond the Rockies.

Smith typified these men and their exploits. Originally from western New York, he had moved west as far as Illinois by 1822. That year he signed on with an expedition bound for the upper Missouri River. In the course of this and later explorations, Smith nearly fell victim to a grizzly bear in South Dakota's Black Hills, crossed the Mojave Desert into California and explored the San Joaquin Valley, and hiked back across the Sierras and the Great Basin to the Great Salt Lake, a forbidding trip. His thirst for adventure led to his death just before his thirty-third birthday at the hands of Comanche Indians. Biographies popularized the exploits of Smith and other mountain men, transforming them into legends in their own day.

The Federal Government and the West

The federal government's growing strength spurred westward expansion. Under the Articles of Confederation, several states had ceded western lands to the national government, creating a bountiful public domain. The Louisiana Purchase had brought the entire Mississippi River under American control. Six million acres of public land had been promised to volunteers during the War of 1812. The **National Road,** a highway begun in 1811 in Cumberland, Maryland, stretched farther westward, reaching Wheeling, Virginia, in 1818 and Vandalia, Illinois, by 1838. People crowded along it.

National Road Federally sponsored highway that crossed the Appalachians and opened the way for families to move west

The same governmental strength that aided whites brought misery to the Indians. Virtually all the foreign policy successes of the Republicans worked to the Native Americans' disadvantage. The Louisiana Purchase and the Adams-Onís Treaty had stripped them of Spanish protection.

Lewis and Clark bluntly told the Indians that they must "shut their ears to the counsels of bad birds" and listen only to the "Great Father" in Washington. The American victory in the War of 1812 deprived the tribes of British protection. Early in the negotiations leading to the Treaty of Ghent, the British had insisted on the creation of an Indian buffer state in the Old Northwest, but they later dropped this demand and abandoned the Indians to their fate.

The Removal of the Indians

Westward-moving white settlers found in their path sizable numbers of Native Americans, especially in the South, home to the **"Five Civilized Tribes"**—the Cherokees, Creeks, Choctaws, Chickasaws, and Seminoles. Years of commercial dealings and intermarriage with Europeans had created in these tribes influential minorities of mixed-bloods who had embraced Christianity and agriculture. The Cherokees had adopted Anglo-American culture to a greater extent than any other tribe. Among them were farmers, millers, and even slave owners; they also had a written form of their language, written laws, and their own bilingual newspaper, the *Cherokee Phoenix.*

"Five Civilized Tribes" Once-powerful southeastern Indians "removed" in 1830s to make way for white settlement

Primary Source: Three Celebrated Ball Players— Choctaw, Sioux, and Ojibbeway

Such "civilization" made little impression on southern whites, who viewed the Civilized Tribes with contempt and their lands with envy. A handful of tribes had sold their lands to the federal government and accepted removal west of the Missis-

Map 9.1   The Removal of the Native Americans to the West, 1820–1840
The so-called Trail of Tears, followed by the Cherokees, was one of several routes along which various tribes migrated on their forced removal to reservations west of the Mississippi.

sippi River by 1830, but most clung to their land and customs. When the Creek mixed-blood chief William McIntosh sold most of the Indians' land to the federal government, the tribal council executed him.

In the 1820s white squatters moved onto tribal lands; southern legislatures, loath to restrain white settlers, moved to expropriate Indian lands. State laws extended state jurisdiction over the tribes and excluded Indians from serving as witnesses in court cases involving whites, which effectively made it virtually impossible for Indians to collect debts owed them by whites.

President Andrew Jackson relished such measures. Himself a frontiersman contemptuous of Native Americans, Jackson believed that the tribes must be subject to the laws of the states, not exist as independent nations. Jackson's belief spelled doom for the Indians, who could neither vote nor hold office. In 1834 Cherokee chief John Ross got a taste of what state jurisdiction meant: Georgia, without consulting him, put his house up as a prize in the state lottery.

In 1830 President Jackson secured passage of the Indian Removal Act, authorizing him to exchange western territory for tribal lands. Thus, during Jackson's eight years in office, the federal government forced Indians to exchange 100 million acres of their eastern lands for 32 million acres of public lands. The Choctaws, Creeks, and Chickasaws began their "voluntary" migration in the late 1820s. In 1836 Creeks who clung to their homes were forcibly removed, often in chains. The bitter war to remove the Seminoles from their Florida lands lasted seven years and cost the federal government $20 million.

Trail of Tears, by Robert Lindneux

Cherokee Nation v. Georgia
Supreme Court decision recognizing Cherokees' claim to their lands; ignored by President Jackson

Worcester v. Georgia Court decision declaring Cherokees entitled to federal protection; ignored by President Jackson

Trail of Tears The death of one-third or more of the Cherokee tribe upon their "removal" to the West

Ironically, the Cherokees, often considered the "most civilized" tribe, suffered the most. Pursuing their claims before the Supreme Court, they won two favorable decisions from Chief Justice John Marshall. In ***Cherokee Nation* v. *Georgia*** (1831), Marshall recognized the Cherokees as a "domestic dependent nation" with a legitimate claim to their lands in Georgia. A year later, in ***Worcester* v. *Georgia*,** Marshall declared them a "distinct" political community entitled to federal protection against Georgia's claims.

President Andrew Jackson reportedly sneered, "John Marshall has made his decision; now let him enforce it" and ignored the ruling. Then in 1835 the U.S. government negotiated the fraudulent Treaty of New Echota with a handful of unauthorized individuals. It ceded most remaining Cherokee lands to the United States for $5.6 million and the Indians' transportation west. The principal signers were killed by other Cherokees in 1839, but by then the tribe's fate was sealed. Sixteen thousand Cherokees straggled west to the Indian Territory between 1835 and 1838 along the so-called **Trail of Tears.** A total of perhaps eight thousand died during and immediately after the hard journey.

Indians in the Northwest Territory fared no better after they signed land-cession treaties. Two uprisings marked their westward removal. The first was quickly crushed, but the second, led by a Sac and Fox chief, Black Hawk, raged along the frontier in Illinois until federal troops and state militiamen virtually annihilated the Indians in 1832. After Black Hawk's defeat, the other northwestern tribes agreed to removal. Between 1832 and 1837 the United States consequently acquired nearly 190 million acres of Indian land in the Northwest for $70 million.

The Agricultural Boom

In clearing the Indians from their territory, the federal government was responding to whites' pressures for land. Depleted soil and overcrowding had long driven farmers west, but after the War of 1812 soaring agricultural commodity prices and rising demand for western foodstuffs sharpened the land hunger. England and France, exhausted by war, were importing substantial amounts of American wheat and corn; New England needed food for its burgeoning industrial population. In short, federal Indian policy, although devastating to Native Americans, made farming possible in the West, and high prices and high demand made it attractive.

Cotton and Eli Whitney's cotton gin provided the impetus for settlement of the Old Southwest, especially Alabama and Mississippi. Indeed, the explosive westward thrust of southern farmers and planters after the War of 1812 resembled a gold rush. By 1817 land prices had shot up from $30 to $50 an acre. By 1820 Alabama and Mississippi produced half the nation's cotton. With a seemingly unlimited British market for raw cotton, production tripled between 1816 and 1831. Between 1831 and 1836 the value of cotton exports rose 300 percent, and cotton accounted for two-thirds of U.S. exports.

CHECKING IN

- The War of 1812 opened the way for several thrusts of westward migration that carried the American population across the Mississippi River.
- Western society evolved its own set of values and prided itself on its democratic nature.
- Expansion multiplied the problems of Native Americans, culminating in the "removal" of tribes in the Southeast and the Old Northwest.
- An agricultural boom fueled the drive west.
- In the South, the cotton gin combined with rich western lands to create a huge surge in cotton production and export.

THE GROWTH OF THE MARKET ECONOMY

What changes were linked to the rise of the market economy?

The high prices of agricultural commodities, such as wheat and cotton, tempted a growing number of farmers to add a cash crop, thus venturing into commercial agriculture or the **market economy.** In the South, the sale of slaves from older states to the new Cotton Belt accelerated rapidly after 1815. However, farmers often launched into the market economy without weighing the risks.

The new commercial farmers encountered serious problems, including wildly fluctuating markets. They also routinely had to borrow money to cover the long interval between harvest and sale of commercial crops. This debt was frequently worse than expected, particularly because many western farmers had also borrowed money to buy their land. The root of this indebtedness was the federal government's inability to transfer the public domain directly to small farmers.

market economy Newly developing commercial economy that depended on goods and crops produced for sale rather than consumption

Federal Land Policy

Federal land policy floundered in this period. In the face of partisan and sectional pressures, the federal government passed various land laws in quick succession, each intended to undo the damage caused by its predecessors.

The Ordinance of 1785 had aimed to ensure the orderly settlement of the public domain by creating townships of 36 square miles, divided into 640-acre sections. Ordinary farmers could not afford such large purchases, but it was assumed that they would pool their money to buy sections. Federalists, with their political base in the East, were reluctant to encourage western settlement but were eager to sell land to raise revenue for the government. They reconciled their conflicting goals by selling huge tracts of land to speculators who waited for its value to rise and then sold off parcels to farmers. By 1796 the minimum purchase was 640 acres at $2 an acre.

Jefferson and the Republicans, sure that the small farmer was the backbone of the

Republic, took a different tack. The land law of 1800 dropped the minimum purchase to 320 acres. By 1832 the minimum purchase had shrunk to 40 acres and the price to $1.25 an acre. Long before then, speculators were already selling land in 40-acre parcels, a size that the small farmer could handle both financially and physically.

The growing availability of credit after the War of 1812 fed speculation. The chartering of the Second Bank of the United States in 1816 increased the amount of money in circulation and stimulated the growth of state banks. Between 1812 and 1817, bank notes in circulation soared from $45 million to $100 million. Stockholders and officers saw banks less as investments than as agencies that could lend them money for land speculation. The result was an orgy of speculation; by 1819 the dollar value of sales of public lands was more than 1,000 percent greater than the average from 1800 to 1814.

The Speculator and the Squatter

Despite these problems, most of the public domain found its way into the hands of small farmers. The desire to recoup investments led speculators to sell quickly, as did the proliferation of squatters.

Squatters had long helped themselves to western land. Proud and independent, they hated land speculators and pressured Congress to allow "preemption" rights—that is, the right to purchase at the minimum price the land that they already lived on and had improved. After passing a series of limited preemption laws, Congress acknowledged a general right of preemption in 1841.

But for farmers who had to purchase land from speculators, interest rates ranged as high as 40 percent. Many western farmers, drowning in debt, had to skimp on food and plant cash crops in the hope of paying off creditors. Having moved west to fulfill dreams of self-sufficiency, they found themselves caught in the cash-crop economy, which quickly exhausted their soil and forced them to move farther westward in search of new land. The phrase "the moving frontier" refers not only to the obvious fact that the line of settlement shifted farther west with each passing decade, but also to the fact that the same people kept moving, chasing their elusive dreams. Typical was Abraham Lincoln's family, who migrated from the East through several farms in Kentucky and then on to Indiana.

The Panic of 1819

In 1819 the land boom collapsed, the victim of a financial panic caused in large part by state banks that issued their own bank notes, little more than a promise to pay the bearer a certain amount of specie (gold and silver coin) on demand. These plentiful notes had helped fuel the land boom after 1815. Farmers also borrowed to buy more land and plant more crops, depending on sales to Europe, to enable them to repay loans. But even as they did so, bumper crops in Europe combined with an economic slump in England to trim foreign demand for U.S. crops.

The result was a cascade of economic catastrophes. In the summer of 1819 the Bank of the United States, holding large amounts of state bank paper, began to insist that the state banks redeem this paper in specie. To pay these debts, state banks demanded that farmers and land speculators repay their loans—in specie. Credit contracted sharply throughout the nation, particularly in the West. Prices for commodities like wheat, corn, cotton, and tobacco sank by 50 percent or more. Hard-pressed farmers could not pay their debts, speculators could not collect their money, and land values collapsed from nearly $70 an acre to barely $2.

The significance of the Panic lay not only in its economic bite but also in the conclusions many Americans reached. First, the Panic left a bitter taste about banks, especially the Bank of the United States, widely blamed for the crash. Second, it demonstrated how dependent farmers had become on distant markets and the extent to which farmers had become entrepreneurs. This in turn accelerated the search for better, cheaper ways to get crops to market.

The Transportation Revolution: Steamboats, Canals, and Railroads

The transportation systems available in 1820 had serious weaknesses. The great rivers west of the Appalachians ran primarily north to south and hence could not by themselves connect western farmers to eastern markets. Roads were expensive to maintain, and horse-drawn wagons were slow and limited in range. Consequently, after 1820 attention and investment shifted to the development of waterways, beginning what became known as the **Transportation Revolution.**

In 1807 Robert R. Livingston and Robert Fulton introduced the steamboat *Clermont* on the Hudson River. They soon gained a monopoly from the New York legislature to run a New York–New Jersey ferry service. Spectacular profits lured competitors, who secured a license from Congress and then filed suit to break the Livingston-Fulton monopoly. In 1824 Chief Justice John Marshall, in *Gibbons* v. *Ogden,* ruled that Article I, Section 8, of the Constitution, which empowered Congress to regulate interstate commerce, applied to navigation as well. In this case, he wrote, the power of Congress to regulate interstate commerce had to prevail over the power of New York; thus the Livingston-Fulton monopoly was void. In the aftermath of this decision, other state-granted monopolies collapsed and steamboat traffic increased rapidly. The number of steamboats operating on western rivers jumped from 17 in 1817 to 727 by 1855.

Steamboats assumed a vital role along the Mississippi-Ohio river system. They were far more useful than rafts, which journeyed only one way, or keelboats, which took up to four months to travel upstream from New Orleans to Louisville; in 1817 a steamboat made the identical trip in just twenty-five days. The development of long, shallow hulls permitted navigation of the Mississippi-Ohio system even when hot, dry summers lowered the river level. Steamboats became more ornate as well as more practical, offering luxurious cabins and lounges, called saloons. For example, the saloon of the *Eclipse,* a Mississippi River steamboat, was the length of a football field and featured skylights, chandeliers, a ceiling crisscrossed with Gothic arches, and velvet upholstered mahogany furniture.

While steamboats proved their value, canals replaced roads and turnpikes as the focus of popular enthusiasm and financial speculation. Although the cost of canal construction was mind-boggling—Jefferson dismissed the idea of canals as "little short of madness"—canals offered the possibility of connecting the Mississippi-Ohio system with the Great Lakes and even the East Coast.

Transportation Revolution Rapid expansion of canals, steamships, and railroads

Clermont First of the steamboats that revolutionized river travel

Map 9.2   Major Rivers, Roads, and Canals, 1825–1860
Railroads and canals increasingly tied the economy of the Midwest to that of the Northeast.

Erie Canal Major canal that linked Great Lakes to New York City, opening upper Midwest to wider development

A canal boom followed the completion in 1825 of the **Erie Canal,** which stretched 363 miles from Buffalo to Albany. For example, Ohio built a network of canals that enabled farmers to ship wheat by water to Lake Erie; the wheat was then shipped to Rochester for milling and finally traveled via the Erie Canal and the Hudson River to New York City. Shipping costs via the canal network were 10 percent of costs via road.

***Erie Canal,* by John William Hill, 1831**
Construction of the Erie Canal was a remarkable feat, all the more so because the United States did not have any engineering school at the time. The project's heroes were lawyers and merchants who taught themselves engineering and brawny workmen, often Irish immigrants, who hacked a waterway through the forests and valleys of New York.

Railroads were soon competing with canals and gradually overtook them. In 1825 the first railroad for general transportation began operation in England. The new technology quickly reached the United States, and by 1840 there were 3,000 miles of railroad track, equal to the total canal mileage. Faster, cheaper to build, and able to reach more places, railroads enjoyed obvious advantages over canals, but Americans realized their potential only slowly.

Early railroads connected eastern cities rather than crossing the mountains and carried more passengers than freight. Not until 1849 did freight revenue exceed passenger revenue, and not until 1850 did railroads link the East Coast to Lake Erie. There were two main reasons for this slow pace of development. First, unlike canals, most railroads were built by private companies that tended to skimp on costs, and as a result produced lines requiring constant repair. In contrast, canals needed little maintenance. Second, shipping bulky commodities, such as iron, coal, and grain, was cheaper by canal than by rail.

The Growth of the Cities

The transportation revolution accelerated the growth of towns and cities. Indeed, the forty years before the Civil War, 1820 to 1860, saw the most rapid urbanization in U.S. history. By 1860 New York City's population had rocketed from 124,000 to 800,000. Even more spectacular was the transformation of sleepy villages into bustling towns.

Urban growth was particularly fast in the West. The War of 1812 stimulated manufacturing and transformed villages into towns, as did the agricultural boom and the introduction of steamboats after 1815. Virtually all the major western cities were river ports. Of these, Pittsburgh, Cincinnati, Louisville, and New Orleans were the most prominent. Pittsburgh was a manufacturing center, but the others were commercial hubs flooded by people eager to make money.

CHECKING IN

- For farmers, the market economy was alluring but risky.
- Federal land policy was aimed at small farmers but helped feed a speculative boom.
- When the speculative bubble burst, the Panic of 1819 created economic havoc and intensified the American distrust of banks.
- The transportation revolution—steamboats, canals, and railroads—played a major role in westward expansion.
- Western cities mushroomed, first along rivers and then on the Great Lakes.

Interactive Map: Major American Cities in 1830 and 1860

What the transportation revolution gave, it could also take away. The completion of the Erie Canal gradually shifted the center of western economic activity away from the river cities and toward the Great Lakes; Buffalo, Cleveland, Detroit, Chicago, and Milwaukee were the ultimate beneficiaries of the canal. In 1830 nearly 75 percent of western city dwellers lived in the river ports of New Orleans, Louisville, Cincinnati, and Pittsburgh, but by 1840 the proportion had dropped to 20 percent. The advent of modern manufacturing would multiply the effect of the transportation revolution on the growth of cities.

INDUSTRIAL BEGINNINGS

Why did industrialization begin to take hold?

Industrialization gave an added boost to the growth of cities and towns. In any way possible, Americans sought to counter Britain's full-generation lead in building factories; Britain in turn banned the emigration of its skilled mechanics. However, one of those mechanics, **Samuel Slater,** was able to reach the United States in 1789. He helped design and build the first cotton mill in the United States the following year. The mill's work force mushroomed from nine to one hundred, and his mills multiplied. The pace of industrialization quickened in the 1810s and 1820s, especially in cotton textiles and shoes.

Samuel Slater British "mechanic" who carried plans for textile mill to United States; began American textile industry

Industrialization was uneven. There was little in the South, where planters preferred to invest in land and slaves, and much in New England, where poor soil made agriculture an even poorer investment. Generally, industrialization involved three steps: the subdivision of tasks, the gathering of workers in large factories, and the use of high-speed machines to replace handwork.

Industrialization changed lives. Many benefited from industrialization as former luxury goods became cheaper. And while cheap machine-made goods brought luxuries within the reach of working people, they also undermined skilled artisans. Most early factory workers were recruited from farms, where they had set their own pace and taken breaks as tasks were completed. In contrast, machines and the clock dictated the factory worker's pace. Finally, industrialization led to specialization; farmers could now concentrate on farming and buy clothes, shoes, and other products they had previously made.

Causes of Industrialization

Multiple factors stimulated industrialization. Merchants barred from foreign trade by the Embargo Act of 1807 redirected their capital into factories. After the War of 1812, acceptance of tariffs was widespread. Protected from foreign competition, New England's textile output rose from 4 million yards in 1817 to 323 million yards by 1840. And the transportation revolution gave manufacturers easier access to markets in the South and West.

Problems in New England's rural economy also stimulated industrialization. Many farm families had always engaged in small-scale manufacturing, and many of these gradually deserted farming worn-out soils for full-time manufacturing.

Technology played a major role. Lacking craft organizations that tied artisans to a single trade, Americans could freely experiment with machines outside their own craft. Americans also improved on foreign ideas and techniques. For example, in 1798 Eli Whitney, inventor of the cotton gin, gained a government contract to produce ten thousand muskets within a two-year period by using interchangeable parts, an idea originally developed in France. Although Whitney missed his deadline by more than a decade, his idea captured the imagination of many American leaders and foreshadowed the rise of a full-scale industrial economy.

Textile Towns in New England

New England became America's first industrial region. The trade wars leading up to the War of 1812 had devastated the Northeast's traditional economy and stimulated capital investment in manufacturing. New England's many swift-flowing rivers were ideal sources of waterpower for mills. The westward migration of New England's young men, unable to wrest a living from rocky soil, left a surplus of young women who supplied cheap industrial labor. The establishment of the Boston Manufacturing Company in 1813 opened a new chapter in U.S. manufacturing. Backed by ample capital, the Boston Company built textile mills in the Massachusetts towns of **Lowell** and **Waltham;** by 1836 the company employed more than six thousand workers.

Lowell, Waltham Massachusetts towns where two large textile mills were established as early experiments in factory manufacturing

Unlike Slater's mills, the Waltham and Lowell factories turned out more finished products, thus elbowing aside Slater's cottage industry. Slater had tried to preserve tradition by hiring entire families to work at his mills—the men to raise crops, the women and children to toil in the mills. In contrast, 80 percent of the workers in the Lowell and Waltham mills were unmarried women fifteen to thirty years old. Hired managers and company regulations, rather than families, provided discipline. Workers had to live in company boarding houses or approved private homes, attend Sabbath services, observe a 10:00 p.m. curfew, and accept the company's "moral police." These regulations were designed to give mills a good reputation so that families would continue to send their daughters to work there.

Mill Girl Around 1850
This girl mostly likely worked in a Massachusetts textile mill, at either Lowell or Waltham. Her swollen and rough hands suggest that she was a "warper," one of the jobs usually given to children. Warpers were responsible for constantly straightening out the strands of cotton or wool as they entered the loom.

Conditions in the mills were dreadful. To prevent threads from snapping, the factories had to be kept humid; windows were nailed shut, and water was sprayed in the air. Flying dust and deafening noise were constant companions. In the 1830s conditions worsened, as competition and recession led mill owners to reduce wages and speed up work schedules. The system's impersonality intensified the harshness of the work environment. Owners rarely visited factories; their agents, all men, gave orders to the workers, mainly women. In 1834 and again in 1836, women at the Lowell mills quit work to protest low wages. The largest strikes in American history to that point, they not only pitted workers against management but also women against men.

The size of the mills was not typical of industrial development in this era; as late as 1860, the average industrial establishment employed only eight workers. "Outwork" characterized most industries other than textiles. For example, prior to the introduction of sewing machines in the 1850s, women often sewed parts of shoes at home and then sent the piecework to factories for finishing.

CHECKING IN

- Multiple factors stimulated industrialization, including protective tariffs, available capital, and advances in technology.
- Textile mills made New England America's first industrial region.
- Mills like those at Waltham and Lowell relied heavily on the labor of young women.
- "Outwork" dominated early industrialization outside the textile industry.
- Industrialization brought mixed results; as many workers' economic position deteriorated, new questions arose about equality in the United States.

Artisans and Workers in Mid-Atlantic Cities

The skilled artisans of New York City and Philadelphia tried to protect their interests by forming trade unions and "workingmen's" political parties. Initially, they sought to restore privileges and working conditions that artisans had once enjoyed, but gradually they joined forces with unskilled workers. When coal heavers in Philadelphia struck for a ten-hour day in 1835, carpenters, cigar makers, leather workers, and other artisans joined in what became the first general strike in the United States. The emergence of organized worker protests underscored the mixed blessings of economic development. Whereas some people prospered, others found their economic position deteriorating. By 1830 many Americans were questioning whether their nation was truly a land of equality.

EQUALITY AND INEQUALITY

In what ways did inequality actually increase?

That one (white) man was as good as another became the national creed in Antebellum (pre-Civil War) America. Servants insisted on being called the "help," not permanent subordinates. Merchants bowed to no one. Politicians never lost an opportunity to proclaim artisans and farmers the equal of lawyers and bankers.

However, the market and transportation revolutions were placing new pressure on the idea of equality. At the same time that improved transportation enabled some eastern farmers to migrate to the richer soils of the West, it became more difficult for those left behind to compete with the cheaper grain now carried east by canals and railroads. Many eastern farmers had to move to cities to take whatever work they could find, often as casual day laborers on the docks or in small workshops. Their willingness to work for low wages undercut the position of skilled artisans. Even as he believed that the wide distribution of land and individuals' insistence on being treated as equals created more real equality in America than in France, Alexis de

Tocqueville worried that the lower classes in the major cities were becoming "a rabble more dangerous even than that of European towns."

Growing Inequality: The Rich and the Poor

The gap between rich and poor continued to widen in the first half of the nineteenth century. Although striking inequalities separated rich and poor farmers, the inequalities were far greater in the cities, where a small fraction of the people owned a huge share of the wealth. In Boston the richest 4 percent of the people owned almost 70 percent of the wealth by 1848, whereas 81 percent of the population owned only 4 percent of the wealth. New York and other major cities mirrored these statistics.

Although commentators celebrated the self-made man and his rise "from rags to riches," few actually fit this pattern. Less than 5 percent of the wealthy had started life poor; almost 90 percent of well-off people had been born rich. Clearly, the old-fashioned way to wealth was to inherit it, to marry more of it, and to invest it wisely. Occasional rags-to-riches stories like that of John Jacob Astor and his fur-trading empire sustained the myth, but it was mainly a myth.

Splendid residences and social clubs also set the rich apart. In New York half the city's wealthy families lived on only eight streets, and they belonged to the same clubs. Tocqueville noted these facts and also observed that the rich feigned respect for equality, at least in public. They rode in ordinary carriages, brushed elbows with the less privileged, and avoided the conspicuous display of wealth that marked their private lives.

At the opposite end of the social ladder were the poor. By today's standards most antebellum Americans were poor; they depended on their children's labor to meet expenses, had little money for medical care or recreation, and suffered frequent unemployment. In 1850 an estimated three out of eight males over twenty owned little more than their clothing. In dealing with economic statistics, it is important to remember that the accumulation of wealth takes place over a lifetime. With its high birthrate, America was a nation of young people with little property. But many of them would gain wealth as they grew older.

Primary Source: Chimney Sweep

Antebellum Americans distinguished between poverty, a common condition, and *pauperism,* which meant both poverty and dependency—the inability to care for oneself. The elderly, the ill, and the widowed often fell into the category of pauperism. Such people were known as the "deserving" poor in contrast to the "undeserving" poor, loafers and drunkards whose poverty was seen as self-willed. Most moralists assumed that since poverty resulted either from circumstances beyond anyone's control, such as age or infirmity, or from voluntary decisions to squander money on alcohol, it would not pass from generation to generation.

It was a comforting but misleading assumption. A class of people who could not escape poverty was emerging in the major cities in the first half of the nineteenth century. One source was immigration. As early as 1801 a New York newspaper bemoaned the arrival of boatloads of immigrants with large families but with neither money nor health.

The poorest white immigrants were from Ireland, where English landlords had evicted peasants from the land in the eighteenth century. These Irish immigrants played key roles in canal construction; others clustered in the Five Points area of New York City, which became the worst slum in America.

As Catholics, the Irish had little appeal to the kindly impulses of American Protestants, but even Protestant poor suffered in the years from 1815 to 1840. As some Americans convinced themselves that success lay within everyone's grasp, they also tended to believe that the poor were responsible for their own poverty. Ironically, even as many Americans blamed the poor for being poor, discrimination mired some groups in enduring poverty. Among the chief victims were northern free blacks.

Free Blacks in the North

Prejudice against African-Americans was deeply ingrained in white society throughout the nation. Although slavery had largely disappeared in the North by 1820, discriminatory laws remained. The voting rights of African-Americans were severely restricted; for example, New York eliminated property requirements for whites but kept them for blacks. There were attempts to bar free blacks from migrating. And segregation prevailed in northern schools, jails, and hospitals. By 1850, blacks could vote on equal terms with whites in only one city, Boston.

Most damaging of all to free blacks was the social pressure that forced them into unskilled, low-paying jobs throughout the northern cities. Although a few free blacks accumulated moderate wealth, free blacks in general were only half as likely as other city dwellers to own real estate.

African Methodist Episcopal Church First American denomination established by and for African-Americans

One important black response to discrimination was the establishment of their own churches. When a group of free blacks was ejected from a Philadelphia church, they ultimately established the first black-run Protestant denomination, the **African Methodist Episcopal Church,** in 1816. The A.M.E. rapidly expanded to encompass a territory bounded by Washington, D.C., Pittsburgh, and New York City. Its members campaigned against slavery, provided education for black children, and formed mutual-aid societies.

Just as northern African-Americans left white churches to form their own, free blacks gradually acquired some control over the education of their children. Northern city governments made little provision for the education of free persons of color, at first leaving northern blacks dependent on the philanthropy of sympathetic whites to educate their children. But the 1820s and 1830s witnessed an explosion of black self-hope societies devoted to encouraging black education and run by graduates of the African Free School.

Richard Allen

First bishop of the African Methodist Episcopal Church, Richard Allen spent much of his time traveling, organizing societies of black Methodists, preaching on Sundays, and cutting wood on other days to earn his living.

The "Middling Classes"

Most antebellum Americans were neither fabulously rich nor grindingly poor but part of the **"middling classes."** Even though the wealthy owned an increasing proportion of wealth, per capita income grew at 1.5 percent annually between 1840 and 1860, and the standard of living generally rose after 1800.

"middling classes" Farmers, artisans, professionals—neither rich nor poor

Americans applied the term *middling classes* to farmers and artisans who held the ideal of self-employment and were considered steady and dependable. Often, however, farmers and artisans led lives considerably less stable than this ideal. Allan Melville, the father of novelist Herman Melville, was an enterprising import merchant who did well until the late 1820s, when his business sagged. By 1830 he was "destitute of resources and without a shilling." Despite loans of $3,500, Melville's downward spiral continued, and he died two years later, broken in spirit.

Artisans shared the perils of life in the middling classes. During the colonial period many had attained the ideal of self-employment, owning their tools, taking orders, making their products, and training their children and apprentices in the craft. By 1850 this self-sufficient artisan class had split into two distinct groups. The few artisans who had access to capital became entrepreneurs who hired journeymen to do the actual work. Without capital, most remained journeymen, working for the artisans-turned-entrepreneurs with little prospect of self-employment.

The emerging middling classes shared with the poor a high degree of transience. Even professionals, such as judges and lawyers, spent part of each year riding from one county courthouse to another. The itinerant clergyman mounted on an old nag and riding the countryside to visit the faithful was a familiar figure.

Transience would affect the lives of most Americans. Farmers exhausted their land by intensive cultivation of cash crops and then moved on. City dwellers moved frequently as they changed jobs—public transportation lagged far behind the spread of the cities. A survey on September 6, 1851, found that on that day 41,729 entered the city of Boston while 42,313 left. Most of these were searching for work, a frequent necessity for the middling classes as well as the poor.

CHECKING IN

- The gap between rich and poor widened, especially in cities.
- Americans generally blamed the poor for being poor.
- Free blacks saw their rights and economic position erode even further.
- The "middling classes" increased, but many did not achieve stability.
- More than ever, transience characterized American society.

THE REVOLUTION IN SOCIAL RELATIONSHIPS

How did the rise of the market economy and industrialization change relationships within families and communities?

Following the War of 1812 the growth of interregional trade, commercial agriculture, and manufacturing disrupted traditional social relationships and forged new ones. Two broad changes took place. First, Americans began to question traditional forms of authority and to embrace individualism; once the term had meant nothing more than selfishness, but now it connoted positive qualities such as self-reliance and the ability of each person to judge his or her own best interests. Wealth, education, and social position no longer received automatic deference. Second, Americans created new foundations for authority. For example, women developed the idea that they possessed a "separate sphere" of authority in the home, and individuals formed voluntary associations to influence the direction of society.

The Attack on the Professions

Intense criticism of lawyers, physicians, and ministers exemplified the assault on and erosion of traditional authority. Between 1800 and 1840 the wave of religious revivals known as the Second Great Awakening (see Chapter 10) sparked fierce attacks on the professions. Revivalists blasted the clergy for creating complex theologies, drinking expensive wines, and fleecing the people. One revivalist accused physicians of inventing fancy Latin and Greek names for diseases to disguise their inability to cure them.

These attacks on the learned professions peaked between 1820 and 1850. Samuel Thomson led a successful movement to eliminate all barriers to entry into the medical profession, including educational requirements. By 1845 every state had repealed laws requiring licenses or education to practice medicine. In religion, ministers found little job security as finicky congregations dismissed clergymen whose theology displeased them. In turn, ministers became more ambitious and more inclined to leave poor, small churches for large, wealthy ones.

The increasing commercialization of the economy led to both more professionals and more attacks on them. In 1765, America had one medical school; by 1860 there were sixty-five. The newly minted doctors and lawyers had neither deep roots in the towns where they practiced nor convincing claims to social superiority. "Men dropped down into their places as from clouds," one critic wrote. "Nobody knew who or what they were, except as they claimed."

This questioning of authority was particularly sharp on the frontier. Easterners sneered that every man in the West claimed to be a "judge," "general," "colonel," or "squire." Would-be gentlemen substituted an exaggerated sense of personal honor for legal or customary claims of authority. Obsessed with their fragile status, these "gentlemen" could react testily to the slightest insult; consequently, duels were common on the frontier. At a Kentucky militia parade in 1819, an officer's dog jogged onto the field and sat at his master's knee. Enraged by this breach of military decorum, another officer ran the dog through with his sword. A week later, the two men met with pistols at ten paces. One was killed, the other maimed for life.

The Challenge to Family Authority

Meanwhile, children quietly questioned parental authority. The era's economic change forced many young people to choose between staying at home to help their parents and venturing out on their own. This desire for independence fueled westward migration as well. Restless single men led the way. Two young men from Virginia put it succinctly: "All the promise of life now seemed to us to be at the other end of the rainbow—somewhere else—anywhere else but on the farm. . . . All our youthful plans had as their chief object the getting away from the farm."

As young antebellum Americans tried to escape close parental supervision, courtship and marriage patterns also changed. No longer dependent on parents for land, young people wanted to choose their own mate. Romantic love, rather than parental preference, increasingly determined marital decisions.

One sign of young people's growing control over courtship and marriage was the declining likelihood that the young women of a family would marry in their birth order. Traditionally, fathers wanted their daughters to marry in the order of their birth to avoid any suspicion that there was something wrong with one or more of them. By the end of the eighteenth century, daughters were making their own decisions about marriage, and the custom of birth order vanished. Another mark of the times was the growing popularity of long engagements; young women were reluctant to tie the knot, fearing that marriage would snuff out their independence. Equally striking was the increasing number of young women who chose not to marry.

Thus young people lived more and more in a world of their own. Moralists reacted with alarm and flooded the country with books of advice to youth, which stressed the same message: newly independent young people should develop self-control, and "character." The self-made adult began with the self-made youth.

Wives and Husbands

Another class of advice books counseled wives and husbands about their rights and duties. These books were a sign that relations between spouses were also changing. Young men and women accustomed to making their own decisions would understandably approach marriage as a compact among equals. Although inequalities within marriage remained—especially the legal tradition that married women could not own property—the trend was toward a form of equality.

One source of this change was the rise of the doctrine of **separate spheres.** The traditional view of women as subordinate in all ways yielded to a separate-but-equal doctrine that portrayed men as superior in making money and governing the world, and women as superior in exerting moral influence on family members. Most important was the shift of responsibility for child rearing from fathers to mothers. Advice books instructed mothers to discipline children by withdrawing love rather than using corporal punishment. A whipped child might obey but would remain sullen and bitter. The gentler methods advocated in manuals promised to penetrate the child's heart, to make the child *want* to do the right thing.

separate spheres Popular doctrine that emphasized women's morality and authoritative role within the home

The idea of a separate women's sphere blended with the image of family and home as secluded refuges from a disorderly society. Popular culture painted an alluring portrait of the pleasures of home in such sentimental songs as "Home, Sweet Home" and such poems as "A Visit from St. Nicholas." Even the physical appearance of houses changed; one prominent architect published plans for peaceful single-family homes to offset the hurly-burly of daily life. "There should be something to love," he wrote. "There must be nooks about it, where one would love to linger; windows, where one can enjoy the quiet landscape at his leisure; cozy rooms, where all fireside joys are invited to dwell." But reality diverged far from this ideal. Ownership of a quiet single-family home lay beyond the reach of most Americans, even much of the middle class. Farm homes, far from tranquil, were beehives of activity, and city dwellers often had to sacrifice privacy by taking in boarders to supplement family income.

The decline of cottage industry and the growing number of men (merchants, lawyers, brokers) who worked outside the home gave women more time to lavish on children. Married women found these ideals sources of power: the doctrine of separate spheres subtly implied that women should control not only the discipline but also the number of children.

In 1800 the United States had one of the highest birthrates ever recorded. Statistically, the average woman bore 7.04 children. Children were valuable for the labor they provided and for the relief from the burdens of survival that they could bring to aging parents. The more children, the better, most couples assumed. However, the growth of the market economy raised questions about children's economic value. Unlike a farmer, a merchant or lawyer could not send his children to work at the age of seven or eight. The birthrate gradually dropped, especially in towns and cities, so that statistically by 1900 the average woman would bear 3.98 children. Birthrates remained higher among African-Americans and immigrants and in the rural West, where land was plentiful.

Abstinence, *coitus interruptus* (the withdrawal of the penis before ejaculation), and abortion were common birth-control methods. Remedies for "female irregularity"—unwanted pregnancy—were widely advertised. The rubber condom and the vaginal diaphragm were familiar to many Americans by 1865. Whatever the method, husbands and wives jointly decided to limit family size. Economic and ideological considerations blended together. Husbands could note that the economic value of children was declining; wives, that having fewer children would give them more time to nurture each one and thereby to carry out their womanly duties.

Most supporters of the ideal of separate spheres did not advocate full legal equality for women. Indeed, the ideal of separate spheres was an explicit *alternative* to legal equality. But the concept enhanced women's power within marriage by giving them influence in such vital issues as child rearing and the frequency of pregnancies.

Primary Source: Portrait of a Woman and a Man

voluntary association Horizontal allegiance (as opposed to superior-subordinate relationship) of individuals with similar interests or circumstances

CHECKING IN

- As the market economy took hold, American society placed greater emphasis on individualism.
- As part of a general questioning of authority, most Americans viewed the professions such as law and medicine with increasing skepticism.
- Young people increasingly rebelled against family authority.
- The doctrine of "separate spheres" appeared as part of a transformation of ideas about gender roles.
- Voluntary associations flourished.

Horizontal Allegiances and the Rise of Voluntary Associations

As some forms of authority weakened, Americans devised new ways by which individuals could extend their influence over others. The antebellum era witnessed the widespread substitution of *horizontal* allegiances for *vertical* allegiances. In vertical allegiances, authority flows from the top down, and people in a subordinate position identify their interests with those of superiors rather than with others in the same subordinate roles. The traditional patriarchal family is an example of vertical allegiance, as is the traditional apprentice system. When social relationships assumed a horizontal form, new patterns emerged. Vertical relationships remained but became less important. New relationships linked those who were in a similar position: for example, in the large textile mills, operatives realized they had more in common with one another than with their supervisors. Wives tended to form associations that bound them with other married women, and young men developed associations with other young men.

Voluntary associations encouraged sociability as transients and newcomers came together, usually in associations based on gender or race. These associations served as vehicles for members to assert their influence. Temperance societies fought to abolish alcohol, while moral-reform societies combated prostitution; both in effect enhanced women's power over men.

Chapter Summary

 DOWNLOAD THE MP3 AUDIO FILE OF THE CHAPTER SUMMARY, AND LISTEN TO IT ON THE GO.

What caused the surge of westward migration after the War of 1812? (page 194)

An agricultural boom lured people west, as did the swelling demand for cotton created by the cotton gin. Westward movement carried the American population across the Mississippi River by 1820, raising both hopes and problems. A new society was rising in the West, one that viewed itself as more democratic and more egalitarian than the East. Native Americans were ruthlessly pushed aside or "relocated" to make room for white settlers.

What changes were linked to the rise of the market economy? (page 199)

Western farmers soon entered the market economy, which was both lucrative and volatile. They began to plant cash crops and to purchase manufactures. Although federal land policy was meant to sell parcels to small farmers, speculators snapped up much of the land. The speculative boom collapsed in the Panic of 1819, but the movement westward continued, with the transportation revolution opening the way for settlers and products. And cities mushroomed, especially in the Great Lakes area.

Why did industrialization begin to take hold? (page 204)

Protective tariffs, technology, and the ready availability of capital stimulated industrial development, especially in New England, where the textile industry led the way. Young women formed the primary work force at many New England mills, but elsewhere a piecemeal system of work predominated. Results of this early industrialization were uneven, particularly in terms of equality and inequality.

In what ways did inequality actually increase? (page 206)

In America's cities, the gap between rich and poor widened; most people held the poor responsible for their poverty. While the "middling classes" increased, free blacks saw even more of their rights slip away.

How did the rise of the market economy and industrialization change relationships within families and communities? (page 209)

Individualism increasingly characterized American society, while most Americans questioned authority in general and viewed the professions with skepticism. Young people more and more defied or ignored familial authority. Women both benefited from and were harmed by the doctrine of "separate spheres." Voluntary, horizontal organizations thrived.

KEY TERMS

Alexis de Tocqueville *(p. 193)*

National Road *(p. 196)*

"Five Civilized Tribes" *(p. 196)*

Cherokee Nation v. *Georgia (p. 198)*

Worcester v. *Georgia (p. 198)*

Trail of Tears *(p. 198)*

market economy *(p. 199)*

Transportation Revolution *(p. 201)*

Clermont (p. 201)

Erie Canal *(p. 202)*

Samuel Slater *(p. 204)*

Lowell, Waltham *(p. 205)*

African Methodist Episcopal Church *(p. 208)*

"middling classes" *(p. 209)*

separate spheres *(p. 211)*

voluntary association *(p. 212)*

Democratic Politics, Religious Revival, and Reform

First State Election in Michigan

CHAPTER PREVIEW

The Rise of Democratic Politics, 1824–1832
How did American politics become more democratic in the first half of the nineteenth century?

The Bank Controversy and the Second Party System, 1833–1840
What were the major factors in the rise of the second party system?

The Rise of Popular Religion
What changes took place in American religious life?

The Age of Reform
In what ways did reform movements attempt to forge a more orderly society?

The 1820s were a period of transition. As the revolutionary generation passed from the scene—both Thomas Jefferson and John Adams died on July 4, 1826—new generations of Americans grappled with new problems born of westward migration, growing economic individualism, and increasing sectional conflict over slavery. Massive social and economic change shattered old assumptions and created a vigorous new brand of politics.

This transformation led to the birth of a second American party system, with Democrats and Whigs replacing Republicans and Federalists. The changes went far beyond names. The new parties organized grassroots support, molded government in response to the people's will, and welcomed conflict as a way to sustain interest in political issues.

Reform movements paralleled, and sometimes replaced, politics as idealistic men and women worked for temperance, abolition, education reform, and equality for women. Strongly held religious be-

CL This icon will direct you to the website where you can Prepare for Class, Improve Your Grade, and Ace the Test:
www.cengage.com/history/boyer/ enduringconcise6e

liefs, often the product of evangelism and nontraditional sects, impelled reformers into these and other crusades, and they soon discovered that their success rested on their ability to influence politics.

Both the political and the reform agendas of the 1820s and 1830s diverged from those of the nation's founders. Those leaders had feared popular participation in politics, left an ambiguous legacy on slavery, and displayed little interest in women's rights. Yet even as Americans shifted their political and social priorities, they continued to venerate the Founders.

THE RISE OF DEMOCRATIC POLITICS, 1824–1832

How did American politics become more democratic in the first half of the nineteenth century?

In 1824 Andrew Jackson and John Quincy Adams were both members of Jefferson's Republican party; by 1834 Jackson was a Democrat and Adams, a Whig. Tensions spawned by industrialization, the rise of the Cotton South, and westward expansion split Jefferson's old party. Generally, supporters of states' rights joined the **Democrats,** and advocates of national support for economic development became **Whigs.**

Democrats Members of the party that emerged from Jefferson's Republican party as one of two dominant parties in second party system

Whigs Initially called National Republicans; members of the other dominant party

Democrat or Whig, leaders had to adapt to the rising notion that politics should be an expression of the will of the common people rather than an activity that gentlemen conducted on the people's behalf. Americans still looked up to their leaders, but the leaders could no longer look down on the people.

Democratic Ferment

Democratizing forces in politics took several forms. One of the most common was the abolition of the requirement that voters own property; no western states had such a requirement, and eastern states gradually liberalized their laws. Moreover, written ballots replaced the custom of voting aloud, which had enabled elites to influence others at the polls. And appointive offices became elective. The selection of members of the Electoral College shifted gradually from state legislatures to the voters, and by 1832 only South Carolina followed the old custom.

The fierce tug of war between Republicans and Federalists in the 1790s and early 1800s had taught both parties to court voters and listen to their will. At grand party-run barbecues North and South, potential voters washed down free clams and oysters with free beer and whiskey.

The pace of political democratization was uneven, however. The parties were still run from the top down as late as 1820, with candidates nominated by caucus; that is, a meeting of party members in the legislature. And political democracy did not extend to allowing either women or free blacks the right to vote.

The Election of 1824

Sectional politics shattered the harmony of the Era of Good Feelings. In 1824, five candidates, all Republicans, battled for the presidency. John Quincy Adams emerged as the New England favorite. John C. Calhoun and William Crawford fought to represent the South. Henry Clay of Kentucky hoped for support from the East as well as his native West. Tennessean Andrew Jackson stunned the four by emerging as a favorite of frontier people, southerners, and some northerners.

A paralyzing stroke soon removed Crawford from the race. Impressed by Jackson's support, Calhoun withdrew to run unopposed for the vice presidency. Jackson won the popular and electoral vote but failed to win the majority of the electoral vote required by the Constitution. When the election went to the House of Representatives, Clay threw his support, and thus the presidency, to Adams; Adams then promptly appointed Clay secretary of state. Jackson's supporters raged that a "corrupt bargain" had cheated their candidate, "Old Hickory," of the presidency. Although no evidence of any outright deal was uncovered, the widespread belief in a corrupt bargain hung like a cloud over Adams's presidency.

John Quincy Adams as President

Failing to understand the changing political climate, Adams made several other miscalculations that would cloak his presidency in controversy. For example, he proposed federal support for internal improvements, although strict Jeffersonians had continued to attack them as unconstitutional. Adams then infuriated southerners by proposing to send American delegates to a conference of newly independent Latin American nations. Southerners opposed U.S. participation because it would imply recognition of Haiti, the black republic created by slave revolutionaries. Instead of building new bases of support, Adams clung to the increasingly obsolete view of the president as custodian of the public good, aloof from partisan politics. Idealistic though his view was, it guaranteed him a single-term presidency.

The Rise of Andrew Jackson

As Adams's popularity fell, Andrew Jackson's rose. His victory over the British at the Battle of New Orleans made him a national hero, and southerners admired him as a Tennessee slaveholder, a renowned Indian fighter, and an advocate of Indian removal. Also, southerners praised Jackson's demand that they be allowed a free hand in pushing the Indians westward as a noble application of Jeffersonian ideals of states' rights—and a way to satisfy their land hunger. Veteran politicians distrusted Jackson's notoriously hot temper and his penchant for duels, but ordinary people seemed

THE ELECTION OF 1824

CANDIDATE	PARTY	ELECTORAL VOTE	POPULAR VOTE	PERCENTAGE OF POPULAR VOTE
John Quincy Adams	Democratic-Republican	84	108,740	30.5
Andrew Jackson	Democratic-Republican	99	153,544	43.1
William H. Crawford	Democratic-Republican	41	46,618	13.1
Henry Clay	Democratic-Republican	37	47,136	13.2

Chronology

1824	John Quincy Adams elected president by the House of Representatives
1826	American Temperance Society organized
1828	Andrew Jackson elected president; "Tariff of Abominations"; John Calhoun anonymously writes *South Carolina Exposition and Protest*
1830	Jackson's Maysville Road Bill veto; Indian Removal Act
1830–1831	Charles G. Finney's Rochester revival
1831	William Lloyd Garrison starts *The Liberator*
1832	Jackson vetoes recharter of the Bank of the United States; Jackson reelected president; South Carolina Nullification Proclamation
1833	Force Bill; Compromise Tariff; American Anti-Slavery Society founded; South Carolina nullifies the Force Bill
1834	Whig party organized
1836	Specie Circular Martin Van Buren elected president
1837	Horace Mann becomes secretary of the Massachusetts Board of Education; Elijah Lovejoy murdered by proslavery mob; Grimké sisters set out on lecture tour of New England
1838	Sarah Grimké's *Letters on the Condition of Women and the Equality of the Sexes* and Angelina Grimké's *Letters to Catharine E. Beecher*
1840	Independent Treasury Act passed; William Henry Harrison elected president; first Washington Temperance Society started
1841	Dorothea Dix begins exposé of prison conditions
1844	Brook Farm community founded; Joseph Smith murdered by anti-Mormon mob
1848	Seneca Falls Convention

to have no such objections. As the only candidate in 1824 not linked to the Monroe administration, Jackson was also in a position to capitalize on discontent after the Panic of 1819. To many Americans, Jackson, who as a boy had fought in the Revolution, was a living link to a more virtuous past.

By 1826 towns and villages across the country buzzed with political activity. Because supporters of Jackson, Adams, and Clay all still called themselves Republicans, few realized that a new political system was being born. The man most alert to the new currents was Martin Van Buren, who would be Jackson's vice president and then president.

Van Buren exemplified a new breed of politician. A tavernkeeper's son, he had worked his way up through New York politics and created a powerful statewide machine, the Albany Regency, composed of men like himself from the middling and lower ranks. A genial man who befriended even his political rivals, Van Buren loved the game of politics.

The election of 1824 had convinced Van Buren of the need for two-party competition. Without the discipline imposed by party competition, the Republicans had splintered into sectional factions. The country would be better served, he thought, by reducing the shades of opinion in the country to just two so that parties could

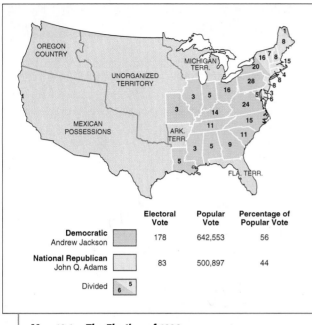

	Electoral Vote	Popular Vote	Percentage of Popular Vote
Democratic Andrew Jackson	178	642,553	56
National Republican John Q. Adams	83	500,897	44
Divided	5 6		

Map 10.1   The Election of 1828

Primary Source: Canvassing for a Vote

clash and a clear winner emerge. Jackson was the logical leader and the presidential nominee, of one new party, becoming known as the Democratic party; its opponents, calling themselves National Republicans, nominated Adams. The second American party system was taking shape.

The Election of 1828

The 1828 campaign was a vicious, mud-slinging affair. The National Republicans attacked Jackson as a murderer, a drunken gambler, and an adulterer. He had in fact killed several men in duels and had several more executed militarily, and in 1791 he had married Rachel Robards, erroneously believing that her divorce from her first husband had become final. Jackson supporters retaliated that Adams was rich and in debt, had tried to gain favor with the Russian tsar by providing him with a beautiful American prostitute, and—perhaps worst of all to westerners—wore silk underwear.

The Adams supporters' charges that Jackson was an illiterate backwoodsman backfired and endeared "Old Hickory" to ordinary people. Jackson's mudslingers proclaimed that Jackson was the common man incarnate—his mind unclouded by learning, his morals simple and true, his will fierce and resolute. Adams, in contrast, was an aristocrat, a scholar whose learning obscured the truth, a man who could write but not fight.

The election swept Jackson into office with twice Adams's electoral votes. The popular vote, much closer, reflected the strong sectional bases of the new parties. Adams doubled Jackson's vote in New England, while Jackson doubled Adams's vote in the South and nearly tripled it in the Southwest.

Jackson in Office

Jackson rode to the presidency on a wave of opposition to corruption and privilege, and one of his first moves was to institute "rotation in office"—the removal of officeholders of the rival party. Nearly half of the higher-ranking civil servants were summarily fired.

"spoils system" Practice of rewarding political supporters with public office

Although his opponents called it the **"spoils system,"** Jackson defended rotation in office on the basis of democracy: the duties of most officeholders were so simple that as many plain people as possible should have the chance to work for the government.

Jackson's use of the spoils system ruffled feathers, but the issues of internal improvements and tariffs ignited real controversy. Like most southerners, Jackson believed that federal support for internal improvements was simply a lavish giveaway. He thought that such funding violated the Constitution, which stated that Congress could appropriate money only for national purposes, not for the benefit of particular sections or interests. Accordingly, in 1830 Jackson vetoed a bill to provide federal support for a road in Kentucky between Maysville and Lexington.

The Maysville Road Bill veto and the almost-simultaneous Indian Removal Act enhanced Jackson's popularity in the South. The tariff issue, however, would test southern loyalty. In 1828, while Adams was still president, Congress passed a high protective tariff favorable to western agriculture and New England manufacturing. Southerners fumed at the tariff, which raised the price of manufactured goods and also created the threat of retaliatory tariffs against southern cotton exports. To the surprise of Jackson and his followers, he, rather than Adams, bore the brunt of southern ire.

***Andrew Jackson,* by Ralph Earl**
Jackson during the Nullification Crisis, looking serene in the uniform of a major-general and determined to face down the greatest challenge to his presidency.

Nullification

The 1828 tariff, the **"Tariff of Abominations,"** laid the foundation for a split between Jackson and his vice president, John C. Calhoun. Although he had entered Congress as a "war hawk" and had championed nationalism early in his career, Calhoun had gradually become a states' rights sectionalist. He had supported the tariff of 1816 but would fiercely oppose that of 1828.

Calhoun burned with ambition to be president. Jackson had stated that he would serve only one term and as vice president Calhoun assumed that he would succeed Jackson. To do so, he needed to maintain the support of the South, which was increasingly taking an antitariff stance. Calhoun's own state, South Carolina, had suffered economic decline throughout the 1820s; its citizens blamed protective tariffs.

Calhoun also accepted the Virginia and Kentucky Resolutions of 1798–1799, which defined the Union as a compact among the states, an association conferring only limited powers on the central government. He insisted that the only constitutional tariff was one that raised money for the common national defense, not one that favored a particular section at the expense of others. Calhoun expressed these views anonymously in the widely circulated ***South Carolina Exposition and Protest*** (1828), which argued not only that the 1828 tariff was unconstitutional but also that states had the right to nullify that tariff within their borders.

More was at stake than the price of manufactured goods. Southerners feared that a government capable of passing tariffs favoring one section over another might also pass laws meddling with slavery. Although this idea seemed far-fetched—Jackson himself was a slaveholder—South Carolina's whites were edgy about the safety of slavery. African-Americans were a majority of their state's population, the slave Nat Turner's bloody rebellion in Virginia in 1831 raised fears of a similar threat to South

"Tariff of Abominations"
Protective tariff of 1828 that infuriated southerners; spawned nullification crisis

South Carolina Exposition and Protest John C. Calhoun's restatement of Virginia and Kentucky Resolutions that justified nullification

***John C. Calhoun,* by Charles Bird King, c. 1825**

The magnetic Calhoun, Jackson's vice president, broke with Jackson over nullification and the Peggy Eaton affair, and resigned the vice presidency in 1832.

Nullification Crisis Controversy over nullification that pitted Jackson against Calhoun and led to talk of secession by Southerners

Carolina, and William Lloyd Garrison's new newspaper, *The Liberator,* advocated immediate abolition. To many South Carolinians, these were ominous signs warning that a line had to be drawn against tariffs and possible future interference with slavery.

Like Calhoun, Jackson was strong-willed and proud. Unlike Calhoun, he already was president and the leader of a national party that included supporters of the tariff. To mollify both protariff and antitariff forces, he devised two policies.

First, he distributed surplus federal revenue, derived largely from the tariff duties, to the states, hoping to remove the taint of sectional injustice from the tariff. Second, he tried to ease tariffs down from the sky-high 1828 rates, and Congress passed slight reductions in 1832. But these measures did little to satisfy Calhoun and the South Carolinians.

By the time the somewhat lower tariff was passed, other issues had ruptured relations between the president and vice president. Jackson learned that in 1818, then–Secretary of War Calhoun had urged that Jackson be punished for his unauthorized raid into Spanish Florida. In 1829 Jackson's secretary of war, John H. Eaton, married Peggy O'Neale Timberlake, the widowed daughter of a Washington tavernkeeper. While still married to a naval officer away on duty, Peggy had acquired the reputation of flirting with Eaton, who boarded at her father's tavern. After her husband's death and her marriage to Eaton, she and Eaton were snubbed socially by Calhoun's wife and his friends in the cabinet in what became known as the "petticoat war." Jackson concluded that Calhoun had initiated the petticoat war to discredit him and advance his own presidential aspirations. A Jefferson Day dinner in April 1830 featured a symbolic confrontation between Jackson and Calhoun. Jackson proposed the toast "Our Union: It must be preserved." Calhoun responded, "The Union next to Liberty the most dear. May we always remember that it can only be preserved by distributing equally the benefits and burdens of the Union."

The stage was set for the **Nullification Crisis.** In November 1832 a South Carolina convention, citing Calhoun's states' rights doctrine, nullified the tariffs of 1828 and 1832 and forbade the collection of customs duties within the state. Jackson reacted quickly. He despised nullification as an "abominable doctrine" that would reduce the government to anarchy and denounced the South Carolinians as "unprincipled men who would rather rule in hell than be subordinate in heaven." He sent arms to Unionists in South Carolina and issued a proclamation that lambasted nullification as unconstitutional; the Constitution, he emphasized, had established "a single nation," not a league of states.

In March 1833 the crisis eased as President Jackson signed "the olive branch and the sword," in one historian's words. The Compromise Tariff of 1833, the olive branch or peace offering, provided for a gradual but significant lowering of tariff duties from 1833 to 1842. The Force Bill, the sword, authorized the president to use arms to collect customs duties in South Carolina. Although South Carolina did not abandon the principle of nullification—in fact, it petulantly nullified the Force Bill—it accepted the Compromise Tariff and rescinded its nullification of the tariffs of 1828 and 1832.

This so-called Compromise of 1833 grew out of a mixture of partisanship and statesmanship. Its chief architect was Henry Clay of Kentucky, who had long favored high tariffs. Clay not only feared the outbreak of civil war but also wanted to keep control of the tariff issue away from the Jacksonians, even if that meant a lower tariff. The nullifiers, recognizing that no other states had supported them, preferred giving Clay, not Jackson, credit for defusing the crisis; they therefore supported the Compromise Tariff and rescinded the Nullification Proclamation.

The Bank Veto and the Election of 1832

Jackson recognized that the gap between rich and poor was widening. Although he did not object to wealth earned by hard work, he believed that the wealthy too often enjoyed privileges granted by corrupt legislatures. Additionally, disastrous speculation early in his life had led him to distrust all banks, paper money, and monopolies—and the **Bank of the United States** was guilty on all counts.

The Bank of the United States had received a twenty-year charter from Congress in 1816. As a creditor of state banks, the Bank of the United States in effect restrained their printing and lending of money by its ability to demand the redemption of state notes in specie (gold or silver coin). Many other aspects of the bank made it controversial. For example, it was widely blamed for the Panic of 1819. Second, as the official depository for federal revenue, it was a privileged institution at a time when privilege was coming under fierce attack. The bank had far greater lending capacity than state banks and thus dominated them. Third, although chartered by the federal government, the bank was controlled by its stockholders, who were private citizens—"moneyed capitalists" in Jackson's view. Finally, its location in Philadelphia, rather than Washington, symbolized the bank's independence of supervision by the national government. The bank's president, the aristocratic Nicholas Biddle, whom Jackson loathed, saw himself as a public servant duty-bound to keep the bank above politics.

Aware of Jackson's opposition, Biddle sought an early rechartering of the bank, urged on by Henry Clay, who hoped to ride the probank bandwagon into the White House in 1832. Congress passed, and Jackson promptly vetoed, the recharter bill. The president denounced the bank as a private and privileged monopoly that drained the West of specie, was immune to taxation by states, put inordinate power in the hands of a few men, and made "the rich richer and the potent more powerful."

By 1832 Jackson had made clear his views on major issues. He was simultaneously a strong defender of states' rights *and* a staunch Unionist. Although he cherished the Union, Jackson believed the states far too diverse to accept strong direction from the federal government. Throwing aside earlier promises to retire, Jackson ran for the presidency again in 1832, with Martin Van Buren as his running mate. Henry Clay ran on the National Republican ticket, stressing his American System of protective tariffs, national banking, and federal support for internal improvements.

Bank of the United States
National Bank created by Alexander Hamilton

CHECKING IN

- During the 1820s politics became increasingly democratic, and voter participation increased dramatically.
- Andrew Jackson emerged as "the common man."
- As president, Jackson opposed the use of federal funds for internal improvements.
- The Nullification Crisis of 1828–1833 exposed deep divisions between the North and the South.
- Jackson saw his veto of the charter of the Bank of the United States as a victory for the common man.

Jackson's overwhelming personal popularity swamped Clay, 219 to 49 electoral votes. Secure in office for another four years, Jackson was ready to finish dismantling the Bank of the United States.

The Bank Controversy and the Second Party System, 1833–1840

What were the major factors in the rise of the second party system?

Jackson's bank veto ignited a searing controversy that threatened to engulf all banks. One major problem was that the United States had no paper currency of its own. Instead, private bankers (widely viewed as sinister figures) issued paper notes, which they promised to redeem in specie. These IOUs fueled economic development by making credit easy. But if a banknote depreciated, wage earners paid in paper would suffer. Further, paper money encouraged speculation, which multiplied both profit and risk. For example, farmers could now buy land on credit in the belief that its value would rise; if it did, they could sell the land at a profit, but if its value fell, the farmers became mired in debt. Would the United States embrace swift economic development at the price of allowing some people to get rich quickly while others languished? Or would the nation undergo more modest growth in traditional molds, anchored by "honest" manual work and frugality?

The War on the Bank

Jackson could have allowed the Bank of the United States, "the monster," as he termed it, to die a natural death when its charter expired, but he and his followers believed that if the bank escaped with a breath of life, "it will soon recover its wonted strength." When Biddle began calling in bank loans and contracting credit to forestall further moves by Jackson, Jacksonians saw their darkest fears confirmed. The bank, Jackson said, "is trying to kill me, but I will kill it." So the president began removing federal deposits from the Bank of the United States and putting them into private banks chartered by individual states, which became known as "pet banks."

In turn, this policy raised new problems. State banks that were depositories for federal funds could use these moneys as the basis for issuing more notes and extending more loans. Jackson hoped to head off the danger of a credit-fueled speculative economy by limiting the number of state banks used for federal revenue. But he discovered that doing so was impossible; indeed, by the end of 1833 there were twenty-three pet banks, chosen in part for their loyalty to the Democratic party. Jackson could not stem the rapid economic expansion fueled by paper money and by foreign specie flowing in to purchase cotton.

The Democratic party split between advocates of soft money (paper) and hard money (specie). The two Democratic camps agreed that the Bank of the United States was evil, but for different reasons. Soft-money Democrats, especially strong in the West, resented the bank's restriction of credit and wanted more paper money. Hard-money Democrats, typically wage-earning urban workers, disliked the speculative economy based on paper money and easy credit, and they deeply feared inflation.

Jackson himself believed that paper money sapped "public virtue" and "robbed honest labour of its earnings to make knaves rich, powerful, and dangerous." Trying to stem the proliferation of soft money, in 1836 Jackson issued a proclamation called the Specie Circular, which provided that only specie—gold or silver—could be accepted in payment for public lands.

The Rise of Whig Opposition

During Jackson's second term the National Republicans changed their name to the Whig party and broadened their base of support in both the North and the South. As Jackson's policies became clearer and sharper, the opposition attracted people alienated by his positions.

For example, Jackson's crushing of nullification led some southerners to the Whigs, as did his war against the bank and opposition to federal aid for internal improvements. Most of the South remained Democratic, but the Whigs made substantial inroads. And supporters of Henry Clay's American System joined advocates of public education and temperance in seeking a more activist, interventionist national government.

Meanwhile, social reformers in the North were infusing new vitality into the opposition to Jackson. These reformers wanted to end slavery and the sale of liquor, improve public education, and elevate public morality. While most Democrats opposed any government attempt to impose uniform standards on the diverse American society, Whigs tended to accept active government intervention, and thus reformers gravitated to the Whig party. Reformers, almost all Protestants, distrusted immigrants, especially the Irish, who viewed drinking as a normal recreation and who, as Catholics, suspected (correctly) that public schools favored by reformers would teach Protestant doctrines. At the same time, reform agitation and its association with the Whigs drove Irish immigrants into the arms of the Democratic party. In turn, many native-born Protestants, contemptuous of the Irish, turned Whig.

The most remarkable source of Whig strength was Anti-Masonry. Masonry had long provided prominent men, including George Washington, with fellowship and exotic rituals. The spark that ignited the Anti-Mason crusade was the abduction and disappearance in 1826 of William Morgan, a New York stonemason who had threatened to expose Masonic secrets. Efforts to solve the mystery of Morgan's disappearance failed because local officials were themselves Masons, seemingly determined to thwart the investigation. Rumors spread that Masonry was a powerful anti-Christian conspiracy of the rich in order to suppress popular liberty and an exclusive retreat for drunkards. Intensely moralistic small farmers and artisans from the Northeast flocked to the Whig party as a bulwark against Masonry.

By 1836 the Whigs had become a national party with widespread appeal. Whigs everywhere assailed Andrew Jackson as an imperious dictator, "King Andrew I," and the name "Whigs" evoked memories of the American patriots who had opposed George III in 1776.

The Election of 1836

Andrew Jackson was a hard act to follow. Democrats nominated Martin Van Buren, proclaiming that he and the Democratic party were Jackson's heirs, the perfect embodiment of the popular will. The Whigs ran four candidates from different sections of

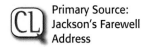

Primary Source: Jackson's Farewell Address

the country. The Democrats accused the Whigs of attempting to split the vote and throw the election into the House, where they could wheel and deal as in 1824. But in fact the Whigs had no strategy, much less such a devious one, and Van Buren carried the popular vote. His margin was narrow, however, and in an ominous sign, the Democrats carried barely half the southern vote—they had won two-thirds of it only four years earlier.

The Panic of 1837

Jackson left office in 1837 in a burst of glory. Yet he bequeathed to his successor a severe depression.

In the speculative boom of 1835 and 1836, born of Jackson's policy of placing federal funds in state banks, the total number of banks doubled, the value of bank notes in circulation nearly tripled, and both commodity and land prices soared skyward. But the overheated economy began to cool rapidly in May 1837. Prices tumbled as bank after bank suspended specie payments. The ensuing depression was far more severe and prolonged than the Panic of 1819. Wages fell by one-third between 1836 and 1842.

The prolonged depression had multiple roots. Domestically, Jackson's Specie Circular of July 1836, declaring that only specie, not paper money, could be used to purchase public lands, dried up credit. Global events played a major role as well. In the 1820s Americans had used freshly-mined silver imported from Mexico to buy tea, silks, and other goods in China. By the early 1830s the Chinese were using increasing amounts of this silver to pay for opium grown in India and peddled by British merchants. In turn, large amounts of silver flowed out of British coffers to invest in canals and other American projects. Worried that British investors were overextended in the United States and determined to keep specie at home, in 1836 the Bank of England drastically raised interest rates. To continue to attract foreign investment, American banks then raised their interest rates.

Making a bad situation much worse, the price paid for American cotton by British merchants plummeted in 1837. Bumper harvests in England had led to cheap food for workers, who then used more of their funds to buy goods spun from American cotton. But in the years 1836 through 1838 poor harvests drove up the cost of food and left workers with little to spend on clothing. Topping things off, in 1839 the United States brought in a record cotton harvest, lowering cotton prices even further. To pay for imported foodstuffs, the Bank of England raised money by raising interest rates. Soaring British interest rates meant that money flowed into England, money that Americans had optimistically assumed would be available to continue financing canals. British investment in the United States dried up, leaving the American landscape littered with half-finished canals to nowhere.

The Search for Solutions

Van Buren, known as "the sly fox" and "the little magician" for his political craftiness, would need those skills to confront the depression, which was battering ordinary citizens and the Democratic party alike. The president called for the creation of an independent treasury that would hold government revenues and keep them from the grasp of corporations. When Van Buren finally signed the Independent Treasury Bill into law on July 4, 1840, his supporters hailed it as a second Declaration of Independence.

The Independent Treasury reflected the basic Jacksonian suspicion of an alliance between the federal government and banking. However, the Independent Treasury Act failed to address banking on the state level, where newly chartered state banks—more than nine hundred in number by 1840—lent money to farmers and businessmen, fueling the speculative economy feared by Jacksonians.

Whigs and Democrats differed sharply in their approach to the multiplication of state banks. Whigs, convinced that Jackson's Specie Circular, not banks themselves, had brought on the depression, supported policies allowing any group to start a bank as long as its members met state requirements. Democrats, who tended to blame banks and paper money for the depression, adopted the hard-money position favored by Jackson and his advisers. After 1837 the Democrats were in effect an antibank, hard-money party.

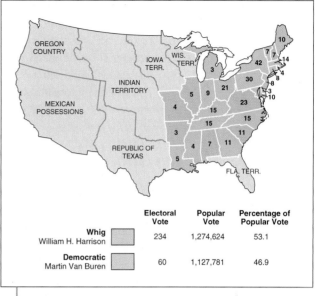

	Electoral Vote	Popular Vote	Percentage of Popular Vote
Whig William H. Harrison	234	1,274,624	53.1
Democratic Martin Van Buren	60	1,127,781	46.9

Map 10.2   The Election of 1840

The Election of 1840

Despite the depression, the Democrats renominated Van Buren. Avoiding the mistake of 1836, the Whigs nominated a single candidate, Ohio's William Henry Harrison, and ran John Tyler of Virginia for vice president.

Early in the campaign the Democrats made a fatal mistake, ridiculing Harrison as "Old Granny," who desired only to spend his declining years in a **log cabin** sipping cider. In so doing, they handed the Whigs the most famous campaign symbol in American history. The Whigs saluted Harrison as a rugged frontiersman, the hero of the Battle of Tippecanoe (tip-pee-cuh-NOO), and a defender of all those people who lived in log cabins. Disdaining a platform, the Whigs ran a "hurrah" campaign using log cabins for headquarters, singing log cabin songs, and ladling out log cabin cider. Instead of a platform, they trumpeted, "Tippecanoe and Tyler, too!" and attacked Van Buren as an aristocrat who lived in "regal splendor."

Harrison was elected in a clear victory. The depression would have made it difficult for any Democrat to win, but many of Van Buren's problems stemmed from his style of campaign. While the Whigs ran a rousing race aimed directly at the "common man," Van Buren quietly wrote letters of encouragement to key supporters. Ironically, the Whigs beat the master politician at his own game.

log cabin Symbol of Whig party in 1840 "hurrah" campaign for the presidency

CHECKING IN

- Jackson's "war" on the bank intensified the difference between the Democrats and the Whigs.

- The new Whig party included reformers and opponents of Jackson.

- The Panic of 1837 exploded during the administration of Martin Van Buren and greatly strengthened the Whigs.

- The election of 1840, the first real "hurrah" campaign, gave the Whigs the White House for the first time.

- After 1840 the second party system was firmly in place.

The Second Party System Matures

The strong contrasts between the two parties and the sharp choices they presented jolted the American electorate. Nearly 2.4 million people voted in 1840, up an astonishing 60 percent from 1836. Prior to 1840 the proportion of white males who voted had ranged from 55 to 58 percent; in 1840 it rose to 80 percent.

Both the depression and the frenzied log cabin campaign had brought voters to the polls in 1840, but voter turnouts stayed high even after prosperity returned. The second party system reached a high plateau in 1840 and remained there for over a decade. The gradual hardening of the line between the two parties stimulated popular interest in politics. However, religion rather than politics was the seedbed of many of the reform movements that burst upon the national scene in the 1830s.

THE RISE OF POPULAR RELIGION

What changes took place in American religious life?

In *Democracy in America,* Alexis de Tocqueville called religion "the foremost of the political institutions" in the United States. Tocqueville was referring to the way religious impulses reinforced democracy and liberty. Just as Americans demanded that politics be accessible to average people, they insisted that ministers preach doctrines that appealed to ordinary men and women. Successful ministers used plain language to move the heart, not theological complexity to dazzle the intellect. Increasingly, Americans put individuals in charge of their own religious destiny, thrusting aside Calvinist predestination in favor of the belief that anyone could attain heaven. A series of religious revivals known as the Second Great Awakening contributed to the growing harmony between religion and politics and to the growing conviction that heaven itself was democratic.

Second Great Awakening
Religious revival that swept the country and fed into reform movements

The Second Great Awakening

The **Second Great Awakening** first flared up in Connecticut in the 1790s, and during the following half-century it set ablaze one section of the nation after another. As the revivals moved westward, they underwent striking changes typified by the rise of camp meetings. Here the members of several denominations gathered together in sprawling open-air camps to hear revivalists proclaim that the Second Coming of Jesus was near and that the time for repentance was now. The most famous camp meeting took place at Cane Ridge, Kentucky, in August 1801. A huge crowd gathered on a hillside to listen to thunderous sermons, sing hymns, and experience divine grace.

These frontier revivals featured "exercises" in which men and women rolled around like logs, jerked their heads furiously, and grunted like animals. Critics blasted the frontier frenzy for encouraging fleshly lust and complained that "more souls were begot than saved" at the camp meetings. But although these early frontier revivals challenged traditional religious customs—indeed, the most successful preachers were farmers and artisans who had experienced powerful conversions and scorned those whose religion came from books—the revivalists promoted law, order, and morality.

Methodists Arose out of revivalism to become largest American Protestant denomination

Methodists, the most successful frontier denomination, became the largest American Protestant denomination, soaring from 70,000 members in 1800 to more than 1 million in 1844. The Methodists emphasized that religion was a matter of the heart rather than the head and relied on itinerant circuit riders—young, unmarried men who traveled ceaselessly and preached in houses, open fields, or wherever else listeners would gather. After the Methodist circuit riders left, their converts held weekly "classes" to provide mutual encouragement and to chastise members for drunkenness, fighting, gossiping, fornication, and even shrewd business practices.

Eastern Revivals

By the 1820s the Second Great Awakening had begun to shift back to the East. The hottest revival fires blazed in an area of western New York known as the Burned-Over District. No longer a frontier, western New York teemed with people drawn by the hope of wealth after the completion of the Erie Canal. It was a fertile field of high expectations and bitter discontent. The man who harnessed these anxieties to religion was **Charles Grandison Finney,** a lawyer-turned-Presbyterian minister. His greatest "harvest" came in the thriving canal city of Rochester in 1830–1831.

Finney's innovations at the Rochester revival justified his reputation as the "father of modern revivalism." First, he pioneered in generating cooperation among Protestants, and all denominations participated in his revivals. In addition, he introduced such novelties as the "anxious seat," a bench where those ready for conversion could be made objects of special prayer, and the "protracted meeting," which ran nightly for a week or more. Finally, although a Presbyterian, Finney rejected the Calvinist doctrine of total depravity, humankind's irresistible inclination to sin. Instead, he proclaimed, sin was a voluntary act, and those who willed themselves to sin could just as readily will themselves not to sin. In theory, men and women could live perfect lives, free of sin. Those converted by Finney or other evangelists (ee-VAN-juh-lists) believed that they were cleansed of past guilt and were beginning a new life. "I have been born again," a young convert wrote. "I am three days old when I write this letter."

Originally controversial, Finney's ideas came to dominate "evangelical" (eh-van-JELL-ih-cull) Protestantism, which focused on the need for an emotional religious conversion. He succeeded because he told people what they wanted to hear: that their destiny was in their own hands. A society that celebrated the self-made individual embraced Finney's assertion that, even in religion, people could make of themselves what they chose. Finney multiplied his success by emphasizing the role of women, who outnumbered male converts nearly two to one. Finney encouraged women to give public testimonials of their conversion, and he often converted men by first winning over their wives and daughters.

Charles Grandison Finney
One of most important revivalists; stressed individual responsibility

Critics of Revivals: The Unitarians

Although some praised revivals for saving souls, others doubted their lasting effects. The **Unitarians** were a small, but influential group of critics. Although their basic doctrine—that Jesus Christ was less than fully divine—had gained acceptance among religious liberals in the eighteenth century, Unitarianism became a formal denomination only in the early nineteenth century. Unitarians won few converts outside New England, but their tendency to attract the wealthy and educated gave them influence beyond their numbers.

Unitarians criticized revivals as uncouth emotional exhibitions and argued that "character building" was more effective than sudden emotional conversion. Yet they and the revivalists agreed in rejecting the Calvinist emphasis on human wickedness. Christianity had only one purpose, a Unitarian leader proclaimed: "the perfection of human nature, the elevation of men into nobler beings."

Unitarians Denomination of generally educated, wealthy New Englanders upset by emotionalism of revivals

Mormons First major denomination founded in United States; persecuted for many years

Joseph Smith Founder of Mormon Church

The Rise of Mormonism

Far more controversial than the Unitarians were the **Mormons** and their church, the Church of Jesus Christ of Latter-day Saints, another new denomination of the 1820s. **Joseph Smith,** its founder, grew up in the heart of the Burned-Over District. Conflict among the various religious denominations that thrived in the region— Methodists, Presbyterians, Baptists—left Smith confused. He wondered who was right and who was wrong or whether they were "all wrong together."

Smith resolved this conflict, which was not uncommon in the Burned-Over District, in a unique way. He claimed that an angel had led him to a buried book of revelation and to special stones for use in translating it. The Book of Mormon, which Smith translated, tells the story of an ancient Hebrew prophet, Lehi, whose descendants migrated to America and created a prosperous civilization. Jesus had appeared and performed miracles in the New World, but Lehi's descendants had departed from the Lord's ways and quarreled among themselves. God had cursed some of these defectors with dark skin; these were the American Indians, who had long since forgotten their history.

Smith quickly gathered followers. Mormonism's appeal lay partly in its placing America at the center of Christian history and partly in its resolving the conflicting claims within Protestantism by additional revelations beyond those in the Bible. The Mormons moved steadily west, both to escape persecution and to draw closer to the Indians, whom they wished to convert. Smith's claim of a new revelation guaranteed a hostile reception for the Mormons wherever they went, because it undermined the authority of the Bible, which, along with the Constitution, contained the ideals on which the American republic rested.

In 1843 Smith added fuel to the fire by proclaiming yet another revelation, this one sanctioning polygyny, the practice of taking multiple wives. Smith's claims that he was a prophet, the "Second Mohammed," also intensified controversy. Smith called himself "Prophet of the Kingdom of God" and announced his candidacy for the presidency of the United States. But in 1844 the state of Illinois charged him with treason and jailed him in the town of Carthage. There, in June 1844, a mob murdered Smith and his brother.

Mormonism is one of the few religions to originate in the United States. Smith initially hoped that Americans would respond to his call, but hostility from non-Mormons soon convinced him that the future of Mormonism lay in separation from society. In this respect it mirrored the efforts of several religious communal societies, among them the Shakers, whose members likewise set themselves apart from society.

Shakers Sect that stressed withdrawal from society; known for craftsmanship

The Shakers

The founder of the **Shakers** (who derived their name from a convulsive religious dance that was part of their ceremony) was Mother Ann Lee, the illiterate daughter of an English blacksmith. Lee and her followers had established a series of tightly knit agricultural-artisan communities in America after her arrival in 1774. Shaker artisanship, particularly in furniture, had quickly gained renown for its simple lines, beauty, and strength. Shaker advances in the development of new farm tools and seed varieties would be a boon to the growing market economy. However, the Shakers were fundamentally otherworldly and hostile to materialism. Lee had insisted that her followers abstain from sexual intercourse, believed that the end of the world was imminent, and derived many of her doctrines from trances and visions. She had also taught that at the Second Coming, Jesus would take the form of a woman.

Shaker missionaries took advantage of revivalism's appeal. At Cane Ridge and other revivals, Shaker proselytizers attracted converts whom the revivals had loosened from their traditional religious moorings. By the 1830s the Shakers numbered about six thousand.

Although the Shakers and the Mormons lived apart from traditional society, most evangelical Protestants taught that religion and the pursuit of wealth were compatible as long as people were honest, temperate, and bound by conscience. By encouraging involvement in society, evangelism provided a powerful stimulus to the multiple social reform movements of the 1820s and 1830s.

CHECKING IN

- "Democratizing" reached religion as well as politics.
- The Second Great Awakening emphasized the emotional aspects of religion.
- Methodism emerged as a major Protestant denomination.
- The Mormon Church and the Shakers were born amid the fever of revivalism, but their members lived apart from society.
- Despite such new sects, revivalists generally encouraged involvement in society and were a powerful stimulus to reform movements.

THE AGE OF REFORM

In what ways did reform movements attempt to forge a more orderly society?

Democratic ferment spilled out beyond politics and religion. During the 1820s and 1830s unprecedented numbers of men and women joined organizations aimed at improving society. The abolition of slavery, women's rights, temperance, better treatment of criminals and the insane, public education, and even the establishment of perfect, utopian communities were on the various reformers' agenda.

At a time when women and blacks alike could not vote, the major parties sidestepped such controversial issues as slavery and women's rights. Reform movements offered both groups the opportunity to influence public issues. White male reformers generally viewed politics as a sorry spectacle that rewarded the sacrifice of principle with victory at the polls. Although they occasionally cooperated with political parties, especially the Whigs, reformers gave their loyalty to their causes, not to parties.

Religious revivalism intensified the righteousness of reformers, who believed that they were on God's side of any issue. Abolitionists and temperance reformers tended to come from evangelical backgrounds, but others, school reformers and women's rights advocates particularly, were often hostile or indifferent to revivals. Yet even reformers opposed to revivalism borrowed evangelical preachers' language and psychology by painting drunkenness, ignorance, and inequality as sins calling for immediate repentance and change.

Reform movements lacked a national scope. New England and those parts of the Midwest settled by New Englanders were hotbeds of reform, while southerners actively suppressed abolition, displayed only mild interest in temperance and educational reform, ignored women's rights, and saw utopian communities as proof of the mental instability of northern reformers.

The War on Liquor

Agitation for **temperance** (TEM-per-enss) intensified during the second quarter of the nineteenth century. Alcohol abuse was a growing problem: per capita consumption of rum, whiskey, gin, and brandy had risen steadily until it exceeded seven gallons per year

temperance Abstinence from alcohol; name of the movement against alcohol by 1830, nearly triple today's rate. The average adult male downed half a pint of liquor a day, and reformers saw alcohol excess as a male indulgence whose bitter consequences (for example, spending money on liquor instead of food) fell on women and children. Not surprisingly, millions of women marched behind the temperance banner.

The movement took off in 1825 when the popular evangelist Lyman Beecher, in six widely acclaimed lectures, thundered against all use of alcohol. Evangelical Protestants established the American Temperance Society the following year, and by 1834 it enjoyed some five thousand state and local affiliates. Women, who found a public outlet for their moral energies in the temperance movement, made up one-third to one-half of their members. The American Temperance Society demanded total abstinence and flooded the country with tracts denouncing the "amazing evil" of strong drink.

The laboring class became a chief target for temperance reformers. Passing a jug around the workplace every few hours had been a time-honored way to relieve on-the-job fatigue, but large factories demanded a more disciplined, sober work force. Manufacturers quickly supported the evangelical temperance reformers. Uninterested in temperance at first, workers flocked to reform after the Panic of 1837, forming the Washington Temperance Societies beginning in 1840. Many workers who joined the Washingtonians were reformed drunkards who had concluded that hard times required temperance and frugality. Because so many of the forces dislocating workers in the late 1830s were beyond their control, they looked to something that they could control: drinking. Take care of temperance, a Washingtonian told his audience, and the Lord would take care of the economy.

As temperance won new supporters, the crusaders shifted their emphasis from the individual drinker to the entire community and demanded that towns and even states ban all traffic in liquor. By the late 1830s prohibition was scoring victories, especially in New England. The steady rise of alcohol consumption halted in the early 1830s and then began to fall; by the 1840s the rate of consumption was less than half that in the 1820s.

Public-School Reform

Like temperance crusaders, school reformers worked to encourage orderliness and thrift in the common people. Rural "district" schools were a main target. Here students ranging in age from three to twenty crowded into a single room and learned to read and count, but little more.

District schools enjoyed considerable support from rural parents. However, reformers insisted that schools had to equip children for the emerging competitive and industrial economy. In 1837 **Horace Mann** of Massachusetts, the most articulate and influential of the reformers, became the first secretary of his state's newly created board of education. He presided over sweeping reforms to transform schools from loose organizations into highly structured institutions that occupied most of a child's time and energy. Mann's goals included shifting financial support of schools from parents to the state, compelling attendance, extending the school term, introducing standardized textbooks, and grading schools (that is, classifying students by age and attainment).

School reformers sought to spread uniform cultural values as well as to combat ignorance. Requiring students to arrive at a set time would teach punctuality, and

Horace Mann Important public-school reformer

matching children against their peers would stimulate the competitiveness needed in an industrializing society. Children would read the same books and absorb the same moral lessons. The McGuffey readers, which sold 50 million copies between 1836 and 1870, preached industry, honesty, sobriety, and patriotism.

Primary Source:
He That Ne'er Learns
His A, B, C

Mann's reforms took root primarily in the North, despite challenges from farmers satisfied with the district school, from Catholics objecting to anti-Catholic and anti-Irish barbs in the textbooks, and from the working poor, who widely saw compulsory education as a menace to families dependent on children's wages. He and other school reformers prevailed in part because their opponents could not cooperate with one another and in part because the reformers attracted influential allies, including urban workers, manufacturers, and women. Reformers predicted that school reform would make teaching a suitable profession for women, and they were right. By 1900, 70 percent of the nation's teachers were women.

School reform also appealed to native-born Americans alarmed by the swelling tide of immigration. The public school became a vehicle for forging a common American culture out of an increasingly diverse society. However, few reformers stressed the integration of black and white children. When black children got any schooling, it was usually in segregated schools; black children in integrated schools encountered such virulent prejudice that African-American leaders in northern cities often preferred segregated schools.

Abolition

Antislavery sentiment had flourished among whites during the revolutionary era but faded in the early nineteenth century. The American Colonization Society, founded in 1817, was the main antislavery organization of this period. It proposed gradual emancipation, compensation for slave owners when slaves became free, and the shipment to Africa of freed blacks. Although these proposals attracted some support from slave owners in the Upper South, they were unrealizable. The growing cotton economy had made slavery more attractive than ever to most southerners, and few owners would have freed their slaves, even if compensated. The U.S. slave population, fed by natural increase, soared in the early nineteenth century from 1.2 million in 1810 to more than 2 million by 1830, but only 1,400 blacks migrated to Africa, and most were already free.

Radical antislavery views flourished primarily among African-Americans themselves. Opposing colonization in Africa—for most American blacks were native born—they formed scores of abolition societies. One free black, David Walker of Boston, even called for a rebellion to crush slavery.

In 1821 Benjamin Lundy, a white Quaker, began a newspaper, the *Genius of Universal Emancipation,* that trumpeted repeal of the Constitution's three-fifths clause, the outlawing of the internal slave trade, and the abolition of slavery in U.S. territories. Seven years later Lundy hired a young New Englander, **William Lloyd Garrison,** as an editorial assistant. The prematurely bald, bespectacled Garrison would become a potent force in the antislavery movement.

William Lloyd Garrison
Outspoken radical opponent of slavery

In 1831 Garrison launched a newspaper, *The Liberator,* to spread his radical antislavery message. "I am in earnest," he wrote. "I will not equivocate—I will not excuse—I will not retreat a single inch—AND I WILL BE HEARD." His battle cry was "immediate emancipation"; his demand, civil and legal equality for African-

Americans. However, even Garrison did not believe that all slaves could be freed overnight. People first had to realize that slavery was sinful and its continued existence intolerable.

Black abolitionists supported Garrison; in its early years three-fourths of *The Liberator*'s subscribers were African-American. Other blacks were emerging as powerful writers and speakers. **Frederick Douglass,** an escaped slave, could rivet an audience with an opening line: "I appear before the immense assembly this evening as a thief and a robber. I stole this head, these limbs, this body from my master, and ran off with them."

Frederick Douglass Escaped slave who became major figure in antislavery movement

Relations between white and black abolitionists were often stormy. Many white abolitionists called for legal, but not civil and social, racial equality; preferred light-skinned to dark-skinned blacks; and hesitated to admit African-Americans to antislavery societies. And widespread white prejudice made the life of any abolitionist precarious. Mobs attacked abolitionists often; one angry crowd in Alton, Illinois, murdered the abolitionist editor Elijah Lovejoy in 1837.

Abolitionists drew on the language of revivals to describe slavery as sin, but Protestant churches did not rally solidly behind abolition. Lyman Beecher roared against the evils of strong drink but whimpered about those of slavery.

As if external hostility were not enough, abolitionists differed passionately with one another. The largest national abolition group, the American Anti-Slavery Society, founded in 1833, was split by disagreements over whether abolitionists should form their own political party and about what role women should play in antislavery. Abolitionists from the Midwest and from the Burned-Over District, most with ties to Charles Grandison Finney, formed the antislavery Liberty party in 1840 and ran a presidential slate. In contrast, Garrison increasingly rejected *all* laws and government. Like slavery, Garrison and his extremist followers argued, all government depended on force, and because force was the opposite of Christian love, Christians should refuse to vote, to hold office, or to have anything to do with government.

Angelina and Sarah Grimké Sisters who were powerful antislavery speakers; later leaders of women's rights movement

Equally divisive to the abolitionist cause were questions over the role of women in the movement. In 1837 **Angelina and Sarah Grimké** (GRIM-kee), the daughters of a South Carolina slaveholder, made an antislavery lecture tour of New England. The Grimké sisters were controversial because they spoke to audiences of both men and women at a time when it was thought indelicate for women to address male audiences. Clergymen chastised the Grimké sisters for lecturing men rather than obeying them.

Such criticism backfired, turning the Grimkés and others to the cause of women's rights. In 1838 Sarah wrote *Letters on the Condition of Women and the Equality of the Sexes;* Angelina penned her equally classic *Letters to Catharine E. Beecher* (a militant opponent of female equality). Many male abolitionists tried to dampen the feminist flames, including the poet John Greenleaf Whittier, who dismissed women's grievances as "paltry" compared to the "great and dreadful wrongs of slavery." Garrison, welcoming the controversy, promptly espoused women's rights and urged equal treatment for women in the American Anti-Slavery Society. In 1840 the election of Abby Kelley to a previously all-male committee split the society, with many profeminists splintering off to form their own groups.

One of the most disruptive abolitionist tactics was to flood Congress with petitions calling for an end to slavery in the District of Columbia. In 1836, southerners secured passage of the gag rule, which automatically tabled abolitionist petitions and thus prevented congressional discussion of them. It was not lifted until 1845.

However, the importance of the gag rule was enormous. It shifted the issue from the abolition of slavery to the constitutional issues of free speech and the right to petition Congress. Members of Congress with little sympathy for abolition attacked the South for suppressing the right of petition. In effect, the gag rule fight vindicated Garrison's tactic of stirring up emotions on the slavery issue. By holding passions over slavery at the boiling point, Garrison kept the South on the defensive. The less secure southerners felt, the more they blundered into clumsy overreactions like the gag rule.

The Antislavery Alphabet
Viewing children as morally pure and hence as natural opponents of slavery, abolitionists produced antislavery toys, games, and, as we see here, alphabet books.

Women's Rights

Women occupied a paradoxical position in the 1830s. They could not vote and, if married, had no right to own property or to keep their own wages. At the same time, reform movements gave women unprecedented opportunities for public activity within their own "sphere"; for example, by suppressing liquor, women could claim that they were transforming wretched homes into nurseries of happiness.

The argument that women were natural guardians of family life was double-edged. It justified reform activities on behalf of the family but undercut women's demands for legal equality. So deeply ingrained was sexual inequality that most women came reluctantly to the issue of women's rights as a result of their experience in other reform movements, especially abolitionism. Among the early women's rights advocates who started their reform careers as abolitionists were the Grimké sisters, Lucretia (loo-CREE-shuh) Mott, Lucy Stone, and Abby Kelley.

Like abolitionism, the women's rights cause emphasized that differences of race and gender were unimportant. "Men and women," wrote Sarah Grimké, "are CREATED EQUAL!" The most articulate and aggressive advocates of women's rights tended to gravitate to William Lloyd Garrison, who stressed the degradation of women under slavery; the entire South was a vast brothel, Garrison wrote, in which slave women were "treated with more indelicacy and cruelty than cattle."

The discrimination within the abolition movement infuriated women and drove them to make women's rights a separate cause. When Lucretia Mott and other American women attended the World Anti-Slavery Convention in London in 1840, they were relegated to a screened-off section. The incident made a deep impression on Mott and on Elizabeth Cady Stanton. In 1848 they organized a women's rights convention at **Seneca** (SEN-ih-cuh) **Falls, New York.** The convention issued a Declaration of Sentiments that began, "All men and all women are created equal." The participants passed a series of resolutions, including a call for the right of women to vote, which would become the centerpiece of women's rights activity after the Civil War.

Seneca Falls, New York Site of first women's rights convention in 1848

The close association of women's rights with abolitionism hampered the women's movement, however. Women would not secure the right to vote throughout the nation until 1920, fifty-five years after the Thirteenth Amendment had abolished slavery. But

Elizabeth Cady Stanton with Sons, 1848

This daguerreotype shows Elizabeth Cady Stanton as she looked the year of the Seneca Falls Convention. Her career as a reformer, which carried her into temperance, antislavery, and women's rights, did not deter her from raising seven children.

Dorothea Dix Leader of crusade to improve conditions for the insane

there were some victories. In 1860, New York met the demand of the early feminists for greater equality in marriage by passing a comprehensive law allowing married women to own property. Many women were satisfied with such piecemeal reforms.

Penitentiaries and Asylums

Nineteenth-century reformers operated from radically new assumptions about the causes of poverty, crime, and insanity. Rather than seeing such deviant behavior as the result of defects in human nature, as earlier Americans had, these reformers concluded that it stemmed from drunken fathers and broken homes. At the root of all evil lay the failure of parental discipline, not the will of God or the wickedness of human nature. Thus secular reformers, like religious revivalists, concluded that the right combination of moral influences could change human nature.

To cure crime, for example, reformers created highly ordered and disciplined penitentiaries (pen-ih-TEN-char-eez) as substitutes for failed parental discipline. Sincere reformation, rather than simple incarceration, became the goal. Solitary confinement would purge offenders' violent habits, reformers believed; at new prisons in Auburn (AW-burn) and Ossining (AWSS-ih-ning), New York, prisoners could neither speak nor look at one another during the day and spent their nights in small, windowless cells.

Antebellum America also witnessed a transformation in the treatment of the poor. The infirm poor crowded into almshouses (AHMS-houses), and the able-bodied poor entered workhouses. Idealistic reformers argued that taking the poor from demoralizing surroundings and putting them into such highly regimented institutions could change them into virtuous, productive citizens. But the results were often dismal. In 1833 a legislative committee found that inmates of the Boston House of Industry were packed seven to a room and included unwed mothers, the sick, and the insane as well as the poor.

Many of the insane were confined in prisons. In 1841 an idealistic Unitarian schoolteacher, **Dorothea Dix,** discovered insane people kept in an unheated room at the East Cambridge, Massachusetts, jail. After visiting other jails and almshouses, an appalled Dix reported that the insane were confined "in *cages, closets, cellars, stalls, pens! Chained, naked, beaten with rods, and lashed into obedience.*" Supported by Horace Mann and other reformers, she encouraged legislatures to create separate insane asylums, and by 1860, twenty-eight states, four cities, and the federal government had built public mental institutions.

Penitentiaries, workhouses, and insane asylums all reflected the optimistic belief that deviancy could be erased by providing the right environment. Reformers believed that the unfettered freedom and individualism of American society were defects and that the poor, criminal, and insane needed regimentation. Although the idealism behind such reforms was genuine, later generations have questioned the assumptions underlying them.

Utopian Communities

The belief in the perfectibility of human nature and conduct found its most extreme expression in the "utopian" (yoo-TOH-pee-ehn) communities that flourished during the reform years. Most of these, founded by intellectuals, were meant to be alternatives to the prevailing competitive economy and models whose success would inspire others.

American interest in utopian communities began in the 1820s. In 1825 British industrialist Robert Owen founded the **New Harmony** community in Indiana. As a mill owner, Owen had improved his workers' living conditions and educational opportunities; he was convinced that the problems of the early industrial age were social, not political. Vice and misery would vanish if social arrangements were perfected, he thought. The key was the creation of small, planned communities—"Villages of Unity and Mutual Cooperation"—with a perfect balance of occupational, religious, and social groups.

New Harmony was to provide a model for the United States. But by 1827 the community, a magnet for idlers and fanatics, had fallen apart. However, Owen's belief that environment shaped character and that cooperation was superior to competition survived and influenced urban workers in particular throughout the nineteenth century.

Experimental communities with hopeful names such as Fruitlands and Hopedale proliferated amid the economic chaos of the late 1830s and 1840s. Brook Farm, the best-known of the utopian communities, which was founded near Boston in 1841, was the creation of a group of religious philosophers called **transcendentalists** (tran-sen-DEN-tuh-lists). Most transcendentalists, including Ralph Waldo Emerson, had started as Unitarians but then tried to revitalize Christianity by proclaiming the infinite spiritual capacities of ordinary men and women. Brook Farm, like other utopias, was both a retreat and a model. Sure that the competitive commercial life of the cities was unnatural, philosophers spent their evenings in lofty musings after a day perspiring in the cabbage patch. Brook Farm attracted several renowned writers, including Emerson and Nathaniel Hawthorne, and its literary magazine, *The Dial,* disseminated transcendentalist ideas about philosophy, art, and literature (see Chapter 11).

The most controversial of the antebellum experiments in communitarian utopianism, the Oneida (oh-NYE-duh) community in New York State, established in 1848 by John Humphrey Noyes (noise), challenged conventional notions about religion, property, gender roles, sex, dress, and motherhood. Renouncing private property, Oneidans practiced communism. Noyes insisted that men perform kitchen duties and allowed women to work in the community's stores and factories. What most upset outsiders was Noyes's application of communism to marriage. After exchanging wives with one of his followers, Noyes proclaimed that at Oneida all women were married to all men and all men to all women.

Although contemporaries dismissed Noyes as a crackpot, Oneida achieved considerable economic prosperity and attracted new members long after less radical utopian experiments, such as Brook Farm, had collapsed. Widely derided as fit only for eccentrics, utopias exemplified in extreme form the idealism and hopefulness that permeated reform in the Jacksonian era.

New Harmony One of most important utopian communities, founded in Indiana by Robert Owen

transcendentalists American religious philosophers who believed in the capacity of the human spirit; included many renowned writers

CHECKING IN

- Reform movements, invigorated by revivalism, swept over the North and West, but had little impact in the South.
- The temperance movement targeted workers and enjoyed considerable success.
- Educational reform aimed both to prepare children for life in an industrializing economy and to reinforce Protestant American culture; reformers also established new institutions to deal with the poor, criminals, and the insane.
- The antislavery movement gained momentum but was split by disagreements.
- The struggle for women's rights emerged from women's participation in the antislavery movement and other reform efforts.
- Reformers established a variety of utopian communities (usually unsuccessful), which sought to create a model for ideal society.

Chapter Summary

 DOWNLOAD THE MP3 AUDIO FILE OF THE CHAPTER SUMMARY, AND LISTEN TO IT ON THE GO.

How did American politics become more democratic in the first half of the nineteenth century? (page 215)

Starting in the 1820s, restrictions on voting for white males dwindled, and politics became increasingly inclusive. Andrew Jackson, seen as the incarnation of democratic politics, won the White House for two terms and fought for what he saw as the causes of the common man, especially in his crusade against the Bank of the United States. However, the Nullification Crisis revealed sharp differences between North and South.

What were the major factors in the rise of the second party system? (page 222)

In waging his "war" against the bank, Jackson intensified differences between the Democrats and the Whigs. This war helped to solidify the second party system but led to the Panic of 1837. The resulting depression engulfed and destroyed the presidency of Martin Van Buren and handed the White House to the Whigs in 1840, putting the second party system firmly in place. New styles of campaigning emerged with the "log cabin" campaign of 1840, and voter participation soared.

What changes took place in American religious life? (page 226)

Revivalism dominated religion for many Americans during the Second Great Awakening; emotionalism and emphasis on personal responsibility became more important. The Mormon Church, the first American-born religion, rose amid the fervor of revivalism. Revivalists generally emphasized the need for involvement in society and thus became a powerful stimulus to reform movements.

In what ways did reform movements attempt to forge a more orderly society? (page 229)

Reform movements targeted a wide range of society's issues, including alcohol consumption, education, the treatment of the mentally ill, prisons, slavery, and women's rights. Often reformers were participants in several crusades simultaneously, and one movement frequently led to another, as antislavery spawned the drive for women's rights. Utopian communities appeared and collapsed with little long-term effect.

KEY TERMS

Democrats *(p. 215)*

Whigs *(p. 215)*

"spoils system" *(p. 218)*

"Tariff of Abominations" *(p. 219)*

South Carolina Exposition and Protest (p. 219)

Nullification Crisis *(p. 220)*

Bank of the United States *(p. 221)*

log cabin *(p. 225)*

Second Great Awakening *(p. 226)*

Methodists *(p. 226)*

Charles Grandison Finney *(p. 227)*

Unitarians *(p. 227)*

Mormons *(p. 228)*

Joseph Smith *(p. 228)*

Shakers *(p. 228)*

temperance *(p. 229)*

Horace Mann *(p. 230)*

William Lloyd Garrison *(p. 231)*

Frederick Douglass *(p. 232)*

Angelina and Sarah Grimké *(p. 232)*

Seneca Falls, New York *(p. 233)*

Dorothea Dix *(p. 234)*

New Harmony *(p. 235)*

transcendentalists *(p. 235)*

CHAPTER 11

Technology, Culture, and Everyday Life
1840–1860

Steam Locomotive Crossing the
Niagara Railway Suspension Bridge

technology The practical
application of science to
improving life

CL This icon will direct you to the website
where you can Prepare for Class,
Improve Your Grade, and Ace the Test:
**www.cengage.com/history/boyer/
enduringconcise6e**

CHAPTER PREVIEW

Technology and Economic Growth
*What technological improvements brought
about American economic growth between 1840
and 1860?*

The Quality of Life
*In what ways did technology transform the lives of
ordinary Americans?*

Democratic Pastimes
*In what new ways did Americans pass their free
time during this period?*

The Quest for Nationality in Literature and Art
*How did the work of American writers and artists
become distinctly American?*

In the mid-nineteenth century, most Americans believed that **technology**—a word coined in 1829 to describe the application of science to improving the conditions of life—was God's chosen instrument of progress. For example, they forecast that the telegraph, a major invention of the age, would bring about world peace.

But progress had a darker side. Revolvers were useless for hunting or in battle, but excellent for the violent settling of private scores. Farmwomen who had traditionally earned money sewing by hand in their homes gave way to women who sewed by machine in sweatshops. Philosophers and artists began to worry about the despoliation of the landscape by factories, and conservationists launched conscious efforts to preserve enclaves of nature as parks and retreats.

237

TECHNOLOGY AND ECONOMIC GROWTH

What technological improvements brought about American economic growth between 1840 and 1860?

To optimistic Americans, technology was both democratic and progressive. Machines would advance civilization because they could perform the work of ten people without needing food or clothing, Daniel Webster contended.

The technology that transformed life in antebellum America included the steam engine, the cotton gin, the reaper, the use of interchangeable parts in manufacturing, the sewing machine, and the telegraph. Some of these inventions originated in Europe, but Americans had a flair for investing in others' inventions and perfecting their own. Sadly, these advances did not benefit everyone. The cotton gin, for example, riveted slavery firmly in place by intensifying southern dependence on cotton. Nonetheless, the improved transportation and increased productivity that technology made possible raised the living standard of many free Americans between 1840 and 1860.

Agricultural Advancement

Although few settlers ventured onto the treeless, semiarid Great Plains before the Civil War, settlement edged west after 1830 from the woodlands of Ohio and Kentucky into parts of Indiana, Michigan, and Illinois where flat grasslands (prairies) alternated with forests. The prairies' matted soil was difficult to break for planting, but in 1837 **John Deere** invented a steel-tipped plow that halved the labor required to clear prairie for planting. Timber for housing and fencing was available near the prairies, and settlement occurred rapidly.

John Deere Inventor of the steel plow

As wheat quickly became the Midwest's major cash crop, technology eased the task of harvesting. The traditional hand sickle consumed enormous amounts of time and labor, and collecting and binding the cut wheat consumed even more. Experiments with horse-drawn machines to replace sickles had failed until **Cyrus McCormick** of Virginia developed the mechanical reaper. In 1834 McCormick patented his machine; in 1847 he opened a factory in Chicago, and by 1860 he had sold 80,000 reapers. During the Civil War, McCormick made immense profits by selling 250,000 reapers. The mechanical reaper, which harvested grain seven times faster than traditional methods with half the labor force, guaranteed that wheat would dominate the midwestern prairies.

Cyrus McCormick Inventor of the mechanical reaper

Ironically, just as Connecticut Yankee Eli Whitney's cotton gin had created the Old South's economy, an invention by Cyrus McCormick, a pro-slavery Democrat, would help the Union win the Civil War. Northern agriculture took advantage of his reaper and copies of it to raise agricultural production; southerners, reliant on slave labor, had little reason to mechanize. The reaper would keep northern agricultural production high despite the mobilization of hundreds of thousands of northern men.

Although Americans generally remained wasteful farmers—abundant cheap land made it more "practical" to move west than to try to improve played-out soil—a movement for more efficient cultivation developed before the Civil War, primarily in the East. Because eastern soils could not compete with fertile western lands, eastern farmers had little choice.

Chronology

1823	Philadelphia completes the first urban water-supply system; James Fenimore Cooper, *The Pioneers*
1826	Cooper, *The Last of the Mohicans*
1833	The *New York Sun,* the first penny newspaper, is established
1834	Cyrus McCormick patents the mechanical reaper
1835	James Gordon Bennett establishes the *New York Herald*
1837	Ralph Waldo Emerson, "The American Scholar"
1839	Edgar Allen Poe, "The Fall of the House of Usher"
1841	P. T. Barnum opens the American Museum
1844	Samuel F. B. Morse patents the telegraph; Poe, "The Raven"
1846	William T. G. Morton successfully uses anesthesia; Elias Howe, Jr., patents the sewing machine
1849	Second major cholera epidemic
1850	Nathaniel Hawthorne, *The Scarlet Letter*
1851	Hawthorne, *The House of the Seven Gables;* Herman Melville, *Moby-Dick;* Erie Railroad completes its line to the West
1852	Pennsylvania Railroad completes its line between Philadelphia and Pittsburgh
1853	Ten small railroads are consolidated into the New York Central Railroad
1854	Henry David Thoreau, *Walden*
1855	Walt Whitman, *Leaves of Grass*
1856	Pennsylvania Railroad completes Chicago link; Illinois Central completed between Chicago and Cairo, Illinois
1857	Baltimore–St. Louis rail service completed
1858	Frederick Law Olmsted is appointed architect-in-chief for Central Park

Virginia wheat growers fertilized their soil with plaster left over from construction of the James River Canal and raised their average yield 250 percent between 1800 and 1860. In the 1840s cotton planters began importing guano (GWAH-no), the droppings of sea birds on islands off Peru, for use as a fertilizer. By applying fertilizers, eastern cotton growers could close the gap created by the superior fertility of soils in the Southwest.

(CL) Primary Source: Anonymous Endorsement of Scientific Agriculture

Technology and Industrial Progress

The early growth of U.S. manufacturing relied primarily on imported technology. That dependence lessened during the 1830s as American industries became more innovative.

Eli Whitney had pioneered in the application of **interchangeable parts** in the United States in 1798, but the manufacture of guns and other products using interchangeable parts still required a great deal of handwork before the components could be fitted together. By the 1840s, however, American factories had eliminated the need for hand-fitting by improving the quality of machine tools.

interchangeable parts Identical components made by machine tools, speeding manufacturing process; pioneered by Eli Whitney

Woman at Singer Sewing Machine

Asked to repair a sewing machine that did not do continuous stitching, Isaac M. Singer invented one that did. Patented in 1851, the Singer machine quickly dominated the market. Although most early sewing machines were used in factories, some had made their way into households by 1860.

— The American system of manufacturing offered multiple advantages. Damaged machines no longer had to be discarded but could be repaired simply by installing new parts. Improved machine tools allowed entrepreneurs to rapidly mass-produce new inventions. By the 1850s Connecticut firms, among them Smith & Wesson, were mass-producing the revolving pistol, which Samuel Colt had invented in 1836. Sophisticated machine tools made it possible to increase production "by confining a worker to one particular limb of a pistol until he had made two thousand." Elias Howe's sewing machine, invented in 1846, entered mass production only two years later.

After Samuel F. B. Morse transmitted the first telegraph message, Americans eagerly seized on the telegraph's promise to eliminate the constraints of time and place. They formed telegraph companies and strung lines with stunning speed. By 1852 more than fifteen thousand miles of line connected cities as distant as Quebec, New Orleans, and St. Louis. The first transcontinental line was completed in 1860. A later historian would christen the telegraph the "Victorian Internet" because of the ways it changed business and personal communication.

The Railroad Boom

Even more than the telegraph, the railroad dramatized technology's democratic promise. In 1790 even European royalty could travel no faster than fourteen miles an hour and then only with frequent changes of horses. By 1850 an ordinary American could travel three times as fast on a train. The swift, comfortable transportation that American railroads provided for the common person dramatized technology's democratic promise. U.S. railroads offered only one class of travel, in contrast to the several classes on European railroads. With the introduction of adjustable upholstered seats that could serve as couches at night, every American in effect traveled first class—except for African-Americans, who often were forced to sit separately.

Americans loved railroads "as a lover loves his mistress," one Frenchman wrote, but there was little to love about the earliest railroads. Sparks from locomotives showered the passengers riding in open cars, which were common. Travelers sometimes had to get out and pull trains to stations. Lacking lights, trains rarely ran at night. Before the introduction of standard time zones in 1883 (see Chapter 18), scheduling was a nightmare; at noon in Boston it was twelve minutes before noon in New York City. Delays were frequent, for trains on single-track lines had to wait on sidings for other trains to pass. Because a train's location was a mystery once it had left the station, these waits could seem endless.

Between 1840 and 1860 the size of the rail network and the power and convenience of trains were stunningly transformed. Railroad track went from three thousand to thirty thousand miles, flat-roofed coaches replaced open cars, kerosene lamps made night travel possible, and powerful engines let trains climb steep hills. Fifty thousand miles of telegraph wire enabled dispatchers to communicate with trains en route and thus to reduce delays.

Nonetheless, problems lingered. Sleeping accommodations remained crude and schedules, erratic. Because individual railroads used different-gauge track, frequent changes of train were necessary: there were eight changes between Charleston and

Bad Things of Railroads

Philadelphia in the 1850s. Yet nothing slowed the advance of railroads or cured America's mania for them. By 1860 the United States had more track than all the rest of the world.

Railroads spearheaded the second phase of the transportation revolution. Canals remained in use, but railroads, both faster and less vulnerable to winter freezes, gradually overtook them, first in passengers and then in freight. By 1860 the value of goods transported by railroads greatly exceeded that carried by canals.

During the 1850s the nation's rail net grew by 22,000 miles, with most of the expansion east of the Mississippi River. Cities such as Chicago, Chattanooga, and Atlanta boomed because of the railroads. Most important, the railroads crossed the Appalachian Mountains to link the East and the Midwest.

Chicago's growth illustrates the impact of these rail links. In 1849 it was a village of a few hundred people with virtually no rail service. By 1860 it had become a metropolis of 100,000, served by eleven railroads. Farmers in the upper Midwest no longer had to send their grain, livestock, and dairy products down the Mississippi to New Orleans; they could now ship their products directly east. Chicago supplanted New Orleans as the interior's main commercial hub.

The east-west rail lines stimulated the settlement and agricultural development of the Midwest. By 1860 Illinois, Indiana, and Wisconsin had replaced Ohio, Pennsylvania, and New York as the leading wheat-growing states. Enabling farmers to speed their produce to the East, railroads increased the value of farmland and promoted additional settlement. In turn, this population growth stimulated industrial development in cities such as Chicago and Minneapolis, for the new settlers needed lumber for fences and houses and mills to grind wheat into flour.

Railroads also spurred the growth of small towns along their midwestern routes. For example, the Illinois Central Railroad, which had more track than any other railroad in 1855, made money by hauling cargo and by real estate speculation. Purchasing land along its path, the Illinois Central laid out entire towns around its stations. The railroad used a template for all such towns, laying them out on a grid with east-west streets named after trees and north-south streets numbered. Soon one rail town looked like any other.

As the nation's first big business, railroads transformed the conduct of business, particularly in finance. State money had helped to finance many lines, but by the 1840s it began to dry up. Federal aid would not be widely available until the Civil War. Although local and county governments tried to fill the void, the dramatic expansion of the rail net in the 1850s required new sources of financing. Private investors had long purchased railroad stock, but the large trunk lines of the 1850s needed far more capital than small investors could generate. Thus the railroads turned to the capital market in New York City. The railroad boom helped to make Wall Street the nation's greatest capital market, as the securities of all the leading railroads were traded on the floor of the New York Stock Exchange. New York also became the center of modern investment firms. These companies evaluated securities issued by railroads in Toledo or Chattanooga and then found purchasers in New York, Paris, London, and Amsterdam. Controlling the flow of funds to the railroads, investment

Map 11.1 Railroad Growth, 1850–1860

Rail ties between the East and the Midwest greatly increased during the railroad boom of the 1850s.

Interactive Map: Population Distribution, 1790 & 1850

bankers soon influenced their internal affairs. A Wall Street analyst noted in 1851 that railroad men seeking financing "must remember that money is power, and that the [financier] can dictate to a great extent his own terms."

Rising Prosperity

Technology also improved life by lowering prices. Clocks that cost $50 to make by hand in 1800 could be made by machine for 50¢ by 1850. Widespread use of steam power led to a 25 percent rise in the average worker's real income (purchasing power) between 1840 and 1860; unlike water wheels, steam engines could run in all seasons, so workers did not have to face long winter layoffs. Although cotton textile workers saw little gain in hourly wages, their average annual wages rose from $160 to $201 between 1830 and 1869.

The growth of towns and cities also contributed to the upward trend in average annual wages. In contrast to rural farming areas, with their heavily seasonal labor, urban settings offered jobs year-round. Towns and cities also provided women and children—who seldom were paid for farm labor—new opportunities for paid work. Children's wages played an important role in family finances for working-class families. An average New York or Philadelphia working-class family spent $500 to $600 per year on food, rent, clothing, and fuel. However, an average male head of household earned $300 a year. Clearly, the survival of many families depended on the wages of children and wives.

The average urban worker was marginally better off than the average rural worker, primarily because of seasonal fluctuations in agricultural work. Most antebellum Americans continued to see farming as the ideal occupation, but comparatively few could raise the $500 or so in cash necessary to purchase, clear, and stock a farm and then wait three to five years for any reward. In many ways, farm workers were worse off than their urban counterparts.

The economic advantages that came with living in cities help explain why so many Americans moved to urban areas in the first half of the nineteenth century. Cities also provided an unprecedented range of comforts and conveniences.

CHECKING IN

- Technology, such as the steel plow, the mechanical reaper, and the cotton gin, revolutionized American agriculture.
- The American system of manufacturing, based on interchangeable parts, grew rapidly.
- The amount of railroad track multiplied tenfold, linking major cities and transforming villages into cities.
- Railroads, America's first big business, revolutionized not only transportation but also financial systems.
- Prices fell and prosperity increased for most white Americans.

THE QUALITY OF LIFE

In what ways did technology transform the lives of ordinary Americans?

Subtle but critical changes in the quality of daily life accompanied the large-scale transformations in transportation, production, and income in the two decades before the Civil War. These changes occurred within the home and affected such routine activities as eating, drinking, and washing. Americans became far more comfortable as machine-made furniture, stoves, and fresh food entered the home.

But change occurred unevenly. Technology made it possible for the middle class to enjoy luxuries formerly reserved for the rich, yet it widened the gulf between middle class and poor. As middle-class homes became increasingly lavish, the urban poor crowded into cramped tenements. And some critical elements—medicine, for example—lagged far behind in the technological explosion.

Dwellings

During the early 1800s the unattached and distinctive wood-frame houses dotting colonial urban skylines yielded to quickly constructed, uniform-looking brick row houses. In response to rising land values, row houses were typically built with narrow facades, and they were often twice as long from front to back as they were from side to side, a design that tended to shut out light. As land values soared (as much as 750 percent in Manhattan between 1785 and 1815), renting, rather than owning, homes became common. By 1815 more than half of the homes in large cities were rented. Skyrocketing land values also led to the subdivision of row houses for occupancy by several families. The worst of these, known as tenements, were usually the home to Irish immigrants and free blacks.

Fashionable urban residences usually faced small parks and boasted a *Park* or *Square* address, not the plebeian *Street*. The wealthy enjoyed elegant doors, curved staircases, carved columns, and fancifully shaped rooms, all beyond the reach of the middle class. However, the rise of mass-produced furniture brought furnishings in the elaborately ornamented French style known as rococo (roh-COH-coh) into middle-class homes by 1860. Technological advances in furniture making tended to level taste between the middle and upper classes while marking those classes off from everyone else.

In rural areas, the quality of housing depended as much on the date of settlement as on social class. In recently settled areas, the standard dwelling was a one-room log cabin with split-log floors that allowed in drafts, a roof that let in snow, a crude chimney made of sticks and clay, and windows covered by oiled paper or cloth. As rural communities matured, log cabins gave way to cheap and simple frame houses of two or more rooms with glass windows and better insulation.

Primary Source: Bowen House, View from the Road

Conveniences and Inconveniences

To us, everyday life in the 1840s and 1850s was primitive; but to contemporaries it was constantly improving. Stoves made it possible to cook several dishes at once, and railroads brought fresh vegetables to the city, an unobtainable luxury in the 1830s. Urban waterworks carried fresh water from rivers and reservoirs to hydrants. In 1823, Philadelphia completed the first urban water-supply system; by 1860, sixty-eight public water systems were operating in the United States.

Such new conveniences existed side by side with squalor. Coal stoves belched out soot to pollute the air and blacken new-fallen snow. Only the rich could afford fruit out of season. And so few homes had iceboxes that salt remained the principal means of preserving meat; Americans ate more pork than beef because salt destroyed the flavor of beef more than that of pork. Although public waterworks were engineering marvels, their impact was uneven; few urban houses had running water, so families carried water from street hydrants into their homes. Because hot running water was rare, the water had to be heated on the stove before one could take a bath. Not surprisingly, people rarely bathed.

Infrequent baths meant pungent body odors, but they mingled with a multitude of other strong scents. Even fashionable residential streets contained stables backed by mounds of manure. Street cleaning was left to private contractors, who often discharged their duties casually, so urban Americans relied on hogs, which they let roam freely to scavenge, to clean public thoroughfares. Stables backed by mounds of manure and outdoor privies added to the stench. Flush toilets were rare outside cities, and within cities, sewer systems lagged behind water systems. Boston had only 5,000 flush toilets in 1860 for a population of 178,000, a far higher ratio of toilets to people than most cities. Expensive conveniences like running water and flush toilets widened the gap between the haves and the have-nots. They also sharpened gender differences. Freed from making articles for home consumption, women were now expected to achieve fulfillment by obsessively making every house a "glorious temple" of spotless floors and gleaming furniture.

Disease and Health

epidemic disease Disease, such as cholera, yellow fever, and other diseases, that spreads rapidly and is difficult to control

Despite the slowly rising living standard, Americans remained vulnerable to disease. **Epidemic diseases** swept through antebellum American cities and felled thousands. Yellow fever and cholera (CAH-luh-rah) killed one-fifth of New Orleans's population in 1832–1833, and cholera alone killed 10 percent of St. Louis's population in 1849.

Ironically, the transportation revolution increased the danger of epidemic diseases. The cholera epidemic of 1832, the first truly national epidemic, followed shipping routes: one branch of the epidemic ran from New York City up the Hudson River, across the Erie Canal to Ohio, and down the Ohio River to the Mississippi and New Orleans; the other branch followed shipping up and down the East Coast from New York.

Major outbreaks of cholera or yellow fever intensified public calls for the establishment of municipal health boards. However, even when such agencies were formed, they were often powerless to require the reporting of diseases.

The inability of physicians to explain epidemic diseases led to general distrust of the medical profession and to making public health a low-priority issue (see Chapter 9). No one understood that bacteria caused cholera and yellow fever. Instead, doctors debated the "contagion" theory versus the "miasm" (MY-az-um) theory of disease. Contagionists, who believed that touch spread disease, called for quarantines of affected areas. Supporters of the miasm theory argued that poisonous gases (miasms) emitted by rotten vegetation or dead animals carried disease through the air. They concluded that swamps had to be drained and streets cleaned. It quickly became apparent that neither theory worked.

Although epidemic disease baffled antebellum physicians, the discovery of anesthesia opened the way for advances in surgery. Laughing gas (nitrous oxide) had long provided partygoers who inhaled it enjoyable sensations of giddiness and painlessness, but it was difficult to handle. Crawford Long, a Georgia physician who had attended laughing gas frolics in his youth, employed sulfuric ether (an easily transportable liquid with the same properties as nitrous oxide) during surgery. Long did not follow up his discovery, but in 1846 William T. G. Morton, a dentist, successfully employed sulfuric ether during an operation at Massachusetts General Hospital. Within a few years, ether was widely used.

The discovery of anesthesia improved the public image of surgeons, who had long been viewed as brutes hacking away at agonized patients. It also permitted longer and thus more careful operations. However, the failure of most surgeons to recognize the importance of clean hands and sterilized instruments partially offset the value of anesthesia. As early as 1843, Oliver Wendell Holmes, Sr., a poet and physician, published a paper on how unclean hands spread puerperal (poo-ER-puh-rul) fever among women giving birth, but disinfection was accepted only gradually. Operations remained as dangerous as the conditions they tried to heal. The mortality rate for amputations hovered around 40 percent, and during the Civil War, 87 percent of soldiers who suffered abdominal wounds died from them.

Primary Source:
Mourning Picture

Popular Health Movements

Doubtful of medicine and skeptical of the benefits of public health, antebellum Americans turned to various therapies that promised a longer, healthier life. Hydropathy (high-DRAW-puh-thee), the "water cure," offered "an abundance of water of dewy softness and crystal transparency, to cleanse, renovate, and rejuvenate the disease-worn and dilapidated system." Well-to-do women flocked to hydropathic sanitoriums both to relieve pain and to enjoy relaxation and exercise in a congenial gathering place.

Sylvester Graham, a temperance reformer turned health advocate, popularized dietary changes as the way to better health. He urged Americans to eat less; to substitute vegetables, fruits, and whole-grain bread (called Graham bread) for meat; to abstain from spices, coffee, tea, and alcohol; and to avoid sexual "excess" (by which he meant most sex).

Reformers became enthusiastic proponents of Graham's ideas. Abolitionists and others agreed with Graham that Americans' unnatural cravings, whether for red meat or for sex, stimulated violence and aggressive impulses. But Graham's doctrines also attracted a broad audience beyond the reform movements. His books sold well, and his public lectures were thronged. His commonsense ideas appealed to Americans wary of orthodox medicine, and he used familiar religious terms to describe disease, which was hell, and health, which amounted to a kind of heaven on earth.

phrenology Belief that one can read a person's character by examining bumps on the skull

Phrenology

The belief that each person was master of his or her own destiny underlay not only evangelical religion and health movements but also the most popular of the antebellum scientific fads: **phrenology** (free-NAHL-uh-jee). Created by a Viennese physician, Franz J. Gall, phrenology rested on the idea that the human mind comprised thirty-seven distinct faculties, or "organs," each localized in a different part of the brain. Phrenologists thought that the degree of each organ's development determined skull shape, so that they could accurately analyze an individual's character by examining the bumps and depressions of the skull.

In the United States two brothers, Orson and Lorenzo Fowler, became the chief promoters of phrenology in the 1840s. Orson Fowler opened a publishing house (Fowlers and Wells) that marketed phrenology books everywhere. The Fowlers met criticisms that phrenology was godless by pointing out a huge organ called "Veneration" to prove that people were naturally religious, and they answered charges that phrenology was pessimistic by claiming that exercise could improve every desirable mental organ.

Phrenology appealed to Americans as a "practical" science. In a mobile, individualistic society, it promised a quick assessment of others. Merchants sometimes used phrenological charts to hire clerks, and some young women even induced their fiancés to undergo a phrenological analysis before marriage.

"The Illustrated Phrenological Almanac, 1859"

By dividing the brain into a large number of "faculties," phrenologists like Lorenzo Fowler, editor of the *Phrenological Almanac* for 1859, made the point that each person, regardless of whether born high or low, had an abundance of improvable talents.

CHECKING IN

- Housing generally improved in the mid-nineteenth century, but class distinctions became more pronounced.
- Improvements in urban living conditions, such as stoves and water systems, were somewhat offset by increased pollution.
- Epidemic diseases still flourished, but anesthesia came into use, and interest in antisepsis stirred.
- Health fads like hydropathy proliferated.
- Phrenology became a popular phenomenon.

penny press Cheap newspapers developed by James Gordon Bennett

Easily understood and practiced, and filled with the promise of universal betterment, phrenology was ideal for antebellum America. Just as Americans had invented machines to better their lives, they could invent "sciences" that promised human betterment.

DEMOCRATIC PASTIMES

In what new ways did Americans pass their free time during this period?

Between 1830 and 1860, technology transformed recreation into a commodity that could be purchased in the form of cheap newspapers and novels and equally cheap tickets to plays, museums, and lectures. Fortunes awaited entrepreneurs who could sense what kind of entertainment people wanted and who could use available technology to satisfy them. James Gordon Bennett, one of the founders of the **penny press,** and P. T. Barnum, the greatest showman of the century, made the public want what they had to sell.

Technology also began the process by which individuals became spectators rather than creators of their own amusements. Americans had also found ways to enjoy themselves—even the gloomiest Puritans had enjoyed games and sports. After 1830, however, the provision of entertainment began to shift from individuals to the entrepreneurs who supplied ways to entertain the public.

Newspapers

In 1830 the typical American newspaper was four pages long, with the front and back pages filled almost completely with advertisements. The interior pages contained editorials, reprints of political speeches, notices of political events, and information about shipping. Even the most prominent papers had a daily circulation of only one thousand to two thousand; subsidies from political parties or factions supported them.

Because they could be profitable without being popular, most early newspapers had limited appeal. Priced at six cents an issue, the average paper was too expensive for a worker who earned less than a dollar a day. Moreover, with few eye-catching news stories or illustrations, papers seemed little more than bulletin boards.

In the 1830s technology began to transform newspapers. Cheaper paper and steam-driven presses drastically lowered production costs, and enterprising journalists, among them James Gordon Bennett, saw the implications: slash prices, boost circulation, and reap vast profits. In 1833 New York's eleven daily newspapers had a combined daily circulation of only 26,500. Two years later, the combined circulation of the three largest "penny" newspapers had soared to 44,000. From 1830 to 1840 national newspaper circulation rose from 78,000 to 300,000, and the number of weekly newspapers more than doubled.

The penny press also revolutionized the marketing and format of newspapers. Newsboys hawked the penny papers on busy street corners, and reporters filled the papers with gripping news stories designed to attract readers. As sociologist Michael Schudson observes, "The penny press invented the modern concept of 'news'." Politics and economics yielded place to human interest stories: rape, robbery, murder, and abandoned children. The penny papers also used the telegraph to speed both news and human-interest stories to readers.

Some penny papers were little more than scandal sheets, but others, such as Bennett's *New York Herald* and Horace Greeley's *New York Tribune,* pioneered modern financial and political reporting. The *Herald* featured a daily "money article" that analyzed and interpreted financial events. "The spirit, pith, and philosophy of commercial affairs is what men of business want," Bennett wrote.

The Theater

Like newspapers, theaters increasingly appealed to a mass audience. Antebellum theaters were large and crowded; cheap seats drew a democratic throng of lawyers and merchants and their wives, artisans and clerks, sailors and noisy boys, and a sizable body of prostitutes. The presence of prostitutes in the audience was only one of many factors that made theaters vaguely disreputable. Theater audiences were notoriously rowdy: they stamped their feet, hooted at villains, and threw potatoes and garbage at the stage when they disliked the characters or the acting.

The plays themselves were as diverse as the audiences. Melodramas, whose plots resembled those of sentimental novels, were popular; vice was punished, virtue was rewarded, and the heroine married the hero. Yet the single most popular dramatist was William Shakespeare. In 1835 Philadelphia audiences witnessed sixty-five performances of his plays. Shakespeare himself might not have recognized some of these performances, adapted as they were for popular audiences. Theatrical managers highlighted swordfights and assassinations, cut long speeches, and changed tragic endings to happy ones. Producers arranged for short performances or demonstrations between acts. In the middle of *Macbeth,* the audience might see an impersonation of Tecumseh or of Aaron Burr, jugglers and acrobats, a drummer beating twelve drums at once, or a three-year-old who weighed one hundred pounds.

minstrel show Blackface show of "Negro" song and dance

Minstrel Shows

The **minstrel shows** that Americans flocked to see in the 1840s and 1850s forged enduring stereotypes that buttressed white Americans' sense of superiority by diminishing blacks. The shows arose in northern cities in the 1840s as white men in "blackface" took the stage to present an evening of songs, dances, and humorous sketches.

Although the performances featured elements of African-American culture, especially dance steps, most of the songs were from white culture. Stephen Foster's "Camp-town Races" and "Massa's in the Cold, Cold Ground," first performed in minstrel shows, reflected whites' notions of how blacks sang, not authentic black music. The images of blacks projected by minstrelsy catered to the prejudices of the working-class whites who dominated the audiences. Minstrel troupes depicted blacks as stupid, clumsy, and obsessively musical, and emphasized their Africanness. At a time of intensifying political conflict over race, minstrel shows planted images and expectations about blacks' behavior through stock characters such as Uncle Ned, the tattered, humble, and docile slave; and Zip Coon, the arrogant urban free black who paraded around in a high hat and long-tailed coat and lived off his girlfriends' money.

Dan Bryant, the Minstrel
Bryant was one of many antebellum popularizers of black minstrelsy.

By the 1850s cities from New York to San Francisco had minstrel theaters, and touring professionals brought minstrelsy to small towns and villages. The craze for minstrelsy even brought minstrels to the White House to entertain Presidents John Tyler, James K. Polk, Millard Fillmore, and Franklin Pierce.

P. T. Barnum Showman who exhibited "natural wonders," real and otherwise

P. T. Barnum

No one understood better than **P. T. Barnum** how to turn the public's craving for entertainment into a profitable business. He was simultaneously a hustler who cheated his customers before they could cheat him, and an idealist who founded a newspaper to attack wrongdoing and who thought of himself as a public benefactor.

After moving to New York City in 1834, Barnum began his career as an entrepreneur of entertainment. His first venture exhibited an African-American woman, Joyce Heth, whom Barnum billed as the 169-year-old former slave nurse of George Washington. In Barnum's mind, the truth or falsehood of the claim was irrelevant. What mattered was that people would pay to see her. It was the start of a lifelong game between Barnum and the public.

In 1841 Barnum purchased a run-down museum in New York City, rechristened it the American Museum, and opened a new chapter in the history of popular entertainment. Avoiding the educational slant of other museums, Barnum concentrated on curiosities and faked exhibits; he wanted to interest people, not to educate them. The American Museum included ventriloquists, magicians, albinos, a five-year-old midget named Tom Thumb, and the "Feejee Mermaid," a shrunken oddity "taken alive in the Feejee Islands." By 1850 Barnum's entertainment emporium was the best-known museum in the nation.

A genius at publicity, Barnum recognized that newspapers could invent as well as report news. Thus he frequently wrote letters (under various names) to newspapers hinting that the scientific world was agog over some astonishing curiosity that the public could soon view at the American Museum. Barnum's success rested on more than people's curiosity, however. A temperance advocate, he provided lectures on the evils of alcohol and gave the place a reputation as a center for safe family amusement. In addition, Barnum tapped the public's insatiable appetite for natural wonders. At a time when each year brought new technological marvels, Americans would believe in anything, even the Feejee Mermaid.

CHECKING IN

- Between 1830 and 1860, entrepreneurs found new business opportunities with popular entertainment.
- James Gordon Bennett revolutionized the newspaper world with the penny press.
- Theater became a major source of entertainment for diverse and often rowdy audiences.
- P. T. Barnum introduced Americans to the wonders of the Feejee Mermaid and other oddities.
- Blackface minstrel shows provided popular entertainment while reinforcing negative stereotypes of African-Americans.

THE QUEST FOR NATIONALITY IN LITERATURE AND ART

How did the work of American writers and artists become distinctly American?

Europeans paid no attention to American poetry or fiction before the 1820s. Although Americans could point with pride to Washington Irving's tales of Sleepy Hollow and Rip Van Winkle, they also had to admit that Irving had done most of his work while living in England.

After 1820 the United States experienced a literary flowering known as the **"American Renaissance."** Leading figures of this burst of creativity included James Fenimore Cooper, Ralph Waldo Emerson, Henry David Thoreau (theh-ROW), Margaret Fuller, Walt Whitman, Nathaniel Hawthorne, Herman Melville, and Edgar Allan Poe. In 1830, 40 percent of books published in the United States were written by Americans; by 1850 this had increased to 75 percent.

This renaissance provided Americans opportunity to use their nation in both literature and art. The quest for a distinctively American literature shaped the writings of Cooper, Emerson, and Whitman. It also revealed itself in the majestic paintings of the Hudson River school, the first home-grown movement in art, and in the landscape architecture of Frederick Law Olmsted.

American Renaissance Literary movement that flourished after 1820

Roots of the American Renaissance

Two broad movements, one economic and the other philosophical, contributed to this development. First, the transportation revolution created a national market for books, especially fiction. First to benefit from this new market was Sir Walter Scott, a British author whose historical novels became wildly popular in the United States and showed that there was a huge market for fiction. Scott became a model for many American authors, including James Fenimore Cooper.

Second, a new philosophical movement, romanticism, saturated the American Renaissance. Romantics emphasized emotion and inner feelings, focusing on the individual and his or her unique response to nature and emotion. This new emphasis on emotion created a more democratic literature, accessible to virtually everyone (unlike earlier classicism, which demanded a knowledge of ancient history and mythology). Women entered the fiction market in large numbers; although barred from higher education and the classics, they could easily access their emotions and tweak the emotions of their readers. Harriet Beecher Stowe's massive best-seller, *Uncle Tom's Cabin,* illustrates how successful women authors were in tugging at their readers' heartstrings. Novels also possessed a subversive quality, a freedom of plot and character not available to the essayist. Authors could create unconventional characters, situations, and outcomes, and left more room for interpretation by the reader, who was far more likely to focus on plot and characters than moral sentiments.

Cooper, Emerson, Thoreau, Fuller, and Whitman

James Fenimore Cooper was a trailblazer in the development of a national literature with distinctively American themes. In his frontiersman Natty Bumppo, "Leatherstocking," Cooper created an American archetype. Natty first appears in *The Pioneers* (1823) as an old man, a former hunter, who blames the farmers for wantonly destroying upstate New York's game and turning the silent and majestic forests into deserts of tree stumps. As a spokesman for nature against the march of civilization, Natty became a highly popular figure, and his life unfolded in several other enormously popular novels, such as *The Last of the Mohicans* (1826), *The Pathfinder* (1840), and *The Deerslayer* (1841).

During the 1830s Ralph Waldo Emerson emerged as the most influential spokesman for those who sought a national literature and art. Emerson, who served briefly as a Unitarian minister and then became a popular lecturer, voiced American intellectual ambitions in his 1837 address "The American Scholar," which called on American writers to break free of European standards.

As the leader of transcendentalism, the American offshoot of romanticism, Emerson contended that ideas of God and freedom were innate, not the result of reason. Knowledge was like sight—an instantaneous and direct perception of truth. Anyone, whether a learned university professor or a common farmer, could glimpse truth by following the promptings of his heart. Thus the United States, young and democratic, could produce as noble a literature and art as any tradition-bound European nation. "Our day of independence, our long apprenticeship to the learning of other lands draws to a close," he proclaimed. Let "the single man plant himself indomitably on his instincts and...the huge world will come around to him."

Although he admired Cooper's fiction, Emerson expressed his own version of literary nationalism in essays characterized by a homely reliance on the individual as well as an interest in broad philosophical questions. The true scholar, he stressed, must be independent. Emerson's essays did not rely on systematic arguments and evidence; with his conviction that truth was intuitive and individual, he relied on a sequence of vivid if unconnected assertions whose truth the reader would instantly see. One of his readers remarked that listening to Emerson was like trying to see the sun in a heavy fog; one could see light but never the sun itself.

Emerson had a magnetic attraction for young intellectuals ill at ease in conventional society. Henry David Thoreau, born in 1817, typified the younger Emersonians. Unlike Emerson, whose adventurousness was largely intellectual, Thoreau was both a thinker and a doer. At one point he went to jail rather than pay poll taxes that would support the Mexican War, a conflict that he saw as part of a southern conspiracy to extend slavery. The experience of jail led Thoreau to write *Civil Disobedience* (1849), in which he defended disobedience of unjust laws.

In spring 1845 Thoreau moved a few miles from Concord, Massachusetts, into the woods near Walden Pond. He constructed a simple cabin on land owned by Emerson and spent the next two years providing for his wants away from civilization. Thoreau's stated purpose for his retreat to Walden was to write a book about a canoe trip that he and his brother had taken, but he soon discovered a larger purpose and undertook a much more important book. *Walden* (1854), although it abounded with descriptions of nature and wildlife, carried a larger, transcendentalist message. Thoreau proclaimed that his woodland retreat had taught him that only a few weeks' work was needed to satisfy material needs; most of the year could be used to examine life's purpose. The problem with Americans, he wrote, was that they turned themselves into "mere machines" to acquire wealth without asking why. Thoreau prodded Americans with the uncomfortable truth that material progress and moral progress were not as intimately related as they liked to think.

One of the most remarkable figures in Emerson's circle was Margaret Fuller, an intellectual whose status distanced her from conventional society. Her father, although disappointed that she was not a boy, gave her the sort of education a young man might have received at Harvard; she read Latin and Greek, the modern German romantics, and the English literary classics. Transcendentalism, with its emphasis on the free life of the spirit

Margaret Fuller

In 1846, Margaret Fuller was sent by Horace Greeley to Europe as the *Tribune*'s foreign correspondent. There she met artists and writers, observed the Revolutions of 1848, and married an Italian nobleman. On her return to America in 1850, she, her husband, and infant son died in a shipwreck off Long Island.

and the need for each person to discover truth on his or her own, opened a new world for Fuller. For five years she supported herself by presiding over "conversations" by Boston's elite men and women. Transcendentalism also reinforced her feminist ideas; in *Women in the Nineteenth Century* (1845) she cast aside the doctrine of "separate spheres" and contended that no woman could achieve personal fulfillment without developing her intellectual abilities and overcoming her fear of being called masculine.

Another unconventional thinker with whom Emerson sympathized was the poet Walt Whitman, self-taught, exuberant, earthy, outgoing, and in love with everything American except slavery. A journalist and fervent Democrat, Whitman had an intimate, affectionate knowledge of ordinary Americans. His reading of Emerson nurtured his belief that the United States would be the cradle of a new citizen in whom natural virtue would flourish. The threads of Whitman's early career came together in his major work, *Leaves of Grass,* a book of poems first published in 1855.

Leaves of Grass shattered existing poetic conventions. Whitman composed in free verse, and his blunt, often lusty words assailed "delicacy." He wrote of "the scent of these armpits finer than prayer" and "winds whose soft-tickling genitals rub against me."

To some contemporary critics, *Leaves of Grass* seemed the work of an escaped lunatic. One derided it as a "heterogeneous mass of bombast, egotism, vulgarity, and nonsense." Emerson and a few others, however, reacted enthusiastically. Emerson had long awaited the appearance of "the poet of America" and knew immediately that Whitman was that poet.

Hawthorne, Melville, and Poe

Three major writers of the 1840s and 1850s strayed far from Emerson's ideals. Nathaniel Hawthorne, Herman Melville, and Edgar Allan Poe wrote fiction that paid little heed to Emerson's call for a literature treating the everyday experiences of ordinary Americans. Hawthorne, for example, set *The Scarlet Letter* (1850) in New England's Puritan past, *The House of the Seven Gables* (1851) in a mansion haunted by memories of the past, and *The Marble Faun* (1859) in Rome. Poe set several of his short stories in Europe; and Melville's novels *Typee* (1846), *Omoo* (1847), and *Mardi* (1849) took place in the exotic South Seas, whereas his masterpiece, *Moby-Dick* (1851), was set aboard a whaler.

In part, these three writers felt that American life lacked the materials for great fiction. Hawthorne bemoaned the difficulty of writing about a country "where there is no shadow, no antiquity, no mystery, no picturesque and gloomy wrong." Psychology, not society, fascinated these writers. Each probed the depths of the human mind rather than the intricacies of social relationships. Their work displayed an underlying pessimism about the human condition and the fundamental irrationality of human nature.

Pessimism led them to create characters obsessed by pride, guilt, a desire for revenge, or a quest for perfection and then to set their stories along the byways of society, where they could explore the complexities of human motivation without the jarring intrusions of everyday life. For example, in *The Scarlet Letter* Hawthorne returned to the Puritan era to examine the psychological and moral consequences of the adultery committed by Hester Prynne (prin) and the minister Arthur Dimmesdale, although he devoted little attention to depicting the Puritan village in which the action takes place. Melville, in *Moby-Dick,* created the frightening Captain Ahab (AY-hab), whose relentless pursuit of a white whale fails to fill the chasm in his soul and brings death to all his crew except the narrator. Poe, in his short story "The Fall of the House of Usher" (1839), interwove the symbol of a crumbling mansion with the mental agony of a crumbling family.

Although these three authors ignored Emerson's call to write about the ordinary life of their fellow Americans, they fashioned a distinctively American fiction. Their works, preoccupied with analysis of moral dilemmas and psychological states, fulfilled Tocqueville's prediction that writers in democratic nations, while rejecting traditional sources of fiction, would explore the abstract and universal questions of human nature.

Literature in the Marketplace

The suspicion that commercialism would corrupt art did not entirely vanish in nineteenth-century America, but it certainly withered. The brilliant poet Emily Dickinson made little or no attempt to publish her work at all. But other authors, hard strapped for cash, entered the marketplace. Poe, for example, scratched out a meager living writing short stories for popular magazines. Thoreau craved recognition and tried to market his poems in New York City; failing that, he turned to detailed narratives of nature that sold very well.

Emerson helped to promote the lyceum (lye-SEE-um), a new institution aimed at bringing culture to a broader public. Local organizations for sponsoring lectures, lyceums blossomed rapidly between the late 1820s and 1860. Taking advantage of the emergence of the railroad, Emerson worked the lyceum circuit, presenting most of his essays as lectures before publishing them, and relied on lecture fees as his principal source of income. Newly built railroads and cheap newspapers that announced his comings and goings enabled others to follow in his path.

Although few women traveled the lyceum circuit, they discovered other ways to tap into the growing market for literature. Writing fiction was the most lucrative occupation open to women prior to the Civil War.

Sentimental novels, written mainly by women for women, dominated popular fiction in the 1840s and 1850s. Susan Warner, one of the most popular writers, used such tearjerkers to elevate herself from poverty to luxury. In her *The Wide, Wide World,* the heroine wept, on the average, every other page for two volumes. Women's fiction could also be subversive, challenging the image of men as steadfast providers and women as delicate dependents. In a typical novel, a female orphan or a spoiled rich girl was thrown into hard times by a drunken father and learned to prevail. The moral was clear: women could overcome trials and improve their lives.

Warner and other writers benefited from technology that drastically lowered the price of books. Before 1830, the enormously popular books of Sir Walter Scott had been issued in three-volume sets that retailed for as much as thirty dollars. By the 1840s, paperbacks costing as little as seven cents flooded the marketplace.

This sea of popular culture threatened to swamp Emerson, Hawthorne, Poe, and Melville. Emerson competed on the lecture circuit against P. T. Barnum; Hawthorne complained bitterly about "female scribblers"; and Poe maintained that the public's judgment of a writer's merit was nearly always wrong. Nonetheless, society by and large did not ignore these major writers. Emerson's lectures made him famous, *The Scarlet Letter* enjoyed strong sales, and Poe's "The Raven" was so popular that some suggested that the raven replace the eagle as America's national bird.

American Landscape Painting   American painters between 1820 and 1860 also sought to develop nationality in their work. Lacking a mythic past of gods and goddesses, they subordinated historical and figure painting to landscape painting. The American landscape, though barren of the "poetry of decay" that Europe's ruined castles and crumbling temples provided, was fresh and relatively unencumbered by the human imprint. These conditions posed a challenge to the painters of the **Hudson River School,** which flourished from the 1820s to the 1870s. Its best-known representatives—Thomas Cole, Asher Durand, and Frederic Church—painted scenes of the unspoiled region around the Hudson River.

Hudson River School Landscape painting that emphasized grandeur, emotion

Although all three men compared the majesty of the Hudson to that of the Rhine, none was exclusively a landscapist. Some of Cole's most popular paintings were allegories, such as *The Course of Empire,* a sequence of five canvases depicting the rise and fall of an ancient city; it implied that luxury doomed republican virtue.

The works of Washington Irving and the opening of the Erie Canal had piqued interest in the Hudson during the 1820s. Then, after 1830, Emerson and Thoreau lauded primitive nature; "in wildness is the preservation of the world," Thoreau wrote. By this time, much of the original American forest had already fallen to pioneer axes, and one writer urgently concluded that "it behooves our artists to rescue from [civilization's] grasp the little that is left before it is too late."

The Hudson River painters did more than preserve a passing wilderness; they also emphasized emotional effect. Cole's rich colors; billowing clouds; massive, gnarled trees; towering peaks; and deep chasms so heightened the dramatic impact of his paintings that poet William Cullen Bryant compared them to "acts of religion." In powerful, evocative canvases, American artists aimed to capture the natural grandeur of their land.

Like Cole, George Catlin tried to preserve a vanishing America through his art. His goal was to paint as many Native Americans as possible in their pure and "savage" state. By 1837 he had created 437 oil paintings and thousands of sketches of faces and customs from nearly fifty tribes. Catlin's romantic view of the Indians as noble savages was a double-edged sword. His admirers delighted in his dignified portrayals of Indians but shared his foreboding that the march of progress had already doomed these noble creatures to oblivion.

Landscape architects tried to create small enclaves of nature to provide spiritual refreshment to harried city dwellers. "Rural" cemeteries with pastoral names like Harmony Grove, placed near major cities, became tourist attractions, designed as much for the living as for the dead. On a grander scale Frederick Law Olmsted and Calvert Vaux (voh) designed New York City's Central Park to look like undisturbed countryside. Drainage pipes carried water to man-made lakes, and trees screened out the surrounding buildings. Central Park became an idealized version of nature, meant to remind visitors of landscapes that they had seen in pictures. Thus nature was made to mirror art.

CHECKING IN

- Romanticism combined with the technological revolution to produce an "American Renaissance."
- American literature took on nationalistic themes with James Fenimore Cooper and his tales of the frontier.
- Ralph Waldo Emerson was the center of the transcendentalist movement, which included Henry David Thoreau and Margaret Fuller.
- American writers such as Poe, Hawthorne, and Melville plumbed the depths of the human psyche.
- The Hudson River School of painting romanticized the American landscape and drenched it in emotion.

Chapter Summary

 DOWNLOAD THE MP3 AUDIO FILE OF THE CHAPTER SUMMARY, AND LISTEN TO IT ON THE GO.

What technological improvements brought about American economic growth between 1840 and 1860? (page 238)

Rapid technological growth revolutionized agriculture and greatly increased productivity in the manufacturing sector as well. Railroads played a vital role, linking cities, spawning new cities, creating markets, and providing a new business model. Prices fell, and prosperity rose.

In what ways did technology transform the lives of ordinary Americans? (page 242)

As cities grew, housing and living conditions improved for better-off residents, but squalor and pollution persisted, and class distinctions sharpened. The inability to control epidemic disease fed such popular fads as hydropathy and phrenology.

In what new ways did Americans pass their free time during this period? (page 246)

Popular entertainment became the realm of entrepreneurs such as James Bennett Gordon with his "penny press" and P. T. Barnum with his stable of wonders. Theater flourished, drawing diverse and rowdy audiences, and blackface minstrel shows reinforced negative stereotypes.

How did the work of American writers and artists become distinctly American? (page 248)

The disappearing frontier elicited a distinctly American literature from James Fenimore Cooper. An "American Renaissance" produced such "democratic" writers as Whitman and Emerson, as well as those fascinated by the darker side of human nature, such as Poe, Hawthorne, and Melville. The Hudson River School emphasized the grandeur and emotion of the American landscape.

KEY TERMS

technology *(p. 237)*
John Deere *(p. 238)*
Cyrus McCormick *(p. 238)*
interchangeable parts *(p. 239)*
epidemic disease *(p. 239)*
phrenology *(p. 245)*
penny press *(p. 246)*
minstrel show *(p. 247)*
P. T. Barnum *(p. 248)*
American Renaissance *(p. 249)*
Hudson River School *(p. 253)*

CHAPTER 12

The Old South and Slavery

1830–1860

African-American Family Group in Virginia

Nat Turner Leader of largest slave rebellion in U.S. history

CL This icon will direct you to the website where you can Prepare for Class, Improve Your Grade, and Ace the Test: **www.cengage.com/history/boyer/enduringconcise6e**

CHAPTER PREVIEW

King Cotton
How did the rise of cotton cultivation affect the South?

The Social Groups of the White South
What major social divisions segmented the white South?

Social Relations in the White South
How did slavery affect social relations in the South?

Life Under Slavery
How did slaves and free blacks respond to their circumstances?

The Emergence of African-American Culture
What were the distinctive features of the culture that developed among slaves?

Slipping through the swampy woodlands of Southampton County, Virginia, in the early morning of August 22, 1831, a band of slaves led by **Nat Turner** embarked on a grisly campaign of liberation. As the death count rose, so did the number of slaves following Turner; by noon more than sixty slaves had taken up axes, hatchets, and muskets, and more than sixty whites had been shot, clubbed, or hacked to death.

Despite Southampton County's isolation, word of the slave uprising soon reached the capital, Richmond, and neighboring North Carolina counties, and thousands of militia and vigilantes poured into the area. Shocking destruction greeted them; dismembered bodies and fresh blood testified to the rage unleashed by the rebels. In turn, the slaves would fall victim to white rage, as scores of blacks were killed, whether or not they had actually been involved. Most of Turner's followers were either shot on sight or jailed, tried, and hanged. Turner himself eluded capture until late October; after a trial he, too, was hanged.

White Virginians were stunned. What had gone wrong? Slavery in Virginia, they believed, was relatively mild, certainly in comparison to the harsh conditions in Alabama and Mississippi. And Nat Turner's background at first glance offered no answers—he did not claim that he had been mistreated by his owners. Far more was known about Nat Turner than any other black slave because of his "Confessions," recorded by his court-appointed attorney.

Nat Turner

By noon Turner's army, which had grown to sixty or seventy followers, had murdered about sixty whites. As word of trouble spread, militia and vigilantes, thousands strong, poured into Southampton from across the border in North Carolina and from other counties in Virginia.

What the "Confessions" did reveal was in many ways more troubling than a simple litany of mistreatment and resentment. The Nat Turner of the "Confessions" was an intelligent and deeply religious man who had learned to read and write in childhood. Although Virginians, like most southerners, thought that Christianity would make slaves more docile, Nat Turner had focused on biblical passages threatening death to anyone who "stealeth" a man, a fair description of slavery. A mystic and prophet, Turner claimed that in his childhood he had seen heavenly visions of black and white spirits fighting each other. A solar eclipse had been, he thought, God's signal that the time had come for him to lead his people to freedom by killing slaveholders.

Asked shortly before his death whether he had been mistaken, Nat Turner replied, "Was not Christ crucified?" White southerners read his confessions and shuddered; many concluded that they were living on a "smothered volcano."

In the short term, Nat Turner's rebellion triggered a fierce debate over emancipation of slaves in the Virginia legislature of 1831–1832; in the long run, it hardened the hold that slavery had on the South. Once Virginia rejected emancipation, the word all but disappeared from the southern vocabulary. As northern states one by one jettisoned slavery, southern states clung to it more fiercely. Although the Upper and Lower South differed tremendously, slavery forged the two sections into a single entity known as the Old South.

KING COTTON

How did the rise of cotton cultivation affect the South?

In 1790 the South was essentially stagnant. Tobacco, its primary cash crop, had lost its economic vitality even as it had depleted the once-rich southern soils, and neither rice nor cotton could replace tobacco's economic importance. Three out of four southerners still lived along the Atlantic seaboard, specifically in the Chesapeake and the Carolinas. One of three resided in Virginia alone.

The contrast between that South and the dynamic South of 1850 was stunning. By 1850 southerners had moved south and west—now only one out of seven southerners lived in Virginia—and cotton reigned as king, shaping this new South. The growth of the British textile industry had created a huge demand for cotton, while Indian removal had made way for southern expansion into the "Cotton Kingdom," a broad swath of land that stretched from South Carolina, Georgia, and northern Florida in the east through Alabama, Mississippi, central and western Tennessee, and Louisiana, and from there on to Arkansas and Texas.

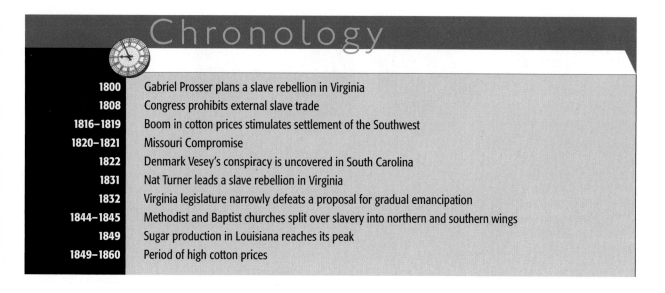

Chronology

1800	Gabriel Prosser plans a slave rebellion in Virginia
1808	Congress prohibits external slave trade
1816–1819	Boom in cotton prices stimulates settlement of the Southwest
1820–1821	Missouri Compromise
1822	Denmark Vesey's conspiracy is uncovered in South Carolina
1831	Nat Turner leads a slave rebellion in Virginia
1832	Virginia legislature narrowly defeats a proposal for gradual emancipation
1844–1845	Methodist and Baptist churches split over slavery into northern and southern wings
1849	Sugar production in Louisiana reaches its peak
1849–1860	Period of high cotton prices

The Lure of Cotton

Southerners extolled **King Cotton.** A warm climate, wet springs and summers, and relatively dry autumns made the Lower (or Deep) South ideal for cultivating cotton. A cotton farmer needed neither slaves nor cotton gins nor the capital required for sugar cultivation. Indeed, perhaps 50 percent of farmers in the "Cotton Belt" owned no slaves, and to process their harvest, they could turn to the widely available commercial gins. In short, cotton profited everyone; it promised to make poor men prosperous and rich men kings.

King Cotton Term expressing southern belief that U.S. and British economies depended on cotton

Yet large-scale cotton cultivation and slavery grew together as the southern slave population nearly doubled between 1810 and 1830. Three-fourths of all southern slaves worked in the cotton economy in 1830. Owning slaves enabled a planter to harvest vast fields of cotton speedily, a crucial advantage because a sudden rainstorm at harvest time could pelt cotton to the ground and soil it.

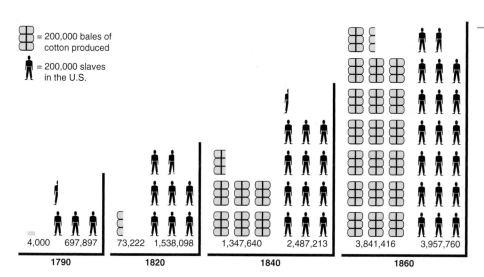

= 200,000 bales of cotton produced

= 200,000 slaves in the U.S.

4,000	697,897	73,222	1,538,098	1,347,640	2,487,213	3,841,416	3,957,760
1790		1820		1840		1860	

Growth of Cotton Production and the Slave Population, 1790–1860

Cotton and slavery rose together in the Old South.

Value of Cotton Exports as a Percentage of All U.S. Exports, 1800–1860

By 1840 cotton accounted for more than half of all U.S. exports.

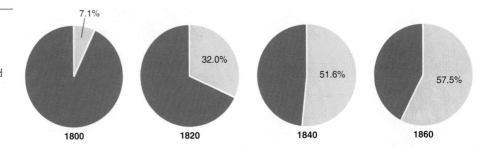

7.1%	32.0%	51.6%	57.5%
1800	1820	1840	1860

CL Interactive Map: The Legal Status of Slavery, from the Revolution to the Civil War

Cotton offered an added advantage: it was compatible with corn production. Corn could be planted either earlier or later than cotton and harvested before or after. Because the cost of owning a slave remained the same regardless of whether he or she was working, corn production allowed slaveholders to shift slave labor between corn and cotton. By 1860 the acreage devoted to corn in the Old South actually *exceeded* that devoted to cotton. Economically, corn and cotton gave the South the best of two worlds. Intense demand in Britain and New England kept cotton prices high and money flowing into the South. Because of southern self-sufficiency in growing corn and raising hogs that thrived on the corn, money did not drain away to pay for food. In 1860 the twelve wealthiest counties in the United States were all in the South.

Ties Between the Lower and Upper South

Two giant cash crops, sugar and cotton, dominated agriculture in the Lower South. The Upper South, a region of tobacco, vegetable, hemp, and wheat growers, depended far less on the great cash crops. Nevertheless, a common dependence on slavery unified the Upper and the Lower South, and made the Upper South identify more with the Lower South than with the nation's free states.

A range of social, political, and psychological factors promoted this unity. First, many settlers in the Lower South had come from the Upper South. Second, all white southerners benefited from the Constitution's three-fifths clause, which let them count slaves as a basis for congressional representation. Third, abolitionist attacks on slavery stung all southerners and bound them together. Fourth, economic ties linked the two Souths. The profitability of cotton and sugar increased the value of slaves throughout the South. The sale of slaves from the declining **plantation** states of the Upper South to the booming Lower South was a huge business.

plantation Large landholding devoted to a cash crop, such as cotton or tobacco

The North and South Diverge

However, the changes responsible for the dynamic growth of the South widened the distance between it and the North. The South remained predominantly rural as the North became more and more urban.

Lack of industry kept the South rural; by 1850 it had one-third of the U.S. population but accounted for only one-tenth of the nation's manufacturing. In 1850 the industrial output of the entire South was less than one-third that of Massachusetts alone.

Some southerners advocated and created factories in the South, but they were a minority. By 1860, cotton-textile mills were scattered throughout the South, and Richmond boasted the nation's fourth-largest producer of iron products, the Trede-

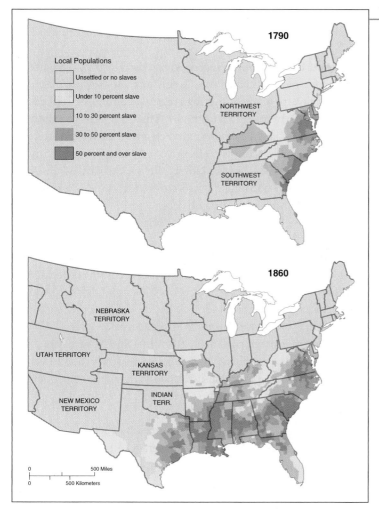

1790

Local Populations

- Unsettled or no slaves
- Under 10 percent slave
- 10 to 30 percent slave
- 30 to 50 percent slave
- 50 percent and over slave

NORTHWEST TERRITORY

SOUTHWEST TERRITORY

1860

NEBRASKA TERRITORY

UTAH TERRITORY

KANSAS TERRITORY

NEW MEXICO TERRITORY

INDIAN TERR.

0   500 Miles
0   500 Kilometers

Map 12.1   Distribution of Slaves, 1790 and 1860

In 1790 the majority of slaves resided along the southeastern seaboard. By 1860, however, slavery had spread throughout the South, and slaves were most heavily concentrated in the Deep South states.

Source: Reprinted with permission of the McGraw-Hill Companies, from *Ordeal by Fire: The Civil War and Reconstruction,* Second Edition, by James M. McPherson. Copyright © 1992 by the McGraw-Hill Companies.

gar (TREH-du-gur) Iron Works. Despite these successes, industrial output in the South trailed far behind that of the New England and mid-Atlantic states.

Most southern factories were small, produced for nearby markets, and were closely tied to agriculture. In the north, factories turned hides into tanned leather and leather into shoes, or cotton into threads and threads into suits. In contrast, southern factories turned grain into flour, corn into meal, and logs into lumber.

Slavery posed a major obstacle to southern industrialization, but not because slaves were unfit for factories; the Tredegar Iron Works was among many factories that employed slaves. However, the prospect of industrial slavery troubled slaveholders. Away from the strict discipline and supervision possible on a plantation, slaves sometimes behaved as if they were free, shifting jobs, working overtime, and even negotiating better working conditions. But the chief brake on southern industrialization was money, not labor. To raise the capital needed to build factories, planters would have had to sell their slaves. They seldom did. Cash crops, such as cotton and sugar, were proven, but the benefits of industrialization were remote and doubtful. Successful industrialization also would disrupt social relations, a southerner contended, by introducing "filthy, overcrowded, licentious factories" and attracting abolitionists. As long as southerners believed that the cash-crop economy remained profitable, they had little reason to plunge into the uncertainties of industrialization.

In education, as in industry, the South lagged behind the North. Where northerners recognized the benefits of an educated work force for their growing manufacturing economy, agriculturally oriented southerners rejected compulsory education and were reluctant to tax property to support schools. They abhorred the thought of educating slaves, and southern lawmakers made it a crime to teach slaves to read. For most whites, the only available schools were private. White illiteracy thus remained high in the South as it declined in the North. Before the Civil War, for example, nearly 60 percent of North Carolinians who enlisted in the U.S. Army were illiterate, compared to 30 percent for northern enlistees.

The primary reason for the South's failure to develop effective public schools was widespread indifference. Agricultural, self-sufficient, and independent, the middling and poor whites of the South remained unconvinced of the need for public education. They had little dependence on the printed word, few complex commercial transactions, and infrequent dealings with urban people. Planters did not need an orderly and disciplined white work force; they already had a black one that they were determined to keep illiterate lest it acquire ideas about freedom.

Because the South diverged so sharply from the North, outsiders often dismissed it as backward. A northern journalist wrote of white southerners in the 1850s, "They work little, and that little, badly; they earn little, they sell little; they buy little, and have little—very little—of the common comforts and consolations of civilized life."

But the South did not lack progressive features. By 1860 white per capita income in the South exceeded the national average. And although southerners lagged behind northerners in general technology, they did advance in the area that concerned them most: scientific agriculture.

Thus the Old South was not economically backward—it was merely different. Cotton was a wonderful crop, and southerners could hardly be blamed for making it their ruler. As a southern senator wrote in 1858, "You dare not make war upon cotton; no power on earth dares to make war upon it. Cotton is king."

CHECKING IN

- By 1830 the cotton economy dominated the South.
- Although cotton production flourished primarily in the Lower South, the Upper South benefited as well.
- "King Cotton" brought great prosperity to the South, but it also made slavery seem ever more vital to white southerners.
- The South nevertheless lagged far behind the North in industrialization and education.

THE SOCIAL GROUPS OF THE WHITE SOUTH

What major social divisions segmented the white South?

There was wide diversity within and between the South's slaveholding and nonslaveholding classes. Although some planters owned hundreds of slaves and lived lavishly, most lived more modestly. In 1860 one-fourth of all white families in the South owned slaves; nearly half of those owned fewer than five slaves, and three-fourths had fewer than ten slaves. Only 12 percent owned twenty or more slaves, and only 1 percent owned a hundred or more. Nonslaveholders were equally diverse. Most owned farms and drew on the labor of family members, but other whites squatted on land in the pine barrens or piney woods and scratched out a living by raising livestock, hunting, fishing, and planting a few acres of corn, oats, or sweet potatoes.

Planters, small slaveholders, family farmers, and pine-barrens folk composed the South's four main white groups. Many southerners—lawyers, physicians, merchants, and artisans—did not fall into any of these four, but they tended to identify their interests with one or another of the agricultural groups.

Planters and Plantation Mistresses

The plantation, with its porticoed mansion and fields teeming with slaves, stands at the center of the popular image of the Old South. This romanticized view, reinforced by novels and movies like *Gone with the Wind,* is not entirely false, for the South did contain plantations that travelers found "superb beyond description." Abundant slaves, the division of labor they afforded, and plentiful land allowed large plantations to generate incomes of $20,000 or more a year, an immense sum in those years.

In the eighteenth century during the initial flush of settlement in the piedmont and trans-Appalachian South, even well-off planters generally had lived in humble log cabins. After 1810, however, elite planters competed with one another to build stately mansions. Yet most planters counted their wealth, not in grand mansions and elegant furnishings, but in the value of their slaves. A field hand was worth as much as $1,700 in the 1850s, and few planters sold their slaves to buy furniture and silver plate.

But in their constant worry about profit, planters enjoyed neither repose nor security. High fixed costs—housing and feeding slaves, maintaining cotton gins, hiring overseers—led them to search for more and better land, higher efficiency, and greater self-sufficiency. Because cotton prices tended to fluctuate seasonally, planters often assigned their cotton to commercial agents in cities who held the cotton until the price was right. The agents extended credit so that the planters could pay their bills before the cotton was sold. Indebtedness became part of the plantation economy and intensified the planters' quest for profitability. Psychological strains compounded economic worries. Frequent moves disrupted circles of friends and relatives, particularly as migration to the Southwest (Alabama and Mississippi) carried families into less settled, more desolate areas. Until 1850 this area was still the frontier.

Migration to the Southwest often deeply unsettled plantation women. They suddenly found themselves in frontier conditions with neither friends, neighbors, nor relatives nearby and surrounded by slaves. Frequent absences by husbands, whether they were looking for new land, supervising outlying plantations, or conducting business in the city intensified wives' loneliness.

Planters and their wives found various ways of coping with their isolation. Employing overseers to run the plantation, some lived in cities; in 1850 half the planters in the Mississippi Delta lived in New Orleans or Natchez. Most planters acted as their own overseers, however, and dealt with the problems of harsh living conditions by opening their home to visitors. The responsibility for such hospitality fell heavily on wives, who might have to entertain as many as fifteen people for breakfast and attend to the needs of visitors who stayed for days. Plantation wives also bore the burdens of raising their children, supervising house slaves, making clothing and carpets, looking after smokehouses and dairies, planting gardens, and, often, keeping the plantation accounts.

Among the heaviest sorrows of some plantation mistresses was the presence of mulatto (moo-LOT-oh) children, constant reminders of their husbands' infidelities.

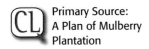

Primary Source:
A Plan of Mulberry
Plantation

Charlestonian Mary Boykin Chesnut, a famous diarist, observed tartly, "Any lady is ready to tell you who is the father of all the mulatto children in everybody's household but her own. These, she seems to think, drop from clouds."

The Small Slaveholders

In 1860, 88 percent of all slaveholders owned fewer than twenty slaves, and most possessed fewer than ten. One out of every five slaveholders worked outside of agriculture, as a lawyer, physician, merchant, or artisan.

Small slaveholders experienced conflicting loyalties and ambitions. In upland regions they absorbed the outlook of the more numerous **yeomen** (YO-men), who owned only a few slaves and rarely aspired to become large planters. In contrast, in the plantation-dominated low country and delta regions, small slaveholders often aspired to planter status. There someone with ten slaves could realistically look forward to owning thirty. And ambitious, acquisitive individuals equated success with owning more slaves. The logic of slavery remained the same: the only way to justify the investment in slaves was to set them to work on profitable crops. Such crops demanded more and better land, and both the planters and the small slaveholders of the deltas were restless and footloose.

The social structure of the deltas was fluid. In the early antebellum period, large planters had been reluctant to risk transporting their hundreds of valuable slaves in a still-turbulent region. It was small slaveholders who led the initial westward push into the Cotton Belt in the 1810s and 1820s. Gradually, large planters, too, moved westward, buying up the land that the small slave owners had developed and turning the region from Vicksburg to Natchez into large plantations. Small slave owners took the profits from selling their land, bought more slaves, and moved on. They gradually transformed the region from Vicksburg to Tuscaloosa (tusk-uh-LOO-suh), Alabama, into a belt of medium-sized farms with a dozen or so slaves on each.

yeoman Independent small farmer, usually nonslaveholding

The Yeomen

Nonslaveholding family farmers, or yeomen, composed the largest single group of southern whites. Most owned land, and many hired slaves to help at harvest. In areas of poor soil, such as eastern Tennessee, yeomen were typically subsistence farmers, but most yeomen grew some cash crops. Their landholdings were comparatively small, ranging from fifty to two hundred acres. Yeomen generally inhabited uplands, such as the piedmont of the East or the hilly upcountry of the Southwest, far from the rich coastal plains and deltas.

Above all, the yeomen valued self-sufficiency. Unlike planters, who were driven to acquire more land and to plant more cash crops, the yeomen devoted much of their acreage to subsistence crops, such as corn, sweet potatoes, and oats. The planter's ideal was profit with modest self-sufficiency; the yeoman's goal, self-sufficiency with modest profit.

Yeomen living in planter-dominated regions were often dismissed as "poor white trash," but in the upland regions that they dominated, the yeomen were highly respected. Upland slaveholders tended to own only a few slaves; like the yeomen, they were essentially family farmers.

Unlike southern planters, yeomen marketed their cash crops locally, trading cotton, wheat, and tobacco for goods and services from nearby artisans and merchants. In some areas yeomen sold their surplus corn to drovers and herdsmen who specialized in raising hogs. Along the French Broad River in eastern Tennessee, for example, twenty thousand to thirty thousand hogs a year were fattened for market. At peak season a traveler would see one thousand hogs a mile. The hogs were penned at night in huge stock stands—veritable hog motels—and fed with corn supplied by the local yeomen.

The People of the Pine Barrens

Independent whites of the wooded "pine barrens" were one of the most controversial groups in the Old South. About 10 percent of southern whites, they usually squatted on the land; put up crude cabins; cleared some acreage, where they planted corn between tree stumps; and grazed hogs and cattle in the woods. They neither raised cash crops nor engaged in the daily routine of orderly work that characterized family farmers. With their ramshackle houses and handfuls of stump-strewn acres, they appeared lazy and shiftless.

Abolitionists cited the pine-barrens people as proof that slavery degraded whites, but southerners responded that, although the pine-barrens folk were poor, they could at least feed themselves, unlike the paupers of northern cities. In general, the people of the pine barrens were both self-sufficient and fiercely independent. Pine-barrens men were reluctant to hire themselves out as laborers to do "slave" tasks, and the women refused to become servants.

CHECKING IN

- The white South consisted of four main social groups: plantation owners, small slaveholders, yeomen, and the people of the pine barrens.
- Plantation owners, who owned most of the slaves, were at the top of the social structure.
- Small slaveholders, including professionals as well as farmers, most often owned fewer than ten slaves.
- Yeomen farmers, who generally owned no slaves, were the largest segment of the white population.
- The fiercely proud and independent "people of the pine barrens" composed 10 percent of the white population.

SOCIAL RELATIONS IN THE WHITE SOUTH

How did slavery affect social relations in the South?

Antislavery northerners often charged that slavery warped the South's entire social structure. By creating a permanent black underclass of bond servants, they alleged, slavery robbed lower-class whites of the incentive to work, reduced them to shiftless misery, and rendered the South a premodern throwback in an otherwise progressive era. Southerners retorted that the real center of white inequality was the North, where merchants and financiers paraded in fine silks and never soiled their hands with manual labor.

In reality, the white South mixed aristocratic and democratic, premodern and modern features. Although the South featured considerable class inequality, property ownership was widespread. Rich planters dominated social life and the legislature, but they did not necessarily get their way, and often their political agenda paralleled that of other whites. Like white northerners, white southerners were restless, acquisitive, eager to make money, and skillful at managing complex commercial enterprises. Yet such practices as slaveholding and dueling thrived in the South when they were dying out elsewhere.

Conflict and Consensus in the White South

Planters tangled with yeomen on several issues. With extensive economic dealings and need for credit, planters inclined toward the Whig party, which generally supported economic development. The independent yeomen, cherishing their self-sufficiency, tended to be Democrats.

Yet few conflicts arose between these groups. An underlying political unity reigned in the South. Geography was in part responsible: planters, small slaveholders, yeomen, and pine-barrens folk tended to cluster in different regions, each independent of the others. There was somewhat more geographical intermingling of groups in the Upper South. With widespread land ownership and few factories, the Old South was not a place where whites worked for other whites, and this tended to minimize friction.

The white South's political structure was sufficiently democratic to prevent any one group from gaining exclusive control over politics. Planters dominated state legislatures, but they owed their election to the popular vote. And the democratic currents that had swept northern politics between 1815 and 1860 had affected the South as well; newer southern states entered the Union with democratic constitutions that included universal white manhood suffrage—the right of all adult white males to vote.

Although yeomen often voted for planters, the nonslaveholders did not give their elected representatives a blank check to govern as they pleased. During the 1830s and 1840s, Whig planters who favored banks faced intense and often successful opposition from Democratic yeomen. The nonslaveholders got their way often enough to nurture their belief that they, not the slaveholders, controlled politics.

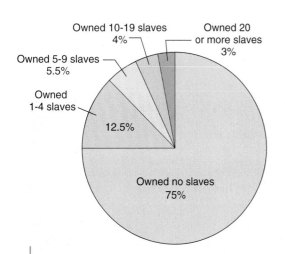

Slave Ownership, 1860

In combination with the impact of Hinton R. Helper's *The Impending Crisis of the South* (1857), which called on nonslaveholders to abolish the institution of slavery in their own interest, this decline left slaveholders worried about the loyalty of nonslaveholders to slavery.

Conflict over Slavery

Nevertheless, considerable *potential* existed for conflict between slaveholders and nonslaveholders. The southern white carpenter who complained in 1849 that "unjust, oppressive, and degrading" competition from slave labor depressed his wages surely had a point. Between 1830 and 1860 the slaveholding class shrank in size in relation to the total white population, but its share of total wealth increased. As a Louisiana editor wrote in 1858, "The present tendency of supply and demand is to concentrate all the slaves in the hands of the few, and thus excite the envy rather than cultivate the sympathy of the people."

Yet although pockets of opposition dotted the South, slavery did not create profound or lasting divisions between slaveholders and nonslaveholders. For example, antagonism to slavery flourished in parts of Virginia up to 1860, but proposals for emancipating the slaves dropped from the state's political agenda after 1832. Kentucky had a history of antislavery activity dating back to the 1790s, but after calls for emancipation suffered a crushing defeat in an 1849 referendum, slavery ceased to be a political issue there.

The rise and fall of pro-emancipation sentiment in the South raises a key question: as most white southerners were nonslaveholders, why did they not attack slavery more consistently? To look ahead, why were so many southerners willing to fight ferociously and to die bravely during the Civil War in defense of an institution in which they apparently had no real stake? There are several reasons. First, some nonslaveholders hoped to become slaveholders. Second, most southerners accepted the racist assumptions on which slavery rested; they dreaded the likelihood that emancipation would encourage "impudent" blacks to entertain ideas of social equality with whites. Third, no one knew where the slaves, if freed, would go or what they would do. Colonizing freed blacks in Africa was unrealistic, southerners concluded, but they also believed that, without colonization, emancipation would lead to a race war.

The Proslavery Argument

Between 1830 and 1860 southerners constructed a defense of slavery as a **positive good** rather than a necessary evil. St. Paul's injunction that servants obey their masters became a biblical justification for some. Others looked to the classical past to argue that slavery was both an ancient and a classical institution; the slave society of Athens, they said, had produced Aristotle (AIR-iss-taht-ul) and Plato (PLAY-toh), and Roman slaveholders had laid the foundations of Western civilization. George Fitzhugh of Virginia contrasted the plight of the northern "wage slaves," callously discarded when they became too ill or too old to work, with the lot of southern slaves, cared for by masters who attended to their health, their clothing, and their discipline.

positive good Southern argument that slavery benefited both black and white

At the same time, southerners increasingly suppressed any open discussion of slavery within the South. Proslavery writers warned that abolitionists wanted to destroy the family as well as slavery by undermining the "natural" submission of children to parents, wives to husbands, and slaves to masters. In the 1830s proslavery southerners seized abolitionist literature from the southern mail and burned it. Although Kentucky abolitionist Cassius Marcellus Clay protected his press with two cannons, in 1845 a mob dismantled it anyway.

THE NEGRO IN HIS OWN COUNTRY.

THE NEGRO IN AMERICA.

The Negro in His Own Country and the Negro in America

Proslavery propagandists contrasted what they believed to be the black's African savagery with the blessings of civilization on an American plantation.

The rise of the proslavery argument coincided with a shift in southern churches' position on slavery. During the 1790s and early 1800s, some Protestant ministers had assailed slavery as immoral, but by the 1830s most clergymen had convinced themselves that slavery was both compatible with Christianity and necessary for the proper exercise of Christian religion. Slavery, they proclaimed, displayed Christian responsibility toward one's inferiors, and it helped African-Americans to develop Christian virtues, such as humility and self-control. Southerners increasingly attacked antislavery evangelicals in the North for disrupting the "superior" social arrangement of the South. In 1837, southerners and conservative northerners had combined forces to drive antislavery New School Presbyterians out of that denomination's main body; in 1844 the Methodist Episcopal Church split into northern and southern wings; and in 1845 Baptists formed a separate Southern Convention. In effect, southern evangelicals seceded from national church organizations long before the South seceded from the Union.

Violence in the White South

Throughout the colonial and antebellum periods, violence deeply colored the daily lives of white southerners. In the 1760s a minister described backcountry Virginians "biting one anothers Lips and Noses off, and gowging one another—that is, thrusting out anothers Eyes, and kicking one another on the Cods [genitals], to the great damage of many a Poor Woman." Gouging out eyes became a specialty of sorts among poor southern whites. On one occasion a South Carolina judge entered his court to find a plaintiff, a juror, and two witnesses all missing one eye. Stories of eye gougings and ear bitings became part of Old South folklore. Mike Fink, a legendary southern fighter and hunter, boasted that he was so mean in infancy that he refused his mother's milk and howled for whiskey. Yet beneath the folklore lay the reality of violence that gave the Old South a murder rate as much as ten times higher than that of the North.

The Code of Honor and Dueling

At the root of most violence in the white South lay intensified feelings of personal pride that reflected the inescapable presence of slaves. White southerners saw slaves degraded, insulted, and powerless to resist. In turn, whites reacted violently to even trivial insults to demonstrate that they had nothing in common with slaves.

Among gentlemen this exaggerated pride took the form of a code of honor, with honor defined as an extraordinary sensitivity to one's reputation. Northern moralists celebrated a rival idea—character—the quality that enabled an individual to behave in steady fashion regardless of how others acted toward him or her. In the honor culture of the Old South, however, even the slightest insult, as long as it was perceived as intentional, could become the basis for a duel.

Formalized by French and British officers during the Revolutionary War, **dueling** gained a secure niche in the Old South as a means by which gentlemen dealt with affronts to their honor. Seemingly trivial incidents—a harmless brushing against the side of someone at a public event, a hostile glance—could trigger a duel. Yet dueling did not necessarily lead to violence. Gentlemen viewed dueling as a refined alterna-

dueling Formal man-to-man fight over a matter of honor

tive to the random violence of lower-class life. Instead of leaping at his antagonist's throat, a gentleman remained cool, settled on a weapon with his opponent, and agreed to a meeting place. In the interval, friends of the parties negotiated to clear up the "misunderstanding" that had provoked the challenge. Most confrontations ended peaceably rather than on the field of honor at dawn.

But many ended violently. Many southerners saw recourse to the law as a way to settle personal disputes involving honor as cowardly and shameless. Andrew Jackson's mother told the future president, "The law affords no remedy that can satisfy the feelings of a true man."

Dueling rested on the assumption that gentlemen could recognize each other and know when to respond to a challenge. Nothing in the code of honor compelled a person to duel with someone who was not a gentleman, for such a person's opinion hardly mattered. An insolent porter who insulted a gentleman might get a whipping but did not merit a duel. Yet it was often difficult to determine who was a gentleman. Indeed, the Old South teemed with would-be gentlemen.

The Southern Evangelicals and White Values

With its emphasis on the personal redress of grievances and its inclination toward violence, the ideal of honor conflicted with the values preached by the southern evangelical churches, notably the Baptists, Methodists, and Presbyterians. These denominations stressed humility and self-restraint, virtues that sharply contrasted with the culture of display that buttressed the extravagance and violence of the Old South.

By the 1830s, however, southern evangelicals had begun to change. They no longer made an effort to reach out to women, blacks, and the poor; instead, women were now expected to remain silent in church, while urban blacks increasingly formed their own churches. Both Methodists and Baptists began to attract the well-to-do, a tendency that increased with the opening of colleges such as Randolph-Macon and Wake Forest. More and more, southern gentry and evangelicals shared values, including a prickly regard for their honor and reputation. By the 1860s the South counted many gentlemen like the Bible-quoting Presbyterian general Thomas J. "Stonewall" Jackson, fierce in a righteous war but a sworn opponent of strong drink, gambling, and dueling.

CHECKING IN

- Southern politics became more democratic.
- White southerners, even those who owned no slaves, united in support of slavery.
- The defense of slavery as a "positive good" emerged after 1830.
- White "gentlemen" had an exaggerated sense of honor, which often led to duels.
- Southern evangelicals became supporters of existing systems, including slavery.

LIFE UNDER SLAVERY

How did slaves and free blacks respond to their circumstances?

Slavery, the institution at the root of the code of honor and other distinctive features of the Old South, has long inspired controversy among historians. Some have seen slavery as a benevolent institution in which African-Americans lived contentedly under kindly masters; others, as a brutal system that drove slaves into constant rebellion. Neither view is accurate, but both contain a germ of truth. There were kind masters, and some slaves developed genuine affection for their owners. Yet

Black Women and Men on a Trek Home, South Carolina

Here African-American women loaded down with cotton join their men on the march home after a day in the fields. (©Collection of The New York Historical Society, ID 47843.)

slavery inherently oppressed its African-American victims by forcibly appropriating their life and labor. Even kind masters exploited blacks in order to earn profits. And kindness was a double-edged sword; the benevolent master expected grateful affection from his slaves and interpreted that affection as loyalty to slavery itself. When northern troops descended on the plantations during the Civil War, masters were genuinely surprised and dismayed to find many of their most trusted slaves deserting to Union lines.

The kindness or cruelty of masters was important, but three other factors primarily determined slaves' experience: the kind of agriculture in which they worked, whether they resided in rural or urban areas, and what century they lived in. The experiences of slaves working on cotton plantations in the 1830s differed radically from those of slaves in 1700, for reasons unrelated to the kindness or brutality of masters.

The Maturing of the Plantation System

Slavery changed significantly between 1700 and 1830. In 1700 the typical slave was a man in his twenties, recently arrived from Africa or the Caribbean, who worked on an isolated small farm. Drawn from different regions of Africa, few slaves spoke the same language. Because slave ships carried twice as many men as women, and because slaves were widely scattered, blacks had difficulties finding partners and creating a semblance of family life. Severe malnutrition sharply limited the number of children slave women bore. Without continuing importations, the number of slaves in North America would have declined between 1710 and 1730.

In contrast, by 1830 the typical North American slave was as likely to be female as male, had been born in America, spoke English, and worked beside numerous other slaves on a plantation. The rise of plantation agriculture in the eighteenth century was at the heart of the change. Plantation slaves found mates more easily than slaves on scattered farms. The ratio between slave men and women fell into balance, and marriage between slaves on the same or nearby plantations increased. The native-born slave population soared after 1750. The importation of African slaves declined, and in 1808 Congress banned it.

Work and Discipline of Plantation Slaves

In 1850 the typical slave worked on a large farm or plantation with at least ten other slaves. Almost three-quarters of all slaves belonged to masters with ten or more slaves, and just over one-half lived in units of twenty or more slaves. Thus understanding the life of a typical slave requires examining plantation routines. On smaller units, slaves usually worked under the task system, a daily or weekly quota of work. On large cotton and sugar plantations, slaves were generally more closely supervised and regulated under the gang labor system.

An hour before sunrise, a horn or bell awakened the slaves. After a sparse breakfast, they marched to the fields. Slave men and women worked side by side in the fields. Those female slaves who did not labor in the fields remained busy. A former slave, John Curry, described how his mother milked cows, cared for children whose mothers worked in the fields, cooked for field hands, washed and ironed for her master's household, and looked after her own seven children. Plantations never lacked tasks for slaves of either gender, and in any season the slave's day stretched from dawn to dusk. When darkness made field work impossible, slaves toted cotton bales to the ginhouse, gathered wood for supper fires, and fed the mules. Weary from their labors, they slept in log cabins on wooden planks.

Although virtually all antebellum Americans worked long hours, no others experienced the combination of long hours and harsh discipline that slave field hands endured. Northern factory workers did not live in fear of drivers walking among them with a whip. Repulsive brutality pervaded American slavery. For example, pregnant slave women were sometimes forced to lie in depressions in the ground and endure whipping on their backs, a practice that supposedly protected the fetus while abusing the mother. Masters often delegated discipline and punishment to white overseers and black drivers. The barbaric discipline meted out by others twinged the conscience of many masters, but most justified it as their Christian duty to ensure the slaves' proper "submissiveness."

Despite the system's brutality, some slaves advanced—not to freedom but to semiskilled or skilled indoor work. Some became blacksmiths, carpenters, or gin operators, and others served as cooks, butlers, and dining room attendants. These house slaves became legendary for their disdain of field hands and poor whites. Slave artisans and house slaves generally enjoyed higher status than the field hands.

The Slave Family

Masters thought of slaves as naturally promiscuous and flattered themselves into thinking that they alone held slave marriages together. Masters had powerful incentives to encourage slave marriages: bringing new slaves into the world and discouraging slaves from running away. James Henry Hammond, governor of South Carolina and a large slaveholder, noted in his diary how he "flogged Joe Goodwyn and ordered him to go back to his wife. Ditto Gabriel and Molly and ordered them to come together."

This picture of benevolent masters holding together promiscuous slaves is misleading. Slavery itself posed the keenest challenge to slave families. Conditions on small farms and new plantations discouraged the formation of families, and even on large plantations, slaves were often dispersed to different sites without any consideration of marriage or family ties. Slave adults were far less likely than whites to marry, and slave children

H. E. Hayward and Slave Nurse Louisa, 1830
Slavery did not prevent white children and their slave nurses from forming attachments to each other.

Map 12.2   Internal Slave Trade, 1810–1860

An internal slave trade developed after the slave trade with Africa ended in 1808. With the growth of cotton production, farmers in the Upper South found it profitable to sell their slaves to planters in the Lower South.

more likely to live with a single parent or even with neither parent. The law provided neither recognition of nor protection for the slave family. Masters reluctant to break slave marriages by sale could neither bequeath their reluctance to heirs nor avoid economic hardship that might force them to sell slaves. The reality, one historian has calculated, was that on average a slave would see eleven family members sold during his or her lifetime.

Inevitably, the buying and selling of slaves disrupted attempts to create a stable family life. Poignant testimony to the effects of sale on slave families appeared in advertisements for runaway slaves. An 1851 North Carolina advertisement said that a particular fugitive was probably "lurking in the neighborhood of E. D. Walker's, at Moore's Creek, who owns most of his relatives, or Nathan Bonham's who owns his mother; or perhaps, near Fletcher Bell's, at Long Creek, who owns his father." Small wonder that a slave preacher pronounced a couple married "until death or *distance* do you part."

Other factors disrupted slave marriages. The marriage of a slave woman did not protect her against the sexual demands of her master or, indeed, of any white. Slave children of white masters sometimes became targets for the wrath of white mistresses. Field work kept slave mothers from their children, who were cared for by the elderly or by the mothers of other children.

Despite these enormous obstacles, relationships within slave families were often intimate and, where possible, long lasting. Lacking legal protection, slaves developed their own standards of family morality. A southern white woman observed that slaves "did not consider it wrong for a girl to have a child before she married, but afterwards were extremely severe upon anything like infidelity on her part." Given the opportunity, slaves solemnized their marriages before members of the clergy. White clergymen who accompanied Union armies into Mississippi and Louisiana during the Civil War conducted thousands of marriage rites for slaves who had long viewed themselves as married and desired a formal ceremony and registration.

On balance, slave families differed profoundly from white families. Many planters divided their holdings into several farms and distributed slaves among them without regard to marriage ties. Conditions on small farms and new plantations discouraged the formation of families. Spouses were always vulnerable to being sold.

Broad kinship patterns—close ties between children and grandparents, aunts, and uncles, as well as parents—had marked West African cultures, and they were reinforced by the separation of children and parents that routinely occurred under slavery. Frederick Douglass never knew his father and saw his mother rarely, but he vividly remembered his grandmother. In addition, slaves often created "fictive" kin networks, naming friends as their uncles, aunts, brothers, or sisters. In this way they helped to protect themselves against the disruption of family ties and established a broader community of obligation. When plantation slaves greeted each other as "brother," they were making a statement not about actual kinship, but about obligations to each other.

Primary Source:
A Slave Perspective
on Family Ties

The Longevity, Health, and Diet of Slaves

Of the 10 million to 12 million Africans imported to the New World between the fifteenth and nineteenth centuries, North America received only 550,000 of them (about 5 percent), whereas Brazil received 3.5 million (nearly 33 percent). Yet by 1825, 36 percent of all slaves in the Western Hemisphere lived in the United States, and only 31 percent in Brazil. The reason for this difference is that slaves in the United States reproduced faster and lived longer than those in Brazil and elsewhere in the Western Hemisphere.

Several factors account for U.S. slaves' longer lives and higher rates of reproduction. First, with the gender ratio among slaves equalizing more rapidly in North America, slaves there married earlier and had more children. Second, because raising corn and livestock was compatible with growing cotton, the Old South produced plentiful food. Slaves generally received a peck of cornmeal and three to four pounds of fatty pork a week, which they often supplemented with vegetables grown on small plots and with catfish and game.

Slaves enjoyed greater immunity from malaria and yellow fever than whites but suffered more from cholera, dysentery, and diarrhea. Lacking privies, slaves usually relieved themselves behind bushes; consequently, urine and feces contaminated the sources of their drinking water. Slave remedies for stomach ailments, although commonly ridiculed by whites, often worked. For example, slaves ate white clay to cure dysentery and diarrhea. We now know that white clay contains kaolin, a remedy for these disorders.

Nonetheless, slaves suffered a higher mortality rate than whites. The very young suffered most; infant mortality among slaves was double that among whites, and one in three African-American children died before age ten. Plantations in the disease-ridden lowlands had the worst overall mortality rates, but overworked field hands often miscarried or bore weakened infants even in healthier areas.

Slaves off Plantations

Greater freedom from supervision and greater opportunities awaited slaves who worked off plantations in towns and cities. Most southern whites succumbed to the lure of cotton and established small farms; the resulting shortage of white labor created a steady demand for slaves outside the plantation economy. Driving wagons, working as stevedores on the docks, manning river barges, and toiling in mining and lumbering gave slaves an opportunity to work somewhere other than the cotton fields. Other African-Americans served as engineers for sawmills or artisans for ironworks. African-American women and children constituted the main labor force for the South's fledgling textile industry.

The draining of potential white laborers from southern cities also provided opportunity for slaves to become skilled artisans. Slave or free, blacks found it easier to pursue skilled occupations in southern cities than in northern ones, where immigrant laborers competed with blacks for work.

Despite slavery's stranglehold, urban African-Americans in the South enjoyed opportunities denied their counterparts in the North. Generally, slaves who worked in factories, mining, or lumbering were hired out by their masters rather than owned by their employers. If working conditions for hired-out slaves deteriorated badly, masters would refuse to provide employers with more slaves. Consequently, working conditions for slaves off the plantation generally stayed at a tolerable level.

Life on the Margin: Free Blacks in the Old South

Free blacks were likelier than southern blacks in general to live in cities. In 1860 one-third of the free blacks in the Upper South and more than half in the Lower South were urban.

Urban specialization allowed free blacks the chance to become carpenters, coopers (barrel makers), barbers, and small traders. Most of the meat, fish, and produce in an antebellum southern market was prepared for sale by free blacks. Urban free blacks formed their own fraternal orders and churches; in New Orleans free blacks also had their own opera and literary journals. In Natchez, a free black barber, William Tiler Johnson, invested the profits of his shop in real estate, rented it out, bought slaves and a plantation, and hired a white overseer.

Despite such successes, free blacks were vulnerable in southern society. They continued to increase in absolute numbers (a little more than 250,000 free people of color lived in the South in 1860), but the rate of growth of the free black population slowed radically after 1810. Fewer masters freed their slaves after that time, and following the Nat Turner rebellion in 1831, states legally restricted the liberties of free blacks. By the mid-1830s most southern states made it a felony to teach blacks to read and write. Every southern state forbade free blacks to enter, and in 1859, Arkansas ordered all free blacks to leave.

Although a free-black culture flourished in certain cities, that culture did not reflect the conditions under which the majority of blacks lived. Most free blacks dwelled in rural areas, where whites lumped them together with slaves, and a much higher percentage of blacks were free in the Upper South than in the Lower South.

Many free blacks were mulattos, the product of white masters and black women, and looked down on "darky" field hands and laborers. But as discrimination against free people of color intensified during the late antebellum period, many free blacks realized that whatever future they had was as blacks, not whites. Feelings of racial solidarity increased during the 1850s, and after the Civil War, the leaders of the ex-slaves were usually blacks who had been free before the war.

Slave Resistance

Fear of slave insurrection haunted the Old South. In lowland and delta plantation areas slaves often outnumbered whites. In the cities, free blacks could have provided leadership for rebellions. Rumors of slave conspiracies flew within the southern white community, and all whites knew of the massive black revolt that had destroyed French rule in Saint Domingue.

But Nat Turner's revolt remained the only slave rebellion that actually resulted in white deaths. Most slave rebellions were conspiracies that never materialized. For example, in 1800 a Virginia slave named Gabriel Prosser plotted an uprising but was betrayed by other slaves and executed. In 1822 Denmark Vesey (VEE-see) and his followers planned to attack Charleston, South Carolina, and seize the city's arms and ammunition, but other slaves informed the authorities, and the conspirators were executed.

Several factors explain this apparent tranquility. First, although slaves formed a majority in South Carolina and a few other areas, they did not constitute a *large* majority in any state. Second, unlike Caribbean slave owners, most southern masters lived on their plantations; they possessed armed force and were willing to use it. Third, family ties among U.S. slaves made them reluctant to risk death and thereby to orphan their children. Finally, slaves who ran away or plotted rebellion had no allies. Southern Indians routinely captured runaway slaves and claimed rewards for them; some Indians even owned slaves.

Unable to rebel, many slaves tried to escape to freedom in the North. Some light mulattos who passed as whites succeeded. More often, slaves borrowed, stole, or forged passes from plantations or obtained papers describing them as free. Frederick Douglass borrowed a sailor's papers to make his escape from Baltimore to New York City. Some former slaves, including Harriet Tubman and Josiah Henson, returned to the South to help others escape. Despite legends of an "underground railroad" of abolitionists helping slaves to freedom, fugitive slaves owed little to abolitionists. The "safe houses" of white sympathizers in border states were better known to slave catchers than to runaways.

Escape to freedom was a dream rather than a realistic alternative for most blacks. Out of millions of slaves, probably fewer than a thousand actually escaped to the North. Slaves who did run away often were seeking, not freedom, but the chance to visit spouses or escape punishment; most remained in the South. During the eighteenth century, African slaves had often run away in groups and tried to create the sort of villages they had known in Africa. But the American acquisition of Florida deprived potential runaways of their major haven, leaving them few uninhabited places to which they could flee.

Despite poor prospects for permanent escape, slaves could disappear for prolonged periods into the free-black communities of southern cities. Slaves enjoyed a fair degree of practical freedom to drive wagons to market and to come and go when they were off plantations. Slaves sent to a city might overstay their leave and pass themselves off as free. This kind of practical freedom did not change slavery's underlying oppressiveness, but it did give slaves a sense of having certain rights, and it helped to channel slave resistance into activities that were furtive and relatively harmless, rather than open and violent. Theft, for example, was so common that planters kept tools, smokehouses, and closets under lock and key. Overworked field hands might leave tools out to rust, feign illness, or simply refuse to work. Slaves could not be fired for such malingering or negligence. And Frederick Law Olmsted even found masters afraid to punish a slave "lest [he or she] should abscond, or take a sulky fit and not work, or poison some of the family, or set fire to the dwelling." Indeed, not all furtive resistance was harmless. Arson and poisoning, both common forms of vengeance in African culture, flourished in the Old South. So did fear. Masters afflicted by dysentery never knew for sure that they had not been poisoned.

Arson, poisoning, theft, work stoppage, and negligence acted as alternatives to violent rebellion, but their goal was not freedom. Their object was merely to make slavery bearable. Most slaves would have preferred freedom but settled for less. "White folks do as they please," an ex-slave said, "and the darkies do as they can."

THE EMERGENCE OF AFRICAN-AMERICAN CULTURE

What were the distinctive features of the culture that developed among slaves?

Enslaved blacks combined elements of African and American cultures to create a distinctive culture of their own, giving a distinctive twist to both the African and American components of slave culture.

The Language of Slaves

Before slaves could develop a common culture, they needed a common language. During the colonial period, African-born slaves, speaking a variety of languages, had developed a **"pidgin"** (PID-jin)—that is, a language that has no native speakers but in which people with different native languages can communicate. Many African-born slaves spoke English pidgin poorly, but their American-born descendants used it as their primary language.

Like all pidgins, English pidgin was a simplified language. Slaves often dropped the verb *to be* (which had no equivalent in African tongues) and ignored or confused

"pidgin" Common language spoken by slaves who spoke many different tongues

---

CHECKING IN

- Plantation field hands often labored under brutal conditions, whereas "house slaves" fared better.

- Nuclear slave families were precarious, but the slave culture of extended families offset this to some extent.

- Although slaves in the United States generally lived longer than slaves elsewhere in the Western Hemisphere, the mortality rate of slave children under the age of ten was 35 percent.

- Free blacks had opportunities but also faced stifling restrictions.

- Although the Nat Turner rebellion was a notable exception, slave resistance generally was subtle, furtive, and widespread.

genders. Instead of saying "Mary is in the cabin," they typically said, "Mary, he in cabin." They substituted *no* for *not,* as in "He no wicked." Some African words, among them *banjo,* moved from pidgin to standard English, and others, such as *goober* ("peanut"), entered southern white slang. Although many whites ridiculed pidgin and black house servants struggled to speak standard English, pidgin proved indispensable for communication among slaves.

African-American Religion

Religion played an equally important role in forging an African-American culture. Africa contained rich and diverse religious customs and beliefs. Despite the presence of a few Muslims and Christians in the early slave population, most of the slaves brought from Africa followed one of many native African religions. Most of these religions drew little distinction between the spiritual and natural worlds—storms, illnesses, and earthquakes were all assumed to stem from supernatural forces.

However, African religions did not unify American slaves. African religions differed greatly, and the majority of slaves in the colonial period were young men who had not absorbed this religious heritage. Remnants of African religion remained, however, in part because, before the 1790s, whites made few attempts to convert slaves to Christianity. Evangelical Christianity, like African religions, drew few distinctions between the sacred and the worldly. Just as Africans believed that droughts and plagues resulted from supernatural forces, revivalists knew in their heart that every drunkard who fell off his horse and every Sabbath breaker struck by lightning had experienced a deliberate, direct punishment from God.

By the 1790s African-Americans formed about one-quarter of the membership of the Methodist and Baptist denominations. The fact that converted slaves played significant roles in the South's three slave rebellions reinforced whites' fears that a Christian slave would be a rebellious slave. These slave uprisings, especially the Nat Turner rebellion, spurred Protestant missionaries to intensify their efforts among slaves. They pointed to the self-taught Turner as proof that slaves could learn about Christianity and claimed that only organized efforts at conversion would ensure that the slaves were taught correct versions of Christianity.

Christian blacks' experience in the Old South illustrates the contradictions of life under slavery. Urban blacks often had their own churches, but rural blacks and slaves worshipped in the same churches as whites. Although African-Americans sat in segregated sections, they heard the same service as whites. Churches became the most interracial institutions in the Old South, and biracial churches sometimes disciplined whites for abusing black Christian members. But Christianity was not a route to black liberation. Ministers went out of their way to remind slaves that spiritual equality was not the same as civil equality.

However, slaves listening to the same sermons as whites often came to different conclusions. For example, slaves drew parallels between their captivity and that of the Jews, the Chosen People. Like the Jews, slaves concluded, they were "de people of de Lord." If they kept the faith, they would reach the Promised Land.

"The Promised Land" could refer to Israel, to heaven, or to freedom. Whites agreed that Israel and heaven were the only permissible meanings, but some African-Americans thought of freedom as well. Many plantations had black preachers, slaves trained by white ministers to spread Christianity among blacks. In the presence of masters or ministers, African-American preachers repeated the familiar biblical command "Obey your master." Often, however, slaves met for services apart from whites, and then the message changed.

Some slaves privately interpreted Christianity as a religion of liberation, but most recognized that their prospects for freedom were slight. Generally, Christianity neither turned blacks into revolutionaries nor made them model slaves. It did, however, provide slaves with a view of slavery different from their masters' outlook. Masters argued that slavery was a benign and divinely ordained institution, but Christianity told slaves that the institution was an affliction, a terrible and unjust system that God had allowed in order to test their faith. For having endured slavery, he would reward slaves. For having created it, he would punish masters.

Primary Source: Henson Recalls Broken Families and Personal Opportunity

Black Music and Dance

African-American culture expressed blacks' feelings. Long after white rituals had grown sober and sedate, the congregation in African-American religious services shouted "Amen" and let their body movements reflect their feelings. Slaves also expressed their emotions in music and dance. Southern law forbade them to own "drums, horns, or other loud instruments, which may call together or give sign or notice to one another of their wicked designs and intentions." Instead, slaves made rhythmic clapping, called "patting juba" (JOO-buh), an indispensable accompaniment to dancing. Slaves also played an African instrument, the banjo, and beat tin buckets as substitutes for drums. Slave music was tied to bodily movement; slaves expressed themselves in a dance that was African in origin, emphasizing shuffling steps and bodily contortions rather than quick footwork and erect backs as in whites' dances.

Whether at work or prayer, slaves liked to sing. Work songs usually consisted of a leader's chant and a choral response. Masters encouraged such songs, believing that singing induced slaves to work harder and that the innocent content of work songs proved that slaves were happy. However, Frederick Douglass, recalling his own past, observed that "slaves sing most when they are most unhappy. The songs of the slave represent the sorrows of his heart; and he is relieved by them, only as an aching heart is relieved by its tears."

Blacks also sang religious songs, later known as **spirituals,** which reflected the powerful emphasis that slave religion placed on deliverance from earthly travails. Whites took a dim view of spirituals and tried to make slaves sing "good psalms and hymns" instead of "the extravagant and nonsensical chants, and catches, and hallelujah songs of their own composing." But enslaved blacks clung to their spirituals, drawing hope from them that "we will soon be free, when the Lord will call us home," as one spiritual promised.

spiritual Slave religious song that stressed liberation from difficult situations

CHECKING IN

- Slaves developed "pidgin" as a way of communicating.
- After 1800 most slaves were Christian.
- Masters tried to use Christianity to encourage submissiveness, but slaves saw it as a faith that promised rewards for them and punishment for their masters.
- Slave music and dance incorporated many African elements.
- Spirituals reflected the slaves' desire for deliverance.

Chapter Summary

 DOWNLOAD THE MP3 AUDIO FILE OF THE CHAPTER SUMMARY, AND LISTEN TO IT ON THE GO.

KEY TERMS

Nat Turner *(p. 255)*
King Cotton *(p. 257)*
plantation *(p. 258)*
yeoman *(p. 262)*
positive good *(p. 265)*
dueling *(p. 266)*
"pidgin" *(p. 274)*
spiritual *(p. 276)*

How did the rise of cotton cultivation affect the South? *(page 256)*

By the 1830s cotton production dominated the South, and southerners spoke proudly of "King Cotton." Although it brought great prosperity, the cotton economy also slowed down the development of industry and education. And it made slavery seem more vital than ever.

What major social divisions segmented the white South? *(page 260)*

Geography and economics divided white southerners into four distinct groups: plantation owners, small slave owners, yeomen, and the people of the pine barrens. Yeomen, the largest group, generally owned no slaves, nor did the people of the pine barrens.

How did slavery affect social relations in the South? *(page 263)*

Whites, although divided politically, were united in defense of slavery, which gave all whites an automatically superior position. They defended slavery as a "positive good," and southern churches became supporters and defenders of slavery as well.

How did slaves and free blacks respond to their circumstances? *(page 267)*

Field hands labored under harsh conditions. Nuclear families were always threatened, but the tradition of extended families somewhat offset this. Free blacks faced a life bounded by severe restrictions. Rebellion against slavery, despite the spectacular example of Nat Turner, was usually subtle, emerging in the form of pretended illness, carelessness, or feigned stupidity.

What were the distinctive features of the culture that developed among slaves? *(page 274)*

Whites tried to use Christianity to preach submission and obedience, but slaves saw it as a faith of hope and liberation. Slave music and dance frequently incorporated African elements, and spirituals expressed the slave desire for deliverance.

Immigration, Expansion, and Sectional Conflict

1840–1848

This icon will direct you to the website where you can Prepare for Class, Improve Your Grade, and Ace the Test: www.cengage.com/history/boyer/ enduringconcise6e

CHAPTER PREVIEW

Newcomers and Natives
How did the massive immigration of the 1840s influence the balance of power between Whigs and Democrats?

The West and Beyond
How did Americans expand into the Southwest and to the Pacific coast in the 1840s?

The Politics of Expansion, 1840–1846
How did "Manifest Destiny" influence American politics?

The Mexican-American War and Its Aftermath, 1846–1848
What were the results of the Mexican-American War?

Gold Miners

The Mormons who trekked westward between 1845 and 1847 were part of the great flood of Americans washing across the continent in the spirit of "Manifest Destiny." Although their goal was the construction of a separate Mormon society, which they achieved in "Deseret," (de-zur-ETTE), as they called the Utah emptiness where they established their colony, the Mormons shared the American dream of expansion and the fervent belief that they could create a better life by moving beyond the boundaries and constraints of eastern settlements.

In barely a thousand days during James K. Polk's administration (1845–1849), the United States expanded by 50 percent. It annexed Texas, gained half of the vast Oregon territory through negotiations with Britain, and claimed California and New Mexico after deliberately provoking war. At the same time, immigrants poured into the United States, largely from Europe.

Expansion and immigration were linked. Most immigrants gravitated to the ardently expansionist Democratic party. In turn, Democrats concluded that more expansion was the solution to widening sectional and ethnic conflict. By bringing more land into cultivation, they believed, America could recapture its Jeffersonian ideal as a nation of self-sufficient farmers. And expansion would offer something for everyone: Oregon would gratify the North; Texas, the South; and California, every region.

It didn't work out that way. In fact, expansion heated sectional antagonisms to the boiling point, split the Democratic party along sectional lines, and set the nation on the path to the Civil War.

NEWCOMERS AND NATIVES

How did the massive immigration of the 1840s influence the balance of power between Whigs and Democrats?

Between 1815 and 1860, 5 million European immigrants reached the United States. Of these, 4.2 million arrived between 1840 and 1860, and 3 million crowded in from 1845 to 1854 alone, the largest immigration relative to population in U.S. history. The Irish and the Germans dominated this wave of newcomers; by 1860 three-fourths of foreign-born Americans were Irish or German.

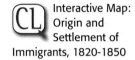

Interactive Map: Origin and Settlement of Immigrants, 1820-1850

Expectations and Realities

Although a desire for religious freedom drew some immigrants to U.S. shores, hopes of economic betterment lured the majority. Travelers' accounts and relatives' letters assured Europeans that America was an ideal world, a utopia. Yet, typically, immigrants faced hard times.

Their problems began at European ports, where hucksters hawked worthless tickets and ships scheduled to leave in June might not sail until August. Countless immigrants spent their precious savings in waterfront slums awaiting departure. The ocean voyage itself could be terrifying. Most immigrants sailed on cargo ships as steerage passengers, crowded into quarters as cramped as slave ships for six weeks or more.

For many, the greatest shock came after landing. In the depression years of the 1840s, immigrants quickly discovered that farming in America was a perilous prospect, radically different from what they had known in Europe. Unlike the compact farming communities of Europe, American agricultural areas featured scattered farms, and Americans' individualism led them to speculate in land and to move frequently.

Clear patterns emerged amid the shocks and dislocations of immigration. For example, most Irish immigrants lacked the capital to purchase land and consequently crowded into urban areas of New England, New York, New Jersey, and Pennsylvania, where they could find jobs. German immigrants often arrived at southern ports, but slavery, climate, and lack of economic opportunity gradually drove them north to settle in Illinois, Ohio, Wisconsin, and Missouri.

Cities, rather than farms, attracted most antebellum immigrants; by 1860 German and Irish newcomers constituted half or more of the population of St. Louis, New York, Chicago, Cincinnati, Milwaukee, Detroit, and San Francisco. These fast-growing cities needed people with strong backs who were willing to work for low wages. In addition to jobs, cities provided immigrants with the community life lacking in farming areas.

The Germans

In 1860 there was no German nation-state, only a collection of principalities and kingdoms. Immigrants from this area thought of themselves as Bavarians, Westphalians, or Saxons, not Germans.

German immigrants spanned a wide spectrum of class and occupation. Most were farmers, but professionals, artisans, and tradespeople made up a sizable minority. For example, Levi Strauss, a Jewish tailor from Bavaria, reached the United States in 1847. When gold was discovered in California the next year, Strauss gathered rolls of cloth and sailed for San Francisco. There he fashioned tough work overalls from canvas. Demand soared, and Strauss opened a factory to produce his cheap overalls, later known as blue jeans or Levi's.

A common language transcended the differences among German immigrants and bound them together. They clustered in the same neighborhoods, formed their own militia and fire companies, and established German-language parochial schools and newspapers. The diversity of the German-speaking population further fostered solidarity. Because Germans supplied their own lawyers, doctors, teachers, and

Figure 13.1   German, Irish, and Total Immigration, 1830-1860

Irish and German immigrants led the more than tenfold growth of immigration between 1830 and 1860.   *Source:* U.S. Bureau of the Census, *Historical Statistics of the United States, Colonial Times to 1970,* Bicentennial Edition I (Washington, D.C., 1975.)

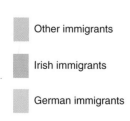

Chronology

1822	Stephen F. Austin founds the first American community in Texas
1830	Mexico closes Texas to further American immigration
1835	Santa Anna invades Texas
1836	Texas declares its independence from Mexico; Fall of the Alamo; Goliad massacre; Battle of San Jacinto
1840	William Henry Harrison elected president
1841	Harrison dies; John Tyler becomes president
1842	Webster-Ashburton Treaty
1844	James K. Polk elected president
1845	Congress votes by joint resolution to annex Texas; Mexico rejects Slidell mission
1846	The United States declares war on Mexico; John C. Frémont proclaims the Bear Flag Republic in California; Congress votes to accept a settlement of the Oregon boundary issue with Britain; Tariff of 1846; Colonel Stephen Kearny occupies Santa Fe; Wilmot Proviso introduced; Taylor takes Monterrey
1847	Taylor defeats Santa Anna at the Battle of Buena Vista; Vera Cruz falls to Winfield Scott; Mexico City falls to Scott; Lewis Cass's principle of "squatter sovereignty"
1848	Gold discovered in California; Treaty of Guadalupe-Hidalgo signed; Taylor elected president

merchants from their midst, they had no need to go outside their neighborhoods. Native-born Americans simultaneously admired German industriousness and resented German self-sufficiency, which they interpreted as clannishness. In a vicious cycle, the Germans responded by becoming even more clannish. In effect, they isolated themselves from gaining the political influence that Irish immigrants acquired.

The Irish

There were three waves of Irish immigration. Between 1815 and the mid-1820s, most Irish immigrants were Protestants, small landowners, and tradespeople drawn by enthusiastic veterans of the War of 1812 who reported that America was a paradise where "all a man needed was a gun and sufficient ammunition to be able to live like a prince." From the mid-1820s to the mid-1840s, Irish immigration became both more Catholic and poorer, comprising primarily tenant farmers evicted by Protestant landlords as "superfluous." Rich or poor, Protestant or Catholic, nearly a million Irish crossed the Atlantic to the United States between 1815 and 1845.

Then, between 1845 and the early 1850s the character of Irish immigration changed dramatically. In Ireland, blight destroyed harvest after harvest of potatoes, virtually the only food of the peasantry, and triggered one of the most gruesome famines in history. The Great Famine killed a million people. Those who survived, a landlord wrote, were "famished and ghastly skeletons." To escape suffering and death, 1.8 million Irish emigrated to the United States in the decade after 1845.

Overwhelmingly poor and Catholic, these newest Irish immigrants entered the work force at the bottom. While Irish men dug streets and canals and railroads, Irish women worked as maids and textile workers. Poverty drove women to work at early ages, and the outdoor, all-season labor performed by their husbands turned many of them into working widows. Because the Irish usually married late, almost half the Irish immigrants were single adult women, many of whom never married.

It sometimes seemed that, no matter what the Irish did, they clashed with other Americans. The poorer Irish who dug canals, took in laundry, or worked as domestics competed with equally poor free blacks. The result was Irish animosity toward blacks and Irish hatred of abolitionists. At the same time, the Irish who secured skilled or semiskilled jobs clashed with native-born white workers.

Anti-Catholicism, Nativism, and Labor Protest

Hostility toward Irish immigrants often took the form of anti-Catholicism, a latent impulse among American Protestants since early Puritan days. The surge of Irish immigrants in the second quarter of the nineteenth century revived anti-Catholic fever. A groundswell of anti-Catholic publications climaxed with Maria Monk's best-selling *Awful Disclosures of the Hotel Dieu Nunnery in Montreal,* which vividly described wild sexual relations between nuns and priests. Although she claimed to be a former nun, Maria Monk was actually a former prostitute.

The surge of Catholic immigration in the 1840s also had political ramifications fueled by **nativism.** Protestants formed anti-immigrant societies with names like the American Republicans and the United Order of Americans. One such secret society, the Order of the Star-Spangled Banner, would become the **"Know-Nothing,"** or American, **party,** a major political force in the 1850s. In the 1840s, nativist parties prospered during flare-ups over local issues, such as whether the Protestant or Catholic version of the Bible should be used in predominantly Catholic schools. In 1844, for example, the "Bible Riots" in Philadelphia, spurred on by the electoral success of American Republican party candidates, led to the deaths of sixteen people and the destruction of thirty buildings at the hands of Protestant mobs.

An explosive mixture of fears and discontents fueled nativism. Protestants generally saw their doctrines, such as the responsibility of each individual to interpret Scripture, as far more democratic than Catholicism, which made doctrine the province of the pope and the hierarchy. Native-born artisans and journeymen, already hard pressed by the subdivision of tasks and the aftermath of the Panic of 1837, feared that desperately poor Catholic immigrants represented a threat to their jobs.

Many Irish immigrants, refugees from an agricultural society, believed that they could gain more through unions and strikes than through farming. Even women workers organized unions in these years; the leader of a seamstresses' union proclaimed, "Too long have we been bound down by tyrant employers."

Probably the most important development for workers in the 1840s was a state court decision. In *Commonwealth* v. *Hunt* (1842), the Massachusetts Supreme Court ruled that labor unions were not illegal monopolies that restrained trade. However, because less than 1 percent of the work force at that time belonged to a union, their impact was sharply limited. Thus Massachusetts employers easily brushed aside the *Commonwealth* decision, firing union agitators and replacing them with cheap immigrant labor.

nativism Reaction against immigrants of different ethnic, religious backgrounds

"Know-Nothing" party Also "Order of the Star-Spangled Banner" or "American Party"; expression of nativism

Primary Source: Philadelphia Mechanics Respond to New Pressures

Ethnic and religious tensions also split the antebellum working class during the 1830s and 1840s. Friction between native-born and immigrant workers inevitably became intertwined with the political divisions of the second party system.

Immigrant Politics

Few immigrants had voted before reaching America, and even fewer had fled political persecution. Political upheavals had erupted in Austria and some German states in the turbulent year of 1848, but among the 1 million German immigrants to the United States, only 10,000 were political refugees, or "Forty-Eighters." Once settled in the United States, however, many immigrants became politically active. They discovered that urban political organizations could help them find housing and jobs—in return for votes. Both the Irish and the Germans identified overwhelmingly with the Democratic party. By 1820 the Irish controlled Tammany Hall, the New York City Democratic organization; Germans became staunch Democrats in Milwaukee, St. Louis, and other cities.

Immigrants' fears about jobs partly explained their widespread Democratic support. Former president Andrew Jackson had given the Democratic party an antiprivilege, antiaristocratic coloration, making the Democrats seem more sympathetic than the Whigs to the common people. In addition, antislavery was linked to the Whig party, and the Irish loathed abolitionism because they feared that freed slaves would become their economic competitors. Moreover, the Whigs' moral and religious values seemed to threaten those of the Irish and Germans. Hearty-drinking Irish and German immigrants shunned temperance-crusading Whigs, many of whom were also rabid anti-Catholics. Even public-school reform, championed by the Whigs, was perceived as a menace to the Catholicism of Irish children and as a threat to the integrity of German language and culture.

The Bible Riots illustrate both the interplay of nativism, religion, and politics, and the way in which local issues shaped the immigrants' political loyalties. Both Democrats and Whigs became adept at attracting voters initially drawn to politics by such local issues as liquor regulations and school laws. Nativists usually voted for Whig candidates rather than those of overtly nativist parties, whereas immigrants followed the Democratic party from local battles into national politics.

The Democratic party schooled immigrants in broad national principals: venerate George Washington, revere Thomas Jefferson and Andrew Jackson, and see "monied capitalists" as parasites who would tremble when the people spoke. By identifying their party with all that they thought best about the United States, the Democrats helped give immigrants a sense of themselves as Americans.

Democrats also introduced immigrants to national interests, redirecting local political loyalties to national politics. In the 1830s, the party had persuaded immigrants that national measures such as the Bank of the United States and the tariff, seemingly remote from their daily lives, were vital to them. Now, in the 1840s, the Democrats would try to convince immigrants that national expansion likewise was in their interest.

CHECKING IN

- Immigrants often found American realities far less attractive than their utopian dreams.
- German immigrants tended to cluster together, cutting off their access to political power.
- Irish immigrants, poor and usually Catholic, triggered an ethnic and religious backlash known as nativism.
- Immigrants often spearheaded early union movements.
- German and Irish immigrants generally became Democrats; most nativists were Whigs.

THE WEST AND BEYOND

How did Americans expand into the Southwest and to the Pacific coast in the 1840s?

As late as 1840 the American West meant the area between the Appalachian Mountains and the Mississippi River or just beyond. West of that lay the inhospitable Great Plains. A semiarid, treeless plateau, the Plains sustained huge buffalo herds and the nomadic Indians who lived off the buffalo. Because the Great Plains presented would-be farmers with formidable obstacles, public interest shifted toward the Far West, the fertile region beyond the Rockies.

The Far West

By the Transcontinental (or Adams-Onís) Treaty of 1819, the United States had relinquished to Spain its claims to Texas west of the Sabine River, and in return Spain renounced its claims to the Oregon Country north of California. Two years later, the Mexican Revolution had brought Mexico independence from Spain and possession of all North American territory claimed by Spain—Texas, California, and the southwest quadrant of the continent. In 1824 and 1825 Russia yielded its claims to Oregon south of Alaska, and in 1827 the United States and Great Britain revived an earlier agreement for the joint occupation of the Oregon Territory. Texas, New Mexico, California, and Oregon stretched over an area larger than Britain, France, and Germany combined. Although this vast region should have tempted them, in the 1820s Mexico, the United States, and Britain all viewed the Far West as a remote and shadowy frontier. The American line of settlement reached only to Missouri, a 2,000-mile trek (allowing for mountains) from the West Coast.

Far Western Trade

After sailing around South America and up the Pacific coast, early merchants had established American and British outposts on the West Coast. Between the late 1790s and the 1820s, for example, Boston merchants had built a thriving trade, exchanging goods from the eastern United States for western sea-otter fur, cattle, hides, and tallow (rendered from cattle fat and used for making candles and soap). The British Hudson's Bay Company developed a similar trade in Oregon and northern California. The California trade generated little friction with Mexico. Californians were as eager to buy as the traders were to sell. Traders who settled in California, such as the Swiss-born John Sutter, learned to speak Spanish and became assimilated into Mexican culture.

Also during the 1820s, trading links developed between St. Louis and Santa Fe. Each spring, Midwesterners loaded wagon trains with tools, clothing, and household sundries, and rumbled westward to Santa Fe, where they traded their goods for mules and silver. Mexico welcomed the trade. By the 1830s more than half the goods trucked west along the Santa Fe Trail trickled into the mineral-rich Mexican provinces of Chihuahua and Sonora, and were exchanged for Mexican silver pesos, which became the principal medium of exchange in Missouri.

Map 13.1   Trails to the West, 1840

By 1840 several trails carried pioneers from Missouri and Illinois to the West.

Some Americans ventured north from Santa Fe to trap beaver in what is today western Colorado and eastern Utah. Americans from St. Louis soon found themselves competing with both the Santa Fe traders and the agents of the Hudson's Bay Company for lucrative beaver pelts. Gradually, the St. Louis traders wrested the beaver trade from their Santa Fe competitors. Although silk hats were overtaking beaver ones in popularity by 1854, more than half a million beaver pelts were auctioned off in London that year.

For the most part, American traders and trappers operating on the northern Mexican frontier in the 1820s and 1830s provided a service to Mexico's provinces. The Mexican people of New Mexico and California depended on American trade for manufactured goods, and the Mexican government in both provinces needed revenues from customs duties. The New Mexican government often had to wait until the caravan of American traders arrived from St. Louis before it could pay its officials and soldiers.

Yet, despite the mutually beneficial relations between Mexicans and Americans, the potential for conflict was always present. Spanish-speaking, Roman Catholic, and accustomed to a hierarchical society, the Mexicans formed a striking contrast to the Protestant, individualistic Americans. Furthermore, American traders returned to the United States with glowing reports about the fertility and climate of Mexico's northern provinces. Consequently, by the 1820s American settlers were moving into eastern Texas. At the same time, the ties binding Mexico's government to its northern provinces were fraying.

The American Settlement of Texas to 1835

Spain and, later, Mexico recognized that the key to controlling their frontier provinces lay in promoting settlement there by Spanish-speaking people—Spaniards, Mexicans, and Indians who had embraced Catholicism and agriculture. Thus, by the early nineteenth century, Spanish missions, which had long been the chief instrument of Spanish expansion, stretched up the California coast as far as San Francisco and into the interior of New Mexico and Texas.

The Spanish missions combined political, economic, and religious goals. Paid by the government, the Franciscan priests who staffed the missions tried to convert Native Americans and to settle them on mission lands. By 1823 more than 20,000 Indians lived on the lands of the twenty-one California missions, most of them protected by a fort, or *presidio,* like that at San Francisco.

In the late 1820s the mission system began to decline, the victim of Mexican independence and the new government's decision to secularize the missions by distributing their lands to ambitious government officials and private ranchers. Many of the Native Americans who fled the missions joined the nomads who had always resisted conversion; lawlessness surged, and few Mexicans ventured into the vast and threatening emptiness of the frontier.

In 1824 the Mexican government began to encourage American colonization of the region as a way to bring in manufactured goods and to gain protection against Indian attacks on lands farther south and west. The government bestowed generous land grants on agents known as *empresarios* (em-pre-SAR-ee-ohs) to recruit peaceful American settlers for Texas, as the Anglo region of Coahuila-Tejas (koh-uh-WHEEL-uh TAY-has) became known. **Stephen F. Austin,** the most successful of the empresarios, brought in three hundred families by 1825. By 1830 seven thousand Americans lived in Texas, more than double the Mexican population there.

Stephen F. Austin Empresario who led first Americans into Texas

Trouble quickly developed. Most of the American settlers were southerners, many of them slaveholders. Mexico abolished slavery in 1829; the next year it closed its borders to importation of slaves and to further American immigration. Neither ban worked. Americans continued to pour into Texas: by 1836 Texas contained thirty thousand Anglo-Americans, five thousand black slaves, and only four thousand Mexicans.

At the same time, Mexican politics grew more and more unstable. When Antonio López de **Santa Anna** became president of Mexico in 1834, he restricted the power of the individual states, including Coahuila-Tejas. His actions ignited a series of rebellions in the Mexican states, the most important of which became the Texas Revolution.

Santa Anna Mexican dictator who helped provoke Texas Revolution

The Texas Revolution, 1836

At first the insurgent Anglo-Texans sought greater autonomy for Texas, not independence. But Santa Anna's brutal treatment of the rebels alarmed the initially moderate Austin and others. When Santa Anna invaded Texas in fall 1835, Austin cast his lot with the radicals who wanted outright independence.

Santa Anna's armies met with initial success. In February 1836, 4,000 of his men laid siege to San Antonio, where 200 rebels had retreated into an abandoned mission, the **Alamo.** On March 6—four days after Texas had declared its independence, although they did not know about it—the defenders of the Alamo were overwhelmed

Alamo Site of famed defeat of Texans during Texas Revolution by Mexican troops. Under Santa Anna's orders, the Mexican army killed all the Alamo's defenders, including the wounded. A few weeks later Mexican troops massacred 350 Texas prisoners at Goliad (GO-lee-add).

Even before the Alamo and Goliad, Texas delegates had met to proclaim Texas independent of Mexico. They chose **Sam Houston,** already a military leader, as their first president. Houston retreated east to pick up recruits, many of them Americans who had crossed the Sabine (suh-BEEN) River border to fight Santa Anna. On April 21, 1836, Houston's army turned and surprised the complacent Mexican forces under Santa Anna, which had encamped on a prairie just to the east of what is now the city of Houston. Shouting, "Remember the Alamo!" and "Remember Goliad!" Houston's army of 1,200 tore through the Mexican lines, killing nearly half of Santa Anna's men in fifteen minutes and capturing the general himself. This engagement, the Battle of San Jacinto (juh-SIN-toh), gave Texas its independence from Mexico, although the Mexican government never ratified the treaty that Santa Anna signed.

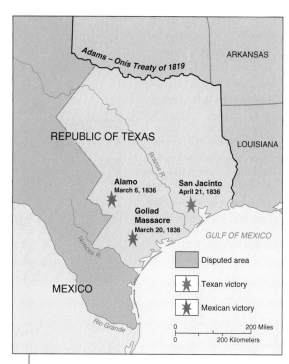

Map 13.2   Major Battles in the Texas Revolution, 1835–1836
Sam Houston's victory at San Jacinto was the decisive action of the war and avenged the massacres at the Alamo and Goliad.

American Settlements in California, New Mexico, and Oregon

Before 1840, California and New Mexico, both less accessible than Texas, exerted only a mild attraction for American settlers. That year, a mere one hundred Americans lived in New Mexico and perhaps four hundred in California. According to a contemporary, these Americans "are scattered throughout the whole Mexican population, and most of them have Spanish wives. . . . They live in every respect like the Spanish."

Yet the beginnings of change were evident. During the 1840s Americans streamed into the Sacramento Valley, lured by favorable reports of the region and welcomed by the Hispanic population as a way to encourage economic development.

To the north, Oregon's abundant farmland beckoned settlers from the Mississippi Valley. By 1840 some 500 Americans had settled there, in what was described as a "pioneer's paradise" where "the pigs are running around under the great acorn trees, round and fat and already cooked, with knives and forks sticking in them so that you can cut off a slice whenever you are hungry."

Sam Houston Military and political leader of Texas during and after Texas Revolution

CL Interactive Map: Texas Revolution

The Overland Trails

Whether bound for California or Oregon, Americans faced a four-month ordeal crossing terrain little known in reality but vividly depicted in fiction as an Indian killing ground. Cautious pioneers stocked up on enough guns to equip an army in jump-off towns such as Independence and St. Joseph, Missouri. In fact, they were more likely to shoot one another than to be shot by the usually cooperative Indians and much more likely to be scalped by Independence or St. Joseph merchants selling their goods at inflated prices.

Emigrant Wagon Train Bedding Down for the Night

Men, women, and children divided the tasks—caring for oxen, feeding horses, drawing water, preparing supper, washing clothes—on the basis of gender and age. (Benjamin F. Reinhart, *An Evening Halt—Emigrants Moving to the West in 1840*, 1867, oil on canvas, 40 x 70 in. In the Collection of the Corcoran Gallery of Art, Washington, D.C. Gift of Mr. and Mrs. Lansdell K. Christie, 59.21.)

Overland Trail Route westward to Oregon and California followed by thousands of Americans

CHECKING IN

- By the 1820s Americans were deeply involved in trade along Mexico's northern frontiers.
- In the 1820s the Mexican government invited Americans to settle in Texas as a buffer against Indians; within a decade more than thirty thousand Americans lived in Texas.
- Texans rebelled against Mexico in 1836 and won their independence.
- In the 1840s Americans began streaming into Oregon and California.
- More than fourteen thousand Americans followed the overland trails west.

Along the **Overland Trail** the emigrants faced hardships and hazards: ornery mules that kicked, bit, and balked; oxen that collapsed from thirst; and overloaded wagons that broke down. Trails were difficult to follow and too often marked by the debris of broken wagons and the bleached bones of oxen. Guidebooks were more like guessbooks. In 1846 the Donner Party, following one such book, lost so much time that it became snowbound in the High Sierras and survived by turning to cannibalism. Emigrants met the challenges of the overland trail by close cooperation with one another, traveling in huge wagon trains rather than alone. Men yoked and unyoked the oxen, drove the wagons and stock, and hunted. Women packed, cooked, and assisted in childbirths.

Between 1840 and 1848, an estimated 11,500 pioneers followed an overland trail to Oregon, and some 2,700 reached California. Such small numbers made a difference, for the British did not settle Oregon at all, and the Mexican population of California was small and scattered. By 1845 California was clinging to Mexico by the thinnest of threads. The territory's Hispanic population, the *californios,* felt little allegiance to Mexico, which they contemptuously called "the other shore." Some of them wanted independence from Mexico, whereas others contemplated British or French rule. By the mid-1840s these *californios,* with their tenuous allegiances, faced a growing number of American settlers with definite political sympathies.

THE POLITICS OF EXPANSION, 1840–1846

How did "Manifest Destiny" influence American politics?

Westward expansion raised the question of whether the United States should annex Texas. In the 1840s the Texas issue sparked political passions and became entangled with other unsettling issues about the West. Between 1846 and 1848, a war with Mexico and a dramatic confrontation with Britain settled these questions on terms favorable to the United States. ·

At the start of the 1840s, western issues received little attention in a nation concerned primarily with issues relating to economic recovery—tariffs, banking, and internal improvements. Only after politicians failed to address the economic problems coherently did opportunistic leaders thrust expansion-related issues to the top of the political agenda.

The Whig Ascendancy

The election of 1840 brought the Whig candidate William Henry Harrison to the presidency and installed Whig majorities in both houses of Congress. The Whigs proposed to replace Van Buren's Independent Treasury (see Chapter 10) with some sort of national fiscal agency, such as the Bank of the United States. The Whig party also favored a revised tariff that would increase government revenues but remain low enough to permit the importation of foreign goods. According to the Whig plan, the states would then receive tariff-generated revenues for internal improvements.

The Whig program might well have breezed into law. But Harrison died after only a month in office, and his successor, John Tyler, a Virginia aristocrat put on the ticket for his southern appeal and the first man to assume the presidency after the death of an incumbent, proved a disaster for the Whigs. A former Democrat, Tyler continued to favor the Democratic philosophy of states' rights. As president, he used the veto to shred his new party's program. In August 1841 a Whig measure to create a new national bank fell to Tyler's veto, as did a subsequent modification.

Tyler also played havoc with Whig tariff policy by vetoing one bill to lower tariffs to 20 percent in accord with the Compromise Tariff and rejecting another to distribute revenue from a higher tariff to the states. Whig leaders were understandably furious; some Whigs talked of impeaching Tyler. In August 1842 the president, needing money to run the government, signed a new bill that maintained some tariffs above 20 percent but abandoned distribution to the states.

Tyler's erratic course confounded and disrupted his party. By maintaining some tariffs above 20 percent, the tariff of 1842 satisfied northern manufacturers, but by abandoning distribution, it infuriated southerners and westerners. The issue cut across party lines. In the congressional elections of 1842, the Whigs paid a heavy price for failing to enact their program; they lost control of the House to the Democrats. Now the nation had one party controlling the Senate, another controlling the House, and a president who appeared to belong to neither.

Tyler and the Annexation of Texas

Although disowned by his party, Tyler ardently desired a second term as president. Domestic issues offered him little hope of building a popular following, but foreign policy was another matter. In 1842 Tyler's secretary of state, Daniel Webster, concluded the Webster-Ashburton Treaty with Great Britain, settling a long-festering dispute over the Maine-Canada border. Tyler reasoned that if he could follow the treaty, which was highly popular in the North, with the annexation of Texas, he could build a national following.

The issue of slavery clouded every discussion of Texas. Antislavery northerners saw proposals to annex Texas as part of a southern conspiracy to extend American territory into Mexico, Cuba, and Central America. Thus an unlimited number of new slave states could be created, but British Canada would eliminate the possibility of free states' expanding to the north. And some southerners talked openly of carving Texas into four or five slave states.

Nevertheless, in summer 1843 Tyler launched a campaign for Texas annexation. He justified his crusade by reporting that he had learned of an attempt to make Texas a British, rather than an American, ally.

In spring 1844, Tyler and John C. Calhoun, who became secretary of state in 1844, submitted to the Senate a treaty annexing Texas. Accompanying the treaty was a letter from Calhoun to the British minister in Washington, defending slavery as beneficial to African-Americans, the only way to protect them from "vice and pauperism." Abolitionists now had evidence that the annexation of Texas was linked to a conspiracy to extend slavery. Consequently, both Whig and Democratic leaders came out in opposition to the annexation of Texas, and the treaty went down to crushing defeat in the Senate. But however ostensibly decisive, the Senate vote simply dumped the annexation question into the upcoming presidential election.

The Election of 1844

Tyler's ineptitude turned the presidential campaign into a free-for-all. Unable to gather support as an independent, he dropped out of the race. Henry Clay had a secure grip on the Whig nomination, but Martin Van Buren's apparently clear path to the head of the Democratic ticket vanished as the issue of annexation split his party. A deadlocked Democratic party finally turned to James K. Polk of Tennessee, the first "dark horse" nominee in American history.

Jeering "Who is James K. Polk?" the Whigs derided the nomination. However, Polk, a wily campaigner, convinced many northerners that annexation of Texas would benefit them. In an imaginative scenario, Polk and his supporters argued that, if Britain succeeded in abolitionizing Texas, slavery would not be able to move westward, racial tensions in existing slave states would intensify, and the chances of a race war would increase. However far-fetched, this argument played effectively on northern racial phobias and helped Polk to detach annexation from Calhoun's narrow, prosouthern defense.

In contrast to the Democrats, whose position was clear, Clay and the Whigs wobbled. After several shifts, Clay finally came out against annexation, but not until September. His wavering alienated his southern supporters and prompted some of his northern supporters to bolt the Whigs for the antislavery Liberty party, formed in 1840. The Whigs also infuriated Catholic immigrant voters by nominating Theodore Frelinghuysen (fray-ling-HIGH-zun) for the vice presidency. A supporter of temperance and an assortment of other causes, Frelinghuysen confirmed fears that the Whigs were the orthodox Protestant party. Catholic immigrants turned out in large numbers to vote for the Democrats.

On the eve of the election in New York City, so many Irish marched to the courthouse to be qualified for voting that the windows had to be opened to allow people to enter and leave. Polk won the electoral vote 170 to 105, but his margin in the popular vote was only 38,000 out of 2.6 million votes cast. A shift of 6,000 votes in New York, where the immigrant vote and Whig defections to the Liberty party had hurt Clay, would have given Clay the state and the presidency.

Manifest Destiny, 1845

The election of 1844 demonstrated the strength of national support for the annexation of Texas. The surging popular sentiment for expansion reflected a growing conviction that America's natural destiny was to expand into Texas and all the way to the Pacific Ocean.

Expansionists emphasized extending the "area of freedom" and talked of "repelling the contaminating proximity of monarchies upon the soil that we have consecrated to the rights of man." Americans needed only a phrase to capture this ebullient spirit. In 1845 John L. O'Sullivan, a New York Democratic journalist, supplied that phrase when he wrote of "our manifest destiny to overspread and to possess the whole of the continent which Providence has given us for the development of the great experiment of liberty and federated self-government entrusted to us."

Because most champions of **Manifest Destiny** were Democrats who favored annexing Texas, northern Whigs dismissed Manifest Destiny as a smoke screen to conceal an evil intent to extend slavery. In fact, many expansionists supported neither slavery nor annexation. Most had their eyes, not on Texas, but on Oregon and California. Blaming the post-1837 depression on the failure of Americans to find markets for their agricultural surplus, they saw California and Oregon as solutions. An Alabama Democrat praised California's "safe and capacious harbors," which "invite to their bosoms the rich commerce of the East."

More than trade was at stake. To many, expansion presented an opportunity to preserve the agricultural character of the American people and thus to safeguard democracy. Fundamentally Jeffersonian, expansionists equated industrialization and urbanization with social stratification and class strife. To avoid the "bloated wealth" and "terrible misery" that afflicted Britain, the United States *had* to expand.

Democrats saw expansion as a logical complement to their support of low tariffs and their opposition to centralized banking. High tariffs and banks tended to "favor and foster the factory system," but expansion would provide farmers with land and with access to foreign markets. Americans would continue to be farmers, and the foundations of the Republic would remain secure.

This message, trumpeted by the penny press, made sense to the working poor, many of them Irish immigrants. Expansion would open economic opportunity for the common people and thwart British plans to free American slaves, whom the poor viewed as potential competition for already-scarce jobs.

Expansionism drew on the ideas of Thomas Jefferson, John Quincy Adams, and other leaders of the early Republic who had proclaimed the American people's right to displace any people, uncivilized or European, from their westward path. Early expansionists had feared that overexpansion might create an ungovernable empire, but their successors had no such qualms. Although they pointed with alarm to the negative effects of industrialization, the expansionists also relied on the technology of industrialization. The railroad and the telegraph, they said, had annihilated the problem of distance and made expansion safe.

Manifest Destiny Phrase coined to describe beliefs of ardent expansionists

 Primary Source: California Dream Railroad Poster

James K. Polk

Lacking charm, Polk bored even his friends, but few presidents could match his record of acquiring land for the United States.

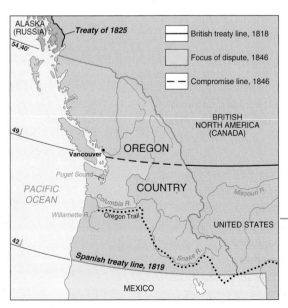

Map 13.3   Oregon Boundary Dispute

Although demanding that Britain cede the entire Oregon Territory south of 54°40', the United States settled for a compromise at the forty-ninth parallel.

Polk and Oregon

The growing spirit of Manifest Destiny intensified the Oregon issue. To soften northern criticism of the pending annexation of Texas, the Democrats had included in their 1844 platform the assertion that American title "to the whole of the Territory of Oregon is clear and unquestionable." Taken literally, this statement, which Polk repeated in his inaugural address, pressed an American claim to the entire Oregon Territory between California and 54°40', the southern boundary of Alaska, a claim never before advanced.

Polk's objectives in Oregon were far subtler than his language. He knew that it would take a war with Britain for the United States to claim the entire Oregon Territory, and he wanted to avoid war. He hoped the belligerent language would persuade the British to accept what they had previously rejected, a division of Oregon at the forty-ninth parallel. This settlement would give the United States the superb deep-water harbor of Puget Sound and the southern tip of Vancouver Island. The British had long held out for a division along the Columbia River, which entered the Pacific Ocean far south of the forty-ninth parallel.

Polk's position roused furious interest in acquisition of the entire territory. Mass meetings adopted such resolutions as "The Whole or None!" and "Fifty-four Forty or Fight!" Each year brought new American settlers into Oregon. John Quincy Adams, although no supporter of the annexation of Texas or the 54°40' boundary for Oregon, believed that American settlements gave the United States a stronger claim than discovery and exploration had given the British. The United States, Adam preached, was the nation bound "to make the wilderness blossom as the rose, to establish laws, to increase, multiply, and subdue the earth all "at the first behest of God Almighty."

In April 1846 Polk forced the issue by notifying Britain that the United States was terminating the joint British-American occupation of Oregon. In effect, this message was that the British could either go to war over the American claims to 54°40' or negotiate. They chose to negotiate. Although raging against that the "ill-regulated, overbearing, and aggressive spirit of American democracy," Britain faced too many other problems to wage war over "a few miles of pine swamp." The ensuing treaty divided Oregon at the forty-ninth parallel, although Britain retained all of Vancouver Island and temporary navigation rights on the Columbia River. On June 15, 1846, the Senate ratified the treaty.

THE MEXICAN-AMERICAN WAR AND ITS AFTERMATH, 1846–1848

What were the results of the Mexican-American War?

Between 1846 and 1848 the United States successfully fought a war that cost Mexico its claims to Texas and the provinces of New Mexico and California. Although many Americans rejoiced over this victory, others foresaw that questions over the status of slavery in the newly acquired territories boded ill for the future.

CHECKING IN

- The death of William Henry Harrison threw Whig control of the national government into turmoil.
- Attempts to bring Texas into the Union raised the volatile issue of slavery.
- Dark horse candidate and expansionist James K. Polk won the 1844 election.
- "Manifest Destiny" became the slogan of expansionists.
- Polk won a treaty dividing the Oregon Territory with Great Britain, giving the United States its first Pacific boundary.

The Origins of the Mexican-American War

While Polk challenged Britain over Oregon, the United States and Mexico moved toward war. The conflict had both immediate and remote causes. One long-standing grievance lay in the failure of the Mexican government to pay $2 million in debts owed to U.S. citizens. Bitter memories of the Alamo and of the Goliad massacre, moreover, reinforced American loathing of Mexico. Above all, the issue of Texas poisoned relations. Mexico still hoped to regain Texas or to keep it independent of the United States.

Still politically unstable—its presidency changed hands twenty times from 1829 to 1844—Mexico was afraid that an aggressive United States—"the colossus of the North"—would trample on anyone in its path while disguising its intentions with high-sounding phrases. Once in control of Texas, Mexicans feared, the United States might seize other provinces, or even Mexico itself, and treat Mexicans as it treated slaves.

Polk's election increased the strength of the pro-annexationists, as his campaign had persuaded many northerners that Texas's annexation would bring national benefits. In February 1845 both houses of Congress responded to popular sentiment by passing a resolution annexing Texas. However, Texans balked, in part because some feared that union with the United States would provoke a Mexican invasion and war on Texas soil.

Polk moved rapidly. To sweeten the pot for Texans, he supported their claim that the Rio Grande (REE-oh GRAN-day) constituted Texas's southern border, despite Mexico's contention that the Nueces (NOO-ay-sess) River, one hundred miles farther north, bounded Texas. Because the Rio Grande meandered west and north nearly two thousand miles, it encompassed a huge territory, including part of modern New Mexico. The Texas that Polk proposed to annex was thus far larger than the Texas that had gained independence from Mexico. On July 4, 1845, reassured by Polk's support, Texas voted to accept annexation. Under Polk's orders, American troops under General Zachary Taylor deployed at Corpus Christi, south of the Nueces River, in territory still claimed by Mexico.

California and its fine harbors influenced Polk's actions, for he had entered the White House with the firm intention of extending American control over that province, too. If Mexico went to war with the United States over Texas, Polk's supporters claimed, "the road to California will be open to us." Reports from American agents convinced Polk that the way lay open for California to join the United States as Texas would—by revolution and then annexation.

Continued turmoil in Mexican politics further complicated this complex situation. In early 1845 a new Mexican government agreed to negotiate with the United States, and Polk decided to give negotiations a chance. In November 1845 he dispatched John Slidell to Mexico City with instructions to gain Mexican recognition of the annexation of Texas with the Rio Grande border. In exchange, the U.S. government would assume the debt owed by Mexico to American citizens. Polk also authorized Slidell to offer up to $25 million for California and New Mexico. However, by the time Slidell reached Mexico City, the government there had become too weak to make concessions and refused to negotiate. Polk then ordered Taylor to move southward to the Rio Grande, hoping to provoke a Mexican attack and unite the American people behind war.

The Mexican government, however, dawdled over taking the bait. Polk was about to send a war message to Congress when word finally arrived that Mexican forces had crossed the Rio Grande and attacked the U.S. army. *"American blood has been shed on American soil!"* Polk's followers jubilantly proclaimed. On May 11, 1846, Polk informed Congress that war "exists by the act of Mexico herself" and called for $10 million to fight the war.

Polk's disingenuous assertion that the United States was already at war provoked furious opposition in Congress. For one thing, the Mexican attack on Taylor's troops had taken place on land never before claimed by the United States. Equally grievous, in announcing that war already existed, Polk seemed to undercut congressional power to declare war. He was using a mere border incident as a pretext to plunge the nation into a general war to acquire more slave territory. But Polk had backed the Whigs into a corner. They could not afford to appear unpatriotic—they remembered vividly what opposition to the War of 1812 had cost the Federalists—so they swallowed their outrage and supported war.

Polk's single-minded pursuit of his goals had prevailed. A humorless, austere man who banned dancing and liquor from the White House, he inspired little personal warmth, even among his supporters. But he triumphed over all opposition, in part because of his opponents' fragmentation, in part because of expansion's popular appeal, and in part because of his foreign antagonists' weakness. Reluctant to fight over Oregon, Britain had negotiated. Too weak to negotiate, Mexico chose to fight over territory that it had already lost (Texas) and where its hold was feeble (California and New Mexico).

The Mexican-American War   Most European observers expected Mexico to win the war. Its army was four times the size of the American forces, and it was fighting on home ground. Having botched its one previous attempt to invade a neighbor, Canada in 1812, the United States now had to sustain offensive operations in an area remote from American settlements. American expansionists, however, hardly expected the Mexicans to fight at all. Racism and arrogance convinced many Americans that the Mexican people, degraded by their mixed Spanish and Indian population, were "as sure to melt away at the approach of [American] energy and enterprise as snow before a southern sun," as one newspaper publisher insisted.

In fact, the Mexicans fought bravely and stubbornly, although unsuccessfully. In May 1846 Taylor, "Old Rough and Ready," routed the Mexican army in Texas and pursued it across the Rio Grande, eventually to capture the major city of Monterrey (mon-ter-RAY) in September. War enthusiasm surged in the United States. Recruiting posters blared, "Here's to old Zach! Glorious Times! Roast Beef, Ice Cream, and Three Months' advance." Taylor's conspicuously ordinary manner—he went into battle wearing a straw hat and a plain brown coat—endeared him to the public, which kicked up its heels in celebration to the "Rough and Ready Polka" and the "General Taylor Quick Step." After taking Monterrey, Taylor, starved for supplies, halted and granted Mexico an eight-week armistice. Eager to undercut Taylor's popularity—the Whigs were already touting him as a presidential candidate—Polk stripped him of half his forces and reassigned them to General Winfield Scott. He was to mount an amphibious attack on Vera Cruz (VEHR-uh-krooz) and proceed on to Mexico City, following the path of Cortés and his conquistadors. Events outstripped Polk's scheme, however, when Taylor defeated a far larger Mexican army at the Battle of Buena Vista (BWAY-nuh VEES-tuh), on February 22–23, 1847.

Farther north, American forces took advantage of the shakiness of Mexican rule to strip away New Mexico and California. In spring 1846 Colonel Stephen Kearny led an army from Fort Leavenworth, Kansas, toward Santa Fe. Having overcome immense natural obstacles to reach New Mexico, Kearny took the territory by a combination of bluff, bluster, and, perhaps, bribery. The Mexican governor, who had said that "it is better to be thought brave than to be so," fled at Kearny's approach. Once he had suppressed a brief rebellion by Mexicans and Indians, Kearny controlled New Mexico securely enough that he could dispatch part of his army south into Mexico to support Taylor at Buena Vista.

California also fell easily into American hands. In 1845 Polk had ordered the Pacific Squadron under Commodore John D. Sloat to occupy California's ports in the event of war. The president had also dispatched a courier overland with secret orders for the colorful **John C. Frémont.** A Georgia-born adventurer, Frémont had taken advantage of his marriage to the daughter of a powerful senator to have accounts of his explorations in the Northwest published as official government documents, and then basked in glory as "the Great Pathfinder." Polk's courier caught up with Frémont in Oregon. Instructed to proceed to California and "watch over the interests of the United States," Frémont interpreted his orders liberally. In June 1846 he rounded up some American insurgents, captured the town of Sonoma (suh-NOH-muh), and proclaimed the independent "Bear Flag Republic." The combined efforts of Frémont, Sloat, and Kearny (who had continued on to California after his successful New Mexico campaign) established U.S. control over California.

John C. Frémont Adventurer who played a role in California rebellion against Mexico; later a force in national politics

The war's final and most important campaign brought Winfield Scott, known as "Old Fuss and Feathers," to glory. In March 1847 Scott carried out a successful amphibious landing near Vera Cruz, pounded the city into submission, and moved inland to attack Mexico City. The U.S. army encountered a Mexican force under

Primary Source: Mexican News

Map 13.4 Major Battles of the Mexican-American War

The Mexican-American War's decisive campaign began with General Winfield Scott's capture of Vera Cruz and ended with his conquest of Mexico City.

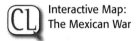

Interactive Map: The Mexican War

Santa Anna at the seemingly impregnable Cerro Gordo (SERR-oh GORD-oh) Pass, but a young captain, Robert E. Lee, helped to find a trail that outflanked the Mexicans and led to a small peak overlooking the pass. The Americans planted howitzers there, stormed the pass, and routed the Mexican army. On September 13, 1847, Mexico City fell to Scott, and he joined Zachary Taylor in the pantheon of new American heroes.

The Mexican army had outnumbered the U.S. forces in virtually every battle. American soldiers died like flies from yellow fever, and they carried into battle the agonies of venereal disease, which they picked up (and left) in every Mexican town they captured. But the Mexican forces could not match the superior artillery and unprecedented weaponry or the superior logistics and organization of the "barbarians of the North."

Treaty of Guadalupe Hidalgo
Agreement ending Mexican-American War; ceded vast amount of land to United States

By the **Treaty of Guadalupe-Hidalgo** (gwah-duh-LOO-pay ee-DOLL-go) (February 2, 1848), Mexico ceded Texas with the Rio Grande boundary, New Mexico, and California to the United States; from the Mexican cession would come the states of New Mexico, California, Nevada, and Utah, most of Arizona, and parts of Colorado and Wyoming. In turn, the United States assumed the claims of U.S. citizens against the Mexican government and paid Mexico $15 million. Although some rabid expansionists denounced the treaty because it failed to include all of Mexico, Polk, like most Americans, was satisfied. Empty territory was fine, but few Americans wanted to annex the mixed Spanish and Indian population of Mexico itself and incorporate into the United States "ignorant and indolent half-civilized Indians," in one writer's words. The virulent racism of American leaders allowed the Mexicans to retain part of their nation. On March 10, 1848, the Senate ratified the treaty by a vote of 38 to 10.

The War's Effects on Sectional Conflict

Despite wartime patriotic enthusiasm, sectional conflict sharpened between 1846 and 1848. Questions related to territorial expansion intensified this conflict, but so, too, did President Polk's uncompromising and literal-minded Jacksonianism.

Polk had restored the Independent Treasury, to the Whigs' dismay, and had eroded Democratic unity by pursuing Jacksonian policies on tariffs and internal improvements. Despite Polk's campaign promise to combine a revenue tariff with mild protection, his administration's Tariff of 1846 slashed duties to the minimum necessary for revenue. Having alienated his northern supporters, Polk then disappointed western Democrats, thirsting for federal aid to fund internal improvements, by vetoing the Rivers and Harbors Bill of 1846.

Important as these issues were, territorial expansion generated the Polk administration's major battles. To Polk, it mattered little whether new territories were slave or free. Expansion would meet its purposes by dispersing the population, weakening dangerous tendencies toward centralized government, and ensuring the agricultural and democratic character of the United States. Focusing attention on slavery in the territories struck him as "not only unwise but wicked." To Polk, the Missouri Compromise, prohibiting slavery north of 36°30', embodied a simple, permanent solution to the question of territorial slavery.

But many northerners were coming to see slavery in the territories as a profoundly disruptive issue that neither could nor should be solved simply by extending the 36°30' line. Abolitionist Whigs, who opposed any expansion of slavery on moral grounds, posed a lesser threat to Polk than northern Democrats who feared that extending slavery into New Mexico and California would deter free laborers from settling those territories. Those Democrats argued that competition with slavery degraded free labor, that the westward extension of slavery would create a barrier to the westward migration of free labor, and that such a barrier would intensify social problems already evident in the East: excessive concentration of population, labor protest, class strife, and social stratification.

The Wilmot Proviso

A young Democratic congressman from Pennsylvania, David Wilmot, galvanized these disaffected northern Democrats. In August 1846 he introduced an amendment to an appropriations bill. This amendment, which became known as the **Wilmot Proviso,** stipulated that slavery be prohibited in any territory acquired by the negotiations. Wilmot represented the Democrats who had supported annexing Texas on the assumption that it would be the last slave state. Like other northern Democrats, he believed that Polk had made an implicit bargain: Texas for slaveholders, California and New Mexico for free labor. But Polk and southern Democrats opposed any barrier to the expansion of slavery south of the Missouri Compromise line; they believed that the westward expansion of slavery would reduce the concentration of slaves in older southern regions and thus lessen the chances of a slave revolt.

Wilmot Proviso Attempt to ban slavery from any territory acquired from Mexico

The proviso raised unsettling constitutional questions. Calhoun and other southerners contended that, because slaves were property, the Constitution protected slaveholders' right to carry their slaves wherever they chose. This position led to the conclusion that the Missouri Compromise was unconstitutional. On the other side, many northerners cited the Northwest Ordinance of 1787, the Missouri Compromise, and the Constitution itself, which gave Congress the power to "make all needful rules and regulations respecting the territory or other property belonging to the United States," as justification for congressional legislation over slavery in the territories. With the election of 1848 approaching, politicians of both sides, eager to hold their parties together and avert civil war, frantically searched for a middle ground.

The Election of 1848

The Whigs watched in dismay as prosperity returned under Polk's program of an independent treasury and low tariffs. Never before had Henry Clay's American System of national banking and high tariffs seemed so irrelevant. But the Wilmot Proviso gave the Whigs a political windfall; originating in the Democratic party, it allowed the Whigs to portray themselves as the South's only dependable friends.

These considerations inclined the majority of Whigs toward Zachary Taylor. As a Louisiana slaveholder, he had obvious appeal to the South. As a political newcomer, he had no loyalty to a discredited American System. And as a war hero, he had broad national appeal. Nominating Taylor as presidential candidate in 1848, the Whigs presented him as an ideal man "without regard to creeds or principles" and ran him without any platform.

The Democrats faced a greater challenge because David Wilmot was one of their own. They could not ignore the issue of slavery in the territories, but if they embraced the positions of either Wilmot or Calhoun, the party would split along sectional lines. When Polk declined to run for reelection, the Democrats nominated Lewis Cass of Michigan, who had formulated the doctrine of "squatter sovereignty," or **popular sovereignty,** as it was later called. Cass argued that Congress should let the question of slavery in the territories be decided by the people who settled there. Squatter sovereignty appealed to many because of its arresting simplicity and vagueness; it neatly dodged the explosive question of whether Congress actually possessed power to prohibit territorial slavery.

popular sovereignty Proposal that settlers in new territories should decide issue of slavery for themselves

In the campaign, both parties tried to avoid the issue of slavery in the territories, but neither succeeded. A pro-Wilmot faction of the Democratic party linked up with the abolitionist Liberty party and antislavery "Conscience" Whigs to form the Free-Soil party. Declaring their dedication to "Free Trade, Free Labor, Free Speech, and Free Men," the Free-Soilers nominated Martin Van Buren on a platform opposing any extension of slavery.

Zachary Taylor benefited from the opposition's alienation of key northern states over the tariff issue, from Democratic disunity over the Wilmot Proviso, and from his war-hero stature. He captured a majority of electoral votes in both North and South. Although it failed to carry any state, the Free-Soil party ran well enough in the North to demonstrate the grassroots popularity of opposition to the extension of slavery. By showing that opposition to the spread of slavery had far more appeal than outright abolitionism, the Free-Soilers sent both Whigs and Democrats a message that they would be unable to ignore in future elections.

The California Gold Rush

When Wilmot had introduced his proviso, the issue of slavery in the West was more abstract than immediate, for Mexico had not yet ceded any territory. The picture quickly changed when an American carpenter discovered gold while building a sawmill in the foothills of California's Sierra Nevada only nine days before the Treaty of Guadalupe-Hidalgo was signed. A frantic gold rush erupted. A San Francisco paper complained that all California "resounds with the sordid cry to *GOLD, GOLD, GOLD!* while the field is left half-planted, the house half-built, and everything neglected but the manufacture of shovels and pickaxes." By December 1848 pamphlets with titles like *The Emigrant's Guide to the Gold Mines* had hit the streets of New York City, and the gold rush was on. Overland emigrants to California increased from 400 in 1848 to 44,000 in 1850.

Arriving by land as well as by sea, gold-rushers swelled California's population from 15,000 in the summer of 1848 to 250,000 by 1852. They came from every corner of the world; one journalist reported that, when she walked through a miners' camp, she heard English, Italian, French, Spanish, German, and Hawaiian. Clashes between Anglo-Americans and Hispanics were frequent. Anglo-Americans particularly resented the Chinese who flooded into California in the 1850s as contract laborers. Rampant prejudice did not stop Americans from hiring Chinese workers, however.

The gold rush transformed the Hispanic hamlet of Yerba Buena (YAIR-buh BWAY-nah) into the "pandemonium" city of San Francisco; population soared from 150 to 50,000. No other American city boasted people from more parts of the world. The ethnic and racial tensions of the gold fields spilled over into the city, and in 1851 merchants organized a Committee of Vigilance to patrol the streets, deport undesirables, and try and hang alleged thieves and murderers.

The gold rush made the issue of slavery in the West an immediate, practical concern. The newcomers to California included Mexicans, free blacks, and slaves brought by southern planters. White prospectors loathed the idea of competing with these groups and wanted to drive them from the gold fields. Violence mounted, and demands grew for a strong civilian government to replace the ineffective military government left over from the war. Polk began to fear that without a satisfactory congressional solution to the slavery issue, Californians might organize a government independent of the United States. The gold rush guaranteed that the question of slavery in the Mexican cession would be the first item on the agenda for Polk's successor and the nation.

"Union" Woodcut by Thomas W. Strong, 1848
This 1848 campaign poster for Zachary Taylor reminded Americans of his military victories, unmilitary bearing (note the civilian dress and straw hat), and deliberately vague promises.

CHECKING IN

- The United States entered into the Mexican-American War by choice rather than by necessity.
- After losing the war, Mexico ceded to the United States the Southwest quadrant of the present United States and recognized Texas's independence.
- Victory in the war again raised the question of the expansion of slavery.
- The election of 1848 revealed the growing strength of opposition to the expansion of slavery.
- The discovery of gold in California guaranteed that, despite politicians' wishes to sidestep the issue, the expansion of slavery would rise to the top of the national agenda.

Chapter Summary

 DOWNLOAD THE MP3 AUDIO FILE OF THE CHAPTER SUMMARY, AND
LISTEN TO IT ON THE GO.

How did the massive immigration of the 1840s influence the balance of power between Whigs and Democrats? (page 279)

As German and Irish immigrants poured into the United States, they gravitated to the Democratic party. Meanwhile, nativism grew stronger among Whigs.

How did Americans expand into the Southwest and to the Pacific coast in the 1840s? (page 284)

Americans had begun trading along Mexico's northern frontiers early in the nineteenth century. In the 1820s Mexico invited Americans to settle in Texas, which sought its independence in the 1830s. In the following decade thousands of people followed the overland trails to California and Oregon.

How did "Manifest Destiny" influence American politics? (page 288)

The issue of annexation of Texas stalled because it raised the vexatious issue of the expansion of slavery. But the pro-expansion sentiment known as Manifest Destiny helped bring ardent expansionist James K. Polk to the White House in 1844 and fueled support for Texas annexation despite the slavery question.

What were the results of the Mexican-American War? (page 293)

In the Treaty of Guadalupe-Hidalgo, the United States gained one-fourth of its present territory, and Mexico recognized Texas's independence. However, once again the question of the expansion of slavery came to the forefront of American politics, despite politicians' attempts to sidestep it.

KEY TERMS

nativism *(p. 282)*

"Know-Nothing" party *(p. 282)*

Stephen F. Austin *(p. 286)*

Santa Anna *(p. 286)*

Alamo *(p. 286)*

Sam Houston *(p. 287)*

Overland Trail *(p. 288)*

Manifest Destiny *(p. 291)*

John C. Frémont *(p. 295)*

Treaty of Guadalupe Hidalgo *(p. 296)*

Wilmot Proviso *(p. 297)*

popular sovereignty *(p. 298)*

CHAPTER 14

From Compromise to Secession

1850–1861

The Last Moments of John Brown

Harpers Ferry Federal arsenal in Virginia; site of John Brown's abortive attempt to fuel a slave uprising in the South

CL This icon will direct you to the website where you can Prepare for Class, Improve Your Grade, and Ace the Test: **www.cengage.com/history/boyer/ enduringconcise6e**

CHAPTER PREVIEW

The Compromise of 1850
Why did the Compromise of 1850 only temporarily resolve the crisis facing the Union?

The Collapse of the Second Party System, 1853–1856
Why did the Whig party disintegrate, and what were the consequences?

The Crisis of the Union, 1857–1860
What major issues dominated American politics from 1857 to 1860?

The Collapse of the Union, 1860–1861
Why did the Civil War ultimately erupt in 1861?

In early July 1859 a man calling himself Isaac Smith rented a dilapidated farmhouse a few miles from **Harpers Ferry,** Virginia, the site of a federal armory. Before long, others arrived, including two young women; soon they were busy unloading fifteen boxes of what Smith termed "hardware." Although the men seemed reclusive, the young women were amiable, chatting with their neighbors, to whom everything seemed normal.

In fact, nothing was normal. "Smith" was actually **John Brown,** a brooding abolitionist with a price on his head for the murder of proslavery settlers in Kansas three years earlier in the Pottawatomie (pot-uh-WATT-uh-mee) Massacre. Brown believed that God had ordained him to "purge this land with blood" to eradicate the evil of slavery. Joining him were a daughter, a daughter-in-law, three of his sons, and a mixed crew of white idealists, free blacks, and fugitive

301

John Brown Self-appointed agent of God to destroy slavery; responsible for Pottawattomie Massacre as well as Harpers Ferry raid

slaves. The "hardware" consisted of rifles and revolvers, which Brown and his followers intended to use to raid the Harpers Ferry arsenal— and ignite a slave insurrection throughout the South.

Although he was in many ways a marginal figure in the abolitionist movement— he had written no stirring tracts against slavery—Brown fascinated many eastern abolitionists, themselves pacifists, who were beginning to suspect that only violence would end slavery. They knew nothing of his plans for Harpers Ferry and accepted his disavowal of any role in the Kansas massacre. With their contributions, they endorsed Brown's plans to carry on the fight against those who would forcibly turn Kansas into a slave state, in effect accepting the use of violence.

On the moonless evening of October 16, 1859, Brown and his army of eighteen seized the arsenal and armory at Harpers Ferry and waited for slaves to rally around them and begin a massive rebellion. Two days later, a contingent of marines under the command of Colonel Robert E. Lee stormed the armory and killed or mortally wounded almost all of Brown's followers. A handful escaped but were eventually captured and executed. Brown himself was seriously wounded and captured. The anticipated—and feared—slave rebellion never happened.

Although the northern abolitionists who had supported him tried to distance themselves from the event, correspondence unearthed at the farmhouse clearly linked them to Brown. During his trial, Brown rejected his own lawyers' claims that he was insane and instead told his captors that he had rendered to God the "greatest service man can." Gradually northern opinion became more and more sympathetic to Brown, seeing him as a martyr. Such opinion reached its apotheosis with the respected Ralph Waldo Emerson, who said that Brown's execution would "make the gallows as glorious as the cross."

Southerners saw matters quite differently. Brown may have botched the operation, but his plan to provoke a slave insurrection was reminiscent of Nat Turner's rebellion a generation earlier. To slaveholders, Brown's vision of uniting nonslaveholding whites, free blacks, and slaves was all too plausible; Brown was not a lunatic but a tool of the abolition movement that would drench the South in blood.

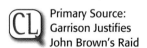

Primary Source: Garrison Justifies John Brown's Raid

THE COMPROMISE OF 1850

Why did the Compromise of 1850 only temporarily resolve the crisis facing the Union?

Ralph Waldo Emerson's grim prediction that a U.S. victory in the Mexican War would be like swallowing arsenic proved disturbingly accurate. When the war ended in 1848, the United States contained an equal number (fifteen each) of free and slave states, but the vast territory gained by the war threatened to upset this balance. Any solution to the question of slavery in the Mexican cession—a free-soil policy, extension of the Missouri Compromise line, or popular sovereignty—ensured controversy. The prospect of free soil angered southerners, whereas extension of the Missouri Compromise line antagonized free-soil northerners as well as southern extremists who proclaimed that Congress could not bar slavery's expansion. Popular sovereignty offered the greatest hope for compromise by taking the question of slavery

Chronology

1848	Treaty of Guadalupe-Hidalgo ends Mexican War; Free-Soil party formed; Zachary Taylor elected president
1849	California seeks admission to the Union as a free state
1850	Nashville convention assembles to discuss the South's grievances; Compromise of 1850
1852	Harriet Beecher Stowe, *Uncle Tom's Cabin*; Franklin Pierce elected president
1853	Gadsden Purchase
1854	Ostend Manifesto; Kansas-Nebraska Act
1854–1855	Know-Nothing and Republican parties rise
1855	Proslavery forces steal the election for a territorial legislature in Kansas; Proslavery Kansans establish a government in Lecompton; Free-soil government established in Topeka, Kansas
1856	The "sack" of Lawrence, Kansas; John Brown's Pottawatomie Massacre; James Buchanan elected president
1857	*Dred Scott* decision; President Buchanan endorses the Lecompton constitution in Kansas
1858	Congress refuses to admit Kansas to the Union under the Lecompton constitution; Lincoln-Douglas debates
1859	John Brown's raid on Harpers Ferry
1860	Abraham Lincoln elected president; South Carolina secedes from the Union
1861	The remaining Lower South states secede; Confederate States of America established; Crittenden compromise plan collapses; Lincoln takes office; Firing on Fort Sumter; Civil War begins; Upper South secedes

out of national politics and handing it to each territory, but this notion pleased neither free-soil nor proslavery extremists.

As the rhetoric escalated, events plunged the nation into crisis. Utah and then California, both acquired from Mexico, sought admission to the Union as free states. Texas, admitted to the Union as a slave state in 1845, aggravated matters by claiming the eastern half of New Mexico, thus potentially opening the door to slavery's extension into other newly acquired territory.

By 1850 other issues had become intertwined with territorial questions. Northerners had grown increasingly unhappy with slavery in the District of Columbia, within the shadow of the Capitol; southerners complained about lax enforcement of the Fugitive Slave Act of 1793. Any broad compromise would have to take both matters into account.

Zachary Taylor at the Helm

President Zachary Taylor believed that the South must not kindle the issue of slavery in the territories, because neither New Mexico nor California was suited for slavery. Taylor's position differed significantly from the thinking behind the still-controversial Wilmot Proviso, which proposed that Congress bar slavery in the territories ceded by Mexico. Taylor's plan, in contrast, left the decision to the states. He prompted

California to apply for admission as a free state, bypassing the territorial stage, and hinted that he expected New Mexico (where the Mexican government had abolished slavery) to do the same. This strategy appeared to offer a quick, practical solution to the problem of extending slavery. The North would gain two new free states, and the South would gain acceptance of the right of the individual state to bar or permit slavery as it chose. This was the very foundation of the South's defense of slavery, its armor against the onslaught of the abolitionists. Nothing in the Constitution forbade a state to act one way or the other on slavery.

But southerners rejected Taylor's plan. Not only would it yield the Wilmot Proviso's goal—the banning of slavery from the lands acquired from Mexico—but it rested on the shaky assumption that slavery could never take root in California or New Mexico. Southerners also protested the addition of two new free states. "If we are to be reduced to a mere handful . . . wo, wo, I say to this Union," John C. Calhoun warned. Disillusioned with Taylor, a slaveholder from whom they had expected better, nine southern states agreed to send delegates to a convention to meet in Nashville in June 1850.

Henry Clay Proposes a Compromise

Had Taylor held a stronger position in the Whig party, he might have blunted mounting southern opposition. But many leading Whigs had never accepted this political novice, and in early 1850 Kentucky senator Henry Clay challenged Taylor's leadership by forging a compromise bill to resolve the whole range of contentious issues. Clay proposed (1) the admission of California as a free state; (2) the division of the remainder of the Mexican cession into two territories, New Mexico and Utah, without federal restrictions on slavery; (3) the settlement of the Texas–New Mexico boundary dispute on terms favorable to New Mexico; (4) as a pot sweetener for Texas, an agreement that the federal government would assume the state's large public debt; (5) continuation of slavery in the District of Columbia but abolition of the slave trade; and (6) a more effective fugitive slave law.

Clay rolled all these proposals into a single "omnibus" bill. The debates over the compromise bill during late winter and early spring 1850 marked the last major appearance on the public stage of Clay, Calhoun, and Webster, the trio who had stood at the center of American political life since the War of 1812. Clay, ever the conciliator, warned the South against the evils of secession and assured the North that nature would check the spread of slavery. Gaunt and gloomy, the dying Calhoun listened as another senator read Calhoun's address for him, a repetition of his warnings that only if the North treated the South as an equal could the Union survive. Webster spoke vividly in favor of compromise, "not as a Massachusetts man, nor as a Northern man, but as an American," and chided the North for trying to "reenact the will of God" by excluding slavery from the Mexican cession. Strident voices countered these attempts at conciliation. The antislavery Whig William Seward (SOO-urd) of New York enraged southerners by talking of a "higher law than the Constitution"—namely, the will of God against the extension of slavery.

Even as the Union faced its worst crisis since 1789, events in summer 1850 eased the way toward resolution. When the Nashville convention met in June, only nine of the fifteen slave states, primarily in the Lower South, sent delegates. Despite the

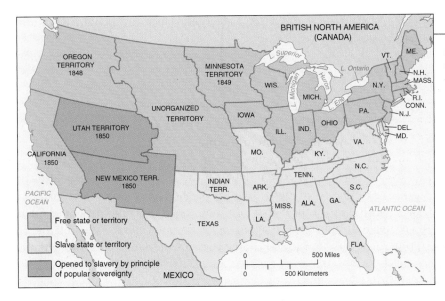

Map 14.1   The Compromise of 1850

The Compromise of 1850 admitted California as a free state. Utah and New Mexico were left open to slavery or freedom according to the principle of popular sovereignty.

reckless pronouncements of the "fire-eaters" (extreme advocates of "southern rights"), moderates dominated. Then Zachary Taylor celebrated too extravagantly on July 4 and died five days later of a stomach ailment. His successor, Millard Fillmore of New York, supported Clay's compromise. Finally, Senator Stephen A. Douglas of Illinois took over stewardship of the compromise. He broke the omnibus into a series of individual measures; to secure Democratic support, Douglas proposed that popular sovereignty settle the slavery issue in New Mexico and Utah. These tactics worked. By summer's end the **Compromise of 1850** had become reality.

Compromise of 1850 Last-ditch attempt to paper over the issue of slavery expansion; ultimately a failure

Assessing the Compromise

Although President Fillmore hailed the compromise as a final settlement of sectional issues, it failed to bridge the underlying differences between North and South. Southerners had voted against the admission of California and northerners against the Fugitive Slave Act.

Each section could claim victories from the compromise. Northern victories were clear: admission of California and abolition of the slave trade in the District of Columbia. However, southern victories, such as the stricter fugitive slave law, were clouded by the legislators' failure to resolve the issue of congressional authority over slavery in territories outside the Mexican cession.

Southerners therefore reacted ambivalently to the Compromise of 1850. In state elections during fall 1850 and 1851, procompromise candidates generally thrashed the law's opponents. At the same time, even Unionists in Georgia wrote the celebrated Georgia platform, which threatened secession if Congress prohibited slavery in the Mexican cession or repealed the Fugitive Slave Act. And the South's one clear victory, the passage of a new, more stringent fugitive slave law, quickly proved a mixed blessing. Few slaves had been taken into the Mexican cession, so the question of slavery there had a hypothetical quality. But the issues raised by the new fugitive slave law were concrete: real southerners would pursue real fugitives—on northern soil. Average northerners to whom slavery had been an abstraction would respond to this new reality with fury.

Fugitive Slave Act Harsh measure allowing recapture of escaped slaves; part of Compromise of 1850; alienated northerners and southerners alike

Enforcement of the Fugitive Slave Act

Northern moderates accepted the **Fugitive Slave Act of 1850** as the price of saving the Union, but the law outraged antislavery northerners. It denied alleged fugitives the right of trial by jury, forbade them to testify at their own trials, permitted their return to slavery merely on the testimony of a claimant, and enabled court-appointed commissioners to collect ten dollars if they ruled for the slaveholder but only five if they ruled for the fugitive. As one commentator noted, the law threatened to turn the North into "one vast hunting ground." It targeted *all* runaways, putting at risk even fugitives who had lived as free blacks for thirty years or more. Above all, the law brought home to northerners the uncomfortable truth of their own complicity in slavery's continuation. By legalizing the activities of slave-catchers on northern soil, the law reminded northerners that slavery was a national problem, not merely a southern institution.

Efforts to catch and return runaways inflamed emotions in both North and South. In 1854 a Boston mob aroused by antislavery speeches killed a courthouse guard in an abortive effort to rescue fugitive slave Anthony Burns. Determined to enforce the law, President Franklin Pierce sent federal troops to escort Burns to the harbor, where a ship carried him back to slavery. As five platoons of troops marched Burns to the ship, fifty thousand people lined the streets. The Burns incident shattered the complacency of conservative supporters of the Compromise of 1850. "We went to bed one night old fashioned conservative Compromise Union Whigs," textile manufacturer Amos A. Lawrence wrote, "and waked up stark mad Abolitionists."

Northerners devised ways to interfere with the enforcement of the Fugitive Slave Act. "Vigilance" committees spirited endangered blacks to Canada, lawyers dragged out hearings to raise slave-catchers' expenses, and "personal liberty laws" hindered state officials' enforcement of the law. These obstructionist tactics convinced southerners that the "victory" represented by the passage of the Fugitive Slave Act was increasingly illusory.

Frederick Douglass

Born into slavery, Frederick Douglass became a commanding orator and writer in the 1840s and 1850s. He bitterly attacked the Fugitive Slave Act. The only way to make the law a "dead letter," he vowed, was to make "half a dozen or more dead kidnappers."

Uncle Tom's Cabin Harriet Beecher Stowe's classic novel about slavery; had enormous political impact

Uncle Tom's Cabin

Harriet Beecher Stowe's novel *Uncle Tom's Cabin* (1852) drummed up wide northern support for fugitive slaves. Stowe, the daughter of famed evangelical Lyman Beecher, greeted the Fugitive Slave Act with horror. In one of the novel's most memorable scenes, she depicted the slave Eliza, clutching her infant son, bounding to freedom across ice floes on the Ohio River. Slavery itself was Stowe's main target. Much of her novel's power derives from its view that good intentions mean little in the face of so evil an institution. The good intentions of a kindly slave owner die with him, and Uncle Tom is sold to the vicious Yankee Simon Legree, who whips Tom to death. Stowe also played effectively to the emotions of her audience by demonstrating how slavery ripped slave families apart.

 Primary Source: Harriet Beecher Stowe Portrays Slavery's Brutality

Uncle Tom's Cabin Theater Poster

With its vivid imagery of slavery, Harriet Beecher Stowe's *Uncle Tom's Cabin* translated well to the stage. Scenes of Eliza crossing the ice of the Ohio River with bloodhounds in pursuit and the evil Simon Legree whipping Uncle Tom outraged northern audiences and turned many against slavery. Southerners damned Mrs. Stowe as a "vile wretch in petticoats."

Three hundred thousand copies of *Uncle Tom's Cabin* were sold in 1852, and 1.2 million by summer 1853. Stage dramatizations reached perhaps fifty times more people than the novel did. As a play, *Uncle Tom's Cabin* enthralled working-class audiences normally indifferent or hostile to abolitionism.

The impact of *Uncle Tom's Cabin* is hard to gauge. Although the novel stirred deep feelings, it reflected prevailing stereotypes far more than challenging them. Only light-skinned blacks were aggressive and intelligent; dark-skinned blacks such as Uncle Tom were docile and submissive.

Surgery on the plot, however, could not fully excise the antislavery message of *Uncle Tom's Cabin*. Although it hardly lived up to the prediction of one abolitionist that it

Sojourner Truth

Sojourner Truth was born into slavery in upstate New York and named Isabella by her Dutch owner. She was illiterate and a mystic given to hearing messages from God, including one in 1843 that told her to change her name to Sojourner Truth. By then she had joined William Lloyd Garrison's band of abolitionists. In the 1840s and 1850s she traveled from New England to Indiana preaching against slavery. Six feet tall and speaking English with a Dutch accent, she cut a striking figure on the platform, sprinkling humorous asides with vivid gestures, gospel songs, and clever put-downs. In one notable instance, when hecklers questioned her femininity, she bared her breasts to silence them.

would convert two million people to antislavery, it did push many waverers toward a more aggressively antisouthern and antislavery stance and forced others at least to look at this uncomfortable issue.

The Election of 1852

The Fugitive Slave Act fragmented the Whig party. Northern Whigs took the lead in defying the law, and southern Whigs had a difficult time explaining away the power of vocal free-soil Whigs.

In 1852 the Whigs' nomination of Mexican-American War hero General Winfield Scott as their presidential candidate widened the sectional split in the party. Although a Virginian, Scott owed his nomination to the northern free-soil Whigs. His single, feeble statement endorsing the Compromise of 1850 undercut southern Whigs trying to portray the Democrats as the party of disunion and themselves as the party of both slavery and the Union.

The Democrats bridged their own sectional division by nominating Franklin Pierce of New Hampshire, a dark-horse candidate whose chief attraction was that no faction of the party violently opposed him. Northern and southern Democrats alike rallied behind the Compromise of 1850 and behind the ideal of popular sovereignty, and Pierce won a smashing victory. In the most one-sided election since 1820, he carried twenty-seven of the thirty-one states and collected 254 of 296 electoral votes.

THE COLLAPSE OF THE SECOND PARTY SYSTEM, 1853–1856

Why did the Whig party disintegrate, and what were the consequences?

Franklin Pierce was the last presidential candidate to carry the popular and electoral vote in both North and South until Franklin D. Roosevelt swept into office in 1932. Pierce also became the last president to hold office under the second party system—Whigs against Democrats. Within four years of Pierce's election, the Whig party would disintegrate, to be replaced by two newcomers, the American (Know-Nothing) party and the **Republican party.**

Republican party Party, opposed to slavery expansion, that emerged after Whig party's disintegration; strong in North, nonexistent in South

Unlike the Whigs, the Republican party was a purely sectional, northern party, drawing its support from both former Whigs and discontented Democrats. The Democrats survived as a national party, but with a base so shrunken in the North that the newborn Republican party captured two-thirds of the free states in the election of 1856.

For decades the second party system had kept the conflict over slavery in check by providing Americans other issues to argue about—banking, internal improvements, tariffs, and temperance. By the 1850s the debate over slavery extension overshadowed such issues and exposed raw divisions in each party. Whigs, with their larger, more aggressive free-soil wing, were much more vulnerable to disruption than the Democrats. Thus, when Stephen A. Douglas put forth a proposal in 1854 to organize the vast Nebraska Territory with no restrictions on slavery, he ignited a firestorm that consumed the Whig party.

The Kansas-Nebraska Act

Signed in late May 1854, the **Kansas-Nebraska Act** shattered the already-weakened second party system and triggered renewed sectional strife. The bill's roots lay in the seemingly uncontroversial desire of farmers to organize the large territory west of Iowa and Missouri. Railroad enthusiasts who dreamed of a rail line linking the Midwest to the Pacific also wanted the territory organized.

In January 1854 Democratic senator Stephen A. Douglas of Illinois proposed a bill to organize Nebraska as a territory. Douglas believed that a railroad to the Pacific would bring national benefits, including a continuous line of settlement, and he thought that a railroad-based western expansion would unite the splintering Democratic factions.

Two sources of potential conflict loomed. First, some southerners advocated a southern-based Pacific route rather than a midwestern one. Second, Nebraska lay north of the Missouri Compromise line in the Louisiana Purchase, a region closed to slavery. Under Douglas's bill, the South would lose the Pacific rail route *and* face the possibility of more free territory in the Union. To placate southerners and win their votes, Douglas made two concessions. First, he proclaimed the Missouri Compromise now void, superseded by the Compromise of 1850 and its doctrine of popular sovereignty. Second, Douglas agreed to divide the territory into northern and southern parts, Nebraska and Kansas. Implicit in this, at least to southerners, was the idea that Nebraska would be free soil but Kansas would be open to slavery.

These modifications to Douglas's original bill set off a storm of protest. Despite Douglas's belief that national expansion was the critical issue, most attention focused on the extension of slavery. Antislavery northerners assailed the bill as "an atrocious plot" to violate the "sacred pledge" of the Missouri Compromise and to turn Kansas into a "dreary region of despotism, inhabited by masters and slaves." Their anger provoked an equal response among southerners and added the issue of sectional pride to the already-volatile mix of expansion and slavery.

Despite the uproar, Douglas guided the bill easily through the Senate. Matters were far more tumultuous in the House, where the bill passed by a narrow margin. Ominously, not a single northern Whig in the House voted for the bill, and northern Democrats split evenly.

The Surge of Free Soil

Amid the clamor over his bill, Douglas ruefully observed that he could now travel to Chicago by the light of his own burning effigies. Neither a fool nor a political novice, he was the victim of a political bombshell—**free soil**—that exploded under his feet.

Support for free soil united many who agreed on little else. Many free-soilers were racists who opposed allowing any African-Americans, slave or free, into the West. Others repudiated slavery on moral grounds and rejected blatantly racist legislation. Although split over the morality of slavery, most free-soilers agreed that slavery impeded whites' progress. Because a slave worked for nothing, free-soilers claimed, no free laborer could compete with a slave. If slavery secured a toehold in Kansas, free-soilers warned, Minnesota would fall to slavery as well.

The Kansas-Nebraska Act, in free-soilers' opinion, was "a part of a continuous movement of slaveholders to advance slavery over the entire North." Free-soilers saw southern planters, southern politicians, and their northern dupes, such as Stephen A. Douglas, entangled in a gigantic conspiracy to extend slavery.

Kansas-Nebraska Act Attempt to allow popular sovereignty in newly organizing territories

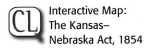 Interactive Map: The Kansas–Nebraska Act, 1854

free soil Movement opposed to any expansion of slavery

The Ebbing of Manifest Destiny

The uproar over the Kansas-Nebraska Act embarrassed the Pierce administration. It also doomed Manifest Destiny, the one issue that had held the Democrats together in the 1840s.

Franklin Pierce had come to office championing Manifest Destiny, but increasing sectional rivalries sidetracked his efforts. In 1853 his emissary James Gadsden negotiated the purchase of a strip of land south of the Gila River (now southern Arizona and part of southern New Mexico), an acquisition favored by advocates of a southern railroad route to the Pacific. Fierce opposition to the Gadsden Purchase revealed mounting free-soilers' suspicions of expansion, and the Senate approved the treaty only after slashing nine thousand square miles from the purchase. The sectional rivalries beginning to engulf the Nebraska bill clearly threatened any proposal to gain new territory.

Cuba provided even more vivid proof of the change in public attitudes toward expansion. In 1854 a former Mississippi governor, John A. Quitman, planned a filibuster (an unofficial military expedition) to seize Cuba from Spain. Pierce wanted to acquire Cuba and may first have encouraged Quitman's plans, but the president backed down in the face of northern opposition. Northerners saw the filibuster as another manifestation of the Slave Power's conspiracy to grab more territory for the South's "peculiar institution."

Events, however, slipped out of Pierce's control. In October 1854 the American ambassadors to Great Britain, France, and Spain, two of them southerners, met in Belgium and issued the unofficial Ostend Manifesto, calling on the United States to acquire Cuba by any means, including force.

Despite the Pierce administration's disavowal of the Ostend Manifesto, the idea of expansion into the Caribbean continued to attract southerners, including the Tennessee-born adventurer William Walker. Between 1853 and 1860, the year a firing squad in Honduras (hahn-DURE-uss) executed him, Walker led a succession of filibustering expeditions into Mexico and Nicaragua (nee-ka-RAH-gwa). Taking advantage of civil chaos in Nicaragua, he made himself the chief political force there, reinstituted slavery, and talked of making Nicaragua a U.S. colony.

Although some southerners were against expansion—among them the Louisiana sugar planters who opposed acquiring Cuba because Cuban sugar would compete with their product—southern expansionists stirred up enough commotion to worry antislavery northerners that the South aspired to establish a Caribbean slave empire. Like a card in a poker game, the threat of expansion southward was all the more menacing for not being played. As long as the debate on the extension of slavery focused on the continental United States, prospects for expansion were limited. However, adding the wild card of Caribbean territory changed all calculations.

The Whigs Disintegrate, 1854–1855

While straining Democratic unity, the Kansas-Nebraska Act wrecked the Whig party. Although Democrats lost ground in the 1854 congressional elections, the Whigs failed to benefit. No matter how furious the free-soil Democrats were at Douglas for introducing the act, they could not forget that southern Whigs had supported him. Northern Whigs split into two camps: antislavery "Conscience" Whigs, led by Senator William Seward of New York, and conservatives, led by former president Millard Fillmore. The conservatives believed that the Whig party had to adhere to the Compromise of 1850 to maintain itself as a national party.

This deep division within the Whig party repelled antislavery Democrats and prompted antislavery Whigs to look for an alternative party. By 1856 the new Republican party would become home for these antislavery refugees; however, in 1854 and 1855 the American, or Know-Nothing, party emerged as the principal alternative to the faltering established parties.

The Rise and Fall of the Know-Nothings, 1853–1856

The **Know-Nothings** evolved out of a nativist organization, the Order of the Star-Spangled Banner (see Chapter 13). (The party's popular name derived from its members' standard response to inquiries about its activities: "I know nothing.") It was one of many such societies that mushroomed in response to the unprecedented immigration of the 1840s. It sought to rid the United States of immigrant and Catholic political influence by pressuring the existing parties to appoint only native-born Protestants to office and to extend the naturalization period before immigrants could vote.

Know-Nothings Nativist party that enjoyed brief surge of power in early 1850s

Winfield Scott's campaign for the presidency in 1852 had alienated many nativists, who had previously voted Whig. Trying to revitalize his badly split party, Scott had courted the traditionally Democratic Catholic vote. Most Catholics had voted for Franklin Pierce, but many nativists bailed out of the Whig party. The Kansas-Nebraska Act cemented nativist allegiance to the Know-Nothings, opposed both to the extension of slavery and to Catholicism. An obsessive fear of conspiracies unified the Know-Nothings. They simultaneously denounced a papal conspiracy against the American republic and a Slave Power conspiracy reaching its tentacles throughout the United States.

The Know-Nothings enjoyed a meteoric rise and an equally rapid fall. For example, in 1854 they captured the governorship, almost the entire state legislature, and all the congressional seats of Massachusetts. Such Know-Nothing successes wrecked Whig hopes of capitalizing on hostility to the Kansas-Nebraska Act.

By 1856 the Know-Nothings had become a falling star soon to plummet below the horizon. They proved as vulnerable to sectional conflicts over slavery as the Whigs. In 1855 southern Know-Nothings, mainly proslavery former Whigs, combined with northern conservatives to make acceptance of the Kansas-Nebraska Act part of the Know-Nothing platform, blurring the attraction of Know-Nothingism to northern voters who were more antislavery than anti-Catholic. Chief beneficiary of the Know-Nothing dilemma was the emerging Republican party, which had no southern wing to blur its antislavery message.

One Whig refugee, Illinois congressman Abraham Lincoln, asked pointedly, "How can anyone who abhors the oppression of negroes be in favor of degrading classes of white people?" "We began by declaring," Lincoln continued, "that 'all men are created equal.' We now practically read it 'all men are created equal except negroes.' When the Know-Nothings get control, it will read 'all men are created equal, except Negroes and Foreigners and Catholics.'" Even most Know-Nothings concluded that "neither the Pope nor the foreigners ever can govern the country or endanger its liberties, but the slavebreeders and slavetraders do govern it, and threaten to put an end to all government but theirs." Consequently the Know-Nothings proved vulnerable to the challenge posed by the emerging Republican Party, which did not officially embrace nativism and had no southern wing to placate.

The Republican Party and the Crisis in Kansas, 1855–1856

Born in the chaotic aftermath of the Kansas-Nebraska Act, the Republican party would become the main opposition to the Democratic party by 1856 and would win each presidential election from 1860 until 1884. In 1855, however, few would have predicted such a bright future. Although united in opposition to the Kansas-Nebraska Act, the fledgling party was host to conservatives who wanted to restore the Missouri Compromise, radicals who had been part of the Liberty party abolitionists, and a sizable middle of free-soilers.

Building organizations at the state level was essential, for state issues often shaped voters' allegiances. The Know-Nothings, for example, linked support for temperance, strong at the state level, with anti-Catholicism and antislavery. Frequently, antislavery voters were also protemperance and anti-Catholic, believing that addiction to alcohol and submission to the pope were both forms of enslavement to be eradicated. Competing with the Know-Nothings for these intensely moralistic voters at the state level, Republicans faced a dilemma: if they attacked the Know-Nothings for stressing anti-Catholicism over antislavery, they might well alienate the voters, but if they compromised with the Know-Nothings, they might well lose their own identity as a party.

Alternately attacking and conciliating, the Republicans succeeded in some state elections in 1855 but lost ground as popular ire against the Kansas-Nebraska Act cooled. By the start of 1856 they were organized in only half the northern states and lacked any national organization. The Republicans desperately needed something to make voters more concerned about the Slave Power than about rum or Catholicism. Salvation for the nascent party came in the form of violence in Kansas, which quickly became known as "Bleeding Kansas." This violence united the party around its free-soil center, intensified antislavery feelings, and boosted Republican fortunes.

In the wake of the Kansas-Nebraska Act, Boston abolitionists had organized a company to send antislavery settlers into Kansas, but most of the territory's early settlers came from Missouri or other parts of the Midwest. Few of these opposed slavery on moral grounds. Some supported slavery; others wanted to keep all African-Americans out of Kansas.

Despite most settlers' racist leanings and hatred of abolitionists, Kansas became a battleground between proslavery and antislavery forces. In March 1855 thousands of proslavery Missouri "border ruffians" crossed into Kansas to vote illegally in the first elections for the territorial legislature. Drawing revolvers, they quickly silenced judges who challenged their right to vote in Kansas. Ironically, proslavery forces probably would have won an honest election. But the proslavery legislature established in 1855 in Lecompton, Kansas, operated under a cloud of fraud. The Lecompton legislature shredded what little good reputation it had by passing a series of outrageous laws, punishing the harboring of fugitive slaves with ten years' imprisonment, and making the circulation of abolitionist literature a capital offense.

The legislature's actions set off a chain reaction. In summer 1855 free-staters, including many who had been aroused to oppose the Lecompton legislature, organized a rival government at Topeka. In May 1856 the Lecompton government dispatched a posse to Lawrence, where some free-staters were organizing a militia. Antislavery minister Henry Ward Beecher had urged that rifles would do more than Bibles to enforce morality in Kansas, and the militias christened their guns "Beecher's Bibles." The Lecompton posse, bearing banners emblazoned "Southern rights" and "Let Yankees tremble and abolitionists fall," tore through Lawrence, burning buildings and destroying two printing presses. There were no deaths, but Republicans immediately dubbed the incident "the sack of Lawrence."

The next move belonged to John Brown, a Connecticut-born abolitionist with an overpowering sense of divinely ordained mission. The "sack" of Lawrence convinced Brown that God now beckoned him "to break the jaws of the wicked." In late May, Brown led seven men, including his four sons and his son-in-law, toward Pottawatomie Creek near Lawrence. They shot to death one man associated with the Lecompton government and hacked four others to pieces with broadswords. Brown's "Pottawatomie Massacre" terrified southerners and transformed Bleeding Kansas into a battleground between North and South.

Popular sovereignty had failed in Kansas. Instead of resolving the issue of the extension of slavery, popular sovereignty had institutionalized the division over slavery by creating two rival governments. The Pierce administration compounded its problems, and Kansas's, by denouncing the antislavery Topeka government and recognizing the proslavery Lecompton government, thus forcing northern Democrats into the awkward appearance of supporting the "Bogus Legislature" at Lecompton. Nor did popular sovereignty keep the slavery issue out of politics. On the day before the proslavery attack on Lawrence, Republican senator Charles Sumner of Massachusetts delivered a wrathful speech, "The Crime Against Kansas," in which he verbally lashed the Senate for its complicity in slavery. Sumner singled out Senator Andrew Butler of South Carolina for making "the harlot, slavery" his mistress. Two days later, a relative of Butler, Democratic representative Preston Brooks of South Carolina, strode into the Senate chamber and beat Sumner with a cane. The hollow cane broke after five or six blows, but Sumner, who required stitches, took three years to recuperate. Brooks immediately became a hero in the South. Fragments of his cane were prized as relics, and the City of Charleston presented him a new cane inscribed "Hit him again."

Now "Bleeding Kansas" and "Bleeding Sumner" united the North. The "sack" of Lawrence, President Pierce's recognition of the proslavery Lecompton government, and Brooks's actions seemed to clinch the Republican argument that an aggressive slaveocracy was in power and holding white northerners in contempt. By denouncing the Slave Power rather than slavery, the Republicans sidestepped the divisive question of slavery's morality. Instead, they focused on portraying planters as arrogant aristocrats, the natural enemies of the laboring people of the North.

The Election of 1856

The presidential race of 1856 revealed the scope of the political realignment of the preceding few years. The Republicans, in their first presidential contest, nominated John C. Frémont, the "pathfinder" of California "Bear State" fame. Northern Know-Nothings also endorsed Frémont, while southern Know-Nothings nominated Millard Fillmore, the last Whig president. The Democrats dumped the battered Pierce for James Buchanan (byoo-CAN-un) of Pennsylvania, who had had the luck to

CHECKING IN

- The Kansas-Nebraska Act set off a fire-storm of controversy.
- The Free-Soil movement strengthened as the Whigs splintered over the act.
- The "Know-Nothings" briefly flourished as an alternative to the Whigs.
- "Bleeding Kansas" boosted the sectional Republican party, which was emerging in the North with former free-soilers, Whigs, and Know-Nothings.
- The election of 1856 showed that the Whigs had vanished as a political force and that the Republicans were on the rise.

be out of the country (as minister to Great Britain) during the Kansas-Nebraska furor. A signer of the Ostend Manifesto, Buchanan was popular in the South.

The campaign became two separate races: Frémont versus Buchanan in the free states and Fillmore versus Buchanan in the slave states. Buchanan was in effect the only national candidate. Although Frémont attracted wide support in the North and Fillmore equal support in the South, Buchanan carried enough votes in both North and South to win the presidency.

The election of 1856 made three facts clear. First, the American party was finished as a major national force. Having worked for the Republican Frémont, most northern Know-Nothings joined that party. Fillmore's dismal showing in the South convinced southern Know-Nothings to abandon their party and seek a new political affiliation. Second, although in existence for barely a year, lacking any base in the South, and running a political novice, the Republican party did very well. A purely sectional party had nearly captured the presidency. Third, as long as the Democrats could unite behind a single national candidate, they would be hard to defeat. To achieve unity, however, the Democrats would have to find more James Buchanans—"dough-face" moderates acceptable to southerners and northerners alike.

THE CRISIS OF THE UNION, 1857–1860

What major issues dominated American politics from 1857 to 1860?

No one ever accused James Buchanan of impulsiveness or fanaticism. Although a moderate who wished to avoid controversy, Buchanan would preside over one of the most controversy-ridden administrations in American history. A Supreme Court decision concerning Dred Scott, a Missouri slave who had resided in free territory for several years; the creation of the proslavery Lecompton constitution in Kansas; the raid by John Brown on Harpers Ferry, Virginia; and secession itself would wrack Buchanan's administration. The forces driving the nation apart were spinning out of control by 1856, and Buchanan could not stop them. By his inauguration, southerners saw creeping abolitionism in the guise of free soil, and northerners detected an ever more insatiable Slave Power. Once these potent images took hold in the minds of the American people, politicians could do little to erase them.

The Dred Scott Case, 1857

Pledged to congressional "noninterference" with slavery in the territories, Buchanan looked to the courts for resolution of the vexatious issue of slavery's extension. A case that appeared to promise a solution had been winding its way through the courts for years; on March 6, 1857, two days after Buchanan's inauguration, the Supreme Court handed down its decision in *Dred Scott* v. *Sandford*.

During the 1830s his master had taken Dred Scott, a slave, from the slave state of Missouri into Illinois and the Wisconsin Territory, both closed to slavery. After his master's death, Scott sued for his freedom on the grounds of his residence in free territory.

The Court faced two key questions. Did Scott's residence in free territory during the 1830s make him free? Did Scott, again enslaved in Missouri, have the right to sue in the federal courts? The Supreme Court could have neatly sidestepped controversy by ruling that Scott had no right to sue, but it chose not to.

Instead, Chief Justice Roger B. Taney, a seventy-nine-year-old Marylander, handed down a sweeping decision that touched off another fire-storm. First, Taney wrote, Scott, a slave, could not sue for his freedom. Further, no black, whether a slave or a free descendant of slaves, could become a U.S. citizen. Continuing his incendiary opinion, Taney ruled that even had Scott been entitled to sue, his residence in free territory did not make him free, because the Missouri Compromise, whose provisions prohibited slavery in the Wisconsin Territory, was itself unconstitutional. The compromise, declared Taney, violated the Fifth Amendment's protection of property (including slaves).

The ***Dred Scott* decision**, instead of settling the issue of expansion of slavery, touched off another blast of controversy. The antislavery press flayed it as "willful perversion" filled with "gross historical falsehoods." Republicans saw the decision as further evidence that the fiendish Slave Power gripped the nation.

Like Stephen A. Douglas after the Kansas-Nebraska Act, James Buchanan now appeared as another northern dupe of an evil slaveocracy. Republicans restrained themselves from open defiance of the decision only by insisting that it did not bind the nation; Taney's comments on the constitutionality of the Missouri Compromise, they contended, were opinions unnecessary to settling the case and therefore technically not binding.

The savage reaction to the decision provided more proof that no "judicious" or nonpartisan solution to slavery was possible. Any doubter needed only to read the fast-breaking news from Kansas.

***Dred Scott* decision** Threw out Missouri Compromise, created political turmoil

The Lecompton Constitution, 1857

While the Supreme Court wrestled with the abstract issues raised by the expansion of slavery, President Buchanan sought a concrete solution to the problem of Kansas, where the free-state government at Topeka and the officially recognized proslavery government at Lecompton regarded each other with profound distrust. Buchanan's plan for Kansas looked simple: an elected territorial convention would draw up a constitution that would either prohibit or permit slavery; Buchanan would submit the constitution to Congress; Congress would then admit Kansas as a state.

Unfortunately, the plan exploded in Buchanan's face. Popular sovereignty, the essence of the plan, demanded fair play, a scarce commodity in Kansas. The territory's history of fraudulent elections left both sides reluctant to commit their fortunes to the polls. In June 1857 an election for a constitutional convention took place, but free-staters, by now a majority in Kansas, boycotted the election on grounds that the proslavery forces would rig it. A constitutional convention dominated by proslavery delegates then met and drew up the Lecompton constitution, which protected the rights of slaveholders already residing in Kansas and provided for a referendum to decide whether to allow more slaves into the territory.

Buchanan faced a dilemma. A supporter of popular sovereignty, he had favored letting Kansas voters decide the slavery issue. But now he confronted a constitution drawn up by a convention chosen by less than 10 percent of the eligible voters. However, there were compelling reasons to accept the Lecompton constitution. The South, which had provided Buchanan's winning margin in the 1856 election, supported it. To Buchanan, the wrangling over slavery in Kansas was a case of extremists' turning minor issues into major ones, especially because only about two hundred slaves resided in Kansas and because prospects for slavery in the remaining territories were slight. The admission of Kansas to the Union as free or slave seemed the quickest way to end the commotion, and so in December 1857 Buchanan endorsed the Lecompton constitution.

Stephen A. Douglas and other northern Democrats broke with Buchanan. To them, the Lecompton constitution, in allowing voters to decide only whether more slaves could enter Kansas, violated the spirit of popular sovereignty. "I care not whether [slavery] is voted down or voted up," Douglas declared. But refusing to allow a vote on the constitution itself, with its protection of existing slave property, smacked of a "system of trickery and jugglery to defeat the fair expression of the will of the people."

Meanwhile, in Kansas, the newly elected territorial legislature called for a referendum on the Lecompton constitution and thus on slavery itself. Two elections followed. In December 1857 the referendum called by the constitutional convention took place. Free-staters boycotted it, and the Lecompton constitution passed overwhelmingly. Two weeks later, the election called by the territorial legislature took place. This time proslavery forces boycotted, and the constitution went down to crushing defeat. Buchanan tried to ignore this second election, but when he attempted to bring Kansas into the Union under the Lecompton constitution, Congress blocked him and forced yet another referendum. In this third election Kansas could accept or reject the entire constitution, with the proviso that rejection would delay statehood. However, Kansans voted down the Lecompton constitution.

Buchanan simultaneously had failed to tranquilize Kansas and alienated northerners in his own party, who now more than ever believed that the southern Slave Power pulled all the important strings in the Democratic party. Douglas emerged as a hero for northern Democrats but saw his cherished formula of popular sovereignty become a prescription for strife rather than harmony.

The Lincoln-Douglas Debates, 1858

Despite the acclaim that he received for his stand against the Lecompton constitution, Douglas faced a stiff challenge in the 1858 Illinois senatorial election. Of his Republican opponent, Abraham Lincoln, Douglas remarked, "I shall have my hands full. He is the strong man of his party—full of wit, facts, and dates—and the best stump speaker with his droll ways and dry jokes, in the West."

Physically and ideologically, the two candidates presented a striking contrast. Tall and gangling at 6'4", Lincoln possessed energy, ambition, and a passion for self-education that had carried him from the Kentucky log cabin where he was born into law and politics in his adopted Illinois. First elected as a Whig, he joined the Republican party in 1856. The New England–born Douglas stood a foot shorter than Lincoln, but to the small farmers of southern origin who populated the Illinois flatlands, he was the "little giant," the personification of the Democratic party in the West. The campaign quickly became more than just another Senate race, for it pitted the

Stephen A. Douglas
Douglas's politics were founded on his unflinching conviction that most Americans favored national expansion and would support popular sovereignty as the fastest and least controversial way to achieve it. Douglas's self-assurance blinded him to rising northern sentiment for free soil.

Abraham Lincoln
Clean-shaven at the time of his famous debates with Douglas, Lincoln would soon grow a beard to give himself a more distinguished appearance.

Republican party's rising star against the Senate's leading Democrat, and, thanks to the railroad and the telegraph, it received unprecedented national attention.

Opening his campaign with his famous "House Divided" speech ("this government cannot endure permanently half *slave* and half *free*"), Lincoln stressed the gulf between his free-soil position and Douglas's popular sovereignty. Douglas dismissed the house-divided doctrine as an invitation to secession. What mattered to him was not slavery but the continued expansion of white settlement.

The high point of the campaign came in a series of seven debates held from August to October 1858. Douglas used the debates to portray Lincoln as a virtual abolitionist and advocate of racial equality. Lincoln replied that Congress had no constitutional authority to abolish slavery in the South. He also asserted that "I am not, nor ever have been in favor of bringing about the social and political equality of the white and black man."

In the debate at Freeport, Illinois, Lincoln tried to make Douglas squirm by asking how popular sovereignty could be reconciled with the *Dred Scott* decision. Lincoln maintained that if Congress had no authority to exclude slavery from a territory, then it seemingly followed that a territorial legislature created by Congress also lacked the power to do so. Douglas responded that, although the Supreme Court had ruled that Congress could not exclude slavery from the territories, the voters in a territory could do so by refusing to enact laws that gave legal protection to slave property. This "Freeport doctrine" salvaged popular sovereignty but did nothing for Douglas's reputation among southerners, who preferred the guarantees of *Dred Scott* to the uncertainties of popular sovereignty. Trying to move beyond debates on free soil and popular sovereignty, Lincoln shifted in the closing debates to attacks on slavery as "a moral, social, and political evil." He argued that Douglas's view of slavery as merely an eccentric and unsavory southern custom would dull the nation's conscience and facilitate the legalization of slavery everywhere. At the same time, however, Lincoln compromised his own position by rejecting both abolition and equality for blacks.

Neither man scored a clear victory in the debates, and the senatorial election, which Douglas won, settled no major issues. Nonetheless, the candidates' contest was crucial. It solidified the sectional split in the Democratic party and made Lincoln famous in the North—and infamous in the South.

The Legacy of Harpers Ferry

Although Lincoln explicitly rejected abolitionism, he called free soil a step toward the "ultimate extinction" of slavery. Many southerners ignored the differences between free soil and abolitionism and saw the entire North locked in the grip of demented leaders bent on civil war.

Two things reinforced southerners' dire image of the North: the evidence of northern complicity in the Harpers Ferry raid in 1859 and the virtual canonization of John Brown by northern preachers. Convinced that many northerners endorsed the use of violence to end slavery, some southerners began refusing to associate with northerners and northern institutions. For example, about 250 southerners studying medicine in Philadelphia withdrew from the city's medical schools and enrolled in southern medical schools. Although Lincoln and Seward condemned the raid, southerners suspected that they regretted the conspiracy's failure more than the attempt itself.

Brown's abortive raid also rekindled southern fears of a slave insurrection. Rumors flew around the South, and vigilantes turned out to battle conspiracies that existed only in their own minds. Volunteers, for example, mobilized to defend northeastern Texas against thousands of abolitionists supposedly on their way to pillage Dallas and its environs. Elsewhere, vigilantes rounded up thousands of slaves, tortured some into confessing to nonexistent plots, and then lynched them. The hysteria generated by such rumors played into the hands of the extremists known as fire-eaters, who encouraged the witch hunts in order to gain political support.

Although fears of a slave insurrection proved groundless, they strengthened southern anxieties about abolitionism. More and more southerners concluded that the Republican party itself directed abolitionism and deserved blame for John Brown's plot as well. After all, had not influential Republicans assailed slavery, unconstitutionally tried to ban it, and spoken of an "irrepressible conflict" between slavery and freedom?

The South Contemplates Secession

A pamphlet published in 1860 embodied a growing southern conviction: *The South Alone Should Govern the South*. Most southerners, however, reached this conclusion gradually and reluctantly. In 1850, insulated from the main tide of immigration, southerners thought themselves the most American of Americans. The events of the 1850s led growing numbers of southerners to conclude that the North had deserted the principles of the Union and had virtually declared war on the South by using such headline-grabbing phrases as "irrepressible conflict" and "a higher law." To southerners, the North, not slavery, was the problem.

As sectional ties frayed, John Brown's raid electrified southern opinion. Secession made no sense as a tactic to win concrete goals, but logic had yielded to emotion in much of the South. Fury at what southerners considered the irresponsible, unconstitutional course taken by Republicans in attacking slavery drove the talk of secession, and so did the belief that the North treated the South as inferior, even as a slave. "Talk of Negro slavery," wrote one angry southerner, "is not half so humiliating and disgraceful as the slavery of the South to the North." Convinced that slavery made it possible for them to enjoy unprecedented freedom and equality, white southerners took great pride in their homeland. They bitterly dismissed Republican portrayals of the South as a region of arrogant planters and degraded white common folk. Submission to the Republicans, declared Democratic senator Jefferson Davis of Mississippi, "would be intolerable to a proud people."

THE COLLAPSE OF THE UNION, 1860–1861

Why did the Civil War ultimately erupt in 1861?

As long as the pliant James Buchanan occupied the White House, southerners only talked of secession. However, once Buchanan declined to seek reelection, they anxiously awaited the next presidential election. By 1860, voters were deciding not just an election but also the fate of the Union. Lincoln's election began the parade out of the Union by southern states. Initially only the Lower South seceded, encouraging moderates to search frantically for a compromise to save the Union. But the time for compromise had passed.

The Election of 1860

Republicans had done well in the elections of 1856 as a single-issue, free-soil party, but they had to broaden their base to win in 1860. Republican leaders needed an economic program to complement their advocacy of free soil. A severe economic slump following the Panic of 1857 provided them an opening. The depression shattered a decade of prosperity and thrust economic concerns to the fore. In response, the Republicans developed an economic program based on support for a protective tariff, federal aid for internal improvements, and grants to settlers of free 160-acre homesteads carved from public lands.

To broaden their appeal, the Republicans chose Abraham Lincoln as their presidential candidate over the better-known William H. Seward. Lincoln offered a stronger possibility of carrying such key states as Pennsylvania and his home state of Illinois, and projected a more moderate image than Seward, whose penchant for phrases like "irrepressible conflict" and "higher law" made him appear radical. In contrast, Lincoln had repeatedly said that Congress had no constitutional right to interfere with slavery in the South and had rejected the "higher law" doctrine.

The Democrats, still clinging to national party status, had to bridge their own sectional divisions. The *Dred Scott* decision and the conflict over the Lecompton constitution had weakened northern Democrats and strengthened southern Democrats. While Douglas still desperately defended popular sovereignty, southern Democrats stretched *Dred Scott* to conclude that Congress now had to protect slavery in the territories.

The Democratic party's internal turmoil boiled over at its Charleston convention in the spring of 1860. Failing to win a platform guaranteeing the federal protection of slavery in the territories, delegates from the Lower South stormed out. The convention adjourned to Baltimore, where a new fight erupted over whether to seat the pro-Douglas delegates hastily chosen to replace the absent delegates from the Lower South. When the convention voted to seat these new delegates, representatives from Virginia and the Upper South walked out. What remained of the original Democratic convention nominated Douglas, but the seceders marched off to yet another hall in Baltimore and nominated Buchanan's vice president, John C. Breckinridge of Kentucky, on a platform calling for the congressional protection of slavery in the territories. The spectacle of two different Democratic candidates for the presidency signaled the complete disruption of the party.

The South still contained a sizable number of moderates, often former Whigs. In 1860 these southern moderates joined former northern Whigs in the new Constitutional Union party. They nominated John Bell of Tennessee, a slaveholder who had opposed the Kansas-Nebraska Act and the Lecompton constitution. Calling for the Union's preservation, the new party took no stand on slavery's extension.

The four candidates presented a relatively clear choice. At one end of the spectrum, Lincoln conceded that the South had the constitutional right to preserve slavery, but he demanded that Congress prohibit its extension. At the other end, Breckinridge insisted that Congress had to protect slavery anywhere it existed. In the middle were Bell and Douglas, the latter still trying to salvage popular sovereignty. In the end, Lincoln won 180 electoral votes; his three opponents, only 123. However, Lincoln's popular votes, 39 percent of the total, came almost completely from the North. Douglas, the only candidate to run in both sections, ran second in the popular vote but carried only Missouri. Bell won most of the Upper South, and Breckinridge took Maryland and the Lower South.

The Movement for Secession

Southerners faced a dilemma. The president-elect was so unpopular in the South that his name had not even appeared on the ballot in many southern states. Lincoln's victory struck many southerners as a calculated insult. The North, a South Carolina planter said, "has got so far toward being abolitionized as to elect a man avowedly hostile to our institutions."

Few southerners believed that Lincoln would fulfill his promise to protect slavery in the South; most feared that he would act as a mere front man for more John Browns. "Now that the black radical Republicans have the power I suppose they will Brown us all," a South Carolinian lamented.

Some southerners had threatened secession at the prospect of Lincoln's election, and now the moment of decision had arrived. On December 20, 1860, a South Carolina convention voted unanimously for secession; in short order Alabama, Mississippi, Florida, Georgia, Louisiana, and Texas followed. On February 4, 1861, delegates from these seven states met in Montgomery, Alabama, and established the Confederate States of America. But uncertainty colored the secession movement. Many southerners, even in the Deep South, had resisted the fire-eaters' call to leave the Union. Jefferson Davis, inaugurated in February 1861 as president of the Confederacy, was a reluctant secessionist who had remained in the Senate two weeks after his own state of Mississippi had seceded.

At first the Upper South rejected secession completely. More economically dependent on the North, it had proportionately fewer slaves and more non–slave-holders, whose loyalty in case of secession was dubious. Finally, if secession precipitated a war, the Upper South was the likely battleground. Consequently, the secession

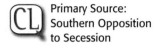

Primary Source: Southern Opposition to Secession

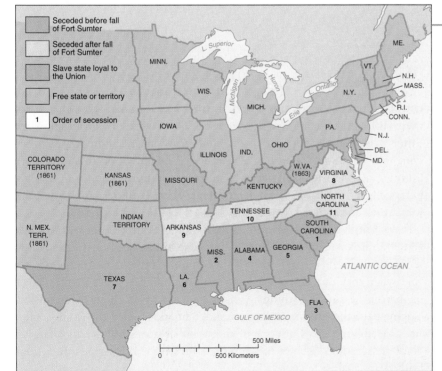

Map 14.2   Secession

Four key states—Virginia, Arkansas, Tennessee, and North Carolina—did not secede until after the fall of Fort Sumter. The border slave states of Maryland, Delaware, Kentucky, and Missouri stayed in the Union.

movement that South Carolina had begun so boldly in December 1860 seemed to be falling apart by March 1861.

The Search for Compromise

The lack of southern unity confirmed the view of most Republicans that the secessionists were more bluster than substance. Seward described secession as the work of "a relatively few hotheads," and Lincoln believed that the loyal majority of southerners would soon wrest control from the fire-eating minority.

This perception stiffened Republican resolve to resist compromise. Moderate John J. Crittenden of Kentucky suggested compensation for owners of runaway slaves, repeal of northern personal-liberty laws, a constitutional amendment to prohibit the federal government from interfering with slavery in southern states, and another amendment to restore the Missouri Compromise line. But in the face of adamant Republican opposition, the **Crittenden plan** collapsed.

Lincoln's faith in a "loyal majority" of southerners exaggerated both their numbers and their dedication to the Union. Many southern opponents of the fire-eating secessionists sat on the fence, waiting for major concessions from the North; their allegiance to the Union was conditional. But compromise would have meant the abandonment of free soil, a basic principle of the Republican party, and Lincoln, who misread southern opinion, resisted.

Beyond the issue of compromise, the precipitous secession of the Lower South had changed the question that Lincoln faced. The issue no longer revolved around slavery's extension but around secession. The Lower South had left the Union in the face of losing a fair election. For Lincoln to cave in to such pressure would violate majority rule, the sacred principle on which the nation had been founded.

Crittenden plan Attempt to find a compromise that would prevent Union from splitting

Fort Sumter Federal fort in Charleston, South Carolina, harbor, where first shots of Civil War were fired when Union attempted to resupply troops

CHECKING IN

- Lincoln's victory in the 1860 presidential election brought matters to a head.
- Fearing they were now at the mercy of abolitionists, states in the Lower South began to secede.
- Moderates sought a compromise, but Republicans resisted.
- An attempt to resupply Fort Sumter, a federal fort in Charleston harbor in South Carolina, met with armed resistance.
- When President Lincoln called for militia to suppress an insurrection, the states of the Upper South seceded.

The Coming of War

By the time Lincoln took office in March 1861, only a spark was needed to set off a war. Lincoln had pledged in his inaugural address to "hold, occupy, and possess" federal property in the states that had seceded, a statement that committed him to the defense of Fort Pickens in Florida and **Fort Sumter** in the harbor of Charleston, South Carolina. Accordingly, the president informed South Carolina's governor of his intention to supply Fort Sumter with provisions but neither reinforcements nor ammunition. Shortly before dawn on April 12, 1861, Confederate shore batteries bombarded the fort, which surrendered the next day.

Proclaiming an insurrection in the Lower South, Lincoln called for 75,000 militia to suppress the rebellion. The outbreak of hostilities ended fence-sitting in the Upper South. "I am a Union man," one southerner wrote, "but when they [the Lincoln administration] send men south it will change my nations. I can do nothing against my own people." In quick succession Virginia, North Carolina, Arkansas, and Tennessee joined the Confederacy. Acknowledging that "I am one of those dull creatures that cannot see the good of secession," Robert E. Lee resigned from the U.S. Army rather than lead troops against his native Virginia.

The North, too, was ready for a fight, less to abolish slavery than to punish secession. Stephen Douglas, exhausted by his efforts to find a peaceable solution to the issue of slavery extension, assaulted "the new system of resistance by the sword and bayonet to the results of the ballot-box" and affirmed, "I deprecate war, but if it must come I am with my country, under all circumstances, and in every contingency."

Chapter Summary

 DOWNLOAD THE MP3 AUDIO FILE OF THE CHAPTER SUMMARY, AND LISTEN TO IT ON THE GO.

Why did the Compromise of 1850 only temporarily resolve the crisis facing the Union? (page 302)

Unlike the Compromise of 1820, the Compromise of 1850 was a medley of different bills supported by shifting coalitions. It temporarily averted disunion, but it failed to resolve underlying divisions between North and South. In particular, the new Fugitive Slave Act alienated the North because of its harshness and the South because of northern resistance.

Why did the Whig party disintegrate, and what were the consequences? (page 308)

The surprising strength of the Know-Nothings and the free-soil movement both undercut the Whigs, already battered into sectional fragments by the Compromise of 1850; the Kansas-Nebraska Act delivered the final blow. Temporarily the Democrats were the only major political party, and when the Republicans emerged as a counterpart, they were a sectional rather than a national party.

What major issues dominated American politics from 1857 to 1860? (page 314)

The last years of the 1850s saw several tumultuous political issues emerge: the Dred Scott decision, Bleeding Kansas, and John Brown's raid on Harpers Ferry. Each one frayed the political fabric of the nation a bit further.

Why did the Civil War ultimately erupt in 1861? (page 319)

Southerners, already feeling besieged, saw Abraham Lincoln's election as a sign that they had lost all influence at the national level. Lower South states seceded quickly, but the Upper South remained in the Union until Lincoln ordered the resupplying of Fort Sumter, a federal fort in the harbor of Charleston, South Carolina, and shooting erupted. Emotion far more than reason dictated these moves.

CHAPTER 15

Crucible of Freedom: Civil War

1861–1865

Soldiers' Photographs

CHAPTER PREVIEW

Mobilizing for War
What major advantages did each side possess at the start of the Civil War?

In Battle, 1861–1862
How was the war fought in its early years?

Emancipation Transforms the War, 1863
Why was emancipation important in the course of the war, and what role did African-Americans play in the conflict?

War and Society, North and South
In what ways did the Civil War affect the two sides?

The Union Victorious, 1864–1865
How did the Union finally win the war?

Soldiers on both sides claimed the ideals of liberty, loyalty, and patriotism as their own, and like them, too, most Americans in 1861 harbored false expectations. Few volunteers expected a long war, and none anticipated the carnage that the war would bring.

One out of every five soldiers who fought in the Civil War died in it. The 620,000 American soldiers killed between 1861 and 1865 nearly equaled the number of U.S. soldiers killed in all other American wars combined. As it became clear that a few battles would not decide the war, leaders on both sides contemplated, and often adopted, previously unthinkable strategies. The Confederacy, despite its states' rights basis, had to draft men into its army and virtually extort supplies from civilians. By the end of the war, the Confederacy was even prepared to arm slaves in a desperate effort to save a society founded on slavery. The North, which began the war with the objective of overcoming secession, explicitly disclaiming any intention of interfering with slavery, found that, to win, it had to destroy slavery. For politicians as well as soldiers, the war defied expectations and turned into a series of surprises. The inseparable connection of Union war goals and the emancipation of slaves was perhaps the most momentous surprise.

MOBILIZING FOR WAR

What major advantages did each side possess at the start of the Civil War?

Neither North nor South was prepared for war. In April 1861 most of the Union's small army, a scant sixteen thousand men, was scattered across the West. One-third of its officers had resigned to join the Confederacy. The nation had not had a strong president since James K. Polk in the 1840s, and many viewed the new president, Abraham Lincoln, as a yokel. It seemed doubtful that such a government could marshal its people for war. The Confederacy was even less prepared: it had no tax structure, no navy, only two tiny gunpowder factories, and poorly equipped, unconnected railroad lines.

During the first two years of war, both sides would have to overcome these deficiencies, raise and supply large armies, and finance the war. In each region, mobilization would expand the powers of the central government to a degree that few had anticipated.

Recruitment and Conscription

The Civil War armies were the largest organizations ever created in America; by the end of the war, more than 2 million men had served in the Union army and 800,000 in the Confederate army.

At first the raising of armies was a local, rather than a national or state, effort. Regiments usually consisted of volunteers from the same locale. Southern cavalrymen provided their own horses, and uniforms were left to local option. In both armies the troops themselves elected officers up to the rank of colonel. This informal, democratic way of raising and organizing soldiers reflected the nation's political traditions but could not long withstand the stresses of the Civil War. As early as July 1861 the Union began examinations for officers. With casualties mounting, moreover, military demand exceeded the supply of volunteers. The Confederacy felt the pinch first and in April 1862 enacted the first **conscription** law in American history, requiring all able-bodied white men aged eighteen to thirty-five to serve in the military. (By war's end the limits would be seventeen and fifty.) The Confederacy's Conscription Act aroused little enthusiasm. A later amendment exempting owners or overseers of twenty or more slaves evoked complaints about "a rich man's war but a poor man's fight."

Despite opposition, the Confederate draft became increasingly difficult to evade, and this fact stimulated volunteering. Only one soldier in five was a draftee, but four out of every five eligible white southerners served in the Confederate army. An 1862

conscription Drafting men to serve in the army

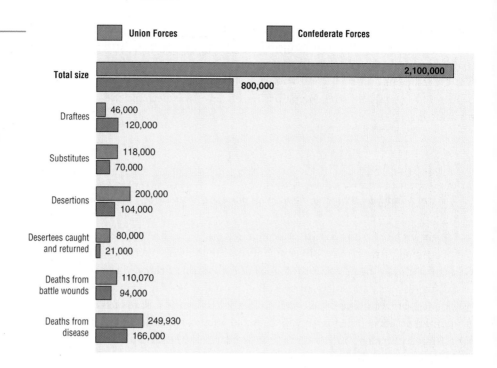

Figure 15.1 Opposing Armies of the Civil War

As this graph shows, the Civil War had profound human costs. In both the North and South, hardly a family did not grieve for a lost relative or friend. Injured veterans became a common sight in cities, towns, and rural districts well into the twentieth century.

law requiring all soldiers to serve for the duration of the war ensured that a high proportion of Confederate soldiers would be battle-hardened veterans.

Once the army was raised, the Confederacy had to supply it. At first the South imported arms and ammunition from Europe or relied on weapons taken from federal arsenals and captured on the battlefield. Gradually, the Confederacy assigned contracts to privately owned factories, such as the Tredegar Iron Works in Richmond; provided loans to establish new plants; and created government-owned industries, such as the giant Augusta Powder Works in Georgia. The South lost few, if any, battles for want of munitions.

Supplying troops with clothing and food proved more difficult. When the South invaded Maryland in 1862, thousands of Confederate soldiers remained behind because they could not march barefoot on Maryland's gravel-surfaced roads. Late in the war, Robert E. Lee's Army of Northern Virginia ran out of food but never out of ammunition. Supply problems had several sources: railroads that fell into disrepair or were captured, an economy that grew more cotton and tobacco than food, and Union capture of the livestock- and grain-raising districts of central Tennessee and Virginia. Close to desperation, the Confederate Congress in 1863 passed the Impressment Act, authorizing army officers to take food from reluctant farmers at prescribed rates and to impress slaves into labor for the army.

The industrial North more easily supplied its troops with arms, clothes, and food, but keeping a full army was another matter. When the initial tide of enthusiasm for enlistment ebbed, Congress turned to conscription with the Enrollment Act of March 1863. Every able-bodied white male citizen aged twenty to forty-five faced the draft.

The Enrollment Act provided some exemptions and offered two ways of escaping the draft: substitution, or paying another man to serve; and commutation, or paying a $300 fee to the government. Democrats denounced conscription as a viola-

Chronology

1861	President Abraham Lincoln calls for volunteers to suppress the rebellion (April); Virginia, Arkansas, Tennessee, and North Carolina join the Confederacy (April–May); Lincoln imposes a naval blockade on the South (April); U.S. Sanitary Commission formed (June); First Battle of Bull Run (July); First Confiscation Act (August)
1862	Legal Tender Act (February); George B. McClellan's Peninsula Campaign (March–July); Battle of Shiloh (April); Confederate Congress passes the Conscription Act (April); David G. Farragut captures New Orleans (April); Homestead Act (May); Seven Days' Battles (June–July); Pacific Railroad Act (July); Morrill Land Grant Act (July); Second Confiscation Act (July); Second Battle of Bull Run (August); Battle of Antietam (September); Preliminary Emancipation Proclamation (September); Battle of Fredericksburg (December)
1863	Emancipation Proclamation issued (January); Lincoln suspends writ of habeas corpus nationwide (January); National Bank Act (February); Congress passes the Enrollment Act (March); Battle of Chancellorsville (May); Battle of Gettysburg (July); Surrender of Vicksburg (July); New York City draft riots (July)
1864	Ulysses S. Grant given command of all Union armies (March); Battle of the Wilderness (May); Battle of Cold Harbor (June); Surrender of Atlanta (September); Lincoln reelected (November); William Tecumseh Sherman's march to the sea (November–December)
1865	Congress passes the Thirteenth Amendment (January); Sherman moves through South Carolina (January–March); Grant takes Richmond (April); Robert E. Lee surrenders at Appomattox (April); Lincoln dies (April)

tion of individual liberties and states' rights, and ordinary citizens resented the substitution and commutation privileges, leveling their own "poor man's fight" charges. Nevertheless, as in the Confederacy, the law stimulated volunteering: only 8 percent of all Union soldiers were draftees or substitutes.

Financing the War

The recruitment and supply of huge armies lay far beyond the capacity of American public finance at the start of the war. During the 1840s and 1850s, federal spending had averaged only 2 percent of the gross national product.* With such meager expenditures, the federal government met its revenue needs from tariff duties and income from the sale of public lands. During the war, however, as annual federal expenditures rose to 15 percent of the gross national product, the need for new sources of revenue became urgent. When neither additional taxes nor war bond sales produced enough revenue, the Union and the Confederacy began to print paper money. Early in 1862 President Lincoln signed into law the Legal Tender Act, authorizing the issue of $150 million in paper **"greenbacks."** Although the North's financial officials distrusted paper money, they resorted to it because, as the Union's treasury secretary bluntly put it, *"The Treasury is nearly empty."* Unlike gold and silver, which had established market

"greenbacks" Paper money used by Union to help finance war

---

* Gross national product (GNP): the sum, measured in dollars, of all goods and services produced in a given year. By contrast, in the 1980s the federal budget averaged about 25 percent of GNP.

values, the value of paper money depended on the public's confidence in the government that issued it. To bolster that confidence, Union officials made the greenbacks legal tender (that is, acceptable in payment of most public and private debts).

In contrast, the Confederacy never made paper money legal tender, so suspicions arose that the southern government had little faith in its own money. The Confederacy raised little of its wartime revenue from taxes, compounding the problem. Northern invasions and poor internal transportation made collecting taxes difficult, and ultimately the South raised less than 5 percent of its wartime revenue from taxes (compared to 21 percent in the North).

Confidence in the Confederacy's paper money quickly evaporated, and the value of paper money in relation to gold plunged. The Confederate response—printing more paper money—merely accelerated inflation. Prices in the North rose 80 percent during the war, but those in the South soared more than 9,000 percent; what cost a southerner one dollar in 1861 cost forty-six dollars by 1864.

By raising taxes, floating bonds, and printing paper money, both North and South broke with the hard-money, minimal-government traditions of American public finance. In the North, Republicans took advantage of the departure of southern Democrats to push through Congress a measure that they and their Whig predecessors had long advocated: a national banking system. Passed in February 1863, the National Bank Act allowed banks to obtain federal charters and to issue national bank notes (backed by the federal government). The North's ability to revolutionize its system of public finance reflected both its long experience with complex financial transactions and its political cohesion.

Political Leadership in Wartime

The Civil War pitted rival political systems as well as armies and economies against each other. The South entered the war with several apparent political advantages. Lincoln's call for militiamen to suppress the rebellion had transformed southern waverers into secessionists. Southerners had a strong leader in Jefferson Davis, the president of the Confederacy, who possessed experience, honesty, courage, and what one commentator called "a jaw sawed in *steel*."

In contrast, the Union's list of political liabilities appeared lengthy. Loyal but contentious northern Democrats wanted no conscription, no national bank, and no abolition of slavery. Even within the Republican party, Lincoln, with little national experience, had trouble commanding respect. A small but vocal group of Republicans known as the Radicals—including Secretary of the Treasury Salmon P. Chase, Senator Charles Sumner of Massachusetts, and Representative Thaddeus Stevens of Pennsylvania—vigorously criticized Lincoln. First they focused on his failure to make the slaves' emancipation a war goal, and later they would assail him for being too eager to readmit the conquered rebel states into the Union.

Lincoln's style of leadership both encouraged and disarmed opposition within the Republican party. Keeping his counsel to himself until ready to act, he met criticism with homespun anecdotes that threw his opponents off guard. Caught between Radicals and conservatives, Lincoln used his cautious reserve to maintain open communications with both wings of the party and to fragment his opposition. He also co-opted some members of the opposition, including Chase, by bringing them into his cabinet.

Abraham Lincoln

When Lincoln became president in March 1861, he faced more severe problems than any predecessor. Washington photographer Matthew Brady captured this image of the solemn president-elect a few weeks after the formation of the Confederacy and shortly before Lincoln's inauguration.

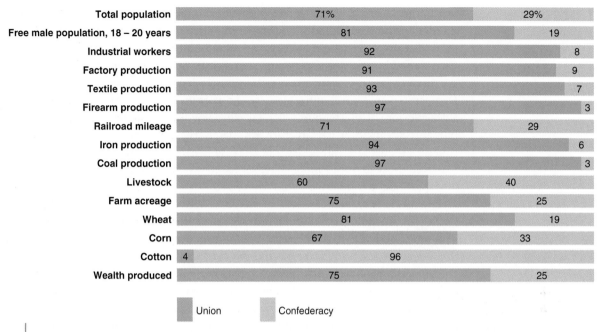

	Union	Confederacy
Total population	71%	29%
Free male population, 18 – 20 years	81	19
Industrial workers	92	8
Factory production	91	9
Textile production	93	7
Firearm production	97	3
Railroad mileage	71	29
Iron production	94	6
Coal production	97	3
Livestock	60	40
Farm acreage	75	25
Wheat	81	19
Corn	67	33
Cotton	4	96
Wealth produced	75	25

Figure 15.2   Comparative Population and Economic Resources of the Union and the Confederacy, 1861
At the start of the war, the Union enjoyed huge advantages in population, industry, railroad mileage, and wealth, and, as it would soon prove, a superior ability to mobilize its vast resources. The Confederacy enjoyed the many advantages of fighting a defensive war.

In contrast, Jefferson Davis had a knack for making enemies. A West Pointer, he would rather have led the army than the government, and he used his sharp tongue to win arguments rather than friends. Davis's cabinet suffered frequent resignations; for example, the Confederacy had five secretaries of war in four years. Relations between Davis and his vice president, Alexander Stephens of Georgia, were disastrous. Stephens left Richmond, the Confederate capital, in 1862 and spent most of the war in Georgia sniping at Davis as "weak and vacillating, timid, petulant, peevish, obstinate."

The clash between Davis and Stephens involved not just personalities but also the ideological divisions that lay at the heart of the Confederacy. The Confederate Constitution explicitly guaranteed the sovereignty of the Confederate states and prohibited the government from enacting protective tariffs or supporting internal improvements. For Stephens and other influential Confederate leaders, the Confederacy existed to protect slavery and to enshrine states' rights. For Davis, the overriding objective of the Confederacy was to secure the independence of the South from the North, if necessary at the expense of states' rights.

This difference between Davis and Stephens somewhat resembled the discord between Lincoln and the northern Democrats. Lincoln believed that winning the war demanded increasing the central government's power; like Stephens, northern Democrats resisted centralization. But Lincoln could control his opponents more effectively than Davis controlled his. By temperament Lincoln was more suited to reconciliation than Davis was, and the different nature of party politics in the two sections favored him as well.

In the South, the Democrats and the remaining Whigs agreed to suspend party politics for the war's duration. Although intended to encourage unity, this decision led to discord. As southern politics disintegrated along personal and factional lines, Davis found himself without organized political support. In contrast, in the Union, northern Democrats' opposition to Lincoln tended to unify the Republicans. After Democrats won control of five states in the election of 1862, Republicans swallowed a bitter lesson: no matter how much they disdained Lincoln, they had to rally behind him or risk being driven from office. Ultimately, the Union developed more political cohesion than the Confederacy, not because it had fewer divisions, but because it managed those divisions more effectively.

Securing the Union's Borders

Even before large-scale fighting began, Lincoln moved to safeguard Washington, which was bordered by two slave states (Virginia and Maryland) and filled with Confederate sympathizers. A week after Fort Sumter's fall, a Baltimore mob attacked a Massachusetts regiment bound for Washington, but enough troops slipped through to protect the capital. Lincoln then dispatched federal troops to Maryland and suspended the writ of habeas corpus (HAY-bee-uss CORE-puss);* federal troops could now arrest Marylanders without formally charging them with specific offenses. Both Maryland and Delaware, another border slave state, voted down secession.

Next Lincoln authorized the arming of Union sympathizers in Kentucky, a slave state with a Unionist legislature, a secessionist governor, and a thin chance of staying neutral. Lincoln also stationed troops just across the Ohio River from Kentucky, in Illinois, and when a Confederate army invaded Kentucky early in 1862, those troops drove it out. Officially, at least, Kentucky became the third slave state to declare for the Union. Four years of murderous fighting ravaged the fourth, Missouri, as Union and Confederate armies and bands of guerrillas clashed. Despite the savage fighting and the divided loyalties of its people, Missouri stayed in the Union. West Virginia was formed in 1861 when thirty-five counties in the primarily nonslaveholding regions west of the Shenandoah Valley refused to secede; it became a state in 1863.

By holding the border slave states in the Union, Lincoln kept open his lines to the free states and gained access to the river systems in Kentucky and Missouri that led into the heart of the Confederacy. Lincoln's firmness, particularly in the case of Maryland, scotched charges that he was weak-willed. The crisis forced the president to exercise long-dormant powers. In *Ex Parte Milligan* (1861), Chief Justice Roger B. Taney ruled that Lincoln had exceeded his authority in suspending the writ of *habeas corpus* in Maryland. Lincoln, citing the Constitution's authorization of the writ's suspension in "Cases of Rebellion" (Article I, Section 9) insisted that he would determine whether a rebellion existed, and simply ignored Taney's ruling.

CHECKING IN

- The North enjoyed enormous manpower and industrial advantages.
- Both sides resorted to conscription, although most soldiers were volunteers.
- The Union was far more successful in raising money to finance the war.
- The Union could rely on established political, military, and economic systems; the Confederacy, although politically unified at the start, suffered from political divisions and conflicting views of the Confederate government's role.
- Abraham Lincoln proved to be a far better leader than Jefferson Davis.

---

* Habeas corpus: a court order requiring that the detainer of a prisoner bring the person in custody to court and show cause for his or her detention.

In Battle, 1861–1862

How was the war fought in its early years?

▎The Civil War was the first war in which both sides relied extensively on railroads, the telegraph, mass-produced weapons, joint army-navy tactics, iron-plated warships, rifled guns and artillery, and trench warfare. Thus there is some justification for its description as the first modern war. But to its participants slogging through muddy swamps and weighed down with equipment, the war hardly seemed modern.

Armies, Weapons, and Strategies

Compared to the Confederacy's 9 million people, one-third of them slaves, the Union had 22 million people in 1861. The North also enjoyed 3.5 times as many white men of military age, 90 percent of all U.S. industrial capacity, and two-thirds of its railroad track. But the North faced a daunting challenge: forcing the South back into the Union. The South, in contrast, fought only for independence. To subdue the Confederacy, the North would have to sustain offensive operations over an area comparable in size to the part of Russia that Napoleon had invaded in 1812 with disastrous results.

Measured against this challenge, the North's advantages in population and technology shrank. The North had more men but needed them to defend long supply lines and to occupy captured areas. Consequently, it could commit a smaller proportion of its overall force to combat. The South, relying on slaves for labor, could assign a higher proportion of its white male population to combat. And although the Union had superior railroads, it had to move its troops and supplies huge distances, whereas the Confederacy could shift its troops relatively short distances within its defense area without railroads. Finally, southerners had an edge in morale, for Confederate troops usually fought on home ground.

The Civil War witnessed experiments with a variety of new weapons, including the submarine, the repeating rifle, and the multibarreled Gatling gun, the predecessor of the machine gun. Whereas smooth-bore muskets had an effective range of 80 yards, the Springfield or Enfield rifles widely in use by 1863 were accurate at 400 yards. The rifle's development posed a challenge to long-accepted military tactics, which stressed the mass infantry charge. Armed with muskets, defenders could fire only a round or two before being overwhelmed. Armed with rifles, however, defenders could fire several rounds before closing with the enemy. Attackers would have far greater difficulty getting close enough to thrust bayonets; fewer than 1 percent of the casualties in the Civil War resulted from bayonet wounds.

As the fighting wore on, both sides recognized the value of trenches, which offered defenders protection against withering rifle fire. In addition, the rifle forced generals to depend less on cavalry. Traditionally, cavalry had been among the most prestigious components of an army, in part because cavalry charges were often devastatingly effective and in part because the cavalry helped to maintain class distinctions within the army. More accurate rifles reduced the cavalry's effectiveness, for the bullet that missed a rider could hit his horse—and often the horse itself was the primary target. Thus the cavalry was increasingly relegated to reconnaissance (reh-CAHN-nuh-sense) and raids.

Primary Source: Wounded Escaping from the Burning Woods of the Wilderness

Nonetheless, the introduction of the rifle did not fundamentally change military tactics. An attacking army still had a good chance of success if it surprised its enemy, and the lush forests of the South offered abundant opportunities for surprise. Lack of the element of surprise could doom an attacking army. At the Battle of Fredericksburg in December 1862, Confederate forces virtually annihilated Union forces charging uphill over open terrain.

Much like previous wars, the Civil War was fought basically in a succession of battles during which exposed infantry traded volleys, charged, and countercharged. The side that withdrew first from the battlefield was considered the loser, even though it frequently sustained lighter casualties than the "victor." The defeated army usually moved back a few miles to lick its wounds; the winners stayed in place to lick theirs. Politicians on both sides berated generals for not pursuing a beaten foe, but was almost impossible for a mangled victor to gather horses, mules, supply trains, and exhausted soldiers for a new attack. Not surprisingly, for much of the war, generals on both sides concluded that the best defense was a good offense.

What passed for long-range Union strategy in 1861 was the **Anaconda plan,** which called for the Union to blockade the southern coast and to thrust, like a huge snake, down the Mississippi River. In theory, sealing off and severing the Confederacy would make the South recognize the futility of secession and end the war as bloodlessly as possible. However, the lack of adequate ships and men to seize the Mississippi in 1861 prevented the implementation of this ambitious plan.

Early in the war, the need to secure the border slave states, especially Kentucky and Missouri, dictated Union strategy in the West, sending northern armies plunging southward from Kentucky into Tennessee. The Appalachian Mountains tended to separate this western theater from the eastern theater, where major clashes took place in 1861.

| **Stalemate in the East** | East of the mountains, the Confederates' decision to locate their capital in Richmond, Virginia, shaped Union strategy. |

"Forward to Richmond!" became the Union's first war cry. But before Union troops could reach Richmond, one hundred miles southwest of Washington, they would have to dislodge a Confederate army brazenly encamped at Manassas (muh-NASS-suss) Junction, Virginia, only twenty-five miles from the Union capital. Lincoln ordered General Irvin McDowell to attack the rebel force. In the resulting **First Battle of Bull Run** (or First Manassas[*]), amateur armies clashed in bloody chaos under a blistering sun in July 1861 as well-dressed, picnicking Washington dignitaries watched the carnage. The Confederates routed the larger Union army.

After Bull Run, Lincoln appointed General **George B. McClellan** to replace McDowell as commander of the Union's Army of the Potomac, its main fighting force in the east. McClellan, a master of administration and training, transformed a ragtag mob into a disciplined fighting force. His soldiers adored him, but Lincoln became disenchanted. To the president, the key to victory lay in launching simultaneous attacks on several fronts so that the North could exploit its advantages in manpower

---

Anaconda plan Early Union strategy to split Confederacy down the Mississippi, force surrender

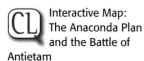 Interactive Map: The Anaconda Plan and the Battle of Antietam

First Battle of Bull Run The war's first full battle, also called First Manassas; fiasco that showed war would be longer and harder than first thought

George B. McClellan Union general very popular with troops; Lincoln thought he had the "slows" and replaced him

---

[*] Because the North often named battles after local landmarks, usually bodies of water, and the South after the nearest town, some Civil War battles are known by two names

Map 15.1 The War in the East, 1861–1862

Union advances on Richmond were turned back at Fredericksburg and the Seven Days' Battles, and the Confederacy's invasion of Union territory was stopped at Antietam.

and communications. McClellan, a proslavery Democrat, hoped for a series of relatively bloodless victories that would result in the readmission of southern states into the Union with slavery still intact.

In the spring of 1862 McClellan got a chance to demonstrate the value of his strategy. After Bull Run, the Confederates had pulled back behind the Rappahannock River to block a Union march toward Richmond. McClellan decided to go around the southerners by transporting his troops down the Chesapeake Bay to the tip of the peninsula formed by the York and James rivers and then to attack Richmond from the rear.

At first McClellan's Peninsula Campaign unfolded smoothly. But after luring the Confederacy to the brink of defeat—Union forces were less than five miles from Richmond—McClellan hesitated; he refused to launch the final attack without the reinforcements he expected. Confederate forces under General Thomas "Stonewall" Jackson had turned back the reinforcements. As McClellan delayed, General **Robert E. Lee** assumed command of the Confederacy's Army of Northern Virginia. An opponent of secession, a man so courteous that he seemed almost too gentle, Lee nevertheless was McClellan's opposite, bold and willing to accept casualties.

Lee immediately took the offensive, attacking the much larger Union forces in the Seven Days' Battles (June–July 1862). Raging through forests east of Richmond, the battles cost the Confederacy nearly twice as many men as the Union, but McClellan, not Lee, blinked. Unnerved by mounting casualties, he sent a series of panicky reports to Washington. Lincoln, who cared little for McClellan's peninsula strategy, ordered him to call off the campaign and return to Washington.

Robert E. Lee Bold and resourceful commander of Army of Northern Virginia

**Primary Source:
Antietam Bridge**

Antietam Union victory in August 1862 that gave Lincoln the opportunity to announce the Emancipation Proclamation

Emancipation Proclamation Freed all slaves in Confederate-held territory; changed nature of Civil War

With McClellan out of the picture, Lee and his lieutenant, Stonewall Jackson, pushed north, routing a Union army at the Second Battle of Bull Run (Second Manassas) in August 1862. Lee followed up this victory with a bold stroke: he took his army across the Potomac and northward into Maryland, hoping that the fall harvest could provide him with desperately needed supplies. The stakes were enormous. By seizing western Maryland, Lee could threaten Washington, relieve pressure on Richmond, improve the prospects of peace candidates in the North's upcoming fall election, and possibly induce Britain and France to recognize and support the Confederacy as an independent nation. McClellan met Lee at the Battle of **Antietam** (an-TEE-tum), also called Sharpsburg, on September 17, 1862. North and South together suffered 24,000 casualties in this bloodiest day of the war. Tactically, the battle was a draw, but strategically it constituted a major Union victory because it forced Lee to withdraw south of the Potomac. Most important, Antietam provided Lincoln the occasion to issue the **Emancipation Proclamation,** freeing all slaves under rebel control. Lincoln complained that McClellan had "the slows" and faulted him for not pursuing Lee after Antietam. McClellan's replacement, General Ambrose Burnside, thought himself unfit for high command. He was right. In December 1862 he led 122,000 federal troops against 78,500 Confederates at the Battle of Fredericksburg (Virginia). Burnside captured the town but then sacrificed his army in futile charges up the heights west of the town. The carnage shook even Lee. "It is well that war is so terrible—we should grow fond of it," he told an aide during the battle. Richmond remained, in the words of a southern song, "a hard road to travel." The war in the East had become a stalemate.

Scenes of Antietam

A painting of the Antietam battlefield by James Pope, a Union soldier of the Second Vermont Infantry, shows three brigades of Union troops advancing under Confederate fire. In the photograph of Antietam, dead rebel gunners lie next to the wreckage of their battery. The building in both painting and photograph, a Dunker (German Baptist Brethern) church, was the scene of furious fighting.

The War in the West

The Union fared better in the West. Unlike the geographically limited eastern theater, the war in the West shifted over a vast terrain that provided access to rivers leading directly into the South. The West also spawned new leadership in the person of an obscure Union general, **Ulysses S. Grant.** A West Point graduate with a reputation for heavy drinking, and a failed farmer and businessman, Grant soon proved one of the Union's best leaders.

In 1861–1862 Grant had stabilized control of Missouri and Kentucky and then moved south to attack Corinth (CORE-inth), Mississippi, a major rail junction. In early April 1862 Confederate forces staged a surprise attack on Grant's army, encamped at Shiloh (SHY-loe) Church in southern Tennessee. Driven back on the first day, Union forces counterattacked on the second day and drove the Confederate army from the field. Of 77,000 men who fought at Shiloh, 23,000 were killed or wounded. Defeated at Shiloh, the Confederates evacuated Corinth.

For the Corinth-Shiloh campaign, the Confederacy had stripped New Orleans of its defenses, leaving its largest city guarded by only 3,000 militia. A combined land-sea force under Union general Benjamin Butler and Admiral David G. Farragut (FAIR-uh-gut) took advantage of the weakened defenses and captured New Orleans in late April. Farragut continued up the Mississippi as far as Natchez. When a Union flotilla moved down the river in June and took Memphis, the North controlled the great river except for a 200-mile stretch between Port Hudson, Louisiana, and Vicksburg, Mississippi.

In 1862 Union and Confederate forces also clashed in the trans-Mississippi West, a vast region that stretched from the Midwest to the Pacific coast. On the banks of the Rio Grande, Union volunteers and Mexican-American companies drove a Confederate army from Texas out of New Mexico. A thousand miles to the east, opposing armies battled for control of the crucial Missouri River. In Pea Ridge, Arkansas, in March 1862, northern troops scattered a Confederate force of 16,000.

These Union victories changed the trans-Mississippi war. As the rebel threat faded, western volunteers who had mobilized to crush Confederates turned to fighting Indians. After 1865, federal troops moved west to complete the rout of the Indians that had begun during the Civil War.

Map 15.2 The War in the West, 1861–1862

By the end of 1862 the North held New Orleans and the entire Mississippi River except for the stretch between Vicksburg and Port Hudson.

Ulysses S. Grant Lincoln-appointed head of Army of the Potomac; ultimately defeated Lee

The Soldiers' War

Civil War soldiers were typically volunteers from farms and small towns who joined companies of recruits from their area. Local loyalties spurred enrollment, especially in the South, as did ideals of honor and valor. Soldiers on both sides saw military life as a transforming experience in which citizens became warriors and boys became men.

Recruits were meshed into regiments and then sent to training camps. Military training was notoriously poor, and much of army life was tedious and uncomfortable. Union troops ate beans, bacon, salt pork, pickled beef, and hardtack—biscuits almost impossible to crack. Confederate forces ate bacon and cornmeal, and they often ran out of food, blankets, shoes, socks, and clothes. Both sides suffered from a multitude of lice, fleas, ticks, flies, and rats, and from the diseases they carried.

Dreams of military glory faded swiftly. War brought appalling casualties, and soldiers quickly learned to inure themselves to the stench of death. The high casualty rates came not from improved technology, such as the rifle, but from the armies' inability to use such technology well. The deadly cost of battle fell most heavily on the infantry, in which at least three out of four soldiers served. A combination of inexperience, inadequate training, and barriers of terrain curbed their impact. Large masses of soldiers faced one another at close range for long periods of time, exchanging fire until one side or the other gave up and fell back. Armies gained in efficiency in battle through experience, and only late in the war.

The motives of these soldiers varied widely. Some Confederates joined in order to preserve slavery, which they paired with liberty. As the war ground on, more and more Union soldiers came to see emancipation as their goal, sometimes for humanitarian reasons. "Since I am down here I have learned and seen more of what the horrors of slavery was than I ever knew before," an Ohio officer wrote from Louisiana. Others had more practical goals. By the summer of 1862 Union soldiers in the South had become agents of liberation. Many who had once damned the "abolitionist war" now endorsed emancipation as part of the war effort. As an Indiana soldier said, "Every negro we get strengthens us and weakens the rebels."

Ironclads and Cruisers: The Naval War

By plunging the navy into the Confederacy like a dagger, the Union exploited one of its clearest advantages. The North began the war with more than forty active warships—the South had none—and by 1865 northern industrial advantages had given the United States the largest navy in the world. Steamships could penetrate the South's river systems from any direction. Yet the Union navy faced an extraordinary challenge in its efforts to blockade the South's 3,500 miles of coastline. Sleek Confederate blockade runners darted in and out of southern harbors with little chance of capture early in the war. Their chances of success gradually diminished, however, as the North tightened the blockade and began to capture key southern ports. In 1861 almost 90 percent of blockade runners made it through; by 1865 the rate had sunk to 50 percent. Union seizure of rebel ports and coastal areas shrank the South's foreign trade even more. In daring amphibious assaults in 1861 and 1862, the Union captured the excellent harbor of Port Royal, South Carolina; the coastal islands off South Carolina; and most of North Carolina's river outlets. Naval patrols and amphibious operations shrank the South's ocean trade to one-third its prewar level.

Despite meager resources, the South made impressive efforts to offset the North's naval advantages. Early in the war the Confederates raised a scuttled Union frigate, the *Merrimac;* sheathed its sides in iron; rechristened it the *Virginia;* and deployed it to attack wooden Union ships at Hampton Roads, Virginia. The *Virginia* met its match on March 9, 1862, when it tangled with the hastily built Union iron-clad *Monitor. The* first battle ever fought between ironclads, the engagement ended in a draw.

The South constructed other ironclads and even the first submarine, which dragged a mine through the water to sink a Union ship off Charleston in 1864. Unfortunately, the "fish" failed to surface and went down with its prey. The Confederacy had more success on the high seas, where wooden, steam-driven commerce raiders like the *Alabama* and the *Florida,* both built in England, wreaked havoc on the Union's merchant marine. No matter how successful, commerce raiding would not tip the balance of the war in the South's favor because the North, unlike its foe, did not depend on imports for war materials. The South would lose the naval war.

The Diplomatic War

While armies and navies clashed in 1861–1862, conflict developed on a third front: diplomacy. At the war's start southerners had confidently opened a campaign to gain swift diplomatic recognition for the Confederacy. They were sure of the support of Britain's and France's upper classes and even more certain that Britain, dependent on the South for four-fifths of its cotton, would have to break the Union blockade.

In 1861, Confederate diplomats James Mason and John Slidell sailed for Europe to lobby for recognition of an independent South, but their ship, the *Trent,* fell into Union hands. When the pair ended up as prisoners in Boston, British tempers exploded. Considering one war at a time quite enough, President Lincoln ordered Mason and Slidell released. Settling the *Trent* affair did not eliminate friction between the United States and Britain. Union diplomats protested the construction in British shipyards of the Confederate commerce raiders *Alabama* and *Florida.* In 1863, the U.S. minister to London, Charles Francis Adams (son of President John Quincy Adams and grandson of President John Adams) threatened war if two British-built ironclads commissioned by the Confederacy were turned over to the South. Britain capitulated to Adams's protests and purchased the ships for its own navy.

The South fell far short of its diplomatic objectives. Neither Britain nor France ever recognized the Confederacy as a nation. Southerners had badly overestimated the leverage of "cotton diplomacy" and the power of King Cotton; their threats to withhold raw cotton supplies failed. Britain had an enormous cotton surplus on hand when the war began and developed other sources of cotton during the war, especially in India and Egypt. Although the South's share of England's cotton imports plummeted from 77 percent to 10 percent during the war, Britain's textile industry never faltered.

The South had exaggerated Britain's stake in helping the Confederacy. As a naval power that had frequently blockaded its own enemies, Britain's diplomatic interest lay in supporting the Union blockade in principle; from Britain's standpoint, to help the South break the blockade would set a precedent that could easily boomerang. Finally, although France and Britain often considered recognizing the Confederacy, the timing never seemed quite right.

Lincoln's issuance of the Emancipation Proclamation, freeing the slaves, effectively preempted any British or French move toward recognition of the Confederacy. By transforming the war into a struggle about slavery, Lincoln won wide support among liberals and the working class in Britain. The proclamation, wrote Henry Adams (diplomat Charles Francis Adams's son) from London, "has done more for us here than all of our former victories and all our diplomacy."

EMANCIPATION TRANSFORMS THE WAR, 1863

Why was emancipation important in the course of the war, and what role did African-Americans play in the conflict?

"I hear old John Brown knocking on the lid of his coffin and shouting 'Let me out! Let me out!'" abolitionist Henry Stanton wrote to his wife after the fall of Fort Sumter. "The Doom of Slavery is at hand." In 1861 this prediction seemed wildly premature. In his inaugural address Lincoln had stated bluntly, "I have no purpose, directly or indirectly, to interfere with the institution of slavery in the states where it exists." Yet within two years both necessity and ideology made emancipation a primary northern goal.

The rise of emancipation as a war goal reflected the changing character of the conflict itself. As the fighting raged on, demands for the prosecution of a "total war" intensified in the North, and many people who were unconcerned about the morality of slavery accepted abolition as a military necessity.

From Confiscation to Emancipation

The Union's policy on emancipation developed in several stages. As soon as northern troops invaded the South, questions arose about captured rebel property, including slaves. Generally, slaves who fled behind Union lines were considered "contraband"—enemy property liable to seizure—and were put to work for the Union army. In August 1861 Congress passed the first Confiscation Act, which authorized the seizure of all property, including slaves, used in military aid of the rebellion. This law did not free slaves, nor did it apply to those who had not worked for the Confederate army.

Several factors determined the Union's cautious approach. For one thing, Lincoln maintained that the South could not legally secede and thus argued that the Constitution's protection of property still applied. Second, Lincoln did not want to alienate slaveholders in the border states and proslavery Democrats. In December 1861 he assured Congress that the war would not become a "remorseless revolutionary struggle." At the same time, however, the Radical Republicans pressured Lincoln to make the Civil War a second American Revolution, one that would abolish slavery. They agreed with African-American abolitionist Frederick Douglass that "to fight against slaveholders without fighting against slavery, is but a half-hearted business."

Emancipation also took on military significance with each Union setback, as northerners began to recognize that slavery permitted the South to commit a higher percentage of its white men to battle. In July 1862, Congress therefore passed the second Confiscation Act, which authorized the seizure of property belonging to all rebels, stipulated that slaves who entered Union lines "shall be forever free," and authorized the use of blacks as soldiers.

Nevertheless, Lincoln continued to stall. "My paramount object in this struggle *is* to save the Union, and is *not* either to save or destroy slavery," Lincoln averred. "If I could save the Union without freeing *any* slave, I would do it, and if I could save it by freeing *all* the slaves, I would do it; and if I could save it by freeing some and leaving others alone, I would also do that." But Lincoln, who had always loathed slavery, gradually came around to the view that the war had to lead to abolition. Reluctant to push the issue while Union armies reeled in defeat, he drafted a proclamation of emancipation and waited for the right moment to announce it. After the Union victory at Antietam, Lincoln issued the Preliminary Emancipation Proclamation (September 1862), which declared all slaves under rebel control free as of January 1, 1863. The final Emancipation Proclamation, issued on January 1, 1863, declared "forever free" all slaves in areas in rebellion.

The proclamation had limited practical impact. It applied only to areas in which it could not be enforced, those still in rebellion, and did not touch slavery in the border states. But the Emancipation Proclamation was a brilliant political stroke. By making it a military measure, Lincoln pacified northern conservatives, and by issuing the proclamation himself, he stole the initiative from the Radical Republicans. Through the proclamation, moreover, Lincoln mobilized support for the Union among European liberals, pushed the border states toward emancipation (both Missouri and Maryland abolished slavery before the war's end), and increased slaves' incentives to escape as Union troops neared.

The Emancipation Proclamation did not end slavery everywhere or free "*all* the slaves," but it changed the war. From 1863 on, the war for the Union was also a war against slavery.

Crossing Union Lines
The attacks and counterattacks of the opposing armies turned many slaves into pawns of the war, free when Union troops overran their area, slaves again if the Confederates regained control. One North Carolina slave celebrated his liberation twelve different times. By 1865 about 500,000 former slaves were in Union hands.

Although in the first year of the war masters could retrieve slaves from Union armies, after 1862 slaves who crossed Union lines were considered free. The continual influx of freed slaves created a huge refugee problem for army commanders. Many freed slaves served in army camps as cooks, teamsters, and laborers. Some worked for pay on abandoned plantations or were leased out to planters who swore allegiance to the Union. Whether in camps or on plantations, freedmen questioned the value of liberation. Deductions for clothing and food ate up most of their earnings, and labor contracts bound them for long periods of time. Moreover, the freedmen encountered fierce prejudice among Yankee soldiers, who widely feared that emancipation would propel blacks northward after the war. The best solution to the widespread "question of what to do with the darkies," wrote one northern soldier, "would be to shoot them."

But this was not the whole story. Contrabands who aided the Union as spies and scouts helped to break down bigotry. "The sooner we get rid of our foolish prejudice the better for us," a Massachusetts soldier wrote home. In March 1865, Congress established the Freedmen's Bureau to provide relief, education, and work for the former slaves. The same law also provided that forty acres of abandoned or confiscated land could be leased to each freedman or southern Unionist, with an option to buy after three years. This was the first and only time that Congress provided for the redistribution of confiscated Confederate property.

Black Soldiers in the Union Army

During the first year of the war, the Union had rejected African-American soldiers. Only after the Emancipation Proclamation did the large-scale enlistment of blacks begin. Prominent African-Americans, including Frederick Douglass, worked as recruiting agents in northern cities. Douglass clearly saw the link between military service and citizenship. "Once let the black man get upon his person the brass letters, U.S.; let him get an eagle on his button, and a musket on his shoulder and bullets in his pocket, and there is no power on earth which can deny that he has earned the right to citizenship." By the war's end 186,000 African-Americans had served in the Union army, one-tenth of all Union soldiers. Half of them came from the Confederate states.

White Union soldiers commonly objected to the new recruits on racial grounds. But some, including Colonel Thomas Wentworth Higginson, a liberal minister and former John Brown supporter who led a black regiment, welcomed the black soldiers. "There is a fierce energy about them [in battle]," he exulted, "beyond anything of which I have ever read, except it be the French Zouaves [(zoo-AHVZ), troops in North Africa]." Even Union soldiers who held African-Americans in contempt came to approve of "anything that will kill a rebel." All African-American soldiers served in segregated regiments under white officers. For most of the war, black soldiers earned far less pay than whites. Not until June 1864 did Congress belatedly equalize the pay of black and white soldiers.

African-American soldiers also suffered a far higher mortality rate than whites. Seldom committed to combat, they were far more likely to die of disease in bacteria-ridden garrisons. The Confederacy refused to treat captured black Union soldiers as prisoners of war; instead, they were sent back to the states from which they had come to be reenslaved or executed. In an especially gruesome incident, when Confederate troops under General Nathan Bedford Forrest captured Fort Pillow, Tennessee, in 1864, they massacred 262 blacks.

Although fraught with inequities and hardships, military service symbolized citizenship for African-Americans. It proved that "black men can give blows as well as take them," Frederick Douglass declared. "Liberty won by white men would lost half its luster." And the Union's use of African-American soldiers, especially former slaves, struck a military as well as a psychological blow at the Confederacy. "They will make good soldiers," General Grant wrote in 1863, "and taking them from the enemy weakens him in the same proportion they strengthen us."

CL Primary Source: Zouave Soldier

Slavery in Wartime

Anxious white southerners on the home front felt as if they were perched on a volcano. "We should be practically helpless should the negroes rise," declared a Louisiana planter's daughter, "since there are so few men left at home." To maintain control over their 3 million slaves, they tightened slave patrols, spread scare stories among slaves, and sometimes even moved entire plantations to relative safety in Texas.

Some slaves remained faithful to their owners, hiding treasured belongings from marauding Union soldiers. Others were torn between loyalty and desire for freedom; one body servant, for example, accompanied his master to war, rescued him when he was wounded, and then escaped on his master's horse. Given the chance to flee to Union lines, most slaves did. Freedom was irresistible. The majority of southern slaves stayed on their plantations under the nominal control of their masters. Despite the fears of southern whites, no general slave uprising occurred, and the Confederate war effort continued to utilize slave labor. Thousands of slaves worked in war plants, toiled as teamsters and cooks in army camps, and served as nurses in field hospitals.

But even slaves with no chance of flight were alert to the opportunity that war provided and swiftly tested the limits of enforced labor. Moreover, wartime conditions reduced the slaves' productivity. With most of the white men off at war, the master-slave relationship weakened and the women and boys who remained on plantations complained of difficulty in controlling slaves. Many refused to work, did their work inefficiently, or destroyed property.

Whether slaves fled to freedom or merely stopped working, they effectively undermined the plantation system. Slavery disintegrated even as the Confederacy fought to preserve it. By 1864 a desperate Confederate Congress considered impressing slaves into the army in exchange for their freedom at the war's end. Although Robert E. Lee himself favored making slaves into soldiers, others were adamantly opposed. "If slaves will make good soldiers," a Georgia general argued, "our whole theory of slavery is wrong." In March 1865, however, the Confederate Congress passed a bill to arm 300,000 slave soldiers.

Although the plan to arm the slaves never took effect, the debate over it damaged southern morale by revealing deep internal divisions over war goals. Even before these conflicts had become obvious, the South's military position had deteriorated.

The Turning Point of 1863

In summer and fall 1863, Union fortunes improved dramatically in every theater of the war. However, the spring had gone badly, as General Joseph "Fighting Joe" Hooker, a windbag fond of issuing pompous proclamations to his troops, suffered a crushing defeat at Chancellorsville, Virginia, in May 1863. Although Chancellorsville cost the South dearly—Stonewall Jackson was accidentally killed by his own troops—it humiliated the North, whose forces had outnumbered the Confederate troops two to one. Reports from the West brought no better news: Grant was still unable to take Vicksburg, and the rebels clung to a vital 200-mile stretch of the Mississippi.

Union fortunes rose when Lee determined to invade the North. The decision provoked dissension within the Confederate government, but Lee needed supplies that war-racked Virginia could no longer provide. He also hoped that Lincoln would move troops from Vicksburg back into the eastern theater, and he believed that a major Confederate victory on northern soil could tip the balance to propeace northern Democrats and gain European recognition for the Confederacy. Lee led his 75,000 men into Maryland and then pressed forward into southern

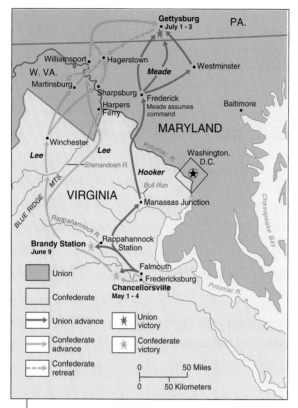

Map 15.3   The War in the East, 1863

Victorious at Chancellorsville in May 1863, Lee again invaded Union territory but was decisively stopped at Gettysburg.

Gettysburg Union victory that halted Confederate invasion of Pennsylvania; turning point in war in East

Vicksburg Union victory that gave North complete control of Mississippi River

Pennsylvania. Lincoln, rejecting Hooker's plan to attack a virtually unprotected Richmond, replaced him with General George G. Meade.

Early in July 1863 Lee's offensive ground to a halt at a Pennsylvania road junction, **Gettysburg.** Confederates foraging for shoes in the town stumbled into Union cavalry, and both sides called for reinforcements. Thus began the war's greatest battle. The Union fielded 90,000 troops against Lee's 75,000, and the struggle raged for the first three days of July. On July 2, Lee rejected advice to plant his army in a defensive position between Meade's force and Washington and instead attacked the Union flanks. But because Confederate assaults were uncoordinated, and some southern generals disregarded orders and struck where they chose, the Union was able to move in reinforcements and regain its earlier losses.

On the afternoon of the third day, Lee ordered a direct frontal assault on the Union lines, and 15,000 men under General George E. Pickett charged across the open field, flags bright in the brilliant sunshine. Union rifles poured volley after volley into the onrushing Confederates, whose line wavered and then broke. More than half of Pickett's force lay dead, dying, or captured. When Lee withdrew to Virginia the next day, July 4, he had lost seventeen generals and more than one-third of his army. Total Union and Confederate casualties numbered 50,000. Although Meade failed to pursue the retreating rebels, the Union men rejoiced that they had parried Lee's stab northward.

Almost simultaneously, the North won a strategically vital battle in the West, at **Vicksburg.** After arduous maneuvering, Grant had besieged Vicksburg, the key to the Mississippi. After six weeks, during which southern soldiers and civilians alike survived by eating mules and even rats, the Confederate commander surrendered his 30,000-man garrison to Grant on July 4, the day that Lee began his withdrawal from Pennsylvania. Port Hudson, the last Confederate stronghold on the Mississippi, soon surrendered. "The Father of Waters flows unvexed to the sea," Lincoln proclaimed.

A second crucial Union victory in the West soon followed, as armies stormed back and forth across Tennessee. By November 1863 the Union forces had finally captured and held Chattanooga, and the way lay open for a Union strike into Georgia.

Coming on the heels of reverses that had driven northern morale to its lowest point of the war, Union successes in the second half of 1863 stiffened the North's will to continue fighting and plunged some Confederate leaders into despair. After the fall of Vicksburg, chief of ordnance Josiah Gorgas lamented, "Yesterday we rode the pinnacle of success—today absolute ruin seems our portion. The Confederacy totters to its destruction."

Totter it might, but the South was far from falling. Lee and his Army of Northern Virginia still defended Virginia and Richmond. Although the loss of Vicksburg had cut the Confederacy in half, southern states west of the Mississippi could still provide soldiers. And the heart of the Confederacy—the Carolinas, Georgia, Florida, Mississippi, and Virginia—remained in southern hands. Few thought the fate of the Confederacy sealed.

WAR AND SOCIETY, NORTH AND SOUTH

In what ways did the Civil War affect the two sides?

The Civil War, engulfing two economies and societies, extended far beyond the battlefields. By 1863 the contrasts between North and South were stark: superior resources enabled the Union to meet wartime demands that the imperiled Confederacy could not. But both sides confronted similar problems: labor shortages, inflation, and disunity and dissent. Families, were disrupted and dislocated, especially in the South. Women on both sides took on new roles at home, in the workplace, and in relief efforts.

CHECKING IN

- The Emancipation Proclamation made the war a conflict about slavery, but it only freed slaves in rebel-held territory.

- The proclamation kept Britain and France from recognizing the Confederacy.

- Confederate slaves posed a refugee problem for Union armies; the refugees suffered discrimination but performed valuable tasks for the federal troops.

- Despite early resistance, 186,000 African-Americans served as soldiers in Union armies; the South ultimately authorized the use of black troops, but too late to take effect.

- Union victories at Gettysburg and Vicksburg in early July 1863 were the turning point of the war.

The War's Economic Impact: The North

The war had a wildly uneven effect on the Union's economy. Deprived of southern markets, the shoe industry in Massachusetts declined; deprived of raw cotton, the textile industry went into a tailspin. But northern industries directly related to the war effort, such as the manufacture of arms and uniforms, benefited from huge government contracts. Railroads flourished. Now an overwhelming majority in Congress, and with no need to balance southern interests against those of the North, the Republican party carried through a vigorous probusiness legislative agenda. Congress hiked the tariff in 1862 and again in 1864 to protect domestic industries. In July 1862 it passed the **Pacific Railroad Act** to build a transcontinental railroad. The government chartered the Union Pacific and Central Pacific corporations and gave each large land grants and generous loans, a total of 60 million acres of land and $20 million. The issuance of greenbacks and the creation of a national banking system brought a measure of uniformity to the nation's financial system.

> **Pacific Railroad Act** Legislation that gave cash and land subsidies to those building the transcontinental railroad

The Republicans designed these measures to help all social classes and partially succeeded. The **Homestead Act** (passed in May 1862), embodying the party's ideal of "free soil, free labor, free men," granted 160 acres of public land to settlers after five years of residence on the land. By 1865 twenty thousand homesteaders occupied new land in the West, forerunners of a human tidal wave. To bring higher education within the reach of the common people, the **Morrill Land Grant Act** of July 1862 gave states proceeds from public land to establish universities emphasizing "such branches of learning as are related to agriculture and mechanic arts [engineering]." It spurred the growth of large state universities, mainly in the Midwest and West. Michigan State, Ohio State, Iowa State, and Purdue along with many others profited from the law.

> **Homestead Act** Measure that provided free land on Great Plains to those willing to live there and develop it

> **Morrill Land Grant Act** law that established funding for agricultural and mechanical colleges, not traditional liberal arts colleges

Despite the idealistic goals underlying such laws, the war benefited the wealthy more than the average citizen. Corrupt contractors grew rich by selling the government substandard merchandise, such as the notorious "shoddy" clothing made from compressed rags, which quickly disintegrated. Speculators made millions in the gold market, profiting more from Union defeats than from Union victories. Dealers with access to scarce commodities reaped astonishing profits. Manpower shortages in agricultural areas stimulated demand for Cyrus McCormick's mechanical reaper. McCormick redoubled his profits by investing in pig iron and watching as wartime demand drove the price of iron from $23 to $40 a ton.

Ordinary workers suffered. Protective tariffs, wartime excise taxes, and inflation bloated the price of finished goods, and wages lagged 20 percent or more behind cost increases. As boys and women poured into government offices and factories to replace men serving in the army, they drew lower pay, and the threat that employers could hire more youths and females undercut the bargaining power of the men who remained in the labor force.

Workers complained about their low wages, and a handful formed unions, a practice that would accelerate after the war. Employers denounced work complaints as unpatriotic hindrances to the war effort, and in 1864 troops were diverted from combat to put down protests in war industries.

The War's Economic Impact: The South

The war shattered the South's economy. In fact, if both regions are considered together, the war retarded *American* economic growth. For example, the U.S. commodity output, which had increased 51 percent and 62 percent in the 1840s and 1850s, respectively, rose only 22 percent during the 1860s. Even this modest gain depended wholly on the North, for during that same decade, commodity output in the South *declined* 39 percent.

Multiple factors offset the South's substantial wartime industrial growth. For example, the war destroyed the South's railroads. Cotton production plunged from 4 million bales in 1861 to 300,000 in 1865. Southern food production also declined because of Union occupation and a shortage of manpower. In areas under Confederate control, the yields per acre of crops like wheat and corn contracted; scarcities abounded. Agricultural shortages compounded the South's already severe inflation. By 1860 salt selling for $1.25 a sack in New York City cost $60 in the South, and food riots erupted in Mobile, Atlanta, and Richmond.

Part of the blame for the South's food shortage rested with the planters. Despite government pleas to grow more food, many planters continued to raise cotton. To feed its hungry armies, the Confederacy impressed food from civilians. Farms and plantations run by the wives of active soldiers provided the easiest targets for food-impressment agents, and the women sent desperate pleas to their husbands to return home. By late 1864, half the Confederacy's soldiers were absent from their units.

The manpower drain that hampered food production reshaped the lives of southern white women; with three of every four white men in the military during the war, southern women faced new challenges and chronic shortages. With manufactured goods in short supply, women wove cloth and improvised replacements for unavailable goods, such as ink, dye, coffee, shoes, and candles. The war made refugees of many women; Texas became an appealing haven for those who sought to preserve their slave property.

In one respect, the persistence of cotton growing aided the South, as cotton became the basis for the Confederacy's flourishing trade with the enemy. In July 1861 the U.S. Congress virtually legalized this trade by allowing northern commerce with southerners loyal to the Union. In practice, it proved impossible to tell loyalists from rebels, and northern traders happily swapped bacon, salt, blankets, and other necessities with whoever would sell them southern cotton. By 1864 traffic through the lines was providing the South with enough food daily to feed Lee's Army of Northern Virginia. A northern congressman lamented that it seemed the Union's policy was "to feed an army and fight it at the same time."

Dealing with Dissent

Both wartime governments faced mounting dissent and disloyalty. Within the Confederacy, dissent assumed two basic forms. First, a vocal group of states' rights supporters persistently attacked Jefferson Davis's government as a despotism. Second, loyalty to the Union flourished among the nonslaveholding small farmers who lived in the Appalachian region. To these people, the Confederate rebellion was a slave owners' conspiracy. An Alabama farmer complained of the planters, "All they want is to get you pupt up and to fight for their infurnal negroes and after you do there fighting you may kiss there hine parts for o they care." On the whole, the South responded mildly to such popular disaffection. In 1862 the Confederate Congress gave President Davis the power to suspend the writ of habeas corpus, but he used it sparingly.

Lincoln faced similar challenges in the North, where the Democratic minority opposed both emancipation and the wartime growth of centralized power. One faction, the "Peace Democrats" (called **Copperheads** by their opponents, to suggest a resemblance to a species of easily concealed poisonous snakes), demanded a truce and a peace conference. They charged that the administration's war policy would "exterminate the South," make reconciliation impossible, and spark "terrible social change and revolution" nationwide.

Copperheads Northern "Peace Democrats" who opposed war

Strongest in the border states, the Midwest, and northeastern cities, the Democrats mobilized farmers of southern background and the urban working class, especially recent immigrants, who feared losing their jobs to free blacks. In 1863 this volatile mix of political, ethnic, racial, and class antagonisms exploded into anti-draft protests in several cities. By far the most violent eruption occurred in July 1863 in New York City, where mobs of Irish working-class men and women roamed the streets for four days until federal troops suppressed them. The Irish loathed the idea of being drafted to fight a war on behalf of slaves who, once freed, might compete with them for jobs. They also bitterly resented the provision of the draft law that allowed the rich to purchase substitutes. The rioters lynched at least a dozen blacks, injured hundreds more, and burned draft offices, the homes of wealthy Republicans, and the Colored Orphan Asylum.

President Lincoln's speedy dispatch of federal troops to quash these riots typified his forceful response to dissent. Lincoln imposed martial law with far less hesitancy than Davis; he suspended the writ of habeas corpus nationwide in 1863 and authorized the arrest of rebels, draft resisters, and anyone engaged in "any disloyal practice." The responses of Davis and Lincoln to dissent underscored the differences between the two regions' wartime political systems. Lincoln and the Republicans used dissent to rally patriotic fever against the Democrats, but Davis lacked the institutionalization of dissent provided by party conflict and thus had to tread lightly lest he be branded a despot.

Yet Lincoln did not unleash a reign of terror against dissent. In general, the North preserved freedom of the press, speech, and assembly. In 1864 the Union became the first warring nation in history to hold a contested national election. Moreover, most of the 15,000 civilians arrested in the North were quickly released.

The Medical War

The Union and the Confederacy alike witnessed remarkable wartime patriotism that propelled civilians, especially women, to work tirelessly to alleviate soldiers' suffering. The **U.S. Sanitary Commission,** organized in June 1861 to assist the Union's medical bureau, depended on women volunteers. The commission raised funds, bought and distributed supplies, and ran special kitchens to supplement army rations. The legendary "Mother" Mary Ann Bickerdyke served sick and wounded Union soldiers as both nurse and surrogate mother. When a doctor asked her by what authority she demanded supplies for the wounded, she shot back, "From the Lord God Almighty. Do you have anything that ranks higher than that?"

U.S. Sanitary Commission Major source of medical aid for soldiers

Women also reached out to aid the battlefront through the nursing corps. Some 3,200 women served the Union and the Confederacy as nurses. Dorothea Dix, famed for her campaigns on behalf of the insane, became head of the Union's nursing corps. **Clara Barton,** an obscure clerk in the Patent Office, found ingenious ways of channeling medicine to the sick and wounded. Catching wind of Union movements before the Battle of Antietam, she showed up at the battlefield on the eve of the clash with a wagonload of supplies. When army surgeons ran out of bandages and started to dress wounds with corn husks, she raced forward with lint and bandages. In 1881 she would found the American Red Cross. The Confederacy had its own legendary nurses. Sally Tompkins was commissioned a captain for her hospital work. Belle Boyd, both a nurse and a spy, once dashed through a field to give Stonewall Jackson information.

Clara Barton Nurse who worked for Sanitary Commission, later founded Red Cross

Danger stalked nurses in hospitals far from the front. Louisa May Alcott, a nurse at the Union Hotel Hospital in Washington, D.C., contracted typhoid. Wherever they worked, nurses witnessed haunting, nightmarish scenes. "About the amputating table," one wrote, "lay large piles of human flesh—legs, arms, feet, and hands . . . the stiffened membranes seemed to be clutching oftentimes at our clothing."

 Primary Source: The Women's War

Pioneered by British reformer Florence Nightingale in the 1850s, nursing was a new vocation for women. In the eyes of critics, it marked a brazen departure from women's proper sphere. Male doctors were unsure about how to react to female nurses and sanitary workers. Some saw a potential for mischief in women's presence in male hospital wards. But other physicians viewed nursing and sanitary work as useful. The miasm theory of disease (see Chapter 11) won wide respect among physicians and stimulated valuable sanitary measures. In partial consequence, the ratio of disease to battle deaths was much lower in the Civil War than in the Mexican-American War. Nonetheless, for every soldier killed during the Civil War, two died of disease. The germ theory of disease was unknown, and arm and leg wounds often led to gangrene (GAN-green) or tetanus (TET-uh-nuss). Typhoid, malaria, diarrhea, and dysentery raged through army camps.

Prison camps posed a special problem. The two sides had far more prisoners than they could handle, and prisoners on both sides suffered gravely. The worst conditions plagued the southern camps. Squalor and insufficient rations turned the Confederate prison camp at Andersonville, Georgia, into a virtual death camp; 3,000 prisoners a month (out of a total of 32,000) were dying there by August 1864. After the war an outraged northern public demanded, and got, the execution of Andersonville's commandant.

The War and Women's Rights

Nurses and Sanitary Commission workers were not the only women to serve society in wartime. In North and South alike, women took over jobs vacated by men. In rural areas, where manpower shortages were most acute, women often plowed, planted, and harvested.

Northern women's rights advocates hoped that the war would yield equality for women as well as for slaves. A grateful North, they contended, should reward women for their wartime service and recognize the link between black rights and women's rights. In 1863, feminists Elizabeth Cady Stanton and Susan B. Anthony organized the National Woman's Loyal League. Its members principally gathered signatures on petitions calling for a constitutional amendment to abolish slavery, but Stanton and Anthony used the organization to promote woman suffrage as well. Despite high expectations, the war did not bring women significantly closer to economic or political equality. Nor did it much change the prevailing definition of women's sphere. Men continued to dominate the medical profession, and for the rest of the century the census classified nurses as domestic help.

This failure to win the vote for women by capitalizing on the rising sentiment for abolition keenly disappointed women's rights advocates. The North had compelling reasons to abolish slavery, but northern politicians saw little practical value in woman suffrage. The *New York Herald,* which supported the Loyal League's attack on slavery, dismissed its call for woman suffrage as "nonsense and tomfoolery."

CHECKING IN

- During the war, northern Republicans pushed several economic development measures through Congress—tariffs, railroad subsidies, national banking, and homestead legislation—and industrialization thrived.
- The Confederate economy, in contrast, crumpled under wartime pressure, and civilians suffered shortages and hardship.
- Lincoln was much quicker than Davis to suppress dissent.
- The war stimulated the use of women as nurses and led to advances in anesthesia and sanitary conditions.
- Women like Elizabeth Cady Stanton pointed to women's wartime service to promote women's rights; however, in the end, the war did not bring acceptance of women's political or economic equality.

THE UNION VICTORIOUS, 1864–1865

How did the Union finally win the war?

Successes at Gettysburg and Vicksburg in 1863 notwithstanding, the Union stood no closer to taking Richmond at the start of 1864 than in 1861, and most of the Lower South remained under Confederate control. The North's persistent inability to destroy the main Confederate armies eroded the Union's will to attack. War weariness strengthened the Democrats and jeopardized Lincoln's reelection in 1864.

The year 1864 was crucial for the North. A Union army under General William Tecumseh Sherman captured Atlanta in September, boosting northern morale and helping to reelect Lincoln. Sherman then marched unimpeded across Georgia and into South Carolina and devastated the states. In Virginia, Grant backed Lee into trenches around Petersburg and Richmond and forced the evacuation of both cities—and ultimately the Confederacy's collapse.

The Eastern Theater in 1864

Early in 1864 Lincoln made Grant the commander of all Union armies and promoted him to lieutenant general. At first glance, the stony-faced, cigar-puffing Grant seemed an unlikely candidate for so exalted a rank, held previously only by George Washington. Grant's only distinguishing characteristics were his ever-present cigar and a penchant for whittling sticks into chips. "There is no glitter, no parade about him," a contemporary noted. But Grant's successes in the West had made him the Union's most popular general. He moved his headquarters to the Army of the Potomac in the East and mapped a strategy for final victory.

Grant shared Lincoln's belief that the Union had to coordinate its attacks on all fronts to exploit its numerical advantage. He planned a sustained offensive against Lee in the East while ordering Sherman to attack the rebel army in Georgia. Sherman's mission was "to break it [the Confederate army] up, and to get into the interior of the enemy's country . . . inflicting all the damage you can."

In early May 1864, Grant led 118,000 men against Lee's 64,000 in a forested area near Fredericksburg, Virginia, called the Wilderness. The Union army fought the Army of Northern Virginia in a series of bloody engagements in May and June. These battles ranked among the war's fiercest; at Cold Harbor, Grant lost 7,000 men in one hour. Instead of recoiling from such an immense "butcher's bill," Grant pressed on, forcing Lee to pull back to trenches guarding Petersburg and Richmond.

Once entrenched, Lee could not threaten the Union rear with rapid moves, as he had done for three years. Lee sent General Jubal A. Early on raids down the Shenandoah (sheh-nan-DOH-uh) Valley, which served the Confederacy as a granary and as an indirect way to menace Washington. Grant countered by ordering General Philip Sheridan to march down the valley from the north and lay it waste. By September 1864 Sheridan controlled the devastated valley and boasted that a crow flying over the once-prosperous area would have to carry its own lunch.

While Grant and Lee grappled in the Wilderness, Sherman led 98,000 men into Georgia. Opposing him with 53,000 men (later reinforced to 65,000), General Joseph Johnston slowly retreated toward Atlanta, conserving his strength for a defense of the city and forcing Sherman to elongate his supply lines. Dismayed by this defensive strategy, President Davis replaced Johnston with the adventurous John B. Hood. He gave Davis what he wanted, a series of attacks on Sherman, but Sherman pressed relentlessly forward against Hood's increasingly depleted army. Unable to defend Atlanta, Hood evacuated the city, which fell to Sherman on September 2, 1864.

The Election of 1864

Atlanta's fall came at a timely moment for Lincoln, in the thick of a tough campaign for reelection. Radical Republicans opposed his renomination, largely because of his desire to restore occupied parts of the Confederacy to the Union, and rallied around

Secretary of the Treasury Salmon P. Chase. The Democrats, meanwhile, had never forgiven Lincoln for making emancipation a war goal, and now the Copperheads demanded an immediate armistice followed by negotiations.

Lincoln, however, benefited from his own resourcefulness and his foes' problems. Chase's challenge failed, and by the time of the Republican convention, Lincoln's managers controlled the nomination. To isolate the Peace Democrats, the Republicans formed a temporary organization, the National Union party, and chose a southern Unionist, Democratic senator Andrew Johnson of Tennessee, for the vice presidency. The Democrats nominated George B. McClellan, former commander of the Army of the Potomac, who advocated military victory and tried to distance himself from the Democratic platform, which called for peace without victory.

Lincoln doubted that he would be reelected and even arranged furloughs so that Union soldiers, most of whom supported him, would be able to vote in states lacking absentee ballots. The fall of Atlanta provided an enormous boost and saved Lincoln's presidency. With 55 percent of the popular vote and 212 out of 233 electoral votes, he swept to victory.

The convention that nominated Lincoln also endorsed a constitutional amendment to abolish slavery, which Congress passed early in 1865. The **Thirteenth Amendment** would be ratified by the end of the year.

|Thirteenth Amendment Ended slavery in all U.S. territory

Sherman's March Through Georgia

Meanwhile, Sherman gave the South a lesson in total war. Refusing to chase Hood back into Tennessee, he decided to abandon his own supply lines, to march his army across Georgia to Savannah (suh-VAN-uh), and to live off the countryside. He would break the South's will to fight, terrify its people, and "make war so terrible . . . that generations would pass before they could appeal again to it."

Sherman began by burning much of Atlanta and forcing the evacuation of its civilian population. This harsh measure freed him of the need to feed and garrison the city. Then he led the bulk of his army, 62,000 men, out of Atlanta toward Savannah. Four columns of infantry, augmented by cavalry squads and followed by thousands of jubilant slaves, moved on a front sixty miles wide and at a pace of ten miles a day, destroying everything that could aid the Confederacy—arsenals, railroads, munitions plants, cotton gins, crops, and livestock. This ruin far exceeded Sherman's orders. Although told not to destroy civilian property, foragers ransacked and demolished homes. Indeed, havoc seemed a vital part of Sherman's strategy. By the time he occupied Savannah, he estimated that his army had destroyed $100 million worth of property. After taking Savannah in December 1864, Sherman's army wheeled north toward South Carolina, the first state to secede and, in his view, one "that deserves all that seems in store for her." Sherman's columns advanced unimpeded to Columbia, where fires set by looters, slaves, soldiers of both sides, and liberated Union prisoners razed the city.

Sherman headed for North Carolina. By spring 1865 his army had left behind four hundred miles of ruin. Other Union armies controlled the entire Confederacy, except Texas and Florida, and destroyed its wealth. "War is cruelty and you cannot refine it," Sherman wrote. "Those who brought war into our country deserve all the curses and maledictions a people can pour out."

Map 15.4 The Final Virginia Campaign, 1864–1865

Refusing to abandon his campaign in the face of enormous casualties, Grant finally pushed Lee into defensive fortifications around Petersburg, whose fall doomed Richmond. When Lee tried to escape to the west, Grant cut him off and forced his surrender.

Interactive Map: Grant's Campaign Against Lee

Appomattox Courthouse Site of Lee's surrender to Grant

Toward Appomattox

While Sherman headed north, Grant renewed his assault on the entrenched Army of Northern Virginia. His main objective was Petersburg, a railroad hub south of Richmond. The fall of Atlanta and the devastation wrought by Sherman's army took a heavy toll on Confederate morale. Desertions reached epidemic proportions. Late in March 1865, Grant, reinforced by Sheridan, swung his army around the western flank of the Petersburg defenders. Lee could not stop him. On April 2 a courier brought the grim news to Jefferson Davis, attending church in Richmond: "General Lee telegraphs that he can hold his position no longer."

Davis left his pew, gathered his government, and fled. On the morning of April 3, Union troops entered Richmond, pulled down the Confederate flag, and raised the Stars and Stripes over the capital. Explosions set by retreating Confederates left the city "a sea of flames." Union troops liberated the jail, which held slaves awaiting sale, and its rejoicing inmates poured into the streets. On April 4 Lincoln toured the city and for a few minutes sat at Davis's desk with a dreamy expression on his face.

Lee led a last-ditch effort to escape westward to Lynchburg and its rail connections. But Grant and Sheridan choked off the route, and on April 9 Lee bowed to the inevitable. He asked for terms of surrender and met Grant in a private home in the village of **Appomattox** (app-oh-MAT-tux) **Courthouse,** east of Lynchburg. As stunned troops gathered outside, Lee appeared in full dress uniform, complete with sword. Grant entered in his customary disarray, smoking a cigar. The final surrender came four days later, as Lee's troops laid down their arms between federal ranks. "On our part," wrote a Union officer, "not a sound of trumpet . . . nor roll of drum; not a cheer . . . but an awed stillness rather." Grant paroled Lee's 26,000 men and sent them home with the horses and mules "to work their little farms." Within a month the remnants of Confederate resistance collapsed.

Grant headed back to a jubilant Washington. On April 14 he turned down a theater date with the Lincolns; his wife found Mrs. Lincoln overbearing. That night at Ford's Theater an unemployed pro-Confederate actor, John Wilkes Booth, entered Lincoln's box and shot him in the head. Shouting the Virginia state motto, "Sic Semper Tyrannis" (Such is always the fate of tyrants), Booth leaped onto the stage and fled. Assassination attempts on the secretary of state and vice president failed, and Booth escaped. Within two weeks Union troops hunted him down and shot him to death. Four accused accomplices were hanged, and four more were imprisoned. On April 15 Lincoln died, and Andrew Johnson became president. Six days later, Lincoln's funeral train left Washington on its mournful journey to Springfield, Illinois. Crowds of thousands gathered at stations to weep as the black-draped train passed.

Grant in 1864

Exuding determination and competence, General Ulysses S. Grant posed in front of his tent in 1864. Within a year, Grant's final assault on Petersburg and the Union army's triumphant march into Richmond would bring the war to an end.

The Impact of the War

The Civil War took a larger human toll than any other war in American history. More than 620,000 soldiers died during the tragic four years of war, nearly equal the number of American soldiers killed in all the nation's earlier and later wars. The death count stood at 360,000 Union soldiers and 260,000 Confederates.. Most families in the nation suffered losses. Vivid reminders remained well into the twentieth century. For many years, armless and legless veterans gathered at regimental reunions, and thousands of communities built monuments to the dead.

The war's costs were staggering, but only the southern economy was destroyed. By war's end the North had most of the nation's wealth and industrial capacity. Spurring economic modernization, the war provided opportunities for industrial development and capital investment. No longer the largest slave-owning power in the world, the United States would become a major industrial nation.

The war had political ramifications as well. States never regained their antebellum range of powers. The national banking system gradually supplanted state banks, and greenbacks provided a national currency. The war also promoted large-scale organization in both the business world and public life.

Finally, the Civil War fulfilled abolitionists' prophecies as well as Union goals, producing the very sort of radical upheaval within southern society that Lincoln had tried to avoid. Beaten Confederates wondered whether blacks and Yankees would permanently take over the South. "Hello, massa," an African-American Union soldier called out when he spotted his former owner among Confederate prisoners whom he was guarding. "Bottom rail top dis time." The nation now shifted its attention to the reconstruction of the conquered South and the fate of 3.5 million newly freed slaves.

CHECKING IN

- Lincoln finally found the general he needed in Ulysses S. Grant, who realized that the South could not withstand the enormous casualties of relentless combat.

- Sherman brought total war to the South with his march through Georgia and the Carolinas.

- Lincoln's triumph in the 1864 election reflected increasing Union confidence in victory.

- Forced to leave Richmond undefended, Lee surrendered in April 1865, effectively ending major combat.

- In the final months of the war, Congress passed the Thirteenth Amendment, abolishing slavery, but the assassination of Lincoln left the postwar future in limbo.

Chapter Summary

 DOWNLOAD THE MP3 AUDIO FILE OF THE CHAPTER SUMMARY, AND LISTEN TO IT ON THE GO.

What major advantages did each side possess at the start of the Civil War? (page 325)

The Union had enormous manpower advantages, as well as a strong industrial base. The South's advantages were few. Although at first the Confederacy was politically unified, political divisions developed over the role of national government in the Confederacy. Lincoln was a far better political leader than Davis.

How was the war fought in its early years? (page 331)

Although new weapons, such as the rifle, appeared, the Civil War was basically fought as a traditional war, with mass infantry charges and large battles. To secure independence, the South needed only to defend itself and fight close to its own resources, whereas the northern armies had to invade and occupy a vast region. The war in the East quickly became a stalemate, but the Union established supremacy west of the Mississippi early in the war. Many Confederate leaders assumed that the British textile industry's need for southern cotton would force Britain to become an ally, but the British remained aloof.

Why was emancipation important in the course of the war, and what role did African-Americans play in the conflict? (page 338)

The Emancipation Proclamation transformed the Civil War from a conflict over secession into a war about slavery, and it effectively prevented Great Britain from openly supporting the Confederacy. Whenever possible, slaves strove to escape from slavery. Slave refugees posed problems for Union armies but also performed valuable tasks for federal troops. Nearly 200,000 African-Americans fought in Union armies, and manpower shortages drove the Confederacy to authorize use of black troops as well.

In what ways did the Civil War affect the two sides? (page 343)

During the war, the federal Congress passed major bills promoting economic development: tariffs, railroad subsidies, national banking laws, and legislation to encourage homesteading. However, the war devastated the South's economy, with resulting shortages and hardships for civilians. Women assumed new roles as nurses and hoped that their service would advance the cause of women's rights.

How did the Union finally win the war? (page 347)

Lincoln found the general he had been searching for in Ulysses S. Grant, who was willing to absorb enormous casualties to inflict the losses he knew the South could not afford. Sherman's capture of Atlanta guaranteed Lincoln's reelection in 1864 and boosted northern determination. By April 1865 Lee was forced to abandon the defense of Richmond and surrendered at Appomattox Courthouse. The Thirteenth Amendment, passed in the final months of the war, ended slavery. However, Lincoln's assassination left the postwar future in limbo.

KEY TERMS

conscription (p. 325)
"greenbacks" (p. 327)
Anaconda plan (p. 332)
First Battle of Bull Run (p. 332)
George B. McClellan (p. 332)
Robert E. Lee (p. 333)
Antietam (p. 334)
Emancipation Proclamation (p. 334)
Ulysses S. Grant (p. 335)
Gettysburg (p. 342)
Vicksburg (p. 342)
Pacific Railroad Act (p. 343)
Homestead Act (p. 343)
Morrill Land Grant Act (p. 343)
Copperheads (p. 345)
U.S. Sanitary Commission (p. 346)
Clara Barton (p. 346)
Thirteenth Amendment (p. 349)
Appomattox Courthouse (p. 350)

CHAPTER 16

The Crisis of Reconstruction

1865–1877

The Devastated South

The end of the Civil War was a time of uncharted possibilities—and unresolved conflicts. While former slaves exulted over their freedom, their former owners were often as grim as the ravaged southern landscape. Several thousand fled to Brazil, Mexico, or Europe, but most remained.

After most wars, victors care little for the mood of the vanquished, but the Civil War was different. The Union had sought not merely victory but the return of national unity. The federal government faced unprecedented questions. How could the Union be restored and the South reintegrated? Who would control the process—Congress or the president? Should Confederate leaders be tried for treason? Most important, what would happen to the

3.5 million former slaves? The freedmen's future was *the* crucial postwar issue, for emancipation had set in motion the most profound upheaval in the nation's history. Slavery had been both a labor system and a means of racial control; it had determined the South's social, economic, and political structure. The end of the Civil War, in short, posed two huge challenges that had to be addressed simultaneously: readmitting the Confederate states to the Union and defining the status of free blacks in society.

Between 1865 and 1877 the nation faced major and often divisive challenges and crises. Conflict characterized congressional debates, the former Confederacy, and the industrializing postwar North. These crises of Reconstruction—the restoration of the former Confederate states and the fate of the former slaves—reshaped the legacy of the Civil War.

RECONSTRUCTION POLITICS, 1865–1868

On what major issues did Radical Republicans and President Johnson struggle over Reconstruction policy?

The end of the Civil War offered multiple possibilities for chaos and vengeance. The federal government could have imprisoned Confederate leaders; former rebel troops could have become guerrillas; freed slaves could have waged a racial war against their former masters. None of this happened. Instead, intense *political* conflict dominated the immediate postwar period. The political upheaval, sometimes attended by violence, produced new constitutional amendments, an impeachment crisis, and some of the most ambitious domestic legislation ever enacted by Congress, the Reconstruction Acts of 1867–1868. It culminated in something that few expected, the enfranchisement of African-American men.

Radical Republicans Former abolitionists who controlled Congress and Reconstruction in late 1860s

In 1865 only a handful of **Radical Republicans** advocated African-American suffrage. But in the complex political battles of Reconstruction, the Radicals won broad support for their program, including African-American male enfranchisement. Just as the Civil War had led to emancipation, so Reconstruction led to African-American suffrage.

Lincoln's Plan

Conflict over Reconstruction began even before the war ended. In December 1863, President Lincoln issued the Proclamation of Amnesty and Reconstruction, which allowed southern states to form new governments if at least 10 percent of those who had voted in the 1860 elections swore an oath of allegiance to the Union and accepted emancipation. This plan excluded most Confederate officials and military officers, who would have had to apply for presidential pardons, as well as African-Americans, who had not voted in 1860. Lincoln hoped both to undermine the Confederacy and to build a southern Republican party.

Radical Republicans in Congress wanted a slower readmission process that would exclude even more ex-Confederates from political life. The Wade-Davis Bill, passed by Congress in July 1864, provided that a military government would rule

Chronology

1863	President Abraham Lincoln issues Proclamation of Amnesty and Reconstruction
1864	Wade-Davis Bill passed by Congress and pocket-vetoed by Lincoln
1865	Freedmen's Bureau established; Civil War ends; Lincoln assassinated; Andrew Johnson becomes president; Johnson issues Proclamation of Amnesty and Reconstruction; Ex-Confederate states hold constitutional conventions (May–December); Thirteenth Amendment added to the Constitution; Presidential Reconstruction completed
	Civil Rights Act of 1866 and the Supplementary Freedmen's Bureau Act over Johnson's vetoes; Ku Klux Klan founded in Tennessee; Race riots in southern cities; Republicans win congressional elections; Howard University founded
	Reconstruction Act of 1867; William Seward negotiates the purchase of Alaska; Constitutional conventions meet in the ex-Confederate states
	Andrew Johnson impeached, tried, and acquitted; Fourteenth Amendment added to the Constitution; Ulysses S. Grant elected president
1869	Transcontinental railroad completed
1870	Congress readmits the four remaining southern states to the Union; Fifteenth Amendment added to the Constitution; Enforcement Act of 1870
	Second Enforcement Act; Ku Klux Klan Act
	Liberal Republican party formed; Amnesty Act; Alabama claims settled; Grant reelected president
1873	Panic of 1873 begins (September–October), setting off five-year depression
1874	Democrats gain control of the House of Representatives
1875	Civil Rights Act of 1875; Specie Resumption Act
1876	Disputed presidential election: Rutherford B. Hayes versus Samuel J. Tilden
1877	Electoral commission decides election in favor of Hayes; the last Republican-controlled state governments fall in Florida, South Carolina, and Louisiana
1879	"Exodus" movement spreads through several southern states

each former Confederate state and that at least half of the eligible voters would have to swear allegiance before they could choose a convention to repeal secession and abolish slavery. In addition, to qualify as a voter or a delegate, a southerner would have to take the "ironclad" oath, swearing that he had never voluntarily supported the Confederacy. The Wade-Davis Bill would have delayed readmission of southern states almost indefinitely.

Lincoln pocket-vetoed* the Wade-Davis Bill, and an impasse followed. Arkansas, Louisiana, Tennessee, and parts of Virginia moved toward readmission under variants of Lincoln's plan, but Congress refused to seat their delegates. Lincoln hinted that he might be moving toward a more rigorous policy than his original one, a program that would include African-American suffrage. But his death foreclosed the possibility that he and Congress might draw closer to agreement, and Radicals now looked with hope to the new president, Andrew Johnson.

---

* Pocket-vetoed: failed to sign the bill within ten days of Congress's adjournment.

Presidential Reconstruction Under Johnson

At first glance, Andrew Johnson seemed a likely ally for the Radicals. The only southern senator to remain in Congress when his state seceded, Johnson had taken a strong anti-Confederate stance, proclaiming that "treason is a crime and must be made odious," and had served as military governor of Tennessee for two years. Self-educated, an ardent Jacksonian, a foe of the planter class, a supporter of emancipation—Johnson carried impeccable credentials. However, as a lifelong Democrat he had his own political agenda, sharply different from that of the Radicals. He neither adopted abolitionist ideals nor challenged racist sentiments. He hoped mainly that the fall of slavery would cripple southern aristocrats.

In May 1865, with Congress out of session, Johnson shocked Republicans by announcing his own program, A Proclamation of Amnesty and Reconstruction, to bring the southern states still without Reconstruction governments—Alabama, Florida, Georgia, Mississippi, North Carolina, South Carolina, and Texas—back into the Union. Virtually all southerners who took an oath of allegiance would receive pardon and amnesty, and all their property except slaves would be restored to them. Confederate civil and military officers would still be disqualified, as would well-to-do former Confederates (anyone owning taxable property worth $20,000 or more). This purge of the plantation aristocracy, Johnson said, would benefit "humble men, the peasantry of the South, who have been decoyed . . . into rebellion." Poorer whites would now be in control, oath takers could elect delegates to state conventions, which would call regular elections, proclaim secession illegal, repudiate debts incurred under the Confederacy, and ratify the Thirteenth Amendment, which abolished slavery.

Presidential Reconstruction began in summer 1865 with unforeseen results. Johnson handed out pardons liberally (some thirteen thousand) and dropped his plans for the punishment of treason. By the end of 1865 all seven states had created new civil governments that in effect restored the *status quo ante bellum* (state of affairs before the war). Confederate officers and large planters resumed state offices, and former Confederate congressmen and generals won election to Congress. Because many of these new representatives were former Whigs who had not supported secession, southerners believed that they genuinely had elected "Union" men. Some states refused to repudiate their Confederate debts or to ratify the Thirteenth Amendment.

"black codes" Laws passed by southern states to limit the rights of freedmen

Most infuriating to the Radicals, every state passed **"black codes"** intended to ensure a landless, dependent black labor force—to "secure the services of the negroes, teach them their place," in the words of one Alabamian. These codes, which replaced earlier slave codes, guaranteed the freedmen some basic rights—marriage, ownership of property, the right to testify in court against other blacks—but also restricted freedmen's behavior. Some states established segregation, and most prohibited racial intermarriage, jury service by blacks, and court testimony by blacks against whites. Most harmful, black codes included economic restrictions to prevent blacks from leaving the plantation, usually through labor contracts stipulating that anyone who had not signed a labor contract was a vagrant and subject to arrest.

Freedmen's Bureau Agency established by federal government to aid former slaves

These codes left freedmen no longer slaves but not really liberated. Although many of their provisions never actually took effect—for example, the Union army and the **Freedmen's Bureau** suspended the enforcement of the racially discriminatory laws—the black codes reflected white southern attitudes and showed what "home rule" would have been like without federal intervention.

To many northerners, both the black codes and the election of former Confederates to high office reeked of southern defiance. When the Thirty-ninth Congress convened in December 1865, it refused to seat the southern delegates and prepared to dismantle the black codes and to lock ex-Confederates out of power.

Primary Source:
Louisiana Black
Code

Congress Versus Johnson

Southern blacks' status became the major issue in Congress. With Congress split into four blocs—Democrats, and Radical, moderate, and conservative Republicans—a politically adroit president could have protected his program. Ineptly, Johnson alienated the moderates and pushed them into the Radicals' arms by vetoing some key moderate measures.

In late 1865 Congress voted to extend the life of the Freedmen's Bureau for three more years. Staffed mainly by army officers, the bureau provided relief, rations, and medical care; built schools for former slaves; put them to work on abandoned or confiscated lands; and tried to protect their rights as laborers. To strengthen the bureau, Congress had voted to allow it to run special military courts that would settle labor disputes and invalidate labor contracts forced on African-Americans under the black codes. In February 1866 Johnson vetoed the bill; the Constitution, he declared, neither sanctioned military trials of civilians in peacetime nor supported a system to care for "indigent persons." Then in March 1866 Congress passed the Civil Rights Act of 1866, which made African-Americans U.S. citizens with the same civil rights as other citizens and authorized federal intervention to ensure African-Americans' rights in court. Johnson vetoed this measure as well, arguing that it would "operate in favor of the colored and against the white race." In April Congress overrode his veto, and in July it enacted the Supplementary Freedmen's Bureau Act over another presidential veto.

These vetoes puzzled many Republicans, for the new laws did not undercut the basic structure of presidential Reconstruction. Although the vetoes gained support for Johnson among northern Democrats, they cost him dearly among moderate Republicans, who began to ally with the Radicals. Was Johnson a political incompetent, or was he merely trying, unsuccessfully, to forge a centrist coalition? Whatever the case, he drove moderate and Radical Republicans together toward their next step: the passage of a constitutional amendment to protect the new Civil Rights Act.

The Fourteenth Amendment, 1866

In April 1866 Congress adopted the **Fourteenth Amendment,** its most ambitious attempt to deal with the problems of Reconstruction and the freed slaves. In the first clause, the amendment proclaimed that all persons born or naturalized in the United States were citizens and that no state could abridge their rights without due process of law or deny them equal protection under the law. Second, the amendment guaranteed that, if a state denied suffrage to any male citizen, its representation in Congress would be proportionally reduced. Third, the amendment disqualified from state and national offices *all* prewar officeholders who had supported the Confederacy. Finally, it repudiated the Confederate debt and maintained the validity of the federal debt. In effect, the Fourteenth Amendment nullified the *Dred Scott* decision, threatened southern states that deprived African-American men of the right to vote, and invalidated most of the pardons that President Johnson had ladled out.

Fourteenth Amendment
Amendment that defines citizenship and guarantees equal protection under the law

Passage of the amendment created a fire-storm. Abolitionists said that it did not go far enough to protect African-American voting rights, southerners blasted it as vengeful, and President Johnson denounced it. The president's unwillingness to compromise solidified the new alliance between moderate and Radical Republicans, and transformed the congressional elections of 1866 into a referendum on the Fourteenth Amendment.

Over the summer Johnson set off on a whistle-stop train tour campaigning against the amendment. Humorless and defensive, the president made fresh enemies, however, and doomed his hope of creating a new political party, the National Union party, opposed to the amendment. Meanwhile, the moderate and Radical Republicans defended the amendment, condemned President Johnson, and branded the Democratic party "a common sewer . . . into which is emptied every element of treason, North and South."

Republicans carried the congressional elections of 1866 in a landslide, winning nearly two-thirds of the House and three-fourths of the Senate. They had secured a mandate for the Fourteenth Amendment and their own Reconstruction program.

Congressional Reconstruction, 1866–1867

The congressional debate over reconstructing the South began in December 1866 and lasted three months. Radical leaders, anxious to stifle a resurgence of Confederate power, called for African-American suffrage, federal support for public schools, confiscation of Confederate estates, and extended military occupation of the South. Moderate Republicans accepted part of this plan, and in February 1867, after complex political maneuvers, Congress passed the Reconstruction Act of 1867. Johnson vetoed it, and on March 2, Congress passed the law over his veto. Three more Reconstruction acts—passed in 1867 and 1868 over presidential vetoes—refined and enforced the first act.

The Reconstruction Act of 1867 invalidated the state governments formed under the Lincoln and Johnson plans; only Tennessee, which had already ratified the Fourteenth Amendment and had been readmitted to the Union, escaped further Reconstruction. The new law divided the other ten former Confederate states into five military districts. It provided that voters—all black men, plus whites not disqualified by the Fourteenth Amendment—could elect delegates who would write a new state constitution granting African-American suffrage. After congressional approval of the state constitution, and after the state legislature's ratification of the Fourteenth Amendment, Congress would readmit the state into the Union. The enfranchisement of African-Americans and disfranchisement of so many ex-Confederates made the Reconstruction Act of 1867 far more radical than Johnson's program. Even then, however, it provided only temporary military rule, made no provisions to prosecute Confederate leaders for treason, and neither confiscated nor redistributed property.

Radical Republican leader Thaddeus Stevens had proposed confiscation of large Confederate estates to "humble the proud traitors" and to provide land for the former slaves. Because political independence rested on economic independence, he contended, land grants would be far more valuable to African-Americans than the vote. But moderate Republicans and others backed away from Stevens's proposal.

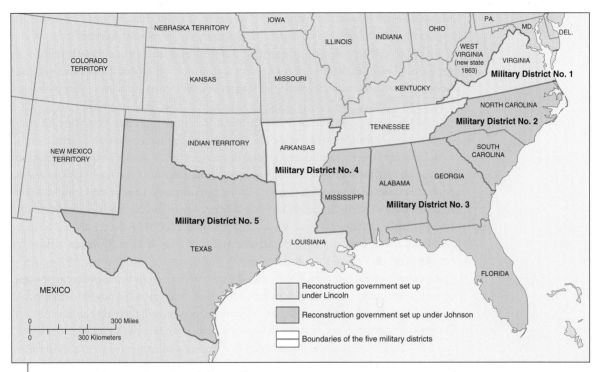

Map 16.1　The Reconstruction of the South

The Reconstruction Act of 1867 divided the former Confederate states, except Tennessee, into five military districts and set forth the steps by which new state governments could be created.

Tampering with property rights in the South might well jeopardize them in the North, they argued, and could endanger the entire Reconstruction program. Thus Congress rejected the most radical parts of the Radical Republican program.

Congressional Reconstruction took effect in spring 1867, but Johnson impeded its implementation by replacing pro-Radical military officers with conservative ones because Reconstruction could not be enforced without military power. Furious and more suspicious than ever of the president, congressional moderates and Radicals again joined forces to block Johnson from further hampering Reconstruction.

Interactive Map:
The Reconstruction

congressional Reconstruction
The four Reconstruction acts that Congress imposed on the South in 1867

The Impeachment Crisis, 1867–1868

In March 1867, responding to Johnson's obstructionist tactics, Republicans in Congress passed two laws to restrict presidential power. The Tenure of Office Act prohibited the president from removing civil officers without Senate consent. Its purpose was to protect Secretary of War Edwin Stanton, a Radical ally needed to enforce the Reconstruction acts. The other law banned the president from issuing military orders except through the commanding general, Ulysses S. Grant, who could not be removed without the Senate's consent. Not satisfied with clipping the president's wings, Radicals also began to look for grounds for **impeachment** and conviction to remove all possible obstacles to Reconstruction. Intense investigations by the House

impeachment Process to remove a president from office; attempted but failed in case of Andrew Johnson

Judiciary Committee and private detectives turned up no impeachable offenses, but Johnson himself soon provided the charges that his opponents needed.

In August 1867 Johnson suspended Stanton and in February 1868 tried to remove him. The president's defiance of the Tenure of Office Act drove moderate Republicans back into alliance with the Radicals. The House approved eleven charges of impeachment, nine of them based on violation of the Tenure of Office Act and the other two accusing Johnson of being "unmindful of the high duties of the office," of seeking to disgrace Congress, and of not enforcing the Reconstruction acts.

Johnson's trial by the Senate, which began in March 1868, riveted public attention for eleven weeks. Seven congressmen, including leading Radicals, served as prosecutors, or "managers." Johnson's lawyers maintained that by violating the Tenure of Office Act, he was merely seeking a court test of a law that he believed to be unconstitutional. They also contended that the law did not protect Stanton, because Lincoln, not Johnson, had appointed him. And they asserted that Johnson was guilty of no crime indictable in a regular court.

Congressional "managers" countered that impeachment was a political process, not a criminal trial, and that Johnson's "abuse of discretionary power" constituted an impeachable offense. Some Senate Republicans wavered, fearful that the removal of a president would destroy the balance of power within the federal government. They also distrusted Radical Republican Benjamin Wade, the president pro tempore of the Senate, who, since there was no vice president, would become president if Johnson were thrown out.

Ultimately, despite intense pressure, seven Republicans risked political suicide by voting with the Democrats against removal, and the Senate failed by one vote to convict Johnson. In so doing, the legislators set two critical precedents: in the future, no president would be impeached on political grounds, nor would he be impeached because two-thirds of Congress disagreed with him. In the short term, nonetheless, the anti-Johnson forces achieved their goals, for Andrew Johnson had no future as president. Republicans in Congress could now pursue their last major Reconstruction objective: guaranteeing African-American male suffrage.

<h2>The Fifteenth Amendment and the Question of Woman Suffrage, 1869–1870</h2>

African-American suffrage was the linchpin of congressional Reconstruction. Only with the support of African-American voters could Republicans secure control of the southern states. The Reconstruction Act of 1867 had forced southern states to enfranchise black men in order to reenter the Union, but most northern states still refused to grant suffrage to African-Americans. The **Fifteenth Amendment,** drawn up by Republicans and approved by Congress in 1869, aimed to protect black suffrage in the South and to extend it to the northern and border states on the assumption that newly enfranchised African-Americans would gratefully vote Republican. The amendment prohibited the denial of suffrage by the states to anyone on account of "race, color, or previous condition of servitude."

Democrats opposed the amendment on the grounds that it violated states' rights, but they did not control enough states to prevent its ratification. However, to some southerners, the amendment's omissions made it acceptable; as a Richmond

Fifteenth Amendment
Amendment guaranteeing men the right to vote

THE RECONSTRUCTION AMENDMENTS

AMENDMENT AND DATE OF CONGRESSIONAL PASSAGE	PROVISIONS	RATIFICATION
Thirteenth (January 1865)	Prohibited slavery in the United States	December 1865
Fourteenth (June 1866)	Defined citizenship to include all persons born or naturalized in the United States Provided proportional loss of congressional representation for any state that denied suffrage to any of its male citizens Disqualified prewar officeholders who supported the Confederacy from state or national office Repudiated the Confederate debt	July 1868, after Congress made ratification a prerequisite for readmission of ex-Confederate states to the Union
Fifteenth (February 1869)	Prohibited the denial of suffrage because of race, color, or previous condition of servitude	March 1870; ratification required of Virginia, Texas, Mississippi, and Georgia for readmission to the Union

newspaper pointed out, it had "loopholes through which a coach and four horses can be driven." Indeed, the new amendment did not guarantee African-American office-holding, nor did it prohibit restrictions on suffrage, such as property requirements and literacy tests, both of which might be used to deny African-Americans the vote.

The debate over black suffrage drew new participants into the fray. Women's rights advocates had tried to promote both black suffrage and woman suffrage, but Radical Republicans rejected any linkage between the two, preferring to concentrate on black suffrage. Supporters of women's rights were themselves divided. Frederick Douglass argued that black suffrage had to receive priority. "If the elective franchise is not extended to the Negro, he is dead," explained Douglass. "Woman has a thousand ways by which she can attach herself to the ruling power of the land that we have not." Women's rights leaders Elizabeth Cady Stanton and Susan B. Anthony disagreed. If the Fifteenth Amendment did not include women, they emphasized, it would establish an "aristocracy of sex" and increase the disabilities under which women already labored.

The battle over black suffrage and the Fifteenth Amendment split women's rights advocates into two rival suffrage associations, both founded in 1869. The Boston-based American Woman Suffrage Association sought state-by-state suffrage, whereas the more radical National Woman Suffrage Association, based in New York and led by Stanton and Anthony, promoted a constitutional amendment for woman suffrage.

Throughout the 1870s the two groups competed for support. Two western states, Wyoming and Utah, extended the vote to women, but the

CHECKING IN

- Lincoln's somewhat lenient plan for Reconstruction died with him.

- President Johnson's even more tolerant plan for Reconstruction infuriated Radical Republicans.

- Congress overrode presidential vetoes of Reconstruction measures such as the Freedmen's Bureau and passed its own harsher version of Reconstruction legislation.

- The Fourteenth Amendment defined citizenship and guaranteed equal protection under the law, and the Fifteenth Amendment guaranteed the right of freedmen, but not of women, to vote.

- The attempt to impeach Johnson on political grounds failed by a narrow margin.

suffrage movement had little to do with it. In 1872 Susan B. Anthony mobilized about seventy women to try to vote nationwide; she was indicted, convicted, and fined. In 1875 the Supreme Court ruled that a state could deny women the right to vote. Woman suffrage advocates braced for a long struggle.

By the time the Fifteenth Amendment was ratified in 1870, Congress could look back on five years of momentous achievement. Three constitutional amendments had broadened the scope of democracy by abolishing slavery, affirming the rights of citizens, and prohibiting the denial of suffrage on the basis of race. Congress had readmitted the former Confederate states into the Union. At the same time, momentum had slowed at the federal level. In 1869 the center of action shifted to the South, where tumultuous change was under way.

RECONSTRUCTION GOVERNMENTS

What impact did federal Reconstruction policy have on the former Confederacy and ex-Confederates?

During the years of presidential Reconstruction, 1865–1867, the southern states faced formidable tasks: creating new governments, reviving war-torn economies, and dealing with the impact of emancipation. Racial tensions flared as freedmen organized political meetings to protest ill treatment and demand equal rights, and deadly race riots erupted in major southern cities. In May 1866 white crowds attacked African-American veterans in Memphis and rampaged through African-American neighborhoods, killing forty-six people.

Congressional Reconstruction, supervised by federal troops, began in spring 1867 with the dismantling of existing governments and the formation of new state governments dominated by Republicans. By 1868 most former Confederate states had rejoined the Union, and within two years the process was complete.

But Republican rule did not long endure in the South. Opposition from southern Democrats, the landowning elite, vigilantes, and most white voters proved insurmountable. Nevertheless, these Reconstruction governments were unique because African-American men, including former slaves, participated in them. Slavery had ended in other societies, too, but only in the United States had freedmen gained democratic political rights.

A New Electorate

The Reconstruction laws of 1867–1868 transformed the southern electorate by temporarily disfranchising 15 percent of potential white voters and by enfranchising more than 700,000 freed slaves. Black voters outnumbered whites by 100,000 overall and held voting majorities in five states.

This new electorate provided a base for the Republican party, which had never existed in the South. To scornful Democrats, the Republicans comprised three types of scoundrels: northern **"carpetbaggers"** who had come south for wealth and power; southern **scalawags,** poor and ignorant, who sought to profit by supporting Republican rule; and hordes of uneducated freedmen, who were easily manipulated. In

"carpetbagger" Northerner who moved south after Civil War, supported Republicans and Reconstruction

scalawag Southerner who supported Reconstruction

fact, the hastily assembled Republican party, crossing racial and class lines, constituted a loose coalition of diverse factions with often-contradictory goals.

To northerners who moved south after the war, the former Confederacy was an undeveloped region, ripe with possibilities. The carpetbaggers included many former Union soldiers who hoped to buy land, open factories, build railroads, or simply enjoy the warmer climate. Holding almost one in three state offices, they wielded disproportionate political power.

A handful of scalawags were old Whigs, but most were small farmers from the mountain regions of North Carolina, Georgia, Alabama, and Arkansas. Former Unionists who had owned no slaves and who felt no loyalty to the old plantation elite, they wanted to improve their economic position and lacked commitment to black rights or suffrage. Most came from regions with small black populations and cared little whether blacks voted or not. Scalawags held the most political offices during Reconstruction, but they proved the least stable element of the southern Republican coalition; eventually, many drifted back to the Democratic fold.

Freedmen, the backbone of southern Republicanism, provided eight out of ten Republican votes. They sought land, education, civil rights, and political equality, and remained loyal Republicans. "We know our friends," an elderly freedman said. Although Reconstruction governments depended on African-American votes, freedmen held at most one in five political offices and constituted a legislative majority only in South Carolina, whose population was more than 60 percent black. No African-Americans won the office of governor, and only two served in the U.S. Senate—the same number as served during the twentieth century. A mere 6 percent of southern members of the House were African-American, and almost 50 percent came from South Carolina.

Black officeholders on the state level formed a political elite. They often differed from black voters in background, education, wealth, and complexion. Many were literate blacks who had been free before the Civil War. In the South Carolina legislature, for example, most black members came from large towns and cities; many had spent time in the North; and some were well-off property owners or even former slave owners themselves. Color differences were evident as well; 43 percent of South Carolina's black legislators were of mixed race, compared to just 7 percent of the state's black population.

Black officials and black voters often had different priorities. Most freedmen cared mainly about their economic future, especially about acquiring land, while black officeholders cared most about attaining equal rights. Still, both groups shared high expectations and prized enfranchisement. "We'd walk fifteen miles in wartime to find out about the battle," a Georgia freedman declared. "We can walk fifteen miles and more to find how to vote."

Republican Rule   Large numbers of African-Americans participated in government for the first time in the state constitutional conventions of 1867–1868. The South Carolina convention had an African-American majority, and in Louisiana half the delegates were freedmen. In general, these conventions instituted democratic changes, such as universal manhood suffrage and public-school systems, almost nonexistent in the antebellum South, but they failed to provide either integrated schools or land reform.

When proposals for land confiscation and redistribution arose in the state conventions, they fell to defeat, as they had in Congress. Southern Republicans hoping to attract northern investment hesitated to threaten property rights or to adopt land-reform measures that northern Republicans had rejected. South Carolina did set up a commission to buy land and make it available to freedmen, and several states changed their tax structures to force uncultivated land onto the market, but in no case was ex-Confederate land confiscated.

Once civil power shifted to the new state governments, Republican administrations began ambitious public-works programs. They built roads and bridges, promoted railroad development, and funded institutions to care for orphans, the insane, and the disabled. Republican regimes also expanded state government and formed state militias in which African-Americans often were heavily represented. These reforms cost millions, and state debts and taxes skyrocketed. During the 1860s, taxes rose 400 percent. Although northern tax rates still exceeded southern tax rates, southerners, particularly landowners, resented the new levies.

Opponents of Reconstruction viewed Republican rule as wasteful and corrupt, the "most stupendous system of organized robbery in history." Indeed, corruption did permeate some state governments, as in Louisiana and South Carolina. The main profiteers were government officials who accepted bribes and railroad promoters who doled them out. But neither group was exclusively Republican. In fact, corruption increasingly characterized government *nationally* in these years and was both more flagrant and more lucrative in the North.

Counterattacks

For ex-Confederates, African-American enfranchisement and the "horror of Negro domination" created nightmares. As soon as congressional Reconstruction began, it fell under attack. Democratic newspapers assailed delegates to the North Carolina constitutional convention as an "Ethiopian minstrelsy . . . baboons, monkeys, mules . . . and other jackasses."

Primary Source:
Mr. Solid South

But Democrats delayed any political mobilization until the readmission of the southern states was completed. Then they swung into action, often calling themselves Conservatives to attract former Whigs. At first, they pursued African-American votes, but when that initiative failed, they switched tactics. In every southern state the Democrats contested elections, backed dissident Republican factions, elected some Democratic legislators, and lured scalawags away from the Republican party.

Vigilante efforts to reduce black votes bolstered Democratic campaigns to win white ones. Antagonism toward free blacks, long present in southern life, grew increasingly violent. As early as 1865, Freedmen's Bureau agents itemized a variety of outrages against blacks, including shooting, murder, rape, arson, roasting, and "severe and inhuman beating." White vigilante groups sprang up in all parts of the former Confederacy, but one organization became dominant. In spring 1866, six young Confederate war veterans in Tennessee formed a social club, the **Ku Klux Klan,** distinguished by elaborate rituals, hooded costumes, and secret passwords. New Klan dens spread rapidly. By the election of 1868, when African-American suffrage

Ku Klux Klan Organization that used terrorism to prevent freedmen from voting and to reestablish white supremacy had become a reality, the Klan had become a terrorist movement directed against potential African-American voters.

The Klan sought to suppress black voting, reestablish white supremacy, and topple the Reconstruction governments. It targeted Union League officers, Freedmen's Bureau officials, white Republicans, black militia units, economically successful blacks, and African-American voters. Concentrated in areas where white and black populations were nearly even and racial tensions greatest, Klan dens adapted their tactics to local conditions. In Mississippi, the Klan targeted black schools; in Alabama it concentrated on Republican office holders. In Arkansas terror reigned in 1868, while it peaked in Georgia and Florida in 1870. Some Democrats denounced Klan members as "cutthroats and riff-raff," but some prominent Confederate leaders, including General Nathan Bedford Forrest, who had commanded Confederate troops at the Fort Pillow massacre, (see p. 340) were active Klansmen. Vigilantism united southern whites of different social classes and drew on the energy of many Confederate veterans.

Republican legislatures tried to outlaw vigilantism, but when state militias could not enforce the laws, state officials turned to the federal government for help. In response, between May 1870 and February 1871 Congress passed three **Enforcement Acts,** each progressively more stringent. The First Enforcement Act protected African-American voters. The Second Enforcement Act provided for federal supervision of southern elections, and the Third Enforcement Act (also known as the Ku Klux Klan Act) authorized the use of federal troops and the suspension of habeas corpus (HAY-bee-us KORP-us), the requirement that cause for detaining a prisoner be shown in court. Although thousands were arrested under the Enforcement Acts, most terrorists escaped conviction.

By 1872 the federal government had effectively suppressed the Klan, but vigilantism had served its purpose. A large military presence in the South could have protected black rights, but instead federal troop levels fell steadily. Congress allowed the Freedmen's Bureau to die in 1869, and the Enforcement Acts became dead letters.

Klan Member in Disguise
The menacing disguise characterized the Ku Klux Klan's campaign of intimidation during Reconstruction. The Klan strove to end Republican rule, restore white supremacy, and obliterate, in a southern editor's words, "the preposterous and wicked dogma of negro equality."

Enforcement Acts Series of laws to protect African-American voters; banned the Klan and similar groups

CHECKING IN

- The Republican party, with a large bloc of freedmen, temporarily dominated the South.

- Reconstruction governments instituted such reforms as public-school systems.

- To many southerners, such reforms seemed a costly waste of money, aggravated by government corruption.

- The Ku Klux Klan and other groups used terrorism against freedmen and their white supporters in an effort to prevent black voting and restore white supremacy.

- The federal government passed laws against such activities but left too few troops in place to protect freedmen.

THE IMPACT OF EMANCIPATION

In what ways did newly freed slaves reshape their lives after emancipation?

"The master he says we are all free," a South Carolina slave declared in 1865. "But it don't mean we is white. And it don't mean we is equal." Yet despite the daunting handicaps they faced—illiteracy, lack of property, meager skills—most former slaves found the exhilaration of freedom overwhelming. Emancipation had given them the right to their own labor and a sense of autonomy, and during Reconstruction they asserted their independence by casting off white control and shedding the vestiges of slavery.

Confronting Freedom

For the ex-slaves, mobility was often liberty's first fruit. Some left the slave quarters; others fled the plantation completely. Emancipation stirred waves of migration within the former Confederacy. Some slaves headed to the Deep South, where desperate planters would pay higher wages for labor, but more moved to towns and cities. Urban African-American populations doubled and tripled after emancipation. The desire to find lost family members drove some migrations. Parents sought children who had been sold; husbands and wives who had been separated reunited; and families reclaimed children who were being raised in masters' homes. The Freedmen's Bureau helped former slaves to get information about missing relatives and to travel to find them, and bureau agents also tried to resolve entanglements over the multiple alliances of spouses who had been separated under slavery.

Once reunited, freed blacks quickly legalized unions formed under slavery, sometimes in mass ceremonies of up to seventy couples. Legal marriage had a tangible impact on family life. In 1870 eight out of ten African-American families in the cotton-producing South were two-parent families, about the same proportion as white families. Men asserted themselves as household heads, and their wives often withdrew from the work force to care for homes and families. "When I married my wife, I married her to wait on me and she has got all she can do right here for me and the children," a Tennessee freedman explained.

Severe labor shortages followed immediately after the war because women had made up half of all field workers. However, by Reconstruction's end, many African-American women had rejoined the work force out of economic necessity, either in the fields or as cooks, laundresses, and domestic servants. (White women often sought employment as well, for the war had incapacitated many white breadwinners, reduced the supply of future husbands, and left families destitute.) Former slaves continued to view stable, independent domestic life, especially the right to rear their own children, as a major blessing of freedom.

African-American Institutions

The freed blacks' desire for independence also led to the growth of African-American churches. The African Methodist Episcopal Church, founded by Philadelphia blacks in the 1790s, gained thousands of new southern members. Negro Baptist churches, their roots often in plantation "praise meetings" organized by slaves, sprouted everywhere.

The Freedmen's School
Supported by the Freedmen's Bureau, northern freedmen's aid societies, and African-American denominations, freedmen's schools reached about 12 percent of school-age African-American children in the South by 1870. Here a northern teacher poses with her students at a school in rural North Carolina.

The influence of African-American churches extended far beyond religion. They provided relief, raised funds for schools, and supported Republican policies. African-American ministers assumed leading political roles until Reconstruction's end and then remained the main pillars of authority within African-American communities.

Schools, too, played a crucial role for freedmen as the ex-slaves sought literacy for themselves and above all for their children. At emancipation, African-Americans organized their own schools, which the Freedmen's Bureau soon supervised. Northern philanthropic organizations paid the wages of instructors, half of whom were women. In 1869 the bureau reported more than four thousand African-American schools in the former Confederacy. Within three more years each southern state had a public-school system, at least in principle, generally with separate schools for blacks and whites. The Freedmen's Bureau and others also helped to establish Howard, Atlanta, and Fisk Universities in 1866–1867 and Hampton Institute in 1868. Nonetheless, African-American education remained limited. Few rural blacks could reach the schools, and those who tried were sometimes the targets of vigilante attacks. Thus, by the end of Reconstruction, more than 80 percent of the African-American population remained illiterate, although literacy was rising among children.

Not only school segregation but also other forms of racial separation were taken for granted. Whether by law or by custom, segregation continued on streetcars and trains as well as in churches, theaters, and restaurants. In 1875 Congress passed the Civil Rights Act, banning segregation except in schools, but in the **1883** *Civil Rights Cases,* the Supreme Court threw the law out. The Fourteenth Amendment did not prohibit discrimination by individuals, the Court ruled, only that perpetrated by the state.

1883 *Civil Rights Cases*
Decisions in which the Supreme Court threw out major laws designed to protect freedmen

White southerners adamantly rejected the prospect of racial integration, which they insisted would lead to racial amalgamation. "If we have social equality, we shall have intermarriage," one white southerner contended, "and if we have intermarriage, we shall degenerate." Urban blacks occasionally protested segregation, but most freed blacks were less interested in "social equality" than in African-American liberty and community. Moreover, the new black elite—teachers, ministers, and politicians—served African-American constituencies and thus had a vested interest in separate black institutions. In addition, rural blacks had little desire to mix with whites; rather, they sought freedom from white control. Above all, they wanted to secure personal independence by acquiring land.

Land, Labor, and Sharecropping

"The sole ambition of the freedman," a New Englander wrote from South Carolina in 1865, "appears to be to become the owner of a little piece of land, there to erect a humble home, and to dwell in peace and security, at his own free will and pleasure." Indeed, to free blacks everywhere, "forty acres and a mule" (a phrase that originated during the war as General William T. Sherman set aside land on the South Carolina sea islands for black settlement) promised emancipation from plantation labor, white domination, and cotton, the "slave crop."

But the freedmen's visions of landownership failed to materialize, for large-scale land reform never occurred. A few slaves did obtain land, with the help of the Freedmen's Bureau or sometimes by pooling resources. The federal government also sought to provide former slaves with land; in 1866 Congress passed the Southern Homestead Act, which set aside 44 million acres of public land in five southern states for freedmen and poor whites. But the soil was poor, and few former slaves had the resources to survive until their first harvest. About four thousand blacks settled on homesteads under the law, but most were unable to establish farms—and poor whites fared little better. By the end of Reconstruction, only a small minority of former slaves in each state owned working farms. In Georgia in 1876, for example, blacks controlled a mere 1.3 percent of total acreage. Without large-scale land reform, barriers to African-American landownership remained overwhelming.

Three obstacles impeded African-American landownership. Freedmen lacked capital to buy land or tools. Furthermore, white southerners generally opposed selling land to blacks. Most important, planters sought to preserve a cheap labor force and forged laws to ensure that black labor would remain available on the plantations.

The black codes written during presidential Reconstruction were designed to preserve a captive labor force. Under labor contracts in effect in 1865–1866, freedmen received wages, housing, food, and clothing in exchange for field work. But cash was scarce, and wages often became a small share of the crop, typically one-eighth or less, to be divided among the entire work force. Freedmen's Bureau agents encouraged African-Americans to sign the contracts, seeing wage labor as a step toward economic independence. "You must begin at the bottom of the ladder and climb up," the head of the Freedman's Bureau told Louisiana freedmen in 1865.

Problems arose immediately. Freedmen disliked the new wage system, especially the use of gang labor, which resembled the work pattern under slavery. Moreover, postwar planters had to compete for labor even as many scorned African-American workers as lazy or inefficient. One landowner estimated that workers accomplished only "two-fifths of what they did under the old system." As productivity fell, so did land values. Plummeting cotton prices and poor harvests in 1866 and 1867 combined with these other factors to create an impasse: landowners lacked labor, and freedmen lacked land.

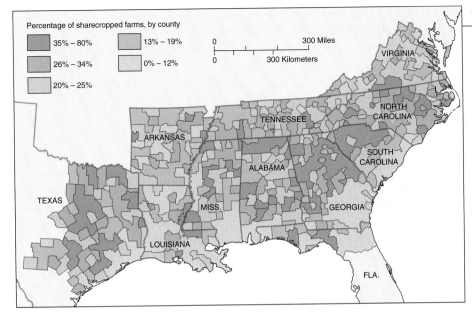

Percentage of sharecropped farms, by county

- 35% – 80%
- 26% – 34%
- 20% – 25%
- 13% – 19%
- 0% – 12%

Map 16.2 Southern Sharecropping, 1880

The depressed economy of the late 1870s caused poverty and debt, increased tenancy among white farmers, and forced many renters, black and white, into sharecropping. By 1880 the sharecropping system pervaded most southern counties, with highest concentrations in the Cotton Belt from South Carolina to eastern Texas.

Source: U.S. Census Office, Tenth Census, 1880, Report of the Production of Agriculture (Washington, D.C.: Government Printing Office, 1883), Table 5.

Southerners began experimenting with new labor schemes, including the division of plantations into small tenancies. **Sharecropping** was the most widespread arrangement. Under this system, landowners subdivided large plantations into farms of thirty to fifty acres and rented them to freedmen under annual leases for a share of the crop, usually one-half. Freedmen liked this decentralized system, which let them use the labor of family members and represented a step toward independence. Planters, meanwhile, retained control of their land. The most productive land thus remained in the hands of a small group of owners; in effect sharecropping helped to preserve the planter elite.

Although the wage system continued on sugar and rice plantations, by 1870 the plantation tradition had yielded to sharecropping in the cotton South. A severe depression in 1873 drove many blacks and independent white farmers into sharecropping. By 1880, sharecroppers, white and black, farmed 80 percent of the land in cotton-producing states. In fact, white sharecroppers outnumbered black, although a higher proportion of southern blacks, almost 75 percent, were involved in the system. Changes in marketing and finance, meanwhile, made the sharecroppers' lot increasingly precarious.

sharecropping System in which tenant farmer paid a share of the crop as rent to the landowner

Primary Source: Barrow Plantation

Toward a Crop-Lien Economy

The postwar South's hundreds of thousands of tenant farmers and sharecroppers needed a local credit system to see them through the growing season until they could harvest their crops. Rural merchants advanced supplies to tenants and sharecroppers on credit and sold their crops to wholesalers. Because renters had no property to serve as collateral, merchants secured their loans with a lien (leen), or claim, on each farmer's next crop. Exorbitant interest rates, 50 percent or more, quickly forced many tenants and sharecroppers into a cycle of indebtedness. The sharecropper might well owe part of his crop to the landowner and another part (the rest of his

crop lien Borrowing against future crops; often created a cycle of debt that tied tenants to sharecropping

crop, or more) to the merchant. Illiterate tenants who could not keep track of their financial arrangements were at the mercy of sometimes-unscrupulous merchants. Once a tenant's real or alleged debts exceeded the value of his crop, he was tied to the land, to cotton, and to sharecropping.

By the end of Reconstruction, sharecropping and **crop liens** had bound the South to easily marketable cash crops, such as cotton, and prevented crop diversification. Soil depletion, land erosion, and outmoded equipment stranded capital-short planters in a cycle of poverty. Trapped in perpetual debt, tenant farmers became the chief victims of the new agricultural order. Cotton remained the only survival route open to poor farmers, regardless of race, but low income from cotton locked them into sharecropping and crop liens. African-American tenants, for whom neither landownership nor economic independence ever materialized, saw their political rights dwindle as rapidly as their hopes for economic freedom. When Reconstruction ended, neither state governments nor the national government offered them protection, for northern politicians were preoccupied with their own problems.

CHECKING IN

- Tens of thousands of freedmen sought missing family members, and former slaves hastened to legalize the marriages they had made under slavery.
- Blacks formed their own communities, churches, and schools as segregation became firmly established in the South.
- Few former slaves achieved land ownership, and sharecropping became the dominant form of agricultural labor for blacks and many poor whites.
- Without economic status, blacks quickly saw their political rights erode.

NEW CONCERNS IN THE NORTH, 1868–1876

Why did northern concern about Reconstruction begin to wane?

The nomination of Ulysses S. Grant for president in 1868 launched a chaotic era in national politics. His eight years in office featured political scandals, a party revolt, a massive depression, and a steady retreat from Reconstruction. By the mid-1870s northern voters cared more about economics, unemployment, labor unrest, and currency problems than about the "southern question." Eager to end sectional conflict, Republicans turned their backs on the freedmen.

Grantism

Republicans had good reason to nominate General Grant. A war hero, he was endorsed by veterans, admired throughout the North, and unscathed by the bitter feuds of Reconstruction politics. To oppose Grant, the Democrats nominated Horatio Seymour, arch-critic of the Lincoln administration and an opponent of Reconstruction and greenbacks. Grant ran on his personal popularity more than on issues. Although he carried all but eight states, the popular vote was close; newly enfranchised freedmen provided Grant's margin in the South.

Grant's presidential leadership proved as weak as his war leadership had been strong, although he lacked Johnson's instinct for disaster. He had little political skill; his cabinet appointments were at best mediocre; and a string of scandals plagued his administration. In 1869 financier Jay Gould and his partner Jim Fisk attempted to corner the gold market with the help of Grant's brother-in-law. When gold prices tumbled, investors were ruined, and Grant's reputation was tarnished. Near the end of Grant's first term, his vice president, Schuyler Colfax, got caught up in the **Crédit Mobilier** (CRAY-dee MOH-bill-yay) scandal, an elaborate scheme to

Crédit Mobilier Scheme to skim profits from the Union Pacific Railroad; one of several scandals to engulf Grant administration skim off the profits of the Union Pacific Railroad. Then in 1875 Grant's personal secretary, Orville Babcock, was found guilty of accepting bribes from the "whiskey ring," distillers who preferred bribery to payment of federal taxes. And in 1876 voters learned that Grant's secretary of war, William E. Belknap, had taken bribes to sell lucrative Indian trading posts in Oklahoma.

Although Grant was not personally involved in the scandals, he did little to restrain such activities, and "Grantism" came to stand for fraud, bribery, and corruption in office. Such evils, however, spread far beyond Washington. The New York City press in 1872 revealed that Democrat boss William M. Tweed led a ring that had looted the city treasury and collected some $200 million in kickbacks and bribes. When Mark Twain and Charles Dudley Warner published their satiric novel *The Gilded Age* in 1873, readers recognized the book's speculators, self-promoters, and opportunists as familiar figures in public life. (The term "Gilded Age" has subsequently been used to refer to the decades from the 1870s to the 1890s.)

Grant did enjoy some foreign policy successes. In 1872 his administration engineered the settlement of the *Alabama* claims with England: an international tribunal ordered Britain to pay $15.5 million to the United States in compensation for damage inflicted by Confederate-owned but British-built raiders. But the administration went astray when it tried to add nonadjacent territory to the Union. In 1867 the Johnson administration had purchased Alaska from Russia at the bargain price of $7.2 million. The purchase had rekindled expansionists' hope, and in 1870 Grant decided to annex the Caribbean island nation of Santo Domingo (the modern Dominican Republic). The president believed that annexation would promote Caribbean trade and provide a haven for persecuted southern blacks. Despite speculators' hopes for windfall profits, the Senate rejected the annexation treaty and further diminished Grant's reputation.

As the election of 1872 approached, dissident Republicans feared that "Grantism" would ruin the party. Former Radicals and other Republicans left out of Grant's "Great Barbecue" formed their own party, the Liberal Republicans.

Boss Tweed

Thomas Nast's cartoons in *Harper's Weekly* helped topple New York Democratic boss William M. Tweed, who, with his associates, embodied corruption on a large scale. The Tweed Ring had granted lucrative franchises to companies they controlled, padded construction bills, practiced graft and extortion, and exploited every opportunity to plunder the city's funds.

The Liberals' Revolt

The Liberal Republican revolt split the party and undermined Reconstruction. Liberals demanded civil service reform to bring the "best men" into government. In the South they demanded an end to "bayonet rule" and argued that African-Americans, now enfranchised, could fend for themselves. Corruption in government posed a greater threat than Confederate resurgence, the Liberals claimed, and they demanded that the "best men" in the South, ex-Confederates barred from holding office, be returned to government.

New York Tribune editor Horace Greeley, inconsistently supporting both a stringent Reconstruction policy and leniency toward the ex-Confederates, received the Liberal Republican nomination, and the Democrats endorsed Greeley as well. Republican reformers found themselves allied with the party that they had recently castigated as a "sewer" of treasonable sentiments.

Despite Greeley's arduous campaigning (he literally worked himself to death on the campaign trail and died a few weeks after the election), Grant carried 56 percent of the popular vote and won the electoral vote handily. But to nullify the Liberals' issues, "regular" Republicans had passed an amnesty act allowing all but a few hundred ex-Confederates to resume office. And during Grant's second term, Republicans' desire to discard the "southern question" grew as a depression gripped the nation.

The Panic of 1873

The postwar years brought accelerated industrialization, rapid economic expansion, and frantic speculation as investors rushed to take advantage of seemingly unlimited opportunities. Railroads led the speculative boom. The transcontinental line reached completion in 1869 (see Chapter 17), and by 1873 almost four hundred railroads crisscrossed the Northeast. But in addition to transforming the northern economy, the railroad boom led entrepreneurs to overspeculate, with drastic results.

In 1869 Philadelphia banker Jay Cooke took over a new transcontinental line, the Northern Pacific. For four years Northern Pacific securities sold briskly, but in 1873 construction costs outran bond sales. In September, Cooke, his bank vaults stuffed with unsalable bonds, defaulted on his obligations. His bank, the largest in the nation, shut down. Then the stock market collapsed, and smaller banks and other firms followed; the Panic of 1873 plunged the nation into a devastating five-year depression. Thousands of businesses went bankrupt. By 1878 unemployment had risen to more than 3 million. Labor protests mounted, and industrial violence spread (see Chapter 18). The depression of the 1870s demonstrated ruthlessly that conflicts born of industrialization had replaced sectional divisions.

The depression also fed a dispute over currency that had begun in 1865. During the Civil War, Americans had used greenbacks, a paper currency not backed by a specific weight in gold. "Sound-money" supporters demanded the withdrawal of greenbacks from circulation as a means of stabilizing the currency. Their opponents, "easy-money" advocates, such as farmers and manufacturers dependent on easy credit, wanted to expand the currency by issuing additional greenbacks. The deepening depression created even more demand for easy money, and the issue split both major parties.

Controversy over the type of currency was compounded by the question of how to repay the federal debt. In wartime the Union government had borrowed astronomical sums through the sale of war bonds. Bond holders wanted repayment in "coin," gold or silver, even though many of them had paid for the bonds in greenbacks. The Public Credit Act of 1869 promised payment in coin.

Senator John Sherman, the author of the Public Credit Act, put together a series of compromises to satisfy both "sound-money" and "easy-money" advocates. Sherman's measures, exchanging Civil War bonds for new ones payable over a longer period of time and defining "coin" as gold only, preserved the public credit, the currency, and Republican unity. His Specie Resumption Act of 1875 promised to put the nation back on the gold standard by 1879.

But Sherman's measures, however ingenious, did not placate the Democrats, who gained control of the House in 1875. Many Democrats, and a few Republicans, were "free-silver" advocates who wanted the silver dollar restored in order to expand the currency and end the depression. The Bland-Allison Act of 1878 partially restored silver coinage by requiring the government to buy and coin several million dollars' worth of silver each month. In 1876 other expansionists formed the Greenback party to keep the paper money in circulation for the sake of debtors, but they enjoyed little success. As the depression receded, the clamor for "easy money" subsided, only to return in the 1890s (see Chapter 20). Although never settled, the controversial "money question" diverted attention away from Reconstruction and thus contributed to its demise.

Reconstruction and the Constitution

During the 1870s the Supreme Court also played a role in weakening northern support for Reconstruction as new constitutional questions surfaced. Would the Court support laws to protect freedmen's rights? The decision in *Ex Parte Milligan* (1866) had suggested not. In *Milligan,* the Court had ruled that a military commission could not try civilians in areas where civilian courts were functioning, thus dooming the special military courts that had been established to enforce the Supplementary Freedmen's Bureau Act. Would the Court sabotage the congressional Reconstruction plan? In 1869, in *Texas* v. *White,* the Court had let Reconstruction stand, ruling that Congress had the power to ensure each state a republican form of government.

However, during the 1870s the Supreme Court backed away from Reconstruction. In the *Slaughterhouse* decision of 1873, the Court ruled that the Fourteenth Amendment protected the rights of *national* citizenship, such as the right to interstate travel, but that the federal government did not have to safeguard such rights against violation by the *states.* The *Slaughterhouse* decision effectively gutted the Fourteenth Amendment, which was intended to secure freedmen's rights against state encroachment.

The Supreme Court retreated even further from Reconstruction in two cases involving the Enforcement Act of 1870. In *United States* v. *Reese* (1876), the Court threw out the indictment of Kentucky officials who had barred African-Americans from voting. Another decision that same year, *United States* v. *Cruikshank,* again weakened the Fourteenth Amendment. In the *Cruikshank* case, the Court ruled that the amendment barred *states,* but not *individuals,* from encroaching on individual rights.

Continuing this retreat from Reconstruction, the Supreme Court in 1883 invalidated both the Civil Rights Act of 1875 and the Ku Klux Klan Act of 1871. Taken cumulatively, these decisions dismantled Republican Reconstruction and confirmed rising northern sentiment that Reconstruction's egalitarian goals were unenforceable.

Republicans in Retreat

The Republicans gradually disengaged from Reconstruction, beginning with the election of Grant as president in 1868. Grant, like most Americans, hesitated to approve the use of federal authority in state or local affairs.

CHECKING IN

- Grant's administration was riddled by corruption, mirroring politics in much of the country.
- The Panic of 1873 devastated the northern economy, plunging the nation into a deep depression.
- Through the 1870s the Supreme Court struck down basic legislation protecting freedmen's rights.
- Most Radical Republican leaders had died by the early 1870s, and commercial and industrial interests began to dominate the Republican party.

MAJOR RECONSTRUCTION LEGISLATION

LAW AND DATE OF CONGRESSIONAL PASSAGE	PROVISIONS	PURPOSE
Civil Rights Act of 1866 (April 1866)*	Declared blacks citizens and guaranteed them equal protection of the laws.	To invalidate the black codes.
Supplementary Freedmen's Bureau Act (July 1866)*	Extended the life of the Freedmen's Aid Bureau and expanded its powers.	To invalidate the black codes.
Reconstruction Act of 1867 (March 1867)*	Invalidated state governments formed under Lincoln and Johnson. Divided the former Confederacy into five military districts. Set forth requirements for readmission of ex-Confederate states to the Union.	To replace presidential Reconstruction with a more stringent plan.
Supplementary Reconstruction Acts		To enforce the First Reconstruction Act.
Second Reconstruction Act (March 1867)*	Required military commanders to initiate voter enrollment.	
Third Reconstruction Act (July 1867)*	Expanded military commanders' powers.	
Fourth Reconstruction Act (March 1868)*	Provided that a majority of voters, however few, could put a new state constitution into force.	
Army Appropriations Act (March 1867)*	Declared in a rider that only the general of the army could issue military orders.	To prevent President Johnson from obstructing Reconstruction.
Tenure of Office Act (March 1867)*	Prohibited the president from removing any federal official without the Senate's consent.	To prevent President Johnson from obstructing Reconstruction.
Omnibus Act (June 1868)[†]	Readmitted seven ex-Confederate states to the Union.	To restore the Union, under the term of the First Reconstruction Act.
Enforcement Act of 1870 (May 1870)[‡]	Provided for the protection of black voters.	To enforce the Fifteenth Amendment.
Second Enforcement Act (February 1871)	Provided for federal supervision of southern elections.	To enforce the Fifteenth Amendment.
Third Enforcement Act (Ku Klux Klan Act) (April 1871)	Strengthened sanctions against those who impeded black suffrage.	To combat the Ku Klux Klan and enforce the Fourteenth Amendment.
Amnesty Act (May 1872)	Restored the franchise to almost all ex-Confederates.	Effort by Grant Republicans to deprive Liberal Republicans of a campaign issue.
Civil Rights Act of 1875 (March 1875)[§]	Outlawed racial segregation in transportation and public accommodations and prevented exclusion of blacks from jury service.	To honor the late senator Charles Sumner.

*Passed over Johnson's veto.
[†]Georgia was soon returned to military rule. The last four states were readmitted in 1870.
[‡]Sections of the law declared unconstitutional in 1876.
[§]Invalidated by the Supreme Court in 1883.

In the 1870s Republican idealism waned. Instead, commercial and industrial interests dominated both the Liberal and "regular" wings of the party, and few wanted any further sectional strife. By 1875, moreover, the Radical Republicans had virtually disappeared. The Radical leaders Chase, Stevens, and Sumner had died, and others had grown tired of "waving the bloody shirt," or defaming Democratic opponents by reviving wartime animosity. It seemed pointless to prop up southern Republican regimes that even President Grant found corrupt. Finally, Republicans generally agreed with southern Democrats that African-Americans were inferior and that to insist on black equality would quash any hope of reunion between North and South. The Republican retreat set the stage for Reconstruction's end in 1877.

RECONSTRUCTION ABANDONED, 1876–1877

What events led the North to abandon Reconstruction?

"We are in a very hot political contest just now," a Mississippi planter wrote his daughter in 1875, "with a good prospect of turning out the carpetbag thieves by whom we have been robbed for the past six to ten years." Indeed, an angry white majority had led a Democratic resurgence throughout the South in the 1870s, and by 1876 Republican rule survived in only three southern states. Democratic victories in state elections that year and political bargaining in Washington in 1877 ended what little remained of Reconstruction.

THE DURATION OF REPUBLICAN RULE IN THE EX-CONFEDERATE STATES

FORMER CONFEDERATE STATES	READMISSION TO THE UNION UNDER CONGRESSIONAL RECONSTRUCTION	DEMOCRATS (CONSERVATIVES) GAIN CONTROL	DURATION OF REPUBLICAN RULE
Alabama	June 25, 1868	November 14, 1874	6½ years
Arkansas	June 22, 1868	November 10, 1874	6½ years
Florida	June 25, 1868	January 2, 1877	8½ years
Georgia	July 15, 1870	November 1, 1871	1 year
Louisiana	June 25, 1868	January 2, 1877	8½ years
Mississippi	February 23, 1870	November 3, 1875	5½ years
North Carolina	June 25, 1868	November 3, 1870	2 years
South Carolina	June 25, 1868	November 12, 1876	8 years
Tennessee	July 24, 1866*	October 4, 1869	3 years
Texas	March 30, 1870	January 14, 1873	3 years
Virginia	January 26, 1870	October 5, 1869[†]	0 years

Source: Reprinted by permission from John Hope Franklin, *Reconstruction After the Civil War* (Chicago: University of Chicago Press, 1962), 231.
*Admitted before the start of Congressional Reconstruction.
[†]Democrats gained control before readmission.

"Redeeming" the South

After 1872 the Republican collapse in the South accelerated. Congressional amnesty enabled virtually all ex-Confederate officials to regain office, divided Republicans lost their grip on the southern electorate, and attrition diminished Republican ranks. Carpetbaggers returned north or joined the Democrats, and scalawags deserted the Republicans in large numbers. Tired of northern interference and seeing the possibility of "home rule," scalawags decided that staying Republican meant going down with a sinking ship. Unable to win new white votes or retain the old ones, the fragile Republican coalition crumbled.

Meanwhile, the Democrats mobilized formerly apathetic white voters. Although still faction-ridden—businessmen who dreamed of an industrialized "New South" had little in common with the old planter elite, the so-called **Bourbons**—the Democrats shared one goal: kicking the Republicans out. The Democrats' tactics varied. In several Deep South states Democrats resorted to violence. In Vicksburg in 1874 rampaging whites slaughtered about three hundred blacks and terrorized thousands of potential voters. Vigilante groups in several southern states disrupted Republican meetings and threatened blacks who had registered to vote. In 1875, the "Mississippi plan" took effect; local Democratic clubs armed their members who broke up Republican meetings, patrolled registration locations, and marched through black areas. "The Republicans are paralyzed through fear and will not act," the anguished carpetbag governor of Mississippi wrote to his wife. "Why should I fight a hopeless battle?" In 1876 South Carolina's "Rifle Clubs" and "Red Shirts," armed groups that threatened Republicans, continued the terrorist tactics that had worked so well in Mississippi.

Terrorism did not completely squelch black voting, but it did deprive Republicans of enough African-American votes to win state elections. Throughout the South, economic pressures reinforced intimidation; labor contracts included clauses barring attendance at political meetings, and planters threatened to evict sharecroppers who stepped out of line.

Redemption, the word that Democrats used to describe their return to power, introduced sweeping changes. States rewrote constitutions, cut expenses, lowered taxes, eliminated social programs, limited the rights of tenants and sharecroppers, and shaped laws to ensure a stable African-American labor force. Legislatures restored vagrancy laws, strengthened crop-lien statutes, and remade criminal law. Local ordinances in heavily black counties often restricted hunting, fishing, gun carrying, and even dog ownership, drastically curtailing the ability of freedmen to live off the land. New criminal codes directed at African-Americans imposed severe penalties for what formerly were misdemeanors: stealing livestock or wrongly taking part of a crop became grand larceny, punishable by five years at hard labor. By Reconstruction's end, a large African-American convict work force had been leased out to private contractors. Freedmen whose hopes had been raised by Republicans saw their prospects destroyed by the redeemers. The new laws, Tennessee blacks stated at an 1875 convention, imposed "a condition of servitude scarcely less degrading than that endured before the late civil war." In the late 1870s an increasingly oppressive political climate gave rise to an "exodus" movement among African-Americans. Nearly fifteen thousand African-American "exodusters" from the Deep South moved to Kansas and set up homesteads. But scarce resources left most of the freed slaves stranded. Not until the twentieth century would the mass migration of southern blacks to the Midwest and North gain momentum.

Bourbons Southern elite who returned to power as Reconstruction wound down

redemption Bourbon term for regaining control of South

The Election of 1876

By autumn 1876, with redemption almost complete, both parties moved to discard the animosity left by the war and Reconstruction. The Republicans nominated Rutherford B. Hayes, the governor of Ohio, for president. Popular with all factions and untainted by the Grant scandals, Hayes, a "moderate," favored "home rule" in the South and civil and political rights for all—clearly contradictory goals. The Democrats nominated Governor Samuel J. Tilden of New York, a political reformer known for his assaults on the Tweed Ring that had plundered New York City's treasury. Both candidates were fiscal conservatives, favored sound money, endorsed civil service reform, and decried corruption.

Tilden won the popular vote by a small margin, but the Republicans challenged pro-Tilden electoral votes from South Carolina, Florida, and Louisiana, and the Democrats challenged one electoral vote from Oregon. Southern Republicans managed to throw out enough Democratic ballots in the contested states to proclaim Hayes the winner.

The nation now faced an unprecedented dilemma. Each party claimed victory, and each accused the other of fraud. In fact, both sets of southern votes were fraudulent: Republicans had discarded legitimate Democratic ballots, and Democrats had illegally prevented freedmen from voting. In January 1877, Congress created a special electoral commission to resolve the conflict. The commission originally consisted of seven Republicans, seven Democrats, and one independent, but when the independent resigned, a Republican replaced him. The commission gave the Republican Hayes the election by an 8-to-7 vote.

Congress now had to certify the new electoral vote. But the Democrats controlled the House, and some planned to forestall approval of the electoral vote. For many southern Democrats, regaining control of their states was far more important than preventing the election of a Republican president—*if* the new Republican administration would leave the South alone. Republican leaders, for their part, were willing to bargain, for Hayes wanted not just victory but also southern approval. Informal negotiations followed, with both parties exchanging promises. Ohio Republicans and southern Democrats agreed that, if Hayes won the election, he would remove federal troops from all southern states. Other negotiations led to the understanding that southerners would receive federal patronage, federal aid to railroads, and federal support for internal improvements. In turn, southerners promised to accept Hayes as president and to treat the freedmen fairly.

Congress thus ratified Hayes's election. Once in office, Hayes fulfilled many of the agreements made by his colleagues. Republican rule toppled in Louisiana, South Carolina, and Florida. But some of the bargains struck in the so-called **Compromise of 1877** fell apart, particularly Democratic promises to treat the freedmen fairly and Hayes's pledges to ensure the freed slaves' rights. "When you turned us loose, you turned us loose to the sky, to the storm, to the whirlwind, and worst of all . . . to the wrath of our infuriated masters," Frederick Douglass had charged at the 1876 Republican convention. "The question now is, do you mean to make good to us the promises in your Constitution?" By 1877 the answer was clear: "No."

Compromise of 1877 Deal that gave northern Republicans the presidency and restored southern Democrats to power, ending Reconstruction

CHECKING IN

- The Republican collapse in the South accelerated after 1872.
- Democrats regained control of southern states.
- "Redeemers" ended reforms and limited or eliminated black rights.
- The election of 1876 resulted in challenges to some electoral votes and charges of fraud on both sides.
- The price of Republican victory in the election was the end of Reconstruction and the virtual abandonment of the freedmen.

Chapter Summary

 DOWNLOAD THE MP3 AUDIO FILE OF THE CHAPTER SUMMARY, AND LISTEN TO IT ON THE GO.

On what major issues did Radical Republicans and President Johnson struggle over Reconstruction policy? (page 354)

Radical Republicans saw Johnson as too lenient on Reconstruction and passed a stringent congressional Reconstruction program over his veto. They even attempted to impeach the president for political reasons, but failed. The Fourteenth and Fifteenth Amendments, which Johnson opposed, were major triumphs for the Radicals.

What impact did federal Reconstruction policy have on the former Confederacy and ex-Confederates? (page 362)

Democrats and ex-Confederates were largely excluded from political power in the South, which fell to Republicans and freedmen. The Reconstruction governments passed costly reform measures, most of which were later abandoned or scaled back. Terrorist organizations such as the Ku Klux Klan flourished briefly. They were outlawed by the federal government but had already intimidated freedmen.

In what ways did newly freed slaves reshape their lives after emancipation? (page 366)

Former slaves sought missing family members, legalized marriages made under slavery, and created schools and churches in large numbers. But without land reform most remained poor and ultimately were caught in the pernicious sharecropping system; their rights were soon eroded.

Why did northern concern about Reconstruction begin to wane? (page 370)

Other concerns soon began to preoccupy Republicans. Corruption, epitomized by the Grant administration, permeated the nation. The Panic of 1873 led to a major depression. The Supreme Court threw out most important measures intended to protect freedmen's rights. Finally, with most Radical Republican leaders gone by the early 1870s, commercial and industrial interests began to dominate the Republican party.

What led the North to abandon Reconstruction? (page 375)

Republican control of the South began to collapse in the early 1870s. As Democrats "redeemed" southern states, they curtailed reforms and eliminated black rights. The price of the Republican victory in the disputed presidential election of 1876 was the end of Reconstruction and the return of the South to Democratic control.

KEY TERMS

Radical Republicans *(p. 354)*

"black codes" *(p. 356)*

Freedmen's Bureau *(p. 356)*

Fourteenth Amendment *(p. 357)*

congressional Reconstruction *(p. 359)*

impeachment *(p. 359)*

Fifteenth Amendment *(p. 360)*

"carpetbagger" *(p. 362)*

scalawag *(p. 362)*

Ku Klux Klan *(p. 364)*

Enforcement Acts *(p. 365)*

1883 *Civil Rights Cases (p. 367)*

sharecropping *(p. 369)*

crop lien *(p. 370)*

Crédit Mobilier *(p. 370)*

Bourbons *(p. 376)*

redemption *(p. 376)*

Compromise of 1877 *(p. 377)*

Appendix

DECLARATION OF INDEPENDENCE

IN CONGRESS, JULY 4, 1776

The Unanimous Declaration of the Thirteen United States of America

When, in the course of human events, it becomes necessary for one people to dissolve the political bands which have connected them with another, and to assume, among the powers of the earth, the separate and equal station to which the laws of nature and of nature's God entitle them, a decent respect to the opinions of mankind requires that they should declare the causes which impel them to the separation.

We hold these truths to be self-evident: That all men are created equal; that they are endowed by their Creator with certain unalienable rights; that among these are life, liberty, and the pursuit of happiness; that, to secure these rights, governments are instituted among men, deriving their just powers from the consent of the governed; that whenever any form of government becomes destructive of these ends, it is the right of the people to alter or to abolish it, and to institute new government, laying its foundation on such principles, and organizing its powers in such form, as to them shall seem most likely to effect their safety and happiness. Prudence, indeed, will dictate that governments long established should not be changed for light and transient causes; and accordingly all experience hath shown that mankind are more disposed to suffer, while evils are sufferable, than to right themselves by abolishing the forms to which they are accustomed. But when a long train of abuses and usurpations, pursuing invariably the same object, evinces a design to reduce them under absolute despotism, it is their right, it is their duty, to throw off such government, and to provide new guards for their future security. Such has been the patient sufferance of these colonies; and such is now the necessity which constrains them to alter their former systems of government. The history of the present King of Great Britain is a history of repeated injuries and usurpations, all having in direct object the establishment of an absolute tyranny over these states. To prove this, let facts be submitted to a candid world.

He has refused his assent to laws, the most wholesome and necessary for the public good.

He has forbidden his governors to pass laws of immediate and pressing importance, unless suspended in their operation till his assent should be obtained; and, when so suspended, he has utterly neglected to attend to them.

He has refused to pass other laws for the accommodation of large districts of people, unless those people would relinquish the right of representation in the legislature, a right inestimable to them, and formidable to tyrants only.

He has called together legislative bodies at places unusual, uncomfortable, and distant from the depository of their public records, for the sole purpose of fatiguing them into compliance with his measures.

He has dissolved representative houses repeatedly, for opposing, with manly firmness, his invasions on the rights of the people.

He has refused for a long time, after such dissolutions, to cause others to be elected; whereby the legislative powers, incapable of annihilation, have returned to the people at large for their exercise; the state remaining, in the mean time, exposed to all the dangers of invasions from without and convulsions within.

He has endeavored to prevent the population of these states; for that purpose obstructing the laws of naturalization of foreigners; refusing to pass others to encourage their migration hither, and raising the conditions of new appropriation of lands.

He has obstructed the administration of justice, by refusing his assent to laws for establishing judiciary powers.

He has made judges dependent on his will alone, for the tenure of their offices, and the amount and payment of their salaries.

He has erected a multitude of new offices, and sent hither swarms of officers to harass our people and eat out their substance.

He has kept among us, in times of peace, standing armies, without the consent of our legislatures.

He has affected to render the military independent of, and superior to, the civil power.

He has combined with others to subject us to a jurisdiction foreign to our constitution, and unacknowledged by our laws, giving his assent to their acts of pretended legislation:

For quartering large bodies of armed troops among us;

For protecting them, by a mock trial, from punishment for any murders which they should commit on the inhabitants of these states;

For cutting off our trade with all parts of the world;

For imposing taxes on us without our consent;

For depriving us, in many cases, of the benefits of trial by jury;

For transporting us beyond seas, to be tried for pretended offenses;

For abolishing the free system of English laws in a neighboring province, establishing therein an arbitrary government, and enlarging its boundaries, so as to render it at once an example and fit instrument for introducing the same absolute rule into these colonies;

For taking away our charters, abolishing our most valuable laws, and altering fundamentally the forms of our governments;

For suspending our own legislatures, and declaring themselves invested with power to legislate for us in all cases whatsoever.

He has abdicated government here, by declaring us out of his protection and waging war against us.

He has plundered our seas, ravaged our coasts, burned our towns, and destroyed the lives of our people.

He is at this time transporting large armies of foreign mercenaries to complete the works of death, desolation, and tyranny already begun with circumstances of cruelty and perfidy scarcely paralleled in the most barbarous ages, and totally unworthy of the head of a civilized nation.

He has constrained our fellow-citizens, taken captive on the high seas, to bear arms against their country, to become the executioners of their friends and brethren, or to fall themselves by their hands.

He has excited domestic insurrection among us, and has endeavored to bring on the inhabitants of our frontiers the merciless Indian savages, whose known rule of warfare is an undistinguished destruction of all ages, sexes, and conditions.

In every stage of these oppressions we have petitioned for redress in the most humble terms; our repeated petitions have been answered only by repeated injury. A prince, whose character is thus marked by every act which may define a tyrant, is unfit to be the ruler of a free people.

Nor have we been wanting in our attentions to our British brethren. We have warned them, from time to time, of attempts by their legislature to extend an unwarrantable jurisdiction over us. We have reminded them of the circumstances of our emigration and settlement here. We have appealed to their native justice and magnanimity; and we have conjured them by the ties of our common kindred, to disavow these usurpations, which would inevitably interrupt our connections and correspondence. They, too, have been deaf to the voice of justice and of consanguinity. We must, therefore, acquiesce in the necessity which denounces our separation, and hold them, as we hold the rest of mankind, enemies in war, in peace friends.

We, therefore, the representatives of the United States of America, in General Congress assembled, appealing to the Supreme Judge of the world for the rectitude of our intentions, do, in the name and by the authority of the good people of these colonies, solemnly publish and declare, that these United Colonies are, and of right ought to be, FREE AND INDEPENDENT STATES; that they are absolved from all allegiance to the British crown, and that all political connection between them and the state of Great Britain is, and ought to be, totally dissolved; and that, as free and independent states, they have full power to levy war, conclude peace, contract alliances, establish commerce, and do all other acts and things which independent states may of right do. And for the support of this declaration, with a firm reliance on the protection of Divine Providence, we mutually pledge to each other our lives, our fortunes, and our sacred honor.

JOHN HANCOCK [*President*]
[*and fifty-five others*]

CONSTITUTION OF THE UNITED STATES OF AMERICA

PREAMBLE

We the people of the United States, in order to form a more perfect union, establish justice, insure domestic tranquility, provide for the common defense, promote the general welfare, and secure the blessings of liberty to ourselves and our posterity, do ordain and establish this CONSTITUTION for the United States of America.

ARTICLE I

Section 1. All legislative powers herein granted shall be vested in a Congress of the United States, which shall consist of a Senate and a House of Representatives.

Section 2. The House of Representatives shall be composed of members chosen every second year by the people of the several States, and the electors in each State shall have the qualifications requisite for electors of the most numerous branch of the State Legislature.

No person shall be a Representative who shall not have attained to the age of twenty-five years, and been seven years a citizen of the United States, and who shall not, when elected, be an inhabitant of that State in which he shall be chosen.

Representatives and direct taxes shall be apportioned among the several States which may be included within this Union, according to their respective numbers, *which shall be determined by adding to the whole number of free persons, including those bound to service for a term of years and excluding Indians not taxed, three-fifths of all other persons.* The actual enumeration shall be made within three years after the first meeting of the Congress of the United States, and within every subsequent term of ten years, in such manner as they shall by law direct. The number of Representatives shall not exceed one for every thirty thousand, but each State shall have at least one Representative; *and until such enumeration shall be made, the State of New Hampshire shall be entitled to choose three, Massachusetts eight, Rhode Island and Providence Plantations one, Connecticut five, New York six, New Jersey four, Pennsylvania eight, Delaware one, Maryland six, Virginia ten, North Carolina five, South Carolina five, and Georgia three.*

When vacancies happen in the representation from any State, the Executive authority thereof shall issue writs of election to fill such vacancies.

Note: Passages no longer in effect are printed in italic type.

The House of Representatives shall choose their Speaker and other officers; and shall have the sole power of impeachment.

Section 3. The Senate of the United States shall be composed of two Senators from each State, *chosen by the legislature thereof,* for six years; and each Senator shall have one vote.

Immediately after they shall be assembled in consequence of the first election, they shall be divided as equally as may be into three classes. The seats of the Senators of the first class shall be vacated at the expiration of the second year, of the second class at the expiration of the fourth year, and of the third class at the expiration of the sixth year, so that one-third may be chosen every second year; and if vacancies happen by resignation or otherwise, during the recess of the legislature of any State, the Executive thereof may make temporary appointments until the next meeting of the legislature, which shall then fill such vacancies.

No person shall be a Senator who shall not have attained to the age of thirty years, and been nine years a citizen of the United States, and who shall not, when elected, be an inhabitant of that State for which he shall be chosen.

The Vice President of the United States shall be President of the Senate, but shall have no vote, unless they be equally divided.

The Senate shall choose their other officers, and also a President *pro tempore,* in the absence of the Vice President, or when he shall exercise the office of the President of the United States.

The Senate shall have the sole power to try all impeachments. When sitting for that purpose, they shall be on oath or affirmation. When the President of the United States is tried, the Chief Justice shall preside: and no person shall be convicted without the concurrence of two-thirds of the members present.

Judgment in cases of impeachment shall not extend further than to removal from the office, and disqualification to hold and enjoy any office of honor, trust or profit under the United States; but the party convicted shall nevertheless be liable and subject to indictment, trial, judgment and punishment, according to law.

Section 4.   The times, places and manner of holding elections for Senators and Representatives shall be prescribed in each State by the legislature thereof; but the Congress may at any time by law make or alter such regulations, except as to the places of choosing Senators.

The Congress shall assemble at least once in every year, and such meeting *shall be on the first Monday in December, unless they shall by law appoint a different day.*

Section 5.   Each house shall be the judge of the elections, returns and qualifications of its own members, and a majority of each shall constitute a quorum to do business; but a smaller number may adjourn from day to day, and may be authorized to compel the attendance of absent members, in such manner, and under such penalties, as each house may provide.

Each house may determine the rules of its proceedings, punish its members for disorderly behavior, and with the concurrence of two-thirds, expel a member.

Each house shall keep a journal of its proceedings, and from time to time publish the same, excepting such parts as may in their judgment require secrecy; and the yeas and nays of the members of either house on any question shall, at the desire of one-fifth of those present, be entered on the journal.

Neither house, during the session of Congress, shall, without the consent of the other, adjourn for more than three days, nor to any other place than that in which the two houses shall be sitting.

Section 6.   The Senators and Representatives shall receive a compensation for their services, to be ascertained by law and paid out of the treasury of the United States. They shall in all cases except treason, felony and breach of the peace, be privileged from arrest during their attendance at the session of their respective houses, and in going to and returning from the same; and for any speech or debate in either house, they shall not be questioned in any other place.

No Senator or Representative shall, during the time for which he was elected, be appointed to any civil office under the authority of the United States, which shall have been created, or the emoluments whereof shall have been increased, during such time; and no person holding any office under the United States shall be a member of either house during his continuance in office.

Section 7.   All bills for raising revenue shall originate in the House of Representatives; but the Senate may propose or concur with amendments as on other bills.

Every bill which shall have passed the House of Representatives and the Senate, shall, before it become a law, be presented to the President of the United States; if he approve he shall sign it, but if not he shall return it with objections to that house in which it originated, who shall enter the objections at large on their journal, and proceed to reconsider it. If after such reconsideration two-thirds of that house shall agree to pass the bill, it shall be sent, together with the objections, to the other house, by which it shall likewise be reconsidered, and, if approved by two-thirds of that house, it shall become a law. But in all such cases the votes of both houses shall be determined by yeas and nays, and the names of the persons voting for and against the bill shall be entered on the journal of each house respectively. If any bill shall not be returned by the President within ten days (Sundays excepted) after it shall have been presented to him, the same shall be a law, in like manner as if he had signed it, unless the Congress by their adjournment prevent its return, in which case it shall not be a law.

Every order, resolution, or vote to which the concurrence of the Senate and House of Representatives may be necessary (except on a question of adjournment) shall be presented to the President of the United States; and before the same shall take effect, shall be approved by him, or being disapproved by him, shall be repassed by two-thirds of the Senate and House of Representatives, according to the rules and limitations prescribed in the case of a bill.

Section 8.   The Congress shall have power

To lay and collect taxes, duties, imposts, and excises, to pay the debts and provide for the common defense and general welfare of the United States; but all duties, imposts and excises shall be uniform throughout the United States;

To borrow money on the credit of the United States;

To regulate commerce with foreign nations, and among the several States, and with the Indian tribes;

To establish an uniform rule of naturalization, and uniform laws on the subject of bankruptcies throughout the United States;

To coin money, regulate the value thereof, and of foreign coin, and fix the standard of weights and measures;

To provide for the punishment of counterfeiting the securities and current coin of the United States;

To establish post offices and post roads;

To promote the progress of science and useful arts by securing for limited times to authors and inventors the exclusive right to their respective writings and discoveries;

To constitute tribunals inferior to the Supreme Court;

To define and punish piracies and felonies committed on the high seas and offenses against the law of nations;

To declare war, grant letters of marque and reprisal, and make rules concerning captures on land and water;

To raise and support armies, but no appropriation of money to that use shall be for a longer term than two years;

To provide and maintain a navy;

To make rules for the government and regulation of the land and naval forces;

To provide for calling forth the militia to execute the laws of the Union, suppress insurrections, and repel invasions;

To provide for organizing, arming, and disciplining the militia, and for governing such part of them as may be employed in the service of the United States, reserving to the States respectively the appointment of the officers, and the authority of training the militia according to the discipline prescribed by Congress;

To exercise exclusive legislation in all cases whatsoever, over such district (not exceeding ten miles square) as may, by cession of particular States, and the acceptance of Congress, become the seat of government of the United States, and to exercise like authority over all places purchased by the consent of the legislature of the State, in which the same shall be, for erection of forts, magazines, arsenals, dock-yards, and other needful buildings;—and

To make all laws which shall be necessary and proper for carrying into execution the foregoing powers, and all other powers vested by this Constitution in the government of the United States, or in any department or officer thereof.

Section 9. *The migration or importation of such persons as any of the States now existing shall think proper to admit shall not be prohibited by the Congress prior to the year 1808; but a tax or duty may be imposed on such importation, not exceeding $10 for each person.*

The privilege of the writ of habeas corpus shall not be suspended, unless when in cases of rebellion or invasion the public safety may require it.

No bill of attainder or ex post facto law shall be passed.

No capitation, or other direct, tax shall be laid, unless in proportion to the census or enumeration herein before directed to be taken.

No tax or duty shall be laid on articles exported from any State.

No preference shall be given by any regulation of commerce or revenue to the ports of one State over those of another; nor shall vessels bound to, or from, one State, be obliged to enter, clear, or pay duties in another.

No money shall be drawn from the treasury, but in consequence of appropriations made by law; and a regular statement and account of the receipts and expenditures of all public money shall be published from time to time.

No title of nobility shall be granted by the United States: and no person holding any office of profit or trust under them, shall, without the consent of the Congress, accept of any present, emolument, office, or title, of any kind whatever, from any king, prince, or foreign state.

Section 10. No State shall enter into any treaty, alliance, or confederation; grant letters of marque and reprisal; coin money; emit bills of credit; make anything but gold and silver coin a tender in payment of debts; pass any bill of attainder, ex post facto law, or law impairing the obligation of contracts, or grant any title of nobility.

No State shall, without the consent of Congress, lay any imposts or duties on imports or exports, except what may be absolutely necessary for executing its inspection laws: and the net produce of all duties and imposts, laid by any State on imports or exports, shall be for the use of the treasury of the United States; and all such laws shall be subject to the revision and control of the Congress.

No State shall, without the consent of Congress, lay any duty of tonnage, keep troops or ships of war in time of peace, enter into any agreement or compact with another State, or with a foreign power, or engage in war, unless actually invaded, or in such imminent danger as will not admit of delay.

ARTICLE II

Section 1.   The executive power shall be vested in a President of the United States of America. He shall hold his office during the term of four years, and, together with the Vice President, chosen for the same term, be elected as follows:

Each state shall appoint, in such manner as the legislature thereof may direct, a number of electors, equal to the whole number of Senators and Representatives to which the State may be entitled in the Congress; but no Senator or Representative, or person holding an office of trust or profit under the United States, shall be appointed an elector.

The electors shall meet in their respective States, and vote by ballot for two persons, of whom one at least shall not be an inhabitant of the same State with themselves. And they shall make a list of all the persons voted for, and of the number of votes for each; which list they shall sign and certify, and transmit sealed to the seat of government of the United States, directed to the President of the Senate. The President of the Senate shall, in the presence of the Senate and the House of Representatives, open all the certificates, and the votes shall then be counted. The person having the greatest number of votes shall be the President, if such number be a majority of the whole number of electors appointed; and if there be more than one who have such majority, and have an equal number of votes, then the House of Representatives shall immediately choose by ballot one of them for President; and if no person have a majority, then from the five highest on the list said house shall in like manner choose the President. But in choosing the President the votes shall be taken by States, the representation from each State having one vote; a quorum for this purpose shall consist of a member or members from two-thirds of the States, and a majority of all the States shall be necessary to a choice. In every case, after the choice of the President, the person having the greatest number of votes of the electors shall be the Vice President. But if there should remain two or more who have equal votes, the Senate shall choose from them by ballot the Vice President.

The Congress may determine the time of choosing the electors and the day on which they shall give their votes; which day shall be the same throughout the United States.

No person except a natural-born citizen, *or a citizen of the United States at the time of the adoption of this Constitution*, shall be eligible to the office of President; neither shall any person be eligible to that office who shall not have attained to the age of thirty-five years, and been fourteen years a resident within the United States.

In case of the removal of the President from office or of his death, resignation, or inability to discharge the powers and duties of the said office, the same shall devolve on the Vice President, and the Congress may by law provide for the case of removal, death, resignation, or inability, both of the President and Vice President, declaring what officer shall then act as President, and such officer shall act accordingly, until the disability be removed, or a President shall be elected.

The President shall, at stated times, receive for his services a compensation, which shall neither be increased nor diminished during the period for which he shall have been elected, and he shall not receive within that period any other emolument from the United States, or any of them.

Before he enter on the execution of his office, he shall take the following oath or affirmation:—"I do solemnly swear (or affirm) that I will faithfully execute the office of the President of the United States, and will to the best of my ability preserve, protect and defend the Constitution of the United States."

Section 2.   The President shall be commander in chief of the army and navy of the United States, and of the militia of the several States, when called into the actual service of the United States; he may require the opinion, in writing, of the principal officer in each of the executive departments, upon any subject relating to the duties of their respective offices, and he shall have power to grant reprieves and pardons for offenses against the United States, except in cases of impeachment.

He shall have power, by and with the advice and consent of the Senate, to make treaties, provided two-thirds of the Senators present concur; and he shall nominate, and by and with the advice and consent of the Senate, shall appoint ambassadors, other public ministers and consuls, judges of the Supreme Court, and all other officers of the United States, whose appointments are not herein otherwise provided for, and which shall be established by law: but Congress may by law vest the appointment of such inferior officers, as they think proper, in the President alone, in the courts of law, or in the heads of departments.

The President shall have power to fill up all vacancies that may happen during the recess of the Senate, by granting commissions which shall expire at the end of their next session.

Section 3. He shall from time to time give to the Congress information of the state of the Union, and recommend to their consideration such measures as he shall judge necessary and expedient; he may, on extraordinary occasions, convene both houses, or either of them, and in case of disagreement between them, with respect to the time of adjournment, he may adjourn them to such time as he shall think proper; he shall receive ambassadors and other public ministers; he shall take care that the laws be faithfully executed, and shall commission all the officers of the United States.

Section 4. The President, Vice President and all civil officers of the United States shall be removed from office on impeachment for, and on conviction of, treason, bribery, or other high crimes and misdemeanors.

ARTICLE III

Section 1. The judicial power of the United States shall be vested in one Supreme Court, and in such inferior courts as the Congress may from time to time ordain and establish. The judges, both of the Supreme and inferior courts, shall hold their offices during good behavior, and shall, at stated times, receive for their services a compensation which shall not be diminished during their continuance in office.

Section 2. The judicial power shall extend to all cases, in law and equity, arising under this Constitution, the laws of the United States, and treaties made, or which shall be made, under their authority;—to all cases affecting ambassadors, other public ministers and consuls;—to all cases of admiralty and maritime jurisdiction;—to controversies to which the United States shall be a party;—to controversies between two or more States;—*between a State and citizens of another State;*—between citizens of different States;—between citizens of the same State claiming lands under grants of different States, and between a State, or the citizens thereof, and foreign states, citizens or subjects.

In all cases affecting ambassadors, other public ministers and consuls, and those in which a State shall be party, the Supreme Court shall have original jurisdiction. In all the other cases before mentioned, the Supreme Court shall have appellate jurisdiction, both as to law and fact, with such exceptions, and under such regulations, as the Congress shall make.

The trial of all crimes, except in cases of impeachment, shall be by jury; and such trial shall be held in the State where said crimes shall have been committed; but when not committed within any State, the trial shall be at such place or places as the Congress may by law have directed.

Section 3. Treason against the United States shall consist only in levying war against them, or in adhering to their enemies, giving them aid and comfort. No person shall be convicted of treason unless on the testimony of two witnesses to the same overt act, or on confession in open court.

The Congress shall have power to declare the punishment of treason, but no attainder of treason shall work corruption of blood, or forfeiture except during the life of the person attainted.

ARTICLE IV

Section 1. Full faith and credit shall be given in each State to the public acts, records, and judicial proceedings of every other State. And the Congress may by general laws prescribe the manner in which such acts, records, and proceedings shall be proved, and the effect thereof.

Section 2.   The citizens of each State shall be entitled to all privileges and immunities of citizens in the several States.

A person charged in any State with treason, felony, or other crime, who shall flee from justice, and be found in another State, shall on demand of the executive authority of the State from which he fled, be delivered up, to be removed to the State having jurisdiction of the crime.

No person held to service or labor in one State, under the laws thereof, escaping into another, shall, in consequence of any law or regulation therein, be discharged from such service or labor, but shall be delivered up on claim of the party to whom such service or labor may be due.

Section 3.   New States may be admitted by the Congress into this Union; but no new State shall be formed or erected within the jurisdiction of any other State; nor any State be formed by the junction of two or more States, or parts of States, without the consent of the legislatures of the States concerned as well as of the Congress.

The Congress shall have power to dispose of and make all needful rules and regulations respecting the territory or other property belonging to the United States; and nothing in this Constitution shall be so construed as to prejudice any claims of the United States, or of any particular State.

Section 4.   The United States shall guarantee to every State in this Union a republican form of government, and shall protect each of them against invasion; and on application of the legislature, or of the executive (when the legislature cannot be convened); against domestic violence.

ARTICLE V

The Congress, whenever two-thirds of both houses shall deem it necessary, shall propose amendments to this Constitution, or, on the application of the legislatures of two-thirds of the several States, shall call a convention for proposing amendments, which, in either case, shall be valid to all intents and purposes, as part of this Constitution, when ratified by the legislatures of three-fourths of the several States, or by conventions in three-fourths thereof, as the one or the other mode of ratification may be proposed by the Congress; provided *that no amendments which may be made prior to the year one thousand eight hundred and eight shall in any manner affect the first and fourth clauses in the ninth section of the first article;* and that no State, without its consent, shall be deprived of its equal suffrage in the Senate.

ARTICLE VI

All debts contracted and engagements entered into, before the adoption of this Constitution, shall be as valid against the United States under this Constitution, as under the Confederation.

This Constitution, and the laws of the United States which shall be made in pursuance thereof; and all treaties made, or which shall be made, under the authority of the United States, shall be the supreme law of the land; and the judges in every State shall be bound thereby, anything in the Constitution or laws of any State to the contrary notwithstanding.

The Senators and Representatives before mentioned, and the members of the several State legislatures, and all executive and judicial officers, both of the United States and of the several States, shall be bound by oath or affirmation to support this Constitution; but no religious test shall ever be required as a qualification to any office or public trust under the United States.

ARTICLE VII

The ratification of the conventions of nine States shall be sufficient for the establishment of this Constitution between the States so ratifying the same.

Done in Convention by the unanimous consent of the States present, the seventeenth day of September in the year of our Lord one thousand seven hundred and eighty-seven and of the Independence of the United States of America the twelfth. In witness whereof we have hereunto subscribed our names.

[Signed by]
G° WASHINGTON
Presidt and Deputy from Virginia
[*and thirty-eight others*]

AMENDMENTS TO THE CONSTITUTION

AMENDMENT I*

Congress shall make no law respecting an establishment of religion, or prohibiting the free exercise thereof; or abridging the freedom of speech, or of the press; or the right of the people peaceably to assemble, and to petition the government for a redress of grievances.

AMENDMENT II

A well-regulated militia being necessary to the security of a free State, the right of the people to keep and bear arms shall not be infringed.

AMENDMENT III

No soldier shall, in time of peace, be quartered in any house without the consent of the owner, nor in time of war, but in a manner to be prescribed by law.

AMENDMENT IV

The right of the people to be secure in their persons, houses, papers, and effects, against unreasonable searches and seizures, shall not be violated, and no warrants shall issue but upon probable cause, supported by oath or affirmation, and particularly describing the place to be searched, and the persons or things to be seized.

AMENDMENT V

No person shall be held to answer for a capital, or otherwise infamous crime, unless on a presentment or indictment of a grand jury, except in cases arising in the land or naval forces, or in the militia, when in actual service in time of war or public danger; nor shall any person be subject for the same offense to be twice put in jeopardy of life or limb; nor shall be compelled in any criminal case to be a witness against himself, nor be deprived of life, liberty, or property, without due process of law; nor shall private property be taken for public use without just compensation.

* The first ten Amendments (Bill of Rights) were adopted in 1791.

AMENDMENT VI

In all criminal prosecutions, the accused shall enjoy the right to a speedy and public trial, by an impartial jury of the State and district wherein the crime shall have been committed, which district shall have been previously ascertained by law, and to be informed of the nature and cause of the accusation; to be confronted with the witnesses against him; to have compulsory process for obtaining witnesses in his favor, and to have the assistance of counsel for his defense.

AMENDMENT VII

In suits at common law, where the value in controversy shall exceed twenty dollars, the right of trial by jury shall be preserved, and no fact tried by a jury shall be otherwise reexamined in any court of the United States, than according to the rules of the common law.

AMENDMENT VIII

Excessive bail shall not be required, nor excessive fines imposed, nor cruel and unusual punishments inflicted.

AMENDMENT IX

The enumeration in the Constitution, of certain rights, shall not be construed to deny or disparage others retained by the people.

AMENDMENT X

The powers not delegated to the United States by the Constitution, not prohibited by it to the States, are reserved to the States respectively, or to the people.

AMENDMENT XI   [Adopted 1798]

The judicial power of the United States shall not be construed to extend to any suit in law or equity, commenced or prosecuted against one of the United States by citizens of another State, or by citizens or subjects of any foreign state.

AMENDMENT XII   [Adopted 1804]

The electors shall meet in their respective States, and vote by ballot for President and Vice President, one of whom, at least, shall not be an inhabitant of the same State with themselves; they shall name in their ballots the person voted for as President, and in distinct ballots the person voted for as Vice President, and they shall make distinct lists of all persons voted for as President, and of all persons voted for as Vice President, and of the number of votes for each, which lists they shall sign and certify, and transmit sealed to the seat of government of the United States, directed to the President of the Senate;—the President of the Senate shall, in the presence of the Senate and House of Representatives, open all the certificates and the votes shall then be counted;—the person having the greatest number of votes for President shall be the President, if such number be a majority of the whole number of electors appointed; and if no person have such majority, then from the persons having the highest numbers not exceeding three on the list of those voted for as President, the House of Representatives shall choose immediately, by ballot, the President. But in choosing the President, the votes shall be taken by States, the representation from each State having one vote; a quorum for this purpose shall consist of a member or members from two-thirds of the States, and a majority of all the States shall be necessary to a choice. And if the House of Representatives shall not choose a President whenever the right of choice shall devolve upon them, before *the fourth day of March* next following, then the Vice President shall act as President, as in the case of the death or other constitutional disability of the President.

The person having the greatest number of votes as Vice President shall be the Vice President, if such a number be a majority of the whole number of electors appointed; and if no person have a majority, then from the two highest numbers on the list the Senate shall choose the Vice President; a quorum for the purpose shall consist of two-thirds of the whole number of Senators, and a majority of the whole number shall be necessary to a choice. But no person constitutionally ineligible to the office of President shall be eligible to that of Vice President of the United States.

AMENDMENT XIII   [*Adopted 1865*]

Section 1.   Neither slavery nor involuntary servitude, except as a punishment for crime whereof the party shall have been duly convicted, shall exist within the United States, or any place subject to their jurisdiction.

Section 2.   Congress shall have power to enforce this article by appropriate legislation.

AMENDMENT XIV   [*Adopted 1868*]

Section 1.   All persons born or naturalized in the United States, and subject to the jurisdiction thereof, are citizens of the United States and of the State wherein they reside. No State shall make or enforce any law which shall abridge the privileges or immunities of citizens of the United States; nor shall any State deprive any person of life, liberty, or property, without due process of law; nor deny to any person within its jurisdiction the equal protection of the laws.

Section 2.   Representatives shall be apportioned among the several States according to their respective numbers, counting the whole number of persons in each State, excluding Indians not taxed. But when the right to vote at any election for the choice of Electors for President and Vice President of the United States, Representatives in Congress, the executive and judicial officers of a State, or the members of the legislature thereof, is denied to any of the male inhabitants of such State, being twenty-one years of age and citizens of the United States, or in any way abridged, except for participation in rebellion, or other crime, the basis of representation therein shall be reduced in the proportion which the number of such male citizens shall bear to the whole number of male citizens twenty-one years of age in such State.

Section 3.   No person shall be a Senator or Representative in Congress or Elector of President and Vice President, or hold any office, civil or military, under the United States, or under any State, who, having previously taken an oath, as a member of Congress, or as an officer of the United States, or as a member of any State legislature, or as an executive or judicial officer of any State, to support the Constitution of the United States, shall have engaged in insurrection or rebellion against the same, or given aid and comfort to the enemies thereof. Congress may, by a vote of two-thirds of each house, remove such disability.

Section 4.   The validity of the public debt of the United States, authorized by law, including debts incurred for payment of pensions and bounties for services in suppressing insurrection or rebellion, shall not be questioned. But neither the United States nor any State shall assume or pay any debt or obligation incurred in aid of insurrection or rebellion against the United States, or any claim for the loss or emancipation of any slave; but all such debts, obligations, and claims shall be held illegal and void.

Section 5.   The Congress shall have the power to enforce, by appropriate legislation, the provisions of this article.

AMENDMENT XV   [*Adopted 1870*]

Section 1.   The right of citizens of the United States to vote shall not be denied or abridged by the United States or by any State on account of race, color, or previous condition of servitude.

Section 2.   The Congress shall have power to enforce this article by appropriate legislation.

AMENDMENT XVI   [*Adopted 1913*]

The Congress shall have power to lay and collect taxes on incomes, from whatever source derived, without apportionment among the several States, and without regard to any census or enumeration.

AMENDMENT XVII   [*Adopted 1913*]

Section 1.   The Senate of the United States shall be composed of two Senators from each State, elected by the people thereof, for six years; and each Senator shall have one vote. The electors in each State shall have the qualifications requisite for electors of [voters for] the most numerous branch of the State legislatures.

Section 2.   When vacancies happen in the representation of any State in the Senate, the executive authority of such State shall issue writs of election to fill such vacancies: Provided, that the Legislature of any State may empower the executive thereof to make temporary appointments until the people fill the vacancies by election as the Legislature may direct.

Section 3.   This amendment shall not be so construed as to affect the election or term of any Senator chosen before it becomes valid as part of the Constitution.

AMENDMENT XVIII   [*Adopted 1919l repealed 1933*]

Section 1.   *After one year from the ratification of this article the manufacture, sale, or transportation of intoxicating liquors within, the importation thereof into, or the exportation thereof from the United States and all territory subject to the jurisdiction thereof, for beverage purposes, is hereby prohibited.*

Section 2.   *The Congress and the several States shall have concurrent power to enforce this article by appropriate legislation.*

Section 3.   *This article shall be inoperative unless it shall have been ratified as an amendment to the Constitution by the legislatures of the several States, as provided by the Constitution, within seven years from the date of the submission thereof to the States by the Congress.*

AMENDMENT XIX   [*Adopted 1920*]

Section 1.   The right of citizens of the United States to vote shall not be denied or abridged by the United States or by any State on account of sex.

Section 2.   The Congress shall have the power to enforce this article by appropriate legislation.

AMENDMENT XX   [*Adopted 1933*]

Section 1.   The terms of the President and Vice President shall end at noon on the 20th day of January, and the terms of Senators and Representatives at noon on the 3d day of January, of the years in which such terms would have ended if this article had not been ratified; and the terms of their successors shall then begin.

Section 2.   The Congress shall assemble at least once in every year, and such meeting shall begin at noon on the 3d day of January, unless they shall by law appoint a different day.

Section 3.   If, at the time fixed for the beginning of the term of the President, the President-elect shall have died, the Vice President-elect shall become President. If a President shall not have been chosen before the time fixed for the beginning of his term, or if the President-elect shall have failed to qualify, then the Vice President-elect shall act as President until a President shall have qualified; and the Congress may by law provide for the case wherein neither a President-elect nor a Vice President-elect shall have qualified, declaring who shall then act as President, or the manner in which one who is to act shall be selected, and such persons shall act accordingly until a President or Vice President shall have qualified.

Section 4.   The Congress may by law provide for the case of the death of any of the persons from whom the House of Representatives may choose a President whenever the right of choice shall have devolved upon them, and for the case of the death of any of the persons from whom the Senate may choose a Vice President whenever the right of choice shall have devolved upon them.

Section 5.   Sections 1 and 2 shall take effect on the 15th day of October following the ratification of this article.

Section 6.   This article shall be inoperative unless it shall have been ratified as an amendment to the Constitution by the Legislatures of three-fourths of the several States within seven years from the date of its submission.

AMENDMENT XXI   [*Adopted 1933*]

Section 1.   The eighteenth article of amendment to the Constitution of the United States is hereby repealed.

Section 2.   The transportation or importation into any State, Territory, or Possession of the United States for delivery or use therein of intoxicating liquors, in violation of the laws thereof, is hereby prohibited.

Section 3.   This article shall be inoperative unless it shall have been ratified as an amendment to the Constitution by conventions in the several States, as provided in the Constitution, within seven years from the date of submission thereof to the States by the Congress.

AMENDMENT XXII   [*Adopted 1951*]

Section 1.   No person shall be elected to the office of President more than twice, and no person who has held

the office of President, or acted as President, for more than two years of a term to which some other person was elected President shall be elected to the office of President more than once. But this article shall not apply to any person holding the office of President when this article was proposed by the Congress, and shall not prevent any person who may be holding the office of President, or acting as President, during the term within which this article becomes operative from holding the office of President or acting as President during the remainder of such term.

Section 2.   This article shall be inoperative unless it shall have been ratified as an amendment to the Constitution by the legislatures of three-fourths of the several States within seven years from the date of its submission to the States by the Congress.

AMENDMENT XXIII   [*Adopted 1961*]

Section 1.   The District constituting the seat of Government of the United States shall appoint in such manner as the Congress may direct:

A number of electors of President and Vice President equal to the whole number of Senators and Representatives in Congress to which the District would be entitled if it were a State, but in no event more than the least populous State; they shall be in addition to those appointed by the States, but they shall be considered for the purposes of the election of President and Vice President, to be electors appointed by a State; and they shall meet in the District and perform such duties as provided by the twelfth article of amendment.

Section 2.   The Congress shall have the power to enforce this article by appropriate legislation.

AMENDMENT XXIV   [*Adopted 1964*]

Section 1.   The right of citizens of the United States to vote in any primary or other election for President or Vice President, for electors for President or Vice President, or for Senator or Representative in Congress, shall not be denied or abridged by the United States or any State by reason of failure to pay any poll tax or other tax.

Section 2.   The Congress shall have the power to enforce this article by appropriate legislation.

AMENDMENT XXV [*Adopted 1967*]

Section 1. In case of the removal of the President from office or of his death or resignation, the Vice President shall become President.

Section 2. Whenever there is a vacancy in the office of the Vice President, the President shall nominate a Vice President who shall take office upon confirmation by a majority vote of both Houses of Congress.

Section 3. Whenever the President transmits to the President pro tempore of the Senate and the Speaker of the House of Representatives his written declaration that he is unable to discharge the powers and duties of his office, and until he transmits to them a written declaration to the contrary, such powers and duties shall be discharged by the Vice President as Acting President.

Section 4. Whenever the Vice President and a majority of either the principal officers of the executive departments or of such other body as Congress may by law provide, transmit to the President pro tempore of the Senate and the Speaker of the House of Representatives their written declaration that the President is unable to discharge the powers and duties of his office, the Vice President shall immediately assume the powers and duties of the office as Acting President.

Thereafter, when the President transmits to the President pro tempore of the Senate and the Speaker of the House of Representatives his written declaration that no inability exists, he shall resume the powers and duties of his office unless the Vice President and a majority of either the principal officers of the executive department[s] or of such other body as Congress may by law provide, transmit within four days to the President pro tempore of the Senate and the Speaker of the House of Representatives their written declaration that the President is unable to discharge the powers and du-

ties of his office. Thereupon Congress shall decide the issue, assembling within forty-eight hours for that purpose if not in session. If the Congress, within twenty-one days after receipt of the latter written declaration, or, if Congress is not in session, within twenty-one days after Congress is required to assemble, determines by two-thirds vote of both Houses that the President is unable to discharge the powers and duties of his office, the Vice President shall continue to discharge the same as Acting President; otherwise, the President shall resume the powers and duties of his office.

AMENDMENT XXVI [*Adopted 1971*]

Section 1. The right of citizens of the United States, who are eighteen years of age or older, to vote shall not be denied or abridged by the United States or by any State on account of age.

Section 2. The Congress shall have power to enforce this article by appropriate legislation.

AMENDMENT XXVII* [*Adopted 1992*]

No law, varying the compensation for services of the Senators and Representatives, shall take effect, until an election of Representatives shall have intervened.

---

* Originally proposed in 1789 by James Madison, this amendment failed to win ratification along with the other parts of what became the Bill of Rights. However, the proposed amendment contained no deadline for ratification, and over the years other state legislatures voted to add it to the Constitution; many such ratifications occurred during the 1980s and early 1990s as public frustration with Congress's performance mounted. In May 1992 the Archivist of the United States certified that, with the Michigan legislature's ratification, the article had been approved by three-fourths of the states and thus automatically became part of the Constitution. But congressional leaders and constitutional specialists questioned whether an amendment that took 202 years to win ratification was valid, and the issue had not been resolved by the time this book went to press.

PRESIDENTIAL ELECTIONS, 1789–2008

Year	States in the Union	Candidates	Parties	Electoral Vote	Popular Vote	Percentage of Popular Vote
1789	11	GEORGE WASHINGTON	No party designations	69		
		John Adams		34		
		Minor candidates		35		
1792	15	GEORGE WASHINGTON	No party designations	132		
		John Adams		77		
		George Clinton		50		
		Minor candidates		5		
1796	16	JOHN ADAMS	Federalist	71		
		Thomas Jefferson	Democratic-Republican	68		
		Thomas Pinckney	Federalist	59		
		Aaron Burr	Democratic-Republican	30		
		Minor candidates		48		
1800	16	THOMAS JEFFERSON	Democratic-Republican	73		
		Aaron Burr	Democratic-Republican	73		
		John Adams	Federalist	65		
		Charles C. Pinckney	Federalist	64		
		John Jay	Federalist	1		
1804	17	THOMAS JEFFERSON	Democratic-Republican	162		
		Charles C. Pinckney	Federalist	14		
1808	17	JAMES MADISON	Democratic-Republican	122		
		Charles C. Pinckney	Federalist	47		
		George Clinton	Democratic-Republican	6		
1812	18	JAMES MADISON	Democratic-Republican	128		
		DeWitt Clinton	Federalist	89		
1816	19	JAMES MONROE	Democratic-Republican	183		
		Rufus King	Federalist	34		
1820	24	JAMES MONROE	Democratic-Republican	231		
		John Quincy Adams	Independent Republican	1		
1824	24	JOHN QUINCY ADAMS	Democratic-Republican	84	108,740	30.5
		Andrew Jackson	Democratic-Republican	99	153,544	43.1
		William H. Crawford	Democratic-Republican	41	46,618	13.1
		Henry Clay	Democratic-Republican	37	47,136	13.2
1828	24	ANDREW JACKSON	Democratic	178	642,553	56.0
		John Quincy Adams	National Republican	83	500,897	44.0
1832	24	ANDREW JACKSON	Democratic	219	687,502	55.0
		Henry Clay	National Republican	49	530,189	42.4
		William Wirt	Anti-Masonic	7	33,108	2.6
		John Floyd	National Republican	11		

Because candidates receiving less than 1 percent of the popular vote are omitted, the percentage of popular vote may not total 100 percent.

Before the Twelfth Amendment was passed in 1804, the electoral college voted for two presidential candidates; the runner-up became vice president.

PRESIDENTIAL ELECTIONS, 1789–2004 (*continued*)

YEAR	STATES IN THE UNION	CANDIDATES	PARTIES	ELECTORAL VOTE	POPULAR VOTE	PERCENTAGE OF POPULAR VOTE
1836	26	MARTIN VAN BUREN	Democratic	170	765,483	50.9
		William H. Harrison	Whig	73		
		Hugh L. White	Whig	26	739,795	49.1
		Daniel Webster	Whig	14		
		W. P. Mangum	Whig	11		
1840	26	WILLIAM H. HARRISON	Whig	234	1,274,624	53.1
		Martin Van Buren	Democratic	60	1,127,781	46.9
1844	26	JAMES K. POLK	Democratic	170	1,338,464	49.6
		Henry Clay	Whig	105	1,300,097	48.1
		James G. Birney	Liberty		62,300	2.3
1848	30	ZACHARY TAYLOR	Whig	163	1,360,967	47.4
		Lewis Cass	Democratic	127	1,222,342	42.5
		Martin Van Buren	Free Soil		291,263	10.1
1852	31	FRANKLIN PIERCE	Democratic	254	1,601,117	50.9
		Winfield Scott	Whig	42	1,385,453	44.1
		John P. Hale	Free Soil		155,825	5.0
1856	31	JAMES BUCHANAN	Democratic	174	1,832,955	45.3
		John C. Frémont	Republican	114	1,339,932	33.1
		Millard Fillmore	American	8	871,731	21.6
1860	33	ABRAHAM LINCOLN	Republican	180	1,865,593	39.8
		Stephen A. Douglas	Democratic	12	1,382,713	29.5
		John C. Breckinridge	Democratic	72	848,356	18.1
		John Bell	Constitutional Union	39	592,906	12.6
1864	36	ABRAHAM LINCOLN	Republican	212	2,206,938	55.0
		George B. McClellan	Democratic	21	1,803,787	45.0
1868	37	ULYSSES S. GRANT	Republican	214	3,013,421	52.7
		Horatio Seymour	Democratic	80	2,706,829	47.3
1872	37	ULYSSES S. GRANT	Republican	286	3,596,745	55.6
		Horace Greeley	Democratic	*	2,843,446	43.9
1876	38	RUTHERFORD B. HAYES	Republican	185	4,034,311	48.0
		Samuel J. Tilden	Democratic	184	4,288,546	51.0
		Peter Cooper	Greenback		75,973	1.0
1880	38	JAMES A. GARFIELD	Republican	214	4,453,295	48.5
		Winfield S. Hancock	Democratic	155	4,414,082	48.1
		James B. Weaver	Greenback-Labor		308,578	3.4
1884	38	GROVER CLEVELAND	Democratic	219	4,879,507	48.5
		James G. Blaine	Republican	182	4,850,293	48.2
		Benjamin F. Butler	Greenback-Labor		175,370	1.8
		John P. St. John	Prohibition		150,369	1.5

*When Greeley died shortly after the election, his supporters divided their votes among the minor candidates.

Because candidates receiving less than 1 percent of the popular vote are omitted, the percentage of popular vote may not total 100 percent.

PRESIDENTIAL ELECTIONS, 1789–2004 (*continued*)

YEAR	STATES IN THE UNION	CANDIDATES	PARTIES	ELECTORAL VOTE	POPULAR VOTE	PERCENTAGE OF POPULAR VOTE
1888	38	BENJAMIN HARRISON	Republican	233	5,477,129	47.9
		Grover Cleveland	Democratic	168	5,537,857	48.6
		Clinton B. Fisk	Prohibition		249,506	2.2
		Anson J. Streeter	Union Labor		146,935	1.3
1892	44	GROVER CLEVELAND	Democratic	277	5,555,426	46.1
		Benjamin Harrison	Republican	145	5,182,690	43.0
		James B. Weaver	People's	22	1,029,846	8.5
		John Bidwell	Prohibition		264,133	2.2
1896	45	WILLIAM McKINLEY	Republican	271	7,102,246	51.1
		William J. Bryan	Democratic	176	6,492,559	47.7
1900	45	WILLIAM McKINLEY	Republican	292	7,218,491	51.7
		William J. Bryan	Democratic; Populist	155	6,356,734	45.5
		John C. Wooley	Prohibition		208,914	1.5
1904	45	THEODORE ROOSEVELT	Republican	336	7,628,461	57.4
		Alton B. Parker	Democratic	140	5,084,223	37.6
		Eugene V. Debs	Socialist		402,283	3.0
		Silas C. Swallow	Prohibition		258,536	1.9
1908	46	WILLIAM H. TAFT	Republican	321	7,675,320	51.6
		William J. Bryan	Democratic	162	6,412,294	43.1
		Eugene V. Debs	Socialist		420,793	2.8
		Eugene W. Chafin	Prohibition		253,840	1.7
1912	48	WOODROW WILSON	Democratic	435	6,296,547	41.9
		Theodore Roosevelt	Progressive	88	4,118,571	27.4
		William H. Taft	Republican	8	3,486,720	23.2
		Eugene V. Debs	Socialist		900,672	6.0
		Eugene W. Chafin	Prohibition		206,275	1.4
1916	48	WOODROW WILSON	Democratic	277	9,127,695	49.4
		Charles E. Hughes	Republican	254	8,533,507	46.2
		A. L. Benson	Socialist		585,113	3.2
		J. Frank Hanly	Prohibition		220,506	1.2
1920	48	WARREN G. HARDING	Republican	404	16,143,407	60.4
		James N. Cox	Democratic	127	9,130,328	34.2
		Eugene V. Debs	Socialist		919,799	3.4
		P. P. Christensen	Farmer-Labor		265,411	1.0
1924	48	CALVIN COOLIDGE	Republican	382	15,718,211	54.0
		John W. Davis	Democratic	136	8,385,283	28.8
		Robert M. La Follette	Progressive	13	4,831,289	16.6
1928	48	HERBERT C. HOOVER	Republican	444	21,391,993	58.2
		Alfred E. Smith	Democratic	87	15,016,169	40.9
1932	48	FRANKLIN D. ROOSEVELT	Democratic	472	22,809,638	57.4
		Herbert C. Hoover	Republican	59	15,758,901	39.7
		Norman Thomas	Socialist		881,951	2.2

Because candidates receiving less than 1 percent of the popular vote are omitted, the percentage of popular vote may not total 100 percent.

PRESIDENTIAL ELECTIONS, 1789–2004 (*continued*)

Year	States in the Union	Candidates	Parties	Electoral Vote	Popular Vote	Percentage of Popular Vote
1936	48	FRANKLIN D. ROOSEVELT	Democratic	523	27,752,869	60.8
		Alfred M. Landon	Republican	8	16,674,665	36.5
		William Lemke	Union		882,479	1.9
1940	48	FRANKLIN D. ROOSEVELT	Democratic	449	27,307,819	54.8
		Wendell L. Willkie	Republican	82	22,321,018	44.8
1944	48	FRANKLIN D. ROOSEVELT	Democratic	432	25,606,585	53.5
		Thomas E. Dewey	Republican	99	22,014,745	46.0
1948	48	HARRY S TRUMAN	Democratic	303	24,105,812	49.5
		Thomas E. Dewey	Republican	189	21,970,065	45.1
		Strom Thurmond	States' Rights	39	1,169,063	2.4
		Henry A. Wallace	Progressive		1,157,172	2.4
1952	48	DWIGHT D. EISENHOWER	Republican	442	33,936,234	55.1
		Adlai E. Stevenson	Democratic	89	27,314,992	44.4
1956	48	DWIGHT D. EISENHOWER	Republican	457	35,590,472	57.6
		Adlai E. Stevenson	Democratic	73	26,022,752	42.1
1960	50	JOHN F. KENNEDY	Democratic	303	34,227,096	49.7
		Richard M. Nixon	Republican	219	34,108,546	49.5
		Harry F. Byrd	Independent	15	502,363	.7
1964	50	LYNDON B. JOHNSON	Democratic	486	43,126,506	61.1
		Barry M. Goldwater	Republican	52	27,176,799	38.5
1968	50	RICHARD M. NIXON	Republican	301	31,770,237	43.4
		Hubert H. Humphrey	Democratic	191	31,270,533	42.7
		George C. Wallace	American Independent	46	9,906,141	13.5
1972	50	RICHARD M. NIXON	Republican	520	47,169,911	60.7
		George S. McGovern	Democratic	17	29,170,383	37.5
1976	50	JIMMY CARTER	Democratic	297	40,827,394	49.9
		Gerald R. Ford	Republican	240	39,145,977	47.9
1980	50	RONALD W. REAGAN	Republican	489	43,899,248	50.8
		Jimmy Carter	Democratic	49	35,481,435	41.0
		John B. Anderson	Independent		5,719,437	6.6
		Ed Clark	Libertarian		920,859	1.0
1984	50	RONALD W. REAGAN	Republican	525	54,451,521	58.8
		Walter F. Mondale	Democratic	13	37,565,334	40.5
1988	50	GEORGE H. W. BUSH	Republican	426	47,946,422	54.0
		Michael S. Dukakis	Democratic	112	41,016,429	46.0
1992	50	WILLIAM J. CLINTON	Democratic	370	43,728,275	43.2
		George H. W. Bush	Republican	168	38,167,416	37.7
		H. Ross Perot	Independent		19,237,247	19.0

Because candidates receiving less than 1 percent of the popular vote are omitted, the percentage of popular vote may not total 100 percent.

PRESIDENTIAL ELECTIONS, 1789–2008 (*continued*)

YEAR	STATES IN THE UNION	CANDIDATES	PARTIES	ELECTORAL VOTE	POPULAR VOTE	PERCENTAGE OF POPULAR VOTE
1996	50	WILLIAM J. CLINTON	Democratic	379	47,401,185	49.2
		Robert Dole	Republican	159	39,197,469	40.7
		H. Ross Perot	Reform		8,085,294	8.4
2000	50	GEORGE W. BUSH	Republican	271	50,456,141	47.9
		Albert Gore Jr.	Democratic	266	50,996,039	48.4
		Ralph Nader	Green		2,882,807	2.7
2004	50	GEORGE W. BUSH	Republican	286	60,608,582	51.0
		John Kerry	Democratic	252	57,288,974	48.0
		Ralph Nader	Independent		406,924	1.0
2008	50	BARACK OBAMA	Democratic	365	66,050,000*	53*
		John McCain	Republican	173	58,010,000*	46*

*Approximations of popular vote and percentages based on available information as volume went to press.

Because candidates receiving less than 1 percent of the popular vote are omitted, the percentage of popular vote may not total 100 percent.

Photograph Credits

Index

Prisons and convicts, 74; in Civil War, 347; debtors, 81; leasing of, 376; reform of, 234

Privateers, 155

Proclamation of 1763, 95–96, 109

Proclamation of Amnesty and Reconstruction (1863), 354, 356

Professions, attack on, 210

Progress, 85; dark side of, 237; Thoreau on, 250

Propaganda, pro-slavery, 265

Property and property rights, 42, 75; in colonial New England, 48; elective office and, 83–84, 132, 133; in South, 358–359, 364; voting and, 68, 132, 133, 136, 208

Prosperity, 242. See also Wealth

Prosser, Gabriel, 273

Prostitution, 212

Protectionism. See Tariffs

Protestant Association, 69

Protestantism, 101, 208; abolition and, 232; anti-immigrant societies and, 282, 311; in England, 67; evangelical, 227, 229, 230, 266, 267, 275; Maryland Catholics and, 40–41, 69; Mexicans and, 285; Mormonism and, 228, 278; as reformers, 223; revival of, 65, 86–88, 210, 226–229; slavery and, 266, 275; Whig party and, 290. See also Puritans; specific sect

Protestant Reformation, 23–24

Protests: anti-draft, in Union, 345; Anti-Masonry, 223; royal centralization and, 66; Stamp Act, 98; strikes, 206, 282; Yamasee, 80. See also Boycotts

Providence, founding of, 47

Public Credit Act of 1869, 372

Publicity, Barnum and, 248

Public lands, 196, 197, 223, 224, 368; land speculation and, 199, 200

Public school reform, 230–231, 283

Public water and sanitation, 243–244

Public works programs, 364

Pueblo Indians, 7, 31, 81, 82; revolt by, 61–62, 79

Puerto Rico, 30

Purdue University, 343

Puritans, 24; Church of England and, 36, 45; "city upon a hill" and, 45–46, 50, 66; economic and religious tensions, 49–50; expansion and Native Americans, 45, 50–52; Glorious Revolution and, 68; in Hawthorne's Scarlet Letter, 251–252; in New England, 36, 45–53, 66; Salem witchcraft and, 52–53; towns, families and farms, 48–49

Put-in-Bay, Battle of, 184, 185

Quakers, 58, 87, 109, 130, 166, 231

Quartering Act: (1765), 102; (1774), 112

Quasi War, 160

Quebec, 60, 94

Quebec Act (1774), 112

Queen Anne's War, 69

Queen's College (Rutgers), 87

Queenston, Battle of, 184, 185

Quids (political faction), 178

Quitman, John A., 310

Race and racism, 26, 166; free-soilers and, 309; Mexico and, 297; minstrel shows and, 247–248; slavery and, 45, 265; in South Carolina, 77–78. See also African Americans; Slaves and slavery

Racial equality, 232. See also Equality

Racial mixing, 29, 79, 296; creoles, 77; Jefferson and, 171–172; mulattos, 261–262, 273

Racial segregation. See Segregation

Radical Republicans, 321, 328, 338, 339; election of 1864 and, 348–349; Johnson impeachment and, 359–360; Reconstruction and, 354, 355, 357, 358, 375

Rags-to-riches stories, 207

Railroads, 203, 240–242, 309; bridges for, 237; in Civil War, 331, 343, 344; expansion and, 291; lyceum circuit and, 252; transcontinental, 343, 372

Raleigh, Walter, 33

Randolph, John, 178–179

Randolph-Macon college, 267

Ratification: of Articles of Confederation, 134; U.S. Constitution, 141–143

Rebellion. See Revolts and rebellions

Recessions, 76; (1808-1810), 182, 183; colonial era, 96, 99; Panic of 1857 and, 319–320

Reciprocity. See Social reciprocity

Reconstruction, 353–377; congressional, 358–359, 362, 364; Constitution and; emancipation and, 356, 366–370; end of, 375–377; Fifteenth Amendment and, 360–361; Fourteenth Amendment and, 357–358, 361, 367, 373; Lincoln's plan for, 354–355; politics of, 354–362; presidential, 355–356; Republicans and, 362–363, 364; state governments during, 362–365; Supreme Court and, 362, 367, 373

Reconstruction Act of 1867, 358, 360, 374

Redemption, of the South, 376

Referendum, in Kansas, 316

Reformation, 23–24

Reform movements, 214–215

Reforms, 223, 229–235; of penitentiaries and asylums, 234; popular health and, 245; utopian communities, 235. See also Abolitionists

Regulator movement, 109–110

Reign of Terror (France), 154

Reinhart, Benjamin F., 288

Religion: challenges to authority of, 210; Enlightenment and, 85–86; Great Awakening and, 86–88; Native American, 13; in Puritan New England, 47; Reformation, 23–24; rise of popular, 226–229; slaves, 275–276; West African, 18. See also Christianity; Clergy and ministers; specific sect

Religious toleration, 41, 47, 59, 87, 134

Renaissance, 19, 21

Report on Manufactures (Hamilton), 150

Report on the National Bank (Hamilton), 150–151

Report on the Public Credit (Hamilton), 149

Representative government, 112, 119; in U.S. Constitution, 139

Republicanism, 133, 151; Southern elites and, 157–158

Republican motherhood, 165

Republican party, 151, 158–159; anti-Catholicism and, 282; Dred Scott case and, 315; factionalism within, 171, 178; farmers and, 199; Federalists and, 160, 176, 215; Kansas crisis and, 312–313; Know-Nothings and, 311; Lincoln and, 316, 330; Reconstruction and, 362–363, 364, 373, 376; secession and, 322; sectional factions in, 217; state sovereignty and, 188–189. See also Elections; Radical Republicans

Republican theorists, 101

Restoration colonies, 54, 57

Revenue Act of 1767. See Townshend duties

Revere, Paul, 107, 113

Revivalism, Protestant, 65, 210, 226–229; Great Awakening, 86–88; Second Great Awakening, 226–227; Shakers and, 228–229; Unitarians and, 227

Revolts and rebellions: Bacon's, 43–44; Leisler's, 68–69; Native American, 95–96; Pueblo, 61–62, 79; Shays's, 137–138; Whiskey Rebellion, 152–153. See also Slave rebellions

Revolution: in France, 91, 145, 153, 154–155, 157; in Texas, 286–287

Revolutionary War, 118–131; blacks and, 119–120, 126, 130–131; casualties in, 114, 122, 124, 126; debt from, 134, 135, 137; debts from, 134, 135, 149–150; French Revolution and, 91; loyalists (Tories) in, 113, 119, 122, 125, 126; Native Americans and, 119, 120, 125–126, 128, 131; in North, 122–125; opposing sides, 120–122; peace of Paris and, 127–128; social change and, 128–131; in South, 126–127; in West, 125–126; white male equality in, 128–129; white women in, 129

Rhode Island, 66, 68, 115, 134; Constitution and, 143; founding of, 47